E/1996/60
ST/ESA/247

DEPARTMENT
FOR ECONOMIC
AND SOCIAL INFORMATION
AND POLICY ANALYSIS

WORLD ECONOMIC AND SOCIAL SURVEY 1996

TRENDS AND POLICIES IN THE WORLD ECONOMY

UNITED NATIONS • NEW YORK 1996

Note

Symbols of United Nations documents are composed of capital letters combined with figures.

E/1996/60
ST/ESA/247

PREFACE

THIS EDITION OF THE **WORLD ECONOMIC AND SOCIAL SURVEY** sees increasing grounds for optimism in the global economy, though considerable problems remain.

Economic growth is spreading, and income per person is rising in the overwhelming majority of developing economies and in almost half the transition economies. Coupled with lower inflation rates, sustained growth provides new opportunities for building a more secure and brighter future.

However, low rates of economic growth and recession still afflict too many economies and, in too many places, unemployment and poverty rates remain inordinately high. Moreover, we live with the continuing social and economic dislocation of violent conflict, civil strife and war.

If we are to overcome these problems, our starting-point must be a realization that peace and prosperity are inextricably linked. Investment forms an essential part of global efforts to achieve these twin goals, and is the focus of Part Two of the Survey. Put simply, investment raises productivity and income; it embodies development and economic transition; it is a central element in post-conflict peace-building.

The 1996 Survey is being issued shortly after the success of the United Nations Conference on Human Settlements (Habitat II), and agreement on the need for a new global urban agenda. In addition to reviewing data and projections on the extent of urbanization, the Survey examines trends in the provision of electric power in developing countries, and alternative institutional arrangements for meeting the world's growing demand for water. Both questions are central to the implementation of the Global Plan of Action adopted in Istanbul.

Habitat II is the latest in a sequence of United Nations global conferences that provide new perspectives on development and a new blueprint for progress. Our intention is that the 1996 Survey will serve as part of the monitoring of that progress towards common social and economic objectives.

BOUTROS BOUTROS-GHALI
Secretary-General

FOREWORD

THE 1996 EDITION OF **WORLD ECONOMIC AND SOCIAL SURVEY** *marks the forty-ninth year that this report or its predecessor publications have surveyed the current situation in the world economy. The Survey is prepared at the request of the Economic and Social Council and the General Assembly of the United Nations to serve as background information and analysis for international deliberations on the world economic and social situation. In the report, the Secretariat of the United Nations seeks to bring to the attention of the international community important and emerging issues of a global nature warranting policy deliberation.*

The Survey was prepared by the Macroeconomics Division of the Department for Economic and Social Information and Policy Analysis, with the collaboration of the Microeconomic and Social Analysis Division, the Population Division and the Statistics Division. The Survey has also benefited from consultations with certain special representatives of the Secretary-General, with the Department of Political Affairs, and with the secretariats of the regional commissions and the United Nations Conference on Trade and Development. The Survey drew upon data and analysis from the United Nations, the Food and Agriculture Organization of the United Nations, the International Monetary Fund, the World Bank, the Organisation for Economic Cooperation and Development, national Governments and regional development banks, as well as individuals in academic, official and private organizations.

CONTENTS

PART THREE. SOME DIMENSIONS OF ECONOMIC AND SOCIAL CHANGE

Page

TABLES

FIGURES

EXPLANATORY NOTES

The following symbols have been used in the tables throughout the report:

..   **Two dots** indicate that data are not available or are not separately reported.

—   **A dash** indicates that the amount is nil or negligible.

-    **A hyphen (-)** indicates that the item is not applicable.

-    **A minus sign (-)** indicates a deficit or decrease, except as indicated.

.   **A full stop (.)** is used to indicate decimals.

/   **A slash (/)** between years indicates a crop year or financial year, for example, 1990/91.

-    **Use of a hyphen (-)** between years, for example, 1990-1991, signifies the full period involved, including the beginning and end years.

   Reference to "tons" indicates metric tons and to "dollars"($) United States dollars, unless otherwise stated.

   Annual rates of growth or change, unless otherwise stated, refer to annual compound rates.

   In most cases, the growth rate forecasts for 1996 and 1997 are rounded to the nearest quarter of a percentage point.

   Details and percentages in tables do not necessarily add to totals, because of rounding.

The following abbreviations have been used:

ACP	African, Caribbean and Pacific (Group of) States
CAP	Common Agricultural Policy (of the European Union)
CEETEs	Central and Eastern European transition economies
CFA	Communauté financière africaine
CIS	Commonwealth of Independent States
CMEA	Council for Mutual Economic Assistance
COMTRADE	Commodity Trade Statistics Database of the United Nations Statistics Division
DAC	Development Assistance Committee (of OECD)
EAP	Enhanced Access Policy (of the International Monetary Fund)
EBRD	European Bank for Reconstruction and Development
EC	European Community
ECE	Economic Commission for Europe
ECLAC	Economic Commission for Latin America and the Caribbean
ECU	European currency unit
EDF	European Development Fund
EMS	European Monetary System
EMU	Economic and Monetary Union
ERM	Exchange Rate Mechanism of the EMS
ESAF	Enhanced Structural Adjustment Facility (of the International Monetary Fund)

EU	European Union
Eurostat	Statistical Office of the European Union
FAO	Food and Agriculture Organization of the United Nations
FDI	foreign direct investment
G-7	the seven major developed countries
GATT	General Agreement on Tariffs and Trade
GDP	gross domestic product
GNP	gross national product
GSP	Generalized System of Preferences
ICP	International Comparison Programme
IDA	International Development Association
IEA	International Energy Agency
ILO	International Labour Organization
IMF	International Monetary Fund
INTRASTAT	system of data collection for intra-EU trade
LIBOR	London Interbank Offered Rate
mbd	million barrels per day
MERCOSUR	Southern Cone Common Market
MFA	Multi-Fibre Arrangement
MFN	most-favoured nation
NIEs	newly industrialized economies
NMP	net material product
ODA	official development assistance
ODI	Overseas Development Institute
OECD	Organisation for Economic Cooperation and Development
OPEC	Organization of the Petroleum Exporting Countries
PPP	purchasing power parity
Project LINK	International Research Group of Econometric Model Builders, with Headquarters at the Department for Economic and Social Information and Policy Analysis of the United Nations Secretariat
SAF	Structural Adjustment Facility
SDRs	special drawing rights (IMF)
SFF	Supplementary Financing Facility (of the IMF)
SITC	Standard International Trade Classification
SOE	State-owned enterprise
TFP	total factor productivity
UEMOA	Union économique et monétaire de l'Afrique de l'ouest
UN/DESIPA	Department for Economic and Social Information and Policy Analysis of the United Nations Secretariat
UNCTAD	United Nations Conference on Trade and Development
UNDP	United Nations Development Programme
UNICEF	United Nations Children's Fund
VAT	value-added tax
WTO	World Trade Organization

The designations employed and the presentation of the material in this publication do not imply the expression of any opinion whatsoever on the part of the United Nations Secretariat concerning the legal status of any country, territory, city or area or of its authorities, or concerning the delimitation of its frontiers or boundaries.

The term "country" as used in the text of this report also refers, as appropriate, to territories or areas.

For analytical purposes, the following country classification has been used:

Developed economies (developed market economies):

North America, southern and western Europe (excluding Cyprus, Malta and former Yugoslavia), Australia, Japan, New Zealand.

Major developed economies (or the Group of Seven):

Canada, France, Germany, Italy, Japan, United Kingdom of Great Britain and Northern Ireland, United States of America.

Economies in transition:

Albania, Bulgaria, Czech Republic, Hungary, Poland, Romania, Slovakia and the former USSR, comprising the Baltic republics and the member countries of the Commonwealth of Independent States (CIS).

Developing countries:

Latin America and the Caribbean, Africa, Asia and the Pacific (excluding Australia, Japan and New Zealand), Cyprus, Malta, former Yugoslavia. For some analyses, China has been shown separately.

South and East Asia:

Unless otherwise stated, South Asia, South-East Asia and East Asia, excluding China.

Mediterranean:

Cyprus, Malta, Turkey, former Yugoslavia.

West Asia:

Bahrain, Iran (Islamic Republic of), Iraq, Israel, Jordan, Kuwait, Lebanon, Oman, Qatar, Saudi Arabia, Syrian Arab Republic, United Arab Emirates, Yemen.

For particular analyses, developing countries have been sub-divided into the following groups:

Capital-surplus countries (or surplus energy exporters):

Brunei Darussalam, Iran (Islamic Republic of), Iraq, Kuwait, Libyan Arab Jamahiriya, Qatar, Saudi Arabia, United Arab Emirates.

Deficit countries (or capital-importing countries) subdivided into the following two subgroups:

Other net energy exporters (or deficit energy exporters):

Algeria, Angola, Bahrain, Bolivia, Cameroon, Colombia, Congo, Ecuador, Egypt, Gabon, Indonesia, Malaysia, Mexico, Nigeria, Oman, Papua New Guinea, Peru, Syrian Arab Republic, Trinidad and Tobago, Tunisia, Venezuela, Viet Nam, Yemen.

Net energy importers:

All other developing countries.

Miscellaneous groupings:

Fifteen heavily indebted countries:

Argentina, Bolivia, Brazil, Chile, Colombia, Côte d'Ivoire, Ecuador, Mexico, Morocco, Nigeria, Peru, Philippines, Uruguay, Venezuela, former Yugoslavia.

Least developed countries (48 countries):

Afghanistan, Angola, Bangladesh, Benin, Bhutan, Burkina Faso, Burundi, Cambodia, Cape Verde, Central African Republic, Chad, Comoros, Djibouti, Equatorial Guinea, Eritrea, Ethiopia, Gambia, Guinea, Guinea-Bissau, Haiti, Kiribati, Lao People's Democratic Republic, Lesotho, Liberia, Madagascar, Malawi, Maldives, Mali, Mauritania, Mozambique, Myanmar, Nepal, Niger, Rwanda, Samoa, Sao Tome and Principe, Sierra Leone, Solomon Islands, Somalia, Sudan, Togo, Tuvalu, Uganda, United Republic of Tanzania, Vanuatu, Yemen, Zaire, Zambia.

Sub-Saharan Africa:

African continent and nearby islands, excluding Nigeria, northern Africa (Algeria, Egypt, Libyan Arab Jamahiriya, Morocco and Tunisia), South Africa.

The designations of country groups in the text and the tables are intended solely for statistical or analytical convenience and do not necessarily express a judgement about the stage reached by a particular country or area in the development process.

I THE WORLD ECONOMY IN 1996

The world economy is in a slowly accelerating growth path. It has not yet attained the more rapid and sustainable rate of growth that it is capable of, although such growth appears to be on the horizon for 1997. Within the global expansion that has already been realized, economic growth impulses are spreading to an increasing number of countries. At least 109 countries, with a combined population of 5.3 billion (all but some 300 million to 400 million of the world's people), are expected to see output per capita rise this year.

Results such as these have been building since the dismal early years of the 1990s. The new numbers reflect a very encouraging and dynamic trend in some countries; for other countries, however, the numbers represent a minor or incipient improvement of the most difficult of circumstances. In certain countries, violent political situations have eased. In many developing and transition economies, domestic adjustment programmes are beginning to bear fruit. Meanwhile, despite rising income per capita, some of the richest countries in the world, especially in Europe, have not been able to significantly reduce their inordinately high unemployment rates, while highly prized social safety nets seem no longer affordable in several developed countries or are seen by Governments as being beyond reach.

THE WORLD ECONOMIC SITUATION

The world's gross output of goods and services is expected to grow about $2\frac{1}{2}$ per cent in 1996 for the third year in a row (see table I.1). This is a lower rate of expansion than the world average of the 1980s. Nevertheless, it represents a considerable improvement compared with the first three years of the decade. Those years were marked by economic recession in the developed economies; economic collapse and some instances of war in the transition economies; and drought, war, violent conflict and difficult economic adjustment in many developing countries (although others grew rapidly).

One year ago, a somewhat higher world growth rate — $3\frac{1}{4}$ per cent — was forecast for 1996,[1] a rate that is now expected to be attained in 1997. The acceleration of world output growth has been postponed in effect by a slower growth trajectory of the developed economies in 1995 and 1996 than was earlier foreseen. That is, instead of growth rates of gross domestic product (GDP) of $2\frac{3}{4}$ per cent in 1995 and 3 per cent 1996, there was an actual growth rate of 2 per cent in 1995 and 2 per cent is now expected in 1996 as well.

The growth rate of GDP of the developing countries in 1995 was very close to the forecast (5.2 per cent achieved, compared with 5 per cent forecast),

[1] See *World Economic and Social Survey, 1995* (United Nations publication, Sales No. E.95.II.C.1), table I.1

Table I.1.
GROWTH OF WORLD OUTPUT, 1981-1997

Annual percentage change								
	1981-1990	1991	1992	1993	1994	1995[a]	1996[b]	1997[b]
World[c]	2.9	0.3	1.1	0.9	2.4	2.4	2 ½	3 ¼
Developed economies	2.9	0.7	1.6	0.7	2.7	2.0	2	2 ½
Economies in transition[d]	2.0	-8.6	-12.0	-6.9	-8.9	-1.8	2	3
Developing economies	3.1	3.5	4.9	5.0	5.5	5.2	5 ½	5 ¾
Memorandum items								
Number of countries with rising per capita output	74	69	73	62	93	103	109	..
Number of countries in sample	122	122	136	137	137	137	137	..
World output growth as seen in *World Economic and Social Survey, 1995*	2.8	0.4	0.7	1.0	2.6	2 ¾	3 ¼	..

Source: UN/DESIPA.

[a] Preliminary estimate.
[b] Forecast, based in part on Project LINK.
[c] Calculated as a weighted average of individual country growth rates of gross domestic product (GDP), where weights are based on GDP in 1988 prices and exchange rates (for contrast with the result when weights are based on GDP conversions at purchasing power parities, which add about 1 percentage point to annual global growth in the 1990s, see introduction to statistical annex).
[d] Based on reported GDP, which seriously underestimates activity in several countries.

while the forecast for 1996 is now even higher (5½ per cent is being currently forecast, compared with 5 per cent forecast one year ago). In addition, the 2 per cent growth rate currently expected in the economies in transition in 1996 equals that forecast one year earlier, while the output decline of 1.8 per cent was less than had been anticipated in 1995.

It is noteworthy that the developing and transition economies have been outperforming the GDP growth rates that were projected one year ago when it was thought that growth in the industrialized countries would strengthen. This suggests that domestic factors have been important sources of economic growth in many developing and transition economies and that some of the developing and transition economies have been relatively successful in the international market-place. Indeed, these countries are increasingly seen as important markets and potential stimuli to growth in the developed economies. Nevertheless, other countries — developing and transition economies — have not yet pried loose from the "low-level equilibrium" trap of high poverty and low growth.

The international economic environment has continued to offer greater opportunities for economic growth to countries that are positioned to take advantage of it. The volume of world merchandise imports grew 10.3 per cent in 1994, and an estimated 8.5 per cent in 1995, and import growth is expected to be buoyant again in 1996 (7¼ per cent), even if less so than last year (see annex table A.19).

In addition, global financial flows continue to mushroom. The world total of international medium-term and long-term credits (bonds, bank loans and related facilities) rose almost one quarter in 1995 to $832 billion (see annex table A.31).

Developing and transition economies together accounted, however, for little over 10 per cent of these arrangements. Many countries do not enjoy access to such funds, as their capacity for additional debt servicing precludes such borrowing. They require direct investment and official financial flows. A special case, and one in which aid delayed or denied is especially costly, is assistance to countries emerging from recent conflict situations. These countries also require official credits and grants. Unfortunately, in general, the prospects for official development assistance (ODA) are bleak.

Developed economies: slow growth but no recession

Several developed economies, such as Canada, the United Kingdom of Great Britain and Northern Ireland and the United States of America, entered the 1990s by slipping into economic recession (see annex table A.2). As these countries began to recover, others went into recession, including France, Germany, Italy and Japan. By 1994, most developed countries were on a path of recovery, although in some cases — that of Japan, in particular — it was closer to economic stagnation. The recovery in Europe and Japan was expected to broaden in 1995, while the growth of GDP was expected to slow somewhat in the countries that were further advanced in their economic cycle.

In the event, growth slowed down more than expected in the countries further advanced in their cycle; it slowed instead of increasing in Western Europe; and output barely rose in Japan. Unanticipated exchange rate appreciation in Japan and Europe seems to have been part of the reason. While the degree of overvaluation of currencies in the first half of 1995 has been reduced, the overall rate of economic growth in 1996 is not expected to surpass the 1995 rate, and only a modest improvement is expected in 1997. In this regard, the current economic cycle is unusually weak: the year of strongest recovery (1994) produced an overall growth rate that was less than the average growth rate of the entire 1980s (table I.1).

In framing their macroeconomic policy stances, Governments have sought to establish conditions for sustainable growth over the medium term. They have thus sought to squeeze inflation from their economies, consolidate fiscal deficits to meet policy goals and strengthen the confidence of financial markets in the soundness of their policies. Japan has been a special case, as its economy has had to absorb a financial crisis that caused massive losses of wealth and rocked the banking system. Large-scale government efforts over several years to restart the economy have had disappointing results.

In some dimensions, the macroeconomic policy strategies of the developed economies have been a success. With the exception of Germany and Japan, fiscal deficits have fallen relative to GDP (annex table A.8) and monetary policy in 1994 and 1995 slowed the growth of demand, as intended. Policy makers then reversed course and cautiously eased monetary conditions during 1995 and early 1996 to avoid pushing their countries into recession. While economic growth was less than expected, it has thus remained positive overall.

Success on the inflation front has been dramatic. Consumer price increases have been held below 2.5 per cent per year on average since 1994, despite recovering demand and substantial increases in petroleum and other international commodity prices (see annex tables A.7 and A.21). A further slowing of inflation is forecast for 1996.

2 Unemployment rates used in this *Survey* are standardized to the extent possible for international comparability and thus may differ somewhat from familiar national definitions (see notes to table A.6).

3 See *World Economic and Social Survey, 1995...*, table A.6.

3 See, for example, *World Economic and Social Survey, 1995...*, chap. XIV; and *World Economic and Social Survey, 1994* (United Nations publication, Sales No. E.94.II.C.1 and Corr.1 translations: E and F only), chap. VI, section entitled "Employment in developed market economies: worsening before improvement".

5 Measurement of economic activity in the economies in transition has been replete with unusual difficulties and thus aggregate output statistics must be interpreted with extreme caution, especially those that span the period extending from the early to the recent transition years. Gross domestic product (GDP) was not the basic measure of aggregate output at the start of transition in most countries and standard methods for collecting national accounts data in market economies were not used. Even had this not been the case, relative prices under central planning would still have borne little relationship to market prices, while sharp changes in the quality and composition of output in several sectors make comparisons over time extremely difficult to interpret (for additional details, see the introduction to the statistical annex).

Meanwhile, progress on other economic fronts has been disappointing. First, there has been virtually no reduction in the overall rate of unemployment in the developed countries since it peaked at 8 per cent of the labour force in 1993 (table A.6),[2] although last year when the economic growth outlook was more optimistic, virtually no gain had been expected in 1995.[3] Unemployment seems to be driven mainly by structural factors.[4]

Second, paralleling the unemployment developments has been a relative stagnation in real wages. Moreover, while this has been a major contributor to the low inflation rate, it has also been a factor in the slow economic growth, since wage income is an important determinant of household expenditure and thus of aggregate demand and production. Furthermore, the investment in high-technology equipment and the policies of companies in "downsizing" their operations — especially in the United States — have raised fears of unemployment, which are hard to assuage when workers who are made redundant cannot find comparable employment opportunities or rising wage levels.

Finally, the fiscal consolidation imperative has reduced prospects for important discretionary government spending on economic, social and cultural activities in many countries. Indeed, several Governments have been reassessing how to fully meet their non-discretionary spending commitments, in particular with regard to social security, broadly defined. These problems do not lend themselves to facile solutions, but instances of labour militancy and voter dissatisfaction are increasingly underlining the incompleteness of the existing policy package.

Transition economies: after the turning point is growth

The depth of the plunge in economic activity that accompanied the collapse of central planning first in Central and Eastern Europe and then in the former Union of Soviet Socialist Republics is hard to grasp and harder to measure. Considering the economies of these countries as a whole, total output measured one third less in 1995 than in 1990.[5] This may well overstate the extent of the decline, but a different signal of the severity of the shock was that, taking all these countries together, population growth abruptly declined in the 1990s (see annex table A.1). This year, however, is expected to mark the end of economic contraction and the resumption of economic growth in the transition economies taken as a whole.

In fact, all the Central and Eastern European transition economies (CEETEs) and the Baltic States had begun growing by 1994. Many — but not all — had strong rates of economic growth in 1995, with further strong growth forecast for 1996 (see annex table A.3). The economic situation has been much more difficult in the countries of the Commonwealth of Independent States (CIS), where output continued to decline in 1995, albeit less rapidly than in earlier years. Only the barest beginnings of growth are foreseen in 1996 and there is so much uncertainty surrounding that prospect that forecasters would not be surprised if the outcome was, instead, a further contraction of output.

The differences in growth rates among the transition economies reflect the different nature, extent and consistency of the policies implemented. All the countries faced sharp inflation jolts when prices were first allowed to rise and the value of credits extended to enterprises — both formal loans and inter-enterprise arrears — exploded, as firms sought to cope with their new, unplanned environment. Policy makers thus had to focus on regaining macro-economic control (on both limiting the growth of the money supply and reining in burgeoning budget deficits) as they at the same time promoted the institutional transformation of their economies — which included turning state enterprises into corporations and privatizing them, rebuilding the banking and financial system on market-oriented principles, overseeing and supporting the foreign-exchange market, reorienting foreign trade, introducing legal reforms and so on — all the while seeking to cope with the social consequences of economic dislocation.

Initially, especially in the CEETEs, the major growth impetus was expected to come from exports to Western Europe. However, there are now solid sources of growth in the CEETEs themselves. Consumer demand, initially satisfied by imports, is increasingly being met by domestic production, and investment is picking up. Industrial productivity is also rising. Yet the unemployment picture remains serious and inflation rates, although falling, remain high (see chap. II).

There is a measure of international market confidence in most of the CEETEs. They have seen considerable inflows of foreign exchange, either as portfolio investment (responding to high local interest rates) or foreign direct investment (attracted by a skilled and relatively low-wage labour force and a relatively developed infrastructure). As a result, foreign-exchange reserves in most countries of the region have jumped.

In many ways, the Russian Federation has also made remarkable progress: inflation has fallen, foreign-exchange reserves are high, private economic activity is advancing strongly. Yet, little economic growth is forecast for 1996 and that with considerable uncertainty. Continued decline should not be completely ruled out. Confidence in the stability of the economic and administrative environment appeared to be weak; for example, significant uncertainty was said to surround the possible economic policy consequences of the presidential election in June 1996. If uncertainty in the business community over future policy was reduced and the country invested the considerable resources that are leaving or being held in the form of foreign exchange, the outlook would be very much brighter. Indeed, the human resources and much of the infrastructure that is so essential for economic growth are for the most part readily available in the Russian Federation. In contrast, the short-term prospects for a resumption of economic growth are small in many other countries of CIS.

Developing economies: economic growth is spreading

GDP per capita rose in 71 developing countries in 1995 out of the 93 countries whose data are regularly monitored, and 75 countries are expected to belong to this group in 1996 (see table I.2). This represents a substantial rise from the 50 countries in 1993. The improvement in the spread of economic growth is also quite dramatic measured in terms of the population. In 1995, almost 90 per cent of the population — or 4 billion people — of developing countries were living in countries experiencing rising average GDP per person. In 1996, 96 per cent of that population — or 4.3 billion — are expected to be in this category.

Table I.2.

NUMBER OF DEVELOPING ECONOMIES AND SHARE OF TOTAL POPULATION WITH RISING PER CAPITA GROSS DOMESTIC PRODUCT (GDP), 1990-1996

	1990		1991		1992		1993		1994		1995[a]		1996[b]	
	Number of countries	Percentage of total population	Number of countries	Percentage of total population	Number of countries	Percentage of total population	Number of countries	Percentage of total population	Number of countries	Percentage of total population	Number of countries	Percentage of total population	Number of countries	Percentage of total population
Developing economies	56	85	55	82	57	84	50	80	60	85	71	90	75	96
of which														
Latin America	15	48	16	58	16	55	16	68	18	89	20	68	23	95
Africa	15	49	16	47	13	46	11	27	17	42	25	67	28	87
South and East Asia	15	99	14	93	15	95	15	95	16	99	15	99	15	99
China	1	100	1	100	1	100	1	100	1	100	1	100	1	100
West Asia	7	73	6	72	9	90	4	15	5	19	6	63	4	61
Least developed countries	12	53	11	41	12	56	15	65	17	57	21	78	22	78

Source: UN/DESIPA.
[a] Preliminary estimate.
[b] Forecast.

Rising per capita output is thus not a phenomenon that is limited mainly to China and the rapidly growing economies of South and East Asia, where, indeed, almost the entire population lives in countries with rising GDP per person. The least developed countries in particular have made significant gains in this regard in 1995 and are expected to advance further in 1996: at least 21 economies out of the 48 least developed countries, with 78 per cent of the total population in the group, registered growth in per capita GDP in each of these two years. This is quite an encouraging development if set against the experience of the early 1990s, when only about a dozen least developed countries, with about half their population, were in this category.

The gain in countries having rising per capita GDP has been most pronounced in Africa, where recovery from very poor conditions began in 1994. By 1995, 67 per cent of the population lived in countries with growing per capita GDP. This proportion is expected to increase to over 87 per cent in 1996. In Latin America, after the sharp economic slow-down in 1995, per capita GDP growth is becoming much more widespread in 1996, extending to 95 per cent of the population.

Interpretation of this development must be tempered, however, by two sobering facts: in many countries the growth of per capita GDP has been small and the average levels of per capita GDP in most regions still remain below what they were in real terms in 1980. At the regional level, per capita GDP growth was negative in Latin America and negligible in Africa in 1995. In 1996, it is expected to average $3/4$ per cent in Latin America and $1 1/2$ per cent

Table I.3.
PER CAPITA GDP OF DEVELOPING ECONOMIES, 1980-1996

	Annual rate of growth of per capita GDP (percentage)				Per capita GDP (1988 dollars)			
	1981-1990	1991-1995	1995[a]	1996[b]	1980	1990	1995[a]	1996[b]
Developing economies	1.0	2.9	3.3	4	770	858	988	1 028
of which								
Latin America	-0.9	0.8	-0.9	¾	2 148	2 008	2 092	2 106
Africa	-0.9	-1.3	-0.0	1 ½	721	700	657	667
West Asia	-5.3	-0.6	0.4	¼	5 736	3 423	3 328	3 335
South East Asia	3.9	4.0	5.0	6	460	674	817	865
China	7.5	10.2	9.1	8	202	411	664	716
Least developed countries	-0.5	-0.9	0.4	1 ¾	261	249	238	243

Source: UN/DESIPA.
[a] Preliminary estimate.
[b] Forecast.

in Africa (see table I.3). In both Latin America and Africa, the rate of per capita GDP growth in the majority of countries experiencing growth was under 2 per cent in 1995 and 1996. In addition, per capita GDP in real terms in both regions in both years has remained below that in 1980. A similar pattern in the magnitude of per capita GDP growth and long-term comparison of the levels of per capita GDP can be seen in the least developed countries.

Another interesting development, as was noted above, is that developing-country growth rates strengthened overall in 1995 despite the slower-than-expected growth of the developed countries, their primary trading partners. Indeed, the volume of developing country exports is estimated to have grown more rapidly in 1995 than in 1994 and if the *Survey* forecast is borne out by events, 1996 will be the third consecutive year of double-digit expansion in export volumes of developing countries (see annex table A.19). This reflects the success of some developing countries in establishing markets for their goods in developed economies — taking advantage in particular of the continued strength of demand for computer-related electronics — as well as the increasing sales of developing countries to other developing countries.[6]

Developing countries have also been assisted by the firming in 1994 and 1995 of international commodity prices, which are expected to remain relatively strong in 1996. In addition, direct foreign investment flows to developing countries have virtually exploded in recent years. In 1995, the net direct investment in the capital-importing developing countries is estimated to have reached $64 billion, although it was highly concentrated in a small number of countries. In 1990, the total investment had been $17 billion.[7]

These developments notwithstanding, international flows of portfolio financing to developing countries were temporarily jolted by the balance-of-payments crisis in Mexico at the end of 1994 and the crisis of confidence it spawned. However, flows, most of which go to the "emerging market" economies — encouraged first by the very quick and strong commitment of the international community to Mexico and other countries with large international financial

6 This reflects particular regional developments: the strong growth of West Asian and other oil exports to rapidly growing developing countries and the substantial growth of a variety of exports from South and East Asia to China and other Asian economies. (See annex table A.15 and, for greater detail, United Nations, *Monthly Bulletin of Statistics*, May 1996, special table D; the weakened link between South and East Asian growth and the growth of the developed economies was observed earlier in, for example, *World Economic and Social Survey, 1994* (United Nations publication, Sales No. E.94.II.C.1 and Corr.1), chap. II, subsection entitled "Developing countries: stronger growth: South and East Asia: keeping up the high pace: weakened link to developed economy growth".)

7 Data are for investment, net of reinvested earnings for a sample of 93 countries (see annex table A.27).

exposure that had been following adjustment regimes, as well as by the sharp policy changes implemented by Mexico itself during 1995 — resumed by the second half of 1995.

All in all, the trade and financial flows that are essential to an internationally open economic development process appear to be evolving in a very promising manner. Certainly, countries are continuing to protect politically sensitive industries from foreign competition, perhaps most persistently in the agricultural sector, and the international regime for trade in services is far from settled. On the other hand, the World Trade Organization is emerging as a significant venue for dispute settlement procedures as well as for negotiation of trade agreements, and developing countries are participating increasingly in its activities; in addition, a more pragmatic approach has also been evolving in the Bretton Woods institutions with regard to alleviating more effectively the debt-servicing burden of some of the poorest developing countries, although concrete proposals have yet to be acted upon (see chap. III).

One essential component of the international package of development cooperation efforts, however, is seriously weakening before its time, namely ODA. All indications attest that the flow of ODA will continue to show a shrinking overall donor commitment to development assistance in coming years. This is not a uniform development, as certain donors are committed to significant increases in their aid effort; but with recent reductions of flows, especially by one of the largest donors, the total amount of concessional resources to be spread among the countries needing and deserving this assistance will be stretched much too thin.

ODA is meant to serve not as income support for poor countries, but as investment support, development support, support in particular for activities that are everywhere the responsibility of the public sector, such as education and health. In addition, aid is warranted for special circumstances — post-conflict situations being a case in point — wherein the private sector bypasses countries because conditions are too unsettled, too dangerous, too risky. In almost all cases, the alternative to ODA financing of a project is no financing, and no project.

ANALYTICAL TOPICS IN THE 1996 SURVEY

In addition to reviewing the current global economic situation, the *World Economic and Social Survey* seeks to foster international discussion of economic and social issues with a significant policy dimension. In this regard, the current *Survey* includes a major study of investment, in particular business fixed investment, the backbone of development in a market economy. The *Survey* also reviews for a general audience selected issues bearing on social and economic development policy that have been a focus of international analysis.

A perspective on investment in the world's economies

Additional investment is the answer — or part of the answer — to most policy problems in the economic and social arena. Investment does not, however, automatically occur in the desired amounts or the desired locations or the desired producing sectors. As investment is a significant policy concern in developed, developing and transition economies, it was made the focus of the main analytical part of the current *Survey*.

The point of departure in this study of investment is the recognition that the subject is rife with such theoretical and statistical complications as the analyst would do well not to ignore, and that to understand investment as a policy issue it is useful to bring to bear upon the subject the broadest variety of considerations, which can best be put forth in the context of a series of case histories. Several such cases were drawn up from the experiences of developed, developing and transition economies, and include discussions of investment in four countries in post-conflict situations that reflect the special concern about this group of countries within the United Nations. Such conclusions as emerged from the various clusters of cases analysed are presented in the appropriate chapters.

Some dimensions of economic and social change

Four issues were singled out for review under the part of the *Survey* that selects specific dimensions of economic and social change for analysis. The first issue pertains to how demographers at the United Nations monitor and project urban growth, a salient topic in light of the extensive analysis based on these data that has been used in papers for presentation at the United Nations Conference on Human Settlements (Habitat II), (Istanbul, June 1996).

The second issue, which also has an urban dimension, concerns how developing countries — where electricity demand is growing fastest — are seeking to expand their electric power supplies and provide electricity more efficiently in a world of increasingly scarce resources. Attention focuses on the efforts to create and utilize economic incentives for efficient energy production, transmission and distribution.

The third issue addressed in this part of the *Survey* raises questions about safe water supply, a matter highlighted by the United Nations Water Conference, held in Mar del Plata, Argentina, in 1977, and the continuing follow-up activities to the Conference in the General Assembly and elsewhere. The emphasis in the water study is on experiences with respect to creating economic structures and institutions that raise the incentives for more efficient use of water and move it most effectively from those places in which it is relatively abundant to those where need is greatest.

Finally, the *Survey* takes up a burgeoning but elusive component of international trade, namely business services (communications, computer software, financial services and so on). Services as a general category constitute a large and rapidly growing share of global economic activity; but as services are "invisibles", they are less readily measured than merchandise. The study thus sought to track the development of the trade in business services by identifying the major suppliers and purchasers, but it quickly became necessary to confront the dilemma arising from the fact that services can be provided across borders in any of several ways, among which only one falls under the traditional rubric of international trade.

PART ONE

STATE OF THE WORLD ECONOMY

II THE CURRENT SITUATION IN THE WORLD'S ECONOMIES

There are two striking features of the present world economic situation. The first is that the growth of economic activity has become more widespread. The second is that growth seems to have the potential to be sustained in a large number of countries.

The geographical spread of economic growth began to manifest itself in 1995. In that year, world economic activity in aggregate grew at the same rate as in 1994, but the growth rates of almost two thirds of the developing countries increased. In addition, five of the seven Central and Eastern European economies grew more rapidly than in 1994. In the Commonwealth of Independent States (CIS), there was a continuation of the decline in output, but the rate of contraction slowed.

Counterbalancing these improvements, there was a slow-down that occurred mainly in the developed countries and, among them, mainly in the seven major economies. In addition, there were especially difficult recessions in certain Latin American economies.

The year 1996 is expected to see a continuation of this pattern of more widespread growth. The rate of growth of output is forecast to rise in about half the developing countries in 1996. The least developed countries in particular are expected to see an overall rate of growth that will be more than twice their average in the 1980s, largely reflecting the improvement in the economic situation in Africa. Growth is expected to continue in the Central and Eastern European countries and output is forecast to rise in each of the Baltic States. It is also possible that rising economic activity will be registered by CIS for the first time since it was created, although considerable uncertainty surrounds the projections in that case. Meanwhile, the developed countries are forecast to have much the same growth rates, as in 1995 albeit distributed differently.

Current international economic conditions are providing an opportunity for growth that many countries have been able to capture. Inflation remains in check in the developed countries and in other countries where it has recently been brought down to acceptable levels. Elsewhere, it is generally on a declining trend, having slowed dramatically in the transition economies and the developing countries as a group. In the world at large, the macroeconomic imbalances that have impeded the struggle against unemployment and poverty in a large number of countries have increasingly been brought under control.

The past few years have demonstrated that the present overall economic environment provides an opportunity for most countries to generate self-sustaining impulses towards national economic growth. Faced with this encouraging prospect, Governments confront two challenges. The first is to translate this growth into reductions in unemployment and poverty. At the same time, policy makers need to ensure that the growth impulses themselves are not short-circuited or derailed.

DEVELOPED ECONOMIES

In the developed economies, the cyclic upswing in economic activity lost some momentum in the course of 1995. The slow-down in Australia, Canada, New Zealand, the United Kingdom of Great Britain and Northern Ireland and the United States of America was not unexpected, as those countries were the first to emerge from the previous recession. In continental Europe, however, the recovery of 1994 and early 1995 virtually stalled in late 1995. Indeed, there was a significant drop in activity at that time in several countries, including Belgium, France, Germany, Sweden and Switzerland. At the same time, after four years of almost no growth in output, the Japanese economy has started showing signs of recovery (see table II.1).

Economic activity has been growing more slowly in the current recovery than during the previous two cyclical expansions. This sluggish pattern could be attributed partly to policies. Governments and central banks have given the highest priority to achieving and maintaining a stable macroeconomic environment and thus have adopted a cautious economic stance.

In countries whose previous recession is further behind them, such as Canada, the United Kingdom and the United States, tighter monetary policy had already been initiated in 1994 by the central banks in order to forestall the overheating of the economy and the strengthening of inflationary expectations. At the same time, the marked rise in interest rates on world capital markets that followed the economic upswing in most industrialized countries in 1994 made itself felt; but market interest rates turned around again at the beginning of 1995. None the less, owing to the usual lag, they provided little stimulus to economic growth last year. Except for Japan, where the Government put together a spending package of record size in September 1995, fiscal policy has been directed at curtailing budget deficits. At least in the short term, this will act as a brake on demand.

The flagging of the upswing in the course of 1995 can be attributed to several factors, besides the tighter policy stances noted above. In Japan, the size of the yen's appreciation in the first months of last year, the continuing need to absorb the losses from fallen land and stock prices in the corporate sector and a weakness of consumer confidence are considered major reasons why the massive fiscal policy stimuli, coupled with record low interest rates, failed to ignite the economy until well into 1995; thus, stagnation persisted much longer than expected. In continental Europe, there were currency turbulences in

Table II.1.
MAJOR INDUSTRIALIZED COUNTRIES: QUARTERLY INDICATORS, 1994-1995

	1994 quarters				1995 quarters			
	I	II	III	IV	I	II	III	IV
	Growth of gross domestic product (GDP)[a] (percentage change in seasonally adjusted data from preceding quarter)							
Canada	4.0	6.8	4.7	5.9	1.1	-0.8	2.1	0.8
France	3.6	5.3	3.2	3.6	2.8	0.4	0.4	-1.6
Germany	4.8	5.0	2.5	2.5	1.0	4.4	0.4	-1.6
Italy	1.2	4.0	5.6	-0.1	5.6	-0.2	7.6	-3.6
Japan	3.2	0.7	3.5	-4.2	0.5	2.6	2.3	3.6
United Kingdom	4.0	5.2	3.9	2.7	1.5	1.9	2.3	2.3
United States	2.5	4.8	3.6	3.2	0.6	0.5	3.6	0.5
Total	3.1	3.9	3.6	1.2	1.2	1.4	2.8	0.7
	Unemployment rate[b] (percentage of total labour force)							
Canad	10.9	10.6	10.1	9.7	9.6	9.5	9.5	9.4
France	12.4	12.4	12.2	12.1	11.8	11.6	11.4	11.6
Germany	8.6	8.6	8.3	8.1	8.1	8.2	8.3	8.4
Italy	11.7	12.5	11.1	11.4	12.2	12.2	12.1	12.1
Japan	2.8	2.8	3.0	2.9	2.9	3.1	3.2	3.3
United Kingdom	9.9	9.8	9.5	9.0	8.7	8.8	8.7	8.6
United States	6.5	6.1	5.9	5.5	5.5	5.6	5.6	5.5
Total	7.3	7.2	6.9	6.7	6.7	6.8	6.8	6.8
	Growth of consumer prices[c] (percentage change from preceding quarter)							
Canada	-1.8	-1.5	2.2	1.1	4.4	2.9	1.1	0.0
France	1.8	2.2	0.7	1.9	2.2	1.8	1.4	2.2
Germany	5.4	2.8	1.4	0.7	3.1	2.1	1.4	-0.3
Italy	5.1	2.7	3.3	4.4	7.0	5.6	5.7	5.4
Japan	0.7	1.5	-1.1	2.3	-2.2	1.5	-1.1	0.0
United Kingdom	0.7	7.3	0.0	2.8	3.6	7.3	1.2	0.5
United States	2.5	2.5	3.6	1.9	3.5	3.5	1.7	2.1
Total	2.2	2.5	2.4	2.1	2.3	3.2	1.2	1.4

Source: UN/DESIPA, based on data of International Monetary Fund (IMF), Organisation for Economic Cooperation and Development (OECD) and national authorities (includes revisions of GDP series, as of 30 April 1996).

a Expressed at annual rate (total is weighted average with weights being annual GDP valued at 1988 prices and exchange rates).

b Seasonally adjusted data as standardized by OECD.

c Expressed at annual rate.

spring 1995, which were at least partly induced by uncertainty about the future of major economic policy parameters in the run-up to Economic and Monetary Union (EMU). These turbulences clouded the economic picture and may have dampened investment activity.

Nevertheless, the late 1995-early 1996 decline in economic activity has likely been a mid-cycle dip rather than the onset of a new recession. The distinct fall in policy-determined as well as long-term interest rates in the course of last year, the fading of the effects of the 1995 currency swings in Europe, and the fall in the exchange rate of the yen since late summer of 1995 have given grounds for expecting that economic activity in the developed countries will pick up gradually during 1996 and show moderate growth at a rate of around 2.5 per cent through 1997. North America, Europe and Japan are likely to follow a similar pattern, though the acceleration in Japanese activity is arriving earlier than in the United States and even earlier than in Europe. Hence, for the first time in many years, all major countries may show a relatively synchronized expansion.

The recovery in the developed economies will continue to be supported by buoyant exports to many developing countries. Indeed, the role of the developing economies as a source of growth for the developed countries has increased steadily.

The increase in real gross domestic product (GDP) in the industrialized countries, although more synchronized, will nevertheless remain quite low. The Western European economy is forecast to grow almost $1\frac{1}{2}$ per cent in 1996, while Japan and the United States are expected to see growth rates of about 2 per cent (see annex table A.2). Indeed, in the United States, it would be unlikely for the monetary authorities or the financial markets to allow much faster economic growth. Moreover, in Europe, fiscal policy will remain tight in order to meet the Maastricht criteria for monetary union, while in Japan, a shift from a stimulative to a neutral fiscal stance cannot be excluded in the remainder of 1996 or 1997 given the widening budget deficit, which is already relatively high as a percentage GDP compared with most other industrialized countries (see annex table A.8).

With moderate growth, consumer price inflation is likely to remain under 2.5 per cent during 1996 (see annex table A.7). This rate of inflation is roughly in line with the long-run target for inflation that is being followed by the major central banks.

A particular feature of the present cycle is that increased output has not led to commensurate increases in real wages. This has been one of the major factors involved in holding inflation down to its present low levels. Yet, this restraint in real wage increases means that consumer spending has not played as large a role in stimulating economic growth as in previous cycles. It also raises questions as to whether businesses that might be encouraged to invest by restrained growth in labour costs will in time be discouraged instead by sluggish consumer demand. In short, contemporary labour-market conditions make households cautious, reduce "consumer sentiment" and hold back the growth of consumption expenditure which accounts for roughly two thirds of GDP in the developed economies.

Persistently high unemployment and growing income inequality are related concerns for policy makers. Indeed, only in the United States and the United

Figure II.1.
CONSUMER CONFIDENCE IN SEVEN MAJOR ECONOMIES

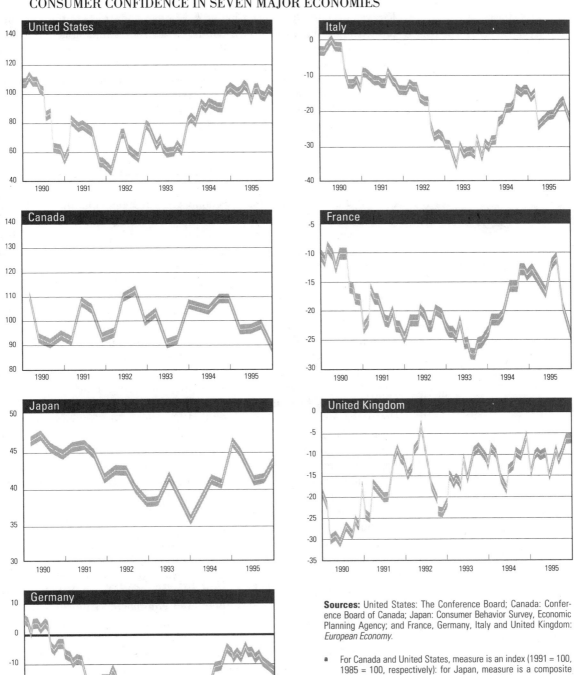

Sources: United States: The Conference Board; Canada: Conference Board of Canada; Japan: Consumer Behavior Survey, Economic Planning Agency; and France, Germany, Italy and United Kingdom: *European Economy*.

a For Canada and United States, measure is an index (1991 = 100, 1985 = 100, respectively): for Japan, measure is a composite index (percentage): for others, measure shows percentage of respondents to a survey who expect an inprovement minus percentage of those who expect a deterioration.

Kingdom, among the seven major developed countries, is the current unemployment rate below its average of the 1980s. The situation is particularly serious in Western Europe where the unemployment rate rose from 8 per cent in 1991 to 11 per cent in 1994 from which point it has barely receded (see annex table A.6). Even in the United States, where the 1995 unemployment rate fell to 5.6 per cent and in Japan, where open unemployment is still quite low compared with that in other countries, a slow growth of wages and a fear of unemployment among those working have come to characterize much of the labour market.

Dimensions of economic performance

In 1995, the United States economy grew by 2 per cent, the slowest increase since the recession year of 1991. After a slow-down in late 1995 and early 1996, caused mainly by weaker consumer spending, lower levels of inventory accumulation and a decline in government expenditures, the economy appears to be moving forward again, albeit at a modest rate. Inventory correction, which was a major drag on growth through much of 1995, has likely run its course. Consumption growth is expected to return to a level close to income growth, at 2 per cent in real terms. Although consumer confidence is down from levels reached in 1995, it is still relatively high (see figure II.1).

Housing has been responding to the declines in interest rates that have taken place over the period to early 1996. The boost from these earlier rate drops may fade, however, fade in the course of the year. Indeed, long-term rates have been subject to upward pressures since January 1996. Business investment has been the main driver of the recovery since the last recession. However, capital spending slowed significantly in late 1995 and is not likely to improve much this year. Nevertheless, it could grow faster than the overall economy. At the same time, exports will likely continue to make strong gains, while imports are expected to slow along with the deceleration in equipment investment. Hence, in 1996, on a net basis, international trade may contribute to growth for the first time since 1991. All told, the United States economy is likely to be on course for sustainable non-inflationary growth at an annual rate of about 2 per cent through 1997.

After recording growth rates of close to 5 per cent in 1994, the economy of Canada slowed markedly to 2 per cent in 1995 owing to the tightening of interest rates. The major source of growth was exports which offset falling final domestic demand. The only domestic demand component that showed relative vigour was investment in machinery and equipment. The external sector and equipment investment are likely to continue making a considerable contribution during the next two years. Besides, a firming trend in jobs and falling interest rates could lead to gains in consumer spending and housing activity. Hence, a gradual increase of growth could be expected.

The slow-down in Australia, unlike that in Canada, was less abrupt. The main factors slowing the economy last year were a deceleration of private fixed investment and inventory correction. The economy seems to be further slowing down slightly in 1996, mainly owing to high interest rates and government spending cuts. It is likely to pick up slightly in 1997, with investment and net exports being the main sources of renewed growth.

Japan is pulling out of the longest economic slump in its post-war history. The combination of low interest rates, a fiscal boost and currency depreciation helped put the economy on a recovery path. GDP grew significantly in the last three quarters of 1993, ending at a rate of 3.6 per cent in the last quarter (see table II.1).

Growth in Japan has accelerated despite a shrinking in its trade surplus. Hence (as was not the case in the past), domestic demand, rather than exports, is leading the expansion. Government spending from a record fiscal package announced last September underpinned much of the growth in late 1995 and early 1996. The impact of this fiscal stimulus will recede significantly towards the end of 1996 as almost 60 per cent of total spending is to be concentrated in the first half of the year. However, the growth of economic activity is becoming more broadly based, as increases in private capital formation and consumer spending appear to be continuing. The private sector has begun to respond to repeated government attempts to revive the economy, thereby providing some assurance that the recovery will not flag once the public spending diminishes. At the same time, Japan has yet to overcome historically high unemployment, weak land prices and, most important, an overhang of bad property loans that are the legacy of the speculative bubble of the late 1980s.

The growth of economic activity in Europe slowed sharply in the second half of 1995 and into early 1996. The recovery from the 1993 recession had largely depended on exports and an early-cycle increase in inventory investment. Subsequently, as final domestic demand remained relatively weak, the slowing in external sources of demand and the deceleration in inventory-building caused the slow-down. Initially, the weakness was concentrated in Germany and France and other countries whose currencies remained closely tied to the deutsche mark.

The easing in both short- and long-term interest rates should encourage a recovery in activity from mid-1996 on, with internal demand increasingly becoming the driving force of the expansion. As was not the case in several previous years, there is likely to be relatively little difference in the growth rates of European economies between this year and 1997. Despite the high level of slackness, Europe's growth is not expected to rebound strongly because fiscal policy is scheduled to stay tight as countries prepare for EMU. Weak growth will keep inflation below 3 per cent and unemployment is likely to recede only marginally if at all.

In France and Germany, the growth of exports and private investment, which sustained demand in 1994 and early 1995, slowed down significantly in the second half of 1995, while private consumption remained sluggish. With inventory drag fading, economic activity seems to have stabilized in the first half of 1996. Reflecting the weak activity at the beginning of the year, GDP growth is likely to be only about $1\text{-}1\frac{1}{2}$ per cent in 1996 and then to accelerate slightly into 1997. In both countries, conditions for an upswing in investment look favourable as profits remain high while interest rates have substantially decreased. In Germany, rationalization, rather than expansion, will continue to be the most important motive for investment, as there continues to be widespread concern over high labour costs. Owing to the soft labour-market conditions, as well as fiscal consolidation measures, consumption growth is likely to be moderate in 1996 and 1997 in these countries. Exports are not likely to make meaningful contributions to growth owing to the strength of their currencies and sluggish foreign demand.

Strong currencies and the slow-down in Europe dampened real GDP growth at the turn of 1995 in Austria, Belgium, Denmark, the Netherlands and Switzerland. Their recovery is likely to proceed in line with that in Germany, with stronger impetus coming from domestic demand.

Contrary to these developments, some of the countries that had earlier undergone a depreciation of their currencies relative to the deutsche mark continued to show solid, albeit slower, GDP growth. In the case of Italy, Spain and Portugal, the fading of the boost from previous devaluations has been partly offset by rising domestic demand as their currencies appreciated and, except in Italy, interest rates moved lower. Indeed, while export growth has been declining, investment is still strong and household spending is picking up. By contrast, currency appreciation in Sweden is undermining growth as falling exports coincide with subdued domestic demand.

The economic upturn in the United Kingdom, another country whose currency had depreciated earlier, was also driven by exports in 1994 and early 1995. Since then, export growth has been held back by a strengthening of the pound, particularly against the deutsche mark. At the same time, there has been a healthy rebound in consumer spending and housing investment, supported by steady growth in real disposable incomes, lower interest rates and, to a lesser extent, a modest reduction in taxation. In addition to already strong investment in machinery and equipment, there is likely to be a pick-up in non-residential construction. Thus, the British recovery is definitely becoming more domestic-based.

Macroeconomic policy stances

Having more confidence that inflation has been brought under control, policy makers in the developed economies have turned their attention to trying to ensure that non-inflationary growth is sustained. This led to a general easing of monetary policy during 1995 and early 1996, when the developed economies paused. Besides, there was a significant decline in market-determined interest rates. By mid-1996, however, amid the signs of improving growth, monetary policy will likely have entered a period of stability; and if the pick-up in growth is sustained, a modest round of tightening through 1997, as well as an upward move in long-term interest rates, could not be excluded. At the same time, fiscal stances remain restrictive in Europe and North America, as deficit reduction policies continue to receive most attention, while in Japan the effects of the earlier fiscal boost to the economy are probably coming to an end.

The monetary authorities of the United States have sought to fine-tune monetary policy, so as to sustain the expansion, yet avoid the inflationary pressures that a more robust rate of growth might produce. As the United States economy has enjoyed since early 1991 both an extended period of positive growth and low inflation, the conduct of monetary policy can be judged to have been very successful. The Federal Reserve raised short-term interest rates a number of times in 1994 to slow the economy. Then from July 1995 through February 1996, when it judged that the economy was decelerating too quickly, the Federal Reserve gradually lowered the federal funds rate 0.75 percentage points to

5.25 per cent. The current low inflation environment has allowed the Federal Reserve the virtually unprecedented move of relaxing monetary policy during a period in which a recession is neither present nor foreseen.

In response to the drop in rates, the United States economy appears to be picking up in the first half of 1996 prompting the monetary authorities to put on hold any further easing. At the same time, there have been some concerns that the current growth rate is too low. It has been argued that the economy can grow faster without inflation accelerating, since (as was not the case in the past) there seems to be little wage inflation at the current rate of unemployment. Hence, it has been suggested that interest rates should be eased further. One consideration that militates against this conclusion is that the new method of measuring GDP growth results in a lower figure than would have obtained using the old method (see introduction to statistical annex). Also, some argue that it is still too early to make judgements as to whether structural changes in the United States economy will allow faster growth than before without risking an increase in inflation.

Fiscal policy has already achieved a reduction in the United States budget deficit in the last three years. At the same time, the budget negotiations for the fiscal year that ends in September 1996 failed to reach a conclusion until April 1996. Agreement has still not been reached on how to balance the budget in the longer term. In the forecast presented in this *Survey*, fiscal policy in the United States is assumed to be essentially neutral in the sense of not imparting an impulse to economic growth.

In the face of a slowing Canadian economy, the Bank of Canada has aggressively eased monetary policy, cutting its key funding rate by 1.25 percentage points since end-October 1995 and leaving monetary conditions at their most accommodative since early 1994. Monetary relief is important as the economy is still weak and as further major fiscal reductions are planned. That is, fiscal policy has been set to achieve a balanced budget in 1998, as against the deficit of 4 per cent of GDP in 1995 and deficits of higher percentages of GDP in each of the two previous years. Indeed, the contractionary effect of fiscal policy in Canada is relatively greater than the much discussed fiscal consolidation in Europe.

Fiscal tightening is also planned in Australia. Yet the inflation picture and the balance-of-payments deficit make it difficult to ease monetary policy there. In New Zealand, after the successful implementation of fiscal consolidation, income taxes will be cut for low- to medium-income working families starting in July 1996. Meanwhile, monetary policy, which tightened at the end of 1994, will stay restrictive. According to the monetary authorities, the continuation of strong growth may bring the inflation rate to the top of the 0-2 per cent target band that the Reserve Bank of New Zealand is required by law to meet.

As already noted, the Japanese authorities have undertaken several demand stimulus measures of unprecedented magnitude in the past several years to alleviate the difficult economic situation. In 1995, the Government introduced three additional emergency fiscal packages; the last one, announced in September, amounted to $132 billion. Once the September fiscal package is completed, the Government may be inhibited from taking further expansionary measures in 1996. Given a sharp deterioration in public finances and the ageing population that will add considerably to the fiscal burden of pensions in future years, the Government is likely to restart fiscal consolidation as soon as possible. The increase in the consumption tax scheduled in 1997 is the first step towards this goal. The economic recovery expected in 1996 and 1997 should also help the consolidation through producing an increase in tax revenues. The public debt has risen relative to GDP because of the deficits incurred in implementing the fiscal packages announced since 1993. This now leaves much less room for fiscal manoeuvre.

The Bank of Japan lowered the official discount rate from 1.75 to 0.5 per cent during 1995. The challenge for the monetary authorities in 1996 is to carefully guide market interest rates towards support of economic growth; that is to say, the sustainability of this recovery should be assured before deciding on the timing of any changes in monetary conditions.

Expectations for economic recovery in 1996 and 1997 have already pushed up long-term interest rates in Japan. This may dampen the still fragile revival of business investment and depress residential investment, which is now showing relatively high growth. On the other hand, there is concern about how long the official discount rate should be kept at the lowest level in the post-war era. As of now, this level seems justifiable and necessary to boost private investment as well as to aid the financial sector, which has been forced to absorb the cost of a wave of bad loans. Besides, consumer price increases are about zero, while the GDP deflator is still falling. In the course of the next two years, however, the recovery is expected to lead the monetary authorities to tighten the currently loose monetary policy.

It is increasingly argued in Japan that deregulation and liberalization of the economy should proceed further to accelerate and smooth the recovery. It is deemed of special importance to introduce more market-based and competition-enhancing policies to the non-tradables sector, whose productivity growth has lagged. The challenge for the authorities is to design policies that would improve the supply capabilities of both the financial and the non-financial sector without a further worsening of the fiscal situation.

In 1995 and early 1996, in most European countries, faced with a rate of growth much slower than the authorities had expected, monetary policy was eased. Initially, interest rates were cut in several steps in Germany as well as in Austria, Belgium, Denmark, France, Ireland, the Netherlands and Switzerland, countries whose monetary policy usually shadows that of Germany, in order to maintain a stable exchange rate against the deutsche mark. The declines have been very significant. For instance, in Germany, the reductions have brought the Bundesbank discount and Lombard rates to levels last reached in December 1987, while in France, the intervention rate of the Banque de France has come down to 3.3 per cent, a level not seen in more than 30 years. Also, in Finland and Norway, monetary policy is assuming an increasingly stimulative stance owing to a very benign inflation outlook.

Monetary policy in several other European countries had been kept tight somewhat longer in order to counter inflationary tendencies and stabilize the exchange rate. By late 1995 or early 1996, however, more positive price movements as well as limited currency appreciation allowed Portugal, Spain and Sweden to begin cutting interest rates. At the same time, in Italy, monetary policy continues to be very tight. Despite official interest rate declines in most developed economies, the Bank of Italy has not loosened monetary policy, as inflation is still running high and fiscal consolidation prospects remain uncertain. Key official interest rates have remained unchanged since May 1995 and as of April 1996 were about 2.5 percentage points above their level in July 1994.

In the United Kingdom, in order to prevent inflationary pressures resulting from relatively fast economic growth, the base rate of the Bank of England was raised in three steps from 5.25 per cent in September 1994 to 6.75 per cent in February 1995. From then until December 1995, a "wait and see" policy on interest rates was maintained as the economy grew more slowly than in 1994, but still above 2 per cent per annum. It was unclear whether the inflation target (2.5 per cent or less) that was set by the Government would be met. The pause ended on 13 December 1995. Between then and April 1996, the base rate was reduced in three steps to 6.0 per cent based on signs that the slowdown in growth might be deeper and last longer than had previously been expected by the Government, as well as on an improvement in the probability of achieving the inflation target. Besides, falling German interest rates lessened the downside risks to sterling. After 75 basis points of monetary easing in four months, the most likely prospect is for an extended period of interest rate stability.

Overall, the monetary stance in Europe will most likely not be changed substantially through 1997. However, although monetary policy is clearly accommodative, the level of real rates may still be too high to permit a self-sustaining recovery, especially in the context of fiscal retrenchment. Indeed, the thrust of fiscal policy in Europe will remain tight in 1996-1997 as countries have been taking steps to put their public finances on course in order to meet the budgetary criteria under the Maastricht Treaty for entering the single European currency area at the start of 1999. A further, although less severe, deficit reduction is planned for 1996 in many countries, including Belgium, Denmark, Finland, France, Greece, Italy, Portugal, Spain, and Sweden. Because these budget cuts are smaller in relation to GDP than those previously effected, and because German fiscal policy will be slightly stimulative, the fiscal impulse in Western Europe as a whole is likely to be less contractionary in 1996 than in the previous year. However, greater fiscal tightening will be seen in 1997, the critical judgement year for meeting the Maastricht criteria for monetary union. This implies a continued bias towards fiscal constriction in Europe.

THE ECONOMIES IN TRANSITION

In 1995, six years after the process of transformation had begun for the countries of Central and Eastern Europe and four years after the process had begun for CIS and the Baltic States, a fairly clear picture emerged of macroeconomic trends in the very disparate group of countries whose common feature is, indeed, this transition.

In most countries of Central and Eastern Europe, the sharpest declines in output took place in 1991, and 1993 was the first year of positive growth (see annex table A.3). The exceptions were Poland which saw the sharpest decline in output in 1990, but positive growth in 1992, and Bulgaria, which first saw output grow in 1994. All these economies grew in 1995. Only two had relatively low growth in output — Hungary at 2 per cent and Bulgaria at 2.5 per cent. All the other countries grew at considerably higher rates than any of the major developed economies and appear set to repeat this relatively favourable performance in 1996. Output growth was restored in the Baltic States in 1994 and, with the exception of Latvia in 1995, those States continued to grow in 1995 and are forecast to grow in 1996.

In CIS, the rate of economic decline slowed appreciably in 1995. It had earlier been expected that 1996 would be the first year of economic growth but, based on recent data for the Russian Federation, this now seems quite uncertain (see below).

Central and Eastern European transition economies (CEETEs)

Of all the Central and Eastern European transition economies (CEETE), and indeed of all the economies in transition, Poland was the only one that by 1995 had come close to regaining its pre-transformation (1989) output level (see table II.2). Even after the strong growth forecast for 1996, all other countries will still be more than 10 per cent below their output level of 1989. Poland shifted rapidly towards market-based decision-making immediately following the beginning of the transformation and is now seeing the results in the form of high growth, improved domestic balances and substantial exports. Perhaps even more significant, the composition and quality of production in Poland, and increasingly in all the CEETEs, are also much improved.

In the CEETEs, the private sector has been rapidly expanding. The overall business environment has improved because of the reduction in inflation, the liberalization of prices, a revival of intraregional trade and stability in policies even after elections produced changes in government.

Table II.2.
REAL GROSS DOMESTIC PRODUCT (GDP) IN CENTRAL AND EASTERN EUROPE, 1990-1996

Index: 1989=100							
	1990	1991	1992	1993	1994	1995[a]	1996[b]
Albania	90.0	65.7	59.3	65.8	70.7	75.0	78.8
Bulgaria	90.9	83.9	79.1	76.2	77.9	79.8	82.4
Czech Republic	8.8	84.7	79.3	78.6	80.7	84.5	89.1
Hungary	96.5	85.2	82.6	82.0	84.4	86.0	88.4
Poland	88.4	82.3	84.3	87.6	91.9	98.6	105.8
Romania	91.8	80.0	72.9	73.9	76.5	81.7	86.5
Slovakia	97.5	83.4	77.6	74.4	78.0	83.8	88.2

Source: UN/DESIPA and Economic Commission for Europe (ECE).
   [a]   Partly estimated.
   [b]   Forecast, based in part on Project LINK.

The positive economic growth rates did not lead to commensurate rises in aggregate employment as productivity increased. Real wages have also risen, but often by less than the increases in productivity. The renewal and expansion of the capital stock and improvements in training and management made possible the increases in productivity that were evident when output expanded.

The expansion in output appears to be broadly based with industry, services and agriculture all growing. Domestic producers of intermediate and investment goods appear to be benefiting from the upturn in fixed investment, particularly in machinery and in the housing sector, while producers of consumer goods appear to be faced with relatively greater competition from imports, particularly in those countries where there has been a significant appreciation of the exchange rate.

Rising investment reflects growing confidence in the stability of the macroeconomic and regulatory environment. It may also reflect export opportunities associated with deepening links with the European Union. With greater macroeconomic stability, domestic and foreign investors are increasingly attracted to the combination in many CEETEs of low labour costs and large, underutilized supplies of skilled labour.

The balance between the demand components underpinning GDP growth has thus shifted from an earlier, almost exclusive reliance on exports to faster-growing consumption and particularly investment.

Inflation has receded further in the area, although rates are still in the double digits in most of the CEETEs. Contributing factors included a slow-down in the growth of nominal wages which, together with higher productivity, has reduced the pressure from unit labour costs; currency appreciation; and exceptionally favourable movements in seasonal food prices.[1] Prospects are for inflation to decelerate further: output and productivity are set to continue rising, wage increases remain moderate, producer prices have increased less than consumer prices and ongoing privatization should increase competitive pressures on prices.

In some countries, however, there are low inflationary pressures coming from rapid growth in output and from the increase in money supply that accompanied substantial capital inflows, attracted by interest rate differentials with Western Europe. In the Czech Republic, Hungary and Poland, the removal of some of the remaining exchange controls facilitated these inflows. As they did not wish to lower interest rates, affected countries had to allow the continuing moderate appreciation of their currencies. One way to achieve this was through a gradual reduction of the cumulative monthly rate of the pre-announced nominal devaluation of the currency, which thus appreciates in real terms. Another of these measures was to widen the band within which the central bank aims to keep the exchange rate.[2] Some central banks also engaged in open market operations to reduce the impact on the money supply.

Official unemployment rates remain at rather high levels ranging from 16 per cent in Poland to 4 per cent in the Czech Republic, although employment growth is picking up.[3] For countries with high shares of employment in agriculture (Albania, Bulgaria, Poland and Romania), a substantial decline in aggregate unemployment will only come about if the labour-shedding expected in this sector is more than offset by the rapid expansion of employment in indus-

[1] A detailed account of these developments has been presented in ECE, *Economic Bulletin for Europe*, vol. 47 (1995); (United Nations publication, Sales No. E.95.II.E.24).

[2] The Czech Republic, Hungary, Poland and Slovakia used this policy tool. In the Polish case, the band has been widened from plus and minus 2 to 7 per cent; on 28 February 1996, the Czech National Bank widened its band from 0.5 to 7.5 per cent.

[3] In fact, aggregate employment was rising, according to official estimates, in 1995 in the Czech Republic, Poland and Romania. In the Romanian case, the rate of unemployment declined from 11 per cent in 1994 to 9 per cent at end-1995 (National Commission of Statistics of Romania, *Monthly Statistical Bulletin*, No. 12 (December 1995), p. XIX).

try and services. In the remaining countries, extended economic growth should be capable of reducing the unemployment rates to single digits.

In 1995, privatization continued to be aggressively pursued in the CEETEs and receipts often exceeded the original targets. Hungary, in particular, sold practically all of its larger telecommunications companies to foreign corporations and received $3.24 billion. It had originally expected the sale to net $1.54 billion.[4] In Bulgaria and Romania, measures were taken to expedite the privatization process,[5] in response to the sluggish implementation of mass privatization laws decided upon previously.[6]

Some CEETEs are seeking to accelerate privatization in the banking sector. With many domestic banks struggling with debt-ridden portfolios, potential demand for their shares when privatized is rather weak. One of the most urgent reasons for privatizing the commercial banks remains the expectation that this will bring greater efficiency and better business practices to the sector.

The policy thrust of the CEETEs towards full market economies is well reflected in their economic integration initiatives. Thus, in November 1995, the Czech Republic became the first transition economy to become a member of the Organisation for Economic Cooperation and Development (OECD), followed by Hungary in April 1996. A major objective of many of the CEETEs goes much further, namely, to meet the conditions for joining the European Union (EU). After a successful conclusion of the Intergovernmental Conference of EU — in late 1997 perhaps — EU negotiations with individual countries seeking entry might be started.[7] In itself, this will give a particular direction to future policy in the CEETEs — sharp limitations on inflation, budget deficits and exchange-rate instability — while working rapidly towards a relatively liberalized environment that allows the state sector only a limited direct economic role. Already by December 1995, the Czech Republic, Hungary, Poland and Slovakia had declared the convertibility of their currencies to be at the level required for accordance with article VIII of the International Monetary Fund (IMF) Articles of Agreement.

The Baltic States

After several years of consistent economic policy and relative political stability, the three Baltic States have also made considerable progress towards becoming market economies. Estonia and Lithuania exhibited stable, if modest, growth of GDP since 1994 (see table A.3), while Latvia's tentative recovery was disrupted by the banking crisis of 1995. As a result, contrary to earlier forecasts, Latvia's GDP declined in 1995. Nevertheless, GDP is expected to grow in all three economies in 1996.

Recovery of output is increasingly driven by internal consumption, fuelled by both investment and consumer demand. For the Baltic countries, this is especially important, since during the early stages of transition, their growth was in a major part predicated on the re-export of Russian oil, metals and raw materials (30-45 per cent of total exports of Estonia and Lithuania) and on off-shore services for Russian capital (Latvia). Neither of the two could provide a stable long-term foundation for sustainable growth. The opportunities for re-exports evaporated with the depletion of accumulated stocks and with the

---

[4] *Népszabadság* (Budapest), 19 January 1996, p.1.

[5] In Bulgaria, the Government prepared major tax breaks for privatized companies on 13 April 1996. It is envisaged that companies that are at least two-thirds privately owned will receive full relief on profit taxes for the first three years, followed by 50 per cent relief for the following two years (see *Duma* (Sofia), 14 April 1996, p.1).

[6] The Bulgarian Parliament on 4 April voted to extend the deadline for selling privatization vouchers. The initial deadline was 8 April, but legislators decided to extend it by one month because so far vouchers have been bought by only 18.4 per cent of those eligible to do so (see *Duma* (Sofia), 5 April 1996, p. 3). The deadline for Romanian citizens for registering their company preferences, which was originally December 1995, was extended to end of March 1996. As of mid-February, only 28 per cent of the citizens had registered their company preferences (see Romania. *Economic Newsletter*, vol. 5, No. 4 (January-March 1996), p. 2).

[7] In an apparent change of policy, the European Union intends to conclude negotiations with the aspiring countries separately and not as a group. This was announced by the President of the Commission of the European Communities, Mr. Jacques Santer, after his trips to the Czech Republic and Hungary extending from 3 to 5 April 1996 *(see Magyar Hirlap* (Budapest), 6 April 1996, p. 1).

Russian Federation's instituting much tougher customs control on its borders. Most important, however, was the almost complete realignment of Russian internal and export prices for oil, metals and other previously lucrative re-export items.

Latvia had taken advantage of another kind of temporarily beneficial, but ultimately detrimental, opportunity. In their quest to make Latvian banks a depository for Russian (and other CIS) offshore capital, the banks offered inordinately high rates of interest on deposits, thus attracting substantial capital inflows. Non-residential short-term deposits constituted about half of total bank deposits. Operating under a very limited supervision by the monetary authorities, the banks pursued a risky lending policy by, for example, not securing their loans with adequate collateral. As a result, a substantial portfolio of bad debts was accumulated. This kind of exposure and the resulting difficulties borne by the banking system proved detrimental to overall economic activity in the country.

Inflation remains disappointingly high in all three countries. Prospects for its significant reduction are remote owing to the forthcoming liberalization of certain sectors (such as utilities in Estonia). Imports, in particular those of capital equipment, are growing rapidly, while exports are constrained by overvaluation of national currencies. The real exchange rate in each country has appreciated considerably since the beginning of the reform; based on consumer prices, the real exchange rate of the Estonian kroon vis-à-vis the United States dollar has appreciated by over 200 per cent from mid-1992 to the end of 1994, and Latvia's lat and Lithuania's litas by nearly 350 per cent.[8]

[8] Tapio O. Saavalainen, *Stabilization in the Baltic Countries: A Comparative Analysis,* IMF Working Paper WP/95/44 (Washington, D.C., IMF, April 1995), p. 18.

Is the Russian federation's economy growing?

By late 1995, the Russian Federation seemed well on its way to macroeconomic stabilization and recovery of output. Some experts, both in the Russian federation and outside, even predicted that the country might attain very rapid growth as early as 1997.[9] These assessments were based on a number of positive developments in the country's economic performance and on the implementation of the Government's economic programme during 1995.

[9] See, for example, OECD *The Russian Federation, 1995,* OECD Economic Surveys (Paris, OECD, 1995), p.23.

Indeed, for the first time since the start of transition, macroeconomic stabilization appeared to be holding consistently. There was no repeat of the negative experience of the earlier years of reform, when progress in reducing inflation during the early part of a year was each time negated by a surge of inflation in the autumn months following a burst of credit creation in late summer and early autumn. In 1995, consumer price inflation was 131 per cent (December over December) compared with 220 per cent in 1994 (see table II.3). In February and March of 1996, monthly inflation was kept at 2.8 per cent — which implies an annual rate of 40 per cent if continued for the year as a whole — the lowest figure since the start of transition.

Containing inflation has been the direct result of the relatively tight monetary policy of the central Government. The federal budget deficit was brought below 3 per cent of GDP compared with almost 11 per cent in 1994. In addition, over the last two years, the Government has significantly reduced the

Table XI.3.

ECONOMIC INDICATORS OF THE SUCCESSOR STATES OF THE UNION OF SOVIET SOCIALIST REPUBLICS (USSR)

	GDP					Consumer prices				
	1991	1992	1993	1994	1995	1991	1992	1993	1994	1995
Armenia	-8.8	-52.3	-14.6	5.5	10.3	140	730	10 900	4 960	25
Azerbaijan	-0.7	-22.6	-23.1	-21.9	-17.4	110	910	1 130	1 660	85
Belarus	-1.2	-9.6	-10.6	-15.8	-16.0	100	970	1 190	2 220	250
Georgia	-20.1	-40.3	-39.4	-30.0	2.4	80	..	..	..	58
Kazakhstan	-11.8	-13.0	-12.9	-24.6	-8.9	80	1 510	1 660	1 880	61
Kyrgyzstan	-7.8	-15.9	-15.5	-20.1	-6.2	110	850	1 210	280	32
Republic of Moldova	-17.5	-29.1	-1.2	-31.2	-3.0	110	1 110	1 180	490	24
Russian Federation[a]	-5.0	-14.5	-8.7	-12.6	-4.0	160	2 510	840	220	131
Tajikistan	..	..	-17.3	-21.3	-12.4	110	910	2 140	240	1 390
Turkmenistan	..	..	..	-20.0	-15.0	110	770	1 630	2 710	..
Ukraine	-11.6	-13.7	-14.2	-23.0	-11.8	90	2 000	10 160	400	182
Uzbekistan	-0.5	-11.1	-2.4	-3.5	-1.0	100	410	1 230	1 550	77

Source: CIS Statistical Committee (1995 data for the Republic of Moldova, Kyrgyzstan, Turkmenistan and Uzbekistan are ECE estimates).
Note: The symbol ".." indicates that data are unavailable.
a   Consumer prices for the Russian Federation show December-to-December changes.

inflationary financing of the budget deficit, in particular by abandoning the traditional reliance on massive credits from the Central Bank of Russia. Instead, the Government is selling bonds on the rapidly expanding market for government securities and drawing extensively on loans from international financial institutions. The financial instruments offered in the domestic market were diversified, and steps were taken to encourage banks to channel their funds into the government securities market. To this end, a currency "corridor" was introduced in summer 1995 which by allowing the exchange rate of the rouble to fluctuate only within set limits instead of freely, thus making profits from currency arbitrage significantly less certain. Also, the increase in bank reserve requirements reduced the funds that banks had available for such speculation.

The decline in output, as recorded in national accounts and industrial production data, seemed to finally bottom out in 1995. The officially reported decline in output notwithstanding, it is widely believed that the economy had in reality already been growing through 1995. That is, a major share of output, in particular that produced by unregistered economic activity, was inadequately reflected in the officially reported data.[10]

Indeed, there are many indications — both in published data and from anecdotal evidence — that the economy of the Russian Federation has begun to grow. There were first, tentative signs of growth of output and productivity in

10 In September 1995, the Government approved revised estimates of the Russian Federation's GDP for the years of transition, prepared by a joint Goskomstat-World Bank team. The revised data indicate that the economy has lost about a third of its output (not more than half as previously reported) since 1990. Moreover, estimates of the magnitude of unregistered output, which cover a wide range, when combined with the officially reported output, raise the level of total economic activity to such an extent as to indicate that growth had already begun in 1995.

a number of industries, both in export-oriented sectors (ferrous metals, chemicals and petrochemicals, fuel and energy) and in primarily domestically oriented ones (engineering, metal-processing, automotive). Housing construction was up 9 per cent in 1995, with privately financed construction becoming the prevalent method of supply. By early 1996, private consumption also showed evidence of increase, as reflected in increased retail sales. Also, the dollar value of exports in 1995 grew by 18 per cent, which after strong growth earlier brought the share of exports in total sales of domestically produced goods to 34 per cent.

In sum, even if contraction of output persists in many sectors of the country's economy, prerequisites of the resumption of growth are there and, if growth picks up later in the year, a small positive rate of growth is possible in 1996 (see annex table A.3). What is urgently needed is adequate investment. As shown in chapter VI of the present Survey, domestic saving is estimated to be adequate to provide this investment; but for this potential to become reality, the economy urgently needs stability in its political, regulatory and administrative environment. Uncertainty, in particular political uncertainty, remains the major obstacle to investment and therefore to an immediate start of sustainable economic growth.

At the same time, evidence of an increased confidence in the economic and financial situation could be seen in the rouble exchange rate. The rouble appreciated 72 per cent against the United States dollar in real terms in 1995, while the ratio of domestic currency in circulation to foreign currency reserves grew for the first time since reforms had begun: from 40 to 77 per cent.[11]

This notwithstanding, the social situation remains very difficult, although it appears to be stabilizing. By early 1996, the process of polarization of incomes reportedly paused, while average real incomes resumed growth. Unemployment growth slowed down, although by February 1996 over 6 million, amounting to 8 per cent of the workforce, were out of work and looking for a job. The share of wages in monetary income continued to drop rapidly — from 40 per cent in 1994 to 30 per cent in 1995, while income from business activity grew to 48 per cent. The number of people reportedly living below the poverty line declined 22 per cent during 1995 and by year-end stood at 36 million. Certainly, the social security system is strained. Arrears in payments to pensioners became a major subject of political discussion. The country now has 37 million pensioners, constituting 20 per cent of the population (compared with 18.5 per cent in 1989).

Thus, four years after economic transformation was launched in the Russian Federation, it is obvious that the social and human costs of the transition have been very high. Though specific qualitative indicators could be questioned, or interpreted in different ways, it is beyond doubt not only that significant groups of the population had seen their real incomes plummet, but that their entire established way of life — with its familiar mainstays, such as accessible medical service, reliable social security system, and guaranteed employment — had crumbled around them.

An intense debate goes on in the Russian Federation on whether these costs were an unavoidable, if painful, component of a long-overdue socio-economic reform that will in the end produce positive results, or rather the unforeseen — at least by the proponents of that reform — outcome of a misguided economic

11 *Interfax Daily Business Report*, Moscow, 20 February 1996.

policy. These very issues are being debated as this Survey goes to press in the context of the presidential elections in the Russian Federation.

It would seem that the first viewpoint is broadly correct. Indeed, amid a constant stream of negative data on the socio-economic situation in the country, it is easy to overlook the impressive path already covered in four years towards establishing a more efficient and flexible economic mechanism. The transformation is far from being over, however, and the fluidity of the situation makes for wide margins of error. However, the potential for the long-range resumption of economic growth is unmistakable.

Other countries in the Commonwealth of Independent States (CIS)

The economic situation in the other countries of CIS is uniformly very difficult. Only two CIS countries reported that their economies grew in 1995; however, these being Armenia and Georgia, their expansion was accounted for primarily by a measure of revival of output after a catastrophic decline in earlier years (see table II.3). In Uzbekistan and Kyrgyzstan, the GDP decline is probably bottoming out. In the other CIS countries, aggregate output continued to shrink at an annual rate of approximately 10 per cent or even worse.[12] .

There was a notable weakening of inflation in a number of CIS countries, in particular Armenia, Kyrgyzstan and the Republic of Moldova, owing to rather strict stabilization policies pursued by their Governments. Other countries (Belarus, Tajikistan) continue to experience high inflation.

In Ukraine, the new leadership that took office in summer 1994 in the midst of a prolonged and steadily worsening economic crisis immediately initiated long-overdue economic reforms. The first steps were aimed at containing the mushrooming budget deficit that had been created, in major part, by credit subsidies to State-owned enterprises. Prices were gradually liberalized, basic market institutions began to be introduced, and a privatization programme was finally launched. These measures have broken the country's slide towards hyper-inflation and a disastrous collapse of output and, perhaps more significantly, generated a perception of the return of positive dynamics in economic policy.

In one of the more visible and important results of the new leadership's effort to reform the economy, monthly inflation was brought down from 72 per cent in November 1994 to single digits by the end of 1995. Consumer prices for the whole of 1995 grew 182 per cent (see table II.3). The first months of 1996 saw inflation pick up speed again, but this time it was largely the result of the intentional upward correction in the levels of prices in service and utility sectors aimed at bringing them closer to cost recovery.

Nevertheless, Ukraine's output continues to shrink in 1996, albeit at a slower rate. In 1995, GDP contracted 12 per cent compared with 23 per cent a year earlier. Industrial output fell 11.5 per cent (27 per cent in 1994), while agricultural production fell 4 per cent.[13]

Ukrainian policy makers have chosen to introduce economic transformation measures gradually, and believe that growth of industrial output should remain a major aim of economic policy.[14] That approach was reiterated in major policy declarations made by the country's President in June 1995.

Accordingly, the Government of Ukraine has developed a 20-25 year Pro-

[12] All the caveats about the incompleteness of data on national output in the Russian Federation apply even more to the other CIS countries. National data should be interpreted as reflecting broad orders of magnitude only.

[13] The country's "shadow economy" is estimated to be even larger proportionately than that of the Russian Federation, so officially reported statistics are believed to seriously underreport output.

[14] See H. Boss, "Ukraine: better, but not good enough", mimeograph (Vienna, Vienna Institute for Comparative Economic Studies, 2 March 1996).

Box II.1

EMERGING FROM TURMOIL IN THE FORMER SOCIALIST FEDERAL REPUBLIC OF YUGOSLAVIA

Five years ago, the Socialist Federal Republic of Yugoslavia began to disintegrate. A middle-income developing country and one of the principal leaders in the non-aligned movement, the Socialist Federal Republic of Yugoslavia had led in the experimentation with market forms of socialism. The descent into political disintegration and war coincided with the entrance onto the path of transition to a full market economy. The scale of intensity and destructiveness of the conflict -- particularly in Bosnia and Herzegovina and, to a lesser extent, Croatia -- has been unequalled in Europe since the Second World War. In 1992, economic sanctions were imposed by the Security Council against the Federal Republic of Yugoslavia (Serbia and Montenegro) for its role in the war in Bosnia and Herzegovina.

Generally speaking, the situation in 1996 in Bosnia and Herzegovina, Croatia, the Federal Republic of Yugoslavia, Slovenia and The former Yugoslav Republic of Macedonia is the most hopeful since the disintegration of the former Socialist federation. Open hostilities ended in Bosnia and Herzegovina with the signature in Paris on 14 December 1995, of the General Framework Agreement for Peace in Bosnia and Herzegovina and the Annexes thereto (collectively the Peace Agreement) (document A/50/790-S/1995/999, attachment); the Basic Agreement on the Region of Eastern Slavonia, Baranja and Western Sirmium (document A/50/757-S/1995/951, annex), signed at Erdut, Croatia, on 12 November 1995, provides for the peaceful reintegration of Eastern Slavonia into Croatia following a period of United Nations Transitional Administration; and sanctions against the Federal Republic of Yugoslavia have been suspended.

The economy of **Slovenia**, the State with the highest per capita income, has experienced the least disruption in the past five years. Following short-lived hostilities in the summer of 1991, this country of about 2 million people[a] has seen its economy grow since 1993. It has undergone an economic transition process akin to that in the rapidly reforming economies of Central and Eastern Europe. Inflation was high in the early years, exceeding 200 per cent in 1992, but macroeconomic adjustment programmes have quickly brought down the inflation rate and single-digit price increases are forecast for 1996 (see table). Unemployment, however, reached 15 per cent of the labour force in 1993 and is expected to remain in double digits this year.

Slovenia's GDP growth in 1995 was driven by exports and investment; labour productivity increased by about 4 per cent[b]. Economic activity in 1996 should be further boosted by the restoration of traditional markets as a result of the Peace Agreement. This will improve prospects for exports and further stimulate investment.

The Federal Republic of **Yugoslavia**, comprising Serbia and Montenegro, with a combined population of about 10.5 million people, was the target of United Nations sanctions from 1992 to 1995. It also suffered the sharpest collapse of production, almost 50 per cent in two years, 1992 and 1993 (see table). Inflation reached almost 9,000 per cent in 1992 and over one fifth of the labour force has been unemployed throughout this period.

A sharp adjustment programme stopped inflation in 1994, albeit temporarily, and output began to recover from the depths of the collapse. Immediately after the suspension of economic sanctions, a 15-point stabilization programme was put in place. Its provisions included lowering the exchange rate of the dinar to its black-market level and moving closer to the time when it could be made convertible, introducing market-determined interest rates, ending state monopolies in foreign trade and industry, accelerating privatization, removing quotas on exports and imports and reducing customs duties.

The restoration of its access to markets should lead to a boom in trade and boost industrial and agricultural output. Five years of unsatisfied demand are likely to fuel strong private consumption growth; investment in the country's damaged infrastructure - especially electric power, railways, roads, water resources, gas supply and heating system networks- will be another stimulus to growth.

[a] Population data from United *Nations,Monthly Bulletin of Statistics,* March 1996.

[b] Franjo Štiblar, "A country report: Slovenia", Project LINK spring meeting, 25-28 March 1996, United Nations, New York..

ECONOMIC INDICATORS OF THE REPUBLICS OF THE FORMER SOCIALIST FEDERAL REPUBLIC OF YUGOSLAVIA

	1991	1992	1993	1994	1995[a]	1996[b]
GDP (Annual percentage change)						
Bosnia and Herzegovina	..	..	..	..	..	..
Croatia	-14.0	-9.7	-3.7	0.8	-1.5	6
The former Yugoslav Republic of Macedonia[c]	-12.0	-13.4	-14.1	-8.2	-3.2	2
Slovenia	-8.0	-5.4	1.3	5.3	4.8	5
Yugoslavia[c]	..	-26.2	-27.7	6.5	6.0	12 ½
Consumer prices (Annual percentage change)						
Bosnia and Herzegovina	..	..	..	..	..	..
Croatia	123	666	1 518	97.5	2.0	2
The former Yugoslav Republic of Macedonia	..	1 691	350	122	17.3	12
Slovenia	118	201	32.3	19.8	12.6	6
Yugoslavia	120	8 990	2 201	3.3[d]	105[e]	60
Registered unemployment (Percentage of labour force)						
Bosnia and Herzegovina	..	..	..	..	..	..
Croatia	14.1	17.8	17.4	17.3	16.9	15
The former Yugoslav Republic of Macedonia	24.5	26.8	30.8	33.2	36.0	30
Slovenia	10.1	13.4	14.8	14.2	14.0	12
Yugoslavia	20.5	22.8	24.0	23.9	23.9	24 ¾

Sources: ECE, Economic Survey of Europe in 1995-1996 (United Nations publication, Sales No. E.96.II.E.1) and European Bank for Reconstruction and Development (EBRD), Transition Report, 1995: Update (London, EBRD, April 1996).

a   Preliminary.
b   ECE forecast.
c   Gross material product (value added in the material sphere, including depreciation).
d   December 1994 over February 1994.
e   November 1995 over December 1994.

Recovery may thus begin in earnest for which reason output has been forecast to grow 12.5 per cent in 1996. However, unless decommissioned military personnel can be rapidly absorbed into the civilian economy, the unemployment rate will not come down substantially in the immediate future.

From 1991 to 1993, the economy of **Croatia** contracted by 25 per cent, in the midst of the disruptions of war and transition. In 1993, inflation exceeded 1,500 per cent and the unemployment rate was over 17 per cent. In two years, however, a credible adjustment programme based on a fixed nominal exchange rate and tight fiscal policy broke inflationary expectations and brought the annual inflation rate down to 2 per cent, albeit at the expense of postponed economic recovery and employment. Continuing implementation of sustainable economic policies and progress towards the peaceful reintegration of Eastern Slavonia following the 1995 Erdut agreement may lead to substantial economic growth in 1996. Inflation is forecast to remain quite low.

The economic prospects of **The former Yugoslav Republic of Macedonia** also brightened in late 1995. It had left the former Yugoslavia under particularly difficult circumstances, as net financial transfers from the former federal Government on the order of 5-7 per cent of GDP were being discontinued, foreign exchange reserves held in Belgrade were being lost, and exports were being hit hard by the dissolution of trade arrangements under the Council for Mutual Economic Assistance and by the imposition of United Nations sanctions on its principal export markets, Serbia and Montenegro.[c] Then, in March 1994, Greece imposed a unilateral trade blockade, which has since been lifted under a United Nations-sponsored Interim Accord between the former Yugoslav Republic of Macedonia and Greece (see document S/1995/794, annex I) in September 1995.

Output in the former Yugoslav Republic of Macedonia has fallen steadily in the 1990s and is roughly half of its 1989 level. Industrial production declined by about 14 per cent in 1995, mainly in the mining, metal-processing, textiles and food-processing branches. More than one third of the labour force are registered as unemployed. Inflation, however, peaked in 1992, at almost 1,700 per cent and was brought down to low double-digit levels under an internationally supported adjustment programme.

It is thus quite significant that output is forecast to begin to rise in 1996, albeit slowly. The suspension of United Nations sanctions against the Federal Republic of Yugoslavia and the improved relations with Greece will allow the re-establishment of economic ties. However, substantial domestic and foreign investments are needed in order to lower the unemployment rate in the economy.

Although data are extremely sparse, the country most affected by the conflict is **Bosnia and Herzegovina**. Its economic situation remains a major concern. In addition to the general destruction and dislocations, the war caused very significant damage to the infrastructure and a brain drain.

The country had not embarked upon the transition before it was overwhelmed by the hostilities, and thus many institutions necessary for a functioning market economy do not exist. Moreover, the success of any national economic policy will depend on healing the divisions between the communities to the extent that Bosnia and Herzegovina can function as an economic entity. There are substantial needs for reconstruction, mine clearance and development.[d]

Multilateral financial institutions, the United Nations and bilateral donors are expected to supply the bulk of the financial resources and technical assistance needed for reconstruction.[e] For the short term, financial support must be on highly concessional terms, considering the limited debt-servicing capacity of the country. Over time, private direct investment and private financial flows can also be expected to play a growing economic role.

[c] World Bank, *Trends in Developing Countries, 1995* (Washington, D.C., World Bank, 1995), p 309.

[d] The matter of investment in post-conflict peace-building situation is discussed in more detail in the context of four case-studies in chap. VIII.

[e] The European Union and the World Bank sponsored two pledging conference, one in December 1995 in Paris and the other on 12 and 13 April 1996 in Brussels. The latter raised commitments of $1.23 billion, assuring the bulk of the $1.8 billion needed for 1996 alone *(World Bank News, 15 April1996)*. In addition, the International Monetary Fund (IMF) extended a loan of $45 million in December 1995, the first under its new emergency credits window for countries in post-conflict situations. The funds were mainly used to repay the Netherlands for a short-terms bridge loan that was used to clear $37 million of arrears to IMF arising from Bosnia and Herzegovina's share of liabilities and assets of the former Socialist Federal Republic of Yugoslavia (IMF press release 95/70 of 20 December 1995, as published in *IMF Survey*, 8 January 1996, pp. 10-11).

15 The Programme is described in "Country report: Ukraine", Project LINK Spring meeting, 25-28 March 1996, United Nations, New York.

gramme of Structural Reconstruction of the Ukrainian Economy.[15]

So far, however, Ukraine seems to be repeating the Russian Federation's 1992-1994 pattern of inconsistency in the implementation of economic reform, in particular in the policies designed to achieve financial stabilization — and with similar results, including persistent inflation, a serious budget deficit, balance-of-payments problems and painfully slow restructuring of enterprises.

THE DEVELOPING ECONOMIES

Developing countries continued to experience relatively strong growth in 1995, with their aggregate GDP increasing by over 5 per cent. In many countries, investment and exports were the main sources of growth during the past year. The aggregate growth rate, however, conceals sharp regional and national differences in economic performance. To a great extent, the high growth rate reflects the performance of South and East Asia and China, which currently originate about 50 per cent of the output of developing countries as a whole. As in recent years, China and South and East Asia registered very fast rates of growth, indeed the highest within the developing regions considered here (see table II.4).

With the exception of Latin America, GDP growth accelerated in other regions in 1995. After several years of declining per capita GDP, output growth in Africa was equal to population growth in 1995. Growth also picked up in Western Asia, while a sharp deceleration in GDP growth in Latin America interrupted the recovery in per capita income that the region had been experiencing since 1991. Among other countries, Turkey rebounded from the sharp contraction of 1994, while the prospects in the former Socialist Federal Republic of Yugoslavia are the best so far this decade, given the cessation of open hostilities (see box II.1).

The aggregate GDP growth rate is expected to increase to about $5\frac{1}{2}$ per cent in 1996 (see annex table A.4). At the same time, inflation will continue to decelerate, with the most significant improvements being made in Latin America and China. This marks a continuation of declining inflation in the developing countries since 1994 (see annex table A.13).

The average rate of increase in GDP in 1996 comprises distinct regional experiences in economic growth. On the one hand, the very rapid economic expansion in South and East Asia and China is moderating. On the other hand, economic recovery is expected to emerge in Latin America and significantly stronger economic growth is foreseen in Africa. For Africa, 1996 will mark the first increase in per capita income since the mid-1980s. With economic conditions improving in a large number of least developed countries in Africa, the average rate of growth of GDP in the least developed countries as a whole is forecast to reach $4\frac{3}{4}$ per cent in 1996.

Africa: export-driven growth

Africa is experiencing the fastest economic growth since the start of this decade. Output grew 2.7 per cent which was about equal to the population growth rate in 1995. The improvement was rather broadly based, as about a dozen countries in Africa recorded GDP growth rates of 5 per cent or higher in

Table II.4.

DEVELOPING COUNTRIES: RATES OF GROWTH OF GDP, 1981-1996

Annual percentage change						
	1981-1991	1992	1993	1994	1995[a]	1996[b]
Developing countries[c]	3.1	4.9	5.0	5.6	5.2	5½
of which						
Latin America and the Caribbean	1.4	2.2	3.0	4.6	0.9	2½
Energy exporters	2.0	3.7	0.8	2.5	-2.6	2
Energy importers	1.0	1.3	4.4	5.8	2.8	2¾
Africa	1.9	0.9	0.4	2.5	2.7	4¼
Energy exporters	2.1	2.7	-0.2	1.6	3.4	3¾
Energy importers	1.7	-1.0	1.0	3.4	2.0	4¾
West Asia	-1.2	5.7	2.6	0.6	3.1	3
South and East Asia[d]	6.0	5.2	5.5	6.7	7.1	6¾
Memo item:						
Sub-Saharan Africa	1.7	0.1	-0.7	1.8	3.1	5
(excluding Nigeria and South Africa)						
Least developed countries	1.9	2.4	1.1	2.5	3.3	4¾
Major developing economies						
China	8.9	13.2	13.4	11.8	10.2	9
Brazil	1.4	-0.8	4.1	5.8	4.2	2½
India	5.0	4.0	3.9	5.4	6.2	6
Republic of Korea	8.7	5.1	5.8	8.4	9.0	7¼
Mexico	1.8	2.8	0.4	3.5	-6.9	2½
Iran (Islamic Republic of)	3.0	6.0	1.8	0.0	3.0	3½
Taiwan Province of China	7.9	6.8	6.3	6.5	6.1	6¼
Indonesia	5.0	6.3	6.5	7.5	8.1	7½
Argentina	-0.5	8.7	6.4	7.4	-4.4	2
Thailand	7.3	7.4	8.0	8.6	8.6	8½
South Africa	1.3	-2.2	1.3	2.7	3.3	4
Saudi Arabia	-2.1	3.0	1.6	-2.7	1.7	1½
Turkey	4.0	6.4	8.0	-6.0	7.9	3

Source: UN/DESIPA.
[a] Preliminary estimate.
[b] Forecast, based in part on Project LINK.
[c] Covering 93 countries that account for 99 per cent of the population of all developing countries.
[d] Excluding China.

1995. In 1996, Africa is expected to see an increase in GDP per capita for the first time since 1985. Prospects have improved under favourable external conditions and ameliorated policy environments. Moreover, after droughts in 1995, good rainfall has generally returned to northern and southern Africa and a favourable agricultural season is predicted for 1996 throughout the continent with the exception of the countries affected by civil strife. Output growth is expected to slow in 1997, however, as demand from developed countries and some commodity prices weaken. The forecast is highly contingent on exogenous factors which can all turn out worse than expected, and thus highlights the vulnerability of the African recovery and the challenges to be overcome.Despite their overall growth performance, most African countries are still among the poorest in the world: 33 out of the 48 least developed countries are African countries. The improved economic performance during the period 1995-1996 is so far only a short-term phenomenon and, unless it continues, will not be sufficient to significantly alleviate poverty, deteriorated social conditions and high unemployment rates accompanying what in some cases have been decades of economic decline or stagnation.

Growth performance in 1995

GDP growth was supported by higher prices and stronger demand in the international commodity markets (see chap. III), mainly from the developed market economies which absorb about two thirds of Africa's exports. Prices of metals and minerals rose faster than the prices of other commodities, providing an important stimulus to increased production in several mineral exporting countries.

Large increases in output of both food and cash crops occurred where normal weather predominated, thus boosting rural incomes. Preliminary data from the Food and Agriculture Organization of the United Nations (FAO) show that African coffee production increased by 10 per cent, cocoa production by 7.6 per cent, tea production by 7 per cent and cotton production by 4 per cent. In Malawi, for instance, the return of favourable weather conditions caused output to rise by 9.5 per cent in 1995, after it had contracted 12 per cent in 1994. In northern and southern Africa, however – in countries such as Morocco, South Africa, the United Republic of Tanzania and Zimbabwe – drought led to a contraction in agricultural output and sluggish growth in agriculture-dependent sectors (such as food processing). In all, total agricultural and food output remained unchanged in 1995 as a result of good crops in some countries being offset by poor harvests in others. African cereal production, however, declined by 13 per cent in 1995. With a number of countries having to cover weather-related shortfalls in food production – at a time when prices for food imports are high – commercial food imports for the 1995/96 marketing year is anticipated to have increased by 7 per cent to 35 million tons. Egypt and Morocco, for example, faced high trade deficits in 1995, in part because of the price increase of imported food.

Oil production increased by 2 per cent in Africa in 1995. With prices also firmer, this bolstered export revenues in the oil-exporting countries in 1995 by 10 per cent, compared with a decline in 1994. The improvement in oil exports contributed to a recovery in Cameroon, the Congo and the Libyan Arab Jamahiriya, countries whose economies contracted in 1994. Nigerian GDP grew by about 2 per cent in 1995. Economic activity in Nigeria has been hindered, inter alia, by deteriorating infrastructure and fuel scarcity owing to the poor conditions of the country's oil refineries.

Strong mineral and metal prices have stimulated mining production — in Ghana and Zimbabwe, for example. However, the poor conditions in the mining sector in Zaire and Zambia limited the ability to take advantage of such factors in these countries. High diamond prices boosted export revenues of Namibia and Botswana, while in Zaire — notwithstanding the above-mentioned poor conditions — officially recorded diamond sales increased by over 20 per cent in real terms.

Non-traditional exports — such as horticultural products from Kenya and Malawi, manufactured goods from export-processing zones in Madagascar and Mauritius and motor vehicles from Botswana — also contributed to growth in these economies. Additionally, tourism revenues increased in 1995 in a number of countries, for example Egypt, Tunisia and Uganda. It contributed to growth in Ethiopia as more destinations became accessible to visitors as a result of the country's progress in the process of transition from civil war to peace. Senegal and the Comoros also witnessed growth in their tourism industry as a result of the devaluation of the CFA franc (see below) which increased these countries' attractiveness to tourists. Namibia, Madagascar and Zimbabwe also enjoyed strong growth in tourism during the year 1995.

The South African economy improved its economic performance in 1995. GDP increased by 3.3 per cent (see table II.4), with investment and exports being the most dynamic components of aggregate demand. The slow recovery in manufacturing employment since 1994 can do little to dent the unemployment rate, which remains alarmingly high (see chap. VIII). This notwithstanding, South Africa's increased trade and investment links with other southern African economies have contributed significantly to the growth performance of the latter. South's Africa trade with these countries had more than doubled since 1993 and direct investment by South African firms in Angola, Bostwana, Lesotho, Mozambique and Namibia, among others, increased dramatically during the same period. Market-oriented reforms in most of these countries, especially the privatization of State-owned enterprises, as well as South Africa's experience and familiarity with regional markets and cultures, improved investment opportunities in these countries and their attractiveness to South African investors.

Several events in 1995 demonstrated once again how vulnerable some African countries remain to the economic consequences of political troubles and instability. Social unrest, civil strife and political crises impeded economic activities in Burundi, Liberia, Rwanda, Sierra Leone, Somalia, the Sudan and Zaire. In Sierra Leone, for instance, rebel attacks caused a severe disruption of agriculture and a virtual cessation of mining, and GDP fell by an estimated 10 per cent in 1995. Policy uncertainty in Nigeria and Zaire remains a dominant factor in their poor economic performance in recent years.

On the other hand, peace agreements have raised economic prospects in Angola and Mozambique. However, the reconstruction of institutions and infrastructure, which suffered extensive damage during the conflicts, will take some time. Moreover, that reconciliation, resettling returnees and providing livelihoods for former combatants are a crucial facet of this process was underlined by the resumed fighting in Liberia in April 1996.

Stabilization and structural reforms

Progress has been made in establishing macroeconomic stability in many African countries. As a result, consumer price inflation has exhibited a declining trend for the region as a whole and reached an estimated 22 per cent in 1995, compared with 24 per cent in 1994 (excluding Zaire).

In Algeria, the budget deficit has been reduced from about 9 per cent of GDP in 1993 to about 1 per cent in 1995 as a result of the reduction of food subsidies, other fiscal reforms and expenditure restructuring. The inflation remained relatively high at about 30 per cent in 1995 owing to the cutback in subsidies and the depreciation of the currency.

Zaire managed to reduce consumer price inflation from 23,773 per cent in 1994 to 542 per cent in 1995. However, inflation resurfaced in Madagascar and remained high in Nigeria. In these countries, the inflation rate was at least 50 per cent in 1995.

Ghana, which over several years maintained fiscal and monetary discipline, has experienced some difficulties lately. Macroeconomic stability has deteriorated since 1992, when the civil servants received an 80 per cent increase in salary, which reversed the budget surpluses of the preceding years. The budget deficits and increases in money supply, coupled with exchange rate depreciation, and weather-related rises in food prices, have led to higher inflation. The Government sought to strengthen the fiscal situation with a new value-added tax (VAT), but riots against the tax and general economic conditions broke out in May 1995. The tax was subsequently withdrawn, but prices were not adjusted downward to pre-VAT levels. The poor implementation of the VAT and a fuel price increase were two additional factors in 1995 that pushed the inflation rate to about 55 per cent.

Structural reforms are progressing in many countries of the continent. In Egypt, to encourage investment, tariffs on imports of capital goods have been reduced, rent controls on new tenancy contracts for housing have been abolished and investment approval procedures have been simplified. Moreover, the new Government — which took office in January 1996 — released a list of several State-owned companies that it intends to privatize in 1996. The new impetus to the privatization programme is expected to soon lead to an agreement with IMF. This will clear the way for the last phase of a large debt relief package agreed with the Paris Club in 1991.[16]

Franc zone

Economic performance has generally improved in the franc zone since the devaluation of the CFA franc in January 1994,[17] The region has benefited from favourable external trade conditions which it was better able to take advantage of after devaluation, as well as a surge in official and private inflows of financial resources, which the devaluation triggered.[18]

As in other parts of Africa, exports have been the driving force behind output growth. Stronger international demand compounded the positive impact of the devaluation of the CFA franc and provided solid incentives for increasing production. The GDP growth rate thus increased in nearly all countries within

[16] On the Egyptian debt relief package, see *World Economic Survey, 1992* (United Nations publication, Sales No. E.92.II.C.1 and Corr.1 and 2), Chap. IV, subsection entitled "Aid, finance and debt of the developing countries: Breaking with convention in official debt restructuring".

[17] This discussion draws in part on Louis M. Goreux, "La dévaluation du franc CFA: Un premier bilan en décembre 1995", mimeo, 28 December 1995, prepared for the World Bank.

[18] Resources from official multilateral and bilateral sources (exceptional and project financing) for the franc zone increased from CFA 828 billion ($2.9 billion) in 1993 to CFA 2,283 billion ($4.1 billion) in 1994.

the zone. Several CFA countries registered GDP growth rates of as high as 5 per cent or more in 1995 (Benin, Burkina Faso, Chad, Côte d'Ivoire, Equatorial Guinea and Togo). Furthermore, investment and manufacturing production have picked up in some countries, particularly in those subsectors that focus on import-substitution and exports. Intrazonal trade expanded as producers from the zone became more competitive than outside suppliers.

Growth performance in the zone was, however, was also partly the outcome of some coinciding factors not related to the devaluation. For instance, new oilfields started production in Côte d'Ivoire and Equatorial Guinea and the sociopolitical situation improved in Chad and Togo.

With the devaluation, inflation at first erupted in the zone but was contained relatively quickly through tight fiscal and monetary policies, price controls, limiting of wage increases in the public sector and reduction of some tax rates. Cumulative prices increase averaged about 50 per cent in the zone from December 1993 to September 1995, with Burkina Faso at the low end at 34 per cent and Benin, Chad and the Congo at the high end at about 60 per cent. Inflation dropped during 1995 but still remained in the double digits in a few countries (Cameroon, Benin, Togo). Some further upward pressure on prices can be expected when the last price controls are relaxed.

The increase in consumer prices has negatively affected living standards, in urban areas in particular. To alleviate the impact of the devaluation on the most vulnerable groups, such as uneducated youth and the unemployed, several countries have initiated public works, and provided training, employment counselling and support for small enterprises. These measures have been partly supported by external finance.[19]

There has been some progress in controlling public finances, as the aggregate budget deficit for the zone declined from 8.3 per cent of GDP in 1993 to 6.1 per cent in 1994. The expectation was that budget deficits would continue to decline in 1995 and 1996 when fiscal and civil service reforms proceeded. Many countries have limited increases in civil servants' salaries and in government expenditure in general. Additionally, substantial debt relief has been granted to a number of countries by official bilateral creditors and this has assisted in containing government expenditures (see chap. III).

Several countries, however, had, as a reflection of financial constraints, accumulated arrears on their domestic payments. Salary arrears, for instance, increased substantially in the Congo and the Niger during 1994 and prompted strikes in both countries in 1994 and 1995. Domestic arrears were essentially eliminated at the end of 1995 in the western part of the franc zone (with the exception of the Niger). The problem persists, however, in the central part.

Reforms have gained momentum in 1995 in a number of countries in the franc zone. Reforms are focusing on privatization, the civil service, government expenditures and revenues, labour codes and agricultural marketing. Reforms addressing institutional and structural constraints are necessary conditions for taking full advantage of the CFA devaluation.[20]

However, structural reforms have barely commenced and it is therefore too early to judge to what extent they will be able to change the production structure and raise the long-term growth potential of the economies. Or to paraphrase Louis M. Goreux:[21] Although the mechanical effects of the devaluation have been realized, there is no reason to feel complacent, because there will be

[19] For example, after the devaluation, France set up a special FF 400 million development fund.

[20] The devaluation and the increase in international commodity prices have given pecuniary incentives to producers. However, several studies have established that price elasticities of supply are rather small, though they increase greatly when non-price factors, such as access to land, credit, roads and fertilizer, are addressed as well (see, for example, Kimseyinga Savadogo, Thomas Reardon and Kyosti Pietola, "Mechanization and agricultural supply response in the Sahel: A farm-level profit function analysis", *Journal of African Economies*, vol. 4, No. 3 (December 1995), pp. 336-377).

21 "La dévaluation du franc CFA: Un premier bilan en décembre 1995", mimeo, 28 December 1995, prepared for the World Bank.

22 See, for one of the latest assessments, Susan Schadler and others, *IMF Conditionality: Experience Under Stand-By and Extended Arrangements*, Occasional Paper, No. 128 (Washington, D.C., IMF, September 1995).

no sustained growth without diversification and investment. Vigorous structural reforms are needed to maintain the current recovery.

Addressing growth constraints

The present upturn in economic performance demonstrates how sensitive Africa remains to external conditions. Policy reforms have contributed to improved economic performance in a number of countries, but the impact on GDP has frequently been rather small and disappointing.[22] Despite the current economic upturn, economic performance remains impeded by long-term structural constraints to development, such as poorly developed institutions, poor infrastructure, a low level of development of human resources and unequal distribution of and access to resources, such as inputs and finance.

African countries continue to suffer from high external indebtedness. Despite international cooperation in attempting to alleviate the external debt burden, the continent still experiences severe difficulties in servicing its debt. Notwithstanding the stronger export performance of the region during 1995, debt indicators remain high. Indeed, in the sub-Saharan region excluding Nigeria and South Africa, the debt service-to-export ratio rose to almost 20 per cent in 1995, from 17 per cent in 1994. This ratio, moreover, does not include arrears which continued to build up in 1995. However, output growth led to a drop in the ratio of debt to gross national product (GNP) as this indicator fell from 136 per cent in 1994 to 121 per cent in 1995. (see table A. 37)

In March 1996, the United Nations launched a system-wide special initiative on Africa to ameliorate a number of these constraints. The United Nations System-Wide Special Initiative of Africa is the United Nations system's most significant mobilization of support ever for Africa as well as its largest coordinated action. The Special Initiative is to focus on such areas as basic education, basic health, water and sanitation. The total costs of the Special Initiative is estimated to be $25 billion over a 10-year period which will come mostly from the reallocation of existing resources at the national and the international level.

Latin America and the Caribbean: renewing adjustment efforts

The year 1995 witnessed positive and negative developments in the Latin American region. Inflation fell to 25 per cent by year-end, a record low in the last 22 years and a major achievement for the region, given its not-so-successful attempts to control inflation in the past. Further slowing of inflation is expected during the current year. The financial crisis that assailed Mexico was contained through concerted international and domestic efforts and has not spread so as to become a major international or regional crisis. Nevertheless, its negative consequences were the interruption of the economic recovery that the region had been experiencing since 1991 and the reverberations that are still being felt by some economies in the region. The regional GDP increased by less than 1 per cent in 1995, well below population growth, and prospects for the current year are for a mild recovery; growth is not expected to exceed 2.5 per cent in 1996 (see table II.4). The slow recovery underlines the possibility of increased social pressure in the region as unemployment has recently expanded or remained high in several countries.[23] Moreover, recent economic developments exposed the fragility of the banking system in some countries, hence signalling a downside risk to the already modest economic performance forecast for the current year.

Price stabilization: is it here to stay?

Most countries in the region continued to make progress in controlling inflation during 1995. In fact, inflation declined in 14 out of 18 countries monitored, and Argentina has now one of the world's lowest inflation rates. Inflation increased somewhat in Bolivia, Costa Rica and El Salvador reflecting fiscal imbalances. Costa Rica is a case in point: the public deficit reached 6.5 per cent of GDP in 1994, although by 1995 it had been brought down to 4.3 per cent. Mexico, on the other hand, was the only Latin American country that experienced a substantial acceleration of its inflation — from 7 per cent in 1994 to 52 per cent in 1995 — as a result of the devaluation of the peso and higher value-added taxes. It is anticipated that Mexican inflation will gradually fall, although it will remain relatively high at 30 per cent during the current year. It is expected that inflation will continue to decline in the region as countries continue to pursue policies aiming at reduced macroeconomic imbalances; much of the fiscal and monetary discipline exerted so far should therefore continue.[24] The lower regional inflation rate in 1995 reflects the success of the Real Plan in Brazil, which heretofore had been an outlier to regional achievement on the inflation front (see figure II.2). The annual inflation rate fell from 930 per cent in 1994 to 22 per cent in 1995.

The Real Plan involved action on the fiscal and monetary levels. Measures leading to the de-indexation of the economy and the introduction of a new currency were taken in 1994 along with policies to restore equilibrium in the

23 Unemployment increased in Argentina, Ecuador, Mexico, Panama, Uruguay and Venezuela in 1995. In Nicaragua, urban unemployment was about 20 per cent in 1995, the same level as in 1994.

24 Inflation, however, is expected to increase in Venezuela as a consequence of the fiscal and exchange rate adjustments currently being considered.

FIGURE II.2. LATIN AMERICAN
CONSUMER PRICE INDEXES: 1989-1995

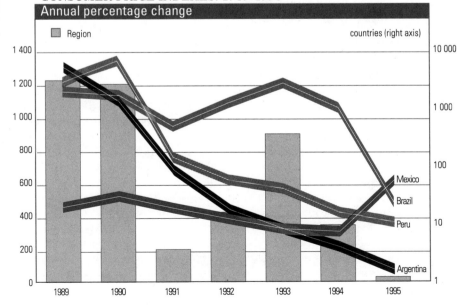

Sources: UN/DESIPA and Economic Commission for Latin America and the Caribbean (ECLAC).

25 On the Brazilian strategy to control inflation see *World Economic and Social Survey, 1995* (United Nations publication, Sales No. E.95.II.C.1), Chap. V, subsection entitled "'Rocky road' to stabilization in Latin America and the Caribbean: Brazil's innovative attack on inflation"; and J. Sachs and A. Zini, "Brazilian inflation and the Plano Real" *The World Economy*, vol. 19, No. 1 (January 1996), pp. 13-37.

26 By the end of 1994, the Mexican current account registered a deficit of some $29 billion, while expected payments on short-term public debt instruments (tesobonos) reached another $29 billion. (On the origins of the Mexican crisis, see *World Economic and Social Survey 1995*, (United Nations publication, Sales No. E.95.II.C.1), Chap. V, subsection entitled "'Rocky road' to stabilization in Latin America and the Caribbean: What happened in Mexico?".

public sector accounts.[25] The consolidated public sector closed the year 1994 with a surplus estimated at 1.2 per cent of GDP (operational concept). During 1995, however, the fiscal position could not be maintained owing to increases in personnel expenditures and interest payments on the domestic debt. Additional pressure on the fiscal accounts has also been brought about by the collapse of some of the country's largest banks, as discussed below. With the relaxation of fiscal discipline, much of the stabilization effort has been relying on the monetary and the exchange rate policy. The continuous decline in inflation demonstrates that this approach has been successful so far. This notwithstanding, the strategy may prove to be unsustainable in the long run, especially as high interest rates continue to attract foreign capital, thus intensifying the problem of excess liquidity in the economy, and discourage an expansion in demand, particularly investment, hence trapping the economy in a slow growth path. Reforms aiming at improved control over public expenditure — pension reform is one case in point — depend on congressional approval and the negotiations between the Government and the Congress have been progressing quite slowly.

Output growth in 1995

The slow-down in the rate of growth of the aggregate regional GDP reflected economic recessions in Mexico and Argentina that had been triggered by the devaluation of the Mexican peso in December 1994 and the temporary reversal of capital inflows to the region.[26] The Mexican economy contracted by 7 per cent, making the recession the worst in the recent history of the country. The Argentine GDP declined 4.4 per cent in 1995, thus interrupting that country's notable period of economic growth: its GDP had increased at an annual average rate of 7.5 per cent during the period 1991-1994. Open unemployment rose severely in both countries, reaching 18 per cent in Argentina — construction and manufacturing were the sectors hardest hit — and 6.5 per cent in Mexico, a record high for the country. Not included in these figures are the estimates for underemployment, which is believed to have soared, particularly in Mexico. The economic performance of these countries would have been much worse had it not been for substantial intensification of their export efforts and favourable international prices (see chap. III).

The Mexican financial crisis exposed the fragility of stabilization efforts based on the use of a fixed exchange rate as a "nominal anchor" when domestic inflation is higher than in major trading partners. It created an appreciating exchange rate which, within a context of trade liberalization, led to increasing trade deficits, financed with short-term foreign capital. Corrective measures were taken in several countries.

Tight monetary policies adopted in Brazil to contain the deterioration of the country's trade balance and prevent runs on the currency led to a sharp deceleration of output growth in that country in the second half of 1995, particularly in manufacturing. Annual GDP growth was reduced to about 4 per cent in 1995, down from 6 per cent in the previous year. Similar policies were adopted in Peru but, given the momentum from the very fast growth in 1994, Peru still produced the second fastest rate of GDP growth in the region in 1995.

Several other economies in the region were less affected by the volatility of short-term capital flows, either because they had not attracted them before in massive amounts and did not have extensive trade links with either Mexico or Argentina (as was the case for most of the Central American and Caribbean countries) or because they were not as vulnerable owing to the implementation of successful structural reforms (as was the case for Chile). In fact, Chile registered the fastest rate of growth in the region — 8.3 per cent — and was supported by increased investment and extremely favourable terms of trade (see chap. VII). These countries could therefore follow their own course, thus registering moderate — albeit on the low side for a developing country — rates of growth of about 2-4 per cent (Paraguay, Bolivia, Panama, Costa Rica, Ecuador and Honduras, among others).

The banking crisis of 1994 (discussed below) is still being felt in Venezuela as public finances have deteriorated sharply and fiscal balance has not been restored. Pressure on its currency has mounted and exchange controls have been imposed. Economic stagnation still affected the non-oil sector of the economy. The economy grew by 2 per cent in 1995

In several of the Caribbean island economies, economic growth slowed down owing to a combination of adverse weather conditions which affected the tourism industry and agriculture (Antigua and Barbuda, Dominica), energy shortages which constrained manufacturing output, and austere fiscal and monetary policies to control inflation (Jamaica, Trinidad and Tobago). On the other hand, growth picked up in the Dominican Republic, and resumed in Cuba and Haiti.

The outlook for 1996

Economic growth should increase in the region in 1996, as Mexico, Argentina and Uruguay slowly emerge from their recessions. These economies are not expected, however, to grow by more than 2 per cent in 1996. Moreover, several of the largest economies of the region — including Brazil, Chile, Colombia and Peru — are expected to have lower growth this year, while the other economies in Central and South America will, on average, repeat their 1995 growth performance. The Caribbean countries are expected to record another year of sluggish growth in 1996.

Growth in Argentina is very much constrained by lack of demand. Household demand has declined in view of increased unemployment, lower real wages and uncertainty. Investment will not provide much boost to the cycle until firms' capacity utilization returns to pre-recession levels, likely not before the end of the year. The country's banking system is overcoming severe difficulties (see box II.2) and, although deposit levels were restored to pre-crisis levels, financial institutions are reluctant to extend credit. Moreover, the Government is committed to fiscal discipline, so it cannot be expected to provide much stimulus to growth. Recently, however, it has lowered taxes on mortgages, the sales of new houses and a few consumer products in order to give some boost to the economy. On the external front, prospects for growth are also uncertain. Though grain prices will remain firm during the year (see chap. III), exports to Brazil — Argentina's main export market — may not be as robust as last year's, as the Brazilian economy is growing more slowly and import demand is thus reduced. Mexico, on the other hand, has shown some signs of recovery, but incomes remain depressed in view of lower real wages and increased unemployment. Additionally, its banking system is still fragile

Box II.2.

THE PROBLEM WITH LATIN AMERICAN BANKS

In several Latin American countries, the banking systems have recently experienced severe difficulties that have impeded the resumption of faster economic growth. The most visible cases are Argentina and Mexico; but banking crises have also been occurring elsewhere in the region, including Bolivia, Brazil, Ecuador, Paraguay and Venezuela. In some countries, the growth of credit needed for economic expansion is being limited by a banking industry that has suddenly become more hesitant to lend; meanwhile, public finances — in any case, stretched tight — are being stressed by costly bailouts.

Vulnerability to shocks

The external financial shocks of 1995 that were absorbed by Argentina and Mexico might have rocked even the most stable and conservative banking systems; but the banks of these countries, like those of many Latin American countries, were quite fragile institutions. The problem began with how the banks undertook their fundamental financial intermediation role.

Banks take deposits — both short-term "demand" deposits and medium-term time deposits — and borrow from other financial institutions and markets, and then they lend out the funds at higher interest rates than they themselves pay. The funds taken in by the Latin American banks have been unusually heavily weighted to short term, liquid deposit instruments, in part reflecting a less-than-solid confidence of depositors. The banks' portfolios of loans, however, tend to have a longer maturity and are usually guaranteed by collateral that cannot immediately be turned into cash. In this type of situation, prudence dictates an extremely conservative bank management and vigilant public supervision of the banking sector. If depositors begin a run on a bank — or all banks — they can seriously deplete bank resources extremely quickly.

In this environment, there have been shortcomings on the part of both management and regulators. It has been argued that the legal framework in which Latin American banks operate is not fully developed and accounting standards are not adequate.[a] Thus, for example, capital-to-asset ratios have not been effectively enforced where accounting practices were inadequate.

Bank lending practices in some countries have evidenced a poor management of risk, particularly over economic cycles. During periods of economic expansion, the volume of bank deposits typically grows and banks naturally lend out these funds. Some of the credits are based on inadequate risk assessments and optimistic expectations of future growth of the economy. When the economic cycle loses steam, borrowers have to cope with declining revenues and liquidity problems and the banks find themselves holding increasing stocks of "bad debt".

At the same time, if depositors perceive the position of the banks to have weakened, they can trigger a liquidity crisis by fleeing the system.[b] The liquidity crisis can also arise without the solidity of the banks being at issue, at least at first, as when fear of an exchange rate devaluation leads to a sharp withdrawal of bank deposits for conversion into foreign exchange.

Argentina is a case in point. During the inflationary period preceding the introduction of the convertibility plan (1991), the demand for bank deposits in local currency was quite modest and the economy was characterized by a low level of monetization. Then, under the new monetary regime, the persistence of high real interest rates and the guaranteed exchange rate attracted short-term external capital and deposits increased, some of which were held in dollar accounts and some converted into pesos.[c] When the December 1994 Mexican crisis arose, Argentine depositors panicked and Argentina's banking system lost about 18 per cent of its deposits during the first three months of 1995. Interest rates soared in order to keep resources in the system, but this compromised borrowers' ability to meet their debt obligations, and the banks had a rush of bad loans.

a   See L. Rojas -Suarez and S.R Weisbrod, *Banking Crisis in Latin America: experiences and issues*, Working Paper Series, no. 321, (Washington, D.C., Inter-American Development Bank (IDB), February 1996

b   See Inter-American Development Bank, *Economic and Social Progress in Latin American*. 1995 report. *Overcoming Volatility* (Washington D.C, IDB October 1995), p.236

c   See G. Rosenwurcel and R. Fernandez, "Argentina" in *Strengthening the Financial Sector in the Adjustment Process*, R. Frenkel, ed., (Washington, D.C., IDB, 1994), pp.39-84.

Similar developments took place in Mexico. The increase of capital inflows in the early 1990s was accompanied by a sharp expansion in domestic credit supply to the private sector.[d] The small and weaker banks became aggressive lenders. Confidence in the future of the economy led these banks to expand credit at much faster rates than the larger banks, which actually became conservative in their credit policies.[e] The appetite for credit was also fed by declining interest rates and optimistic expectations about the economy both by business and by households. Lack of strict supervision compounded the problem, as riskier banks were allowed to expand. When the Mexican crisis emerged, depositors started to run towards more solid institutions or away from the peso, interest rates skyrocketed and an over-indebted private sector started to default on its loans at a high rate.[f]

Changes in the macroeconomic environment underlay some of the recent bank failures in Brazil. Brazilian banks had grown used to an inflationary environment in which demand deposits did not earn any remuneration and the banks could earn easy profits by using the cash from their deposits to purchase fully indexed government securities. With deregulation of the system in 1988 and the ending of restrictions on the establishment of financial institutions, the number of banks increased from 106 in 1988 to 207 in 1992.[g] With the Real Plan, inflation was sharply reduced, but banks lost their lucrative business and the institutions that were not flexible enough had problems adjusting to the new environment, that is, acting like regular banks.

However, this explains only part of the Brazilian problem.The Government tightened monetary policy so as to restrain consumption in view of a rapidly deteriorating trade balance and this pushed up interest rates. Many borrowers then became insolvent, further jeopardizing the banks' situation.

At the same time, several State-owed banks purchased considerable amounts of mostly unserviceable state and municipal bonds and in this way they acted as de facto money issuing centres.In the process, the banks holdings of risky assets exceeded the limits of risk concentration. Although the Central Bank had closed some of the smaller of these institutions in the past, there has recently been considerable pressure to bail them out. Even Banco do Brasil, the largest Latin American bank, suffered huge losses and required a bailout as a result of non-performing loans that had been contracted by the agricultural sector and by some State-owned enterprises.

Lax supervision and poor regulation were behind the Venezuelan banking failures in 1994. The country's second largest bank in terms of deposits fell in 1994 owing to its very weak capital position and growing illiquidity. It was common practice to extend loans to its own shareholders on projects of questionable quality at "friendly" interest rates. The crisis quickly spread to other institutions as they began to be affected by withdrawal of deposits.

Bolstering the banking sector

Monetary authorities had no choice but to act to prevent the collapse of the banking system in their respective countries. The strategy, broadly applied, was to infuse funds to bolster confidence and force bank consolidations so as to make them more viable. Many banks have been liquidated or restructured through mergers and acquisitions, including through increasing participation of foreign banks as partial owners.

In the case of Argentina, the rules governing the fixed exchange regime meant that the Central Bank had limited capacity to act as a lender-of-last-resort to banks.However, Argentina did grant rediscounts to banks in 1995 and established a trust fund to support troubled banks, funded with resources of the multilateral financial institutions. Nevertheless, many banks, particularly the small banks that had riskier portfolios, were closed. As a result, the number of banks operating in the economy declined from 200 by the end of 1994 to about 160 by December 1995 and further consolidation is expected.

[d] Credit extended to the private sector by the banking system jumped from about 17 per cent of GDP in 1990 to 40 per cent in 1994 (Banco de Mexico, "Indicadores economicos", June 1995).

[e] Part of their asset increases was financed by credits from the Central Bank particularly during 1994 when difficulties in capturing additional deposits emerged (see L. Rojas-Suarez and Steven, R. Weisbrod, *Financial Fragilities in Latin America: the 1980s and 1990s*, Occasional Paper, No. 132 (Washington, D.C., IMF, October 1995)).

[f] Non-performing loans were already 9 percent of bank loans in september 1994 and reached 17 per cent one year later (see Economic Commission for Latin american abnd the Caribbean (ECLAC), "Preliminaary ovrview of the Latin American and Caribbean economy, 1995", *Notas sobre la economia y el.desarrollo*, No 585/586 (December 1995)).

[g] D.D Carneiro and others, "Brazil". in *Strengthening the Financial Sector in the Adjustment Process*, R. Frenkel ed. (Washington, D.C., IDB, 1994 pp. 85-146.

Banking deposits have been restored to their pre-crisis level but, as of April 1996, this has yet to be paralleled by an expansion of bank credit.

In Mexico, a temporary capitalization programme (*Programa de Capitalización Temporal* (PROCAPTE)) was put in place to lend funds to undercapitalized banks so as to increase the ratio of capital to loans in their portfolio. A programme to deal with the restructuring of overdue loans was also launched (*Fondo Bancario de Protección al Ahorro* (FOBAPROA)) that aimed at inducing banks to increase their capital and sell their bad debts. Additionally, a programme to cut interest cost on consumers' and small enterprises' loans was devised (*Acuerdo de Apoyo Inmediato a Deudores* (ADE)). Costs of all these programmes have been estimated at about 5 per cent of Mexican GDP. Financing will come from issuing public debt in the domestic market. The total cost may exceed the revenues to the Government earlier in the decade from privatizing the banks.

In Brazil, a programme to support mergers and acquisitions with fiscal incentives and credit subsidies has been launched (*Programa de Estímulo a Restruturação do Sistema Financeiro Nacional* (PROER)), capital adequacy requirements were increased, and a deposit insurance mechanism was introduced. The Venezuelan bailout has been the most costly so far. In order to avoid a generalized run on the banking system, the Central Bank, through the Deposit Insurance Fund (*Fondo de Garantía de Depósitos* (FOGADE))[h] injected a considerable amount of financial aid – albeit without proper supervision – into the system; but then FOGADE began to run out of resources (the unsuccessful bailout had cost an estimated 11 per cent of GDP) and no advances in recapitalizing the banks were made. The Government ended up having to bring the banks under its control.

h At the early stages of the crisis, the government guarantee given by FOGADE on deposits was increased by four times its original value (from about $9,000 to $36,000) in order to reinforce confidence in the banking system by protecting a larger deposit value.

despite government efforts to support the industry, as discussed below. Moreover, as interest rates have remained high and the economy has not yet taken off, additional Mexican enterprises may become insolvent, thus compromising any faster economic recovery.

Growth is expected to slow down among the other large economies of the region. In Brazil, despite some relaxation of monetary policy by the end of 1995, credit conditions remain tight and real interest rates are still high, thus discouraging consumption and investment. Further monetary loosening depends on progress in controlling the fiscal deficit.

The Peruvian growth rate is also expected to decelerate as austere fiscal and monetary measures are adopted owing to the need to correct a growing external imbalance.[27] Additionally, the Government will not be able to provide much stimulus as fiscal revenues decline as a result of reduced economic activity and privatization proceeds decline.

Colombia's economic performance is also expected to deteriorate this year as business confidence is being negatively affected by the political crisis. Much of past year's growth was brought about by increased investment (particularly in the oil sector) and expansionary fiscal policy which will gradually subside this year. The Chilean economy will gradually slow down in 1996 and 1997 as a result of less favourable prices for its major exports and some tightening in its monetary policy. Nevertheless, Chile will still grow strongly in 1996, at 6 per cent.

In a departure from previous interventionist policies, Venezuela is undergoing a new structural adjustment programme aimed at stabilizing the economy.

27 The current account deficit was estimated at 7.5 per cent of GDP by the end of 1995.

The programme entails the abolition of all existing foreign-exchange controls, the liberalization of interest rates, a fivefold rise in gasoline prices and an increase in the wholesale tax. The Government plans to cut this year's deficit from 7 to 2 per cent of GDP and to eliminate the deficit altogether next year. Despite strong institutional support for the programme, the inevitable devaluation (following a 41 per cent devaluation in December 1995) is likely to cause a sharp inflationary upturn, aggravating social unrest. An increase in social spending equivalent to 3 per cent of GDP was announced to limit the social cost of the adjustment. The programme is supported by a financial package from multilateral institutions including a US$ 1.4 billion standby credit from IMF. The non-oil sector is forecast to contract by 4 per cent in 1996. Such a dismal performance will be partially offset by the oil sector, which is expected to grow by 6 per cent and thus contribute to reducing the overall decline of the economy to about $1\frac{1}{2}$ per cent.

West Asia: continued contraction of the public sector

Economic growth in West Asia so recovered as to reach 3.1 per cent in 1995, following a year of near stagnation in 1994 (table II.4). Oil-importing economies expanded at 6.4 per cent while the oil-exporting economies grew 2.6 per cent. Higher oil prices and export revenues boosted economic recovery in most oil-exporting countries; but efforts to implement economic reforms and reduce budget deficits, while reducing fiscal imbalances, restrained growth in most of these countries. Growth in the output of the oil-exporters has thus failed, for a third consecutive year, to keep pace with their rapidly growing populations. In the oil-importing countries, strong growth in private investment and consumption helped boost economic recovery. The progress being made towards peace in the Middle East stimulated growth of new investment, tourism and construction, particularly in Israel, Jordan and Lebanon.

Developments in the oil market and the peace process will continue to dominate the region's economy in 1996. Economic activity is expected to expand by about 3 per cent as the effects of the recent rise in oil prices and private investment filter through local economies. However, this forecast is contingent on maintaining the 1995 levels of oil production and prices, continuation of economic reforms, and progress in the peace process. Fiscal reform in oil-exporting countries, mainly associated with reductions in government expenditure, is expected to subdue economic growth in the near term, with economic in growth unchanged at 2 per cent in 1996. This and the general opening of economies to private investment are expected to enhance the contribution of private economic activity to output growth.

Economic growth in Saudi Arabia recovered in 1995 with GDP expanding by 1.7 per cent, following a contraction of more than 2 per cent in the previous year. Fiscal consolidation, in effect since 1994, will continue to restrain economic growth, which is expected to remain at the same level in 1996 as in 1995. In the Islamic Republic of Iran, economic activity rose by 3 per cent in 1995. It had recovered in spite of large cuts in government spending. Economic reforms, which had been launched six years ago, continued to have a positive impact on the country's balance of payments, leading to a sharp increase in the current account surplus for the third consecutive year. Controlling imports will remain a priority over the next few years as the government continues to generate the current account surpluses needed to finance its debt-servicing obligations. In the United Arab Emirates, output expanded by only 1.3 per cent in 1995 owing to the effects of restrained oil production and falling oil revenues over the past few years, while the still small non-oil sectors of the economy expanded rapidly. Economic growth in Kuwait slowed to 3 per cent in 1995 and is expected to slow further in 1996 as the contraction of government expenditures is continued in order to reduce the large budget deficit created by expenditures during the Persian Gulf conflict. The Government plans to reduce subsidies on petroleum products and services such as water and electricity, increase customs levies and introduce telephone charges for domestic calls, which were previously free.

Against a background of an inflation rate of over 100 per cent, GDP growth in Yemen was barely positive in 1995, reflecting increased petroleum activity. The economy is expected to improve over the next few years as a result of financial assistance to support structural reforms and economic stabilization. In the Syrian Arab Republic, economic expansion, helped by economic reforms and boosted by increasing oil production, is expected to remain strong, with GDP rising by about 5 per cent in 1996.

In the oil-importing countries, economic activity, stimulated by private investments and helped by the prospects of peace, is expected to remain buoyant with GDP growing at 4 per cent in 1996. Private investment has responded to reduced political uncertainties, and foreign investment in these countries has also increased significantly, helping to finance reconstruction, production and infrastructure projects. Continuation of the peace process is expected to mitigate major impediments to the region's economic growth and prosperity, most notably, by allowing the possibility of reducing the large defence budgets and the risks and uncertainties that have traditionally discouraged investment and inhibited regional economic integration in trade, energy and tourism.

The economy of Israel grew about 7 per cent and unemployment dropped to a low level of 6 per cent in 1995. This strong performance continued to be driven primarily by private sector growth. The high growth in domestic demand resulted in a considerable increase in the trade deficit and the current account deficit rose to more than $4 billion, or 5 per cent of GDP. Policies instituted to correct this imbalance are expected to temporarily slow economic growth to 4 per cent in 1996. Economic activity in Jordan expanded at 6.3 per cent and is expected to improve further in 1996 because of sound fiscal and monetary policies. Jordan also began to benefit from its peace treaty with Israel, with tourism arrivals rising and tourism-related construction and private investment surging. Debt cancellation and debt rescheduling also reduced the country's debt-servicing burden. In Lebanon, economic recovery, driven mainly by the rehabilitation and reconstruction of the country's infrastructure, continued to be strong for the third consecutive year, with GDP rising at 7.0 per cent in 1995. Like Israel and Jordan, Lebanon experienced renewed interest from foreign investors, with direct investment flows amounting to $35 million in 1995. A pause in growth momentum is now expected in 1996, as a consequence of the recent conflict in the southern part of the country, but the momentum will resume over the next few years as a large number of reconstruction projects are be launched.

All in all, economic activity in the region continues to suffer from the lingering consequences of the Persian Gulf conflict, particularly in Iraq, Jordan, Kuwait and Yemen. The United Nations sanctions against Iraq, in effect since August 1990, continue to cripple the country's economic and social development and curtail trade and interregional flows of capital investment.

High rates of unemployment also continue to be problematic in many countries, particularly Yemen and the West Bank and Gaza Strip, where 30 per cent of the workforce is unemployed. Unemployment is also beginning to affect nationals of the member countries of the Gulf Cooperation Council[28] (GCC). This is quite unusual, as these countries have traditionally been destinations of an expatriate labour force used to supplement short supplies of domestic labour. It is estimated that expatriate labour represents an average of 60 per cent of the total labour force in those countries.[29] Government policies have aimed at replacing expatriates by nationals, but such policies have proved difficult to implement.

Several oil-exporting countries, including the Islamic Republic of Iran, Kuwait, Oman, Saudi Arabia and the United Arab Emirates, initiated reform programmes involving measures to reduce budget deficits, restructure the public sector, and promote private sector participation. As a result, government subsidies of public utilities and health services were reduced slightly and fees have been charged or raised for a number of government services in some of these countries. Nevertheless, with still large budget deficits,[30] there remains a clear need for a sustained policy to further rationalize spending, reform public enterprises, reduce subsidies and raise non-oil revenues.

Despite some efforts directed at reducing the dominant role of oil in the economy, the production structures of most of the countries in the region remain largely undiversified. This is particularly pronounced in the case of the oil-exporters, where oil provides over 80 per cent of government revenues and accounts for close to 50 per cent of GDP. Because of this high dependence on oil, their economies remain highly vulnerable to the fluctuations in oil prices, which affect not only the oil-exporting countries, but also the oil-importing countries through employment opportunities for expatriate workers, workers' remittances and trade in goods and services.

South and East Asia: high and more sustainable growth

Economic growth in South and East Asia is expected to moderate slightly to 6 per cent in 1996 from 7 per cent in 1995. This reversal in the trend of accelerating growth since 1992 is largely the result of a deceleration in economic expansion in most of the high-growth countries — the Republic of Korea, Singapore, Indonesia, Malaysia and Thailand. Among the other economies in the region, Hong Kong and Taiwan Province of China are expected to maintain their 1995 rates of growth of 5-6 per cent in 1996. The positive trend in economic growth of the last several years in the Philippines, Viet Nam and India is expected to continue. Here, as well as in the high-growth economies, the policy objective is to restrain inflation while maintaining or strengthening the rate of economic growth. In Pakistan, Bangladesh and Sri Lanka, economic growth in 1996 is likely to be restrained by political instability which has deteriorated since last year.

28 The members are Bahrain, Kuwait, Oman, Qatar, Saudi Arabia and the United Arab Emirates.

29 The proportions are 90 per cent in the United Arab Emirates, 83 per cent in Qatar, 82 per cent in Kuwait, 59 per cent in Saudi Arabia and about 60 per cent in Bahrain and in Oman (see Economic and Social Commission for Western Asia (ESCWA), *Survey of Economic and Social Developments* in the *ESCWA Region*, 1994 (United Nations publication, Sales No. 95.II.L.4)

30 The equation can be derived from the fact that the increase in debt is the overall budget deficit and that deficit can be separated into the primary deficit and the interest payment (which itself can be expressed as the debt level times the average interest rate).

The expected deceleration of economic growth in the high-growth economies is the result of tightening monetary policies implemented last year. GDP growth rates will be reduced from a range of 8-10 per cent in 1995 to 7-8 per cent in 1996. After several years of continued high growth, demand began to push against productive and infrastructure capacity constraints, resulting in increasing upward price pressure. The change in policy stance in 1995 was directed at slowing economic expansion to a more sustainable rate, with lower inflation and reduced current account deficits.

Investment, which has been an important impetus for economic growth, has begun to slow in response to more restrictive monetary conditions in Malaysia and Thailand. The investment boom in the Republic of Korea in the last two years is also subsiding. However, the burden of restraint in credit creation in the Republic of Korea has fallen disproportionately on small and medium-sized enterprises, which have less access to, and pay more for, financing than the conglomerates. Investment in Singapore is expected to be less buoyant as well, as the strong currency and rising manufacturing costs make investment in domestic labour-intensive industries less attractive than investment in similar industries in neighbouring Association of South-East Asian Nations (ASEAN) countries. The exception is Indonesia, where monetary policy has not restrained domestic investment and very strong foreign direct investment has boosted total investment. Higher interest rates and curbs on consumer credit growth have restrained private consumption growth in many of these economies as well.

The expansion of exports, which benefited from the appreciation of the yen, was particularly robust in the high-growth economies (except Singapore) in 1995. A significantly lower rate of growth of exports is expected in 1996 because of exchange rate realignments due to the yen depreciation. This effect is expected to be accentuated in the Republic of Korea because its currency is expected to appreciate against the dollar. Growth in export value in Singapore slowed in 1995 from exceptionally high rates in 1994 because of the declining price of electronics, its major export. This trend in export growth in the high-growth economies is expected to continue in 1996, as the weakening of demand from the developed market economies is going to further dampen demand for overall exports. As a result of tight monetary policy, inflation is expected to moderate, to about 5 per cent or lower, in most of the high-growth countries in 1996. The monetary policy stance is expected to remain contractionary this year but the recent resurgence in short-term capital inflows in some countries — Thailand and Indonesia — has expanded liquidity and could undermine the effectiveness of monetary policy. In response, these countries have instituted sterilization measures and temporary controls, such as increased reserve requirements on foreign deposits, to stem the inflow, as they have been reluctant to allow their currencies to appreciate significantly. However, continued inflows at the current pace could reduce the efficacy of these measures, pushing policy makers to allow currency appreciation.

Current account deficits have been rising rapidly in the high-growth economies (except Singapore). The deficits in Malaysia and Thailand (9 per cent and 7.5 per cent of GDP, respectively, in 1995) were particularly large but were adequately financed by capital inflows. However, the structure of capital inflow in Thailand has become potentially more volatile as the short-term debt component has grown rapidly. The resource gap is expected to be reduced only somewhat in 1996 with slower economic expansion. Progress in Malaysia has been promising, with the recent substantial slow-down in industrial growth and car sales, both major sources of demand for imported capital goods and parts. Thailand's adjustment is expected to be slower, although investment growth has slowed significantly. The current account deficit of Indonesia (3.5 per cent of GDP) is expected to continue to widen, with continued high import growth generated by continued strong investment as well as recent trade liberalization. The external imbalance of the Republic of Korea, which deteriorated substantially in 1995, is expected to improve with the slowing of domestic demand. Because of its heavy reliance on imported capital goods from Japan, the improvement in the Republic of Korea's terms of trade from the appreciation of its currency against the yen will also be an important factor.

The economies of Hong Kong and Taiwan Province of China, which have been expanding at relatively moderate rates of 5-6 per cent since the early 1990s, are expected to maintain these rates of growth in 1996. Their ongoing transition from manufacturing to service economies and the political uncertainties surrounding the return of the sovereignty of Hong Kong to China in 1997 are major factors restricting growth to these levels. Lower property prices and political uncertainties are expected to continue to depress consumer and business confidence in Hong Kong. This negative effect will be offset to an extent by continued high levels of infrastructure investment. In Taiwan Province of China, the easing of tensions with China after the recent presidential elections is expected to improve private consumption and business confidence later this year and offset the decline in the first quarter. Furthermore, export growth of both economies will moderate this year because of continued economic slowing in China and, as with most of the region, depreciation of the yen and weakening of demand from developed market economies.

In contrast with the deceleration of economic growth in the high-growth countries, growth in the Philippines is expected to accelerate; moreover, Viet Nam will be able to maintain its high rate of growth and India will sustain its current rate of economic expansion. These economies are benefiting from improved macroeconomic stability and the results of economic reforms implemented since the end of the 1980s and early 1990s. Economic reforms are expected to continue, although with some adjustment in pace and priority compared with earlier years. The major macroeconomic challenge will be restraining inflation while maintaining or strengthening economic growth.

Economic growth in the Philippines will continue to accelerate in 1996 to 6 per cent. Strong expansion of exports and investment will remain the primary stimuli to growth. The competitive exchange rate and continued liberalization in trade and foreign direct investment have been important factors in the dynamism of exports and direct investment inflows. Manufacturing growth is expected to remain strong and has been facilitated by the success of government policies in improving the power supply situation. Recovery of agriculture from last year's natural disasters will also boost production.

Price increases moderated in the latter part of 1995 with the average rate of inflation for the year declining to just over 8 per cent from 9 per cent. Prospects for continued decline in inflation are uncertain because of the effect of large capital inflows on the expansion of credit. As noted above for Thailand

and Indonesia, currency appreciation is the least preferred option for dealing with these capital inflows. In addition, continued reduction of the fiscal deficit in the Philippines is dependent on the implementation of politically unpopular fiscal reform measures, namely, the further reduction of oil price subsidies and the institution of comprehensive tax reform. There is also the one-time effect on prices of the extension of the VAT at the beginning of the year.

Economic growth in Viet Nam is expected to remain at approximately 9.5 per cent in 1996, but at the cost of deteriorating internal and external imbalance. Strong growth in public and private investment is a major stimulus to the economy. Private and official capital inflows have become an important source of financing. Foreign direct investment, primarily from Japan and the Asian newly industrialized economies (the Republic of Korea, Hong Kong, Singapore and Taiwan Province of China) has increased significantly in the last two years. Exports will remain buoyant, with continued strong growth of agricultural exports and gradual diversification into manufactured exports. Import growth due to the strength of investment and consumption and trade liberalization will be even higher, resulting in a larger current account deficit. On the supply side, agricultural output growth is expected to remain strong, barring any natural disasters.

Control of the budget deficit (5.5 per cent of GDP in 1995) will remain a challenge because of difficulties in increasing government revenues through tax reform and a pressing need for development/infrastructure projects. Money supply growth is expected to continue at a high rate, owing to continuing credit creation to finance the state enterprise sector and the inflow of funds. Inflation in 1996 is therefore expected to worsen from about 13 per cent in 1995.

GDP growth in India is expected to be just over 6 per cent in 1996, continuing the pace in 1995. Here too, the major impetus to growth is expected to be investment and exports, as the currency depreciation in late 1995 will maintain export growth at high levels. Investment is also expected to remain strong in response to strong final demand and a more accommodative monetary policy in 1996. Growth in agricultural output and food prices are expected to be stable pending favourable weather conditions. Inflation moderated during 1995 because of the decline in food prices due to increased supplies. Because of the still high budget deficit (almost 6 per cent of GDP), control of inflation in 1995 depended on a tightening of monetary policy, which restrained the growth of private investment.

Economic liberalization and reform since 1991 have contributed importantly to India's robust economic growth in the last two years. To date, most progress has been made in the reform of private investment regulation, the liberalization of exports and imports of intermediate goods, convertibility in the current account and the beginning of reform in the financial sector. The nature and pace of the next wave of reform await the results of the April 1996 elections.

The rates of growth of other South Asian countries — Bangladesh, Pakistan and Sri Lanka — are expected to remain almost unchanged in 1996, in the range of 5-6 per cent, with little improvement in, and even some deterioration of, their domestic and external imbalances. The recent intensification of political conflicts and widespread strikes in Bangladesh and continued sectarian violence and labour unrest in Pakistan can be expected to hold down economic growth because of the resulting disruption of different sectors of the economy. Worsening ethnic strife in Sri Lanka has undermined investor confidence and put a halt to foreign direct investment, damaging prospects for strengthening economic growth in the near term. The difficulty of implementing fiscal reform in an environment of political instability and the pressure to increase military expenditures as a result of internal strife — in the case of Sri Lanka — have kept the budget deficits of these countries above 6 per cent of GDP.

China: consolidation of macroeconomic stabilization

During 1995, China maintained a contractionary policy stance and its economic growth rate slowed to 10 per cent, while inflation slowed also. Reducing inflation was a priority: to achieve this goal, the Government continued its relatively tight monetary policy, while financing its fiscal deficits by bond issues. The growth of fixed investment decelerated from over 30 per cent in 1994 to about 19 per cent in 1995. The rise in retail sales slowed to about 10 per cent in real terms over 1994. As a result, the rate of inflation was reduced to about 17 per cent from 24 per cent in 1994.

The reduction in the rate of inflation was the result of several factors. Macroeconomic policy, as already noted, was one such factor. A record year in grain production helped to contain the rise in food prices, which had been an important factor in overall inflation in recent years. Moreover, the Government took specific measures to curtail price increases. This included liberalization in the wholesale and retail sectors which promoted competition. Also, the central Government used its foreign-exchange reserves to import goods in short supply and restrain price increases in the domestic market. Local Governments adjusted their food stocks to support price stability. Price increases for goods and services still under government price control were postponed. Other measures such as official price inspections were also employed to discourage price increases.

Losses of State-owned enterprises (SOEs) increased as their financial difficulties intensified in a restrictive macroeconomic environment. As a tight monetary policy restrained the amount of credit available to enterprises, the problem of "chain debts" (the term refers to a situation where enterprises are indebted to one another for supplies of materials and intermediate inputs) worsened. Indeed, the problems that the SOE sector posed to overall economic efficiency and to the central Government's budget remained unresolved. Recognizing the crucial role of state enterprise reforms at this juncture of China's economic development, the Government identified the area as a priority in future reforms.

Controlling inflation will also remain a policy priority for 1996 and the Government intends to continue its tight monetary stance as well as to employ more direct means of restraining the growth of fixed investment (for an analysis of China's investment policy, see chap. VII). That priority will be given to financing investment in agriculture and infrastructure would help relax bottlenecks in the economy and thus reduce inflationary pressures. As a result, further moderation in economic growth and the rate of inflation can be expected this year.

The Government has set the target GDP growth rate at 8 per cent and inflation at 10 per cent for 1996. Based on economic data on the first two months of 1996 and an assessment of the policy environment in terms of the response to mounting pressure for increased credit to many SOEs, GDP growth could approach 9 per cent this year, as there may be some monetary loosening later in the year as inflation continues to moderate.

Declining domestic inflation, a relatively tight monetary policy and significant inflows of foreign exchange resulted in a mild appreciation of the domestic currency during 1995. If continued, currency appreciation could dampen the competitiveness of China's exports in 1996. In addition, trade liberalization measures combined with a less contractionary macroeconomic policy can be expected to stimulate the demand for imports. As a result, the trade surplus may narrow somewhat in 1996, although this would follow the much expanded trade surplus of 1995, which reached almost $17 billion. China's foreign-exchange reserves increased by $22 billion during 1995, with total reserves reaching $74 billion by the end of the year.

For the near future, the transition from input-driven economic growth to growth based on efficiency improvement has been identified by the Government as the overarching goal. Economic reforms will be implemented to facilitate this transformation. Financial sector reforms to strengthen the development of financial institutions and prudential supervision as well as trade liberalization will be carried out. At the same time, reforms aimed at establishing a system of social security, unemployment insurance and medical insurance will continue in order to cushion the social impact of the eventual reform of state enterprises. Thus, barring major political changes, the Chinese economy can be expected in 1997 to maintain its relatively high rate of growth while continuing to restrain the rate of inflation.

III THE INTERNATIONAL ECONOMY

The international economy in the mid-1990s contains several encouraging features and presents at least one major difficulty. On the positive side, world trade in 1996 is in its third consecutive year of unusually strong growth. The prices of many commodities exported by developing countries have remained strong. The World Trade Organization, the new international organization established to oversee the operation of the international trading system and handle disputes and in which virtually all the world's nations wish to participate, is now a year old. International financial flows continue to spread rapidly around the globe and foreign direct investment (FDI) is reaching new highs. Immediately after the shock of the Mexican balance-of-payments crisis, Mexico took strong adjustment steps, which the international community supported financially, that facilitated Mexico's return after only a few months to the international financial markets. In addition, the international community formulated a strategy to prevent future emergencies, while setting up special financing as a fall-back. Moreover, substantial progress finally seems to be on the near horizon as regards addressing the severe debt difficulties of a number of low-income countries in a more comprehensive manner.

The most worrisome feature of the international situation, however, is the fact that recent trends and future prospects are bleak for marshalling the concessional international financial resources that are needed in many countries for economically and socially important projects yet are not usually provided on a commercial basis. These are the resources for official development assistance (ODA), that is, for financial and technical cooperation with the poorest countries and the poorest people.

THE SUSTAINED BUOYANCY OF WORLD TRADE

The total value of world merchandise trade was about $5 trillion in 1995. Developed countries supplied almost two thirds of world exports, selling more than 70 per cent to other developed countries. Developing countries provided about 29 per cent of the world total, almost half of which originated in South and East Asia (excluding China). Economies in transition accounted for the remainder of world exports, about 4 per cent of the total (see annex table A.15).

This is a snapshot of world trade, but it should be borne in mind that trade is also very dynamic. Only five years earlier (when international petroleum prices were at a temporary peak), the total value of world trade was less than $3.5 trillion and the developed countries accounted for over 70 per cent of it. Five years hence, world trade will again be a far larger magnitude and the proportions of different countries and country groups in total trading activity will have again evolved appreciably.

Developed countries in the recent growth of world trade

In the first three years of the 1990s, the volume of world exports grew 3.5 per cent a year on average. World export volume then grew by over 10 per cent in 1994, and by almost 9 per cent in 1995, and it is forecast to grow $7\frac{3}{4}$ per cent this year (see annex table A.19). The main reason for the change is that imports of the largest buyers, the developed economies, grew slowly in the early 1990s, but they have been growing rapidly since.

The volume of imports of developed economies grew relatively slowly in the first three years of the decade and then speeded up in the period 1994-1996 for several reasons. The first is that 1991 was a recession year for Australia, Canada, New Zealand and the United States of America, while 1991 and 1992 were recession years for the United Kingdom of Great Britain and Northern Ireland and 1991, 1992 and 1993 were recession years for Finland, Sweden and Switzerland. Japan and much of continental Western Europe entered into recession in 1993. From 1994 on, all the developed countries were in various stages of economic recovery and this raised the demand for imports. However, the slow-down in economic growth during 1995 and continuing into 1996, especially in Europe, as discussed in chapter II, slowed the growth of import demand and is a major factor behind the slower growth of import volume forecast for 1996.

An exception to this story is the case of Japan. The recovery in Japan has been particularly weak, but its import volume rose 13.6 per cent in 1994 and then by over 10 per cent in 1995. A prime reason was the sharp appreciation of the yen, as may be seen in figure III.1. By 1995, the inflation-adjusted purchasing power of the yen had risen more than 25 per cent above the 1990 level, making imports very attractive to Japanese residents.

Exchange-rate changes have been significant in other countries as well. In Italy, for example, the real effective exchange rate of the lira in 1993 was about 14 per cent lower than in 1992, reflecting the depreciation of the lira after Italy left the exchange-rate mechanism of the European Monetary System in the fall of 1992. This loss in foreign purchasing power seems to have aggravated the effect of the recession in Italy in that year: the volume of imports contracted by 11 per cent in 1993. Exports, however, began to surge, stimulated by the exchange-rate effect. They rose 8 per cent in 1993, almost 12 per cent in 1994 and 15 per cent in 1995. Similar factors were at work in the United Kingdom and several smaller European economies.

Additional factors have of course also been at work. In Canada and the United States, for example, the strong role of investment in their recoveries from recession – and in particular the growth of machinery and equipment investment – found a counterpart in their import figures. Thus, while world imports of machinery and equipment (other than passenger road vehicles and

Figure III.1.
SEVEN MAJOR INDUSTRIALIZED COUNTRIES: IMPORTS, OUTPUT AND REAL EXCHANGE RATES, 1991-1996

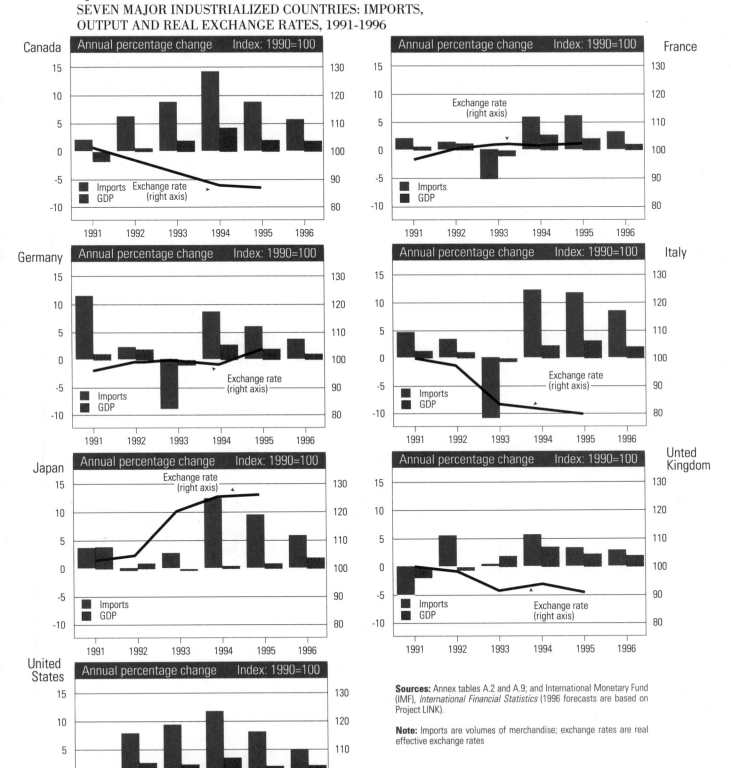

Sources: Annex tables A.2 and A.9; and International Monetary Fund (IMF), *International Financial Statistics* (1996 forecasts are based on Project LINK).

Note: Imports are volumes of merchandise; exchange rates are real effective exchange rates

1 See United Nations, *Monthly Bulletin of Statistics*, May 1996, special table D.

2 Developing countries also took 25 per cent of the exports of developed countries in a previous period, that is, in the early 1980s, before the developing-country debt crisis erupted and during the time that oil prices were high; today the most dynamic markets are in Asia (see annex table A.15).

parts) grew by one eighth from 1992 to 1994, Canada's imports of these items grew 20 per cent and those of the United States grew 26 per cent.[1] In addition, one of the factors in the growth of imports in Japan has been the technological advances in new computers exported by the United States, which have the power to easily run the graphics-based software used in Japanese language programmes. In fact, the volume of imports of machinery and equipment, including computers and semiconductors, rose 36 per cent in 1995. Also, the value of semiconductor imports alone rose 54 per cent (these had been the object of bilateral negotiations between Japan and the United States).

The major export markets of the developed countries are other developed countries and the growth of their exports has risen with the growth of their imports. Thus, Western Europe's export volume grew 11 per cent in 1994, the first year of economic recovery, and over 7 per cent in 1995; but they are forecast to grow only 5 per cent in 1996, owing to the economic slow-down in Europe discussed earlier.

The main exception with respect to the recent export growth buoyancy has been Japan, where as a consequence of the yen appreciation noted above, the volume of exports grew less than 2 per cent in 1994 and 6 per cent in 1995. Export volume is forecast to increase only $2\frac{1}{2}$ per cent in 1996.

The over-8 per cent-a-year export volume growth of the United States in 1994 and 1995 and forecast for 1996 reflects both the flip side of the Japanese import expansion noted above and increased United States sales to developing countries. Indeed, this is a broader phenomenon. Developed countries have been increasingly selling to developing countries, as well they would be since the markets of the latter have been growing so rapidly. Developing economies now purchase about 25 per cent of developed-country exports, up from 20 per cent in 1990.[2]

Dynamics of trade of the developing countries

The volume of developing-country imports has grown by over 9 per cent a year or more since 1991 and it is forecast to rise by $12\frac{1}{4}$ per cent in 1996 (annex table A.19). This is, as usual, the result of a broad mix of outcomes. The growth of Latin America's import volume was dramatically curtailed in 1995 by the financial crisis in two of its three largest economies, while the continuing adjustment programmes in the large West Asian economies once again reduced their import levels. Other Asian economies thus accounted for most of the growth of imports in 1995, although Africa also participated in import volume growth, if in a modest way.

Except in South Africa, the volume of Africa's imports rose only slightly in 1995, although a stronger growth is forecast for 1996 (see annex table A.19). South African imports grew rapidly, fuelled by the country's investment boom (see chap. VIII). While Africa's average import increase was not large by global standards, it was fairly widespread. Imports were stimulated by trade liberalization policies and by expanded food imports owing to drought conditions in northern and southern Africa. The rise in imports was made possible in part by higher commodity export earnings, owing to stronger prices in 1994 and 1995 and the encouragement that this gave to expanding export volumes – abetted, for the countries of the franc zone, by the salutary effects of the devaluation of the CFA franc in early 1994 (see chap. II). Export volumes were thus boosted by almost 5 per cent in 1995 and double that increase is forecast for 1996.

Import growth has been consistently strong in South and East Asia and in most years in China. This is paralleled – and made possible – by the rapid growth of exports. Economies in this region have been particularly successful in expanding into the most dynamic sectors of merchandise trade – into the "new" manufactured products, the highly sophisticated "information-age" goods.[3] They have also spread more traditional manufacturing export capacities around the region (see box III.1 for a case in point).

The Asian region, moreover, has become a significant market for its own products, reflecting its increasing economic integration, much of it fostered by intraregional FDI. The main pattern has been for investment to flow from Japan and the newly industrialized economies – the Republic of Korea, Hong Kong, Singapore and Taiwan Province of China – to Indonesia, Malaysia and Thailand. This, in turn, has generated a demand in the host countries for imported capital goods and other inputs.

More recently, there has been an extension of such regional economic integration to the Philippines and Viet Nam. This has been in response to the significant progress in overall economic reform, particularly the liberalization of FDI regulations, as well as substantially stabilized macroeconomic conditions. Viet Nam is a special case in which the transition to a market-oriented economy has opened up new opportunities for investment as well as a potentially large domestic market.

China is also a major destination for FDI, the gross inflow reaching $38 billion in 1995. Indeed, with strong growth of the volume of exports - estimated at 17 per cent in 1995 (annex table A.19) – and substantial capital inflows, the exchange rate began to appreciate. If continued, currency appreciation could dampen the competitiveness of China's exports in 1996.[4]

The trade situation in Latin America reflected the dramatic events occurring there in 1994 and 1995, mainly in the three largest economies (which together account for about 60 per cent of the region's trade). While Latin American exports grew very strongly in 1995, import growth was sharply curtailed. The latter mainly reflected the sharp adjustments in Argentina and Mexico, as deficits in the balance of payments on current account which many observers had privately feared could not be sustained suddenly became unsustainable in fact in late 1994 and 1995 when the requisite financing disappeared. In 1996, with moderate recovery forecast for Argentina and Mexico, regional import volumes are expected to resume a stronger rate of growth.

In Brazil, the largest economy in the region, import growth was encouraged by a liberalization policy, as part of the anti-inflation programme. Dramatic progress was indeed made in reducing inflation and this boosted confidence and helped to attract large capital inflows that underwrote strong domestic demand and thus the import growth. However, the financial inflows were so large that a substantial build-up of foreign exchange reserves was required to limit the appreciation of the currency.

In the case of Mexico, the exchange-rate peg had to be abandoned before the end of 1994.[5] For 1995, the annual real effective exchange rate of the Mexican peso was 30 per cent below its 1994 level, leaving it almost 20 per cent below the level in 1991 when the latest bout of overvaluation had begun (see

[3] See *World Economic and Social Survey, 1995* (United Nations publication, Sales No. E.95.II.C.1), chap. XI.

[4] A change in tax policy in 1995 underlined how sensitive exports are to price incentives: the Government announced early in the year that the rebate of the value-added tax on exports would be reduced by 3 percentage points in the second half of the year, as a result of which there was a 44 per cent increase in the value of exports in the first half of 1995 compared with the same period of 1994, and a depletion of supplies for export and thus lower exports in the second half of the year, continuing into 1996.

[5] For a brief description of the events, see *World Economic and Social Survey, 1995* (United Nations publication, Sales No. E.95.II.C.1), chap. V, subsection entitled "'Rocky road' to stabilization in Latin America and the Caribbean: what happened in Mexico?".

Box III.1.

POLICY, INVESTMENT AND EXPORTS: HOW BANGLADESH BECAME AN EXPORTER OF READY-MADE GARMENTS

[a] A caveat: exports of ready-made garments are substantially larger than the net foreign exchange earnings from this industry, owing to heavy use of imported textiles, as well as patterns and equipment.

[b] The fiscal year in Bangladesh ends on 30 June of the year named.

[c] Data of Bangladesh Bureau of Statistics, *Statistical Bulletin*, various issues.

[d] Not surprisingly, the United States share of Bangladeshi garments exports fell from 80 per cent in 1984 to about 50 per cent a decade later, the balance going largely to Western Europe.

READY-MADE GARMENTS AND OTHER EXPORTS OF BANGLADESH, 1983-1995

Over some 15 years, exports of ready-made garments rose from insignificance to constitute over half the exports of Bangladesh (see figure).[a] It is an industry that employs a relatively standardized technology (based essentially on sewing machines) with no major economies of scale. Yet it was an industry that at first did not "take off" in Bangladesh. In this case, national policy changes provided an enabling condition and international policy created an incentive for producers in other countries to look to Bangladesh. That policy involved the quota limits on exports of individual developing countries under the Multi-Fibre Arrangement (MFA). The operation of the MFA created a strong incentive to producers in other countries whose exports were being limited to shift their production elsewhere, and Bangladesh became an attractive "elsewhere". The result has been considerable investment in the garment sector, first foreign, but then mainly Bangladeshi.

The industry in its present form began in the early 1980s as a joint venture, Daewoo-Desh, between a large enterprise of the Republic of Korea and a Bangladeshi partner, in which the firm of the Republic of Korea supplied technology through overseas technical training of Bangladeshi employees in the designing of patterns and the cutting of textiles to conform to particular garment styles. By fiscal 1983,[b] 21 enterprises had registered with the newly established Bangladesh Garment Manufacturers and Exporters Association (BGMEA) and reported gross export sales of almost $11 million. By fiscal 1985, 134 firms were registered with BGMEA and export receipts reached $116 million, 12 per cent of total export earnings for the year. The number of registered garment manufacturers has since fluctuated widely (exit as well as entry is very easy in this industry), but export earnings reached $300 million in fiscal 1987, $600 million in 1990 and almost $2 billion by 1995.[c]

Three factors seem to have accounted for the success of the industry in Bangladesh. First was the fact that no major export marketing system was needed, as the industry utilizes instead a much simpler international subcontracting arrangement in which the buyer brings the orders together with the raw materials and the design and cutting specifications to a Bangladeshi garment manufacturer. Second was the establishment of a special bonded warehouse scheme, which made possible the financing on international commercial terms of the material inputs to the manufacturing process. Third was the favourable situation of Bangladesh under the Multi-Fibre Arrangement. Up to 1985, the United States had not imposed any MFA quota ceiling on imports of Bangladeshi garments. Ten years later, the European Union still allowed unrestricted entry.[d]

Low labour costs in Bangladesh satisfied a major requirement for competitiveness in the industry; but it was the international subcontracting system, in conjunction with the offshore financing scheme, that enabled the industry to circumvent the constraints on access to technology, input supply, finance and marketing that sometimes bedevil emerging export industries. Investment requirements have also been quite modest, with as little as $175,000 said to have been needed for fixed capital to set up a small firm. Thus, although the industry was initially largely foreign -- as firms of the Republic of Korea and Sri Lankan firms in particular sought to evade quota limitations on their exports under the MFA -- it has since become mainly Bangladeshi. Indeed, about 90 per cent of the enterprises registered with the BGMEA are owned by Bangladeshis.

Billions of dollars

Total Exports

Garments

Others

1983 1984 1985 1986 1987 1988 1989 1990 1991 1992 1993 1994 1995

Source: Data supplied by World Bank, based on data of Bangladesh.
Note: Data for fiscal years ending 30 June of year cited.

annex table A.14). Coupled with the sharp economic contraction that followed the financial crisis and adjustment programme, Mexico's import volume fell 15 per cent; but Mexico's sales to its major foreign markets, especially the United States, responded briskly to the new price situation: Mexican export volume jumped one quarter for the year.

Argentina maintained its fixed exchange rate to the dollar in 1995, withstanding a major economic contraction in the process; its import volume fell by more than Mexico's. Argentina's exports were robust, however, mainly because import demand in its largest trading partner, Brazil, was surging, as noted above. Indeed, Brazil now takes about a quarter of Argentina's exports, up from less than an eighth in 1990.

Buoyant trade of transition economies

The foreign trade of the Central and Eastern European transition economies (CEETEs) mirrored the buoyant economic growth in most of these economies. The volume of exports grew an estimated 9.5 per cent in 1995 and imports expanded 11 per cent. Similar, if slightly lower, rates of growth are forecast for 1996 (see annex table A.19). In the Baltic States and in countries of the Commonwealth of Independent States (CIS), there also appears to have been a considerable increase in trade flows.

Throughout the transition economies, the changes in trade flows reflect the transformation of production structures – a central element of the transition process. In almost all cases, since 1990, when the process started in earnest, the pattern has been for the shares of trade with other economies in transition to shrink and the shares going to developed countries to grow. This change accelerated with the collapse of the Council for Mutual Economic Assistance (CMEA) in 1991.

It could be expected that the share of manufactures in total exports would rise over time, but the loss of the captive markets of the former CMEA has also meant a temporary decline in demand for manufactured exports. In the case of the Czech Republic in particular, the share of manufactured exports, particularly machinery and transport equipment, first fell in the 1990s, as it ceased to supply the CMEA markets, but it has grown since. In the case of Hungary and Poland, the share of manufactures has risen during the 1990s, reflecting the expansion of trade in intermediate goods.[6]

CEETE exports are still limited to a relatively few agricultural and industrial products. The latter include clothing, steel products, chemicals, footwear and wood products, produced mostly in the framework of "outward processing" trade. That is, lower labour costs, easier access to developed-country markets and, in some cases, less strict environmental regulations than in the developed countries make it attractive for producers from those countries to send primary or semi finished products to the CEETE countries for processing and export. There has, though, been some movement in Hungary and Poland away from traditional export commodities towards locally designed and skill intensive products, including small mechanical and electrical engineering goods.

In the case of almost all the CEETEs, the most dynamic element of exports has been sales to developed economies, especially to the European Union (EU).[7] The EU accounts for about 50 per cent of CEETE exports and imports,

6 See Economic Commission for Europe (ECE), *Economic Bulletin for Europe*, vol. 47 (1995), p. 48; and ECE, *Economic Survey of Europe in 1995-1996* (United Nations publication, Sales No. E.96.II.E.1), table 3.5.4.

7 The share of Czech exports going to developed countries, for example, was 55 per cent in 1991 and 60 per cent in 1994; for Hungary the respective shares were 54 per cent and 71 per cent; and for Poland 66 per cent and 76 per cent.

with Germany being the major partner. Indeed, the deceleration in growth in some of the EU countries in 1995 and early 1996 is one factor behind the slower export growth forecast for 1996.

However, the growing import volume of the CEETEs themselves – 1996 will mark the third consecutive year of annual growth on the order of 10 per cent – is beginning to turn the CEETEs into a significant market for each other's products once again, albeit this time the phenomenon is based on market prices rather than negotiated arrangements. The upturn in intra-group trade first appeared in 1994. In 1995, the value of intra group trade flows grew by 25 per cent. Trade between the CEETEs and the CIS countries also expanded. Exports to developing countries increased compared with 1994.

By the same token, for several years following the dissolution of the Union of Soviet Socialist Republics (USSR), trade among its former constituent republics – now sovereign States – declined. This was due both to the general economic contraction in the region and to the dramatic efforts of many of these countries to reorient their foreign economic ties away from their erstwhile sister republics in the USSR. Thus, by 1995 Azerbaijan was sending over 80 per cent of its exports to the Islamic Republic of Iran and obtaining over 60 per cent of its imports from the Islamic Republic of Iran and Turkey. China took almost half of Kyrgyzstan's exports and Romania was the destination for half of the Republic of Moldova's exports.

However, by the end of 1995 a certain revitalization of intra-CIS trade became noticeable. In January-February 1996, trade among the CIS countries increased 50 per cent, compared with a year earlier, to reach over $5 billion. In the first quarter of 1996, the dollar value of the Russian Federation's exports to the CIS countries grew nearly 40 percent, while imports jumped 70 per cent compared with the same period of 1995.

More generally, in the case of the Russian Federation and several other States of the former Soviet Union, foreign trade remains one of the most dynamic sectors of the economy. In the Russian Federation, where trade volume data are not available, the value of exports in dollars grew 18 per cent in 1995 and imports grew 15 per cent.

Although exports do not appear to have been severely affected as yet, one concern in the Russian Federation has been the real effective appreciation of the rouble. With inflation slowing in the Russian Federation, the real value of the exchange rate of the rouble against the dollar has appreciated, although with considerable oscillation. In late summer of 1995, the Russian authorities sought to reduce the fluctuations in the exchange rate by introducing a rouble trading "corridor" within which the exchange rate has since been allowed to move, with some modifications in the corridor's limits and in the procedures for setting the exchange rate. With a gradual managed devaluation of the rouble – which is the declared policy of the Government and the Central Bank of Russia – exports may get an additional boost.

A peak in non-fuel commodity prices

The international prices in dollars of the non-fuel commodities that developing countries export were on average about 11 per cent higher in 1995 than in 1994 (see annex table A.21). However, these prices peaked in the first quarter of 1995 and then slowly retreated (see figure III.2). The recent commodity "boom" thus lasted from the start of the recovery in prices in the second half of 1993 through the dramatic increases of 1994 to the peak, from which point they retreated slightly by the end of the year. Dollar prices in 1996 are expected to remain at roughly the end-year levels if demand keeps pace with the expected steady-but-moderate growth in the global economy.

Average dollar prices can be a misleading measure by themselves, as exchange rates of the dollar change and the dollar prices of other goods change. Indeed, the 1995 increase in average dollar prices of 11 per cent becomes an increase of only 4 per cent when expressed in units of special drawing rights (SDRs), which are a basket of five major currencies (annex table A.21). Alternatively, if the average dollar prices are expressed as a ratio to the dollar prices of the manufactured exports of the developed economies – sometimes called the "real" price of the commodities – the 1995 increase was only about 2 per cent (annex table A.21). Indeed, although the dollar price peak in 1995 was higher than the previous peak in 1989, it was lower than the 1989 level when expressed in real terms (figure III.2).

The largest price gains in 1995 were for industrial raw materials owing to strong demand. The price index for the minerals and metals group rose 20 per cent, compared with agricultural raw materials which rose by 14 per cent. Increases for individual commodities, such as lead, tin, aluminium, copper, nickel and natural rubber, ranged from 11 to 40 per cent. Producer agreements were successful in reducing excess supplies and strengthening prices of aluminium and tin in global markets.

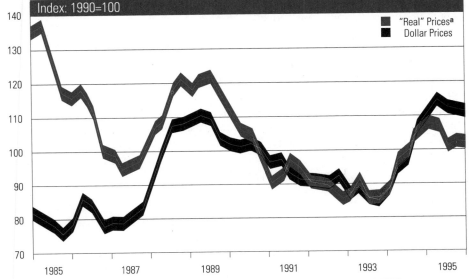

Figure III.2.
NON-FUEL COMMODITY EXPORT PRICES
OF DEVELOPING COUNTRIES, 1985-1995

Index: 1990=100

"Real" Prices[a]
Dollar Prices

Sources: Data of United Nations Conference on Trade and Development (UNCTAD) and UN/DESIPA.
[a] "Real" prices are dollar prices deflated by unit value of manufactured exports of developed economies.

Food prices increased by 6 per cent as a result of increased demand and supply shortages in global markets. The strongest growth in demand came from developing countries where incomes have been growing steadily in recent years. Lower import tariffs and lower domestic food production in countries undergoing rapid industrialization have contributed to the growing worldwide demand for food commodities such as wheat, rice, beef, poultry, vegetable oils and oilseeds, as well as feed grains such as corn and soy meal. China, in the clearest indication of this trend, became a large net importer in 1995 of rice and corn (commodities that the country used to export in large quantities). Wheat and corn prices escalated to 15-year highs in March 1996, because of severe weather related damage to crops in the United States amid low stocks and supply shortages among major producers elsewhere in the world. The Food and Agriculture Organization of the United Nations (FAO) estimated that import costs for 88 low-income grain-importing countries would rise by $3 billion in 1996 as a result of the higher prices.[8]

Tropical beverage prices rose only 1 per cent in 1995 under more normal supply conditions than in 1994, when coffee prices had more than doubled following a severe frost in Brazil's coffee-growing region. Prices remained high during the first half of 1995, but declined rapidly after it became apparent that the damage to Brazil's 1995 crop had been less extensive than originally estimated. Increased exports – triggered, in part, by the high prices – provided a welcome boost in foreign exchange receipts of some low-income suppliers, but also renewed fears of a return to global market conditions of chronic excess supply and low prices. However, an export-retention scheme of the Association of Coffee Producing Countries – comprising major producers in Africa, Asia and Latin America, accounting for 80 per cent of global production – prevented a more precipitous collapse of prices.

The 1995 results more accurately reflected underlying demand and supply conditions in global markets compared with the 1994 situation, when market prices of some commodities were significantly distorted by transactions in commodity-based financial instruments. Speculators were accused by market participants of trading coffee more in futures contracts than in actual supplies of the physical commodity, thus inducing significant volatility. Similarly, the run-up in prices of key industrial minerals and metals in 1994 was partly attributed to record purchases of corresponding futures contracts by investment funds and speculators in anticipation of further price increases. Prices dropped sharply in early 1995, however, as economic growth in the United States slowed, inflationary fears receded and investors retreated from commodity-linked assets to more traditional investments in bond and equity markets.

International petroleum market

Demand on the international petroleum market strengthened in 1995 and into early 1996. Average oil prices climbed to $16.90 a barrel in 1995, about 9 per cent higher than their level in 1994.[9] As a result, total oil revenues of the member countries of the Organization of the Petroleum Exporting Countries (OPEC) rose in 1995 by an estimated $13 billion, or 11 per cent over their level in 1994 (see annex table A.43). Notwithstanding this rise, OPEC oil revenues in 1995 remained at no more than one half the 1974 level in inflation-

[8] Statement of the Director-General of the Food and Agriculture Organization of the United Nations (FAO) at the Twentieth FAO Regional Conference for Europe, Tel Aviv, 29 April 1996.

[9] The price indicator employed here is the average spot price of the Organization of the Petroleum Exporting Countries (OPEC) basket of seven crude oils.

adjusted terms.[10] Indeed, apart from the temporary run-up in oil prices associated with the Iraqi invasion of Kuwait, oil prices have been relatively stable in dollar terms (see figure III.3).

By April 1996, crude oil prices were at their highest level since 1991. There were several special circumstances, including low inventory and uncertainty over whether the United Nations would allow Iraq to export some oil to buy food and medicine. Such uncertainty coincided with a surge in world demand for oil owing to the unexpectedly cold winter across the northern hemisphere and the rapid growth in consumption in Asia. At the same time, expectations in the first half of the year that Iraq would soon resume exporting some oil led refiners to lower their inventories; but when those expectations did not materialize, refiners rushed to buy crude oil to meet the rapid rise in demand, particularly for gasoline. When demand for oil increased (partly to build inventories), prices went up. The rise in prices was a boosted further by speculative commodity traders.

In the period ahead, with the onset of warm weather in the northern hemisphere and the anticipated expansion of output from OPEC and non OPEC producers, prices are expected to decline. The extent of the decline will

[10]   See *World Economic and Social Survey, 1995...*, figure III.4 and associated text.

Figure III.3.
AVERAGE SPOT PRICES OF OPEC BASKET OF CRUDE OILS, 1988-1996

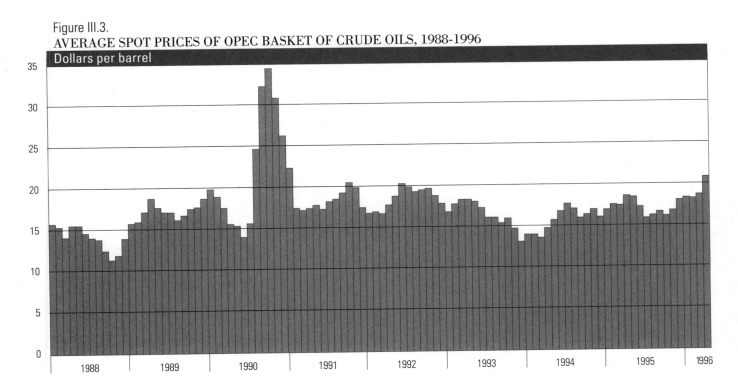

Source: Data of the Organization of the Petroleum Exporting Countries (OPEC).

depend on whether or not Iraq reaches an agreement with the United Nations to export oil. However, because of the sharp and unanticipated rise of oil prices in the first four months of 1996, the average price of oil is likely to be higher for the year as a whole than in 1995. Prices are nevertheless still expected to decline during the remainder of 1996 and into 1997, reflecting mainly the expectations of a partial return of Iraqi oil to the market. Oil prices are thus expected to average $17.50 a barrel in 1996, a rise of almost 4 per cent over the level in 1995.[11]

World oil demand rose by 1.6 million barrels per day, or 2.3 per cent in 1995 (see annex table A.40). Most of the growth came from developing countries, where demand rose by 5 per cent. There was a particularly sharp growth in the countries of South and East Asia (8 per cent) and little or no growth in Africa. Oil consumption in Africa remained nearly static over the past five years, reflecting slow economic growth and, in some cases, shortages of supply. In the developed economies, oil demand grew 1 per cent, while in the economies in transition, the sharp declines in the demand for oil in each year since 1989 finally ended.

World oil production grew in 1995 almost in line with demand, rising by 1.6 million barrels per day, or 2.3 per cent, over output in 1994 (see annex table A.41). Most of the growth was accounted for by the North Sea and non-OPEC developing countries. Total production from OPEC, including natural gas liquids, rose only marginally, reflecting the slow growth of demand for its oil. OPEC's decision to maintain the crude oil production ceiling that it had set more than two years ago (24.52 million barrels per day) was in line with the desire of the majority of OPEC members to ensure price stability even at the cost of losing market share to non-OPEC producers.

The rapid growth in non-OPEC supply, combined with the likelihood of a continuation of this trend for the next several years, has begun to change perceptions of the medium-term outlook for oil market developments. The prevailing view in the late 1980s and early 1990s was that declining supplies of some non-OPEC oil and projections of near-term peaks for other sources, particularly in the North Sea, would lead to a sharp rise in the call for OPEC oil. That view neglected the positive impact of technological progress on oil supply and underestimated the potential for additions to supply from non-OPEC sources.[12]

Indeed, the sharp rise in oil production owing to the commissioning of several new oilfields, resulting from technology-driven cost reductions, made Norway in 1995 Western Europe's biggest oil producer and the world's second largest oil exporter behind Saudi Arabia. Alongside continuing production growth from the North Sea and certain developing countries, the steep decline of production in the United States and the former Soviet Union subsided.

Thus, in spite of an anticipated rapid rise in oil demand, the international oil market will most likely continue to experience excess supplies, as Norway, the United Kingdom, the CIS countries and a large number of developing countries continue to add reserves and capacity, as well as absorb a significant share of the increase in world oil demand. Such developments are expected to keep real oil prices constant for the next decade, albeit with temporary fluctuations.

Another dimension of the changed prospects of the international oil industry is that it has been encouraged by changes in government policies. The growth in non-OPEC supply was helped by more attractive fiscal incentives in

[11] The unexpected extent of the recent price increase thus far in 1996 means that the oil price in the Project LINK forecast, as given in the introduction to the statistical annex, is $0.50 per barrel lower than that expected as the Survey goes to press.

[12] For additional details, see *World Economic and Social Survey, 1995...* chap. X.

a number of oil-exporting developing countries aimed at foreign oil companies. These changes have also brought a progressive shift in the policies of a number of OPEC countries that are seeking to tap into the capital, technology and expertise of international oil companies, thus reopening the way for private investment and ending the monopoly of their State-owned oil companies over oil exploration and development. A number of countries, including Algeria, China, Indonesia, the Islamic Republic of Iran, Malaysia, Nigeria, Venezuela, Viet Nam and countries of the CIS, are allowing foreign companies to engage in new exploration as well as participate in further development of already producing oilfields. Thus, a new relationship is emerging between oil-exporting countries eager to make supplies available to a growing market and international oil companies looking for investment opportunities.

THE INTERNATIONAL TRANSFER OF FINANCIAL RESOURCES

At the end of each year, when national statisticians add up their country's total value of exports and imports — whether of merchandise trade, as has been discussed above, or the more inclusive trade in goods and services — the export and import figures are rarely equal. Either some financial flows intervened to provide the foreign exchange to purchase more imports than could be afforded from export earnings or there are extra foreign exchange earnings not spent on imports that were invested or even held in bank accounts. The net amount of these financial flows in a year, the value that is equal in amount and opposite in sign to the balance of trade in goods and services, is called the net transfer of financial resources.[13]

In 1995, the developing countries imported an estimated $38 billion more in goods and services than they exported; that is, the net transfer of financial resources to them was estimated to be $38 billion. On a net basis, the financial resources came from the developed economies. The net transfer of the transition economies taken together, which can be measured only in part, might have been a net inflow or outflow but in either case it was a small amount.[14]

Net transfers and financial flows of the developed economies

Much of the net transfer of financial resources of the developed economies takes place among themselves. The United States has long been the largest recipient of net financial transfers and Japan the largest single source of net transfers to other countries; but while the United States' absorption of foreign resources has grown continuously since 1992, the supply of resources from Japan peaked in 1994. Moreover, while Germany has traditionally been a large source of resource transfers to other countries, this ceased to be the case in 1991 when the cost of integrating the eastern Länder (States) into the Federal Republic of Germany absorbed the normally available surplus.

Other developed countries have together taken over the role of supplying resources in large volumes. In 1995, the developed countries excluding Germany, Japan, the United Kingdom and the United States transferred $128 billion, on a net basis. Only $40 billion of this, however, was in the form of net capital flows. Unlike Japan, which is a net creditor country and earns over $40 billion in interest and dividends a year, these countries are net debtors. In

13 As per the convention established in the fifth edition of the *Balance of Payments Manual* of the International Monetary Fund (IMF) (Washington, D.C., IMF, 1993), services are defined to exclude factor income and the term "services" is restricted to denoting what used to be called "non-factor services", namely, transportation, travel and a variety of business and government services (see chap. XII for more details on international trade in services). Investment income is grouped here as part of the financial flows that make up the net transfer, along with capital flows and unrequited grants (see the introduction to the statistical annex).

14 A general caveat: owing to incompleteness and non-comparabilities in the data of different countries, the sum of measured sources and recipients of net financial transfers is not zero, as it should be. Indeed, the world balance of trade is not zero; in 1995 it amounted to a deficit of $84 billion (see annex table A.22).

1995, they paid almost $71 billion on a net basis to residents of other countries as interest and dividends (see annex table A.26).

The world's largest net debtor is the United States economy; and with the trade deficit having grown in each year since 1992, the net transfer of financial resources to the United States has also grown, reaching $119 billion in 1995 (see annex tables A.23 and A.26). The net capital flow to the United States was in fact much larger ($185 billion), since in order to obtain the net transfer to the United States of $119 billion, the capital inflow had to be large enough to offset the net foreign payment of interest and dividends, which came to almost $57 billion in 1995.

The dominant vehicle for the financial inflows to the United States in 1995 was portfolio flows (bonds, equities and related financial instruments). The United States received $141 billion in net portfolio inflows in 1995, up from $91 billion in 1994 and an outflow of $31 billion in 1993 (annex table A.26). A good deal of these inflows did not represent net additions to financing of the trade deficit, however, but a substitution for short-term financial inflows.

Meanwhile, Japan's merchandise trade surplus fell by $11 billion in 1995 and its services deficit rose by $10 billion, making for a decline of $21 billion in Japan's surplus on trade in goods and services and thus a decline in Japan's net financial transfer of $21 billion. However, this was brought about in the most unusual of ways: net capital outflows from Japan dropped not by $21 billion but by over $100 billion (annex table A.26). Indeed, they virtually disappeared. The reason is that there were large net short-term capital inflows, as the Japanese private sector brought home foreign short-term funds, owing, inter alia, to domestic liquidity problems associated with "bad debt", depressed real estate prices and so on (see chap. V). These short-term dollar inflows, in turn, were absorbed into official reserves, which rose by $110 billion, in an effort to stop the appreciation of the yen to which the inflows were contributing. Combined with small changes in other components of the net transfer, this brought about the $21 billion reduction in the net transfer.

External financing of transition economies

The external financial situation of the transition economies is a mixture of very different experiences. It is estimated that the CIS countries together had a current account surplus and a trade surplus and were thus in effect transferring resources abroad that in a more settled economic environment might instead have been invested domestically (annex table A.24). On the other hand, the CEETEs, where more headway has been made in economic growth (as discussed in chapter II), have been absorbing resources from abroad on a net basis, albeit in modest amounts.

One of the sources of uncertainty facing potential suppliers of funds to CIS, although certainly not the only one, has been the foreign debt of the former USSR, whose disposition had been unresolved. After the dissolution of the Soviet Union, the Russian Federation inherited the foreign debt of the USSR, which totalled $103 billion (including accumulated arrears) as of the end of 1995. The Russian Federation also borrowed about $17 billion under its own name in the intervening years, mainly from official sources, on which it has kept its debt servicing current.[15]

15   Data of Goskomstat, as per *Interfax Daily Business Report*, Moscow, 19 April 1996, p.2.

In November 1995, after four years of intensive negotiations, the Russian Federation reached an agreement with the commercial bank creditors of the ex-USSR to reschedule the payment of interest and principal on $32.5 billion of bank loans. Under the terms of the agreement, which did not include any debt forgiveness, the $25.5 billion of principal was to be repaid over 25 years after a 7-year grace period. The $1.5 billion of accrued and unpaid interest for 1994-1995 would be paid by the end of 1996, with the rest of the outstanding interest being converted into 20-year bonds with a 7-year grace period. Then, in April 1996, the Russian Federation reached an agreement with its government creditors (the Paris Club) on the comprehensive rescheduling of about $38 billion of debt over the next 25 years. These two debt rescheduling agreements should remove at least this one impediment to new capital inflows.

Although the bulk of the debt restructuring among the CEETEs took place in earlier years, there were certain additional arrangements in 1995. In July, with grants from the World Bank's Debt-reduction Facility and bilateral donors, Albania was able to buy back some $371 million of outstanding commercial bank debt at 26 cents on the dollar.[16] In addition, at the end of 1995, Hungary used part of the proceeds of its privatization deals in 1995 to prepay $1.7 billion of its debt to commercial bank creditors. It planned to prepay $4.5 billion owed to multilateral creditors in 1996.[17]

Hungary, which has perhaps the longest experience of the transition economies in the international financial markets, arranged $3.8 billion in gross credits in 1995, mainly in bond issues.[18] This accounted for more than half the medium- and long-term private credits of all the transition economies taken together last year (see annex table A.31). In 1994, however, Hungary raised 70 per cent of these funds, which is to say that more transition economies are gaining access to the markets. These economies are also becoming increasingly successful in attracting foreign direct investment flows, which the World Bank estimates rose by almost 50 per cent in 1995.[19]

The transition economies are also major recipients of official financial resources. The International Monetary Fund (IMF) made net disbursements of almost $5 billion to transition economies in 1995 ($9 billion had been committed, two thirds of it to the Russian Federation). These were the largest flows to these countries thus far (annex table A.30); however, with a $10 billion loan to the Russian Federation in 1996, that amount could be surpassed this year. The European Bank for Reconstruction and Development (EBRD) also committed its largest volume of resources thus far, $3.3 billion (annex table A.34). In addition, in April 1996, the shareholders of EBRD agreed to double its capital base to 20 billion European currency units (ECUs) ($25 billion) and to redirect its lending away from the main recipient countries, the higher-income Central European economies, towards the other transition economies. Moreover, of course the transition economies have drawn a significant volume of resources from the World Bank and from bilateral arrangements. In time, all but the lowest-income countries among the economies in transition will draw external financial resources primarily from commercial sources; but for the time being the economies in transition are likely to remain significant users of international official flows.

[16] World Bank, *World Debt Tables 1996*, vol. 1 (Washington, D.C., March 1996), table 2.6.

[17] Report by the Governor of the Hungarian National Bank, in *Napi Gazdaság*, Budapest, 11 March 1996.

[18] Data of Organisation for Economic Cooperation and Development (OECD), *Financial Statistics Monthly*, part 1, sect. 1, January 1996.

[19] World Bank, *World Debt Tables 1996*, vol. 1, p. 162.

Net financial transfers and flows to developing countries

One concern of high political sensitivity to the developing countries in the 1980s – owing to the economic stress with which it was associated – was that as a group they were making large net foreign transfers of financial resources. Since 1991, however, the developing countries as a group have been large net recipients of resource transfers, a pattern that continued in 1995 (see table III.1). Among the regions, South and East Asia attracted the largest share of the transfers, following West Asia and Sub-Saharan Africa. Net financial transfers to the least developed countries rose to $12.3 billion.

In Latin America, the positive net transfer of the previous three years was virtually extinguished in 1995, reflecting the import contraction and export expansion in the region that was discussed above. However, when all the standard net financial inflows and investment income payments are added together, it indicates a net inflow of $25 billion, far more than in 1994 and not much below the inflows in the financial "boom" years of 1992 and 1993 (see annex table A.27). Virtually all of those resources, however, were added to official foreign reserves (see annex table A.28).

There were essentially two reasons for this. First, a large part of the resources were official flows, mainly associated with the unprecedented international assistance package for Mexico and a smaller one for Argentina, as well as official flows to other countries, including $600 million to Haiti. While

Table III.1.

NET TRANSFER OF FINANCIAL RESOURCES OF GROUPS OF DEVELOPING COUNTRIES, 1985-1995[a]

Billions of dollars

	1985	1986	1987	1988	1989	1990	1991	1992	1993	1994	1995[b]
Africa of which	-7.4	2.1	-3.3	3.5	0.4	-10.8	-6.4	-1.4	1.3	6.3	5.8
Sub-Saharan Africa[c]	3.1	6.0	6.0	7.8	6.3	8.1	8.7	10.8	8.7	6.6	7.7
Latin America and the Caribbean	-30.6	-11.9	-18.1	-21.8	-27.3	-27.1	-8.9	8.4	14.3	6.4	0.4
West Asia	18.3	34.4	22.1	27.3	19.1	4.3	51.9	39.8	34.3	17.2	10.1
Other Asia of which	4.1	-11.1	-29.9	-18.2	-11.0	-8.6	-7.2	-7.3	9.1	0.8	14.6
China	12.5	7.4	-0.3	4.1	4.9	-10.7	-11.6	-5.0	11.5	-7.6	-5.5
Four exporters of manufactures[d]	-12.1	-22.7	-3.0	-26.4	-21.7	-11.5	-7.1	-8.6	-12.6	-13.0	-7.1
All developing countries	-17.6	11.0	-32.7	-16.6	-24.7	-38.5	30.1	38.7	66.6	35.6	38.4
Memorandum items											
Sample of 93 countries[e] of which	-17.3	-4.1	-34.0	-32.4	-29.7	-28.1	-5.2	14.2	47.3	35.6	38.0
Least developed countries[f]	6.5	7.7	7.8	9.2	9.4	11.2	11.5	13.3	11.7	10.2	12.3

Source: UN/DESIPA, based on data of IMF, official national and other sources (for memorandum items, see annex table A.27).
a Expenditure basis (negative of balance of payments on goods, services and private transfers).
b Preliminary estimate.
c Excluding Nigeria and South Africa.
d Hong Kong, Republic of Korea, Singapore and Taiwan Province of China.
e Ninety-three capital-importing countries, for which sufficient data are available. For more detailed information, see annex table A.27.
f Covering 43 out of the 48 least developed countries.

the Haitian package was mainly for essential imports in the post-conflict, peace-building conditions in that country (see chap. VIII), the massive flows to the other countries did not add to import capacity.

In the case of Mexico, they helped the Government of Mexico to redeem the tesobonos (short-term government securities) that began to fall due in February 1996, thereby preventing a new international debt crisis. They also provided a means to add urgently needed liquidity to the Argentine banking system, given the severe limitations on the actions that the Central Bank could take under its currency board system (see box II.2). In addition, as the loans were to support the central banks of Argentina and Mexico, which had lost considerable foreign exchange reserves during their financial crises, they would naturally be added to reserve levels.

Second, the other major source of inflow to the region was short term capital, attracted especially to Brazil. As already noted, in order to limit the appreciation of its currency, Brazil's Central Bank purchased large volumes of foreign currencies (and sterilized these transactions in order to limit the inflationary impact).

The largest increase in reserves, however, was recorded by China. The monetary authorities in China had adopted a tight monetary policy to fight against double-digit inflation (see chap. II), while strong financial flows continued to be attracted to the country. Thus, as in Brazil, China's Central Bank absorbed a substantial part of the foreign exchange inflows, increasing official reserves in the process.

China shared with other Asian economies strong inflows from the two main sources of long-term private funds, namely foreign direct investment and lending in the form of bonds and syndicated bank credits. In fact, the virtual explosion in direct investment flows in Asia has been such that the net transfer on direct investment in South and East Asia rose above $40 billion – six times the level of 1990 – and accounted for over 90 per cent of the net transfer to the capital-importing developing countries that is associated with direct investment (see annex table A.27). In fact, the direct investment flow has been quite concentrated. Nine developing countries accounted for about three quarters of the total in 1995; China's share alone was about 45 per cent.[20]

Inflows to Indonesia, among the traditionally preferred destinations of foreign investment, increased significantly in the past year, also as a result of recent further liberalization of FDI. In contrast, the growth of FDI in Malaysia and Thailand has moderated as costs have risen. Both countries are seeking to shift their investment mix to higher value-added industries.

The same group of countries that has attracted the bulk of direct investment have also comprised the dominant developing-country recipients in the international market for long-term private credits. These countries are a key reason that the total amount of such forms of lending to developing countries continued to grow unabated in 1995, despite the difficulties in Latin America (see figure III.4).[21] Indeed, with reduced private lending to Latin America on this account in 1995, the region's net transfer associated with bond and loan finance became negative. Moreover, the terms of new loans issued to Latin American borrowers toughened in 1995, in line with changed market perceptions of country risk. Yield spreads widened despite the fact that only the best credit risks had access to the market. At the same time, average maturities shortened from four to three years.

20 World Bank, *World Debt Tables 1996*, vol. 1, table 1.4.

21 As with direct investment, the borrowing by developing countries on international financial markets is mainly by a small groups of countries. Thirteen countries raised $1 billion or more on these markets last year, accounting for 73 per cent of the funds raised by the developing countries as a whole. Ten of the thirteen were South or East Asian economies (including China). This notwithstanding, many developing economies do have access to the market; in 1995, 43 countries either floated bond issues or tapped international bank facilities (data of OECD, *Financial Statistics Monthly*, part 1, sect. 1, January 1996).

Among financial instruments, portfolio equity flows – that is, shares of stock purchased as a financial investment rather than as a direct investment – fell almost 40 per cent in 1995 after dropping a quarter in 1994 from the unprecedented level in 1993. The main reason was the shrinking flows to Latin America that roughly halved in 1994 and then again in 1995. Latin American firms had been the leading beneficiaries of such financing from 1991 to 1993; in the latter year, foreign purchases of Latin American shares peaked at $25 billion. In 1995, they were estimated to have been a little over $6 billion (see table III.2).[22] In any event, this has been a highly concentrated form of finance, with only three countries accounting for 80 per cent of the flows to Latin America (Argentina, Brazil and Mexico) and four countries receiving three fourths of the flows to South and East Asia (Indonesia, the Republic of Korea, Malaysia and Thailand).

Official financing also figured prominently in the developing countries in 1995. Net official credit flows jumped by more than $25 billion, mainly owing to the swift implementation early in 1995 of the emergency financial package for Mexico provided mainly by IMF, the Bank for International Settlements and the United States and another package for Argentina. Indeed, the Mexican loan accounted for $17.8 billion and an Argentine loan for another $2.4 billion of the $23 billion in total IMF commitments to developing countries in 1995, while the drawing down of the Mexican and Argentine loans was the major reason that IMF disbursed $12.5 billion net of repayments to developing countries in 1995, as opposed to the net payments to IMF that characterized most of the previous 10 years (see annex table A.29).

The one other large IMF lending operation for a developing country in 1995 was noteworthy in that it helped raise that year's net concessional flows to developing countries to $1.5 billion (annex table A.29). That operation involved $1.3 billion in Structural Adjustment Facility and Enhanced Structural Adjustment Facility loans to Zambia. However, even though the loans were quickly drawn down, Zambia's indebtedness to IMF rose by only $434 million. The loans were mainly used, in other words, to repay the outstanding non-concession-

[22] The data in table III.2 are not on a balance-of-payments basis and do not necessarily equal the foreign exchange gain to the countries of the firms whose equity shares were purchased.

Table III.2.
GROSS PORTFOLIO EQUITY FLOWS TO DEVELOPING COUNTRIES, BY REGION, 1990-1995

Millions of dollars						
Region or country	1990	1991	1992	1993	1994	1995[a]
Latin America and the Caribbean	896	5 757	8 048	25 149	13 160	6 200
Africa	0	0	144	144	938	501
West Asia	0	0	0	0	26	13
South and East Asia	1 676	419	4 266	17 854	14 920	12 363
China	0	653	1 194	2 278	3 915	1 297
Mediterranean	35	0	0	178	1 059	500
All developing countries	2 607	6 799	13 652	45 603	34 018	20 875
Memo						
Sub-Saharan Africa	0	0	0	17	625	158

Source: Data of World Bank, *World Debt Tables 1996* (Washington, D.C., World Bank, 1996).
Note: The numbers are derived from market transactions and often available only on a gross basis, except for direct purchases of stocks in local markets, which are on a net basis.
[a] Preliminary.

Figure III.4.
FINANCIAL MARKET LENDING TO DEVELOPING COUNTRIES, 1981-1995

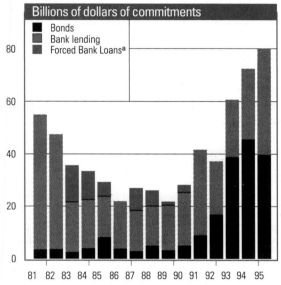

Billions of dollars of commitments

- Bonds
- Bank lending
- Forced Bank Loans[a]

Source: OECD, *Financial Statistics Monthly.*
a Loans accorded as part of debt-restructuring excercises.

Figure III.5.
MULTILATERAL RESOURCE COMMITMENTS TO DEVELOPING AND TRANSITION ECONOMIES, 1970-1995.

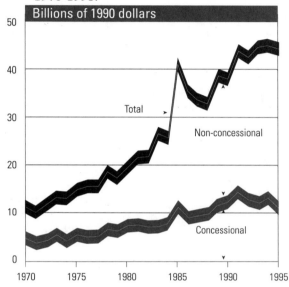

Billions of 1990 dollars

Total
Non-concessional
Concessional

Source: UN/DESIPA, based on annual reports and information supplied by individual institutions.

al obligations of Zambia that had been in arrears. Zambia has thus completed its "rights accumulation programme" to eliminate arrears to IMF. In effect, Zambia was allowed to refinance its $805 million in overdue debt on concessional terms, while it added new borrowings of over $400 million.[23]

Excluding IMF, the dollar value of multilateral lending and grant arrangements also rose in 1995, although with two disturbing features. First, operations that are mainly for low-income countries declined, in particular, loans of the African Development Bank and the International Development Association of the World Bank and operational programmes of the United Nations system (see annex table A.34). Second, taking all the arrangements together, the total volume measured in constant 1990 dollars fell. In fact, the real value of concessional lending and grant programmes peaked in 1991 and was down 5 per cent by 1995 (see figure III.5).

There are other indicators of disappointing developments in concessional flows to developing countries. In particular, the volume of official grants to developing countries is estimated to have remained at the low level of 1994, approximately the same level as in the mid-1980s (annex table A.27). Although grants cover a broader category than development assistance, these data seem to reflect the absolute decline in ODA measured in constant prices that began in 1994. While direct estimates of the flow of ODA in 1995 will be released after this Survey goes to press, available budget data from the major donors suggest that ODA declined again in 1995 in real terms. The primary

23 For background on the rights accumulation programme and the Fund and World Bank mechanisms for handling the Zambian case, among others, see *World Economic Survey, 1991* (United Nations publication, Sales No. E.91.II.C.1), chap. VII, section entitled "Policy on debt owed to multilateral creditors".

reason is the sharp decline in aid from the United States. Having already dropped from being the largest donor to the second largest, following Japan (see annex table A.32), the United States is now on track to drop to third place behind France, a country with less than a quarter of the population of the United States. The United States is not, however, the only retrenching donor.

SELECTED ISSUES IN INTERNATIONAL COOPERATION

International economic relationships may be largely market-generated and market-determined, but Governments have never taken a completely passive or "hands off" approach to their functioning. Two issues among the many that are in the active agenda of Governments seem to have been particularly salient in 1995 and 1996 and are discussed below.

A multiplicity of trading arrangements

If there is a common theme in trade policy measures undertaken by Governments in 1995 and 1996, it seems to be the negotiation of multiple international linkages, linkages that tend to be more open than exclusionary. One can see instances of this in the new trade agreement between the Russian Federation and China signed in April 1996, or the August 1995 agreement of the Central European Free Trade Area to accelerate the elimination of duties on most industrial products, followed by its agreement to admit Slovenia, or the first meeting at summit level between the 15 members of the European Union and 10 Asian nations in March 1996, or the July 1995 summit of the Caribbean Community (CARICOM) which cleared the path to a single regional market with a common external tariff by 1997, or the decision by Suriname to join CARICOM, or the agreement reached by the Presidents of Kenya, the United Republic of Tanzania and Uganda in March 1996 to seek to relaunch the East African Community (EAC), which has been dormant since 1977, or the enlargement of the European Union from 12 to 15 member countries on 1 January 1995 and the growing list of new applicants to the European Union, or the individual trade and cooperation agreements signed in 1995 and 1996 by the European Union and Israel, Morocco and Tunisia. The list of such events could be much longer and could include a large number of the countries of the world.

These agreements are being negotiated in an increasingly liberal international environment, as the commitments in the Uruguay Round of multilateral trade negotiations begin to be implemented, reducing tariff and non-tariff barriers to trade, and as the World Trade Organization develops. The World Trade Organization has already begun to act as a forum for multilateral negotiations, even if sometimes not all the major trading nations with an interest in a particular subject participate in the negotiations. The World Trade Organization is also becoming a mechanism for dispute settlement to which countries – and increasingly developing countries – seem more and more willing to bring their trade policy complaints.[24]

This notwithstanding, the new negotiations seek to strengthen regional groupings and explicit linkages are emerging between regional groupings. For example, the Southern Cone Common Market (MERCOSUR) of Argentina, Brazil, Paraguay and Uruguay became a customs union in January 1995. The

24 See "WTO's first year: 'An encouraging start'", *WTO Focus*, December 1995.

harmonization or elimination of non-tariff barriers was largely completed and a common external tariff, albeit with some exceptions, was put in place. Then in December 1995, the members of MERCOSUR signed a landmark agreement with the 15 members of the European Union, which commits the two groups to the gradual establishment of, potentially, the world's largest free trade zone. Moreover, in June 1996, Chile is to join MERCOSUR as an associate member, with this leading to the reciprocal elimination of tariffs within a maximum of 18 years. In addition, negotiations are under way between MERCOSUR and Bolivia.

Activities have been intense as well among looser groupings of countries, such as the Asia Pacific Economic Cooperation (APEC) forum. APEC is a regional grouping of 18 economies that aim to create a free trade area.[25] The third annual APEC summit was held in Osaka, Japan, in November 1995. APEC members committed themselves there to work for free and open trade and investment within the Asia and Pacific region by the year 2010 for industrialized countries and by the year 2020 for developing economies. The key principles guiding their liberalization efforts include pledges to free trade in all industrial sectors, to allow less advanced economies to meet the plan flexibly and to make any APEC trade concessions ultimately available to the rest of the world on a non-discriminatory basis. While the APEC leaders currently disagree on the depth and speed of tariff reductions, they have agreed to develop individual five-year trade liberalization plans and to present them at the 1996 summit in Subic, the Philippines, in November.

There are also instances of overlapping regional arrangements of different degrees of intensity. For example, regional integration strategies in eastern and southern Africa were pursued most actively through the Common Market for Eastern and Southern Africa (COMESA) and the Southern African Development Community (SADC). COMESA is a formal common market, while SADC plans to convert its trade and regional integration strategies into a southern African economic community by the year 2000. The SADC proposals contain provisions for trade liberalization, the free movement of capital, labour and services among member countries and a common currency. Other groupings in the region include the Southern African Customs Union (SACU), EAC as noted above, and the Cross Border Initiative (CBI), or more formally, the Initiative for Promoting Cross-Border Trade, Investment and Payments in Eastern and Southern Africa. Currently, however, there is relatively little trade among member countries of these groups (for example, 6 per cent of trade of COMESA members and 10 per cent among SADC members is with other members of the same group) and the overlapping memberships, divided loyalties and different goals of each group require a sorting-out and harmonization process as part of future negotiations.[26]

International financial cooperation in a lean period

This is a period of re-examination and retrenchment in financial cooperation for development. As discussed one year ago in the 1995 Survey, searching questions were being raised about the goals and efficacy of ODA and about the role of multilateral cooperation in particular.[27]

In the ensuing year, the severity of the cut-back in the overall volume of development assistance was becoming unmistakable, and was particularly clear in the replenishment negotiations for multilateral assistance — which

[25] The economies are Australia, Brunei Darussalam, Canada, Chile, China, Hong Kong, Indonesia, Japan, Malaysia, Mexico, New Zealand, Papua New Guinea, the Philippines, the Republic of Korea, Singapore, Taiwan Province of China, Thailand and the United States of America.

[26] Membership of the regional groups discussed in this paragraph are as follows: COMESA: Angola, Burundi, the Comoros, Djibouti, Eritrea, Ethiopia, Kenya, Lesotho, Madagascar, Malawi, Mauritius, Mozambique, Namibia, Rwanda, the Seychelles, Somalia, the Sudan, Swaziland, Uganda, the United Republic of Tanzania, Zaire, Zambia and Zimbabwe; SADC: Angola, Botswana, Lesotho, Malawi, Mauritius, Mozambique, Namibia, South Africa, Swaziland, the United Republic of Tanzania, Zambia and Zimbabwe; SACU: Botswana, Lesotho, Namibia, South Africa and Swaziland; EAC: Kenya, Uganda and the United Republic of Tanzania; founding members of the CBI: Burundi, the Comoros, Kenya, Madagascar, Malawi, Mauritius, Namibia, Rwanda, the Seychelles, Uganda, the Unied Republic of Tanzania, Zambia and Zimbabwe.

[27] See *World Economic and Social Survey, 1995...*, chap I, section entitled "The new orientation of international policy for development", and chap. VII, section entitled "Difficult times for official finance for development".

commit donors to shared goals for assistance over a period of years – as well as in annual budget appropriations in several donor Governments. Indeed, in the case of the African Development Fund (ADF), the concessional lending arm of the African Development Bank, there were no new lending arrangements for African countries in 1994 and 1995 because of an inability of the Governors of the Bank to agree upon a replenishment of the Fund (the sixth replenishment had been exhausted at the end of 1993). Since 39 of the 52 African member countries of the Bank were eligible to draw only from the concessional window of the Bank, owing to their poverty and limited debt-servicing capacity, this represented a very costly policy deadlock. Nevertheless, with new management in place at the Bank, prospects for completing the replenishment exercise improved.

Perhaps the most closely watched of the multilateral refunding exercises has been that of the International Development Association (IDA) of the World Bank. IDA is the largest concessional lender to low income developing countries, having committed $7.3 billion in 1994, but only $6 billion in 1995 (annex table A.34). IDA credits are given on financially very advantageous terms: loans have a maturity of 35 to 40 years with a 10-year grace period and a service charge of only 0.75 per cent per year. IDA provides credits to 78 of the world's poorest countries.

The period for lending under the tenth replenishment of IDA was set to expire on 30 June 1996 and no agreement for the eleventh replenishment was in place as 1995 ended. Finally in March 1996, donors agreed to a new financing package for the three-year period that the eleventh replenishment was meant to cover. The package broke formerly fixed rules of burden-sharing among the donors, but at least it allowed IDA to remain an active lender after 1 July.

The IDA package began with a one-year interim fund of about $3 billion to which the United States would not contribute. It would consequently not take part in the decision-making on the loans extended from these funds, nor would its firms be eligible to compete for procurement contracts under the new loans. The United States Administration instead undertook to pay $934 million that was owed under the tenth replenishment of IDA. For the second two years, all IDA donors would contribute about $4 billion in each year. If these funds had been the only ones available for IDA lending, the arrangement would have entailed a major cut-back in the value of IDA lending. However, it was expected that principal repayments on older IDA loans plus contributions from the World Bank would enable IDA to lend a total of about $22 billion over the three-year period.[28]

While the outlook for ODA has become bleak, it seems that the debt situation of some of the low-income developing countries is being seen in a new light. After all, another way to increase the net transfer of resources to a country besides increasing aid inflows is to reduce debt servicing outflows. Significant progress has been made recently in the international debt strategy for handling the debt difficulties of a group of low-income heavily indebted countries.

Indeed, one issue for discussion at the June summit meeting of the seven major industrialized countries (G-7) is a set of proposals for alleviating the debt-servicing burden of 8 to 20 developing countries.[29] The proposals had been discussed by finance ministers of these and other countries at the April meetings in Washington, D.C., of the IMF Interim Committee and the IMF/World Bank Development Committee, but only a framework was agreed upon at that time. Ministers requested that the Bank and the Fund in close collaboration with all

[28] See *World Bank News*, 21 March 1996.

[29] Eight countries are identified as having "unsustainable" debt burdens: Burundi, Guinea-Bissau, Mozambique, Nicaragua, Sao Tome and Principe, the Sudan, Zaire and Zambia; twelve countries are listed as "possibly stressed": Bolivia, Cameroon, the Congo, Côte d'Ivoire, Ethiopia, Guyana, Madagascar, Myanmar, the Niger, Rwanda, Uganda and the United Republic of Tanzania (*World Bank News*, 25 April 1996).

involved creditors and donors put forward specific proposals by their next meeting in September. The G-7 summit is thus an important opportunity to forge agreement among the major creditors and donors on such specifics.

The main advance at the April meeting was the formal recognition of a point, argued by the United Nations[30] and others, that for some countries the "existing mechanisms appear inadequate to secure a sustainable external debt position over the medium term".[31] Also, since the outstanding debt for the countries in question is owed mainly to Governments and multilateral institutions,[32] both would need to accord relief in order to adequately help those countries.

The proposals before the G-7 thus involve greater relief from the Paris Club, the creditor forum in which bilateral debt is restructured, and some mechanism for relief from multilateral debt servicing. The best terms currently available from the Paris Club (called the Naples terms, after the G-7 summit at which they were agreed) allow 67 per cent of "eligible" debt to be written off. The new proposal could raise that proportion to 90 per cent. As to multilateral debt, there is no possibility of formally forgiving such debt, owing to the "preferred creditor status" of the Bank and the Fund, and so proposals have focused on how to help the debtors make their payments. One proposal is to use profits from World Bank operations to help service World Bank loans (comparable arrangements could be made at the regional development banks); another is to sell some of the gold held by IMF, set up a fund with the proceeds and use the earnings of the fund to help pay the interest on IMF loans. In any case, these are the kinds of issues on which decisions could be advanced at the G-7 summit.

The issue at stake in the new stringency of ODA flows and in the difficult replenishments of the multilateral facilities was of course a budgetary one for many donors; however, setting the amounts in question against the total expenditures or even, say, only the military expenditures of the donor countries underlines just how small those amounts are. The financial constraint cannot have been the dominant factor. Indeed, certain donors, such as Denmark, the Netherlands, Norway and Sweden, find it possible to budget more than 0.7 per cent of their gross domestic product (GDP) for ODA. Rather, a major reassessment among donors is occurring – including the contributors at the high end of the league tables of aid effort – concerning what the multilateral institutions and ODA in general should do and their effectiveness in doing it.

The World Bank had been studying its own operations – non concessional as well as concessional lending programmes – for several years and the IMF/World Bank Development Committee in April 1994 agreed to establish a task force on multilateral development banks to review the operation of the World Bank and the four main regional banks. In its April 1996 meeting, the Committee generally endorsed the conclusions and recommendations of the task force and called for wide dissemination of its report.[33]

Developing-country finance ministers in the Group of 24 also reviewed the report and, while commending it, they expressed reservations about some conditions that might increasingly be attached to lending programmes as a result of the report, in particular concerning issues of good governance and civil society, matters that traditionally fall within the jurisdiction of borrowing Governments. Moreover, "ministers expressed serious concerns about the use of environmental, governance, human rights, labour standards or other issues to further protectionist interests in industrial countries".[34]

[30] See, for example, the report of the Secretary-General entitled "The developing country debt situation as of mid-1995" (A/50/379 and Corr.1), of 31 August 1995.

[31] Communiqué of the Interim Committee of the Board of Governors of IMF, Washington, D.C., 22 April 1996, para. 6.

[32] For the 20 countries, 58 per cent of the debt is owed to Governments, 22 per cent to multilateral institutions and the rest is private.

[33] Communiqué of the Joint Ministerial Committee of the Boards of Governors of the World Bank and the International Monetary Fund on the Transfer of Real Resources to Developing Countries, Washington, D.C., 23 April 1996, paras. 12-15.

[34] Communiqué of the Ministers of the Intergovernmental Group of 24 on International Monetary Affairs, Washington, D.C., 21 April 1996, para. 22.

Certainly, the developing-country ministers have identified a possible serious misappropriation of what would in general be laudable concerns of the international community. Indeed, these concerns seem to have taken a major place in the thinking of the donor countries. The Development Assistance Committee (DAC), the donor forum of the Organisation for Economic Cooperation and Development (OECD), has been reviewing strategic requirements for development cooperation over the next two decades. The DAC High-Level Meeting in early May 1996 of development ministers, heads of aid agencies and other senior officials responsible for development cooperation was expected to try to agree on concrete, realizable goals for development cooperation in the twenty first century. The goals would emphasize working with recipient countries to improve specific indicators of economic, social and environmental well-being and foster self-sustaining capacity development for effective, democratic and accountable governance. The possible new strategy was expected to be taken up at the ministerial meeting of OECD later in May and by the summit meeting of the seven major industrialized countries in June.

PART TWO

A PERSPECTIVE ON INVESTMENT

IV A FOCUS ON INVESTMENT: WHY, WHAT, HOW

Investment is an important concern in today's world, and most observers want to see more of it. It can bring about important and desirable economic and social changes, most dramatically in helping post-conflict societies to find a practical basis for peace-building and social reintegration. Investment can also speed the adoption of new labour-saving technologies, although for workers that can be a legitimate source of anxiety. In transition economies, one of the key concerns is to overcome the transition shock, caused when central planning was discarded and suddenly much capital stock was rendered obsolete and relatively worthless. In developing countries, policy makers have experimented with a variety of strategies and approaches to increasing investment and making it more productive, and they have met with very different degrees of success.

Investment in the context of the present part of the *Survey* may be understood in various ways, so that a definition is called for in order to give a degree of precision to the discussion. Although finance influences both the levels and direction of investment (see chap. V below), financing decisions and financial instruments are not part of investment *per se*. Thus, investment in the present discussion refers to the "real" economy, that is, to production of and expenditure on real goods and services, or to put it another way, it refers to changes in the stock of capital. And while the term "capital", may refer to a variety of phenomena, in the present discussion it refers in the conventional sense to "produced means of production". This is a narrower definition than may be suitable for other types of analysis, such as studies of environmental degradation, questions of biodiversity or human capital.

The term "capital" as used here, then, is quite precise: "gross fixed capital formation". It is an activity of producers, which may be firms, Governments or households; it is the value of the fixed assets acquired during a given period, such as one year, less the proceeds from disposals; the assets in question are produced assets, such as machinery, equipment, buildings, other structures and various forms of intellectual property; and the assets must be usable over more than one period.[1]

[1] This is the national accounting definition of fixed investment (see Commission for the European Communities, International Monetary Fund, Organisation for Economic Cooperation and Development, United Nations and World Bank, *System of National Accounts,* 1993 (United Nations publication, Sales No. E.94.XVII.4), para. 1.49). A more inclusive term, "gross investment" is the sum of gross fixed investment and the change in inventories.

Even in limiting the discussion to the traditional concept of fixed investment, the matter remains extremely complex. The essence of investment is that it involves the purchase, production or other acquisition of a very diverse group of assets that are intended to increase the production of consumption or investment goods or services in future periods. Investment stubbornly resists straightforward measurement, as will be discussed below, and has also been difficult to conceptualize at the theoretical level. The simplifications that mainstream economists have employed to make their models tractable — as if capital were a single homogeneous mass that could be bought and sold for a price in a market — are not readily translated into the real world. One of the foremost theorists of modern economics and and a Nobel laureate, the late Sir John Hicks, gave a relevant warning:

"[The theorist's simplifying assumption is not] wrong if it is regarded as no more than a device for preliminary exploration...[But] when a model of this kind...is directly applied to real problems, the result is likely to be misleading. The 'capital substance', which has a definite meaning *in the model* (so many bushels of corn, so many machines), becomes in application a metaphysical entity. Like other metaphysical entities, it is a boat that is loose from its moorings. It is the big thing that is wrong with classical theory."[2]

Analysis of the role of investment in economic growth has come a long way from earlier, more mechanistic approaches. But studies undertaken at the United Nations and elsewhere in recent years have raised new questions about our understanding of investment, such as whether investment data are statistically comparable as measured across countries and over time, thus challenging analysis that is based on such data. They also reflect a greater appreciation that policy prescriptions have seen swings in fashion and that policy-making is a subtle art.

The considerations that enter into policy analysis are generally quite complex, as will be demonstrated below. Policy analysis is not readily amenable to elegant theoretical exercises, nor is it reducible to instruction manuals. Policy analysis is perforce a matter of looking at the experiences of others and learning from them. It is about decision-making in an often highly charged political environment. It is a matter of capturing opportunities and evading limitations that can be created by other players. It is, finally, a matter of weighing pros and cons, of finding compromises between the desirable and the doable. In short, it is far more an art than a science.

The methodology for a deeper understanding of policy issues in the realm of investment requires substantial efforts in comparative description. Much of what is contained in the chapters in the present part of *World Economic and Social Survey* is meant as a contribution in that direction. The present chapter thus seeks to highlight the inevitable data difficulties that should be kept in mind in reading subsequent chapters.

WHY INVESTMENT LEVELS ARE HARD TO COMPARE

One of the perils for a policy analyst to avoid is drawing conclusions from erroneous data and then giving misleading policy recommendations. The most basic assessments that an analyst of investment in a country seeks to make — such as whether the amount of investment is high or low or whether it is growing or shrinking — are not straightforward assessments to make. An analyst

2   John Hicks, *Capital and Growth* (Oxford, Clarendon Press, 1965), p. 35.

should not simply take the aggregate data for a given country at face value, for two basic reasons: (a) coverage may not be complete; and (b) observations may not be comparable.

A good working hypothesis to apply in the very first examination of an investment policy question is that the basic macroeconomic data on investment in any country are incomplete. Investment data in national accounts are generally gathered from the formal economy, that is, legally established enterprises, professions and public-sector activities. Sometimes, estimates are also made of the rest of the economy, the informal sector. All economies have informal sectors, and in the developed economies they are typically considered a relatively minor part of economic activity.[3] However, in some cases — transition economies being a case in point, as discussed in the introduction to the statistical annex — the informal economy can account for a substantial share of gross output and of investment.

In many developing countries, the informal economy may be a subsistence sector that only participates at the margin in the larger market economy. Like output, capital formation in the subsistence sector can be expected to be underestimated as well because it escapes the recording authorities, particularly in countries where investments in such activities as land improvements or cattle raising are often not included in national accounts statistics.[4]

A second pitfall in the measurement of investment lies in the comparability of investment data over time. Again, like output, investment is generally measured for national accounts in both current prices and prices of a base year. Measuring investments in prices of a base year allows inferences to be drawn about changes in the volume of investment. In other words, the total expenditure in different years on machinery, equipment, new structures and capital improvements can be calculated in terms of the prices at one point in time. But that practice gives rise to index-number problems, which are inherent in all efforts to measure real changes in a composite value made up of changing quantities and prices.

The difficulty is that if you want to measure the change in "real" investment between two years, then the measured amount of the change will differ depending on whether you use the first year's prices as the base year or the second year's prices. If the two years are close together in time, the differences may be trivial; but the greater the separation in time, the greater the potential for differences will be. In national accounts data, the typical practice is to fix a base year and then calculate the volume measure for the full series of available years in the prices of the base year. As time passes and the base year slips further and further into the past, it becomes less and less meaningful to the current period.

Statistical methods exist to address that problem, the most notable recent example of which is the annual chain-weighted volume measures for GDP and its components adopted by the Government of the United States of America, wherein the volume change between two adjacent years is the average of the change as expressed in the prices of each separate year, a technique to be recommended, albeit a demanding one in terms of timeliness of information and expenditures by statistical services.[5]

But the measurement problem is actually broader than that. Many capital goods are built to order and are thus unique, such as ships, aircraft, special-

[3] That is not to say that the size of the informal sector is easily measured, since it is not observed in standard data series. Estimates of its size tend to vary widely depending on the methodology employed; for example, estimates for Australia have ranged from 8 to 13 per cent of measured output, and for the United States from 4 to 27 per cent (see Michael Carter, "Issues in the hidden economy: a survey", *The Economic Record,* vol. 60, No. 170 (September 1984), pp. 209-221).

[4] For a discussion of measurement problems, see Alan Heston, "A brief review of some problems in using national accounts data in level of output comparisons and growth studies", *Journal of Development Economics,* vol. 44, No. 1 (June 1994), pp. 29-52; and Partha Dasgupta, *An Inquiry into Well-Being and Destitution* (Oxford, Clarendon Press, 1993), pp. 245-249.

[5] In addition, chained indices have certain undesirable properties; for example, indices for components do not add up to the index for the whole (for additional details on the methodology of index numbers and the pros and cons of chain weighting, see *System of National Accounts, 1993 ...,* chap. XVI).

ized machinery and factory buildings. The creation of a standard price index over time for unique goods is thus impossible by definition; indirect indices must be created if such goods are to be included in a measure of real investment. For that reason, the volume of construction, in particular, is sometimes estimated by deflating construction expenditures by indices of input costs, many of which are simple averages of wage rates and list prices, a procedure which assumes that there has been no change in construction technology over the period indexed.

Sometimes, construction cost indices are adjusted for estimated changes in labour productivity, again depending on available data. Thus, price indices for residential housing may be based on labour costs calculated from an index of earnings and data on material inputs and hours worked. Assuming that the amount of materials used per worker is a measure of output produced per worker, a price index can be calculated. In order to arrive at an index for all construction, it may then be further assumed that price movements in one area of the construction industry are indicative of those occurring in all types of construction, and that construction cost movements in the public sector are the same as in the private sector.

Comparable problems arise when new standard products are introduced and old products disappear, or when the quality of a product changes so dramatically as to make it essentially a different product. The virtual disappearance of manual typewriters and the burgeoning use of personal computers are cases in point and a source of major measurement difficulties pertaining to investment. One measurement problem that leaps out at the analyst arises when national accountants update the base year of their data and recalculate the volume of investment over the historical period using the new base year: what happens is that the historical data change!

For all the above-mentioned reasons, data on investment at constant prices from many countries must be considered only a rough indication of the underlying real volume of capital formation. Sometimes, however, even highly unreliable data do not exist. Economists and policy makers, by default, must then rely instead on the measurement of investment in current prices, which will say something about the value of expenditures but nothing about the amount of investment goods purchased. In highly inflationary environments, such statistics would be virtually impossible to interpret. In any event, economists commonly seek to avoid dealing with a pure value total by normalizing the values, such as by expressing them as a share of GDP, with both variables measured at current prices.

The ratio of investment to GDP would give a reasonable indication of changes over time in the unmeasurable volume of investment if the average prices of the goods and services in GDP and in investment moved in parallel; there is no reason, however, to presume that that is the case. For example, when a country devalues its currency and investment goods are largely imported, the prices of investment goods may increase more than the prices of other GDP components, with the result that the measured ratio of investment to GDP in nominal terms will rise even if there has been no change in the volume of investment (see box IV.1).

When a country devalues and most of its investment goods are imported, it is very likely that the measured share of investment in GDP at current prices will increase even if the quantity of investment remains unchanged. The following exercise illustrates that phenomenon with the help of a table, taking as as an example the experience of Côte d'Ivoire after the devaluation of its currency (the CFA franc) relative to the French franc (FF) in January 1994.[a]

The starting point of the exercise is a breakdown of the main expenditure components of GDP in 1993, which, have been normalized so that the total value of GDP equals 100 units instead of 2,640 billion CFA francs. Thus, the values in the first column of the table represent the shares of the main expenditure components in 1993.

In January 1994, the exchange rate fell from 50 CFA francs per FF to 100 CFA francs per FF. Assuming that quantities stayed the same and only prices changed (which is of course unrealistic since demand would have declined when prices increased), then the prices and thus the values of exports, imports and imported investment and consumption goods would all have doubled in 1994 in terms of domestic currency.

The actual GDP deflator of Côte d'Ivoire increased by 39 per cent in 1994. If the tradable goods prices doubled as assumed above, it would mean that the prices of non-tradables in GDP would have had to rise by 14 per cent in order to get the 39 per cent for the country as a whole. Because the quantities are assumed to remain constant, the nominal values of each category of expenditure are given in the third column of the table as the product of the initial values and the new prices. The fourth column shows what would have been the shares of the GDP components at the assumed new prices: investment as a share of GDP is shown to have increased by 2 percentage points.

Had that been an actual increase, it would have represented a considerable accomplishment, but the increase was entirely spurious since all volumes were assumed not to have changed. The last column indicates the actual 1994 shares of the expenditure components of GDP in Côte d'Ivoire; it shows that the actual investment share was only about 1 percentage point larger than the one predicted by the present exercise, suggesting that the 1994 increase in investment share at current prices was largely a price effect.[b] In 1995, however, the investment share rose again and this time there was no comparable distortion from a price effect (see chap. VII).

Box I V.1.

MEASURING THE RISE IN INVESTMENT AFTER DEVALUATION

a   For additional details, see the Côte d'Ivoire case study in chap. VII.

b   About 66 per cent ((11.4 - 9.3) / (12.5 - 9.3)) of the increase in the investment share was accounted for by the price increase.

THE EFFECT OF DEVALUATION ON THE COMPONENTS OF GDP AT CURRENT PRICES: THE CASE OF CÔTE D' IVOIRE

	1993 normalized values (total = 100)	Assumed 1994 percentage increase in prices	1994 values with 1993 volumes	Implied percentage shares in current prices	Actual 1994 percentage shares in current prices
GDP	100.0	39.4	139.4	100.0	100.0
Investment[a]	9.3	71.2	15.9	11.4	12.5
Imported goods	6.2	100.0	12.4	8.9	..
Non-tradables	3.1	13.6	3.5	2.5	..
Private consumption[b]	63.4	30.9	83.0	59.5	57.9
Imported goods	12.7	100.0	25.4	18.2	..
Non-tradables	50.7	13.6	57.6	41.3	..
Government consumption[b]	20.4	30.9	26.7	19.2	16.8
Imported goods	4.1	100.0	8.2	5.9	..
Non-tradables	16.3	13.6	18.5	13.3	..
Exports	34.2	100.0	68.4	49.1	47.5
Imports	-27.3	100.0	-54.6	-39.2	-34.7

Source: UN/DESIPA, based partly on World Bank data.
a   Assuming that in 1993, two thirds of investment were imported goods.
b   Assuming that in 1993, 20 per cent of consumption was imported; for private consumption, based on David E. Sahn, "Economic reform in Africa: are there similarities with Latin America", mimeo, 1991, and World Bank, *African Development Indicators 1994-1995* (Washington, D.C.).

All the difficulties that arise in comparing investment volumes over time also arise in comparing investment volumes across countries, that is, there are inherent index number problems. In fact, price surveys in a broad range of countries indicate that in developing countries, investment goods are expensive relative to the other components of GDP, and the poorer the country the more expensive they are. Thus, for 12 poor countries (out of a sample of 60 countries), investment accounted for 21 per cent of GDP in 1980 when measured in actual national prices but only 13 per cent when measured in average prices of the full range of countries. At the other extreme, for the richest 14 countries, investment accounted for about 24 per cent of GDP when measured in national prices and about 26 per cent of GDP when measured in average prices.[6]

The solution to the problem in this case is not necessarily to carry out the comparison in terms of the global average prices. Since the weight of the developed countries counts so heavily in the global average, the recalculation of their investment expenditure in the common prices does not change their investment ratio very much from the level found using national prices. But for the low-income developing countries, the "common" prices were not common at all. It is thus not at all clear how to interpret the large mark-down of the ratio of investment to GDP of poor countries once their data are converted to common world prices. Certainly if the example were for a time series and the comparison was of 1970 data in 1990 prices, the analyst would greatly discount the usefulness of the result.

The question of unique goods and comparability of goods also applies to comparisons among developed economies. A case in point is the different intensities of use in Japan and the United States of America of two communication technologies: local area networks (LANs) of personal computers and fax machines. Whereas 52 per cent of personal computers in the United States were connected to LANs in 1993, less than 9 per cent were so connected in Japan. And while there were an estimated 24 fax machines per 1,000 residents in the United States in 1992, there were 33 per 1,000 residents in Japan. The lower LAN share in Japan partially reflected higher costs of LAN services in that country, but an important factor that is often neglected is the nature of Japanese writing. The Japanese language employs thousands of characters, compared with less than 100 characters and often about 25 letters in European languages. Handwriting has been much more common in Japan than using a keyboard, which has led to the wider use of fax machines to send messages in Japan than in the United States. The functionality of each piece of equipment has thus been very different in the two countries, so that it would make little sense to say that the price of personal computers relative to the price of fax machines in Japan should bear a close relationship to the same price ratio in the United States.[7]

In other words, intercountry as well as inter-temporal comparisons of investment expenditure involve significant index number problems that are in their nature insoluble. Thus, the analyst would do well not to rush to a policy conclusion from observing that, say, a given country has a 21 per cent investment ratio as calculated from national data but a 13 per cent investment ratio as calculated using international prices. Instead, it would be advisable to examine the composition of investment expenditure, the degree of new capital formation

6 See Robert Summers and Alan Heston, "The Penn World Table (Mark 5): an expanded set of international comparisons, 1950-1988", *The Quarterly Journal of Economics,* vol. 106, No. 2 (May 1991), pp. 327-368. For an analysis of factors that can account for such phenomena, see Henk-Jan Brinkman, "Price levels of investment across countries", paper presented at an annual meeting of the Allied Social Sciences Association, San Francisco, January 1996 (UN/DESIPA, unpublished).

7 See Jun Fujitani, "Amerika niokeru Howaitokara Shokuba no henyo ni tsuite (On the changes in the workplace of white-collar workers in US enterprises)", *Monthly Labour Statistics and Research Bulletin* (Ministry of Labour of the Government of Japan), August 1994, pp. 19-23; International Telecommunication Union, database on world telecom indicators; and Egil Juliussen and Karen Petska-Juliussen, *The Seventh Annual Computer Industry Almanac 1994-1995* (Incline Village, Nevada, 1994).

and replacement, the capacity expansion and productivity enhancement of the investment and so on. In short, it is necessary to go beyond aggregate numbers to assess the actual situation.

INVESTMENT AND PRODUCTIVITY MEASUREMENT: THE UNITED STATES OF AMERICA AND THE "SOLOW PARADOX"

In the late 1980s, Robert Solow, an American economist and Nobel laureate, pointed to the paradox that the computer revolution had not led to a surge in productivity measured as output per hour of work.[8] Updated versions of the statistics then being used indeed show that productivity in the non-farm sector of the United States economy rose by 0.7 per cent per year from 1980 to 1990, the same as the 0.7 per cent annual rate for 1974-1979, and considerably less than the 2.6 per cent recorded during 1960-1973.[9] Then, in 1991-1994, there was a recovery in productivity growth to 1.6 per cent per year, which would seem to have partially resolved the paradox (see table IV.1).

However, that was something of a statistical illusion. The recent change in the method used by the United States Government for calculating "real" output, which seeks to minimize the index-number problems noted above, has had the effect of increasing the measured growth of output in the relatively distant past and decreasing it in relatively recent years. As a result, the average growth of productivity for the period 1991-1994 fell to 1.2 per cent, while the rate for 1980-90 rose to 0.9 per cent. Moreover, not only has the recent growth of productivity now been seen to be slower than previously measured, but a comparison of the growth of productivity in the 1990s period with the 1960s period now shows an even sharper slow-down than before; the Solow paradox remains.

[8] In Solow's words, "You can see the computer age everywhere but in the productivity statistics"; see R. M. Solow, "We'd better watch out", New York *Times Book Review*, 12 July 1987, p. 36, as cited in S. D. Oliner and D. E. Sichel, "Computers and output growth revisited: how big is the puzzle?", *Brookings Papers on Economic Activity*, No. 2 (1994), p. 273

[9] See Edwin Dean, Michael Harper and Phyllis Flohr Otto, "Improvements to the quarterly productivity measures", United States Department of Labor, *Monthly Labor Review* (October 1995), pp. 27-32; data cited measure productivity from the output instead of the income side of the national accounts, as was formerly the practice.

Table IV.1

GROWTH OF LABOUR PRODUCTIVITY IN THE NON-FARM BUSINESS SECTOR OF THE UNITED STATES OF AMERICA, 1960-1994

Average annual percentage change		
	"Real" output per hour worked, with output measured using:	
	1987 weights	Annual weights
1960-1973	2.6	3.0
1974-1979	0.7	1.0
1980-1990	0.7	0.9
1991-1994	1.6	1.2
1991	1.3	1.2
1992	2.8	2.6
1993	1.2	0.5
1994	1.3	0.7

Source: United States Department of Labor, Bureau of Labor Statistics, *Monthly Labor Review* (October 1995), p. 31.

Why United States productivity growth should have accelerated

The analyst seeking to explain the Solow paradox might begin by examining whether a fall in investment could provide an explanation. The first place one might look for systematic data would be aggregate investment as reported in the national accounts. The share of investment in GDP did indeed fall in the 1980s, reaching a low in the 1991 recession (see table A.5). Thus, perhaps there was less integration of computers into the workplace than had appeared.[10] Nevertheless, the same data show that the share of investment in GDP has been rising since the recovery began.

In fact, the investment data just cited, which were in current prices, underestimated the actual performance of investment even in the 1980s, owing to the falling price of investment goods relative to the general goods and services that comprise GDP.[11] Moreover, for purposes of an analysis of productivity growth in the business sector, data for a narrower category of investment is most appropriate, that is, data for the performance of private fixed investment in constant prices are most relevant. As may be seen in figure IV.1, the share of real private fixed investment in GDP in the United States of America, based on the recently revised data, has remained fairly constant over 35 years, cyclical movements notwithstanding. In addition, the share of residential and non-residential construction has fallen over time, while that of producers' durable equipment has risen. Indeed, real expenditure on equipment — the category of investment spending that includes the computer investment the effects of which Professor Solow was expecting to find — has been the most dynamic component of business investment.

10 Similar statistics in other industrialized economies prompted concerns in the early 1990s about whether the developed economies were investing and saving too little and whether a global capital shortage was looming (see Should industrialized countries promote saving?", *World Economic Survey, 1992* (United Nations publication, Sales No. E.92.II.C.1), pp. 89-98).

11 That has been a global phenomenon (see *World Economic Survey, 1992* ..., pp. 67-69).

Figure IV.1
REAL BUSINESS FIXED INVESTMENT IN THE UNITED STATES OF AMERICA, 1960-1995

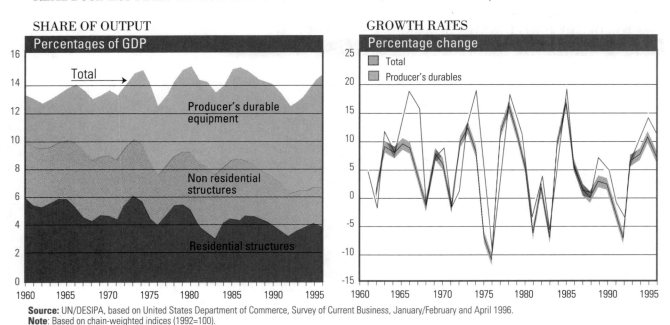

Source: UN/DESIPA, based on United States Department of Commerce, Survey of Current Business, January/February and April 1996.
Note: Based on chain-weighted indices (1992=100).

Information-processing and related equipment, moreover, accounted for about one third of expenditures on producers' durable equipment in 1995, while computers and related equipment comprised about one third of the information-processing expenditures. About the same proportions applied in 1985, albeit for qualitatively different equipment.[12]

According to the Organisation for Economic Cooperation and Development, much of the business fixed investment that has taken place in recent years in the United States of America and other industrialized countries has been geared to replacing spent or obsolete equipment,[13] which is as expected since in more mature economies like the United States long-term growth is more likely to depend on the country's ability to adopt increasingly productive technologies than on capital deepening *per se*.[14] The replacement of old machinery would thus be expected to be associated with higher productivity growth since the new inventions and techniques are embodied in the new machinery. Computer-related investment provides the most striking case in point.

The advances in information-processing technology have changed the types of machinery and equipment purchased and their uses, with purchases increasingly concentrated in computer-assisted equipment. Increasingly, technologies of processing, creation and assembly are coordinated by computers. The merging and synthesis of advanced technologies in the areas of telecommunications, computer networking and automation have encouraged a trend away from highly specialized machinery towards the use of more flexible equipment that can be redesigned, reprogrammed or retooled easily and quickly. The result has been more customized, higher quality products than were produced by the traditional assembly-line approach. Manufacturers are increasingly using more flexible machinery that can be adapted quickly to the production of new products. Computer-aided design equipment and new communication technologies are enhancing firms' abilities to re design products quickly so as to produce customized output in response to changing customer demand.

Indeed, industry-level studies suggest that in manufacturing the expected productivity increases have been taking place. In the manufacturing of the new high-technology equipment itself, large productivity gains have been registered: in all the major economies, labour productivity in the office and computer machinery sector has been growing at an annual average rate of 17-26 per cent in the period 1980-1990.[15] Moreover, in the manufacturing sector of the United States as a whole, productivity rose at the average annual rate of a 3.1 per cent from 1991 through 1994, a distinctly better performance than the 2.6 per cent improvement in the 1980-1990 period.[16]

Many segments of the service sector are also experiencing a wave of new production processes, similar to that of the manufacturing sector. Indeed, in the period from 1985 to 1990, banks in the United States increased their equipment by approximately 75 per cent and securities firms increased theirs by more than 200 per cent. Those figures cover only physical equipment and not the substantial expenditures on software and on software maintenance. Overall, technology expenditures by American banks and securities firms rose from less than 5 per cent of total expenditures in 1980 to about 20 per cent in the early 1990s.[17]

12 Data for 1995 from United States Department of Commerce, *Survey of Current Business*, April 1996 and historical series from United States, *Economic Report of the President*, 1996 (Washington, D.C., Government Printing Office), table B-14.

13 "Investment in the current upswing in a longer-term context", in *OECD Economic Outlook*, No. 57, June 1995, p. 32.

14 See, for example, J. Eaton and S. Kortum, "Engines of growth: domestic and foreign sources of innovation", *NBER Working Paper*, No. 5207, August 1995; A. S. Englander and A. Mittelstadt, "Total factor productivity: macroeconomic and structural aspects of a slow-down", *OECD Economic Studies*, No. 10, Spring 1988, pp. 7-56; G. M. Grossman and E. Helpman, "Endogenous innovation in the theory of growth", *The Journal of Economic Perspectives*, vol. 8, No. 1 (Winter 1994), pp. 23-44; N. G. Mankiw, D. Romer and D. N. Weil, "A contribution to the empirics of economic growth", *Quarterly Journal of Economics*, No. 107 (1992), pp. 407-437; and P. M. Romer, "The origins of endogenous growth", *The Journal of Economic Perspectives*, vol. 8, No. 1 (Winter 1994), pp. 3-22.

15 See, for instance, A.W. Wyckoff, "The impact of computer prices on international comparisons of labour productivity", *Economic Innovation and New Technology*, vol. 3 (1995), p. 285.

16 United States Department of Labor, Bureau of Labor Statistics, "Productivity and costs, third quarter 1995", press release of 8 February 1996.

17 Federal Reserve Bank of New York, *International Competitiveness of U.S. Financial Firms*, A Staff Study, May 1992, p. 64.

New technologies, which are more flexible and multipurpose, are not simply automating traditional activities but are causing a complete redesign of the entire array of services available to clients. Related activities are being combined. One example is the unified bank statement sent to retail clients that contains information about all of their business with the bank. In addition, mortgages are now processed much more quickly and in much greater volume. Client service has been further enhanced by the widespread introduction of automatic teller machines and by automatic deposit and withdrawal services.

Possible explanations for the Solow paradox

There is no single explanation that convincingly explains why the productivity increases at the aggregate level that might have been expected from the shift of investment to high technology capital goods have not yet been seen. Many of the partial explanations say, in essence, that the problem is one of measurement and that the productivity gains have actually taken place.

It is difficult to measure accurately at the aggregate level the effect of the many rapid changes in the prices and quality of both inputs and outputs, a difficulty that has increased over the past decade owing to an increase in the share of output that reflects ideas and services rather than physical substances. For instance, when compiling aggregate measures for output and productivity, the growth of real output in the banking and other financial services sectors is assumed equal to the increase in hours worked in those industries, with other inputs being ignored. Therefore, growth in their labour productivity is zero by assumption. Yet, according to estimates of the United States Bureau of Labor Statistics, which are not used in the construction of aggregate measures, productivity growth in the banking industry has averaged more than 2 per cent per year in the 1990s.[18]

Measurement issues are also important in other service areas, including health care. Here current productivity measures would not reflect explicitly the effect of technological advances that allowed a patient to be treated and to recover in a much shorter time than previously.

A possible reason why computers may not yet have brought about a major increase in measured output and productivity growth is that they are still a small component of the capital stock.[19] In the United States, computing equipment by 1994 accounted for only 2 per cent of the net current-dollar stock of private non-residential equipment and structures. Hence, it has been suggested that computing equipment can be productive at the level of the firm and yet make little contribution to aggregate growth.

The measurement of the capital stock is itself fraught with difficulties. The shift to shorter-lived capital goods has been reflected in an increase in the estimated depreciation of the capital stock. Depreciation in 1990 accounted for about 75 per cent of United States gross investment, as against 60 per cent in 1970. The share of depreciation in gross fixed capital formation has also risen in the other major developed countries. If inadequate allowance were made for the rate at which equipment loses value as a result of obsolescence, as might be expected at a time of rapid technological advance, then the slow-down in the growth of the capital stock would be even greater than the official figures suggest, which could help explain the Solow paradox.[20]

[18] *Economic Report of the President*, 1995 (Washington, D.C., Government Printing Office, 1995), p. 110.

[19] For an extensive discussion of the computer paradox, see S. D. Oliner and D. E. Sichel, loc. cit., pp. 273-334.

[20] For a discussion of changing patterns of investment, see, for instance, A. S. Englander and C. Steindel, "Evaluating recent trends in capital formation", *Federal Reserve Bank of New York Quarterly Review*, vol. 14, No. 3 (Autumn 1989), pp. 7-19.

Other factors unrelated to measurement difficulties have also been suggested as possible explanations of the paradox. One is that productivity statistics have accurately captured the sectoral differences in productivity growth and that those differences have been important. In that argument, as industries with high-wage workers are downsized and new equipment is substituted for labour, redundant workers pour into lower-wage and lower-productivity jobs. The larger number of workers in those sectors holds down wage growth there, leaving employers without a strong incentive to invest in productivity enhancement.[21]

Another argument is that the productivity gains from the new technology have not fully materialized because such impediments as inadequacies in training, the lack of appropriate application software or a failure to undertake organizational restructuring have slowed down their diffusion.[22] For instance, the incorporation of a major new technology may not be very effective unless production processes as well as firms' organizational structures are thoroughly rethought. But it may take some time for re-engineering efforts to be translated into increased production; and besides, some existing production systems simply cannot be integrated easily with the new information and communication equipment. In those circumstances, it might be preferable to delay updating the existing physical capital until it has come to the end of its economic life. That argument suggests, in other words, that productivity will rise as experience with new equipment grows.

Weak demand is another factor that, in principle, could explain the sluggish growth in measured productivity. The productivity numbers reflect how many pieces of output workers actually make in an hour; they do not reflect how many pieces they could make if demand were sufficient for the plant to be operated at full capacity.

According to that argument, since investment has been an early expenditure component to emerge from recession — or was maintained to an unusual degree during the recession — firms may have been investing ahead of demand when they might have postponed their equipment purchases until demand pressures warranted it. In the case of Canada, the strength of investment by Canadian firms during the second half of the 1980s and the early 1990s actually contributed to the fall in the measured productivity of capital during the last recession, as the continued rapid growth in capital inputs exceeded the increase in production.[23]

The question to ask of that argument is why the tendency to invest ahead of demand would only arise now. One answer might be that many of those investments constituted a massive renewal of production processes, and given the observations made above about training and software and the general matter of breaking in new equipment and routines, a period of slow sales might have been seen as having advantages for investment in the new processes. The high rate of modernization of machinery and equipment may mean that firms expected a vigorous recovery in demand to emerge and thus wanted to be positioned to meet it with higher productivity production processes at the appropriate time.

Perhaps the answer to the paradox is indeed that it is too early to judge because the lag in the acceleration of productivity growth is relatively insignificant.

21   See Robert J. Gordon, "Problems in the measurement and performance of service-sector productivity in the United States", NBER Working Paper, No. 5519 (March 1996).

22   It has been argued that in Canada the strong investment in technologically more advanced machinery and equipment increased the need for firms to retrain labour and that the delay in doing so delayed productivity gains (see Statistics Canada, " Productivity, hourly compensation and unit labour costs". *The Daily*, 21 April 1995)

23   For a discussion of productivity and investment trends in Canada, see M. Allard-Saulnier, "Productivity of manufacturing industries in Canada and the United States", *Canadian Economic Observer*, July 1993, pp. 4.1-4.23.

Future figures would then reveal the full extent of the productivity enhancements spurred by technological advances and embodied in the wave of investments. For the moment, however, that is only speculation. The frank answer is: "We do not know".

DATA FOR POLICY ANALYSIS

One conclusion from the preceding discussion seems to be that the policy analysis of investment requires working with data that only very imperfectly capture the real underlying economic relationships in an economy. That problem was demonstrated in the above analysis of the Solow paradox, in spite of the fact that the United States has one of the best statistical systems in the world.

In many countries, funding limitations and a lack of expertise have prevented statistical services from contributing as much as they might to policy analysis. It is extremely shortsighted, however, to curtail important statistical activities in order to contribute what are typically small amounts to governmental budget consolidation. Better statistical data may not by themselves solve many problems, but poorer data will certainly increase the burden on decision makers.

V FINANCIAL SECTOR CONSIDERATIONS IN INVESTMENT

For much of the post-war era, economists have relegated most policy discussions of financial sector operations in developed and developing, centrally planned and transition economies to "microeconomic" analyses of investment. These are questions that concern the composition of investment expenditures and involve issues such as differential access to investment credit of large versus small firms, big-city versus rural needs, established versus start-up companies, public versus private sector borrowers, and so on. Yet "macroeconomic" investment questions — those concerning the total amount of investment in an economy — also can involve financial sector issues, such as arise when financial factors change the capacity or willingness of banks to lend to the business sector in a boom or recession, or during economic transition, or after an economic "shock".

The question of the relevance of finance in explaining investment at the macroeconomic level extends to the operations of the normally working developed economy. Theorists who view businesses as exhibiting behaviour close enough to that of a model firm making investment decisions in a frictionless, competitive environment with no policy distortions tend to treat the investment decision as separable from the financing one. Those who say that asymmetries in the information available to borrowers and lenders are a fundamental aspect even of today's highly sophisticated financial sector argue that financial conditions should affect the level of investment. Both camps see financial conditions as playing a role in cases where markets are imperfect and economies are developing or in transition.[1]

In the chapters that constitute the bulk of the present part of the *Survey*, financial sector determinants of investment — in their macroeconomic and microeconomic dimensions — will enter the discussion at many points, although they certainly do not tell the entire story in any of the case studies. As a prelude to those discussions, it seems useful to examine a case of which it can be said, with the benefit of hindsight, that financial sector operations had much to do with an unusual set of investment outcomes. This is the case of investment in Japan from the late 1980s to the present.

1   For a review of current theoretical views and their application to forecasting models, see Pingfan Hong and Peter Pauly, "Modelling private investment: investment functions in the LINK Model", Project LINK spring meeting, 25-28 March 1996, United Nations, New York.

It also seems useful to consider in a frank way a financial sector policy measure affecting the composition of investment that in broad debates is often held in low repute, but that in practice is still regarded as having a role to play, namely, policy interventions in credit markets and in particular "directed credit". The conclusion of this discussion will be that blanket condemnation of the policy is unwarranted and unrealistic, and that such a policy option is best considered in a limited and time-bound manner. To consider how the use of a given policy instrument should evolve over time — with the understanding that in many cases its life should be limited — might be a general prescription for policy makers. A policy that works well in one period of a country's development might be superseded by a different policy for a new era.

INVESTMENT IN JAPAN: AFTERSHOCK OF A FINANCIAL BOOM

The success of the Japanese economy has traditionally depended on high rates of growth of investment, leading to large increases in labour productivity. Japan developed investment opportunities through its imaginative exploitation of the possibilities that technological advances either in Japan or in other countries were opening up. Japanese companies excelled in the design and manufacture of high-quality and high-technology products. However, while technological advances and the declining relative price of capital goods were raising investment in other countries in the 1990s, Japanese investment growth slowed down and then investment levels began to fall in 1992.

In part, this was an expected element of the economic recession in Japan that had begun in 1992; but the depth and duration of the low levels of investment were a cause of some concern. The recent decline in investment can only be compared with the decline of 20 years ago, after the first oil crisis (see figure V.1). Even so, the recent decline has lasted longer and the contraction in private, non-residential investment has been deeper than in the 1970s episode. Also, the earlier decline had been triggered by the sharp rise in oil prices. It was a purely external shock. In this case, it seems that much of the decline in investment can be explained in terms of traditional economic relationships in Japan. The delayed recovery, however, constitutes a new dimension and a clue that more than the usual factors were at work.

Conventional factors in recent investment behaviour

To a degree, the recent behaviour of investment in Japan can be explained by the operation of traditional macroeconomic determinants of investment in that country. In particular, a simple "accelerator model" seems to explain recent Japanese investment behaviour reasonably well, at least up to a point.[2]

This model assumes that firms have a desired or target stock of plant and equipment that they wish to maintain in order to produce an expected level of output under normal conditions. The ratio of the desired level of capital stock to the expected level of output is fixed by technical and cost factors and is called the capital coefficient or capital-output ratio. At any point in time, the current level of any firm's capital stock would usually not equal the desired

2 The explanation draws upon the analysis of the Economic Planning Agency (EPA) of Japan, *Heisei 6 Nendo Nenji Keizai Hōkoku* (The annual report on the Japanese economy, 1994) (Tokyo, EPA, 1994), chap. 2.

Figure V.1.

GROWTH OF REAL FIXED INVESTMENT IN JAPAN, 1971-1995

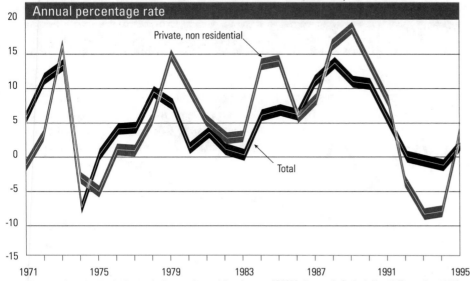

Source: Organisation for Economic Cooperation and Development (OECD), *Economic Outlook*, No. 58 (December 1995).
Note: Underlying data are in terms of 1985 yen.

level and thus firms would seek to adjust their capital stock towards the desired level.

In practice, the model is applied not to individual firms or industries, but to the economy as a whole, with output being measured as gross domestic product (GDP). That is to say, the capital coefficient that drives this model is thought of as an average for the country as a whole or, more precisely, for the private sector as a whole.[3] It is also considered to be a medium-term phenomenon (referring to normal output produced under normal conditions and costs). In particular, the capital coefficient is expected to rise over time, reflecting the increasing research and capital intensity of production by an increasingly productive workforce.

When the current level of capital stock is less than the desired level, investment rises to fill the gap. The desired higher level reflects the need for additional capital to produce a larger flow per year. The term "acceleration" comes from the hypothesis that investment responds to changes in the flow of output, to the acceleration or deceleration in the demand. In any event, investment fills only part of the gap and the speed of gap-filling is itself something to be analysed.

In fact, throughout the 1980s, the actual capital coefficient as calculated from data on Japan's private capital stock and aggregate output remained fairly close to the trend over the same period (see figure V.2). If the trend had in fact been the target level over time, then the result shown in figure V.2 would mean that the actual level was in some periods slightly above, and in other periods slightly below, the desired level. The first case would imply that there had been excess capacity at the time and the second case that plants had been operated at more than usual intensity, for example, with workers doing extra shifts.

[3] Calculating a time-series of the capital coefficient of an economy entails measuring the total capital stock at different points in time in constant prices and this is of course open to the same host of measurement problems as were discussed in chapter IV with respect to investment data.

Figure V.2.
CAPITAL COEFFICIENT AND GROSS DOMESTIC PRODUCT (GDP) OF JAPAN, 1980-1995

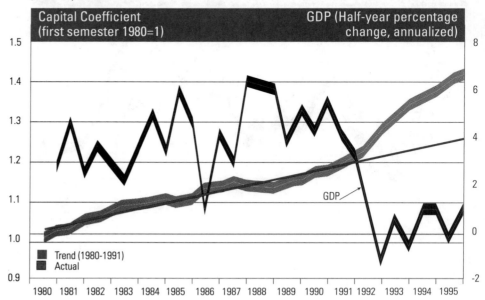

Source: Data of OECD, *Economic Outlook*, No. 58 (December 1995).
Note: Underlying data are in terms of 1985 yen.

Beginning in the second half of 19876, however, as may be seen in figure V.2, the capital coefficient fell under the trend and remained there for several years. It can be seen from the figure that the growth of output was relatively strong in this period and thus that the capital stock was used relatively intensively. This seemed to be a signal to firms to increase their rate of investment, at least that would have been the characteristic response if they had expected the strong growth of the volume of sales to continue, and the investment data in figure V.1 and the closing of the gap in figure V.2 indeed suggest that their response was exactly the characteristic one. Then, in 1992, the recession and subsequent economic stagnation brought demand sharply down and productive capacity became underutilized. Not surprisingly, investment fell. Indeed, private, non-residential investment fell about 9 per cent in 1993 and fell again by 6 per cent in 1994. These drops were, however, somewhat larger than expected.

Another viewpoint on the relationship between investment and the desired capital stock considers at a different aspect of the evolution of the gap between the long-run and the actual capital coefficient. That is, instead of seeking to measure a "normal" relationship between the capital stock and output, this other approach begins with an estimate of the output that would be produced by the "normal" use of the capital stock, referred to as the "potential output". The ratio of the actual output to the potential output is referred to in turn as the "utilization rate". In the above exercise, a utilization rate above 1 corresponds to a capital coefficient below the trend line, and vice versa.

Figure V.3.

INVESTMENT IN AND UTILIZATION OF PLANT AND EQUIPMENT IN JAPANESE MANUFACTURING 1980-1994

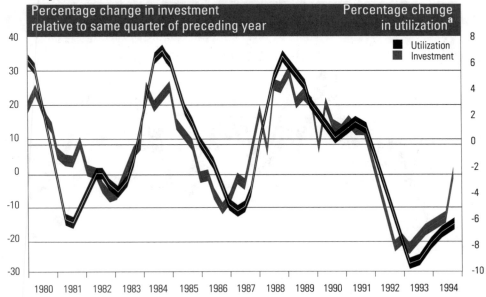

Source: UN/DESIPA, based on data of Government of Japan

a Change in utilization rate is calculated as the average over the previous four quarters of the change in utilization in one quarter versus that in the same quarter of the preceding year.

Figure V.3 suggests that in Japan there has been a close relationship between changes in the utilization rate and investment. Actually, the relationship as depicted in the figure does not assume an instantaneous reaction of investment to changes in utilization, as the figure's utilization data are averages of the utilization rates in each of the four quarters before the quarter shown. This result suggests that when Japanese enterprises observe that their capacity utilization rates are rising and remaining high they then invest in expanding capacity. By the same token, when they observe that the utilization rate is falling, they cut back on investment.

This exercise suggests, in other words, that the investment boom in the late 1980s and the following slow-down in the 1990s may have been mainly the result of enterprise responses to rapid demand expansion in the late 1980s and the sluggish demand conditions in the early 1990s. In this view, entrepreneurs in Japan undertook investment according to conventional business plans. The strong investment exhibited in figure V.1 cannot then be seen as some sort of unexplained investment frenzy (at least according to the above analysis).

Unusual dimensions of recent investment behaviour

Something unusual could be detected, however, in the last cycle of rising and then falling investment. The Economic Planning Agency of Japan (EPA) has looked at changes over time in the rate of return on real assets in the manufacturing sector taken as a whole.[4] The Agency found a relatively simple relationship that seemed to be able to explain (at least until the end of the 1980s) changes in the rate of return. Thus, figure V.4 shows actual rates of return in

4   "Real" assets are distinguished from financial assets and, similarly, the rate of return is with respect to profits from manufacturing operations.

Figure V.4.

RATE OF RETURN ON MANUFACTURING IN JAPAN, 1973-1994

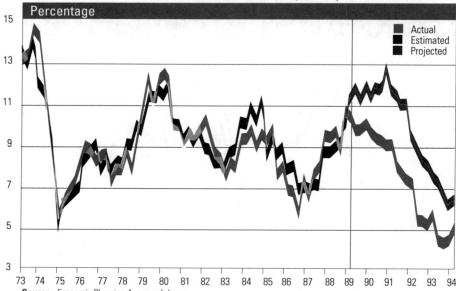

Source: Economic Planning Agency of Japan.
Note: Rate of return is the ratio of operating profits to non-financial assets of manufacturing firms; estimated data are given by an equation fitted to data of 1973-1988.

[5] The equation fits the rate of return on real assets to a linear function of the capacity utilization rate and a dummy variable for the yen's appreciation that followed the Plaza Agreement in 1985.

manufacturing from 1973 to 1988 and the rates of return given by an econometric equation based largely on the capacity utilization rate.[5] Beginning in 1989, however, the relationship no longer held. The actual rate of return was markedly less than expected based on extrapolating the relationship of the earlier period into the later period.

An explanation for the behaviour of the rate of return on real assets since 1989 is somewhat elusive. The predicted time path of the rate of return takes account of the effect of the recession and in this sense the parallel falling lines in 1991 and 1992 suggest that the historical relationship still has considerable predictive power. However, something happened in 1989 and 1990 that the model did not pick up — something that reduced the profitability of manufacturing operations. It was not the exchange rate of the yen (¥), whose appreciation did not begin until 1991 and was strongest in 1993; indeed, the real effective exchange rate of the yen depreciated in 1989 and 1990 (see annex table A.9), and this increased the competitiveness of the tradable goods sector.

What had thus changed in the operations of Japanese enterprise? In particular, might the investment plans of the late 1980s have been chosen less prudently than in earlier years? Japanese firms had grown rapidly in the 1980s. The fact that the average number of subsidiaries owned by a parent company increased from 67 in 1987 to 81 in fiscal 1990, and to 88 in fiscal 1992, suggests that Japanese companies might have overstretched their business operations and been consequently led into unfamiliar and unprofitable fields of business. In short, while the quantity of investment in the late 1980s did not seem to go beyond what might have been expected based on the growth of demand, the "quality" of investments might have deteriorated.

Figure V.5.
ASSETS AND LIABILITIES OF NON-FINANCIAL ENTERPRISES IN JAPAN, 1970-1993

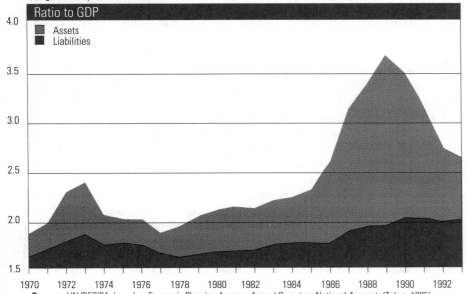

Source: UN/DESIPA, based on Economic Planning Agency, *Annual Report on National Accounts* (Tokyo, 1995)
Note: Assets and liabilities as per standard balance sheet accounting.

The one factor that needs to be introduced into the discussion at this point is the financial "bubble" that developed in Japan in the late 1980s and burst in the early 1990s, causing great disruption of financial markets and the banking system. Figure V.5 indicates the dimensions of the bubble. Through the 1970s and the first half of the 1980s, the growth of financial assets and liabilities in Japan essentially kept pace with the growth of nominal GDP. Thus, the ratios of assets and liabilities to GDP were relatively constant. Then, however, the speculative buying of equity shares and real estate exploded.

Share prices had risen strongly on the stock markets of the major economies in the 1980s and most were thought to be overvalued before they underwent a sharp contraction in October 1987; the Japanese market correction was smaller than in other cases, however, even though the estimated degree of overvaluation was substantially greater.[6] Nevertheless, the Japanese contraction was only delayed and once finally begun, was truly an economic shock.

It was estimated that the gains in stock value in 1987 alone had been equivalent to about 50 per cent of nominal GDP. By the end of 1990, the total value of real and financial assets reached almost three times the 1980 level. The losses in stock values after the fall were correspondingly high and amounted to a value that was equivalent to 38 per cent of GDP in 1992.[7]

Debt also rose relative to its past relationship to nominal GDP, as figure V.5 indicates, even if not nearly as much as assets. The quality of borrowing, however, may have changed. Borrowing became relatively easy to arrange in the speculative environment. Indeed, Japanese firms became large issuers of bonds with equity warrants, wherein the interest rates on the bonds were relatively low because the buyer had an option to convert the bond into equity shares in a rising market.

[6] See *World Economic Survey, 1988* (United Nations publication, Sales No. E.88.II.C.1), Chapter IV, section entitled "Causes and consequences of the stock market crash of October 1987, and annex II.

[7] Annual gains in stock and land combined were equivalent to about 140 per cent of nominal GDP in 1987, while the losses in asset values in 1992 were estimated to be 87 per cent of GDP that year (see Economic Planning Agency *Heisei 7 Nendo Nenji Keizai Hōkoku* (The annual report on the Japanese economy, 1995) (Tokyo, Economic Planning Agency, 1995), p. 197).

Even straight borrowing became easier. Borrowers had to put up collateral against the possibility that they would not be able to service their loans. With asset prices high, companies had more value in their holdings of shares in other companies or in landholdings to pledge as collateral. At the same time, banks saw the risk of default — or more precisely, the possible consequences of default, given the collateral — as being low and they tended to charge lower interest spreads over their costs in the competition to arrange more loans. Indeed, as the value of bank reserves — these included stocks valued at rising market prices — and deposits rose, loan officers of banks were under pressure to expand their lending.

This was the environment in which firms sought borrowing in support of their efforts to expand plant and equipment capacity. It is easy to believe that loan officers in banks might have made less rigorous assessments of projects than were warranted. In short, during the financial bubble period, firms could have become more aggressive risk takers.

In any event, when the crash and recession came more or less on top of each other, the market value of collateral on loans evaporated and then profits from operations disappeared. First, stock prices collapsed, followed by land prices, and together these collapses had a devastating effect on corporate balance sheets. Those assets that firms held in the form of shares in other companies and land lost much of their value, while their obligations to their creditors — both bank borrowing and financial market obligations, such as commercial paper — did not.

The implication of these developments for the capacity of firms to finance investment was a straightforward one: such capacity was reduced sharply. First, the fact that, in order to improve its weakened balance sheet position, a firm might use its current profits to repay its creditors would reduce its internal funds for investment. Second, firms were constrained in terms of obtaining outside finance. There are two main channels for such funds. One channel is new borrowing, whether from banks or the market, which further increases company liabilities, while declining creditworthiness pushes up the cost of new borrowing. The other channel is an equity issue. Firms however, are generally reluctant to create new equity shares when the market is depressed and more shares have to be issued in order to raise a given amount of new funds. The chief reason is that the larger the number of new shares issued, the more the equity stake of the existing shareholders is diluted.

Econometric studies by the Economic Planning Agency confirmed the negative effects of the worsening of balance sheets on investment. Although balance sheet deterioration was found to reduce investment in both the manufacturing and the non-manufacturing sectors, the negative effect was greater in the non-manufacturing sector. This was the case for both debt-position and land-value indicators.[8]

In past cycles, investment in the non-manufacturing sector recovered more quickly than that in other sectors and became the main engine of overall investment activities. The need to undergo balance sheet adjustment may have been one reason that the recession was so prolonged in Japan.

The sharp decline in asset prices has also negatively affected financial institutions, the major suppliers of investment finance in Japan.[9] For them, the collapse of asset prices not only wiped out the earlier capital gains on their

8   More precisely, in the case of the manufacturing sector, in the period extending from the first quarter of 1975 to the fourth quarter of 1994, investment in plant and equipment would on average be depressed by 0.9 per cent in response to a 1 per cent increase in the ratio of long-term debt (bonds and credit from commercial banks) to the total value of tangible fixed assets (excluding land). For the non-manufacturing sector, the decline is estimated to have been 1.2 per cent during the period extending from the first quarter of 1980 to the fourth quarter of 1994. In addition, a 1 per cent decline in the ratio of the value of industrial land to GDP would push investment down by 0.6 per cent in the manufacturing sector and by 1.4 per cent in non-manufacturing, for the respective periods. By the same token, increased investment in the late 1980s was associated with opposite changes in these financial ratios (Economic Planning Agency, *Heisei 7 Nendo Nenji Keizai Hōkoku* (The annual report of the Japanese economy, 1995,) (Tokyo Economic Planning Agency, 1995), appendices 1-3-1 and 1-3-8).

9   This could clearly be seen at the global level where, from 1986 to 1989, 7 of the 10 largest banks in the world in terms of assets were Japanese, holding about three quarters of the combined assets of the 10; by the end of 1990, Japanese banks accounted for 5 of the 10 largest banks in the world, accounting for 57 per cent of the combined assets of the 10 (data of *Institutional Investor*, various issues).

stock and land holdings, but also increased the amount of "bad loans", that is, loans that the borrowers could not fully service. Loans are the basic assets in a bank's balance sheet and the accumulation of bad loans requires a bank to either set aside additional reserves against non-payment or reduce the reported value of the loans on its books, with either course of action reducing the value of its assets. At the end of September 1995, the total amount of bad loans among all the Japanese commercial and trust banks was ¥37 trillion, almost 8 per cent of GDP.[10]

A deterioration in its balance sheet weakens a bank's ability to make loans. When asset prices continued to decline, banks became even more cautious about making loans because the future value of the collateral had become uncertain. At the same time, banks may have become more stringent when assessing investment projects proposed by borrowers. The annual growth rate of total private financing (non-bank borrowing, bonds and commercial paper) and borrowing from commercial banks declined substantially in the 1990s. It is difficult to identify the extent to which banks' inability to lend had the effect of squeezing demand for investment financing. However, the fact that bank lending grew more rapidly than total private financing in the boom years of the late 1980s and then contracted more rapidly in the early 1990s suggests that the inability to lend did have such an effect.

Next steps: investment in non-tradables and tradables

As Japan moves more solidly, if still slowly, into the recovery phase of its current business cycle, private investment is expected to strengthen. Indeed, the 2 per cent growth of GDP forecast in this Survey for Japan in 1996 embodies an expansion of real, private, non-residential investment of $3\frac{3}{4}$ per cent. With the yen's having appreciated 27 per cent since 1990 in real effective terms (see annex table A.9), a substantial portion of this investment should shift into the non-tradables sector, and this would in any case help Japan reduce its persistent balance-of-trade surplus. However, what seems to be occurring, based admittedly on indirect indicators, is that investment in non-tradables is lagging.

In other words, while investment in manufacturing has begun to rise, that in the non-manufacturing sector (mainly services) has been less strong. Moreover, the investment in manufacturing seems to be responding to price signals from the exchange-rate appreciation in that investment has been relatively buoyant in technology-intensive fields, such as semiconductors, personal computers and communications technologies. Investment in more standardized products, such as steel, non-ferrous metals and textiles, has been plunging.[11] In the technology-intensive sectors, Japanese exports have to compete on the basis not so much of price (such competition is made difficult by the appreciation of the yen) as of product and process innovation.

The question, then, is why investment has not also shifted into non-tradables. One reason may have to do with balance sheet developments of firms in the manufacturing sector versus the non-manufacturing sector. The latter seem to have made their balance sheet adjustments relatively more slowly, in part because they have had more of their assets tied up in landholdings than manufacturing firms and land prices have continued to fall. That is, despite a moderate rebound of stock prices in late 1995 and their stability thereafter, land

10 As a reflection of these conditions — and the uncertainty over the full extent of the bad loan problem — Japanese banks had to pay a so-called "Japan premium" in 1995 when they borrowed internationally; that is, Japanese banks had to pay a higher interest rate on international borrowing than did comparable banks from other industrialized countries at the time.

11 "*1996 Nendo Setsubi Tōshi Keikaku Chōsa*" (Report on trends in plant and equipment investment for fiscal 1996), *Nihon Keizai Shimbun*, 15 February 1996.

12 National Land Agency, *Tanki Chika Dōkō Chōsa* (Short-term land prices outlook) February, 1996.

13 See Economic Planning Agency, *Business Cycles in Japan and U.S.A.* (Tokyo, Economic Planning Agency, November 1995).

14 For aspects of the relationship between technologies and Japanese labour management practices, see Hiroshi Kawamura, "Technology and labour: the case of Japan", mimeo (UN/DESIPA, July 1995).

prices have continued to be weak. In February 1996, for example, 95 per cent of land prices designated for commercial usage in the three largest metropolitan areas in Japan (Tokyo, Osaka and Nagoya) were still falling.[12]

This argument should apply, however, only in the short run, as manufacturing firms that had strengthened their balance sheets might be expected at some point to diversify into non-tradables if the profit possibilities were sufficiently attractive. There is another argument, however, namely, that profits in the non-tradables sector have perhaps been relatively weak. Indeed, profit rates in the non-tradable sector have been consistently below those in the manufacturing sector, and the fact that the gap between the two sectors widened after mid-1993, was thought to have dragged down investment in the non-manufacturing sector.[13]

One element connected with this may have been the relatively weak productivity growth registered by the non-manufacturing sector. During the period 1975-1990, labour productivity of the manufacturing sector more than doubled. Over the same period, however, the financial industry increased its productivity by only 35 per cent and the transportation and communications industry by less than 34 per cent. There is, though, anecdotal evidence that the non-tradables sector, particularly wholesale and retail distribution, and banking and insurance services, has recently accelerated its computer and communications-related investment to improve productivity and raise profitability.

However, these computer and communications-driven productivity increases may take some time to manifest themselves. The introduction of computers and communications-related technologies requires a measure of reorganization of management structures, and could result in workers' becoming redundant. This would conflict with Japanese industry's lifetime employment principle which may be declining in importance, but still remains strong.[14]

The final question, then, is whether policy measures might raise the rate of investment in the non-tradables sector of Japan. The massive public investment programme being implemented by the Government of Japan as part of its anti-recessionary fiscal package certainly contributes directly to investment in this sector; but it does not seem that the regional and sectoral allocation of public funds was aimed particularly at encouraging or supporting private investment in non-tradables. Furthermore, the Government can only pursue such an expansionary fiscal policy for a limited period owing to increasing public deficits now and — given burgeoning future social security commitments — in the future.

The deregulation of the services sector, however, can be an important element of a policy to foster investment in non-tradables. The services sector accounts for about 70 per cent of Japan's GDP. Stimulating competition and thereby increasing productivity in this sector are an essential element in raising the long-run potential output of the country as a whole. In fact, the Government is now in the second year of a three-year economic deregulation programme running to April 1998, and covering about 1,800 points of regulation. The programme covers all the major services industries, from banking and insurance to retail and wholesale industries; but so far it has only tackled minor technical measures and has not yet produced visible improvement in investment in the services sector.

In dealing, however, with one specific component of the non-tradables sector, namely, the bankrupt *jusen*, or housing loan companies, the Government has had to take a more active role. The fiscal 1996 budget contained a public rescue plan which was approved by the Japanese parliament in April 1996, but it is still unclear how and to what extent the monetary and legal authorities will resolve the mounting debts owned by the jusen.

In conclusion, what seems clear from this analysis, is that the financial structure that had developed in Japan under the influence of the market, policy, history and social structure revealed, during the "bubble economy" episode, serious weaknesses having macroeconomic as well as sectoral consequences. That financial structure had once helped Japan to become the high-income and internationally competitive exporter of sophisticated manufactures that it is today. Few would dispute, however, that by the early 1990s it was in need of major reforms.

THE ROLE OF GOVERNMENT IN CREDIT MARKETS

There is a wide range of opinion on how intensively government should seek to involve itself in the financial sector. A rather sceptical view, reflecting one strain of opinion that has been influential in terms of the advice proffered to developing countries, can be stated succinctly: "Government intervention in a country's financial sector takes many forms, some benign, some debilitating."[15] Clearly, when Governments act in the financial arena, they intend their policies to be more than merely benign.[16]

It is clear, in any event, that the banking system and financial markets of a country do not make up just another industry, like steel or computer software development. The banking system is responsible for almost all economic payments and originates most of the money circulating in an economy. When the banking system is not sound — or is perceived not to be sound — it can severely disrupt the economy.[17] Governments thus rarely hesitate to limit entry into banking by requiring that banks be licensed. Government policy is generally to supervise banks closely (which supervision may or may not in fact be carried out). Governments also seek to build confidence in the safety of funds placed with banks through government-sponsored deposit insurance.

Besides ensuring the smooth operation of the monetary and financial system, Governments typically also take a growth and development perspective and sometimes an income-distribution or equity perspective concerning the financial sector. That is, Governments typically look to the financial sector as a tool for carrying out policy meant to guide and bolster the flow of investment in the economy. Sometimes Governments participate directly in the financial sector through government-owned financial institutions and sometimes they foster the development of particular financial markets or institutions (the policy to develop a venture capital system in the Republic of Korea is a case in point, as discussed in box V.1). Frequently, however, Governments seek to influence the resource allocation decisions of the private financial sector by altering the credit allocation decisions of banks.

Commentators on policy do not have a common position on whether, or how, Governments should intervene in credit markets, but the fact is that most Governments do so. The intervention can of course take any of several forms. Instruments include subsidized credit, government loan guarantees, special tax treatment of income from loans and other incentives.

[15] Maxwell J. Fry, *Money, Interest, and Banking in Economic Development*, 2nd ed. (Baltimore, Maryland, Johns Hopkins University Press, 1995), p. 353.

[16] This, of course, is only one part of the panoply of possible policies to influence investment, tax policy being a major other option (see, for example, Charles L. Schultze, *Memos to the President* (Washington, D.C., Brookings Institution, 1992), pp. 278-289; for a more general review, see J. A. Kay, "Tax policy: a survey", *Economic Journal*, vol. 100, No. 399 (March 1990), pp. 18-75).

[17] Cases in point include the economic difficulties that several Latin American countries experienced in 1995 and that were associated in part with domestic banking crises (see box II.1).

The Governments of most developing economies influence credit allocation to one degree or another. Developed countries like Canada, France, Germany and the United States of America have used directed credit programmes at some point in time. It has been suggested that government intervention in credit allocation was responsible for the success of several economies on the Pacific Rim, particularly Japan and the Republic of Korea. Most countries, however, cannot boast of the same prowess, despite an abundance of allocation schemes.

In transition economies, the issue is rather delicate, given their objective of moving away from state control. Yet should the State withdraw from capital markets before the completion of enterprise privatization and of banking reform? The Russian Federation and Poland, for example, chose the credit allocation route, whereas the Czech Republic did not (see chap. VI).

The goals of developed and developing countries, in terms of directing credit, generally differ. In developed countries, these programmes are today more often than not tools of social policy or regional development. In developing countries, they have also been used as broader industrial policy tools to achieve higher growth of GDP.

A traditional growth-oriented argument for government involvement in the financial system begins with the observation that the State would raise the growth of output to a more desired level if it encouraged more long-term investment. The view is that if people decided to act collectively rather than individually, they would invest more for the benefit of their own generation and future generations. (In other words the social "rate of discount" is lower than the individual one.) The State could thus assist in situations where long-term finance was warranted but creditors were unwilling to put their resources at risk for long enough periods except at forbidding rates of interest. State guarantees (or borrowing by the State itself) are a common mechanism for extending the maximum maturity of private credits.[18]

Another argument, however, extends its scope beyond the lengthening of maturities to affirm that the State is also needed to help guide credit in specifically desired directions in so far as financial markets are inherently imperfect. Not only do financial institutions commonly have a significant measure of monopoly power, but there is a fundamental asymmetry and incompleteness in the information available to potential lenders about the intentions and capacities of borrowers. The asymmetry is of course a matter of degree, depending on the sector and the type of finance. In any event, it is argued that Governments can help overcome the reluctance of financial institutions to place funds in the "right" places.

A prime example concerns the financing of investments in new industries. The first financial backer of an innovator bears greater uncertainty than later lenders who can "free ride" on the information gained from the first loans. The expected rewards of lending to the innovator have to be great enough to overcome the greater uncertainty, or the costs of the uncertainty might be lowered by policy. An extreme case of this "initial bank" problem has affected the transition economies. As discussed in chapter VI, banks have been reluctant to lend to new firms (or even old firms) operating in the new market economies. In situations where the State largely withdrew from supplying finance, the credit crunch has been severe.[19]

[18] This, essentially, is the financial function of the World Bank, which sells bonds in international capital markets, essentially on the strength of the credit rating of its industrialized-country shareholders, and lends the proceeds for 20 years to developing and transition economy Governments which could not borrow on such terms themselves.

[19] See István Ábel and John P. Bonin, "State desertion and credit market failure in the Hungarian transition", *Acta Oeconomica*, vol. 46, Nos. 1 and 2 (1994), pp. 97-112; and John P. Bonin, "On the way to privatizing commercial banks: Poland and Hungary take different roads", *Comparative Economic Studies*, vol. 35, No. 4 (winter 1993), pp. 103-119.

At the opposite end of the spectrum from the financing of little-known innovators are the government restrictions that require financial institutions to place a percentage of their resources in credits to the government that is beyond what can be justified on a prudential basis. In other words, one of the biggest abuses of central credit direction occurs when it becomes a "low-cost" means of financing the public sector deficit. As these funds would otherwise be lent to the private sector, this constitutes a case of the public sector literally "crowding out" the private.

Directed credit programmes can also be subject to private sector abuse. If privileged borrowers do not themselves have the highest marginal returns on investment, there will be arbitrage incentives to on-lend the resources to more profitable uses. This was the case, for example, in Greece, where the obligatory investment ratios of banks provided incentives for "round tripping" of funds. Industrial and agricultural firms that had access to earmarked credit obtained the credit and lent it to other firms that had higher rates of return but were not eligible under the Government's schemes. Until 1985, 75 per cent of all commercial bank deposits in Greece were earmarked. The privileged sectors included the public sector, which garnered nearly 50 per cent of the deposits, and industrial and small-scale firms, which obtained another 25 per cent. Not until 1993 were these allocations significantly reduced as part of a reform begun in 1987. [20]

Avoiding abuses has required rigorous monitoring of directed credit programmes. Indeed, the success of such schemes in Japan and the Republic of Korea has to some extent been attributed to their monitoring schemes. The Republic of Korea's "export-financing ceiling system" of 1976 based financing decisions on past export performance of potential borrowers. [21] Moreover, diversification of exports and the utilization of new export opportunities were rewarded as well. Mechanisms were also needed to convey information on performance and opportunities to and from the credit recipients and the decision makers. In the case of the Republic of Korea, the Ministry of Commerce and Industry set up monthly meetings attended by senior policy makers and leading businesses.

Another consideration separating successful directed credit programmes from less successful ones is how well defined the targets of the programmes are. The Republic of Korea again provides an instructive example. [22] Between 1961 and the mid-1970s, export-oriented sectors had been targeted and high growth achieved; but over time the number of sectors that were targeted grew and economic growth became increasingly unbalanced. In this case, emphasis on large firms tended to accentuate the power of conglomerates (*chaebols*). This ultimately led to a redirection of credit to small borrowers as well as an effort to try to develop a venture capital sector (see box V.1). [23]

Pollution of objectives of directed credit programmes by political factors is yet another danger. The Republic of Korea contained this problem by granting the credit on a non-discretionary basis. All export-oriented firms that were successful were automatically granted credit, and political discretion could not mar this targeting. On the other hand, the power of large firms was bolstered by the programmes and it was not a simple step, politically speaking, to restructure the programmes. In some other countries, the situation was more difficult, government allocation being rife with abuse: credit was largely provided on a discretionary basis and specification of priority recipients was vague.

[20] Data of the Bank of Greece. For background on directed credit in Greece, see *OECD Surveys: Greece*, (Paris, OECD, 1985).

[21] See Byung-Sun Choi, "Financial policy and big business in Korea: the perils of financial regulation", in *The Politics of Finance in Developing Countries*, Stephen Haggard, Chung H. Lee and Sylvia Maxfield, eds. (Ithaca, New York and London, Cornell University Press, 1993).

[22] The cases of China, Indonesia and Tunisia as presented in chapter VII below also bear on these considerations.

[23] See Yoon Je Cho and Joon-Kyung Kim, "Credit policies and the industrialization of Korea", mimeo (World Bank, December 1994).

Box V.1.

BRINGING VENTURE CAPITAL TO THE REPUBLIC OF KOREA

a   This description draws heavily upon Rodney Clark, *Venture Capital in Britain, America and Japan* (New York, St. Martin's Press, 1987), pp. 5-26; and *Investing in Venture Capital*, Donald E. Fischer, ed. (Charlottesville, Virginia, Institute of Chartered Financial Analysts, 1989).

b   The Act aimed, *inter alia*, to encourage technological innovation in small companies through the commercialization of technology owned by the federal Government, in part via the use of funds of departments of the Government and affiliated institutions with substantial research and development budgets.

c   The following analysis is based on information supplied by the Ministry of Finance and Economy of the Republic of Korea.

A set of institutions have evolved in the United States of America for promoting innovations through the creation of new enterprises. These institutions, known as "venture capital" companies, have played a part in the creation of some of the most famous names in the United States computer industry, including Apple, AST, Compaq, Digital Equipment, Intel and Seagate. The venture capital system in the United States was not designed by policy makers, but arose as a market-based phenomenon. In other countries (the Republic of Korea being a case in point), Governments have sought through policy to emulate the function carried out by the United States system, especially given how much importance, for innovation and competition and thus for economic progress, independent new firms are viewed as having.

The core institution in the venture capital system of the United States is the venture capital partnership or fund.[a] It consists of a small group of entrepreneurs, often with engineering and management backgrounds, who come together to search for start-up investment opportunities. These "general partners" invest in new firms, taking an equity stake (usually a majority of shares) and actively participating in the management of the new firm.

Actually, the general partners conventionally put up only about 1 per cent of the money they invest. The rest is supplied by "limited partners", usually institutional investors, who take a more passive role. The limited partners pay an annual management fee (amounting to a small percentage of the assets invested) to the general partners and also agree that when the partnership is wound up they will take, typically, only 80 per cent of the value to which their original funds have grown.

The goal of the venture fund is to participate actively in new firms and help them grow, but only for a limited number of years, after which time the venture fund exits from an ownership and management role. A common feature of the exit is the firm's "going public" through an initial public offering of shares that will then be traded on the large over-the-counter market that exists in the United States for small company stocks. The firm might also be acquired by another firm through a merger or a leveraged buyout.

As the value of a venture enterprise grows, so does the value of the partners' original investments. Of course, many — actually, most — of the new firms fail. Finally, after a time, the partners wind up the venture partnership itself and divide up the value of their holdings, which, if successful, will be many times greater than the original funds.

The system in the United States has been supported by government policies, including military procurement and support of applied research. It has also benefited from state and local policy packages to lure and nurture innovative firms and federal policies to promote small business, through, for example, the Small Business Administration, which, *inter alia*, lends to small business investment companies for on-lending to small enterprises. Investment incentives were also created under the Small Business Innovation Development Act of 1982,[b] not to mention such broad tax and related incentives, as stem from the relatively low rates of taxation of capital gains in the United States income tax system.

However, the dynamism of the United States venture capital system seems mostly related to the mode of operation of the economy of the United States. The relevant main dimensions seem to include a high level of technological sophistication, allowing for ready development of products that embody new technologies; a large domestic market with high purchasing power, allowing for rapid growth of sales within a short period of time; a well-developed set of financial markets, smoothly providing funds for relatively small companies as well as large firms; and a skilled labour market from which the human resources for new companies can be garnered. In addition, the social environment values inventive entrepreneurship highly and there is strong legal protection for intellectual property.

Venture capital in the Republic of Korea, in contrast, has been much more of a public initiative.[c] Indeed, it was initiated in part as a response to the growth — even the dominance — of large corporations that it was felt had become too big and unwieldy to adapt adequately to the rapidly changing market situations of today. The Government of the

Republic of Korea thus decided to encourage the establishment of many small and medium-sized companies, especially in the technology-intensive industries. Essential to achieving this goal would be the mobilization of considerable amounts of financial resources for venture capital.

Thus, in 1986, the Government began a policy to promote venture capital through incentives for the establishment of venture capital companies. From 15 such companies in 1986 providing $330 million in loans and investments, the sector grew to 55 companies in 1995. Total financing provided in 1995 came to $41 billion.

The system of the Republic of Korea embodies two types of venture companies: one to provide start-up financing of small and medium-sized companies (that is to say, those with 300 or fewer employees) and another to provide expansion financing after start-up. Applicants wishing to establish venture companies for start-up enterprises, called "small business creation investment companies" (SCICs), first register with the Ministry of Trade and Industry. They then become eligible for subsidized long-term loans from the Government, through its Start-up Promotion Fund, to be utilized in investment in new companies.[d] The limited partnership arrangement is also utilized to tap corporate pension funds and insurance companies for resources to invest in new ventures; indeed, within five years the SCICs must invest more than the amount that they received in government funding. The SCICs provide consulting services as well as funds for the new enterprises. Their role is limited, however, to starting enterprises and they must exit from the individual firms in their portfolio within seven years.

For the enterprises that survive, post-SCIC financing and assistance are available from institutions of the second type, the "new technology business finance corporations" (TBFCs). These are non-banking financial institutions, licensed by the Ministry of Finance and Economy, that are empowered to invest, lend, lease or provide factoring services for new technology businesses. To be eligible to receive support from the TBFCs, firms have to have fewer than 1,000 employees and less than $40 million in assets. The government role in financing the TBFCs is mainly through the Technology Credit Guarantee Fund, which guarantees borrowings of TBFCs from financial institutions. The TBFCs, like the SCICs, also draw on limited partnership arrangements; also like the SCICs, the TBFCs provide management consulting services.

The system of the Republic of Korea has not been without problems. Some arise from the dual-institution system, as well as from the thin "over-the-counter" market for new equity listings and the complexities involved in gaining listings on the main stock exchange. However, there is also thought to be an insufficient institutional culture for venture capital and too few experts available to serve as consultants for venture companies. In particular, business people of the Republic of Korea traditionally tend to be reluctant to run their businesses together on a co-ownership basis. Indeed, the owners of venture businesses are said to regard venture capital companies only as fund-supplying institutions and not as partners.

In 1995, the Government further strengthened its policies to encourage the venture capital industry so that more than 10,000 start-ups can be established every year. The Government is expanding its funding for venture capital and also is seeking to develop the over-the-counter market. In addition, the Government is strengthening the legal protection of intellectual property rights and developing the patent system.

Eventually, the Government's aim in this sector is to make itself unnecessary. That is to say, the policy will be considered a success when venture capital companies emerge from dependence on the Government, cultivate their own expertise, find promising investment prospects and support them effectively. The Republic of Korea's approach to the development of a venture capital sector is, in other words, in the nature of an "infant industry" approach to financial development, which is a far cry from the ever-present financial role that the Government and many other governments elsewhere assumed over the years in fostering and channelling investment.

[d] The Fund also supports start-up consulting companies.

24 See Charles W. Calomiris and Charles P. Himmelberg, "Directed credit programmes for agriculture and industry: arguments from theory and fact", *Proceedings of the World Bank Annual Conference on Development Economics, 1993*, Michael Bruno and Boris Pleskovic, eds. (Washington, D.C., World Bank, 1994).

25 Charles W. Calomiris and Charles P. Himmelberg, "Government credit policy and industrial performance: Japanese machine tool producers, 1963-1991", mimeo (World Bank, Financial Sector Development Department, December 1994).

26 Dimitri Vittas and Yoon Je Cho, "Credit policies: lessons from East Asia, Summary", mimeo (World Bank, Financial Sector Development Department, December 1994).

Another lesson derives from the fact that some countries have used credit allocation with more restraint than others. In Japan, for example, it was only one of many policy instruments. Moreover, there was more restraint as regards the degree to which credit was directed, in terms both of amounts and of specification of firms, than in most developing countries.[24] Even in the 1950s, directed credit in the industrial sector formed less than 5 per cent of total funding of the sector; by 1980, this figure had declined to less than 1 per cent. In the machine tool industry at least, directed credit was provided to a firm only once and lasted for a brief period.[25] At the other end of the spectrum, around 50 per cent of funds in the Indian financial system have been subject to statutory reserve or priority credit requirements and the Government directed more than 70 per cent of the resources of the Indian commercial banks.[26]

A final consideration is that the use of directed credit presumes a closed capital market, where financial outflows can be controlled. That is, assuming that the result of a credit programme is a different allocation than the market would have chosen — which is the whole point of the programme — the returns to lenders who participate in the programme may be less than the earnings of non-participants. Then, either the Government will make up the difference to the participating lenders through a subsidy or they (but more likely their depositors) will seek to evade the programme through capital outflows. With financial markets being increasingly globalized, the viability of prolonged central credit allocation would seem to be in question. This does not mean that programmes will not work, only that maintaining them may be difficult if at the same time there is pressure to liberalize the capital account. In any case, it is a good working hypothesis that any large policy-induced distortion will ultimately be evaded.

In sum, experiences under a variety of directed credit programmes suggest that those programmes can indeed achieve their intended goals, at least for a certain time and under certain conditions. When they work well, they seem to be part of an array of tools that a government employs, as other factors are required in combination with direction of credit for such mechanisms to be successful. In the case of the export promotion policy of the Republic of Korea, for example, directed credit was combined with monitoring of the exchange rate to maintain the competitiveness of exports, and domestic price controls were limited so that domestic price distortions would not be widespread. Indeed, as the chapters that follow will demonstrate, the most striking feature in this regard is the multiplicity of policy considerations affecting investment performance.

VI FIXED CAPITAL INVESTMENT AND ECONOMIC TRANSFORMATION

As the countries in transition move from the centrally planned economic model to a market-driven model of economic organization, they fully expect that a new capital stock will be created to enable them to generate wealth by producing goods that their citizens — and foreign purchasers — might actually wish to buy. Investment is central to reaching this goal and has been an increasing focus of attention internationally. It is also our focus in the present chapter.

First to be reviewed will be the investment experiences of a number of Central and Eastern European countries, then those of the *Treuhandanstalt* (the German privatization agency) in what are now the eastern *Länder* (States) of Germany, and finally those of the Russian Federation. The survey is selective, in that the required data are not available for all countries in transition, especially in the Russian Federation's partners in the Commonwealth of Independent States (CIS). However, conclusions may be drawn based on the diversity of country studies that could be prepared.

WHY THE INVESTMENT PROBLEM IN TRANSITION ECONOMIES IS SPECIAL

The economic transition is the second economic revolution in these countries in the twentieth century. The first change was from a market economy to a centrally planned one. This took place in the case of the former Soviet Union after 1917, and in the other countries after 1945. To be able to fully appreciate the difficulties and opportunities that these countries are encountering in making the new transition and the role of investment in the transition, it is useful to go back to what their previous leaders thought the results of the earlier change would be, what they were initially and why the eventual results differed so markedly from expectations.

At the risk of simplification, it can be said that central planning was based upon the concept of economic progress as entailing the production of physical "things" — ships, railways, wheat, clothing. The total value produced in an economy in one year was the sum of the things produced. Services — such as legal services and distribution — were needed too, but they were a charge against the value of production and not production itself; they were thus non-productive.[1]

Once central planning was adopted as the means to organize production, this perspective determined not only what economists studied and wrote about, but also what was in fact produced. Thus, after 1927, a prime objective of the Government of the Union of Soviet Socialist Republics (USSR) was to use its

[1] The terminology of the centrally planned economic model reflected the underlying socio-economic theory. There is no direct translation from the centrally planned terminology to market terminology in all cases. In this chapter, the market terminology is used whenever possible. During the period studied, the accounting system was changing in the various countries from the centrally planned to the market system. Consequently, "even more than price or output data ... investment statistics are bedevilled by problems of definitions, accounting and coverage. As a result, estimates from the same source can differ substantially in repeated revisions, and cross-country comparisons should be viewed with more than the usual degree of scepticism" (European Bank for Reconstruction and Development (EBRD), *Transition Report, 1995* (London, 1995), p. 69).

natural resources and vast supplies of labour to fully industrialize its economy in a way that had never been attempted before — through systematic and concerted planning. A very large proportion of current investment was put into producing more investment goods — in Lenin's words, "using capital to produce capital" — so that production — at least the production of material goods — could be further increased.

The system appeared to have achieved its goal. Table VI.1 gives figures for pig iron production which was once an important determinant of a country's power and wealth: machines, railways and so on were constructed out of iron. On the eve of the First World War, Russian production, which had expanded rapidly since the turn of the century, was slightly behind that of France and considerably behind that of Germany. By the start of the Second World War, the Soviet Union's production was only slightly behind that of Germany. Whereas 1939 production levels in France, Germany and the United States of America were not much above their 1913 levels, and the level of the United Kingdom of Great Britain and Northern Ireland was even lower, the Soviet Union had expanded production dramatically over the period. Although the human costs involved were enormous, the Soviet Union appeared to have devised a system that could ensure growth irrespective of what occurred in the rest of the world, which had not yet emerged from the Great Depression. After the Second World War, further production increases were achieved and by 1970, the Soviet Union was drawing level to the United States in pig iron production.

Centrally allocated and directed investment programmes had thus proved effective for rapid industrialization in selected sectors, as well as for industry retooling for war needs, after-war reconstruction and nuclear arms and space programmes. Yet, as the post-war era went on, faults began to be perceived in the capital accumulation model on which the industrial success of central planning had been based. It became increasingly apparent that a model that catered not directly to consumer demand, but rather to what planners thought consumer demand would be over the planning period — and one that also relied upon the central authorities to direct research — was failing to keep abreast of technological developments in the world at large. One sign of how

Table VI.1.
PRODUCTION OF PIG IRON, 1900-1990

Thousands of metric tons					
	France	Germany	Russia[a] and USSR	United Kingdom	United States
1900	2 714	7 550	2 937	9 104	14 010
1913	5 207	16 761	4 641	10 425	30 876
1939	7 376	17 478	14 500	8 108	32 321
1950	7 838	9 511	19 200	9 819	60 217
1970	19 592	33 897	85 933	17 895	85 141
1990	14 718	30 206	111 385	12 463	50 543

Sources: B. R. Mitchell, *European Historical Statistics, 1750-1970* (New York, Columbia University Press, 1976); U.S. Department of Commerce, *Historical Statistics of the United States: Colonial Times to 1970, Part I)* (Washington, D.C., 1975); and United Nations, *Statistical Yearbook,* various years.
[a] Russian Empire before 1914.

the Soviet Union had remained wedded to a model that did not fit the period is that from 1970 to 1990, pig iron production shrank in the developed countries, particularly the United States, while it increased in the Soviet Union. In 1990, Soviet production was double that of the United States. That statistic was a sign less of success than of something's being wrong.

The investment process under central planning

The reasons that the planning model became discredited can help explain why relatively little value was placed on the capital stock held by the centrally planned economies when they began their transition to market economies.

Capital accumulation (investment) was centrally determined.[2] In its original form, neither meaningful prices, interest rates nor profit was considered in the decision on which sectors would gain which assets. Decision makers focused on physical production capacities and engineering relationships at the micro-economic level and political and socio-economic dimensions at the level of overall accumulation. The model was based on the continuous growth of all factor inputs, including stocks and fixed capital assets. This strategy is often referred to as the "extensive path" of economic growth.[3]

A supposed advantage of the central planning model was that, as accumulation was planned over a multi-year horizon, it would be much more stable from year to year than was normally the case in market economies.[4] It was also thought that investment would be greater than under a market system and so would enable such long-run objectives as industrialization, defence prepared-ness and a high rate of economic growth to be reached. The proportion of net material product (NMP) devoted to net accumulation was usually fixed within the range of 20-30 per cent.[5]

In the 1960s, central planners emphasized investment, even at the expense of the growth of consumption. In the 1970s, the picture changed: accumulation was slower than the growth of income and consumption growth was stronger than accumulation, except in the former Czechoslovakia (see table VI.2). For-eign borrowing in the 1970s helped boost consumption and made available imported consumption goods that were of a much higher quality than those produced by domestic industries. In the 1980s, in Hungary and Poland, accu-mulation actually declined in order to allow growth in consumption and in the exports needed to service foreign debt at a time when income growth had decelerated sharply. By the late 1980s, the fact was inescapable that earlier sacrifices in consumption had been followed by slower — not faster — output growth and that consumption demand could not be satisfied. The central plan-ning model had been totally discredited.

That model had assumed that planners would be able to judge in advance the future requirements of the consumer market, decide the best technical means of producing the output required, construct the machines to produce it, and then actually enter into production. This method worked rather well with the production of a fairly homogeneous and simple good like pig iron, yet it could not anticipate the vast array of goods required to satisfy the increasingly varied and changing consumer demand of competitive market economies.

The flexibility of production that could be observed in private enterprises was lacking in the centrally planned economies. Indeed, the centrally planned

2   In the central planning terminology, "accumulation" included much more than is encompassed, in market terminology, by "fixed capital formation". Accumula-tion over a given time period consisted of (a) fixed assets added in the sphere of material production, (b) fixed assets added in the non-productive sphere, (c) net additions to the stocks of circulating assets in the process of production, (d) net additions to reserves (held idle as an insurance against unex-pected contingencies) and (e) the foreign trade bal-ance. In certain centrally planned economies, the foreign trade balance was not treated as part of accumulation, but rather constituted the difference between net material output produced and net material output distributed.

3   J. Kornai, *Economics of Shortage* (Amsterdam, North Holland Publishing Company, 1980).

4   However, research by Bauer and Ickes detected a special investment cycle: after an increase of invest-ment, financial resources and supply bottlenecks held back further strong economic growth, and this was followed by a deliberate policy to slow down new fixed capital investment. Realizing that this was still not enough to regain the balance of the domes-tic economy both internally and externally, policy makers might stop the most important — and most influential — investment projects. After the econo-my "cooled down", a new investment cycle began, building on postponed demand (see T. Bauer, *Overin-vestment, Growth Cycles and Economic Reform in Some CMEA countries* (Budapest, Institute of Eco-nomics, 1975), p. 296; *Tervgazdaság, beruházás, cik-lusok* (Planned economy, investment, cycles) (Budapest, Közgazdasági és Jogi Könyvkiadó, 1981), p. 632; and B. W. Ickes, "Cyclical fluctuations in cen-trally planned economies", *Soviet Studies*, vol. 38 (1986), pp. 36-52. Several researchers have ques-tioned the validity of this theory for all the transition economies at all times (see P. Mihályi, *Socialist Investment Cycles: Analysis in Retrospect* (Dor-drecht, Netherlands, Kluwer Academic Publishers, 1992), pp. xvi and 233; A. Bajt, "Investment cycles in European socialist economies: a review article", *Journal of Economic Literature*, vol. IX, No. 1 (1971); and K. A. Soós, *Terv, kampány, pénz* (Plan, cam-paign, money) (Budapest, Közgazdasági és Jogi Könyvkiadó, 1986), p. 321. On different approaches to these analyses, see M. Lackó, "Cumulations and easing of tensions", *Acta Oeconomica* (Budapest), vol. 24 (1980), pp. 357-378; and A. Simonovits, "Investment limit cycles in a socialist economy", *Economics of Planning*, vol. 24 (1991), pp. 27-46.

5   These officially given proportions were in fact under-stated, because producer goods were relatively undervalued in comparison with most consumer goods in the NMP valuation, as the former were not subject to turnover taxes.

Table VI.2.

MAIN COMPONENTS OF GROWTH IN FIVE CENTRALLY PLANNED ECONOMIES, 1961-1990

Percentage change

	1961-1970	1971-1980	1981-1990
Bulgaria			
Consumption	6.8	5.8	2.2
Accumulation	9.6	3.8	2.8
Export	14.2	11.4	3.8
National income	7.7	7.0	3.1
Czechoslovakia			
Consumption	4.3	3.5	2.7
Accumulation	4.4	4.4	6.0
Export	6.8	6.4	3.3
National income	4.4	4.6	1.7
Hungary			
Consumption	5.0	3.9	0.9
Accumulation	7.6	2.4	-7.4
Export	10.2	8.3	4.0
National income	5.4	4.5	1.1
Poland			
Consumption	5.3	6.5	0.2
Accumulation	7.5	2.7	-0.8
Export	9.9	7.4	2.9
National income	7.1	5.2	0.8
USSR			
Consumption	5.0	2.5	-3.6
Accumulation	6.3	2.5	1.6
Export	9.3	4.9	1.1
National income	7.2	5.0	2.7

Sources: National statistical data; Organization for Economic Cooperation and Development (OECD) electronic database; Economic Commission for Europe (ECE), *Economic Survey of Europe in 1991-1992* (United Nations publication, Sales No. E.92.II.E.1) and *Economic Survey of Europe in 1992-1993* (United Nations publication, Sales No. E.93.II.E.1); and *Ekonomika stran chlenov SEV* (Economy of member States of the Council for Mutual Economic Assistance (CMEA) (Moscow).

[a] Average annual rate of growth.

system used production processes that usually were out of date compared with those of the advanced market economies even at the moment production began, and enterprises in the planned economies were thus always striving to catch up. The difficulties encountered by the centrally planned system in producing goods of quality standards comparable with those of the developed economies were underlined by the differences between the products of the former German Democratic Republic and those of the former Federal Republic of Germany.[6] These products came from the two parts of what was before the Second World War a single country whose different regions had not been at markedly different levels of technological development.

Not only did the system result in much investment's going to produce increasingly obsolete products, but there was also an almost constant pressure to increase investment. If the expected output growth did not materialize, the remedy entailed not a re-examination of investment programmes in terms of their feasibility and efficiency, but rather another series of "organizational measures", such as decisions to concentrate resources on near-completed facilities so as to bring down the volume of overdue unfinished construction, or to improve management discipline. The result inevitably was to allot more to investment because the plan always stipulated increased volumes of production and construction.

Another upward pressure stemmed from the fact that leaders at all levels of the bureaucracy considered that their power and prestige grew in accordance with the expansion of the unit that they led. Their financial rewards also increased accordingly in many cases. In addition, the difficulties encountered by company management in obtaining its own inputs prompted management to produce these inputs within the firm or branch, which again required investment. In this way, state enterprises became conglomerates, establishing various technologically unrelated divisions such as Construction, Machinery Maintenance, Instruments and Transport. It was safer, even if more costly, to ensure that various renovations, repairs and other activities unrelated to a given enterprise's profile were implemented in-house.[7]

The fact that the costs of investments were always paid from the state budget eliminated any financial consequences to the enterprises of failed investments.[8] There was little resistance to political pressure for more expansion and this forced planners to increase the volume of investments even more. Thus, plan targets for accumulation were overly ambitious in light of the limitedness of the real resources needed for their fulfilment. Meanwhile, the supply of materials, machinery and equipment did not meet needs, causing serious bottlenecks in the domestic economy with important external effects, as rising imports raised trade deficits to unsustainable levels.[9]

Investment was thus pushed up at much faster rates than national income. As summed up by Ota Šik,[10] enterprises and departments, relying on the experience of the previous extensive development, demanded the greatest possible volume of investments, the most manpower and the lowest production targets they could, so as to fulfil the plans easily. As a result, the incremental capital-output ratio rose sharply. By almost any measure, these economies were not efficient.

However, the central planning model did change over time as its defects became more apparent. Indexes of investment efficiency were worked out to aid planners and enterprises in selecting the most "effective" investment projects.

6   Through accession of the German Democratic Republic to the Federal Republic of Germany with effect from 3 October 1990, the two German States united to form one sovereign State. In the text, the present western *Länder* of Germany are often referred to as the "former Federal Republic of Germany" and the eastern *Länder* as the "former German Democratic Republic".

7   J. Winiecki, "The applicability of standard reform packages to eastern Europe", *Journal of Comparative Economics*, vol. 20 (1995), p. 351.

8   J. Kornai, "Transzformációs visszaesés" (Recession in transformation), *Közgazdasági Szemle* (Economic observer), vol. XL, Nos. 7 and 8 (1993), p. 586.

9   The political economy of shortage in the socialist economies has been analysed by J. Kornai in *Economics of Shortage* (Amsterdam, North Holland Publishing Company, 1980).

10   O. Šik, *Plan and Market under Socialism* (Prague, Czechoslovak Academy of Sciences, 1967), p. 86.

With progress made in the mathematics of optimal planning and computerization, planners hoped to achieve a more appropriate allocation of investment resources. The role and responsibilities of investment banks (in some reforming countries, commercial banks) were strengthened so that they would systematically evaluate investment efficiency before extending credits.

In addition, the planned economies embarked on a consistent policy of standardization of capital equipment and processes, systematic exchanges of technological data and specialization among the USSR and the countries that were its partners in the Council for Mutual Economic Assistance (CMEA). "Capital charges", which were annual payments in lieu of interest that were made by enterprises to the State on fixed assets in their possession, were introduced. Profit became the main criterion for enterprise performance in several economies, meaning that enterprises were no longer as extravagant in terms of endeavouring to secure and hoard equipment that they could not utilize profitably.[11]

Still, under a system of administered prices rather than of market-determined prices, distortions in these economies were abundant. It was almost impossible to deduce whether a given branch was really profitable for the national economy or not and it was therefore immensely difficult for the authorities to allocate investment resources according to their relative efficiency in different spheres. Not surprisingly, under such conditions, a good deal of highly inappropriate investment took place.

In the end, it proved impossible to reform the system. A considerable capital stock had been built up at considerable sacrifice; but while it could generate large physical volumes of output, it had proved unable to create the kind of living standards that the citizens of these countries expected to enjoy, which were enjoyed by citizens in many neighbouring countries. This was the legacy left to the economies in transition.

INVESTMENT IN CENTRAL AND EASTERN EUROPE

At the outset of the transition, enterprises in Central and Eastern European transition economies (CEETEs) faced the following conditions. First, there were immediate demands for modernization of the outdated economic structure described above. Second, new enterprise management and organizational forms had to be worked out. Third, rapid modernization of the product mix was called for. These requirements demanded a large volume of high-quality investments. Yet investment contracted and that made the situation worse: much of the most necessary maintenance and replacement investment could not be implemented. The turnaround would not begin until some years later (see table VI.3).[12]

The early years of the transition: the "destructive phase"

The early years of transition in Central and Eastern Europe were generally a time of economic and political uncertainty and macroeconomic instability. In all cases, not just investment but also consumption declined either in 1990 or in 1991. In some cases, investment fell by nearly 30 per cent in a single year (see table VI.3). All of the countries had to take emergency stabilization measures right after the start of the transition process.

11 For a review and assessment of the economic reforms in these economies in the 1980s, see *Journal of Development Planning, No. 20, 1990: Economic Reforms in Centrally Planned Economies and their Impact on the Global Economy*, guest ed. Jozef M. van Brabant (United Nations publication, Sales No. E.90.II.A.9).

12 The account set forth in the present section is fairly general, but as data are not available on a fully comparable basis for all countries in the region, the discussion and tables below refer to the countries for which such data were available.

Table VI.3.
CHANGES IN CONSUMPTION, FIXED INVESTMENT AND GROSS DOMESTIC PRODUCT (GDP) IN CENTRAL AND EASTERN EUROPE, 1990-1995

Annual Percentage Change

		1990	1991	1992	1993	1994	1995[a]
Bulgaria	Consumption	0.6	-8.3	-4.7	-4.6	-2.7	2.3
	Fixed investment	-18.5	-19.9	-23.2	-29.7	-20.2	0.7
	GDP	-9.1	-6.9	-5.7	-3.7	2.2	2.5
Czech Republic	Consumption	6.7	-28.5	15.1	2.9	5.3	1.3
	Fixed investment	-2.1	-17.7	8.9	-7.7	17.3	15.7
	GDP	-1.2	-14.2	-6.4	-0.9	2.6	4.8
Hungary	Consumption	-3.5	-5.2	-0.6	5.4	-2.5	-3.4
	Fixed investment	-7.1	-10.4	-2.8	-0.7	27.0	8.7
	GDP	-3.3	-11.9	-3.0	-0.8	2.9	2.0
Poland	Consumption	-11.7	7.5	3.5	5.1	4.0	4.3
	Fixed investment	-24.8	-4.4	2.3	2.9	8.0	18.9
	GDP	-11.6	-7.0	2.6	3.8	5.0	7.3
Romania	Consumption	9.0	-11.8	-5.5	-1.2	4.7	7.2
	Fixed investment	-35.6	-31.6	13.1	8.2	20.1	10.5
	GDP	-8.2	-12.9	-8.8	1.3	3.5	6.9
Slovakia	Consumption		-25.1	11.0	2.4	-1.7	3.7
	Fixed investment	11.7	-25.2	-15.3	-16.0	-14.3	3.5
	GDP	-2.5	-14.5	-7.0	-4.1	4.8	7.4

Sources: National statistics and LINK estimates; ECE, *Economic Survey of Europe in 1994-1995* (United Nations publication, Sales No. E.95.II.E.1), tables 3.2.7, 3.2.10 and 3.2.13; and ECE, *Economic Survey of Europe in 1995-1996* (United Nations publication, Sales No. E.96.II.E.1), table 3.2.11.

[a] Preliminary.

Even in the early stage of the transition, however, there were warnings of the need to protect, at least temporarily, some of the infant or senile industries during the period of radical changes. It was feared that in the necessarily deep restructuring, CEETEs might lose irreversibly their potential comparative advantages in certain sectors.[13] Yet the centrally planned system was so discredited that it was not politically feasible to adopt measures of state intervention. The introduction of elements of industrial policy or protection of domestic production was out of the question.

While much of the capital stock was obsolete, some of the irreversible scrapping of capacities and closing of enterprises that took place might have been avoided had the domestic short-term conditions not deteriorated so rapidly. Part of this reflected consumer demand, that is to say, sales of domestic products contracted sharply as imports became readily available. On the other hand, had the process of "constructive destruction" been slower than it was, it

13 M. A. Landesmann and P. I. Székely, *Industrial Restructuring and Trade Reorientation in Eastern Europe* (Cambridge, United Kingdom, Cambridge University Press, 1995), p. 5.

would have absorbed considerable resources (in maintaining activities that would never have become competitive) and thus delayed the transfer of resources into more promising lines of production. Indeed, one of the benefits of the sharp break was that some of the investments launched before the transformation according to very different economic policy goals were not completed, thereby freeing some resources for other uses.

External conditions during the early stages of transition were difficult for enterprises. The breaking up of the trade relations of the former CMEA was a major jolt to enterprises that lost well-established and assured markets; so was the new openness of CEETEs towards the global economy. Without any "filtering mechanism" to dampen the shock, these economies were extremely vulnerable to external changes.

On the other hand, openness to external trade and finance also offered benefits. Newly attracted direct investment — and other foreign financing (indirectly) — contributed to new domestic investment. This afforded the opportunity to tap the "productivity reserves" that had been locked up in the form of underutilized human capital and help close a technology and management gap. Moreover, the skill and technology content of some CEETE production in traditional branches had been undervalued in domestic prices relative to international prices. As prices moved closer to international norms, potential returns to investment rose, making investment and its financing more attractive.[14]

Another development in the shake-out of the early years that might, with hindsight, be seen in a positive light is that the CEETEs increased the write-off rates of fixed assets that had suddenly become obsolete, thereby reducing the average age of equipment. Finally, in some countries, the decline in the average age of fixed assets was furthered by the pick-up in investment after 1993 which raised the share of fixed assets that were less than five years old. Both these aspects — rapid scrapping and rapid replacement and modernization — have become integral parts of the current investment strategy.

Recent investment performance: signs of a productivity revival

After the "destructive phase" came the second task of modernization, namely to purchase machinery and equipment of the more advanced specifications demanded, which largely depended upon the availability of external resources. When there was an easing of external constraints, imports of machinery and equipment increased. In the context of the large technological gap between the developed economies and the CEETEs, the increased import of machinery and equipment, which enables new processes or products to be substituted for technologically obsolete ones, may be seen as allowing productivity to rise even when only replacement investment takes place.[15]

Evidence is accumulating of considerable productivity gains in CEETE countries, as is shown in table VI.4. Countries have experienced annual increases of as much as 10 per cent, and often over 15 per cent, in labour productivity in a single year. The economies in transition had another advantage besides their abundant, but underexploited, human resources — a large stock of structures. As described above, output had been increased under the previous system primarily by expanding the number of productive units. Concentrating investment resources on the replacing of obsolete by more productive

14   M. A. Landesmann and P. I. Székely, op. cit., p. 4.

15   Investment-related ("embodied") productivity gains are discussed in more detail in EBRD, *Transition Report*, 1995 (London, 1995), pp. 76-90.

machinery in modernized albeit already existing structures, would increase output per worker. Table VI.5 shows that the share of machinery and equipment in total fixed capital investment increased strongly in the Czech Republic and Poland after 1990. Poland, which saw very fast increases in labour productivity after 1991, had started from a very low base of only about a third of investment being devoted to machinery and equipment; yet by 1995, its share was the largest among the countries examined.

There has also been a marked shift in the direction of investment in the years of transformation, as shown in table VI.6. In agriculture, the countries where the investment share was already small saw a further decline. However, Romania's much larger share fluctuated. The share of investment going to the extractive industries declined as expected, except in Poland where it was broadly stable. Investment in the extractive industry of Romania was higher than in the other countries, mainly owing to petroleum. As production declined substantially in Romania, largely because of demand factors, investment suf-

Table VI.4.
CENTRAL AND EASTERN EUROPEAN ECONOMIES: LABOUR PRODUCTIVITY IN INDUSTRY,[a] 1991-1995

Annual percentage change

	1991	1992	1993	1994	1995[b]
Bulgaria	-5.2	-3.1	-2.8	8.6	11.3
Czech Republic	-21.4	-0.2	-0.5	4.7	10.5
Hungary	-8.1	-0.3	16.4	14.8	13.3
Poland	-4.2	13.7	11.3	12.9	10.4
Romania	-19.3	-14.2	13.7	9.1	16.0
Slovakia	-10.7	-3.6	-5.0	9.9	8.2

Source: *Economic Survey of Europe in 1995-1996* (United Nations publication, Sales No. E.96.II.E.1), table 3.2.7.

[a] Measured as industrial/manufacturing output per employee in the industrial/manufacturing sector.
[b] Provisional, based on partial data.

Table VI.5.
SHARE OF MACHINERY AND EQUIPMENT INVESTMENT IN FIXED CAPITAL INVESTMENT IN FOUR CENTRAL AND EASTERN EUROPEAN TRANSITION ECONOMIES (CEETES), 1990-1995

Percentage

	Czech Republic	Hungary	Poland	Slovakia
1990	46.2	46.4	35.2	46.1
1991	46.4	46.3	35.3	51.2
1992	46.1	48.3	39.3	..
1993	47.3	40.1	49.3	47.7
1994	49.9	36.7	50.0	43.9
1995[a]	52.5	44.1	55.3	48.6

Source: *Główny Urząd Statystyczny, Česky Statistický úřad, Štatistický úrad SR* and *Központi Statisztikai Hivatal* (Central Statistical Office (Poland), Czech Statistical Office, Statistical Office of the Republic of Slovakia, and Central Statistical Office of Hungary), *Statistical Bulletin* No. 3 (1995), p. 24.

[a] First three quarters.

fered not only in this sector but also in the manufacturing branches producing equipment for the industry. In the other countries, there was no such abrupt change in the share of investment going to the manufacturing sector.

Table VI.6 also shows that large relative changes were seen in the construction, post and telecommunications, and finance branches. The increases in the construction sector point to the modernization that was needed for this sector to be able to refurbish existing buildings and erect structures to meet the higher standards now required. Two sectors that most urgently needed modernization were post and telecommunications, and finance. In all countries, the share of total investment going to the former sectors rose substantially. The banking sector had been neglected in the previous system, and the sharp increases in

Table VI.6.
FIXED CAPITAL INVESTMENT OF FOUR CEETES IN SELECTED SECTORS AS A SHARE OF FIXED CAPITAL INVESTMENT, 1991-1994

Percentage		1991	1992	1993	1994
Agriculture	Czech Republic	..	3.3	3.0	4.1
	Hungary	3.9	2.1	1.9	2.6
	Poland	4.4	3.2	3.1	3.0
	Romania	9.5	10.2	6.6	18.7
Extractive	Czech Republic	..	4.9	3.3	2.8
	Hungary	1.1	0.8	0.7	0.6
	Poland	4.1	4.4	4.2	4.3
	Romania	14.0	12.5	10.4	8.0
Manufacturing	Czech Republic	..	20.8	22.3	21.0
	Hungary	26.2	29.7	24.7	22.6
	Poland	27.2	27.3	25.5	29.1
	Romania	24.6	27.3	23.6	16.0
Construction	Czech Republic	..	3.1	2.2	1.2
	Hungary	1.9	2.0	2.0	2.5
	Poland	4.0	4.7	4.1	4.6
	Romania	2.1	2.6	2.8	5.4
Post and telecommunications	Czech Republic	..	2.5	4.1	3.7
	Hungary	7.6	9.8	10.2	12.5
	Poland	1.7	3.8	6.0	5.1
	Romania	0.8	2.3	4.8	3.7
Finance	Czech Republic	..	6.4	9.1	7.3
	Hungary	5.0	5.6	5.9	4.9
	Poland	2.4	3.6	3.9	4.7
	Romania	0.8	2.1	2.9	3.9

Source: National statistical yearbooks, various years.

the low shares of investment in this sector in the cases of Poland and Romania reflect the rapid development of the modern banking system in these countries.

In the first destructive phase of the investment process described above, the demand for machinery and equipment of the standards required to produce for the market economy could only be — and were — supplied by imports. Domestic suppliers have begun to succeed, however, in capturing a larger share of this market: in Hungary, domestic supplies of machinery grew by 18.5 per cent in 1993 and 7 per cent in 1994, while imports grew by 11 per cent in 1993 and declined by 9 per cent in 1994.[16] Similarly, in the Czech Republic, the share of domestically produced equipment in total equipment purchases rose from 37 per cent in early 1993 to 43 per cent in 1994.

These encouraging developments at the sectoral level are being mirrored in a rise in investment at the macrolevel (see table VI.3). Investment growth in several countries, albeit not all, was strong in 1994, and it was positive in all the CEETE countries — and particularly strong in the Czech Republic, Poland and Romania — in 1995.

The privatization process and the growth of new private enterprises resulted in the increasing over the period of the share of private investment in total investment (see table VI.7). Many of the new private enterprises are quite small, as the initial capital requirement for entry into the private sector can be quite low.[17] They can, however, subsequently reinvest a substantial portion of their profits.

Government (budgetary) investment has, in contrast, remained relatively weak, in line with the collapse of budgetary revenues. However, while there are certain measurement difficulties regarding the decline in government investment as a share of GDP since transition began,[18] the role of government-initiated investment seems poised to increase. The need for structural change is probably most intensely felt in the field of infrastructure — roads, telecommunications, educational and health infrastructure. As of the present, the emerging private sector does not have the necessary financial means to participate in these projects; moreover, far less foreign capital than anticipated has been attracted to major infrastructure projects. Future infrastructure development is therefore likely to depend heavily on the state budget. The average government investment/GDP ratio in the CEETEs was 5 per cent in 1995, only slightly above the average ratio of OECD in that year.[19] It may thus be expected to rise, owing to the backlog of public investment needs.

Table VI.7 also shows a decline in state-sector corporate (non-government) investment as a percentage of GDP in many CEETEs after 1989. The main reason for the decline, apart from the severe recession of 1990-1993, was the transition itself. State-owned enterprises had no clear owners, and managers were left without incentives to invest. Even the future of the enterprises as such was uncertain. Managers yielded to wage pressures and used most income flows or even sold off machinery to pay for higher wages.

Why was investment slow to pick up?

The policy environment in the CEETEs has clearly changed dramatically compared with what it was under central planning; but it took several years for the investment environment to improve and for enterprises to begin to respond.

[16] *Statisztikai Havi Kozlemenyek, Monthly Bulletin of Statistics* (Budapest, Statisztikai Kiado), Nos. 2 and 3 (1995), p. 94.

[17] Of the 796 entrepreneurs in a Polish sample survey, 31 per cent started their firms with less than $100, 57 per cent had less than $500 and 65 per cent had less than $1,000 (see S. Johnson and G. Loveman, "Private sector development in Poland: shock therapy and starting over", *Comparative Economic Studies*. vol. 36. No. 4 (winter 1994), p. 179.

[18] That is, for the pre-transition period and for several countries, the statistics may include investment actually undertaken not by the government but by state enterprises, and this would exaggerate the downward tendency in government investment recorded since 1989. In several countries, government investment is overstated because the data also include capital transfers from the State.

[19] For comparison of investment shares in CEETEs and OECD countries, see Heliodoro Temprano, "Saving and investment in transition countries", *European Economy, Supplement A, Economic trends*, No. 7 (July 1995), p. 10.

Table VI.7.
STATE AND PRIVATE INVESTMENT IN CEETES AS A PROPORTION OF GDP, 1989-1995
Percentage

		1989	1990	1991	1992	1993	1994	1995
Albania	Government	..	..	6.0	4.0	8.0	8.0	10.0
	Non-government	..	..	0	1.0	6.0	7.0	9.0
Bulgaria	Domestic investment	32.9	25.6	22.6	19.9	14.2	14.6	15.2
	Private investment	1.5	0.9	0.6	0.4	3.1	3.4	3.7
	State-sector investment	31.4	24.7	22.0	19.5	11.0	11.2	11.5
	Government (budget)	6.9	3.1	2.0	2.7	1.9	1.7	2.0
	Non-government	24.5	21.6	20.00	16.8	9.1	9.5	9.5
Czech Republic	Domestic investment	26.8	28.6	29.9	24.0	17.0	20.4	22.1
	Private investment	1.1	1.5	2.8	3.3	4.1	6.1	6.7
	State-sector investment	25.7	27.1	27.1	20.7	12.9	14.3	15.4
	Government (budget)	6.2	6.1	5.6	6.5	4.2	4.9	5.6
	Non government	19.5	21.0	21.5	14.2	8.7	9.4	9.8
Slovakia	Government	..	..	..	..	4.1	4.2	4.8
	Non-government	..	..	..	..	17.7	12.9	14.1
Hungary	Domestic investment	26.1	24.0	20.8	19.5	23.1	22.9	23.4
	Private investment	9.8	6.6	8.4	9.7	7.4	6.7	6.7
	State-sector investment	16.3	17.4	12.4	10.2	15.7	16.2	16.7
	Government (budget)	5.9	3.6	4.4	6.3	4.7	4.1	4.4
	Non government	10.4	13.8	8.0	3.9	11.0	12.1	12.3
Poland	Government	4.0	3.6	4.1	3.7	3.4	3.2	3.6
	Non-government	24.7	23.9	15.8	11.4	13.0	13.4	13.8
Romania	Domestic investment	25.8	30.2	28.0	32.3	30.1	28.7	27.2
	Private investment		3.8	4.1	4.8	4.9	5.4	5.8
	State-sector investment	25.8	26.4	23.9	27.5	25.2	23.3	21.4
	Government (budget)	8.9	7.7	7.2	7.1	6.6	5.7	5.1
	Non government	16.9	16.7	16.7	20.4	18.6	16.6	16.3

Sources: National statistics; OECD data; EBRD, *Transition Report*, 1995 (London, 1995), p. 72; and DESIPA estimates for 1994 and 1995 (all countries).

The broad policy framework, however, was established rather early. In it, the government has a major role to play in nourishing the budding private and privatized sector. It also was expected to create structures conducive to entrepreneurial activity in the economy, including incentives for investors to channel their savings to enterprises and for enterprises to reinvest their own profits. Governments were also expected to limit the absorption of resources by inflexible and inefficient State-owned enterprises. Implementing this vision was not, however, a straightforward matter.

It was widely understood that, for a sustainable growth of investment, domestic saving had to rise. The component under most direct government control is the government's own saving. In many countries, public saving turned negative as revenues evaporated, while current expenditures rose. The contraction of public saving had typically been translated into substantial increases in public deficits, despite the fact that public investment also fell in most countries. The only CEETEs that avoided this fiscal deterioration were the Czech Republic, Slovenia and the Baltic States.

Savings in CEETEs not only fell abruptly but also were allocated inefficiently. The small part of saving that was not absorbed by the State was often channelled by a weak, non-competitive and largely State-controlled banking system into loss-making enterprises and sectors. Enterprises, in particular small and medium-sized enterprises, perforce relied heavily on the savings of their owners and on their own profits. External financing represented only a small fraction of total investment financing.

Put another way, the challenge was to make the banking sector play its proper role as a financial intermediary. Although the State hived off to new entities such as commercial banks some of the functions previously performed by the sole State-owned bank, it still retained substantial ownership of these bodies. These restructured banks inherited problems from the former system that impeded the banking system's ability to supply finance to a viable enterprise needing investment funds.

During the early years of transition, when both domestic and external markets collapsed, the State-owned enterprises (SOEs) were not able to generate funds to repay their loans to the banks. Subsidies from the State to the SOEs were also reduced. Thus, banks quickly became burdened with a portfolio of non-performing debt of SOEs. The banks in turn had little reason to refuse refinancing and new credits (or even to monitor the use of newly extended credit), as they assumed that they would eventually be repaid by the State. This build-up of SOE debt to banks took place while monetary policy was tightened to counter the burst of inflation that accompanied the early stages of transition. The high interest rates that resulted raised even further the payments due to the banks.

The solution to the SOEs' incurring further non-performing loans was to privatize them, although this was not the only motive for privatization. However, they could be made attractive prospects for privatization only if part or all of their non-performing loans were not treated as obligations of the new owners. This was facilitated by the fact that the banks were State-owned and so would not have insisted on repayment of the debts from the proceeds of privatization in the way that a privately owned bank would have.

Box VI.1.
FOREIGN DIRECT INVESTMENT IN CENTRAL AND EASTERN EUROPE

Foreign direct investment (FDI) in the transition economies had started even before the transition began. Only Hungary, however, had accumulated a substantial FDI stock by 1989, as a result of its reforms in the 1970s and 1980s. Since 1994, Hungary's head start seems to have faded as direct investment in both the Czech and Polish economies speeded up considerably. The dollar value of FDI inflows to CEETEs as a whole increased in each of the last six years (see table).

These growing FDI inflows seem to reflect a number of factors. First and foremost, investors' concerns about political stability in the region seem to have eased. This is a major consideration for the many international companies that are seeking to spread their operations among emerging markets. Second, investors are seeing that these countries have achieved or are on the way to achieving macroeconomic stability. Third, with improving macroeconomic performance, the CEETE countries are enjoying an improvement in their credit ratings. Fourth, trade barriers between the CEETEs and other European States are coming down under the terms of the association agreements with the European Union and agreements among members of the Central European Free Trade Area. Under these two initiatives, the exports of some goods produced in the region are subject to lower import duties and in most parts of the continent are even exempt from them.

The strategies of the direct investors appear to be aimed at establishing a long-term presence in these countries. According to a survey of investments made by a sample of Western European companies in the countries of Eastern Europe, the main reasons for investing had to do more with the general desire to develop new markets in Central and Eastern Europe than with a wish to obtain immediate profits or to exploit competitive positions arising from the specific features of those markets. [a]

About half of the accumulated FDI is concentrated in manufacturing, including engineering, automobile assembly, and the chemical industry. There have also been investments in services: for example, direct investors targeted the antiquated telecommunications system of the region, and this led to large individual agreements. One of the effects of the high share of FDI in manufacturing has been an increase in the role of joint ventures in the external trade of the countries concerned. [b]

In the beginning, FDI was mostly directed towards those industries (and factories) that operated above the average technological productivity and efficiency level. The firms most in need of technological reconstruction and new management techniques were thus largely neglected by potential FDI partners. More recently, however, foreign investors have expressed interest in a broader array of industries. Part of this diversification can be attributed to the strategy of privatization, which gave foreign investors substantial new markets where domestic competitors were not present — as for instance, in telecommunications, where the monopoly public concern was privatized and foreign investors took an interest. There have also been instances of FDI-related imports of new products rising while the domestic supply from the privatized enterprise in which foreign investors participated fell.

In spite of instances of anticompetitive behaviour, the overall effect of FDI has been positive. While overall employment in the economies of the region increased only slightly — or declined — during the years of transition, that in FDI-related businesses increased substantially. Companies with foreign participation have tended to invest actively, [c] and the performance of foreign-owned, especially wholly foreign-owned companies, in terms of per employee wages, net company income and value added, is superior to that of the average domestic enterprise.

a   See Pietro Genco, Siria Taurelli and Claudio Viezzoli, *Private Investment in Central and Eastern Europe: Survey Results*, European Bank for Reconstruction and Development Working Paper, No. 7 (London, July 1993).

b   In the case of Hungary, the share of joint ventures in export earnings was 50% by 1993 (see Judit Hamar, *Foriegn Direct Investment and Joint Ventures in Hungary* (Budapest, Kopint-datorg. December 1993). p. 16)

c   See Pietro Genco, Siria Taurelli and Claudio Viezzoli, op. cit.; and Judit Hamar, *Foreign direct investment and Joint Ventures in Hungary* (Budapest, Kopint-datorg, December 1993).

The disruptions of the transition itself, with relative prices changing rapidly, made it very difficult for the often inexperienced managers of new and privatized companies to make accurate profit forecasts, and so many of the loans that they incurred with the banks have not been repaid.

The result of all these factors is that the State-owned banking system is the least attractive sector of the economy in terms of privatizing and that only some forgiveness of the non-performing loans in the banks' portfolios can make them

FOREIGN DIRECT INVESTMENT IN CENTRAL AND EASTERN EUROPE, 1989-1995
Millions of Dollars

	1989	1990	1991	1992	1993	1994	1995	1995 Stock per capita (dollars)	1995 Share (percentage)
Bulgaria	10	20	100	130	200	200	220	98	3
Czech Republic	10	166	200	1 210	600	800	2 500	552	21
Hungary	120	311	1 538	1 317	2 152	1 511	4 500	1 250	42
Poland	60	88	470	830	1 100	1 300	2 400	164	24
Romania	20	18	187	240	221	600	250	67	6
Slovakia	5	20	53	130	350	400	200	205	4
Central and Eastern Europe	225	623	2 548	3 857	4 623	4 811	10 070	271	100

Sources: For 1989-1994 data, see ECE, *East West Investments and Joint Venture News*, Geneva, various issues, 1989-1994; for 1995 data, see ECE, *East-West Investment News*, Geneva, various issues, 1995-1996.

saleable prospects. For this reason, the banking sector was the last to be —
and in some countries has not yet been — privatized.

Meanwhile, the existing stock of non-performing loans makes the banks
very reluctant to extend any further loans to viable enterprises. In addition,
banks in transition economies have been hard-pressed in terms of assessing
loan applications. They have expected their customers to provide effective
guarantees in the form of real property and movables, cash, government securities, bank guarantees, and so forth. The experience of Hungary, moreover, was
that after the development of bankruptcy procedures and the liquidation of a
number of companies, creditworthy customers found it more difficult to obtain
loans, even at high interest rates.

Such reform of the banking sector as can allow it to perform successful
financial intermediation between savers and investors is of crucial importance.
Financial institutions matter for growth by not so much directly affecting the
rate of capital formation, as evaluating, managing and funding the entrepreneurial activity that leads to growth.

In addition, neither domestic bond nor equity markets are significant alternative sources of funds, as the institutional structures of these markets are
quite primitive and the information requirements for use of market finance are
usually greater than for bank loans. The only alternative — and one that in fact
imparts an advantageous access to credit — comprises foreign direct investment (see box VI.1) and cross-border borrowing, including from the parent
company, and this has grown to sizeable proportions in the Czech Republic
and Hungary.

THE EXPERIENCE OF THE TREUHANDANSTALT
(TREUHAND) IN GERMANY

Many of the difficulties encountered by the CEETEs in their first half-
decade of transition, in particular as regards investment, took a different form
in the context of the reintegration of the German economy. In contrast with the
case of the financially constrained transition economies, the German experi-

ence might be termed (with apologies to the ghost of W. Arthur Lewis) "transition with unlimited supplies of finance".

The setting for the Treuhand

From 2 July 1990, under the terms of the German Economic and Monetary Union, the two Germanies shared the deutsche mark as a common currency. The economic integration of the two Germanies fused together a wealthy region, well endowed with both human and physical capital, with a relatively depressed region, albeit one rich in labour and land. In 1989, the population of the former German Democratic Republic (GDR) was 16 million, and that of the former Federal Republic of Germany (FRG) 62 million. Because the former GDR's capital was relatively outdated, as was its technology, labour productivity was much lower than that of the former FRG.

Although the east mark would have been worth considerably less than the deutsche mark in a truly fluctuating market for the east mark, price contracts, wage contracts and pension claims were converted at a rate of 1 east mark to 1 deutsche mark.[20] This was a political decision that would make it all the more difficult for eastern enterprises to become competitive. Wages in the former GDR had been well above the full employment, market-clearing level to begin with. Moreover, from the first quarter of 1990 to October 1990, average industrial wages per full-time worker rose by about 40 per cent.[21] The result was that labour in the eastern Länder was being paid much higher wages than was justified on the basis of a productivity comparison with the western Länder.

On 3 October 1990, the former GDR became constituent Länder of Germany. As a result, practically all of the former FRG's laws and institutions were almost immediately applicable in the eastern Länder. These laws covered requirements in a variety of areas, such as workplace standards and environmental protection, that many of the existing enterprises in the eastern Länder could not possibly have met. Unlike the CEETEs, there was no "breathing-space" in which laws and regulations could gradually be tightened to conform to the normally much higher standards prevailing in the European Union. Germany decided that, as one country, it could not have a second-class zone where the full protection of German laws did not apply. This was a political decision, but it had profound economic consequences.

Reunification also brought other unique developments. The eastern Länder acquired a new and well-developed institutional infrastructure and automatic access to developed country markets, thanks to Germany's position in the European Union and in the global economy. In contrast to the wage rate issue, these considerations made investment in the eastern Länder a relatively attractive proposition.

The Government also decided to privatize the State-run enterprises in the eastern Länder as rapidly as possible.[22] It entrusted the task to the Treuhandanstalt (Treuhand). The Treuhand had actually been founded on 1 March 1990 by the Government of the former GDR for the purpose of revitalizing its economy. To this end, all industrial enterprises in the GDR were transferred to it and it was charged with administering and preserving the State-owned assets of the GDR on a trust basis.

The former FRG entered the picture in mid-July 1990 at the time of the German Economic and Monetary Union. Against the background of the acceler-

20 Most financial claims, including company debts, were exchanged or converted at a rate of 2 to 1. For further details, see H. Sinn, *Macroeconomic Aspects of German Unification*, Working Paper, No. 3596 (Cambridge, Massachusetts, National Bureau for Economic Research, 1991).

21 A variety of explanations have been forwarded for this dramatic increase in wages in the eastern *Länder*. One such explanation is that the increases reflected the behaviour of strong unions bargaining on behalf of eastern workers. Another hypothesis is that western unions pushed for east-west parity in order to enhance union solidarity and slow migration. See G. Akerlof and others, "East Germany in from the cold: the economic aftermath of currency union", *Brookings Papers on Economic Activity*, No. 1 (1991), p. 25.

22 The desire for haste emanated from the perception articulated by a member of the Chairman's Committee of the *Treuhandanstalt* that either people would go to the West or capital had to flow to the East. In the first phase, the capital flowed to the East in the form of social payments. The second phase had to entail investing in businesses and in infrastructure (see A. Leysen, "Privatization: East Germany", *Eastern European Economics* (fall 1991), p. 35).

ating collapse of the centrally planned economic system of the GDR, the Treuhand was entrusted with a different legal mandate — namely, transforming the industrial sector of the former GDR command economy into a market-driven economy. This mandate was threefold: first, to privatize firms wherever possible; second, to restructure companies where necessary to make them competitive and attractive to investors; third, to maintain employment in so far as this was compatible with the first two objectives. Following the formation of the German Economic and Monetary Union, the Treuhand's supervisory board was expanded to incorporate members from the FRG. With the dissolution of the GDR in October 1990, managerial control shifted decisively to the former FRG.

Headquartered in Berlin, the Treuhand's size peaked in 1992 with some 4,100 employees (roughly two-thirds of whom were citizens of the former GDR) in 15 regional offices.

An overview of Treuhand operations

The Treuhand had a management structure similar to that of a German public company: a two-tier board consisting of a Management Board (*Vorstand*) and a Supervisory Board (*Verwaltungsrat*). The Supervisory Board consisted of 23 members.[23] The Management Board, which was responsible for carrying out the Treuhand's daily affairs, consisted of nine members — eight individuals from the former FRG and one from the former GDR.[24]

The Treuhand was provided with some DM 7 billion in start-up capital in June 1990 to "pre-finance" expected proceeds. This sum was supplemented by DM 10 billion the following year. It was expected initially that further revenues would be derived from privatization returns and borrowing. Through 1991, the Treuhand's annual limit on borrowing was DM 25 billion, a figure that was increased to DM 30 billion annually for 1992-1994. The Treuhand's deficit was DM 20 billion in 1991. By 1992, it was obvious that the Treuhand's revenues would cover no more than 38 per cent of its expenditures. The deficits increased steadily, and the Treuhand closed down operations on 30 December 1994. Its revenues from the sale of companies had amounted to DM 76 billion (approximately $47 billion), yet expenditures had totalled over DM 330 billion (approximately $203 billion). Of this, DM 153 billion had been spent on subsidies and privatization, DM 20 billion had covered the outstanding credits and interest payments of the enterprises, DM 43 billion had been spent on environmental clean-up measures and DM 37 billion had been disbursed on other expenditures.[25] (Besides privatizing enterprises, the Treuhand had sold buildings and plots of land, including farmland and forests.) Contrary to initial hopes that it would be largely self-financing, it had thus accumulated a deficit of DM 250 billion (approximately $154 billion). This deficit alone distinguishes the German experience from that of the CEETEs — none of which could possibly have accumulated such debts to finance its transition. For instance, DM 250 billion was about five times the GDP of the Czech Republic in 1994, but one tenth of the GDP of Germany.

Following its closure, the Treuhand was, in 1995, split into four units. Two of the most important are the *Bundesanstalt für Vereinigungsbedingte Sonderaufgaben* (BVS) (the Federal Agency for Special Tasks Resulting from Unification) and the *Beteiligungs Management Gesellschaft* (BMG) (the Participatory Management Agency). BVS is responsible for what had been the core activities

---

[23] These were the premiers from the five new *Bundeslände* (federal States), government officials from the ministries of finance and economics in Bonn, a representative from the Bundesbank, a manager from a GDR *Kombinatt* or enterprise, seven members of the board of large German companies, and two from foreign corporations, as well as a number of trade union representatives.

[24] See A. Leysen, "Privatization: East Germany", *Eastern European Economics* (fall 1991), p. 29; and W. Carlin and C. Mayer, "Restructuring enterprises in eastern Europe", *Economic Policy: A European Forum*, vol. 15 (1992), pp. 312-346.

[25] Figures from Deutsche Bundesbank, *Monthly Report*, vol. 48, No. 3 (March 1996), p. 50.

of the Treuhand, namely, regulating contractual obligations initially agreed upon by the Treuhand and purchasers, liquidating the remaining unsaleable companies and providing financial assistance for environmental clean-up and improvement schemes. It is slated to operate through 31 December 1996. A major difference with respect to the Treuhand, however, is that BVS is not allowed to raise capital in the financial markets, but rather must rely on funds allocated to it out of the federal budget. Meanwhile, BMG supervises the sale of the remaining viable companies that were still available for purchase. The budget for the two agencies together was DM 5.5 billion for 1995 and DM 5.5 billion for 1996.

In the first phase of the Treuhand's activities, some 8,000 enterprises — with over 4 million employees (or roughly 45 per cent of the total employment of the former German Democratic Republic) in 65,000 plants — were transferred to it. The stated asset value of these firms was DM 620 billion, though in reality it was much less — an issue that will be discussed below. A second phase, which began almost a year later, involved an additional property transfer of almost 10 million acres of land — which is about 40 per cent of the territory of the former GDR. In addition, all properties formerly belonging to the State Police, the former ruling party and the unions were shifted to the Treuhand. The Treuhand was in effect disposing of what had been the tangible productive assets of a country.

The first step undertaken by the Treuhand was an assessment of the viability of the enterprises entrusted to it. Roughly one third of the firms under the Treuhand's control were deemed economically viable in a market economy, another third were judged potentially viable after being restructured, and the final third were considered non-viable under all circumstances. The strategy adopted was to attempt to privatize the first group as quickly as possible, to restructure and then privatize the second set, and to liquidate the last group. The underlying premise in this approach was that the Treuhand could accurately determine which group any given firm belonged in.

Restructuring, while superficially a single process, actually comprised several phases.[26] The first phase may be termed "legal reorganization" and involved such activities as the choice of a legal structure for the firm, splitting up the enterprise where necessary, and the reallocation of enterprises' real estate. The second stage involved evaluating the potential of the enterprise and covered such activities as developing individual enterprise plans for rehabilitation and making decisions as regards closure of lines of activity. Financial reorganization was yet a third phase. This required recalculating enterprise accounts using western norms, redeeming debt, increasing equity capital, guaranteeing bank loans to the firms and providing redundancy payments to reduce employment. Finally, economic restructuring comprised activities such as investing in fixed capital, scrapping obsolete fixed capital, recruiting new personnel, training staff, making personnel cut-backs and, (in other ways) increasing productivity.

The Treuhand's approach was to involve itself intimately in the first two steps of the process (namely, legal reorganization and evaluation), to concern itself only partially with the third phase (financial reorganization) and to leave the fourth phase of economic restructuring almost entirely up to the private investors who were the new owners. Following these principles, privatization

26 See, for example, J. Priewe, "Privatisation of the industrial sector: the function and activities of the *Treuhandanstalt*", *Cambridge Journal of Economics*, vol. 17 (1993), pp. 333-348.

was achieved predominately by way of sale or donation to outside investors, as the outcome of individual negotiations on enterprises regarding investment and employment potential. Where this was not possible, other methods — such as management buyouts or sales to intermediaries — were employed.

The responsibility for finding a buyer for a Treuhand firm rested jointly with its management and the Treuhand. For industries in which international participation was crucial (such as chemicals), the Treuhand looked to international investment banks to seek out buyers.[27]

Once interested parties were identified, the Treuhand sought to establish whether the potential buyer had the means and management skills to purchase and to continue to operate the enterprise. This assessment was made on the basis of a written business plan that the potential buyer had to provide, indicating product markets, investment and employment plans and the likely relationship with local suppliers and customers.

Embedded in the Treuhand's method was the objective of safeguarding a company as far as possible. Successful investors were therefore those who proposed plans that demonstrated convincingly that they would be able to continue operating a company with reasonable prospects of profit. The interpretation of "continue" was very narrow. It was taken to mean "retain the main emphasis of the business, as well as its location". This of course greatly restricted the range of privatization possibilities. Generally speaking, potential investors were rejected if they signified their intention of turning a company to another use or reselling it. This insistence on the preservation of companies and production locations when virtually the entire economy was being restructured may have represented misplaced concreteness, at least on purely economic grounds.[28] The Government's main goal, however, was business continuity.

A Treuhand priority was thus to enforce investors' commitments to keeping companies running. This held true even when companies were good candidates for bankruptcy. The Treuhand stipulated that buyers present not only future business plans, but also the prospects for important strategic variables, in particular employment and investment levels. Moreover, compared with other goals, the negotiation over the purchase price, which would be the primary concern in a normal market acquisition, was a secondary consideration and was frequently shaped more by investors' promises than by the value of companies' assets.[29]

A firm's accounting net worth would be a first indicator of the sale price that the Treuhand might seek from the sale. However, the actual price demanded reflected three further variables: the amount of investment the buyer pledged to undertake, the number of jobs guaranteed, and the speed with which the adjustment plan could be implemented. As a rule of thumb, the purchase price was reduced by between DM 20,000 and DM 50,000 for each worker the buyer was prepared to retain.[30]

The law governing the Treuhand's operations stated both that State-owned companies should be privatized "as quickly as possible" and that they should be put into a condition in which they would henceforth be competitive. However, no hierarchical relationship between these two objectives was specified and the Treuhand was criticized for putting its overriding emphasis on rapid privatization.[31]

By the end of its operations, the Treuhand had privatized 14,000

[27] For further details, see W. Carlin and C. Mayer, "Restructuring enterprises in eastern Europe", *Economic Policy: A European Forum*, vol. 15 (1992), pp. 312-346.

[28] See K. Schmidt, *Requirements for Successful Privatization — Lessons from the Treuhandanstalt's Approach*, Kiel Working Paper, No. 696 (Kiel, Germany, Kiel Institute of World Economics, 1995).

[29] Ibid.

[30] W. Carlin and C. Mayer, loc. cit.

[31] See K. Schmidt, op. cit.

32 This was a larger number than the original 8,000, as the Treuhand had broken up many large enterprises into smaller and more economically viable firms.

33 *Focus on the Treuhandanstalt* (New York, German Information Center, January 1995).

34 Carlin and Mayer, loc. cit., p. 332.

35 For further details, see H. Brezinski, "Privatisation in East Germany", *Moct-Most*, No. 1 (1992), pp. 11-21.

36 H. Sinn, *Macroeconomic Aspects of German Unification*, Working Paper, No. 3596 (Cambridge, Massachusetts, National Bureau for Economic Research, 1991).

37 J. Roesler, "Privatisation in Eastern Germany — experience with the Treuhand", in *Europe-Asia Studies*, vol. 46, No.3 (1994), pp. 505-517.

38 See D. Gros and Alfred Steinherr, *Winds of Change: Economic Transition in Central and Eastern Europe* (London, Longman Group UK, Limited, 1995).

39 In 1989, the last leader of the GDR put his country's net worth at DM 1.5 trillion. In 1990, a successor revised this estimate downward to DM 880 billion. After unification, the first head of the Treuhand supplied an estimate of DM 600 billion for the assets on his books. In 1991, he conceded that assets and liabilities would just balance each other, yielding a zero net worth. In fact, the opening balance sheet estimate of a net worth of minus DM 209 billion turned out to be on the conservative side. When the Treuhand closed down operations at the end of 1994, its deficits had amounted to DM 250 billion (see D. Gros and Alfred Steinherr, op. cit. p. 271).

enterprises [32] and liquidated, or had ready for liquidation, 3,340 others. The successor agencies were to attempt to save some enterprises that were on the point of liquidation. [33]

The degree of difficulty encountered in carrying out this privatization process had varied. For instance, banks, construction firms, hotels and restaurants were privatized rather easily, as were industrial firms with locational advantages. Small firms were sold more easily than larger ones. Large industrial firms that had exported mainly to Central and Eastern Europe — such as automobile manufacturers, railway-carriage makers and shipbuilders — were difficult to sell (or even donate). Chemical industries, electronics firms, machine tool making firms and steel mills posed even more of a problem and, in some instances, were marketable only if production and employment could be cut back by 80 or 90 per cent and additional financial support offered.

Sales to citizens of the western *Länder* accounted for some 75 per cent of all sales and part-sales of firms. Only some 5-10 per cent of sales, or part-sales, were to non-Germans and less than one fifth were management buyouts (MBOs). It has been noted that this latter statistic may in fact overstate the participation of the eastern *Länder's* citizens, since many MBOs actually involved a western *Länder* partner. [34] Non-German investors were initially very wary: In 1990, only some 1,000 foreign investors responded to the Treuhand's solicitations to invest in the former GDR and those foreign entities that did invest often did so via the German subsidiaries of their company. [35]

Treuhand finances

When the Treuhand commenced its operations, it expected revenues from sale of its portfolio of firms of some DM 600 billion. [36] What became unmistakable by 1992, however, and of increasing concern, was that the basic premise of the whole operation — namely, that the privatization of property previously belonging to the State would create the conditions for an immediate economic upswing in the eastern *Länder* and that only a certain, limited amount of initial money would be necessary to set the wheels of recovery into motion — was proving to have been false. [37]

Over time, the Treuhand's financial position was marked by decreasing net privatization receipts and rising expenditures for financial restructuring, interest payments on old and new debts and payments for legal obligations. The mode of privatization gradually shifted from sales to donations.

The Treuhand's balance sheet for its opening day (1 July 1990) — which was presented only in October 1992 in light of the magnitude of the task that the Treuhand had faced in preparing it — cited a "negative net worth" of DM 209 billion. This was at the very least surprising. [38] It was not obvious how the assets of an economy that, according to many internationally accepted statistics, produced enough to give its citizens a higher average per capita income than Greece or Portugal in the late 1980s had not only no value, but a negative one. [39]

Several reasons have been given to explain this negative net worth. First, the centrally planned economies of Eastern Europe had paid scant attention to the environmental impact of their activities. Thus, certain industrial sites could be sold under the newly applicable German law only if cleaned up or restored. Second, the value of the output of many firms was less than the cost of producing it when assessed at prices of the former FRG, with the one-to-one east-west exchange rate. Such firms were worthless, in essence, if they had to operate at prices of the former FRG. Third, the Treuhand had taken over enterprises inclusive of their debts and guaranteed their reimbursement. It has been argued that those who gained from this strategy were the banks in the eastern *Länder*. Their loan portfolios were rehabilitated and they became attractive takeover prospects for banks in the former FRG. Fourth, most enterprises were undercapitalized, as the concept of "net worth" had played no significant role in the centrally planned system. The fact that the Treuhand had taken over these enterprises' debts and recognized compensation claims had the accounting effect of a large initial infusion of capital.[40]

It has been suggested that the size of the Treuhand's deficits were partly caused by its sales strategy. It is argued that, as the Treuhand did not sell equity shares but only whole companies, such institutional investors and individuals as were ready, willing and able to bear the risks of resurrecting the eastern *Länder* by incorporating shares of Treuhand companies into their portfolios were unable to do so. They could participate only by becoming entrepreneurs and buying whole companies. Had the Treuhand opted for a longer time-horizon for privatization, it might have pursued a strategy of, (for instance) capitalizing enterprises and selling part of the shares to a "strategic" investor and part on financial markets. Also, it could have spread out the dates of sale.

A second absorption problem lay in the severe credit constraints faced by potential buyers of Treuhand assets. Unresolved property disputes[41] and the absence of equity capital made it practically impossible for citizens in the eastern *Länder* to borrow for the purpose of buying Treuhand assets. Moreover, the condition that buyers make full and immediate payment in effect required the buyer to finance the purchase with its own new borrowing, increasing the demand for funds in capital markets of the western *Länder*. In addition, the surge in demand and growth in the western *Länder* that accompanied the reintegration strategy prompted the Bundesbank to tighten monetary policy. This boosted interest rates in Germany and thereby lowered the capitalized value of the assets that the Treuhand wished to dispose of, and this resulted in potential buyers' reducing their bids.[42]

Investment in the eastern Länder

The Treuhand was a major part of Germany's transition strategy for the eastern *Länder*. It was — and had to be — a unique approach for a unique situation. After the fact, the Treuhand has been accused of making mistakes, although this was almost inevitable in view of the prime objective of accomplishing its task quickly. This insistence on speed was an integral part of the overall strategy which did accomplish its main mission. Today, the economies of the eastern *Länder* are growing rapidly, even while the rest of Germany struggles with a very sluggish situation. Furthermore, capital formation is now high, with strong private as well as continuing public investment. The outlook is encouraging, although the eastern unemployment rate is still considerably above the western rate (see table VI.8).

In terms of understanding the Treuhand experience, the context of the period is important. The Government was particularly concerned about preventing

[40] See D. Gros and Alfred Steinherr, op. cit., p. 251.

[41] The Treuhand did not in fact immediately have a clear title to all its holdings. Properties that had been expropriated after the establishment of the GDR in October 1949 could be claimed by their original owners, as could properties that had been taken between 1933 and 1945 for religious or political reasons. The possibility that claims of this sort might present themselves — which would have made it impossible for the Treuhand to transfer legal title in the event of a sale — complicated its work through 1992. The fact that 30 per cent of industry had not yet been nationalized at the time of the GDR's founding indicates what the scope of the problem was. For further details, see Akerlof and others, "East Germany in from the cold: the economic aftermath of currency union", *Brookings Papers on Economic Activity*, No. 1 (1991), p. 66.

[42] For a presentation of these arguments in greater detail, see Sinn, op. cit.

large population movements from the eastern to the western Länder, owing to the attraction of higher wages in the latter. Living conditions in the east had thus to be supported by the Government as the economic structure was at the same time being largely remade. In the event, the Government chose to fix the eastern exchange rate at a high level, thereby making much of eastern output even less competitive than it might otherwise have been. Also, the environmental standards and social insurance precepts of the west had to be extended to the east. With rapidly rising eastern wage rates, unemployment — open as well as disguised — would soar. Large fiscal transfers were thus inescapable, but they would diminish as the economy of the eastern *Länder* revived. The economic transition thus had to be quick. Economic structures had to be changed and enterprises reborn. A new class of entrepreneurs had to be created, or managers that had previously responded to bureaucratic incentives needed to be given, and needed to respond to, market-based incentives. Here lay the Treuhand's role.

The Treuhand accomplished what it had set out to do — namely privatize the industry of the eastern *Länder*. This was accompanied by a rapid rise in unemployment, despite the employment guarantees that were often required of prospective buyers of firms. In place from the beginning was of course a "safety net" — the unemployment and other benefits that the citizens of the eastern *Länder* enjoyed as citizens of a unified Germany.

Because firms tended to be closed down rather than reorganized if no buyers could be found, critics of the Treuhand have accused it of incurring unnecessary economic costs by promoting massive de-industrialization. The rebuttal was that privatization represented the only way companies could obtain managers and markets. Accordingly, the Treuhand was actually a buyer of management, technology and access to markets for the companies in its portfolio, rather than (as generally perceived) a seller of assets.[43]

Sceptics of this approach maintain that only rapid modernization of often outdated equipment would have given former GDR enterprises a chance to compete in their new markets; but the Treuhand consciously left this to others wherever possible, letting speed of privatization be its guiding principle. The German Government thought that private owners would be the best ones to make decisions on investment and that it should involve itself as little as possible in this process.

The Treuhand's operating strategy is also said to have raised unemployment. However, the national decision to bring wages in the eastern *Länder* into line with those in the western Länder rendered a large number of enterprises unprofitable. Labour had to be shed in order for these to be sold. However, it has also been argued that the dramatic rundown of industrial employment can be traced to the Treuhand's efforts to contain its expenditure. From the Treuhand's perspective, it was prudent to lay off workers who would then go into retraining or job-creation schemes, or collect unemployment insurance — all at the expense of a federal agency other than the Treuhand.[44]

In the event, both the number of jobs guaranteed per firm (or part of firm) sold, and the total numbers in industrial employment, dropped rapidly. Roughly 200 jobs were guaranteed per sale in the Treuhand's first year of operation, and only about 50 jobs per sale in the first half of 1993.[45] Table VI.8 shows how the employment situation in the eastern Länder deteriorated after 1990.

43 K. Schmidt, Kiel Institute of World Economics, as cited in *The Economist*, 24 December 1994-6 January 1995, p. 83.

44 See W. Carlin, *Privatization and Deindustrialization in East Germany*, Discussion Paper, No. 892 (London, Centre for Economic Policy Research, 1993).

45 Ibid.

Table VI.8.

UNEMPLOYMENT IN THE EASTERN LÄNDER, 1990-1995

Year	Quarter	Unemployment in eastern Länder		Memorandum item: unemployment in western Länder (percentage)
		Thousands	As percentage of labour force	
1990	Second	83	1.0	6.6
	Third	309	3.5	6.4
	Fourth	556	6.3	6.1
1991	First	756	8.6	5.7
	Second	835	9.5	5.6
	Third	1 023	11.6	5.7
	Fourth	1 037	11.8	5.7
1992	First	1 254	..	5.6
	Second	1 172	14.4	5.8
	Third	1 158	14.2	6.0
	Fourth	1 097	13.5	6.3
1993	First	1 165	15.2	6.8
	Second	1 115	14.6	7.1
	Third	1 165	15.3	7.5
	Fourth	1 205	15.8	8.0
1994	First	1 214	16.1	8.2
	Second	1 193	15.9	8.3
	Third	1 114	14.8	8.3
	Fourth	1 043	13.9	8.2
1995	First	1 032	13.8	8.2
	Second	1 027	13.8	8.2
	Third	1 039	13.9	8.3
	Fourth	1 063	14.2	8.3

Source: Deutsche Bundesbank, *Monthly Report*, various issues.

46 See V. N. Balasubramanyam, "*The Treuhandanstalt, FDI and employment in Germany*", *International Journal of Manpower*, vol. 15, No. 6 (1994), pp. 72-84.

47 See H. Siebert, "The integration of Germany: real economic adjustment", *European Economic Review*, vol. 35, No. 2/3 (1991), pp. 591-602.

48 Data of Federal Statistical Office, as per Deutsche Bundesbank, *Monthly Report*, March 1996, table IX.3.

49 See Deutsche Bundesbank, *Monthly Report*, vol. 47, No. 7 (July 1995), p. 42.

50 Ibid., p. 39.

51 Deutsche Bundesbank, *Monthly Report*, October 1995, p. 51.

The increase in unemployment was scarcely avoidable because of the low productivity of labour, which was itself largely due to outdated capital.[46] Seventy-six per cent of the equipment in industry in the eastern *Länder* was older than 5 years, some 55 per cent was older than 10 years, and some 20 per cent was older than 20 years.[47] Many factories were not suitable for modern production methods, warehouses were overly large, and production techniques were geared to the member countries of CMEA. Some 75 per cent of the former GDR's exports had been directed to the CMEA countries prior to 1990. However, the volume of imports of the ex-CMEA area declined by fully 30 per cent in 1991 (see annex table A.20). Many products that might have supplied these markets could not begin to compete internationally in other markets because of poor quality. Finally, personnel was not adapted to modern production processes.

The turnaround in the eastern *Länder* came about fairly soon and the economy has seen positive growth since early 1992. The transfer payments from the western *Länder* helped support the revival, but recovery became more solidly based as a more up-to-date capital stock came into being in the new *Länder*. Indeed, the capital goods-producing industry in the east is itself strengthening. Order books in the capital goods sector grew 21 per cent in 1995 and were 35 per cent above the 1991 level. Foreign orders for eastern manufactures grew 24 per cent, pointing to improving productivity.[48]

The gap between wage and productivity levels in the western and eastern *Länder* has narrowed. In the second half of 1994, average wages and salaries in the new *Länder* reached 70 per cent of western *Länder* gross earnings (compared with 34 per cent in the second half of 1990); but average productivity amounted to only 54 per cent of the western *Länder* level. This was, however, an increase from 26 per cent in the second half of 1990.[49]

The output of the distribution, transport, telecommunications and other services sectors in the eastern *Länder* also expanded rapidly after having been impeded (having been deemed "unproductive") under the former system.[50] Their contribution to value added rose from 30 per cent of GDP in the second half of 1990 to 37 per cent in the first half of 1995.[51]

INVESTMENT IN THE RUSSIAN FEDERATION

If the economic transition in eastern Germany accompanied reintegration into a large developed economy, the transition in the countries of the Commonwealth of Independent States (CIS) accompanied political and economic break-up — that of the Soviet Union. This made for a different experience or, more properly, several different ones. There is simply not enough experience nor data to separate the transient phenomena, caused by general confusion and institutional disarray in the initial stages of transition, from the more stable emerging trends that will eventually shape each country's individual pattern of change and adjustment. The Russian Federation, however, owing to its role in the region, as well as to the greater availability of statistics, provides an especially important case-study of investment under transition.

Investment reforms in the Soviet Union before 1991

Even before the dissolution of the Soviet Union, reforms were being attempted so as to make investment more efficient as the limitations of the centrally planned system became more grave. The share of centralized funds in gross investment had been declining steadily since the early 1980s in accordance with the policy of increasing the independence of enterprises through "self-financing". Before the reforms, enterprises had to remit to the central ministries a part of their notional "depreciation allowance", as determined by the central authorities. The ministries then decided what part of these sums would be returned to each enterprise to enable it to maintain the value of its assets. In practice, loss-making enterprises tended to receive part of the "depreciation allowance" of more successful enterprises. Under the new dispensation, enterprises were permitted to retain a significant share of depreciation funds.

A further step was contained in the Enterprise Law of 1987. Enterprises were to retain the bulk of their "depreciation allowances" and a much larger part of their profits, with which they were expected to finance investment. It was expected that the new procedure would create incentives for more efficient decisions on the microeconomic level. There was a degree of success in this drive towards self-financing — between 1987 and 1991, the share of "centralized resources" (funds allocated centrally by the State) in total investment declined from 82 to 35 per cent.[52]

It was also believed that the State could effectively conduct its policy of restructuring industries primarily through government investment credits for priority sectors on favourable terms, as well as through off-budget funds for specific programmes. In practice, the policy proved marginal, as inadequate funds were allocated to the programmes.

More centrally, this policy of extending "financial independence" to enterprises came into conflict with the unchanged principles of state ownership and control. The hierarchical state structures continued to allocate inputs and outputs, assign business partners, set all prices and, even more significantly, provide supplementary budget financing wherever an enterprise's own funds proved insufficient (in other words, "soft budget constraints" were not hardened).

Moreover, the decentralization of the financing system dramatically weakened mechanisms of accountability and control. Enterprises became financially "independent" without becoming accountable — either to state planning bodies or ministries (as in the standard practice under central planning) or to a board of directors or shareholders (as in market economies). This lack of financial accountability prompted numerous enterprises to channel their newly obtained additional resources into their wage bills to the detriment of investment. Since enterprises were certain of budget support even if their investment proved to be misguided, they began a multitude of inappropriate investment projects, and this was followed by the growth of overdue and unfinished construction. In short, overall investment efficiency, which had not been very high to begin with, declined further.

Investment in the Russian Federation since 1992

Were one to look at the data for investment as a share of GDP, it might appear that the Russian economy had not suffered notably since 1992. Indeed, for the USSR, the average investment ratios for the period 1980-1989 were over 30 per cent of GDP, a figure significantly above the world average for 1977-1988 of about 24 per cent and even more significantly above the devel-

52 See *Rossiiskiy statisticheskiy ezhegodnik, 1994* (Russian statistical yearbook, 1994) (Moscow, Goskomstat 1994), p. 372.

53 See Heliodoro Temprano, "Saving and investment in transition countries", *European Economy, Supplement A, Economic trends*, No. 7 (July 1995), p. 5.

oped economies ratio of 21.5 per cent.[53] The data for the post-1992 period show that the investment ratio remains, despite its falling, higher than typical (see table VI.9). Nevertheless, investment has represented a falling share of a falling GDP and a significant portion of that investment might well be deemed inappropriate today for capital formation.

Indeed, the transition to a market mechanism dramatically changed the investment picture. Hard budget constraints were first introduced in 1992, and output in state enterprises plummeted, income fell, and a contraction in investment occurred in that year and in subsequent years. One reason for the fall in investment was the abrupt and massive contraction in the share of one of the principal figures in investment activity, namely the State, without there being other actual or potential sources of investment either available or ready to fill the void.

The State's withdrawal was the result of two policy developments that, while part of the strategy for the transition to a market economy, were disruptive to investment in the short run. These were the rapid and wide-scale privatization of State-owned enterprises and the discontinuation of direct budget subsidies, even for enterprises that remained wholly or partly owned by the Government.

A temporary fall in the volume of investment was not entirely a misfortune, as many projects were inappropriate to begin with, as noted above. Indeed, the recent trend of new fixed investment by sector is more consistent with data on capacity utilization for these sectors, implying that new investment has been better related to demand. The ratio of investment in services to investment in the goods-producing sectors has risen, for example, while there has been a sharp decline in investment in agriculture, machine-building and light industry. The collapse of state procurement had a particularly severe effect on machine-building with its traditionally very high share of defence-related production. The sectors that are seeing stronger investment activity are primarily services, retail trade and residential construction. As in Central and Eastern Europe, the service and trade sectors had been neglected under the centrally planned model and their rehabilitation is essential to the performance of the market economy. The upsurge in construction, including the refurbishment of offices, has already transformed the appearance of many city centres. New construction and assembly in gross fixed investment grew from 44 per cent in 1990 to 65 per cent in 1994.

However, the degree of distortion in the production structure of the Russian economy that investment will have to overcome is substantial. One indication is that, with the liberalization of foreign trade, the Russian market for both durable and non-durable consumer goods was increasingly being satisfied by imports, as consumers demanded higher-quality products. This import surge smothered non-competitive domestic production, but the phenomenon suggests as well the vast market awaiting high-quality producers.

This notwithstanding, the economy is showing signs of responding to market incentives; for example, the increased openness of the Russian economy has brought a relative boom in several export-oriented sectors — fuel and energy, chemicals and metallurgy. With higher exports, the rate of output decline in the energy sector was about half, and in non-ferrous metallurgy one third, of the industrial production average. As a result, the share of mining and other primary sectors in aggregate industrial production increased from 15.5 to 23.5

Table VI.9.
INVESTMENT ACTIVITY IN THE RUSSIAN FEDERATION

	1990	1991	1992	1993	1994
Gross investment (percentage of GDP)	30.1	36.3	34.3	31.3	28.9
Including					
Fixed investment	28.7	23.3	23.7	22.7	25.1
Inventory change	1.4	13.0	10.6	8.6	3.8
Gross saving (percentage of GDP)	31.0	38.8	52.2	39.3	31.5
Memo item					
Current account balance (billions of dollars)	..	..	4.2	6.4	4.8
Real GDP (1990=100)	100.0	95.0	81.2	74.2	64.8

Source: UN/DESIPA, based on national data.

per cent. It is important to note, however, that while maintenance of production required certain investment expenditures, it did not involve any major domestic funding of these sectors. Instead, new investment was largely financed by tied foreign credits.

Sources of investment finance

While the most recent information indicates that there is considerable pent-up demand that could be satisfied from domestic production and that investment is being reallocated to sectors essential for the market economy, it may still be asked why the overall amount of investment activity has so far not been stronger. Certainly, the initial fall in investment after the start of transition was not unique to the Russian Federation as the discussion of the experiences of other countries presented above has shown. However, investment in those countries strengthened after some years.

As previously noted, when central planning ended in what is now the Russian Federation, firms were already expected to finance the bulk of their investment needs from their own internal resources. Table VI.10 shows that internal funds covered about two thirds of investment in the post-planning years. The remaining third, in which government investment outlays were prevalent, was financed externally with funds mainly passed through the commercial banks.

As part of the general and protracted economic decline that followed the breakup of the USSR and the start of transition, a quarter of industrial enterprises were reported to be in the loss-making category in 1995 compared with less than 10 per cent in 1993, and enterprises' liquid assets covered less than a quarter of overdue accounts payable (compared with over 50 per cent in 1993). The savings of enterprises were in many instances financing an accumulation of inventories in the form of unsaleable goods. Also, the enterprises were not receiving payments for their goods and services and so some of their "savings" were locked up in involuntary credits to customers. In these circumstances, firms were thus not in a position to finance investment projects, especially middle- and long-range ones necessary for restructuring. Even enterprises that managed to realize a profit tended to direct a diminishing share of profits to investment. The share of retained profits in total investment fell from 23 per cent in 1991 to 12 per cent in 1993.[54]

At the same time, the share of depreciation allowances in total investment dropped from 29 per cent in 1991 to 7 per cent in 1993.[55] This was caused by the progressive undervaluation of the book value of fixed assets in the high inflation environment of the early transition period. Several revaluation exercises were undertaken to raise the book value of assets in industry across the board, but this did not keep pace with inflation and the Government now plans to make valuation indexation regular and transparent. Enterprises, however, have not always welcomed the revaluation of their fixed assets, preferring to boost their distributable profits through inadequate depreciation charges. This too reduces the resources at the disposal of firms for replacing inventories and capital stock.

Nevertheless, even if internal funds were adequate, there were general and serious discouragements to investment. As with many of the CEETEs, macroeconomic instability in the early years of transition, manifested most clearly in high rates of inflation, made businesses reluctant to invest. It was not just the high level of inflation, but also its unpredictability, that was important.

The course of the privatization programme and the continuing uncertainty about its future direction have also had a significant discouraging effect on investment. Management is unlikely to take a long-term view in running an enterprise whose ownership is unclear and perceived as unstable. Indeed, uncertainty regarding the terms of ownership plus ineffective accountability led to widespread misuse of assets for short-term purposes (like asset-stripping to service the wage bill) and even, in some reported instances, for the personal enrichment of the managers. In general, the uncertainty of changes in the legal, regulatory and administrative environment, plus the high degree of discretion on the part of officials in implementing and enforcing the often unstable and non-transparent rules and procedures, has encouraged corruption and rent-seeking. The combination of these factors has created a nearly hostile environment for enterprise managers willing to invest in production. Finance external to the firm that managers might tap for investment programmes also shrank, owing primarily to the fall in government investment outlays described above. The precarious state of the federal budget did not permit the State to become a decisive provider of investment for the economy nor to contribute significantly to the sluggish demand for domestically produced investment goods. In 1992-1995, the federal budget financed less than 15 per cent of gross investment in the Russian Federation.[56]

The Government's 1994 programme envisaged creating a mechanism to stimulate investment in what it considered priority sectors by financing at least 20 per cent of a project's overall cost from the budget. The decision to allocate state funds for investment support was to be made on a case-by-case basis from among the competitive tenders submitted by enterprises to an investment tender commission of the Ministry of Economics. The criterion for selection of a

54 *Foreign Investment in Russia: Salient Features and Trends* (Second Report) (Moscow, Bank Imperial, 1995), p. 21.
55 Ibid.

56 See *Investment Policy in Russian Economy: Trends and Perspectives* (Moscow, Institute for the Economy of Transition, January 1996).

Table VI.10.
SOURCES OF INVESTMENT FINANCING
IN THE RUSSIAN FEDERATION

Percentage			
	1992	1993	1994
Centralized investment funds	29.8	37.6	31.8
Including from			
Federal budget	16.6	19.2	13.4
Local budgets	10.3	15.1	10.6
State off-budget funds	2.9	3.3	5.8
Priority sectors support fund			2.0
Enterprises' own funds	69.3	57.4	64.2
Households	0.9	2.6	2.3
Foreign direct investment	..	2.4	1.7
Total	100.0	100.0	100.0

Source: *Rossiiskiy statisticheskiy ezhegodnik, 1995* (Russian statistical
yearbook, 1995) (Moscow, Goskomstat, 1995), p. 378.

project and the State's share in its financing was "the importance of the new production for the country's economy".[57]

However, so far the programme has not lived up to expectations for a number of reasons. One is the shortage of budget funds, which led to delays in disbursements for those projects that were selected, and thereby to a loss of confidence of major potential non-government participants in the programme. Another reason is that, given the state of broad decline in industry, it was particularly difficult to select specific projects for government investment support.

The State's investment support remains traditionally oriented: in 1994, 37 per cent of investment in material production sectors was directed towards fuel and energy, while machine-building received only 5 per cent. The same priority subsists in the Government's programme for 1995-1997: fuel and energy, metallurgy, construction, chemical and petrochemical, timber, machine-building, defence and, finally, light industry, agriculture and transportation, in that order.

Government funds are made available to enterprises for investment through the intermediation of commercial banks. These funds were in fact one of the major initial sources of the banks' liquidity. One common practice was to deliberately delay disbursement to enterprises of the funds received from the budget, and to use the money for currency arbitrage or other short-term speculation. Profits from these activities have bolstered the financial position of many commercial banks.

Another potential source of funds for the banks is household saving. Under central planning, the household sector played a minor role in the financing of investment. Household savings were simply not a part of the equation. Such traditional motivations for individual saving in market economies as financial security after retirement, access to health care and education were not present: the State took care of literally everything and provided a comprehensive and reliable, if modest, social support system. Even real estate, the major vehicle of intergenerational transfers in market economies, did not involve substantial individual savings since, in an absolute majority of cases, housing was provided by the State either directly or through employers that were of course State-

[57] See statement of the Deputy Minister of Economics in *Segodnya*, 7 December 1995, p. 2.

58 Whatever individual real estate acquisitions were made — dachas (country houses), for example — were effected without a financial intermediation system such as mortgage banks.

59 The spike of 1991 in table VI.11 represents what was a temporary phenomenon of rapidly growing monetary incomes and a general shortage of consumer goods.

60 The net accumulation of foreign currency balances is a component of net foreign investment of the Russian economy; in effect, it is a net transfer of resources on grant terms to the currency-issuing country, which buys more goods from the Russian Federation than it sells, with the difference's being accounted for by the currency exported.

owned.[58] There was only one institution to service household saving, the Sberbank, which had an extensive network of branches throughout the country. Its primary function was to accumulate individual savings and channel the funds into the state budget.

With the move to a market economy, households acquired a stronger motivation to save. Their savings in financial form grew from 7.5 per cent of GDP in 1990 to 17 per cent in 1994 (see table VI.11).[59] The composition of those savings has changed rapidly since 1992: the share of cash on hand has fallen and that of foreign currency purchases has grown rapidly. In 1994 and 1995, households devoted more than twice as much of their saving to foreign currency purchases as to bank deposits and securities. This suggests that there is a significant level of household savings that is lost to intermediation by the domestic financial sector. Indeed, as it is held in the currency of another country, it is lost to the Russian economy.[60] The attraction exerted on households by foreign currency seems to be explainable mainly in the following terms: The general macroeconomic instability and concomitant inflation made it more attractive to hold savings in foreign currency or to send those savings abroad — legally or illegally — than to place them in the financial sector.

In addition, with the exception of Sberbank, which has over 30 thousand retail outlets throughout the country, most commercial banks created during the transition — even the largest and most sophisticated — have a very rudimentary retail presence even in Moscow. Retail operations are costly to build (although they are a major source of funds in the long run) and have not resulted in immediate and large profits, as have dealings on currency exchanges and operations in government securities. Recently, however, several major commercial banks have started to develop networks of retail operations; nevertheless, as of the end-1995, household deposits constituted less than 1 per cent of the commercial banks' liquid funds.

Another side of the problem is that the confidence in financial intermediation is very low among the country's population, in particular after nearly 40 million people were robbed of their savings in 1994 by the many fraudulent financial companies which in most cases proved to be nothing but "pyramid schemes" that collapsed without ever making any contribution to productive investment. In the light of this experience, the forthcoming law on deposit insurance is highly relevant. Moreover, numerous investment funds either are in the process of being transformed into bona fide mutual funds and commercial banks, or have folded. In addition, the mechanisms and procedures of stock trade registration and custody are only now being put in place. In sum, it will be some time before household saving becomes an actual rather than a potential major source of investment funds.

The one player in investment activity that has a potentially large role is the country's commercial banking system. Along with being an intermediary in the flow of government, enterprise and now household funds, the banks have accumulated substantial funds of their own. They have nevertheless been quite reluctant to commit them to investment in the real economy.

Clearly, the factors that discouraged managers and owners of enterprises from using retained earnings to finance new investment can readily explain why in many instances even highly developed financial institutions would be unwilling to supply investment capital to a particular enterprise. Yet in the

Table VI.11.
SELECTED ASPECTS OF FINANCIAL SECTOR
ACTIVITY IN THE RUSSIAN FEDERATION

Percentage of GDP	1990	1991	1992	1993	1994
Household activity					
(net increase during the year)					
Bank deposits and	4.5	11.6	1.8	2.9	3.9
security purchases					
Foreign currency purchases	..	..	0.2	3.8	10.6
Cash on hand	3.0	5.8	5.0	4.4	2.7
Total	7.5	17.4	7.0	11.1	17.2
Bank sector activity					
Credits to enterprises	..	34.4	26.5	14.4	10.5
and households					
Short-term			24.0	14.0	9.9
Long-term			1.3	0.5	0.6
Interbank credits	..	..	1.8	1.3	1.5

Source: UN/DESIPA, based on *Rossiiskiy statisticheskiy ezhegodnik*, 1995 (Russian statistical yearbook, 1995) (Moscow, Goskomstat, 1995), pp. 78 and 290.

same way as many obstacles have to be removed before the full potential of retained earnings as a source of investment finance in the emerging market environment can be realized, so also must progress in financial intermediation be made before these institutions will play their full role.

With the start of transition, a new financial system was needed. Financial intermediation became the fastest growing and fastest evolving sphere in the country's economy. A two-tier bank system was created (a Central Bank and separate commercial banks) and other mechanisms and tools of financial intermediation grew in number, in sophistication and in the range of financial services offered. A relatively elaborate, and rapidly developing, financial intermediation industry, a more realistic price structure resulting from progress in price liberalization, and the current account convertibility of the rouble created a totally new environment, and mechanisms, procedures and incentive matrices for money flows.

The credit activity of the commercial banks grew very rapidly after the transition started, but, as far as corporate financing is concerned, the credits mostly financed working capital. The fact that they did not invest in the real economy in any meaningful volume is explained by a combination of factors. First of all, alternatives to investing their available resources in the real economy — like currency arbitrage and operations with government securities — were until very recently significantly more profitable (for more detail, see chap. II). Second, many-faceted uncertainty dampened investment demand. Third, even had the demand existed, establishing credit risk would have been nearly impossible since widespread non-payment has obfuscated the real financial

61 For a discussion of this problem as "an acute asymmetric information problem between insiders and outsiders", see P. Dittus and S. Prowse, *Corporate Control in Central Europe and Russia. Should Banks Own Shares?*, Policy Research Working Paper, No. 1481 (Washington, D.C., World Bank, June 1995).

62 Market capitalization of the top 85 publicly traded Russian companies at the end of 1994 was slightly over $23 billion, including $6.3 billion for Gazprom (natural gas), $3 billion for LUKoil-Holding (oil) and less than $2 billion for Unified Electric Systems (the nationwide electric grid company) (data of *Skate-Press Consulting Agency*, Moscow).

63 *Finansovye Izvestia*, 23 February 1996.

64 *Interfax Daily Business Report*, 31 January 1996, p. 5.

status of enterprises.[61] As a result, potential creditors have been very wary of extending new finance.

Moreover, since the mechanism of collateral, although enacted into law, was not yet operational, high-risk premiums were perceived by the enterprises' creditors as the principal insurance against default. This, in conjunction with the monetary tightness that was part of the anti-inflationary struggle, raised real interest rates quite high, thus effectively cutting many potential borrowers out of the credit market. The banks have continued to seek very large spreads between borrowing and lending rates even though inflation has receded.

The banks are not unique in their reluctance to provide finance for investment. On a more general level, it remains a serious problem for willing financial agents to find acceptable placements for their investment funds. At the same time, many parts of industry are hungry for finance. In theory, market forces would mainly direct investment flows in an appropriate way. In reality, the rapid marketization of the economy, without the creation of many of the institutions needed for the efficient functioning of market forces, created an often chaotic situation in which clear signals of where investment would be most profitable were often not given.

Yet, commercial banks, even while reluctant to lend to potential investors, have moved towards involvement in capital formation in the real economy: they have acquired privatized domestic enterprises. This process, which took off in 1995, became feasible and extremely profitable owing to the severe undervaluation, in terms of a normal international comparison, of the fixed assets of Russian enterprises, including the huge energy and high-tech producers.[62]

A new form of conglomerate has thus been created with state encouragement — the financial-industrial groups (FIGs). The FIGs usually comprise banks (or investment funds), and industrial and trading enterprises. Some groups concentrate their activities and holdings in a specific sector like oil and gas, metallurgy, or automotive production with the objective of concentrating the control of all aspects of the production cycle within the FIG. Others are more diversified and have cross-holdings in a number of industries. A typical group's components are interlinked by a network of cross-holdings, credits and other financing, stocks, and business links with outside suppliers and customers.

By mid-February 1996, there were 30 officially registered FIGs, up from 15 in August 1995. All together, they controlled nearly 300 industrial enterprises, and 70 banks and other financial companies and employed 2.5 million people. The State is a partner in each of these FIGs; its holding varies but is below 25 per cent in every case.[63] It is believed that the actual number of conglomerates is much higher and could well be in the hundreds, but that many prefer to remain unofficial.

It remains to be seen whether the FIGs will prove to be merely another means to redistribute assets or whether they will provide a means to overcome the impediments to financial intermediation noted above. In this regard, some positive developments have already been observed. One example is that the Menatep group has invested over $35 million in its eight food plants in the Moscow region through Rosprom, Menatep's industrial holding company. An investment programme was also designed to increase domestic food production capacity.[64] All together, nearly 200 major investment projects with an aggregate investment of over $3 billion were reportedly in various states of preparation by the FIGs.

The most plausible explanation for this burst of investment activity in the midst of hesitation, reluctance to invest, currency hoarding, and capital flight is that, out of nearly 2,500 banks that appeared in the Russian Federation since the start of economic reform, nearly 80 per cent had been created by industrial enterprises that combined their funds with those of partners from wholesale and retail trade, insurance and sometimes even local Governments. These banks were specifically created to meet their sponsors' financial needs, naturally on preferential terms. With the explosive growth of the financial intermediation business, the roles reversed and the banks evolved: From being auxiliary financial branches of their corporate sponsors, they became in effect the principals in new, diversified conglomerates. So far these banks have limited their financing to the companies that originally were their founders and shareholders (and which they now control). This process acquired new scope and intensity after the introduction of the loans-for-shares programme in the second half of 1995. Under this scheme, which has attracted some controversy, the Government took the equity shares that it had retained in privatized companies and sold some of the shares to large commercial banks in exchange for loans that these banks made to the Government.

Finally, other recent developments may supply the element that has still been missing to foster a recovery of investment activity. Yields on three-month Treasury bills, after remaining in the 90-140 per cent range for most of 1995, dropped sharply in the last months of the year, removing the last major high-yielding sector from the financial market. The banks, faced with the task of finding profitable employment for their funds, were forced to look at investment in the real economy. According to the head of one of the Russian Federation's largest commercial banks, "the time of speculative operations is over; now the priority is investment".[65]

65   Quoted in *The Moscow Tribune*, 12 February 1996, p. 1.

CONCLUSION

The economies in transition have been in the midst of an economic and political revolution and revolutions are by nature neither smooth nor predictable. In all the cases examined in this chapter, an old order crumbled — a political order as well as an economic one — as the previous model had proved unable to satisfy either political or economic aspirations. Different strategies were adopted by the new authorities for recovery and reform, depending on the particular histories and situations of each country, but they all anticipated a major role for new capital formation under principles that bore little relationship to the model of the old regime.

In all cases, the centrally planned model was rejected and there was a widespread desire to move towards a market economy as rapidly as possible. After decades of detailed government direction, there was no longer a majority in the nascent democracies for maintaining an overwhelming degree of direct government control over the economy. The government's role was to be reduced as firms were privatized. The rapid and broad liberalization of foreign trade did not allow government a role in choosing which infant or senile industries to support during the transformation.

At the beginning of the transformation, it was popularly anticipated that economic agents would react quickly to the incentives that sprang up from the rapid marketization of the economy and that a surge in investment would help satisfy the very large domestic demand for higher-quality products. Although foreign investment was to be welcomed, especially for introducing new technology, it was generally thought that domestic resources would be sufficient.

In the event, the new authorities had to contend with a worsening of the already serious economic situation. The influx of imports threatened the viability of domestic competitors. Prospects were truly unclear at first and this deterred private investors who have to balance perceived risks against anticipated rewards before making commitments. As a result, investment was at first not forthcoming.

Although the main direction of change — the rapid move to the market system — was established at the beginning, policy in the years of transformation can still be seen as offering an example of learning by doing, involving a great deal of experimentation. Nevertheless, it seems there have been certain common features of transformation, at least as regards investment and the enterprise sector.

One such feature was the sharply negative reassessment with regard to the value of enterprise assets once countries had abandoned central planning and begun their transition to market economies. Almost overnight, many going concerns became hopeless failures. Critics argue that to some degree Governments made the situation worse than it had to be (for example, by forcing firms in the eastern *Länder* of Germany to absorb the consequences for relative prices of an overvalued exchange rate and a quick march towards wage parity with the western *Länder*, not to mention the imposition of strict environmental standards). It was also argued that some of the assets could have had more years of productive life had the changes been phased in over a longer period.

In view of the discrediting of the old system, the case for a slow adaptation was lost from the start of the transformation, and government plans revolved around how soon the transformation process could be completed. In any event, the strategy of swift privatization generally embodied the expectation that, although the new owners would scrap obsolete equipment, they would also breathe new life and new investment into firms and rescue the assets that could be salvaged. Also, the formation of new private enterprises was anticipated.

On the whole, in the CEETEs and eastern *Länder* of Germany that began the transformation before the Russian Federation, these expectations were realized after the destructive phase: investment has picked up, new enterprises are being formed, more marketable goods are being produced and labour productivity has risen sharply. These achievements were facilitated by past investments in human capital and also in structures. There are many signs that the Russian Federation, too, is following on the path set by the earlier transformers. Its destructive phase, however, has been severe.

Another common feature was the government's being expected to play a major role in the move towards the market economy, in the sense not only of withdrawing from exerting direct economic control and of establishing macroeconomic stability, but also of building new institutions. The Governments were not merely passive observers of markets, but actively sought to maintain employment and promote export competitiveness. Support for the privatization process took many forms. This entailed in some cases direct financial support, including absorbing of old debts to make enterprises more attractive propositions, and in other cases special efforts to close agreements with "strategic" direct foreign investors.

A final common feature was the recognition that virtually an entirely new financial sector would be needed, one that operated on completely different principles for those prevailing under central planning where the financial sector had been essentially a conduit for government financial flows to enterprises. The main failure of the financial sector is that for the most part it has not yet become the main intermediary from private saving to enterprise investment. This failure is partly explained by the fact that the institutions that had been called commercial banks under the previous regime were suddenly expected to behave like banks in market economies — and could not. The new financial-industrial groups in the Russian Federation seem to have arisen as one method of coping with the problem, but they appear to constitute only a partial solution.

All in all, a reasonable hypothesis would recognize that a lack of saving is not the major constraint on investment in the transition economies and that the problem is rather one of bringing the savings that are available into an efficient financial sector that works at arm's length with enterprise borrowers. However, pressure to make the financial sector work more effectively in this way is likely to grow as the legal and macroeconomic situation normalizes and as enterprises, stimulated by the increases in output and productivity that the new economic environment has already made possible, undertake more fixed capital formation, and look increasingly for resources to utilize.

VII INVESTMENT IN DEVELOPING COUNTRIES

During the past 15 years, developing countries have witnessed dramatic changes in the environment in which their economies operate and in their thinking about the foundations of development policy. Policy makers have increasingly recognized that sustained economic growth requires macroeconomic stability and diversification of the economic structure away from dependency on a few export commodities, including oil, which does not allow for sufficient flexibility to adjust quickly to an ever changing economic environment and compounds their countries' vulnerability to exogenous shocks. As ever, investment has been seen as a key vehicle for spreading and deepening development. There has also been greater reliance on the private sector and on market forces: the role of Government in directly providing and in guiding investment has been retrenched, while private investment - under broad policy guidelines - has taken centre stage. Policies instituted have been wide ranging, and have had to respond to a sometimes accommodating and sometimes unforgiving external environment. However, since policies also reflect the particular domestic conditions operating in each country, the pattern of investment in this period has been markedly varied among developing countries.

In the light of the economic, political and social complexities at work, the analysis of investment and its determinants in developing countries has been carried out by means of a set of country case studies with the objective of highlighting the wide array of determinants of investment in the countries considered, as well as the scope of their policy treatments.

The six countries examined below - Bolivia, Côte d'Ivoire, Tunisia, Chile, Indonesia and China - are not intended to be a statistically representative sample of developing countries. Rather, they have been selected because of their diversity in terms of their success in bolstering investment, as well as to capture a range of economic structures, political conditions and levels of economic development and natural endowment. Factors pertinent to investment are discussed in the context of prevailing economic conditions, policies implemented, and political and social constraints.

Analysis of the case studies shows that despite the diversity of country experiences, a number of characteristics in terms of their policy direction and investment determinants seem to be shared by the six countries considered here, which may give some indication of the nature of the challenges that developing countries confront in their quest for higher investment levels and sustained growth.

BOLIVIA: WHEN STABILIZATION IS ONLY HALF THE BATTLE

In the early 1980s, Bolivia experienced a severe economic deterioration that culminated in an uncontrollable inflationary process and significant GDP losses[1]. In August 1985, drastic measures were adopted to put an end to hyper-inflation. The Government of Bolivia also embarked on a process of liberalization and restructuring of the economy. By controlling inflation and eliminating price distortions, the Government has sought to create a stable macroeconomic environment that would be conducive to investment. Private investment, however, has not responded as anticipated.

The key question is, why not? The answer seems to be that control over the major macroeconomic balances has not been assured enough, while the lack of consensus among the major players concerning the future direction of the economy has cast a measure of uncertainty on the sustainability of policies adopted so far. Moreover, a series of structural problems have depressed profitability and discouraged investment.

The sequence of reforms

Over the past 10 years, reforms in Bolivia have been adopted in waves, each corresponding to a change in administration. The first wave occurred in the period 1985-1987, when policy was directed towards price stabilization and adjustment, i.e., towards the restoration of an enabling environment in which investment and growth could resume. The second wave of reform occurred in 1989-1992, when the economy was further liberalized and new opportunities for private - including foreign - investment were created. Finally, the current wave of reforms, initiated in 1993, has deepened past efforts and further opened up the economy to private initiatives.

Eliminating hyper-inflation was undoubtedly the place to start, since the economy was dysfunctional. Measures to correct the fiscal deficit were adopted: prices of goods and services provided by the State were increased, wages were temporarily frozen, subsidies were abolished, government personnel were laid off and a tax reform was introduced. The dual exchange-rate system was abandoned and rates were unified, but at a rate that entailed a de facto devaluation of 93 per cent. Most price controls were abolished, including controls on interest rates, and a process of trade liberalization was initiated[2].

In addition, the Government addressed its external debt. A heavy debt burden was viewed as a disincentive to investment since future debt servicing could heavily tax future returns that investments would generate. A strategy to reduce the debt burden was put in place, entailing buy-backs of commercial bank debt and the rescheduling of bilateral governmental loans on a concessional basis under the Paris Club, followed by a series of individual agreements with Bolivia's major bilateral official creditors[3].

The second cycle of reforms (1989-1992) concentrated on creating greater opportunities for the private investor. A more liberal regulatory framework was adopted, including the 1990 investment code, the 1990 hydrocarbons law, changes in the mining code and the 1992 privatization law. Restrictions on external trade were cut back further (fewer and simplified licensing procedures), while taxes on exports were reduced and import tariffs declined once

[1] Per capita GDP contracted by 4.3 per cent per year on average during the period 1981-1985. The inflation rate, measured by the December to December change in the consumer price index, jumped from 24 per cent in 1980 to 8,170 per cent in 1985, while the consolidated central government deficit reached 41 per cent of GDP in 1985, up from an already high deficit of 8 per cent in 1980.

[2] For the origins of the Bolivian hyper-inflationary process and specific measures adopted in 1985, see J.A. Morales, "La inflación y la estabilización en Bolivia", in *Inflación y Estabilización: la Experiencia de Israel, Argentina, Brasil, Bolivia y México*, M. Bruno, G. di Tella, R. Dornbusch and S. Fischer, eds., (México D.F., Fondo de Cultura Económica, 1988); J. Sachs, "The Bolivian hyperinflation and stabilization", *National Bureau of Economic Research Working Paper*, No. 2073 (Cambridge, Massachusetts, November 1986); and *World Economic Survey, 1989* (United Nations publication, Sales No. E.89.C.II.1).

[3] For an assessment of the Bolivian plan to buy back commercial bank debt, see *World Economic Survey, 1989...*, pp. 72 and 73.

more. Tariffs on imported capital goods were cut to 5 per cent to boost the investment effort in the economy.

The latest round of reforms were adopted by the current Administration, whose head, President Gonzalo Sánchez de Louzada, was one of the architects of the 1985 stabilization plan. Commitment to price stability was maintained, while the restructuring of the economy was taken one step further, as will be discussed below.

Trends in investment

Investment in Bolivia during the second half of the 1970s had been high by historical standards, averaging 22 per cent of GDP during the period 1975-1979[4], reflecting the favourable conditions to which the economy was then exposed: international prices of tin, one of Bolivia's major export commodities, were quite strong; large amounts of natural gas had begun to be exported to Argentina; and inexpensive international finance was available. Mining was the country's most dynamic activity and was dominated by the State. Consequently, a great deal of the investment effort had been originated by the public sector, particularly through its enterprises operating in the mining, hydrocarbon and energy generation sectors.

Economic conditions changed in the early 1980s, when the level of investment fell, averaging only 11 per cent of GDP during the period 1980-1984. The hyper-inflationary process imposed a heavy toll on both public and private investment. In 1985, the stabilization package was announced, but an additional blow was inflicted on the country when tin prices collapsed on the London Metals Exchange in October 1985. By 1985, fixed investment had fallen to about 7 per cent of GDP, shared about equally between the private and the public sectors.

Price stabilization was achieved quickly and major macroeconomic imbalances were reduced during the years following initial reforms, but private investment failed to recover as expected, although the overall investment level in the economy did rise after 1985 thanks to the public sector effort. While private investment remained flat at about 4 per cent of GDP, public investment increased from 3.5 per cent in 1985 to 8.4 per cent in 1989, largely financed by concessional official flows.

Private investment rates finally began to recover in 1990 (see figure VII.1) but remain low in terms of their relative share in GDP (8.6 per cent in 1995), and it is still not clear whether high rates of private investment will be sustained in the future.

Besides their impact on the total volume of investment, the reforms also had an impact on the composition of capital formation in the private sector. As table VII.1 shows, since 1990 private fixed investment has moved away from construction into machinery and equipment. Import liberalization seems to have encouraged greater imports of such goods, with tariffs on them being reduced to 5 per cent in January 1990 from an average level of 20 per cent[5].

Another dimension of the private investment upswing was the contribution of direct investment. Incentives aimed at foreign investors appear to have produced results: net inflows of foreign direct investment recovered during the first half of the 1990s from their very low or even negative levels in the 1980s.

[4] Investment ratios mentioned in the present section were calculated on the basis of national accounts data in current prices, given the unavailability of a complete and consistent series of investment in constant prices for the period analysed here.

[5] Alternatively, it is possible that such imports were not adequately registered before (see IDB, *Ahorro Privado e Inversión en Bolivia* (Washington, D.C., January 1996)).

Figure VII.1
BOLIVIA: GROSS DOMESTIC FIXED INVESTMENT, 1980-1995

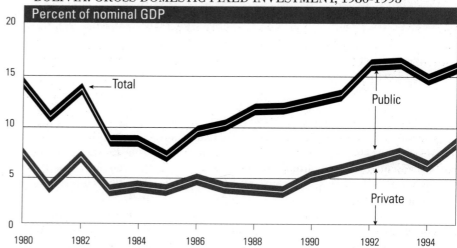

Source: World Bank and IDB.

Table VII.1.
BOLIVIA: COMPOSITION OF GROSS FIXED CAPITAL FORMATION, 1988-1995

Percentage

	Public sector		Private sector		Total	
	Machinery and equipment	Construction	Machinery and equipment	Construction	Machinery and equipment	Construction
1988	45.3	54.7	34.0	66.0	41.8	58.2
1989	46.0	54.0	23.6	76.4	39.3	60.7
1990	44.0	56.0	44.8	55.2	44.3	55.7
1991	47.6	52.4	53.5	46.5	50.0	50.4
1992	47.7	52.3	54.3	54.3	50.4	49.6
1993	41.4	58.6	66.1	33.9	49.2	50.8
1994	41.0	59.0	61.2	38.8	45.4	54.6
1995	43.2	56.8	63.4	36.6	51.1	48.9

Source: Government of Bolivia, Instituto Nacional de Estadísticas.

Net foreign-direct-investment flows reached $140 million in 1995, up from $30 million in 1988, representing about 2 per cent of GDP or about one quarter of the private investment effort in the country. Most of that investment has gone into mining; the export processing zones, particularly gold jewelry; and a number of agriculture sectors, especially soya cultivation, in the Santa Cruz region.

Notwithstanding the above and despite all the incentives, about half of the investment effort in the economy still came from the public sector in 1995, roughly the same share as it had contributed in 1980. Moreover, renewed pressures on the public budget have caused the Government to reduce public-sector investment since 1993. Consequently, 10 years after the initial reforms, gross fixed capital formation in Bolivia is only about 16 per cent of GDP.

The question of confidence in macroeconomic stability

The lack of a strong response from the private sector and the anaemic rates of growth registered by the Bolivian economy are very puzzling to those who monitor economic trends in that country. After all, Bolivia has been praised for being a model adjuster and its economy has shown signs of economic stability. But while Bolivia's status as a model adjuster requires no comment, its apparent economic stability requires further analysis.

Two commonly used indicators of macroeconomic stability are changes in the consumer price index and changes in the real exchange rate.[6] Price stability was achieved rather quickly, as noted above: inflation reached the single-digit level in 1993 and 1994, and stood at about 12 per cent in 1995, one of the lowest levels in Latin America. Changes in the exchange rate also point to stability: since the drastic devaluation of 1985 and the introduction of the new exchange regime, the real exchange rate has remained relatively stable and at a competitive level.

Nevertheless, such apparent stability rests on a fragile base. The fiscal balance has been difficult to control owing to increased current expenditures (mainly for personnel) and a very weak revenue base, a problem that has been intensified by tax evasion and inefficiencies in the tax collection system. Furthermore, Government revenues have been heavily dependent on the hydrocarbon sector. Thus, price reductions in 1992 on gas exports to Argentina meant less funds for the Bolivian Treasury and a rise in the deficit.[7] The deficit of the non-financial public sector had declined from 7 per cent of GDP in 1987 to 3.7 per cent of GDP by 1991, but it climbed back to 6 per cent of GDP in 1993. The fiscal deficit was cut back in 1994 and 1995, mostly as a result of cuts in public investment (see figure VII.1), which in the long run is a costly but unavoidable strategy.

In short, although the response of the Government to fiscal shocks has been to counter their impact, and although monetary policy has maintained a firm grip on domestic credit expansion, the economy remains very vulnerable in the perception of investors.

Evidence for that perception can be found in the financial sector. High interest rates are common in stabilization efforts, as credit conditions are tightened in order to curb demand and actual inflation falls faster than expected inflation. That phenomenon should be temporary, however, unless the authorities do not regain sufficient policy credibility.[8] Yet Bolivian real interest rates have been high for the past 9 years and remain so (see figure VII.2); moreover, most investments in the banking system are deposited in foreign currency (dollars) and placed at very short term, a further indication of the lack of confidence in policy sustainability.

[6] See L. Serven and A. Solimano, "Economic adjustment and investment performance in developing countries: the experience of the 1980s", in *Striving for Growth After Adjustment: The Role of Capital Formation*, L. Serven and A. Solimano, eds., (Washington D.C., World Bank, 1993); and J. Greene and D. Villanueva, "Private investment in developing countries", *IMF Staff Papers*, vol. 38, No.1 (March 1991), pp. 33-58.

[7] Bolivia initially sold large quantities of natural gas to Argentina (220 million cubic feet per day) under a 20-year sales agreement that expired in 1992. Prices paid by Argentina ranged between $2.30 and $2.80 per thousand cubic feet. The sales contract has been renewed but at a substantially lower price: about $1 per thousand cubic feet (see Inter-American Development Bank, *"Bolivia: informe socioeconómico"*, IDB Report No. DES-13 (Washington, D.C., May 1993).

[8] See A. Bennett, "Behaviour of nominal and real interest rates", in *"IMF conditionality: experience under stand-by and extended arrangements, part II, background papers"*, S. Schadler, ed., IMF Occasional Paper No. 129 (Washington, D.C., September 1995), p. 50.

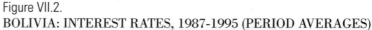

Figure VII.2.
BOLIVIA: INTEREST RATES, 1987-1995 (PERIOD AVERAGES)

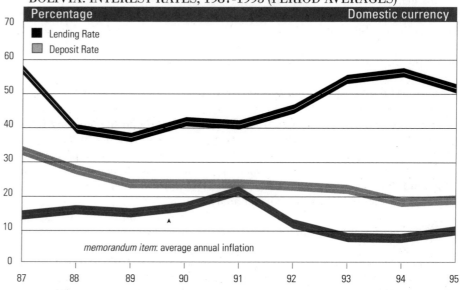

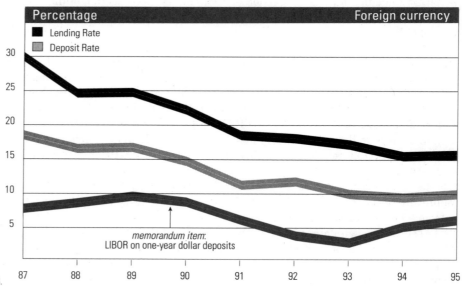

Source: IMF and IDB.

The lack of confidence in the Bolivian economy in spite of policy consistency may be explained in terms of the political economy of the reforms. Although the Government has shown its de facto commitment to price stability and restructuring of the economy, it has faced strong opposition, and by introducing changes to or reversing measures already adopted, has unintentionally sent wrong signals about the continuity of such measures. Moreover, the negotiation process on the adoption of the reforms has been far from smooth. Many reforms have required a long time to be approved by the Congress, and delays in implementation have occurred. A case in point is the privatization programme:

although announced 1990, its legal instrument was approved only in April 1992, its implementation has been slow and marred by controversies, and it was temporarily interrupted in June 1993. Finally, the fine tuning of the economy has also taken its toll in the maintenance of uncertainty. For example, changes introduced to the tax system as well as to the export promotion incentive system may have contributed to the "wait-and-see" attitude that private investors have shown.[9]

Overall, there is apparently no consensus among the major political parties on the general lines that the economy is supposed to be following. Every time elections approach, there is much uncertainty about whether reforms adopted to date will remain in place after a new administration takes over. Businessmen representing some of the major Bolivian private companies have articulated that viewpoint in a recent survey, stating that the lack of policy consensus or what they termed an agreed State policy (*políticas de Estado*) is detrimental to the establishment of a favourable investment climate.[10]

Structural impediments to investment

Even if uncertainties related to macroeconomic policy implementation were minimized and full credibility restored, Bolivia would probably still be disappointed in the level of private investment, because it faces considerable structural constraints that tend to reduce expected profits and thus investment activity.

Financial markets, in particular, are poorly developed in Bolivia. Most of the credit to the private sector is extended through the banking system, which is composed of a limited number of institutions. Interest rates charged are quite high (see figure VII.2), not only because of restrictive monetary policy but also owing to the oligopolistic character of the sector. In addition, administrative inefficiencies have led to large margins being charged. Credit is usually restricted to a number of preferred clients and is legally subject to the presentation of real estate guarantees. Most small farmers and businessmen thus do not have access to credit.[11] In fact, loans are extended on the basis of very poor or incomplete financial information on the borrower, since guarantees are perceived to provide enough of a hedge against eventual default. Hence, credit is not necessarily given on the basis of the soundness of the project to be financed and the banking system carries a very weak loan portfolio; indeed, two major Bolivian banks recently collapsed. An additional problem is that most deposits are in foreign currency and are overwhelmingly placed in short-term instruments. Consequently, only a small share of the loans extended by banks are long-term (13 per cent in 1994). The deposit profile also compels banking institutions to maintain a high degree of liquidity, again helping to push loan rates up. In addition, Bolivia's hyper-inflation led to a contraction in domestic saving, which has started only a slow recovery since 1988, and that reduced supply of savings may be another factor underlying the persistence of high interest rates. All in all, the lack of available finance and high interest rates compromise the expected profitability of a given investment: anticipated rates of return would have to be quite high to justify borrowing.

Infrastructure is also rather poor, which increases costs and compromises the competitiveness of enterprises serving either domestic or foreign markets. The transport system, for instance, is poorly developed and poorly maintained,

9   Additional revisions to the tax system were introduced by the end of 1994, owing to the capitalization processes of a number of key State-owned enterprises.

10   See *Ahorro Privado e Inversión en Bolivia,....*

11   Inventory, accounts receivable, livestock or industrial equipment are not accepted as collateral unless there is a supplemental guarantee based on the ownership of real estate (see World Bank, *How legal restrictions on collateral limit access to credit in Bolivia*, Report No. 13873-BO (Washington, D.C., December 1994).

and moreover is concentrated in the economically decaying mining areas of the *altiplano*, while the most dynamic sectors located in the valleys and lowlands are not adequately served.

Public investment in recent years has emphasized public enterprises, particularly enterprises in the mining and hydrocarbon sector that have direct implications for foreign-exchange earnings. Investment in infrastructure actually declined from 40 per cent of total public investment in 1987 to 35 per cent in 1990, although it increased somewhat to reach 37 per cent in 1994. Besides physical infrastructure, the human infrastructure of Bolivia is not competitive. The lack of an adequately trained and healthy labour force compromises the productivity and profitability of investment. Given the resources available to the Treasury and the fact that until recently the Government focus was elsewhere, human resources have been poorly developed in Bolivia.[12]

Finally, as a domestic market Bolivia also holds limited attraction for investors. Though hard-working and enterprising, most of the 7 million people that comprise the Bolivian population are poor: 70 per cent of the country's households were classified as poor in the 1992 Census. In addition, with GDP growing slowly Bolivia is not a very dynamic market. About 50 per cent of the labour force is engaged in small-scale activity in the informal sector (retail trade, self-employment, family business, domestic services and wage employees of small business). The manufacturing sector (about 14 per cent of GDP) is dominated by small producing units that have less than 15 employees, located in the food processing, textiles and garment sectors, the output of which is mostly channeled to the domestic market.

In other words, with most economic activities other than mining restricted by the small domestic market and with inadequate physical and human infrastructure and credit, few sectors of the Bolivian economy have been seen as a promising opportunity for private investment.

The new policy initiative

The Administration that took office in August 1993 sought to change the above-mentioned stagnation. Its strategy was given in the *Plan de todos* (Plan for all). Of particular relevance for the present chapter are the Plan's programmes for the capitalization and privatization of public enterprises, decentralization and pension reform.

The Capitalization Law (*Ley de Capitalización*) was designed to attract large-scale investments and increase efficiency in six major State enterprises through the injection of new equity capital and technology,[13] which, inter alia, would begin to address the infrastructure problem.

What distinguishes the new capitalization programme from traditional privatization is that it envisages financial resources not being paid to the Treasury but being invested directly in the company. While the private investors - the so called strategic partners - would have complete management control over the company, they would only have up to 50 per cent ownership of the enterprise. The remaining 50 per cent, belonging to the State, would be divided up and transferred to the individual pension accounts of all Bolivians who had reached legal majority (18 years) by December 1995. In parallel with the capitalization process, the Government also envisaged reactivating its privatization pro-

12 Inefficiencies in the management of social programmes and inequities in their distribution have compounded the problem (see IDB, "Bolivia desarrollo diferente para un país de cambios: salir del círculo vicioso de la riqueza empobrecedora", Informe Final de la Misión Piloto sobre Reforma Socio-económica en Bolivia), (February 1995).

13 The six enterprises earmarked for capitalization were the State oil company, the national electricity company, the national telephone company, the national railways, the national smelter company and the national airlines.

gramme, so that it would transfer the remaining public enterprises, which are smaller than the six mentioned above and total about 180 companies, to the private sector.

The magnitude of the proposed change cannot be easily grasped. It required amendments to the Constitution, the design of a new regulatory system for all sectors concerned, and the introduction of specific sectoral legislation, including revisions to the taxing system. By December 1995, four of the six enterprises mentioned above had been capitalized, with the remaining two scheduled for capitalization in mid-1996. The programme is expected to channel to the Bolivian economy a flow of investment equivalent to 30 per cent of GDP during the next 7 years,[14] which may boost economic activity with the additional spending it sets in motion domestically; the long-term benefit, however, will be the improved goods and services and the more effective infrastructure that the programme is expected to create.

Difficulties in the realm of human infrastructure are to be addressed by the decentralization programme, which will guarantee a minimum amount of investment in social sectors. The centrepiece of decentralization is the Popular Participation Law (*Ley de Participación Popular*), which transfers to the municipalities the responsibility for administering, maintaining and renovating the infrastructures of education, health, local roads, irrigation systems and sports. It also establishes a new fiscal revenue sharing system through which 20 per cent of national tax revenues are to be transferred to the municipalities, in proportion to the number of their respective inhabitants. Furthermore, the Law specifies that at least 90 per cent of such resources must be allocated to public investment.[15]

The pension reform programme aims to raise the coverage rate of the Bolivian pension system (only 5 per cent of the population are currently covered) and improve old age benefits. The programme also aims to promote an increase in the domestic saving effort and, by amassing a considerable amount of resources, to contribute to the development of a capital market in the country.

The pension reform programme was largely inspired by Chilean reforms. The current pay-as-you-go system is to be replaced by an individually capitalized and contribution-determined system that is to be privately administered.[16] Private pension administrators will also manage the accounts that will be created from the resources arising from the capitalization process discussed above. Access to the funds in such accounts will be allowed only when the beneficiary reaches age 60, as they are intended to provide an extra economic support for old age. Resources from the capitalization process that would feed such accounts have been estimated to total about $1 billion, representing about 18 per cent of GDP in 1994.

CÔTE D'IVOIRE: WHAT DEVALUATION TOLD INVESTORS

Côte d'Ivoire has known periods of investment boom and bust, but since the late 1970s, it has mainly experienced a bust period. While buffeted by a volatile international economy, like so many other developing countries, Côte d'Ivoire, as a member of the franc zone, had a special constraint on adjustment (as well as special benefits), namely its commitment to maintain the exchange rate at a fixed parity with the French franc. As with any other fixed exchange

14 See CEPAL, *Balance Preliminar de la Economía de América Latina y el Caribe* (Santiago, 20 de diciembre de 1995), p. 17.

15 On the basis of the budget for 1994, resources to be transferred to the municipalities amounted to 600 million bolivianos (more than 2 per cent of GDP).

16 For the Chilean model, see *World Economic and Social Survey, 1995* (United Nations publication, Sales No. E.95.II.C.1), pp. 278 and 279.

rate arrangement, in normal times it is perceived as a pillar of stability and a basis for confidence and for investment decisions. But when the exchange rate is seen to have become fundamentally misaligned and when correcting relative prices without changing the exchange rate is not politically feasible, fixed parity becomes a millstone around the neck of the policy maker, which was the case in Côte d'Ivoire by 1993. Thus, when the CFA franc was devalued in January 1994, it was perceived not just as a necessary adjustment of an economic parameter but as a break with the past and an opening to a more growth-enhancing economic strategy.[17]

Macroeconomic policy during adjustment cycles

Between 1960 and 1980 - the period of the Ivorian "miracle" - GDP grew about 7 per cent annually. A number of exogenous shocks, however, triggered a decline in economic performance in the late 1970s. Prices of cocoa and coffee - Côte d'Ivoire's main exports - started to decline in 1978 after reaching a record high in 1977. Large current account and budget deficits developed quickly, exceeding 10 per cent of GDP in the late 1970s and early 1980s. Foreign borrowing increased, and the total debt stock rose from about $1 billion in 1974 to nearly $9 billion in 1982. With higher interest rates in the early 1980s, total debt service payments reached 54 per cent of exports of goods and services in 1982. The economic situation was clearly not sustainable.

Starting in the late 1970s the Government implemented a number of reform measures to alleviate the impact of those external shocks and restore macroeconomic balance. However, it did not make the standard adjustment measure of changing the parity of the exchange rate, which was fixed to the French franc as part of the franc zone.[18] Instead, the Government had to rely only on fiscal, monetary and wage policies. The budget and current account deficits were eliminated by the mid-1980s, and growth resumed, although there is no agreement on the relative contribution to that recovery of policies and exogenous factors, such as the return of good rainfall after a severe drought in 1983, the depreciation of the French franc against the United States dollar, which indirectly depreciated the CFA franc, and a recovery in commodity prices in the mid-1980s.

After the recovery of GDP in 1985 and 1986, the economy began a long recession in 1987, which was mainly prompted by three exogenous events: the decline of the terms of trade by 28 per cent between 1987 and 1993, the appreciation of the French franc against the United States dollar after 1985, and the sharp devaluation of the currencies of Ghana and Nigeria, which made Côte d'Ivoire relatively less competitive.

As a result, the real effective exchange rate - the trade-weighted average exchange rate corrected for inflation differences with its trading partners - became overvalued. In other words, despite a fixed exchange rate *vis-à-vis* the French franc, Côte d'Ivoire currency depreciated in real effective terms by 29 per cent between 1980 and 1985, and then appreciated by one third between 1986 and 1990. Double-digit current account and budget deficits re-emerged in 1987 and 1991, respectively.

Adjustment efforts this time were clearly unsuccessful. At first, the Government viewed the terms-of-trade fall as temporary, and producer prices for

[17] The following analysis draws upon Jean-Paul Azam and Christian Morrison, *The Political Feasibility of Adjustment in Côte d'Ivoire and Morocco* (Paris, OECD, 1994); Lionel Demery, "Côte d'Ivoire: fettered adjustment", in: Adjustment in Africa: *Lessons From Country Case Studies*, Ishrat Husain and Rashid Faruqee, eds. (Washington, D.C., World Bank, 1994); Louis M. Goreux, "La dévaluation du franc CFA: Un premier bilan en Decembre 1995", mimeo, (28 December 1995); Bart Raemaekers, "Exchange rate policy and economic performance in developing countries: lessons from experiences in WAMU countries", MA thesis, (Tilburg University, the Netherlands, 1996, mimeo); Hartmut Schneider, *Adjustment and Equity in Côte d'Ivoire* (Paris, OECD, 1992); and World Bank, *Republic of Côte d'Ivoire: private sector assessment*, Report No. 12885-IVC (Washington, D.C.), 29 December 1994.

[18] Côte d'Ivoire is a member of the Communauté Financière Africaine (CFA) franc zone, a monetary agreement between France and 14 African countries. Two different regional currencies, both known as the CFA franc, are pegged to the French franc. One is issued by the Central Bank of West African States (Banque centrale des Etats de l 'Afrique de l 'Ouest (BCEAO)) for the seven member countries of the Union monétaire Ouest-africaine (UMOA), namely Benin, Burkina Faso, Côte d 'Ivoire, Mali, Niger, Senegal and Togo. Six other countries have a second issuing authority, the Bank of Central African States (Banque des Etats de l 'Afrique centrale (BEAC)), namely Cameroon, the Central African Republic, Chad, Congo, Equatorial Guinea and Gabon. The fourteenth country, the Comoros, has its own issuing authority, the Banque centrale des Comores, but its currency is also pegged to the French franc. France guarantees the convertibility of the CFA franc into French francs, and keeps an operations account for that purpose at the French Treasury, that mediates between the central banks and centralizes the exchange reserves of member countries.

coffee and cocoa were not lowered until 1989. With foreign-exchange earnings scarce, the Government announced in June 1987 that it would stop interest payments on external debt to official and commercial creditors. To try to raise more tax revenue, a number of indirect taxes were raised during 1987 and 1988, particularly on imports, which was counter to adjustment objectives. The revenue from fiscal measures was disappointing, however, and payment arrears mounted. By 1987, the Government's capital expenditures were already reduced to 3.9 per cent of GDP, down from 23 per cent in 1978, and attempts to cut nominal civil service salaries set off waves of strikes and other social unrest, especially in 1990.

The commodity boom of the mid-1970s fueled a sharp increase in public investment in Côte d'Ivoire (see figure VII.3). The Government launched a large public investment programme for the period 1976-1980, part of which was financed by increased revenues from cocoa and coffee, but more than 50 per cent was financed by foreign loans. Public fixed investment thus rose from 8 per cent of GDP in 1973 to 18 per cent in 1978.[19] Public investment mainly consisted of large agricultural (such as sugar) and infrastructural projects. After the collapse of coffee and cocoa prices in 1978, however, public investment had to be reduced. In fact, the cost of reducing fiscal expenditures during the adjustment period was mainly borne by public investment, although the cuts were not implemented swiftly enough to pull in the burgeoning deficits. In any event, public fixed investment fell to 7 per cent of GDP by 1985, and remained at about that level until 1988, after which it dropped to about 4 per cent of GDP into the 1990s.

Private investment also collapsed after 1978: private fixed investment declined from 22 per cent of GDP in 1978 to 5 per cent in 1984 and stayed between 4 and 6.5 per cent of GDP during the period 1985-1993, a fall so steep that it resulted in net disinvestment. A number of factors contributed to

[19] Investment ratio estimates are based on national accounts data in current prices.

Figure VII.3.
CÔTE D'IVOIRE: GROSS DOMESTIC FIXED INVESTMENT, 1970-1994

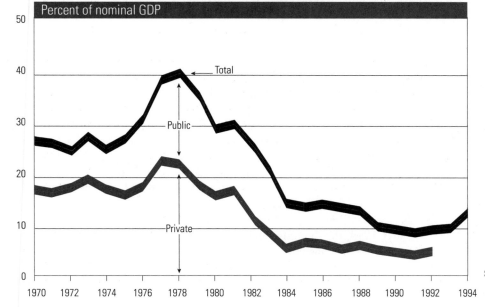

Source: World Bank data.

[20] For an econometric assessment of those factors, see David Fielding, "Determinants of investment in Kenya and Côte d 'Ivoire", *Journal of African Economies*, vol. 2, No. 3 (December 1993), pp. 299-328.

[21] There is disagreement about whether public investment crowded in or crowded out private investment in Côte d 'Ivoire. Crowding in proponents are Lance Taylor, in *Varieties of Stabilization Experience: Towards Sensible Macroeconomics in the Third World* (Oxford, Clarendon Press, 1988), pp. 80-83; and Oussou Kouassy and Bouabre Bohoun, in "Fiscal adjustment and growth in Côte d 'Ivoire", *World Development*, vol. 22, No. 8 (August 1994), pp. 1119-1128. On the other hand, the World Bank in *Republic of Côte d 'Ivoire: private sector assessment...*, annex II, reviewed a number of reasons why the public sector might have crowded out the private sector.

[22] See Demery, Loc. cit., p. 105.

[23] It is estimated that the total stock of flight capital amounted to $ 4.3 billion in 1989 (see Niels Hermes and Robert Lensink, "The magnitude and determinants of capital flight: the case for six sub-Saharan African countries", *De Economist*, vol. 140, No. 4 (1992), pp. 515 530). Capital flight is believed to have accelerated after 1989, particularly in 1993 in anticipation of the devaluation. Indeed, convertibility of the CFA franc outside the CFA zones was suspended in August 1993 to stem capital flight, which also meant that a BEAC-issued CFA franc could no longer be converted into a BCEAO-issued CFA franc. Apparently, the restrictions applied only to the physical outflow of CFA notes and not to bank transactions related to trade, travel or profit remittances.

[24] In mid-1991, consolidated arrears of Government, public enterprises and the *Caisse de stabilisation et soutien des prix des produits agricoles* to the banking system amounted to CFA 300 billion (10 per cent of GDP), compared with CFA 250 billion in demand deposits. This was in addition to non-performing private loans (see "Republic of Côte d 'Ivoire: private sector assessment"..., p. 12). Financial reforms implemented since the late 1980s involved the liquidation of five development banks between 1988 and 1991, the recapitalization of other banks, the abolition of the preferential discount rate, the strengthening of bank supervision and measures to solve the arrears.

[25] The regional central bank raised the discount rate by four percentage points in January 1994.

the decline of private investment.[20] First, the economic recession reduced domestic demand, lessening the need for the expansion of capacity. The fall in public investment might also have been a factor.[21] In part, however, they both declined as a result of the same exogenous factors.

Second, and related to the first factors, between 1980 and 1984 the profitability of private firms collapsed. The return on permanent capital declined from a positive 7 per cent in 1980 to a negative 12 per cent in 1984. The drop in the return on equity was even more dramatic, falling from a positive 13 per cent in 1980 to a negative 145 per cent in 1984. After 1985, profitability was very volatile.

Third, large payment arrears by the Government, reaching 18 per cent of GDP by 1989, hindered private investment.[22] Franc Zone membership limits Government borrowing from the Central Bank and bars monetary financing of the fiscal deficit. Hence, when the Government runs a fiscal deficit, accumulation of payment arrears is the only option once possibilities for borrowing abroad or from commercial banks are exhausted. Such arrears meant that the domestic private sector was not being paid, which seriously affected not only its liquidity but also its confidence.

Fourth, limited supplies and high costs of credit curtailed private investment. Several surveys conducted before the devaluation pointed to finance as one of the most important constraints on investment, even among large firms. Real interest rates on loans were in double digits between 1984 and 1993 (except for the period 1986-1988). Credit to the private sector was restricted because the regional central bank annually sets overall credit ceilings for each member country, and the share of net domestic credit going to the Government increased from 6 per cent in 1981 to 29 per cent in 1993. Moreover, Côte d'Ivoire suffered from capital flight during the 1980s and early 1990s, which was seen in falling domestic and rising foreign bank deposits.[23] Compounding all this was the near collapse of the financial system at the end of the 1980s. Banks suffered from payment arrears of the Government and public enterprises and declining deposits, and in addition were not adequately supervised.[24]

Devaluation

In the early 1990s, it became increasingly clear that economic adjustment was not succeeding under the model that had guided policy since the end of the Second World War. Thus, a devaluation from 50 CFA francs per French franc to 100 CFA francs per French franc was announced on 11 January 1994. Several policy measures were taken following the devaluation, so that for the first time a fully comprehensive approach could be attempted.

First of all, inflation had to be contained since the devaluation itself raised tradable goods prices immediately. Monetary policy was quickly tightened,[25] prices of a number of basic goods were temporarily frozen and subsidized, certain indirect taxes were reduced, and the nominal increase in the base wage of the civil service was limited to 10 per cent for 1994. As a result, after rising steeply in early 1994, the monthly inflation rate slowed down later in the year, so that the increase in consumer prices was limited to 26 per cent for 1994 as a whole, and it slowed further to an estimated 8 per cent in 1995 despite the lifting of price controls. The real effective exchange rate declined by

30 per cent between 1993 and August 1995, but that gain could have been larger were it not for the appreciation of the French franc against the United States dollar.

Reductions of the value-added tax, petroleum taxes, tariffs and other taxes were offset by the reintroduction of export taxes on coffee and cocoa, resulting in smaller budget deficits and even primary balance surpluses for 1994 and 1995. The improvement in the fiscal situation has allowed the Government to clear arrears and increase public investment. Capital expenditures rose from 10 per cent of total expenditures in 1993 to 17 per cent in 1994, and were planned to rise to 25 per cent by 1997. And by July 1995, domestic arrears had been significantly reduced; they are expected to be eliminated by the end of 1996. Total external debt arrears were reduced from $4.1 billion at the end of 1993 to $1.1 billion at the end of 1995, partly due to aid from donors. Côte d'Ivoire received substantial debt relief after the devaluation, which helped to check the rise in debt service payments in terms of local currency.[26] In short, many of the factors that had shaken the private sector were being alleviated.

Structural reforms also gained new momentum after the devaluation. A privatization law as well as new labour, mining and investment codes were adopted, and non-tariff barriers were reduced. In addition, reforms of the agricultural marketing system were announced in August 1995. Producer prices will no longer be guaranteed to farmers but will only serve as guidelines, and export contracts will be awarded by a computer-based competitive bidding system. The Government's stabilization fund will therefore lose its monopoly. Rice imports were liberalized in early 1995, and privatization of, for instance, the rubber and palm oil industry has commenced.

The supply response to the devaluation was generally positive but still moderate in 1994. GDP grew 1.8 per cent in 1994, the first rise in GDP since 1986. In 1995, the recovery spread to virtually all sectors of the economy; GDP is estimated to have increased by 6.5 per cent. Industrial output and construction expanded strongly in 1995, and capacity utilization increased from 76 per cent in 1993 to 86 per cent in the second quarter of 1995. Domestic demand is increasing, particularly as a result of rising purchasing power in rural areas. Exports also increased both to the developed market economies and to the other franc zone countries, where imports from the European Union have been more expensive since the devaluation.

Investment begins to recover

The devaluation, related reforms and the stimulus from international commodity prices have together raised prospects as well as output itself, stimulating investment, although the increase in investment was rather small in 1994 as a result of the fall in demand and uncertainty surrounding the impact of the devaluation. Investors were generally described as having a "wait and see" attitude. None the less, investment increased from 9.3 per cent of GDP in 1993 to 12.5 per cent of GDP in 1994.[27]

Preliminary estimates show that investment strengthened further in 1995, triggered by higher capacity utilization and by improved domestic economic prospects and regional and other export possibilities. In a small informal survey conducted in Abidjan in 1995, companies were optimistic about the

26 In 1994, a total of $0.6 billion of debt was rescheduled, while $1.1 billion of principal and $0.2 billion of interest was forgiven.

27 The increase, however, may be partly a price effect. The prices of investment goods, which are mostly imported, increased more than the prices of other components of GDP, which are partly domestically produced, so that the share of investment in GDP rose (for more detail on those phenomena, see box IV.1).

28 See Raemaekers, op. cit.

long-term economic perspectives, and half of them planned investment for 1995, mostly for expanding capacity, while an even greater percentage planned to invest in 1996.[28]

Foreign direct investment (FDI) is also increasing, in particular in energy, mining and privatized State-owned enterprises. FDI had fluctuated but never collapsed during the worst years of the 1980s, perhaps reflecting confidence in the guaranteed convertibility at a fixed parity with the French franc: investment in oil, gas and electricity was expected to amount to CFAF 80 billion in 1995. Several foreign firms are also involved in the exploration and development of the country's mineral deposits. Moreover, as the privatization programme accelerates, FDI is expected to increase in such areas as agro-industry and telecommunications.

The Government is implementing several measures to encourage investment in order to increase the share of investment in GDP to 20 per cent by 2000, of which 14 percentage points would represent private investment. The new investment and mining codes are specifically designed to simplify procedures and accelerate the approval process. To that end, the *Centre de promotion des investissements en Côte d'Ivoire* was established in 1995 to act as a "one-stop shop". The new codes include several incentives, such as tax holidays and guarantees, and the Government is also planning to provide a range of tax incentives to increase local processing of primary commodities. For example, only 13 per cent of the cocoa it produces is processed in Côte d'Ivoire; the goal is to increase that figure to 50 per cent by 2000.

It appears that, as usual, the increase in investment has been mostly financed with retained earnings or other internal funds, and more funds have become available from exports as a result of the devaluation and the rise in international commodity prices. Indeed, the above-mentioned informal survey in Abidjan confirmed that investments in 1994 and 1995 were largely financed by retained earnings and depreciation provisions.[29] The amount of credit extended to the private sector declined from CFAF 896 billion at the end of 1993 to CFAF 686 billion at the end of September 1994, but recovered to surpass the end-1993 level by November 1995. Lending increased only slowly despite a significant rise in demand and time deposits in commercial banks after the devaluation - on the order of CFAF 426 billion between the end of 1993 and November 1995. The increase in liquidity was largely caused by the return of flight capital, some of which might also have financed investment directly.

29 Ibid.

The slow expansion in private credit despite the rapid increase in liquidity might be explained by the uncertainty generated by the devaluation and the weak financial situation of some banks, making them particularly risk-averse,[30] so that the reduction of the discount rate by the regional central bank by 6 percentage points between June 1994 and June 1995 has not been translated into equivalent cuts in interest rates on loans.

30 Ibid.

Several initiatives have been taken in the financial sector, in part to overcome such impediments to private financing for private investment. The *Banque ouest-africaine de développement* (BOAD) had two bonds issues in 1995 to absorb some of the excess liquidity into investment. In addition, BOAD and the European Investment Bank established at the end of 1994 the *Fonds de Garantie des Investissements Privés en Afrique de l'Ouest*, with a number of donor countries and regional private banks also participating. The aim of the fund is to guarantee 50 per cent of medium-to-long-term loans given by banks to the private sector. Moreover, a number of investment funds have been created by such bodies as the World Bank and BOAD. Finally, France is providing guarantees for bonds issued by banks to raise long-term capital. Finance for investment by small enterprises, however, remains difficult to obtain, in particular since the liquidation of five small development banks in the late 1980s and early 1990s.

TUNISIA: INVESTMENT REVIVES AFTER REFORMS

From the early 1960s to the mid-1980s, the Government of Tunisia intervened extensively in the economy by controlling prices, production, credit and investment. Investment was high, and output grew by 6 per cent per year. Indeed, one could argue that during that period, the foundations were created for the successful response of the economy to the adjustment policies that followed the balance-of-payments crisis of 1986.

That crisis triggered a policy reorientation. The Government liberalized many facets of the economy while restoring macroeconomic stability. During the post-1986 period, Tunisia also underwent a political transition to democracy, which contributed to political stability and reinforced business confidence in the Government's economic policy. Those economic and political reforms contributed to a general improvement in economic performance, a significant change in the structure of the economy and a revival of investment, although investment remains below historical averages.[31]

Investment controls and incentives up to the mid-1980s

During the 1960s, when the Government embarked upon an import-substitution strategy, industrialization - and hence investment - was mainly driven by public enterprises. Between 1962 and 1971, 78 per cent of gross domestic fixed investment (GDFI) by enterprises took place in public enterprises[32] and public enterprises dominated export activity. However, the Government implicitly encouraged the private sector and never discouraged it. Up to the mid-1980s, investment was very much under Government control by means of various investment codes, licensing and regulations: law 69-35 of 1969 stated that any investment had to obtain Government approval. The code also involved several fiscal, financial and other incentives, including the granting of monopoly power, which were in principle not discriminatory between sectors.

Between 1972 and 1974, a number of policies and institutions were initiated to stimulate exports by the private sector. A number of institutions, such as the *Centre de Promotion des Exportations* and *Agence Foncière Industrielle*, were created in the early 1970s. In 1972, specific investment incentives for the promotion of exports were implemented, and in the 1980s various investment codes and regulations were adopted that - in contrast to the 1969 code - did discriminate between sectors. Investment in exports, tourism and lagging regions were particularly favoured.

Until the early 1980s, the volume and direction of credit and interest rates were very much under the control of the Government as well. For example,

[31] Use has been made of Mustapha K. Nabli, "Alternative trade policies and employment in Tunisia", in: *Trade and Employment in Developing Countries: Individual Studies*, Anne O. Krueger and others, eds. (Chicago, University of Chicago Press, 1981), pp. 435-498; *The New Institutional Economics and Development: Theory and Applications to Tunisia*, Mustapha K. Nabli and Jeffrey Nugent, eds. (Amsterdam, North Holland, 1989); Saleh M. Nsouli, Sena Eken, Paul Duran, Gerwin Bell and Zühtü Yücelik, "The path to convertibility and growth: the Tunisian experience", IMF Occasional Paper No. 109 (Washington, D.C., December 1993); World Bank, *Republic of Tunisia: towards the twenty first century*, Report No. 14375-TUN, two volumes (Washington, D.C, October 1995); and *Tunisia: The Political Economy of Reform*, I. William Zartman, ed. (Boulder and London, Lynne Rienner Publishers, 1991).

[32] See Eva Bellin, "Tunisian industrialists and the State", in *Tunisia: The Political Economy of Reform* ..., p. 50.

banks were required to lend 43 per cent of their total deposits (excluding foreign currency deposits of non-residents and convertible dinar deposits) in the form of medium- and long-term loans, 25 per cent in public sector bonds and 18 per cent for the private sector and certain public enterprises. Moreover, credit was controlled through ceilings on rediscounting. However, credit for certain activities, such as export financing, was not limited. Interest rates were subsidized either by the Governments's budget or by the preferential rediscount of the Central Bank.

Tunisia has had a rather well-developed banking system,[33] and aside from retained earnings, finance for investment mainly came from commercial banks during the 1960s and 1970s.[34] Until the mid-1980s, banks were able to remain profitable partly because the rediscount rate of the Central Bank was lower than the lending rate. But profitability decreased between the mid-1970s and the early 1980s. Banks had suffered from negative real interest rates, controls on asset composition and credit controls; according to one estimate, non-performing loans amounted to 20 per cent of their collective portfolio at the end of 1988.[35]

Investment during the 1960s and 1970s was also encouraged by an overvalued exchange rate, which made the import of capital goods cheaper, and low tariffs (less than 10 per cent on average) on intermediate and equipment imports. Non-tariff barriers and import controls, however, were extensive in the 1960s; they were relaxed (but not abolished) in the 1970s.

The above-mentioned policies were successful. Thus, in the two and a half decades up to 1986, investment was relatively high in Tunisia and GDP grew on average by 6 per cent annually. GDFI rarely fell below 30 per cent of GDP (both at constant prices), with public investment usually accounting for one

[33] In 1956, Tunisia counted 79 bank branches, which had increased to 100 by 1970 and 496 by 1988 (see Clement Henry Moore, "Tunisian banking", in *Tunisia: The Political Economy of Reform* ..., p. 87. In mid-1994, the banking system consisted of 12 commercial banks, of which six are publicly owned and provide about 70 per cent of commercial bank loans. In addition, there are eight development banks - all public - and eight offshore banks.

[34] Between 1979 and 1987, only 20 per cent of investment by public and private enterprises was financed by internal funds.

[35] See Moore, loc. cit., p. 77.

Figure VII.4
TUNISIA: GROSS DOMESTIC FIXED INVESTMENT, 1970-1994
(1990 PRICES)

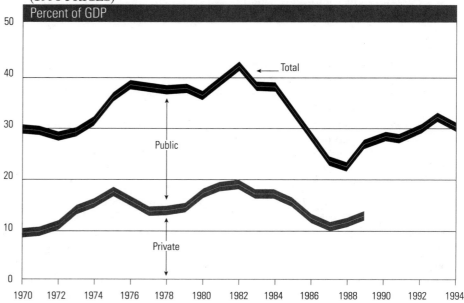

Source: World Bank data.

half to two thirds of GDFI (see figure VII.4). More importantly, the structure of the economy changed. In the 1960s, 83 per cent of GDFI in the textile sector was in public enterprises and 17 per cent in private enterprises; in the 1970s, those percentages were reversed. Textiles showed the most significant shift, but in all sectors except chemicals a similar change took place, reflecting a division of labour between the private and the public sector in which the public sector focused on capital-intensive and technologically advanced industries and the private sector on the more labour-intensive and less technologically advanced sectors. In effect, the number of private firms doubled during the 1970s, even if firms producing only for export markets are excluded.[36] Thus, the share of the manufacturing sector increased from 7 per cent of GDP in the early 1960s to 15 per cent of GDP in the mid-1980s. The structure of trade changed even more dramatically. The share of manufacturing exports in total merchandise exports increased from about 19 per cent in the late 1960s to 45 per cent in 1985, and the share of textile exports in total merchandise exports increased from 2 per cent in 1970 to 21 per cent in 1978.

Adjustment to a crisis

During the first half of the 1980s, export revenues from petroleum and phosphates declined, as prices fell and oil reserves dwindled. Debt-service payments rapidly increased, swelling the current account deficit and culminating in a crisis in mid-1986. Foreign exchange reserves dropped to a few days of imports, which triggered a comprehensive structural adjustment programme supported by the Bretton Woods institutions. Macroeconomic stability was restored, the currency was devalued, and prices, current account foreign-exchange transactions, investment, trade and interest rates were all substantially liberalized. Other areas that underwent reform included the tax system, the financial sector and State-owned enterprises.

Since 1986, economic performance has improved, although GDP growth has been slightly lower than its historical average between 1987 and 1995, partly because of a number of droughts and a drop in tourism revenues in 1991 owing to the Gulf War.[37] The inflation rate, never really high, declined by a few percentage points.[38] But the budget deficit was reduced from over 7 per cent of GDP in 1986 to about 2 per cent in 1994, and the value of merchandise exports increased from $1.8 billion in 1986 to $5.3 billion in 1995, with their volume increasing over the same period by about 50 per cent after a monotonic decline from 1980 to 1985 of 24 per cent. Partly because of the increase in exports, the current account deficit (before official transfers), which amounted to about 8 per cent of GDP during 1982 to 1986, was transformed into a surplus in 1988, after which the deficit averaged 5 per cent of GDP. External debt-servicing payments fell from 28 per cent of exports of goods and services in 1987 to 18 per cent in 1994, owing to the rise in exports earnings, so that Tunisia never had to seek to reschedule its debt-service payments.

Significant economic reforms affecting investment have been introduced since the mid-1980s. The first phase of the trade liberalization programme (1986-1988) focused on raw materials, semi-processed materials, spare parts and capital goods. During the first half of the 1980s, trade restrictions were tightened in response to the looming current-account crisis and by 1986 94 per

36   See Bellin, loc. cit., pp. 51 and 52.

37   GDP grew by 5.5 per cent annually during the period 1962-1995, and by 4.6 per cent during the period 1987-1995.

38   The rate of increase of consumer prices was above 8 per cent for every year between 1980 and 1985 but never higher than 14 per cent; prices rose about 6 per cent in 1995.

cent of the tariff lines were on the restricted list, requiring an annual import authorization, semi-annual import license or import card.

Then the reforms began, and although between the mid-1980s and the early 1990s, total charges (tariffs and para-tariffs) on imports of machinery and equipment slightly increased, non-tariff barriers were significantly reduced. The volume of equipment imports then rose rapidly.

Starting in 1987, investment codes have been significantly liberalized. Sectoral investment codes were revised, and prior approval was abolished for nearly all investments that did not request incentives, and was replaced with a registration obligation. Targeting and simplified procedures were also improved. In December 1993, the Chamber of Deputies approved a new unified investment code, covering all sectors with the notable exception of mining, energy and finance; the new code harmonized incentives and reduced discrimination against certain sectors, such as manufacturing production for the domestic market. Incentives that were previously mainly aimed at export promotion and regional development were extended to such areas as environmental protection, the promotion of technology, research and development and energy savings, the development of entrepreneurship and the development of human capital. The new code and an additional decree reinforced the principle of freedom to invest. Investment has been substantially deregulated, except for certain activities, mostly services, such as transportation and restaurants.

The new code is also more open to foreign direct investment (FDI), demonstrating the importance that the Government is attaching to attracting FDI. In addition, foreign portfolio investment was partially liberalized in June 1995, and the Agency for the Promotion of Foreign Investment was created in July 1995. In fact, even before those recent measures, fiscal and financial incentives for FDI in Tunisia were among the most attractive among 53 developing and developed countries covered by a survey conducted in the late 1980s.[39] In addition, free-trade zones are being created, one of which became operational in late 1995.

With the liberalization of investment came the liberalization of credit and interest rates as well. Liberalization of the financial sector started in the early 1980s, but reforms only became comprehensive with the structural adjustment programme of 1986, which actually focused on the financial sector. Already in January 1987, interest rates were partially liberalized, although banks, under the aegis of *Association Professionelle de Banques*, immediately colluded to fix interest rates. About a year later, prior approval requirements for loans, rediscounting and all refinancing facilities, except in priority sectors, were abolished. Preferential interest rates were increased, and the number of activities eligible for preferential credit was reduced in 1990 and 1992.[40] By 1994, financial reforms had significantly progressed, thanks to the introduction of several new financial instruments since 1988; the issuance of new prudential regulation and the strengthening of Central Bank supervision in 1991; the adoption of a new banking law in 1994 that increased the competition between development and commercial banks; and the removal of the last significant interest control in 1994: a cap on the spread of lending rates over the money market rate.

It is perhaps too early to assess the full impact of the above-mentioned financial sector reforms. Nonetheless, some observations are warranted. First,

[39] Reported in World Bank, *Republic of Tunisia: changing the structure of incentives*, Report No. 9620-TUN (Washington, D.C., November 1991).

[40] By the end of 1992, only 10 per cent of total credit was granted at the preferential rate.

lending rates do not seem to have had a major impact on investment: both have increased steadily since 1987. Second, the extension of domestic credit, excluding net credit to the central Government, more than doubled between 1986 and 1994 but decreased from 64 per cent of GDP in 1986 to 60 per cent in 1994. Moreover, the share of total loans going to public enterprises remained basically the same: it was 17 per cent in 1989 and 16 per cent in 1993.[41] Third, the profitability and operating costs of banks for the period 1987-1993 were broadly in line with those of banks in OECD countries. Finally, there is a danger that the liberalization of the financial sector will negatively affect the amount of credit made available to small and medium-sized enterprises. Hence, publicly supported funds will play an increasingly important role in providing financing for such enterprises since they lack access to formal credit.[42]

Investment revives

In 1988, total GDFI reached its lowest point since 1960 at 22 per cent of GDP. During the first half of the 1980s, the Government had reduced public investment in response to the deteriorating economic situation.[43] Private investment fell as well, as a result of the increasing policy uncertainty and weak domestic demand. The increase in private investment started already in 1988 and public investment followed in 1989, pushing GDFI from 22 per cent of GDP in 1988 to 31 per cent in 1993 (see figure VII.4). FDI increased also but remains moderate outside the energy sector, despite generous incentives, combined with current account convertibility of the Tunisian dinar, macroeconomic and political stability, and the easy transfer of invested capital.[44] Investment ratios remain below the level of the 1960s and 1970s, but there is some indication that the efficiency of investment is improving. Thus, the five-year incremental capital-output ratio declined from a high of 10 in 1987 to 6 in 1992.

An important aspect of any adjustment programme is the restructuring of the economy, in which, of course, investment plays a crucial role. The diversification of the economy after 1986 away from traditional export products is particularly notable, in part because it reduces vulnerability to terms-of-trade shocks. The share of manufacturing exports in total merchandise exports increased from 45 per cent in 1985 to 75 per cent in 1993, with the share of textiles and machinery and equipment in 1985 exports increasing from 20 and 4 per cent, respectively, to 40 and 9 per cent, respectively, in 1992 exports. On the down side, energy, phosphates and derivatives accounted for 46 per cent of total merchandise exports in 1986 but only 15 per cent in 1994.

It is not clear how large a direct effect liberalization has had on investment; the growth of investment is probably as much related to general macroeconomic and political stability and the presence of other necessary conditions, such as export capabilities, infrastructure and an educated labour force, so that, striking as the post-1986 changes are, they were by no means unexpected. Tunisia has expanded its infrastructure and improved educational attainment substantially since independence in 1956, and it has had a long history of providing incentives for exporters and the private sector, going back at least to the early 1970s. The increase in exports in the 1970s was almost as dramatic as it was in the second half of the 1980s. The incentives contained in the investment codes, however, appear to have had an effect on the allocation of invest-

[41] The definition of public enterprises was changed in 1989; hence, no comparison is possible with data before 1989.

[42] A recent compilation of surveys conducted in seven countries (Algeria, Ecuador, Jamaica, the Niger, Swaziland, Thailand and Tunisia), showed that bank finance does not play a significant role in the financing of micro-enterprises in any of those countries. Self-financing and loans from family or friends typically accounted for 80 to 90 per cent - 91 per cent in Tunisia - and bank finance for less than 5 per cent. Regarding bank finance, Tunisia was among the exceptions since the *Fonds National pour la Promotion de l 'Artisanat et des Petits Métiers* provided the bulk of the formal finance, which amounted to 8.6 per cent of the total finance (the percentages do not add up as multiple answers were possible) (see Christian Morrison, Henri-Bernard Solignac Lecomte and Xavier Oudin, *Micro-Enterprises and the Institutional Framework in Developing Countries* (Paris, OECD Development Centre, 1994).

[43] The cuts in the budget were even larger after 1985: capital expenditures by the Government were cut from 30 per cent of total government expenditures in 1985 to about 20 per cent in 1994.

[44] About 90 per cent of FDI between 1991 and 1993 went into the energy sector.

ment; combined with export promoting institutions, they have contributed to change in the structure of exports and to their rapid increase.

The next challenge of liberalization

In July 1995, Tunisia and the European Union (EU) signed a trade and cooperation accord which will, inter alia, create a free trade zone for industrial goods over a 12-year period. Under the 1976 agreement, which the new agreement will replace, Tunisia already had largely free access to the EU for industrial goods. EU firms will now have greater access to the Tunisian market. One study estimated that unless restructured, a third of the Tunisian industrial sector would fail and another third would face serious difficulties. The Government is assisting the industrial sector in preparing for the increased competition, and an initial 100 firms have been selected for a pilot assistance programme, the total cost of which is estimated at $2.4 billion over the next five years. Increased EU assistance and World Bank support is available for such restructuring. But in addition, FDI is considered crucial, and could be stimulated by the agreement because it reduces the likelihood that reforms will be reversed.[45] On the other hand, the agreement gives Tunisia little additional access to the EU, and considering its small market and relatively high transportation costs, firms might as well choose to invest in the EU.[46] For instance, unit labour costs, energy and transportation costs, and illiteracy are still relatively high compared with its competitors, and might be factors in the low level of non-energy FDI. The challenge is for Tunisian firms to rise and meet the competition.

CHILE: THE FRUITS OF REFORM AND STABILITY

Chile can be categorized as a developing economy that has achieved a relatively high level of investment in the 1990s. The ratio of investment to GDP has been increasing since 1985 (see table VII.2). Together with exports, investment is one of the most dynamic components of aggregate demand in the Chilean economy. Private investment is the leading component of total investment. The Chilean investment performance is in clear contrast with that of most Latin American economies. What has made the difference for Chile?

The improved environment for private investment in Chile in the 1990s is the outcome of a long and difficult transition process to achieve sustained macroeconomic and political stability while undertaking deep structural reforms. That process, which began earlier in Chile than in the rest of Latin America, was consolidated by the return to democracy in 1990 and by the recent attention to the social costs of reforms. After almost two decades of implementing, sequencing and fine-tuning liberalization reforms, the long-awaited rewards are emerging.

Growth strategy: a costly experiment, then reform

In the early 1970s, a relatively inward-oriented and interventionist economic policy was discarded and an extreme laissez-faire policy was imposed by a new Government.[47] The economic strategy was based on a radically liberalized

[45] Policy uncertainty and the risk of policy reversal are among the most severe deterrents to FDI (for a survey in Eastern Africa, see Paul Collier, "The marginalisation of Africa", *International Labour Review*, vol. 134, Nos. 4 and 5 (1995), pp. 541-557). It has been argued that trade agreements with the EU will function as an agent of restraint, and will greatly enhance policy credibility and stimulate investment (see Paul Collier and Jan Willem Gunning, "Trade policy and regional integration: implications for the relations between Europe and Africa", *The World Economy*, vol. 18, No. 3 (May 1995), pp. 387-410).

[46] See "Tunisia concludes association agreement with EU", *IMF Survey*, (4 March 1996), pp. 77-79.

Table VII.2.
CHILE: GROSS FIXED CAPITAL FORMATION, 1980-1994[a]

Year	Percentage of GDP
1980	16.6
1981	18.6
1982	14.6
1983	12.0
1984	12.3
1985	16.8
1986	17.1
1987	19.4
1988	20.3
1989	23.0
1990	23.3
1991	20.9
1992	22.7
1993	25.6
1994	24.3

Source: IMF, International Financial Statistics, various issues.

[a] Based on current prices.

[47] See *The Macroeconomics of Populism in Latin America*, Rudiger Dornbusch and Sebastian Edwards eds. (Chicago, NBER-University of Chicago Press, 1991); and Sebastian Edwards and Alejandra Cox Edwards, *Monetarism and Liberalization: The Chilean Experiment*, (Chicago, University of Chicago Press, 1991).

market economy model that placed excessive confidence in automatic market corrections and inflexible rules for money supply growth, leading to the implementation of policies that proved to be unsustainable. Trade liberalization was followed by the opening up of capital-account transactions within a context of an appreciating exchange rate. A consumption boom took pace, fed by cheap external credit and imported goods (as a result of the foreign exchange policy and the drastic lowering of import tariffs), which undermined national industry.[48] The trade balance thus deteriorated, while high domestic interest rates, as a consequence of the monetary policy, led to massive inflows of foreign capital and increased indebtedness of the economy, mainly of its private sector.

The vulnerability of the Chilean economy became evident in the early 1980s in the face of several external shocks: terms-of-trade shocks (higher oil prices and lower copper prices), the leap in real international interest rates and the end of foreign financial inflows. The economy collapsed in 1982, with GDP contracting by 14 per cent and unemployment reaching 33 per cent in that year. The Government reacted to the crisis by adopting emergency measures (austere fiscal and wage policies), while rescheduling and guaranteeing private foreign debts. The exchange rate collapsed and was sharply devalued. The fixed nominal exchange rate policy was abandoned, and a steady real depreciation of the currency was pursued.

A structural adjustment programme was adopted in 1985. It included a more expansionary macroeconomic policy intended to promote the recovery of output, employment, domestic saving and investment, while gaining control over inflation and managing the exchange rate.[49] The country's growth strategy was now to be based on a major restructuring of its economy away from the copper industry and towards more diversified exports.[50] A flexible exchange rate within a crawling band was adopted and managed by a more autonomous Central Bank. Initially, it devalued the currency - aided by the international depreciation of the dollar - and then sought to avoid extreme currency appre-

[48] Average effective import tariffs fell from 150 per cent in mid-1974 to 14 per cent in 1979.

[49] By 1985, Chilean annual inflation was still high by international standards (26 per cent) but was considerably lower and more stable than before. It has followed a declining trend, and reached single digit levels in 1994.

[50] See ECLAC, "La transformación de la producción en Chile: cuatro ensayos de interpretación", *Estudios e Informes*, No. 84 (Santiago, 1993), pp. 275-372.

Figure VII.5
CHILE: REAL EFFECTIVE EXCHANGE RATE, 1983-1995

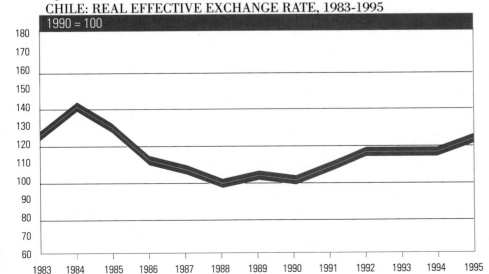

1990 = 100

Source: Same as table A.14

51   See Sebastian Edwards, "Trade policy, exchange rates, and growth", in *Reform, Recovery and Growth: Latin America and the Middle East*, Rudiger Dornbusch and Sebastian Edwards eds. (Chicago, NBER University of Chicago Press, 1995), pp. 13-49.

52   See Vittorio Corbo and Stanley Fischer, "Lessons from the Chilean stabilization and recovery", in *The Chilean Economy: Policy Lessons and Challenges*, B.P. Bosworth and others, eds. (Washington, D.C., The Brookings Institution, 1994), pp. 29-80.

53   Chile 's dependence on the copper industry has declined over the past 10 years, but copper still generates over 30 per cent of its export revenues.

54   "Except for export activities, the investors of the 1960s up to the early 1980s had lost their productive assets through expropriation, through takeovers at low prices or through bankruptcy" See M. Marfan and B. P. Bosworth, "Saving, investment and economic growth", in *The Chilean Economy...*, pp. 194 and 195.

ciation, which would have been adverse to export sectors. The effective exchange rate has indeed remained quite stable during the past 10 years[51] (see figure VII.5).

Import tariffs, temporarily raised during the crisis, were reduced between 1985 and 1988. Those measures radically reoriented incentives in favour of non-traditional export sectors, which began to increase their efficiency through improved quality control and a more aggressive marketing strategy.[52] Consequently, the reforms initiated in 1985, together with improvement of the Chilean terms of trade as international copper prices improved after 1987, contributed to the recovery of the economy.

Investment responses

Investment was very much affected by the crisis and declined in the early 1980s. The decline of private investment was more pronounced than that of public investment. Multilateral financing, the only significant source of foreign currency besides exports, supported some large public investment projects after the crisis.

The overall investment level in the economy recovered somewhat in the middle and late 1980s. Most of the investment effort in that period was foreign direct investment (FDI). Foreign investors had been attracted to Chile by the introduction of a more liberal mining code in 1983, which granted security of tenure to companies operating large concessions. Although policy makers realized how vulnerable Chile would be if its economic development were to be based solely on its mining sector, it was precisely the mining sector that had the capacity to attract foreign capital and help to build some momentum in the economy.[53] Debt-equity swaps and privatization of some infrastructure service (for example, telecommunications) contributed to an expansion of investment during that period.

Private domestic investment took some more time to respond to the new environment. Limitations to higher investment included depressed demand conditions; diminished national saving due to the loss of foreign saving as a source of finance and the slow recovery by domestic private saving owing to the 1982 crisis; past experience with losses and bankruptcy during recessions;[54] and low domestic savings until 1991. Furthermore, changes in policy orientation accompanying the democratization process were also a possibility, thus creating a great deal of uncertainty about the future of the economy. Those conditions changed in the 1990s.

The dramatic decline of unemployment and the parallel rise in wages may have increased the demand for investment to offset rising labour costs and expand capacity. Open urban unemployment was only 4 per cent in 1993 (it increased somewhat later), down from almost 12 per cent in 1987, while average real wages rose by 20 per cent during the period 1989-1995.

The peaceful political transition and the continuity of policy strategy in the 1990s had a positive effect on private investment, including both foreign direct investment and domestic investment. After the change to democracy in 1990, the new administration remained committed to the macroeconomic policy and management of the previous regime. The stable conditions of an open economy gave

Chile the highest rating in terms of investors' confidence in Latin America.[55] The private sector reacted positively to this and investment picked up.

Public finance and private investment

An important component of the Chilean strategy has been fiscal and financial reforms pursued over a long period, which have had a positive impact on investment. The radical deregulation of the economy, a comprehensive round of privatization (1974-1978) and the quick reduction of public deficits in the 1970s brought about a dramatic reduction of public intervention in the economy. Moreover, a sustained practice of budget balancing yielded consistent fiscal surplus during the period preceding the 1980s crisis. In fact, it was precisely the pursuit of a budget surplus - despite deteriorating overall social conditions - that allowed Chile to conduct the well-known reform of its social security system in 1981 from a pay-as-you-go system to a privately managed, contribution-determined, pension system.[56] Moreover, because the public sector was running a fiscal surplus, the savings accumulated in the new pension system could go completely into investment.

Thus, unlike the rest of Latin America, Chile entered its foreign crisis in the 1980s with a strong fiscal position but an unmanageable private foreign debt,[57] which allowed the public sector to rescue the debt-burdened private sector. The 1982-1983 crisis had rendered insolvent many of the enterprises that were privatized in the late 1970s, and they were thus taken over by their local creditor banks. The latter, however, also fell into a dire financial situation owing to capital losses associated with the currency depreciation. Between 1982 and 1984, the official banking supervisory agency intervened in 14 banks and eight other financial institutions, lending them $9 billion.[58] The ensuing debt, owed by ailing banks to the central bank, eased their recovery. By 1995, six banks still owed $4.5 billion, with a 40-year maturity for repayment.

As the treatment of the banking crisis highlighted, the public sector clearly affirmed its role in support of the private sector. Social demands, however, went basically unattended, despite the Government's notable emergency employment programme, which absorbed about 13 per cent of the Chilean labour force at the height of the economic crisis in 1983.[59] Its costs, however, pale next to the central bank's rescue programme. At its peak, the employment programme cost 1.5 per cent of GDP, while the bailout of the private sector peaked at 5.8 per cent of GDP.[60]

With the change to a democratic administration, the State has increased expenditure on social programmes and raised its investment in infrastructure, backed by additional revenues from a tax reform in 1990. The additional public expenditures the tax reform thus enabled are estimated to have a positive, crowding-in, effect on private investment and social stability seemed more assured.[61]

Financial sector development

Chile's experiment with financial liberalization in the 1970s had attracted an abundance of foreign credit to the private sector through the intermediation of local banks. Banks lent those funds to private conglomerates - some linked to the banks themselves - to finance the purchase of enterprises being priva-

[55] For example, Chile was recently accorded the highest sovereign creditworthiness rating in Latin America by *Institutional Investor*, at 59.2, while Colombia placed second at 46.7 (see *Institutional Investor* (March 1996), p. 92).

[56] On the eve of the reforms, Chile 's social security fund had a deficit equivalent to about 2 per cent of GDP. During the first years of the reform, as the State lost contributors to the new system but still had to honour payments to current retirees, the deficit widened and reached more than 6 per cent of GDP in 1984. This deficit has since been narrowing but is still about 4 per cent of GDP. Those costs have been absorbed by the substantial primary fiscal surplus (see *World Economic and Social Survey*, 1995 (United Nations publication, Sales No. E.95.II.C.1), pp. 278 and 279).

[57] See Carlos Díaz-Alejandro, "Goodbye financial repression, hello financial crash", *Journal of Development Economics*, vol. 19 (1985), pp. 1-24. Nevertheless, reduced fiscal revenues owing to lower copper prices led to the resurgence of a deficit in consolidated public-sector accounts during the period 1983-1986.

[58] See ECLAC, "Shock externo y desequilibrio fiscal, la macroeconomía de América Latina en los ochentas: los casos de Argentina, Bolivia, Brasil, Colombia, Chile y México", (LC/R.1469), Santiago, 1994.

[59] The programme was discontinued in 1989, when open unemployment dropped to a more manageable level.

[60] See R. Ffrench-Davis and D. Raczynski, "The impact of global recession and national policies on living standards: Chile, 1973-89" CIEPLAN Notas Técnicas, No. 97 (November 1990); and P. Meller, "Adjustment and social costs in Chile during the 1980s", *World Development*, vol. 19, No. 11 (1991), pp. 1545-1561.

[61] See Osvaldo Larrañaga, "Casos de éxito de la política fiscal en Chile: 1980-1993", *Serie Política Fiscal*, No. 67 (Santiago, ECLAC, 1995).

tized and other investments, most in the non-tradeables sector of the economy (such as real estate). Some were of questionable quality, however; poor risk assessment and lack of proper regulation and supervision thus led to the deterioration of the banks' loan portfolios. When the Chilean peso was devalued and the local currency cost of foreign debt servicing soared, the financial system crashed. As noted above, the Government then bailed out the banking system.

Policy makers were henceforth more conscious of the volume and nature of capital inflows. Domestic financial regulation was reintroduced to avoid excessive financial concentration, and the seized banks were reprivatized by publicly offering their stock in the domestic market. Moreover, when foreign capital inflows started to come back in the late 1980s, the central bank sought to sterilize their impact on the domestic economy so as to avoid financial volatility, increased inflationary pressures and the appreciation of the currency,[62] and a number of controls were imposed on them. However, high domestic interest rates still attract foreign capital inflows, which continue to cause some degree of upward pressure on the exchange rate. Additional capital controls were introduced in 1995 to discourage short-term speculative flows.

Domestic capital markets are burgeoning with the contribution of pension funds being managed by the *Administradoras de Fondos de Pensiones* (AFPs). Given the nature of pension fund investing, this has boosted the supply of long-term project financing, which was very scarce in the past. Moreover, the recent Law 19415 allows institutional investors such as AFPs and insurance companies to buy equity shares in development projects. They may contribute to allocating up to $4 billion for investment in infrastructure. In sum, foreign finance is now playing a much smaller role in investment finance. Indeed, the restructured Chilean banks and other domestic firms themselves have been investing in neighboring countries (total Chilean investment abroad is estimated at about $5 billion).

Favourable external factors

As in other cases in which policy reforms since the late 1980s have been associated with strong economic growth, favourable external factors have been conducive to an increase in investment. Since the second half of the 1980s, foreign private finance has been available for placement in Chile on a steadier basis than it has for other Latin American economies. The improved access to foreign finance was bolstered by a substantial reduction in Chile's foreign indebtedness through pioneering debt-equity conversions of commercial bank debt and substantial prepayments of multilateral debt. Between 1985 and 1990, some $9.6 billion in foreign debt were retired through debt-equity swaps that often involved domestic investors bringing back funds from overseas, which contributed to finance privatization and reinforced the liberal environment for foreign direct investment.[63] At the same time, indicators of external indebtedness declined as the debt overhang eased.[64]

In addition to financial sector developments, declining international prices of capital goods are also having positive effects on the quantity and quality of investment in Chile in the 1990s. Additionally, favourable developments in the terms of trade since the late 1980s and an extremely positive export performance in the past years have supported the growth of foreign reserves while

[62]   See Guillermo Calvo, L. Leiderman and C. Reinhart, "Capital inflows and real exchange rate appreciation in Latin America: the role of external factors", *IMF Staff Papers*, vol. 40, No. 1 (1993), pp. 108-151; and Vicente Galvis, "Sequencing of financial sector reforms: a review", IMF Working Paper No. WP/94/101 (Washington, D.C., 1994).

[63]   See *Debt-Equity Swaps and Development* (United Nations publication, Sales No. E.93.II.A.7), pp. 43-81.

[64]   The ratio of total debt service to exports of goods and services fell from about 50 per cent in 1984 to 19 per cent in 1994, while the ratio of total external debt to GNP declined from 115 per cent to 46 per cent during the same period (see World Bank, *World Debt Tables* (Washington, D.C., 1996)).

allowing for import growth. FDI originally boomed owing to the debt conversions and the mining projects, and more recently owing to the overall healthy conditions of an economy that offered considerable advantages and is likely to continue to do so in the coming years. Santiago is now seen as a low-risk financial, services and operations centre for transnational corporations investing in other South American countries.[65]

In conclusion, the Chilean case shows the considerable advantage offered by the establishment of a competitive environment - as a result of the opening of the economy to ensure increases in productivity - and by intense reform, export orientation and sustained stability in increasing the efficiency and quantity of investment. With the stabilization of the economy, some predictability of the inflation rate and exchange rate has been possible, thus facilitating long-term planning. Import liberalization has created pressure to increase productivity and facilitated investment through a supply of less expensive inputs and capital goods. Given those favourable conditions and the continuous respect for the rules of the game by the Government, a virtuous cycle has settled in.

INDONESIA: INVESTMENT AND ECONOMIC DIVERSIFICATION

A new long-term economic development strategy stressing economic reform and macroeconomic stabilization was adopted in Indonesia following the plunge in world oil prices in 1986. The new strategy was aimed at economic diversification, and has brought about substantial structural change in the Indonesian economy over the past decade. Private investment has expanded particularly sharply in response to the restructuring of domestic economic incentives and macroeconomic stability as well as to the favorable international environment for investment in the region. The expansion of the manufacturing sector, in particular manufactured exports, has been the focus of much of the new investment. The present case study examines the rising trend of public and private investment in Indonesia since the early 1980s and the factors that have contributed to that trend.

Investment trends and productivity

Several years of economic instability in the early 1980s had a depressing effect on investment. Plunging oil and commodity prices significantly weakened the balance of payments and sparked a severe tightening of macroeconomic policy. Public investment declined substantially under fiscal restraints, while private investment stagnated. In the mid-1980s, however, Indonesia embarked on a new development strategy that emphasized liberalization and industrial diversification along with macroeconomic stabilization. That reorientation of stabilization policy was followed by a rapid recovery in investment. The rate of fixed investment in current prices increased from an average of 24 per cent of GDP for 1983-1986 to 27 per cent in 1987-1994 (see table VII.3).

The revival of investment has been one of the most notable results of Indonesia's new development strategy. It has been underpinned by the sustained double digit annual growth in private investment in response to the reorientation of economic incentives in the system (discussed below) and an

65 See ECLAC, "Inversión extranjera y empresas transnacionales en la economía de Chile (1974-1989)", 2 vols., *Estudios e Informes, Nos.* 85-87 (Santiago, 1992).

Table VII.3.
INDONESIA:
GROSS FIXED
INVESTMENT RATE,
1983-1994

Percentage of GDP at current prices			
	Total	Private	Public
1983	25.1	13.2	11.9
1984	22.4	12.5	9.9
1985	23.6	13.5	10.1
1986	24.2	16.2	8.0
1987	24.8	17.3	7.5
1988	25.9	17.7	8.2
1989	27.3	18.7	8.6
1990	28.4	19.2	9.2
1991	28.1	18.5	9.6
1992	27.3	17.7	9.6
1993	25.9	16.1	9.8
1994	27.2	17.8	9.4

Sources: National accounts statistics of the Central Bureau of Statistics of Indonesia (1983 base); and World Bank estimates.

66 IMF data; FDI was equivalent to approximately 5 per cent of gross fixed investment.

67 See H. Soesastro, "Foreign direct investment in Indonesia" in *The Indonesian Quarterly*, Vol XXI, No. 3 (1993), pp.315 and 316.

68 The combined share of the priority sectors in total public investment increased from an average of 68 per cent in the late 1980s to 83 per cent in the early 1990s. The share of investment in physical infrastructure rose from 43 per cent to 59 per cent (based on World Bank estimates).

69 See A. Bhattacharya and M. Pangestu, *Indonesia: Development Transformation and Public Policy* (Washington, D.C., World Bank, 1993), p.13.

70 Within manufacturing, the main export sectors had the highest rates of TFP growth, but the capital-intensive and domestic market oriented industries had low to negative TFP growth (see H. Osada, "Trade liberalization and FDI incentives in Indonesia: the impact on industrial productivity", *The Developing Economies*, vol. 32, No. 4 (December 1994), pp.481-483).

71 See Bhattacharya and Pangestu, op. cit., pp.14 and 15.

increase in aggregate savings. The increase in private fixed investment has outstripped that of public investment; private investment represented 18 per cent of GDP in 1994 compared to only 13 per cent in 1983 (see table VII.3).

The sectoral composition of private investment has also changed significantly since the early 1980s. The most salient feature of the reallocation of investment across industries has been the rapid growth of investment in labour-intensive and in many cases export-oriented manufacturing industries. There are several indicators of that shift: the rapid increase in manufacturing output, which grew at an annual average rate of 11 per cent between 1984 and 1993, almost double the growth rate of GDP; the sharp rise in the share of manufacturing output in GDP from 13 per cent to 21 per cent; the rise of non-oil exports from 32 to 75 per cent of total exports, and the increase in the share of manufactures in non-oil exports from 38 per cent in 1986 to 63 per cent in 1994.

Foreign direct investment (FDI) has increased significantly since the mid-1980s, with inflows increasing nine fold between 1986 and 1994 (reaching $2 billion in 1994).[66] Two thirds of FDI has been concentrated in manufacturing, and about 70 per cent of FDI projects have been in export-oriented sectors.[67]

Public investment declined sharply from the early 1980s through 1986, largely because of the need to reduce government expenditure as part of macroeconomic adjustment programmes. Since 1988, the rate of public investment has averaged approximately 9 per cent of GDP (see table VII.3). Investment in physical infrastructure, human resource development and the reduction of poverty has remained a priority in public investment. At the same time, there has been a significant decline in public investment in directly productive activities.[68]

There was a positive trend in industrial productivity since total factor productivity (TFP) growth was significant - 2.2 per cent annually - between 1988 and 1991.[69] There are indications that TFP growth was more substantial - 3.8 per cent annually - in the non-oil manufacturing sectors, particularly in the export-oriented industries, in the second half of the 1980s.[70]

The reorientation of long-term development strategy

For almost three decades, Indonesia has enjoyed a high level of political stability. In addition, the Government's record in economic management, including the priority it has traditionally placed on macroeconomic stability and long-term economic development since its establishment, have contributed to the credibility of its economic policies.[71] Successful macroeconomic adjustment programmes followed the severe swings in terms of trade from oil and other commodity prices, which first rose steeply at the end of the 1970s and then dropped sharply in the early 1980s, after which oil prices plunged again in 1986. Both adjustment programmes involved sharp currency devaluation and contractionary macroeconomic policies. The 1986 policies included a devaluation of approximately 35 per cent against the dollar, monetary tightening and significant contraction of Government expenditure, including public investment. By undertaking those drastic adjustment programmes, however, the Government demonstrated its commitment to macroeconomic stability.

Aggregate data since the institution of those programmes is indicative of their success. Annual inflation has fluctuated within a relatively narrow range, between 5 and 12 per cent, since the late 1980s. Economic growth has also been sustained at a high rate, between 5 and 7.5 per cent annually. Supporting growth while limiting inflationary pressures has created highly favorable conditions for investment and a firm foundation for long-term policy.[72]

Long-term economic development policies during the 1970s emphasized agricultural and rural development, the improvement of social conditions, human resource development, infrastructure and the expansion of industry.[73] The Government also significantly expanded its direct involvement in production, including public investment in heavy industry, petroleum and mining. Those development efforts were supported by substantial earnings from oil exports; in fact, during the period of high oil prices, the production structure of the Indonesian economy became increasingly concentrated in oil-related industries.

With the initial oil price decline at the beginning of the 1980s and its significant negative effect on Government revenues and the current account balance, the Government recognized the need for diversification of the economy. However, it relied on import substitution policies and a continued strong role of Government to expand the manufacturing sector since the political consensus to implement major economic reforms did not yet exist.[74] It was only after the plunge in oil prices in 1986 and its severe impact on the economy that the political will emerged to put in place development policies that departed radically from the past.

The new long-term economic development strategy was based on economic diversification, and was to be guided by reliance on the private sector and market mechanisms. Furthermore, Indonesia's integration with the international economy was to be greatly expanded. Programmes of extensive liberalization and reform have since been instituted in the domestic financial sector, the foreign trade sector, and in the regulations governing investment in domestic industries. Those programmes have tended to be complementary and supported by appropriate macroeconomic policies.

The implementation of liberalization and reform has followed a gradualist approach. On the one hand, that approach can be seen as contributing to the credibility of those policies since the positive results of each phase bolstered the sustainability of reform. On the other hand, distortions are still pervasive in the economy as a result of partial reforms and remain obstacles to improving economic efficiency.

Financial reform and investment financing

Programmes of financial liberalization and reform were begun in 1983 but were intensified from the late 1980s onward. Those reforms expanded the financing available for private investment and reduced the cost of financing for the private sector. The cost of credit increased for the public sector, as subsidies and directed credit were scaled down or eliminated.[75]

Initial measures were primarily focused on the liberalization of the financial sector, with the deregulation of interest rates, the elimination of central bank ceilings on commercial bank credit and the end of subsidies for the State-owned bank. Those measures succeeded in significantly increasing the placement of private savings in the financial system and the extension of credit to

---

[72] One area of concern has been the growth of foreign debt. The stock of external debt has risen sharply, although debt service remains at a manageable level because of the continued strong growth in exports. Nevertheless, concern about the sustainability of the debt burden constrains the rate of overall external borrowing.

[73] See Bhattacharya and Pangestu, op. cit., pp. 14 and 15.

[74] For an in depth discussion of policy formulation and management, see M. Pangestu, "Managing economic policy reforms in Indonesia", in *Authority and academic scribbles*, S. Ostry, ed. (San Francisco, ICS Press, 1991), pp. 93-120,

[75] See T. Fukuchi, "Liberalization effect in a financially repressed economy: the case of Indonesia, 1982-1990", *The Developing Economies*, Vol. XXXIII, No.3 (September 1995), p.291.

76 See D. Cole and B. Slade, "Financial development in Indonesia", in *Growth and Structural Transformation in the New Order: Aspects of Economic Liberalization Problems for the Future*, A. Booth, ed. (Singapore, Oxford University Press, 1992), p. 92.

77 See Cole and Slade, loc. cit., p.93.

78 The spread declined from over 6 per cent in 1986 to about 3.5 per cent in 1992 (see T. Fukuchi, loc. cit., pp. 306-307).

the private sector. The growth in deposits was primarily in response to the swing to positive real deposit rates that occurred when interest rates were deregulated, and included the repatriation of funds that had flowed out during the macroeconomic shock in the early 1980s.[76]

Much more far-reaching reforms have been implemented since 1988, which have succeeded in changing the structure of the financial system and significantly enhancing financial intermediation,[77] including the opening of the system to private banks and a significant reduction in reserve requirements.[78] In addition to the banking sector, capital markets have developed rapidly since 1987 and have become an important source of financing for large firms. Reform measures that brought this about included an increase in withholding tax on interest on time deposits, reduction in the costs of issuing new stock, permission for foreign purchases of up to 49 per cent of shares of listed stocks, a change in pension law to allow the investment of pension funds in the stock market and the privatization of the stock market in 1992.

Private savings in the banking system increased over 300 per cent between 1986 and 1990. The share of private sector loans rose from 30 per cent in the mid-1980s to 45 per cent in 1992, while the real growth of total bank loans averaged 15 to 20 per cent annually. Real lending rates declined significantly in 1987 with the easing of monetary policy and have subsequently maintained steady levels (see table VII.4). At the same time, real deposit rates rose as a result of the narrowing spread between real deposit and lending rates in response to growing competition in the banking sector.

Despite the above-mentioned reforms, the access of private investors to credit and capital has been very unevenly distributed. Private conglomerates, which dominate the private sector, grew rapidly and relied heavily on bank credit in the 1980s. More recently, the domestic and international capital markets have become important sources of financing. Although small firms have also benefitted from increased access to credit, they have remained largely

Table VII.4.
INDONESIA: SOURCES OF LOANS
AND REAL INTEREST RATES, 1984-1993

Percentage					
	Share of loans (percentage)		Real interest rate (percentage)		
	State banks	Other banks	Deposit	Loan	Spread
1984	71	29	6.9	..	..
1985	69	31	13.5	..	..
1986	67	33	9.4	15.5	6.1
1987	66	34	7.0	11.9	4.9
1988	65	35	8.4	12.8	4.4
1989	62	38	10.5	13.6	3.1
1990	55	45	9.2	12.5	3.3
1991	53	47	10.0	..	..
1992	55	45	8.6	12.3	3.7
1993	..	..	..	10.2	..

Sources: T. Fukuchi, "Liberalization effect in a financially repressed economy: the case of Indonesia, 1982-1990", *The Developing Economies*, vol. XXXIII, No. 3 (September 1995), pp.306-307, compiled from Bank Indonesia, *Indonesian financial statistics*, various issues and IMF, *International Financial Statistics Yearbook*, various issues.

dependent on retained earnings to finance investment.[79] Those firms, particularly those in rural areas and including exporters, continue to experience difficulty in gaining access to credit.[80]

The development of the financial sector is still in the early stages. Because of the lag in development of financial infrastructure - prudential regulation, accounting standards and business law - significant inefficiencies and instability persist in the sector, as reflected in the decline in the quality of bank portfolios in the early 1990s and incidents of bank failures, which have adversely affected efficiency in the allocation of financial resources to investment.

Deregulation of domestic investment and the growth of private investment

Since 1985, restrictions on domestic private investment have been greatly reduced as investment opportunities have been significantly expanded with the streamlining of the investment licensing system, the progressive elimination of monopolies and the opening up of industries to private investment. The growth of the financial sector has provided the capital necessary to exploit those new opportunities.

The response of private investment has been very strong, with the majority of domestic investment projects concentrated in export-oriented industries.[81] Investment growth has been concentrated in private conglomerates that engage in highly diversified and transnational economic activities.[82] Investment growth in small enterprises, however, has lagged behind that of the large conglomerates.

Investment in large conglomerates can potentially be more efficient than investment in smaller firms. Because of their greater access to financial resources, conglomerates can exploit economies of scale and have a greater capacity for supporting large-scale investment. In addition, because of their higher level of technology and access to markets, they can also have a greater capability for absorbing new technology and better marketing know-how for competing internationally. However, they can also present obstacles to improving investment efficiency if they are protected from competition by administrative barriers to entry created by the Government or receive preferential treatment in access to Government contracts or financial support. Examples of such problems in Indonesia range from the creation of monopoly power in industries by the Government to bail-outs in the event of failure of large investment projects. Another example is the preferential access of businesses within a conglomerate to credit from banks that are members of the same conglomerate; while that practice could be justified by the lower transaction cost of such loans because of the lower cost of obtaining credit information on the borrower, it has also been found to have been based on financially unsound decisions and has contributed to defaults.

Investment in export sectors

Exchange-rate policy, trade liberalization and foreign investment reforms have been key factors in raising investment in the export sector.[83] The 35 per cent devaluation in 1986 drastically increased the ratio of prices of tradables to nontradables, reversing the decline in the profitability of the tradables sec-

[79] See M. Gultom-Siregar, "Econometric evidence of effects of financial reforms on firms' financing and investment behavior", *Ekonomi dan Keuangan Indonesia*, vol. 40, No.4, (December 1992).

[80] In response, the Government established a directed credit scheme for small-scale borrowers in 1990, whereby all banks are required to provide 20 per cent of their credit to small businesses (see M. Pangestu, "Financing of small scale business: the Indonesian experience", *The Indonesian Quarterly*, vol. XXI, No.1 (1993)).

[81] See Soesastro, loc. cit., p.316.

[82] See H. Hill, "Manufacturing industry", in *Growth and Structural Transformation in the New Order...*, pp.233 and 234.

[83] See W.T. Woo and others, *Macroeconomic Policies, Crises and Long-Term Growth in Indonesia 1965-90* (Washington, D.C., World Bank, 1994), pp. 111-117.

84 See P. Warr, "Exchange rate policy, petroleum prices and the balance of payments", in *Growth and Structural Transformation in the New Order...*, p.155.

85 World Bank, *Indonesia: improving efficiency and equity, changes in the public sector's role*, Report No. 14006-IND (Washington, D. C., 1995), pp.9 and 10.

86 Included the deregulation of foreign investment in manufacturing sectors, duty exemptions on imported manufactured inputs, liberalized divestiture and local content requirements, more favorable treatment of foreign-invested firms in access to domestic financing, 100 per cent foreign ownership and extended terms for land-use rights.

87 H. Soesastro, loc. cit., 1993, p. 316.

88 For example, between 1970 and 1990 installed capacity of the State electrical company increased eighteenfold, the number of telephone lines increased sevenfold and the length of paved roads increased nearly sixfold.

89 That finding is consistent with the results of studies of two other South-East Asian economies - Malaysia and Thailand - which found that public investment had a significant positive effect on private investment because it raised productivity in the private sector. See F. Larrain and R. Vergara, "Investment and macroeconomic adjustment: the case of East Asia", in L. Serven and A. Solimano, *Striving For Growth After Adjustment: The Role of Capital Formation* (Washington, D.C., World Bank, 1993), p. 264.

tor.[84] Since then, the managed floating rate system has succeeded in maintaining a competitive real effective exchange rate.

Trade reforms, which have been phased in since the mid-1980s, have reinforced the impact of exchange-rate policy. The liberalization of export licensing has significantly reduced the barriers to entry into the export sector. The institution of duty exemptions and drawbacks on imports of inputs for export production and across-the-board tariff reductions have lowered the costs of the export sector. The average tariff rate has been reduced from 37 per cent in 1985 to its current level of 15 per cent. The continued reduction of non-tariff barriers has also had a favorable impact on the cost of imported inputs. By the early 1990s, the proportion of domestic output covered by non-tariff barriers was reduced from 32 per cent to 25 per cent.

The rapid growth since the late 1980s in non-oil exports, particularly manufactured exports, was the result of a strong response of investment to trade sector reforms. The value of non-oil exports increased by an average of 21 per cent annually between 1985 and 1993. Besides the strong expansion of traditional exports (textiles, garments and plywood), there has been diversification into new exports, such as footwear, furniture and electrical machinery.[85]

The ongoing reform of rules governing FDI has been an integral part of Indonesia's policies for promoting exports.[86] In addition, the devaluation in 1986 and continued real depreciation reduced the cost of production in Indonesia for foreign investors. At the same time, there was a transformation of manufacturing competitiveness in Asia (including Japan) in the late 1980s due to the sharp decline in the dollar-yen exchange rate and rising wage costs in the Asian newly industrialized economies (NIE). As the high-cost economies of Japan and the NIEs sought to relocate their more labour-intensive manufacturing industries to lower-cost countries in the region, policy changes in Indonesia made it an attractive destination, along with Thailand and Malaysia. The primary sources and sectors of FDI have changed over time: whereas Japan was by far the largest foreign investor prior to 1988, the Asian NIEs have since emerged as the major investors. Furthermore, investment from the NIEs has been concentrated in labour-intensive export industries.[87] Foreign direct investment has been an important force in product diversification of exports.

Infrastructure and public investment

Infrastructure investment has been a priority in Government investment since the 1970s, when the rapid build-up of infrastructure capacity was concentrated in power generation, telephone lines, paved roads and irrigation.[88] That investment has facilitated the surge in private investment since the late 1980s.[89] In particular, power development has been critical to the growth of manufacturing. From the mid-1980s to 1994, investment in physical infrastructure continued to be substantial, constituting approximately 4 per cent of GDP. Public investment has remained dominant in infrastructure investment. Although there has been some privatization of public infrastructure enterprises since the implementation of a privatization programme at the beginning of the 1990s, the scale remains relatively small.

Demand for infrastructure has continued to rise, due to the sizeable backlog of unmet demand linked to rapid economic growth since the late 1980s and the new demand from anticipated future economic growth. However, given the relatively modest domestic savings rate (26 per cent of GDP) and the level of external debt, there is a constraint on how much of that demand can be met before serious imbalances occur. Thus, the physical infrastructure sector could remain a bottleneck to continued high economic growth and improvement in efficiency.

To date, Indonesia's macroeconomic policies and reform programmes have successfully revitalized private investment and contributed to economic diversification and growth. Their effectiveness appears to have been the result of their appropriateness and complementarity, reinforced by the credibility of the Government in an environment of political stability. They have, therefore, been able to generate the necessary economic adjustment in response to severely adverse turns in the international economic environment, as well as to restructure the economic system to take advantage of favorable international economic developments. Nevertheless, continued economic reform remains central to improvement in economic efficiency, which is critical to maintaining a sustainable high rate of economic growth.

CHINA: INVESTMENT QUANTITY AND QUALITY ISSUES

Since the inception of economic reforms in 1978, China has achieved great success in its economic growth. GDP has grown at an average annual rate of approximately 10 per cent for 15 years.[90] While the market-oriented reform policies that were gradually adopted have created the necessary favourable conditions for the dynamism of the economy, the high investment ratio has been considered as the leading factor in most of the high growth.[91] However, large fluctuations in the growth rate of fixed investment have also been seen as the main cause of the "stop-and-go" macroeconomic cycles that the Chinese economy has experienced in the post-reform period. In addition, the majority of fixed investment has been in the less efficient State-owned enterprise (SOE) sector, so that statistics showing the high rate of fixed investment have embodied signs of continuing policy concerns as well as successes. The Government, as a result, continues to try to balance policies in order to achieve the multiple objectives of a desirable pace of economic reform, a sustained high growth rate and macroeconomic stability.

Accounting for high aggregate investment

The ratio of real fixed investment to real GDP has been rising steadily since almost the beginning of the economic reform process, from 20 per cent in 1981 to above 35 per cent in 1994 (see figure VII.6). Major factors responsible for the acceleration of investment in the last 15 years include reforms that have promoted decentralization in both the investment system itself and in the overall economic system; the high domestic saving rate; and increasing foreign capital inflows.

Reforms in the investment system have made significant changes in the investment decision process, investment financing and capital goods distribution. Prior to those reforms, decision-making regarding fixed investment was strictly controlled by the central planning agencies and implemented by the

[90] Unless otherwise specified, all data used in the present section are based on State Statistical Bureau of China, *Statistical Yearbook of China*, (China Statistical Publishing House), various years.

[91] See Shahid Yusuf (1994) "China 's macroeconomic performance and management during transition", *Journal of Economic Perspectives*, 8(2), 1994; the author estimates that increasing capital investment was responsible for about 40 per cent of GDP growth in China during the post reform period, a higher level than that of Japan during 1960-1970, about the same as that of the Republic of Korea and lower than that of Singapore.

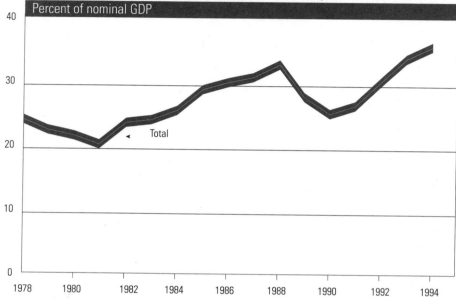

Figure VII.6
CHINA: GROSS DOMESTIC FIXED INVESTMENT, 1978-1994

Percent of nominal GDP

Total

Source: State Statistical Bureau of China, *Statistical Yearbook of China*, (China Statistical Publishing House), various years.

92 In China, the definition of SOE has an administrative dimension. Enterprises owned by the central Government and provincial governments are State-owned. All others, even those entirely owned by local governments below the provincial level, are classified as collectives.

93 Earmarked funds are raised through special levies on prices of goods and services. Typically, they are collected and managed by Government agencies but not included in the budget. This component of the "self-raised fund" is the result of fiscal decentralization, and is a more significant source of investment financing for State and some collective enterprises than for private and other smaller collective enterprises. For more details, see World Bank, *China: public investment and finance*, Report No. 14540-CHA (October 1995), pp.11 and 33.

Ministry of Finance, with investment financed mostly through budgetary grants to SOEs. Capital goods were supplied directly through the central material allocation system. Through reforms, investment decision-making has been gradually decentralized to local governments and enterprises. Although the final decision has remained with the central Government on investment projects that exceed a certain threshold level - anywhere from 30 million to 50 million yuan renminbi (Y), depending on the sector - the autonomy of local governments and enterprises in making investment decisions has increased significantly.

Meanwhile, the financing of investment has been changed substantially, along with reforms in the financial sector and in the SOE sector.[92] Financing through grants from the central budget has been gradually replaced by interest-bearing lending from State banks under the credit plan. More importantly, "self-raised" funds raised by local governments and enterprises have become the dominant source of investment financing, in the form of extrabudgetary resources, including retained earnings; capital depreciation funds; workers' contributions; funds earmarked[93] for investment in particular sectors, such as electricity generation and railroad construction; informal borrowing from the local population; and money raised through the rapidly emerging capital market. By 1994, self-raised funds accounted for 51 per cent of total investment financing for SOEs (see table VII.5). The increasing importance of self-raised funds in financing fixed investment undoubtedly reflects the decentralization of investment decisions in China; the earmarked fund component in self-raised funds, however (about 10 per cent of total investment in 1993 by the World Bank's estimate), is still largely influenced by the central Government.

Table VII.5.
INVESTMENT FINANCE IN CHINA, 1985 AND 1994

Percentage of total fixed investment									
Budgetary allocation		Bank loans		Foreign investment		Self raised funds		Other[a]	
1985	1994	1985	1994	1985	1994	1985	1994	1985	1994
SOE	26.4	5.0	23.1	25.7	2.8	7.2	40.4	51.0	7.3	11.6
Non-State	0.6	0.9	14.3	18.6	0.4	15.6	84.6[b]	46.1	..	20.7

Source: Calculations based on State Statistical Bureau of China, Statistical Yearbook of China 1986 and 1995 (China Statistical Publishing House).

a The definition of "other" source of investment financing is very vague; it is a catchall for all sources not included in the previously named groups.

b Investment by private enterprises in 1985 – 62 per cent of all non-State investment in that year – were financed by self raised funds alone. Data for investment by collective enterprises in that year lumped together self-raised funds and the category "other". As a result, the "self-raised fund" share in non-State investment fell between 1985 and 1994.

The centralized channel for allocating capital goods has been gradually replaced by the market, increasing direct access to those goods by enterprises. For instance, the number of categories of capital goods under State pricing control was reduced from 700 in the pre-reform period to about 30 in 1994, and the number of capital goods under direct State allocation was reduced from 250 to about 10 over the same period.

With those reforms in the investment system, combined with an expansion of the non-State sector (see below), the demand for fixed investment in the post-reform period has become increasingly less determined by central planning and increasingly more determined by local governments, enterprises and individuals. However, the decentralization of investment decisions has not been complemented by increased financial accountability of SOEs, and thus has not created incentives for local governments and State enterprises to take sufficiently into account investment risks and the cost of capital in their decision making. As a result, the demand for investment in the SOE sector is constrained only by the availability of funds.

On the supply side, the increasing investment rate has been accommodated by the high rate of domestic savings. The gross domestic saving ratio was estimated to be about 35 per cent of GDP in the post-reform period, with a slight upward trend. As household income rose, domestic savings shifted from the Government to households in the same period. Moreover, a rapidly developing financial sector that is more active than the old mono-bank system helped to mobilize household savings more effectively. It is also significant that with the share of household savings increasing dramatically and the share of Government savings declining, the supply of financing has also become greatly decentralized.

Accompanying the acceleration in domestic investment has been the increase in foreign investment in China. Attracted by China's high rate of economic growth and its potentially vast market, and encouraged by the preferential treatment accorded by China's open-door policies, foreign capital inflows have surged in recent years. In 1994, the total foreign capital inflow reached

$43 billion, of which 80 per cent was direct foreign investment. The development experience of the coastal provinces, where most foreign capital has been concentrated, suggests that domestic investment and foreign investment have complemented each other. Indeed, some domestic investment has been directly tied to foreign investment in the form of joint-venture projects. As a source of investment financing, foreign investment accounted for roughly 15 per cent of total investment in 1994.

The fact that the rapid economic growth in the post-reform era has been largely accompanied by an increasing investment ratio and that the investment ratio has reached such a high level have naturally led analysts to question the sustainability of such performance in the future. Limited by the infeasibility of further increases in the investment ratio, future growth will have to rely more on improvement in the quality or efficiency of investment. However, because of the low level of efficiency of investment in the SOE sector and the low likelihood of radical reform of the sector in the near term, efficiency improvement in the rapidly growing non-State sector becomes the main focus of analysis.

Investment by non-State entities

Since the onset of economic reforms, the non-State sector[94] has been growing rapidly in China. The share of the non-State sector in total industrial output reached 66 per cent by 1994, compared to 24 per cent in 1980. During the period 1984-1994, the growth rate of China's total industrial output averaged 18 per cent per annum, while that of SOEs averaged only 8 per cent per annum.

Policy reforms have greatly facilitated the development of the non-State sector. The gradual decentralization of enterprise decision-making regarding production, distribution and pricing of a growing group of products has allowed non-State firms to supply and obtain capital goods and materials outside the State plan. Financial reforms have also created a commercial banking system and other non-bank financial institutions that have provided the non-State sector with greater access to financial resources. Rural reforms have released a large number of peasants from farming, thus generating readily available labour for employment in non-State enterprises. Rising rural income has not only created a demand for products of non-State enterprises but has also provided a pool of savings that can be tapped into via rural credit cooperatives or informal arrangements. Furthermore, fiscal decentralization has created financial incentives for local governments to foster the development of urban collectives as well as township and village enterprises, which form the base of an important part of their revenues. The change in development strategy that has accompanied economic reforms, relying less on the direct role of the central Government, has also created a favourable environment for the growth of the non-State sector.

Although national data on the sectoral break-down of investment by non-State entities are not available, it can be deduced that most of that investment goes into labour-intensive manufacturing and services. In 1994, in the five coastal provinces of Jiangsu, Zhejiang, Fujian, Shandong and Guangdong, where the share of the non-State sector in total provincial industrial output was significantly greater than the national average (approximately 80 per cent versus 66 per cent), the share of investment by non-State firms in total investment

94 The non-State sector comprises all economic entities under various forms of ownership other than the State, including collectives (some may even be owned partially or wholly by local governments), private establishments and partly or entirely foreign-owned companies (for a more detailed survey of the development of the non-State sector in China, see *World Economic Survey*, 1993 (United Nations publication, Sales No.E.93.II.C.1, chap. VII).

is also much higher than the national average (65 per cent, 68 per cent, 54 per cent, 52 per cent and 59 per cent, respectively, versus 43 per cent). Those same provinces have experienced a phenomenal growth of township and village industries, which engage in labour-intensive manufacturing or assembly of goods, such as garments, electrical and electronic goods.

The dynamism of the non-State sector is also reflected in its efficiency relative to the State sector. Some measures of productivity can be used to gauge the relative efficiency of the non-State sector. Several studies have estimated the growth of total factor productivity (TFP) in China's industrial sector, and have concluded that non-State firms performed significantly better than their counterparts in the State sector. Using both aggregate industrial data (1980-1988) and regional survey data (1980-1989 and 1980-1992), the studies found TFP growth in non-State industries to be at least 50 per cent higher than in SOEs.[95] Relative profitability measures can also be used to compare the performance of the State and non-State sectors for the effectiveness of their investment. According to estimates published by the State Statistical Bureau, in 1994, State-owned enterprises earned Y12.45 of pre-tax profit for every Y100 of fixed assets, while the comparable figure for village and township enterprises was Y20.45.[96] Although definitions and methods of estimation can be debated, those figures suggest that there may be a significant gap between the efficiency achieved by SOEs and that of their non-State counterparts.

The rise of the non-State sector has influenced the volatility as well as the level of aggregate investment. The share of investment by non-State entities in total investment increased (albeit intermittently) from 30.5 per cent in 1981 to 43 per cent by 1994, but with intervening fluctuations. As illustrated in figure VII.7, from 1982 to 1994 the growth rates of investment by the non-State sector were greater than those of the State sector, except in 1985 and during the period 1989-1992, which were periods of macroeconomic tightening in economic cycles that became observable in post-reform China. The cycle in the first half of the 1980s was rather mild (especially compared to the one in the second half of the 1980s), and its effect on the share of non-State investment in total investment was small and short-lived. In response to the overheating of the economy in 1988, however, the Government applied severe restrictions on credit and investment projects to slow down the economy and curb the high rate of inflation. Total investment was scaled back in 1989, and although the central Government relaxed its strict control over investment in subsequent years while maintaining an overall tight macroeconomic policy stance, non-State investment did not recover as quickly as the State sector. In other words, the growth of investment by the non-State sector was disproportionately affected when the Government pursued stabilization measures.

In addition, political developments in 1989 led to some uncertainty regarding the continuity of reform policies that supported the development of the non-State sector, which may have been a factor in the slow recovery of non-State investment in 1990. An examination of the sources of investment finance and the means of macroeconomic control during this period, however, point to more tangible variables that explain why investment in a more dynamic and more profitable segment of the economy was cut back more severely during the macroeconomic retrenchment of 1989-1990.

[95] See, for example, G. Jefferson, T. Rawski and Y. Zheng, "Growth, efficiency, and convergence in China 's State and collective industry", *Economic Development and Cultural Change*, vol. 40, No. 2 (1992), pp. 239-266; F. Perkins, Y. Zheng and Y. Cao, "The impact of economic reform on productivity growth in Chinese industry: a case study of Xiamen Special Economic Zone", *Asian Economic Journal*, vol. 7, No. 2 (1993), pp. 107-146; and, F. Perkins, "Productivity performance and priorities for the reform of China's State-owned enterprises", *Journal of Development Studies*, vol.32, No. 3 (1996), pp. 414-444.

[96] Unfortunately, no similar data are available for urban collectives and foreign-invested enterprises.

Figure VII.7
CHINA: INVESTMENT BY STATE AND NON-STATE ENTITIES, 1981-1994

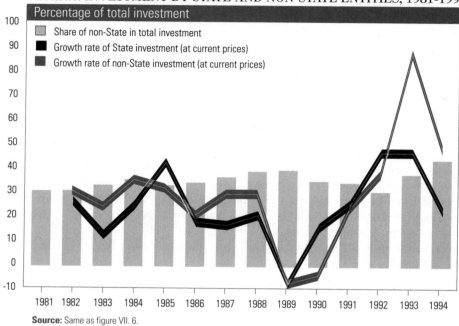

Percentage of total investment

☐ Share of non-State in total investment
■ Growth rate of State investment (at current prices)
■ Growth rate of non-State investment (at current prices)

Source: Same as figure VII. 6.

Investment decisions in non-State-owned enterprises are generally more responsive to changes in profitability, since they are accountable for their financial results. Thus, higher interest rates and credit tightening raise the opportunity cost of funds and deter investment. Moreover, non-State-owned firms are covered by administrative restrictions that the Government still relies on to curb total investment in periods of inflation-fighting, such as tighter control over and stricter enforcement of credit ceilings, and even administrative orders to ban certain investment projects (see below). Non-State firms are more likely to fall victim to such measures, because State banks will inevitably give priority to State-owned enterprises, even if they are relatively less efficient, because such banks are themselves not under full financial accountability. As a result, investment by non-State firms was supplanted by investment in the State sector during macroeconomic stabilization. Because of that bias in credit allocation, the recovery in non-State investment in the years immediately following the period of stabilization was slower than that in the less efficient State sector.

The cyclical pattern of investment growth in the non-State sector is very similar to that in the State sector, the pattern of relative growth rates, which reveals the disproportionate cutbacks in the non-State sector during periods of macroeconomic stabilization, further highlights the inefficiency in the allocation of investment in China in the 1980s. As illustrated in figure VII.7, however, that pattern seems to have changed in the latest round of macroeconomic stabilization, in which the Government has refrained from excessive administrative measures and has employed indirect macroeconomic controls instead in order to engineer an economic "soft landing".

An economic system in transition and the concern about investment efficiency

One increasingly prominent concern in China is whether its high levels of investment are adequately efficient. The overall efficiency of investment can be judged by the resource cost of investment. Using the stock of incomplete investment projects as an indicator of delays between investment and capital formation, and its ratio to total GDP as an indicator of the resource costs of investment, the World Bank found systemic inefficiency of investment in China and a lack of improvement in the post-reform years.[97]

In addition, with increased competition from the non-State sector, the profitability of many SOEs has been deteriorating. For example, more than one third of the SOEs incurred losses in 1994, compared with 10 per cent in 1985 (when structural reforms started in the non-agricultural sector). Moreover, although the share of the State sector in total industrial output declined from about 75 per cent in the early 1980s to 34 per cent in 1994, its share in total investment in the industrial sector decreased much less over the same period, from 85 to about 75 per cent. Those facts suggest a significant discrepancy between the efficiency of investment in the State and non-State industrial sectors, even after taking into consideration that SOEs tend to be large enterprises in capital-intensive sectors.[98]

Nevertheless, the Government intends to preserve the State enterprise sector. One indication is that owing to Government concerns about the consequences of mass unemployment and related social stability issues, the Bankruptcy Law that was enacted in 1986 has never been applied to large SOEs and privatization of SOEs has been kept off the reform agenda, so that efficiency is not the highest priority. As a result, investment in the State sector still goes to loss-making firms. The overall quality of investment at the national level is thus dragged down by the continued investment in an increasing number of inefficient firms in the State sector.

That is not to say that reforms of the SOEs have not been attempted, but reform programmes mounted in the 1980s to create market-like incentives for SOEs to operate more efficiently did not fundamentally improve their overall economic performance. Moreover, while reforms in the formal investment system have contributed to the strong increase in investment demand in the post-reform period, there have also been weaknesses. In particular, the decentralization of investment decision-making has not been accompanied by increased financial accountability. The replacement of most budgetary financing of investment by planned bank-loan financing did not automatically enhance the link between investment and the cost of capital either, because of the incomplete nature of reforms in the financial system as well as in the State enterprise sector. Today, reform plans for the SOEs focus on the separation of the role of the State as owner from its role as manager of the enterprises by converting SOEs into share-holding corporations; so far, however, no fundamental change has been made in enterprise governance that would increase the financial accountability of SOEs.

[97] See World Bank, *China: public investment and finance*, Report No. 14540-CHA (October 1995), pp.40-42.

[98] See ibid. and the *Statistical Yearbook of China*, according to which capital efficiency of the SOEs - as measured by the ratio of original value of fixed assets over net output - has been significantly higher than that of the non-State sector in every one of 40 industrial subsectors.

The financial sector is itself a special case of State-owned enterprises. Although there have been significant reforms in the banking system, they have yet to create competition or the commercialization of State banks. The pre-reform mono-bank system has been transformed into a system currently consisting of one central bank, four specialized State banks, about 10 commercial banks, thousands of credit cooperatives and hundreds of non-banking financial institutions. Until recently, the whole financial sector was subject to credit plans and credit ceilings determined by the central Government based on its investment priorities. Some indirect policy instruments, such as a discount rate, reserve requirements and money-market operations, have been newly created. However, all interest rates on deposits and loans have been set by central authorities that establish a narrow band within which banks can adjust their rates. As a result, the granting of investment loans and interest charges are not determined by the banks solely based on a profitability assessment of investment projects.

As has been learned in the case of the transition economies discussed in chapter VI above, unless enterprises bear the consequences of their investment decisions, the demand for investment will not be responsive to market conditions. Thus, enterprise reform that will improve enterprise governance and change the incentive structure is necessary in order to alter demand for investment at the enterprise level. And unless banks have the autonomy to make loans based on their evaluation of the profitability of projects, fund allocations for investment will remain inefficient. Therefore, reforms of the banking sector that will guarantee such independence and accountability of commercial banks are an integral part of an effort to improve investment efficiency.

Recognizing the importance of improving the quality of investment in sustaining long-term economic growth, the Government of China announced a new reform programme for the investment system in 1994, under which all investment projects are to be divided into three categories: projects with social benefits or of a non-profit nature, such as education, sciences, culture etc.; large infrastructure projects; and commercial (competitive) projects. Investment in the first category will continue to be financed by the budget. Investment in the second category will still be controlled by the Government but will be financed by newly established State policy banks. Investment in the last category, which will make up a large share of total investment, will be financed mainly by commercial banks, non-bank financial institutions and the capital market. Investment without funding from the State, including official borrowing abroad, will only need to be registered with the State Planning Commission; no approval by the Commission is required. Banks and enterprises will bear the full risk of investment projects.

CONCLUSION

The case studies presented above have analysed the most salient issues in the long-term growth of investment gleaned from the experiences of developing countries since the 1980s. Investment has been inextricably linked to the process of structural adjustment and economic reform. It was thought valuable, therefore, to examine the actual experience of individual countries so as to enhance understanding of the forces that shaped investment in that period. A number of patterns have emerged, and are described below.

Structural adjustment and changing role of Government

Investment decisions reflect a positive assessment by a rational economic agent of the future state of the economy. An adverse economic environment that is expected to generate negative results in investments will deter investors. The economic environment deteriorated in much of the developing world in the early 1980s. Durable terms-of-trade shocks, the reversal of financial flows, the emergence of the debt crisis in many developing economies, and the recession in the developed market economies resulted in an unfavorable economic climate for some time. The need to quickly regain equilibrium in their external accounts led some countries to adopt drastic measures in order to reduce domestic absorption. The exchange rate was depreciated and imports were severely compressed, adversely affecting industries that were dependent on imported inputs, and output fell in several countries despite the incentives to exports created by the currency devaluation. Excess capacity developed, which discouraged or at least postponed investment. The public sector had to adjust as well, and cuts in public investment rather than in current expenditure were the usual initial instruments of fiscal adjustment. Public investment was reduced in several of the countries discussed above, such as Bolivia and Côte d'Ivoire, thus lowering the overall level of investment in the economy. With few exceptions, the economic conditions in the early 1980s were not favourable for investment.

While the external balances of many developing economies had improved by the mid-1980s, adjustment was incomplete in terms of domestic balances and problems of inflation (hyper-inflation in the case of Bolivia), and low growth persisted. The servicing of the external debt had become too burdensome, and several countries started to build up arrears on their debt payments. Moreover, an additional terms-of-trade shock was inflicted on the developing economies (Bolivia in 1985; Côte d'Ivoire, Indonesia and Tunisia in 1986), revealing that the economic vulnerabilities of the early 1980s had not been adequately addressed and that most of those economies were suffering not from a liquidity problem but from more deeply rooted structural problems. The need for a more comprehensive policy change emerged in the mid-1980s in many developing countries, and it marked the beginning of a period of deepening policy reforms.[99]

The general thrust of the reforms launched in the second half of the last decade was the creation of a stable and predictable macroeconomic environment, further opening up the economy to market forces, including a deepening of trade liberalization and the creation of opportunities for the private sector so that it could become the engine of growth. The measures that were adopted varied from country to country, as the case studies have demonstrated. But in general, they pointed to a decline in government participation in the economy through deregulation, the abolition of public monopolies and privatization. The State therefore adopted a more indirect role that was supportive of private initiative through sound policies and the creation of new effective institutions.

Policy credibility and continuity

Besides the complex task of formulating an appropriate policy package that is conducive to sustained growth, policy makers need to send clear signals to

[99] Not that changes in policy were adopted only by the mid-1980s - some countries had already started the process of liberalizing and further restructuring and deregulating their economies by then (China and Chile), while others would adopt similar policies only much later (Brazil, India and Venezuela) - but for most of the countries considered here, the mid-1980s seemed to mark a period of deepening policy reforms.

100 As noted on another occasion, policy reforms that appear to be desirable on standard economic grounds will backfire if they indicate doubts about their likely survival. (see "Dilemmas of macroeconomic management: stabilization and adjustment in developing countries", in *Supplement to the World Economic Survey 1990-1991* (United Nations publication, Sales No.E.92.II.C.2), p. 20.

101 E. Malinvaud, "About investment in macroeconomics", in J.P. Fitoussi, *Economics in a Changing World*: Proceedings of the Tenth World Congress of the International Economic Association , Moscow (London, St. Martin 's Press, 1995), vol. 5.

economic agents that the measures adopted can be expected to be sustained.[100] Anticipated policy changes contribute to the "wait-and-see" attitude that private investors have shown in many of the case studies presented here.

Since fixed capital is not easily mobile or tradable, and since the decision to invest entails risks that the expected outcome may not be realized, the investor may postpone investment that is perceived to be profitable if it is known that new information that might lead to a revision of expected profitability will be available at some time in the future.[101] In Côte d'Ivoire, for example, when the Government retreated on politically unpopular adjustment measures it detracted from the potential positive effect on investment of the progress in macroeconomic stability. In contrast, when Governments have demonstrated their commitment to avoiding macroeconomic instability, as in Indonesia and China, it has enhanced their effectiveness. At the same time, it is important to maintain a high degree of flexibility and adaptability in policy-making when policies are clearly unsustainable. Adherence to policies that result in increasing imbalance, such as the commitment to the fixed parity of the CFA franc to the French franc through 1993, have undermined policy credibility.

Changes in Government can also create considerable uncertainty about the future direction of the economy. Certainly, protracted political conflict and instability can have a disruptive effect on an economy as well as adverse effects on expectations of profitability for investment. However, consensus on the soundness and/or general orientation of current policies preserves continuity and reduces uncertainty. Chile is a good case in point: its return to democracy was peaceful and was achieved through a consensus-building process. The new Government remained committed to existing economic policies, while giving higher priority to social sectors, which itself was a result of a new consensus among the Chilean people. Investment boomed in Chile after 1990.

Stabilization and investment

A stable macroeconomic environment, with a low and predictable inflation rate, a competitive exchange rate and a well managed public deficit[102] is crucial for attracting investment. Since investment is about results that will materialize in the future, if uncertainties surrounding the major determining economic variables are reduced and the behavior of those variables can be anticipated with some degree of confidence, then the decision of economic agents to invest is facilitated. Econometric analyses have consistently shown the positive and statistically significant effect of macroeconomic stability on investment. More recently, there have been some changes in the perception that stabilization will automatically lead to increased private investment and growth. It has been argued that in many countries, macroeconomic adjustment has not improved the response of private investment and that even in countries that have made substantial progress in correcting imbalances and restoring profitability – often through drastic cuts in real wages – the effect on private investment has been weak and slow to appear.[103] That observation affirms that investment decisions are actually influenced by an array of factors, macroeconomic stability being one of them. In fact, the revitalization of private investment after successful stabilization is still dependent, among other things, on the improvement of investment profitability and access to investment opportunities and financing, as discussed below.

102 M. T. Hadjimichael and others, "Sub-Saharan Africa: growth, savings and investment, 1986-93", *IMF Occasional Paper* No. 118 (Washington, D.C., January 1995).

103 See L. Serven and A. Solimano, "Private investment and macroeconomic adjustment: a survey", in *Striving for Growth After Adjustment*..., pp. 11 and 12.

The debt overhang

Several developing countries entered the last decade with external debt levels that were well beyond the capacity of their economies to service, particularly in a context of very limited foreign financial inflows. External debt represents repayment obligations that were incurred when funds were borrowed. Economic agents must assume that the obligations will be met and that resources to do so will be mobilized. Thus, debt acts as a tax over the domestic economy, reducing the expected returns an investment may bring. In other words, with most of the debt owed by the public sector or guaranteed by it, high levels of external indebtedness entail risks of increased taxation, devaluation and overall policy instability, which do not provide the right incentives for increased investment. Such risks affect not only domestic investors but also foreign investors and private creditors as well, all of whom assume that economies that are facing severe debt problems lack creditworthiness, and thus opt not to extend credit and resources. A vicious circle settles in: growth is reduced, investment is further compromised, the servicing capacity of the economy subsequently deteriorates, and arrears in some cases accumulate, leading to the validation of the initial negative expectations. Some of the economies analysed above have suffered from that problem, which is known in the literature as the "debt overhang" problem (Côte d'Ivoire and Bolivia).

That line of reasoning led to a change in the international debt management strategy in the late 1980s, when a series of debt reduction approaches were launched to covering both commercial debt (the Brady plan) and official bilateral debt (the Toronto and Houston and, more recently, the Naples terms in the Paris Club).[104] The conclusion of debt rescheduling agreements under the Brady Plan initiative provided a boost of confidence for the economies concerned. Other countries, while choosing not to follow the Brady route, have embarked on a strategy of debt reduction by a series of buy-backs and debt conversions that have reduced their debt burdens and helped to channel flight capital and other external resources to their economies in a rather successful way; Chile is a good example of that approach.

Structural reforms and changes in incentives

There is no accepted standard for the pace, scope and sequencing of reform that would result in investment growth, as can be seen in the different experiences of some countries with high levels of investment, such as Chile, China, Indonesia and Tunisia.[105] What appears to be important is the complementarily and consistency of stabilization policies, on the one hand, and of liberalization and reform measures, on the other hand.

For example, when assessing the effect of the devaluation of the real exchange rate on investment and growth, the potential for higher returns for the tradeable goods sector as a result of the resulting change in relative prices may stimulate investment, so that the devaluation of the CFA franc in January 1994 proved to be a boost for investment in Côte d'Ivoire, as analysed above, because of increased domestic prices in the exportable sector and some stimulus to import-competing industries. But by the same token, devaluation raises the cost of imported capital and other inputs, and also increases the local cur-

[104] For an account of the progress achieved by the international debt strategy, see the report of the Secretary-General on the developing country debt situation as of mid-1995 (A/50/379), 31 August 1995.

[105] There seems to be a degree of consensus on the idea that policy sequencing depends on initial conditions, and that there is a path dependence for policy options, in the sense that each measure taken will condition what the next appropriate action will be (see *World Economic and Social Survey, 1995...*, p.68.

106 See Serven and Solimano, "Private investment and macroeconomic adjustment: a survey", loc. cit., pp. 11-30.

107 The effect of higher interest rates on saving in developing countries has not yet been established in the literature. In addition, it has been argued that since private savings are determined by the interaction of a number of factors it has been difficult to design policies to raise their level. (see Hadjimichael and others, loc. cit.; and Bennett, loc. cit.)

108 For a discussion of the effect of liberalization on interest rates, see R. Clarke, "Equilibrium interest rates and financial liberalization in developing countries", *Journal of Development Studies*, vol. 32, No.3, (February 1996), pp.391-413.

rency costs of firms with external debt, reducing their cash flow while the replacement cost of imported capital goes up.[106] Hence, the net effect of devaluation on investment is unclear.

Nevertheless, when combined with a concurrent reduction of tariffs and non-tariff barriers to offset the increase in the price of imported capital goods and inputs, devaluation seems to produce a positive effect on investment, as in the cases of Indonesia and Tunisia. In countries in which reforms are only partially implemented and import restrictions are still extensive, tariff exemptions and reductions granted to selected sectors have been effective in reducing the cost of imported inputs, as in China and Indonesia.

The effect of access to financing and the level of interest rates on investment is another example of the need for complementarily of policies. With the adoption of stabilization policies, interest rates have remained high because of policies for curbing inflation - particularly in the stabilization programmes anchored to the exchange rate - or to increase financial savings.[107] High real interest rates are often a deterrent to investment since they raise the cost of borrowing, thus reducing expected returns. Where investment is financed by the firm's own resources, a high interest rate increases the opportunity cost of retained earnings and makes financial investments more attractive than fixed investment.

In addition, the persistence of high interest rates, by rendering borrowers insolvent, aggravated the financial weakness of the banking sector of several developing countries and greatly reduced the availability of bank financing.

Until quite recently, the financial sectors in most developing countries were highly centralized and regulated, and were geared towards funding public investment and other priority sectors such as agriculture, with limited financing for private investors. Furthermore, government-imposed interest-rate ceilings within a context of accelerating inflation produced negative real interest rates and an outflow of funds from the banking system. Private investment, under such conditions, was constrained not by the high cost of finance but by the unavailability of credit. In China, the formal financial sector has been regulated to provide credit primarily for the high level of investment of the large State enterprise sector at the expense of the newly developing non-State sector.

With the easing of monetary and fiscal austerity, banking deregulation and the development of non-bank financial institutions and capital markets, there has been increased financing for private investors, which has had a significant positive effect on private investment in many countries. Real lending rates after financial deregulation and reform have declined in some but not all countries (they have not, for example, in Tunisia and Bolivia).[108] Where real interest rates have fallen, the effect on investment has been positive (Chile and Indonesia). As the development of the financial sector is still in the early stages in most developing countries, there are many remaining distortions, such as barriers to the access of small firms and preferential access and terms for conglomerates or public enterprises (Indonesia and China), which have reduced the efficiency of the allocation of financial resources and of investment.

Public divestiture and stabilization have also been interrelated, but the reduction of public investment has not always led to an increase in private investment. Under pressure to reduce public deficits to contain inflationary pressures, public investment was reduced in many countries. It was argued that cuts in public investment were not completely detrimental for the economy since there had been enough evidence of ineffective public projects that failed to yield expected results. Moreover, since public deficits resulting from excessive public investment had also crowded out private investors, the control of public investment could have a positive effect on private investment. However, public investment can be important in supporting private investment. Synergies between public and private investment have been found: public investment in infrastructure and human capital development increases the profitability of private investment.[109] In fact, as the case of Bolivia illustrates, one of the reasons for the limited expansion of investment activities in the country is the lack of adequate public investment in infrastructure. Indonesia, on the other hand, is a case in which public infrastructure and social development investment was shielded from reduction during the 1986 stabilization programme, when public enterprise investment and other Government expenditures were reduced.

Creating investment opportunities

The deregulation of private investment and the demonopolization of industries have been important measures used to promote investment. While they reduce the administrative costs of private investment and increase the range of possibilities for investment, their effect on investment varies, depending on the capital and technology requirements of the sector. The opening of labour-intensive manufacturing sectors (in conjunction with other conducive factors) has led to quick responses of private investment (Indonesia and Tunisia). In China, as discussed above, because of the extremely small base of private producers, it was investment by the rural collective enterprises that soared as a result. The demonopolization of capital and technology-intensive industries, such as infrastructure and mining, has required the participation of large domestic investors and, to a greater degree, of foreign investors. Chile, for example, has been successful in attracting foreign investment in the mining industries, which has proved to be a boost for private investment.

The privatization of existing public enterprises has been used in some developing countries, particularly in Latin America, to shift investment from the public to the private sector and to improve fiscal balances. In comparison, the pace of such privatization has been slow in Asia, and much of the growth in private investment has been in new productive capacity.

The promotion of FDI has been important in increasing the inflow of investment and related technology into a number of sectors in many developing countries. In most of those countries, the significance of FDI has been not in its share of total investment but in its contribution to investment in specific sectors. Many countries have adopted a more liberal foreign investment legislation, under which the foreign investor is given rights comparable to those enjoyed by the domestic investor: profit and capital repatriation have been guaranteed after certain minimum periods, and areas that were once closed to foreign private initiatives have been opened. Access to large domestic markets, such as in Indonesia and China, is also a major attraction. In addition, increased access through the host country to international markets, through regional trade agreements or access to developed economy import quotas (such as garment quotas for Bangladesh, see box III.1), as well as growing regional economic integration (China and Indonesia), have been shown to stimulate foreign investment.

[109] See Supplement to the World Economy Survey 1990-1991...

VIII INVESTMENT IN POST-CONFLICT SITUATIONS

Investment is particularly important for economies that are emerging from civil war, domestic chaos or other political turmoil. The public infrastructure, farms and factories are likely to have suffered from years of damage or neglect. At the very least, expenditure on national security will have crowded out public investment and even basic maintenance. In addition, private investment will have suffered from capital flight because of the natural tendency of local and foreign entrepreneurs to seek safe havens for their capital in times of high risk and uncertainty. The key question for policy makers is how to undertake and encourage the necessary investment in an economic and political environment that is still delicate.

The present chapter examines four countries that are in the process of transformation from societies of conflict to societies of peace and democracy. In two of the countries — Cambodia and El Salvador — that transformation has come after more than a decade of civil war, with considerable loss of human life. The other two countries — Haiti and South Africa — are undergoing a transition to democracy after enduring years of political turmoil, along with the burden of international sanctions. The authors believe that the experience of those four countries embodies lessons for other countries that are currently facing — or will face in the future — the welcome but difficult transition from civil strife to civil peace.

CAMBODIA: FIRST PUBLIC, THEN PRIVATE INVESTMENT

With the overthrow of the Government in 1970, Cambodia entered a state of civil war. Its economy and people suffered greatly.[1] More than 20 years later, Cambodia was still devastated, with a destabilized society. Government expenditure was highly concentrated on military activities as a result of continuing conflict. But Cambodia had also developed a legacy of dependency on foreign donors for balance-of-payments support and government budgetary aid.

Economic policy had changed radically under the rule of the Khmer Rouge (1975-1978). Money was abolished and all forms of financial institutions and transactions were banned. The country also lost a large portion of its literate population, both on the "killing fields" and through emigration.

Under the subsequent Government, money was reintroduced in 1980 and a mono-bank system (typical of centrally planned economies) was established at the same time.[2] By 1982, Cambodia had formally adopted an economic model of socialist planning. Due to continuing civil war, however, it never functioned well as a centrally planned economy. The Government initiated limited market reforms in 1985, when it encouraged private-sector activities in light industry

[1] Statistics on the national economy did not exist for most of the 1970s, itself a reflection of the economic destruction. Data used in the present section are based on estimates of the United Nations Transitional Authority in Cambodia, the World Bank and IMF.

[2] A mono-bank system consists of a State-owned monopoly bank and its branches. The bank functions as the central bank, while its branches also perform the functions of a commercial bank. The system is a tool of central planning, and it passively carries out monetary transactions to facilitate the implementation of the national economic plan.

and agriculture. Farmers were allowed to sell a portion of their output at market prices above the State procurement price. The private sector was permitted to export in 1987.

Starting in 1989, the scope of reform was broadened, prompted partly by the collapse of socialist ideology and partly by crises in the balance of payments and fiscal balance brought on by the termination of financial support from the former USSR. Faced with large fiscal deficits, the Government increasingly used new money creation to cover expenses, and inflation had climbed to more than 150 per cent by the end of 1990. The official exchange rate of the riel (CR) was devalued by 150 per cent in that year against the dollar.

During this period, State enterprises were given more autonomy and private property rights were restored to allow private production in non-plantation agriculture. A two-tier banking structure consisting of the central bank and commercial banks was introduced in 1989. Joint ventures between the State and private sectors were legalized, and a foreign investment law was passed in 1989, allowing joint ventures and entirely foreign-owned operations. A privatization programme was introduced in 1991.

Thus, when the peace agreement sponsored by the United Nations was signed in Paris in October 1991, Cambodia was already moving away from central planning. But reconstruction of the country did not begin until peace was established; in that sense, the transition from conflict to peace coincided with the transition from a centrally planned economy to a market-based one.

The international community became deeply involved in the economy of Cambodia. Because of international concern that one of the four Cambodian political parties might employ control over international aid to its own advantage in the elections that were to take place in 1993, the United Nations

Table VIII.1.

CAMBODIA: SELECTED ECONOMIC INDICATORS, 1989-1996

	GDP growth	Consumer prices	Devaluation of official exchange rate (riels per dollar)	Exchange rate gap[a]	Total investment	Government investment	Non-Government investment
	(annual percentage change)			*(percentage)*	*(percentage of GDP)*		
1989	3.5	..	..	19.0	11.0	1.5	9.5
1990	1.2	..	150	17.8	8.2	1.2	7.0
1991	7.6	150.4	68	11.7	9.4	0.4	9.0
1992	7.0	112.5	78	16.8	9.8	0.3	9.5
1993	3.9	41.0	97	6.6	14.2	4.2	10.0
1994	5.2	17.9	5	1.1	19.2	5.0	14.2
1995[b]	7.0	8.7	12	..	21.5	5.7	15.8
1996[c]	7.5	5.0		..	23.3	6.7	16.6

Source: World Bank and IMF, estimates based on data provided by Cambodian authorities.
a   Defined as the gap between the parallel market rate and the official rate, divided by the official rate; calculations based on World Bank estimates.
b   Estimates.
c   Targets.

Transitional Authority in Cambodia (UNTAC) was given responsibility for the financial operations of the Government in March 1992. UNTAC also coordinated the international aid effort and set in place the basic structure of macroeconomic operations. The World Bank and the International Monetary Fund introduced economic adjustment programmes to stabilize the economy and speed up the country's economic transformation.

The prospect for peace brought financial support from the international community to Cambodia. Aid from Western donors had reached $90 million in 1991, before the arrival of the United Nations in 1992. Estimated local spending of the United Nations Cambodia mission amounted to $200 million, about 10 per cent of Cambodia's GDP in 1992. The sudden injection of demand backed by foreign exchange added fuel to domestic inflation, while helping to slow the rise in the price of the dollar. As a result, inflation remained above 100 per cent in 1991 and 1992, while the price of the dollar increased at a slower pace, which entailed real appreciation of the riel (see table VIII.1), since the price of non-tradables increased sharply relative to the price of tradables.

Because of the overvalued riel and the direct demand of UNTAC, production of non-tradables boomed, especially in the construction and services

Table VIII.2

CAMBODIA: GROWTH OF GDP BY INDUSTRIAL ORIGIN, 1990-1995

Percentage change in volume, 1989 prices

	1990	1991	1992	1993	1994[a]	1995[a]
Agriculture	1.2	6.7	1.9	-2.0	1.4	5.6
Crops and rubber	-5.4	7.2	-0.4	-5.6	-5.8	
Rice	-2.9	-4.0	-1.9	-5.5	-11.1	
Other crops and rubber	-10.0	29.9	2.0	-5.7	2.0	
Livestock	5.6	1.2	6.9	6.3	3.1	
Fishing	31.9	8.9	-5.9	-5.5	0.0	
Forestry	15.0	24.6	15.3	-0.2	50.5	
Industry	-2.2	8.8	15.7	15.0	14.3	9.4
Mining	12.0	7.1	5.9	8.0	5.0	
Manufacturing	-4.4	7.0	3.1	8.0	7.9	
Electricity and water	-16.7	0.0	26.0	6.0	4.8	
Construction	-1.3	11.4	30.3	22.1	20.0	
Services	2.7	8.5	11.1	7.2	5.6	7.4
Transport and communication	-1.5	9.4	15.0	10.0	5.0	
Wholesale and retail trade	-2.2	12.8	15.9	6.0	6.0	
Hotels and restaurants	75.0	42.9	29.5	8.0	7.3	
Government administration, education and health	18.3	0.0	-0.2	5.0	2.4	
Home ownership	2.6	2.5	7.0	8.0	7.2	
Other services	3.3	10.3	9.7	9.0	5.2	
Gross domestic product	1.2	7.6	7.0	3.9	5.2	7.0

Source: World Bank and Ministry of Economics and Finance of the Government of Cambodia.
[a] Preliminary estimates.

sectors, while there was little growth in output of tradables, such as agriculture (see table VIII.2). Geographically, economic growth has been very much concentrated in the national capital and to a lesser degree in provincial urban centres, leaving vast rural areas backward and isolated.

The differential pattern of growth can be seen clearly in table VIII.2. Agriculture, which accounts for about half of GDP, derived most of its growth from forestry and livestock. Rice production, which is the staple food of the population and accounts for a large part of agricultural output, has been declining. Security concerns and the presence of land-mines in the countryside are the two major obstacles to increased production of rice and other crops. The growth of forestry is largely a result of increased timber exports by the Government as part of its effort to increase non-tax revenues. In industry, construction accounts for most of the growth, fuelled by the influx of large numbers of international personnel and government expenditure on infrastructure. Transport, commerce and tourism dominate growth in the service sector.

Considerable progress was made in macroeconomic stabilization during 1993. The inflation rate was cut by two thirds in 1993 and halved again in 1994, while the exchange rate was devalued in real terms in 1993 and then stabilized (see table VIII.1). International aid replaced monetary emission as a method of financing the fiscal deficit. In addition, the elections removed some of the political uncertainty: the question of Khmer Rouge participation in the political process had threatened to unravel the newly established peace.

Since the departure of UNTAC in October 1993, there has been no reversal of economic reforms; in fact, the Government of Cambodia implemented additional fiscal and financial reform measures. Economic growth has been maintained and some confidence has been restored in the country, as reflected in increased investment (see table VIII.1).

Investment in Cambodia

Once peace was restored, Cambodia needed investment in practically every sector of the economy. Twenty years of war had severely damaged its physical infrastructure, and its human capital was depleted. The capacity of the Government to manage the macroeconomic environment and the institutions necessary for a market economy were both very weak.

In the circumstances, financing for investment had to come from abroad, and international support for Cambodia has been strong. At the Ministerial Conference on the Rehabilitation of Cambodia in Tokyo in June 1992, the September 1993 meeting of the International Committee on the Reconstruction of Cambodia (ICORC) in Paris and the March 1994 ICORC meeting in Tokyo, the international community pledged approximately $1.6 billion to rehabilitate Cambodia. Pledges by multilateral and bilateral donors for the period 1992-1995 totalled $2.3 billion, of which $1.3 billion had been disbursed over the same period.

Of the total international aid disbursed to Cambodia between 1992 and 1995, 19 per cent was for technical assistance; 6.5 per cent for investment-related technical assistance; 28 per cent for investment project assistance; 19 per cent for budgetary and balance of payments support; and 27 per cent for food and emergency relief. Aid disbursed for transport, communications, education and health accounted for 29.5 per cent of the total,[3] while capital expenditure in total government outlay increased from 13.7 per cent in 1990 to 35.6 per cent by 1995.

Public investment, mostly in infrastructure rehabilitation financed by international aid, has increased steadily since 1992, enlarging its share of a growing GDP. Public investment also provided some of the necessary physical and institutional infrastructure for the recovery of private investment, which began to respond in 1994 (see table VIII.1).

There is anecdotal evidence that investment by private domestic sources (mostly in rehabilitating the capital, Phnom Penh, and housing construction) and the flow of foreign direct investment (FDI) to the country began soon after the restoration of peace in October 1991. In any event, gross investment (public and private) increased from less than 10 per cent of GDP in 1992 to more than 14 per cent in 1993 and 19 per cent in 1994, with large increases in non-government investment in 1993 and 1994.

Aside from the broader efforts at political and macroeconomic stabilization, the Government took measures to create an environment conducive to private investment. In the financial sector, a central bank with autonomous powers over monetary policy and the regulation of the operations of all financial institutions was formally created by legislation in 1992. A commercial banking sector also emerged. The newly-created banking sector provided an institutional framework to channel savings into private investment in the country.

As adjustment measures worked to stabilize the foreign-exchange market and the gap between the official rate and the market-determined parallel rate narrowed to 1 per cent, exchange rates were unified to the market rate, which paved the way for the liberalization of the current account to encourage investors.

In order to further boost private investors' confidence in the country and to provide incentives for foreign investment, the Government of Cambodia passed a new foreign investment law in August 1994. By early 1995, approximately $2.2 billion in direct foreign investment had been approved by the Government, although the actual amount of foreign investment is not known. However, based on information on approved projects, FDI is concentrated in tourism and financial services, which account for two thirds of the total approved investment. Manufacturing attracted about 15 per cent of total investment, while agriculture received only 3 per cent.

So far, most FDI has come from countries or areas in the Asia and Pacific region: Malaysia, Singapore, Taiwan Province of China, and Thailand. Investors from those neighbouring countries are more familiar with the political, cultural and legal background of Cambodia, and geographic proximity gives them the advantage of knowing the rules of the game, including the informal rules.

Domestic private investment and FDI have been concentrated in sectors with prospects of high immediate returns and in which the investment is reversible, reflecting investors' reactions to uncertainty in Cambodia;[4] a floating hotel and later a floating casino outside Phnom Penh were extreme examples of that type of investment.

Personal security constitutes the most important source of uncertainty. Residual Khmer Rouge forces fight on in parts of the country, and robberies committed by unemployed ex-combatants and underpaid government police

[3] Council for the Development of Cambodia and UNDP, *Development Cooperation Report*, 1994/1995.

[4] An investment is said to be reversible if the entrepreneur can easily recover his assets and exit the industry or country.

forces also pose a security threat. In addition, there is some doubt among residents about the stability of a coalition Government that is perceived to be weak, giving rise to the fear that present policies might be reversed by a future Government.

Unresolved internal security problems have also had an indirect impact on investment through the Government's budget. Because of security concerns, the Government continues to spend large sums on the military and defense (one third of total expenditure in the revised budget for 1995, and 29 per cent in the proposed budget for 1996), which crowds out investment in such areas as the rehabilitation of infrastructure, education and health, which are crucial for the country's development.

The fragility of peace and the complexity of social and economic development in Cambodia indicate that the full transition from conflict to peace and growth will take some time. International aid will thus remain necessary, in particular, to assist in the integration of the country. It is already clear, however, that private-sector investors and resources — both domestic and foreign — can be mobilized in Cambodia and can be expected to commit to longer-term projects as the situation in the country stabilizes further. Public funds and international support in a broad sense are thus an important complement to the domestic political and economic processes that will ultimately determine the pace of recovery and development in Cambodia.

EL SALVADOR: FINANCIAL INFLOW AND INVESTMENT STRUCTURE

Armed conflict in El Salvador is said to date from the end of 1980, but the country had been on the verge of civil war since 1978.[5] A wave of kidnappings and politically motivated murders had continued unabated, even after a military coup by junior officers established a civilian-military junta in October 1979, promising political and economic reforms. At the beginning of 1980, civilian members of the junta changed, and on 6 March 1980 the new junta imposed a state of siege and ordered army troops to expropriate all farms larger than 500 hectares (ha), turning most of them into worker-owned cooperatives. The expropriated farms contained nearly 200,000 ha, more than 14 per cent of the country's arable land. In addition, the junta threatened to expropriate the land of farms measuring 100 to 500 hectares in size, nationalized all financial institutions and established Government agencies for overseas sales of coffee and sugar.

Investment and output were the immediate casualties of those policies and of the armed conflict that erupted between the Government and the Frente Farabundo Martí para la Liberación Nacional (FMLN), a leftist guerrilla movement formed in November 1980 out of the political-military organizations active in El Salvador in the late 1970s. The ratio of gross private investment to GDP dropped from more than 13 per cent in 1978 and 1979 to 6.4 per cent in 1980. Between 1979 and 1982, real GDP fell by 21 per cent and real per capita GDP by 25 per cent.

Over the ensuing years, security expenditures crowded out spending on basic maintenance and expansion of telecommunications, electrical power, transport, water and waste services. The guerillas, in a war of attrition, struck repeatedly at the country's infrastructure, especially telephone exchange boxes

[5] For additional details on the period, see Tommie Sue Montgomery, *Revolution in El Salvador: from Civil Strife to Civil Peace* (Boulder, Colorado, Westview Press, second edition, 1995). For details on agrarian issues in particular, see R. Rubén, "El problema agrario in El Salvador: notas sobre un economía polarizada", *Cuadernos de Investigación*, No. 7 (San Salvador, Centro de Investigaciones Tecnológicas y Científicas, Año II, April 1991); and J. Strassma, "Land reform in El Salvador" (University of Minnesota, mimeo, 1989).

and electrical transmission towers. The authorities were usually able to repair the damage quickly but had to spend vast sums merely to maintain an infra-structure in operation, sums that in time of peace could have been deployed to modernize and expand infrastructure.

El Salvador received a large amount of foreign aid in the 1980s, but its external environment was otherwise unfavourable for a number of reasons: a decline in world coffee prices, higher international interest rates and a break-down of trading arrangements within the Central American Common Market.

The government budget was in continual deficit and its financing by mone-tary emission of the central bank fuelled inflation. That put pressure on the fixed exchange rate, so a dual exchange rate was introduced: an overvalued offi-cial rate in effect at all financial institutions, with strict controls for collecting earnings from exports, and an unregulated, informal black-market rate. Inflation caused the black-market rate to diverge more and more from the official rate.

Although private investment and output grew modestly after 1982, they never recovered the levels of 1979 during the period of civil war. As a percent-age of GDP, private investment in current prices increased steadily from its 1980 low of 6.4 per cent, reaching 9.8 per cent in 1989 and 12.3 per cent in 1991. Public investment was an even greater casualty of war, but instead of a sharp decline followed by a slow recovery, it decreased almost steadily from more than 6 per cent of GDP in the period 1975-1980 to less than 3 per cent by 1990, and remains depressed even today.

More than 75,000 people, mostly civilians, died in the civil war, and about 1 million people, an estimated 20 per cent of the population, left the country. The United States of America was the destination of choice for most, but sig-nificant numbers also went to Costa Rica, Belize, Mexico, Canada and other countries. More than 80 per cent migrated illegally, so that official statistics underestimate the number of emigrants. El Salvador lost many of the best and brightest of its workers: analysis of household survey data reveals 42 per cent of emigrants to have 10 years or more of schooling, compared to 13 per cent of the non-emigrant labour force.[6]

The land issue in El Salvador

El Salvador is the most densely populated country of the American conti-nent, with only 0.25 ha of agricultural land per capita.[7] Land distribution has historically been extremely uneven. At one time, 14 families reputedly owned almost all the fertile land, leaving hundreds of thousands of families landless; access to land has thus long been a source of tension in the countryside. Indeed, the Government chose to continue with land reform despite and to some extent because of the civil war. By 1989, 48,700 former tenants had received a title to the small plots they tilled, increasing to nearly 82,000 the number of families benefiting from agrarian reform and increasing to more than 290,000 ha (a fifth of all agricultural land) the amount of farm land affected.[8]

Numerous estates had been expropriated in 1980 under the initial land reform programme, but for the most part they were sugar and cotton plantations since coffee farms rarely reach 500 ha in size. However, despite the official commitment to land reform, after 1980 the Government did not expropriate the land of the large estates, except for plots rented to landless tenants. The consti-

[6] See Segundo Montes, *El Salvador 1987: Sal-vadoreños Refugiados en los Estados Unidos* (San Salvador, Instituto de Investigaciones, Universidad Centroamericana Jose Simeon Canas, 1987), cited in Edward Funkhouser, "Remittances from international migration: a comparison of El Salvador and Nicaragua", *Review of Economics and Statistics*, vol. 76, No. 1 (February 1995), p. 140.

[7] Population density is, however, much higher in the Caribbean islands and in many countries of Asia.

[8] See ECLAC, "La economía salvadoreña en el proceso de consolidación de la paz" (document LC/MEX/R.414/Rev.1, 29 June 1993), tables 18 and 19.

tution of 1983 increased the 100 ha limit for private holdings promised by the reformist junta to 245 ha, which would still have resulted in the expropriation of a large number of coffee plantations, but implementation of the measure was delayed until 1987, giving farmers ample time to transfer legally —and sometimes also in fact — land in excess of the limit to unrelated buyers and to members of their families.

It is hardly surprising that land also figured in the peace accords, albeit outside the context of a general agrarian reform.[9] In October 1992, as an implementing supplement to the negotiations under the peace accords, the Government and the FMLN agreed to a proposal of the Secretary-General of the United Nations on how to transfer approximately 12 per cent of El Salvador's agricultural land to 7,500 former FMLN combatants, 15,000 former soldiers and 25,000 occupants of private land in zones that had been controlled by the FMLN.[10] The Government was to obtain the land by purchasing plots at market prices from willing sellers. Targeted beneficiaries were to receive plots of 1.4 to 5 ha in size, depending on the quality of the land, in addition to technical assistance and a mortgage equal to the market value of the property. The plots could be located anywhere in the country; landless farmers in zones formerly controlled by the FMLN sometimes received a title to the land that they farmed, but only if the legal owner was willing to sell.

The land transfer has proceeded much more slowly than planned, partly because of implementing delays and partly because of the high costs that are borne by beneficiaries.[11] Land is purchased at market prices, and neither peasants nor ex-combatants are eager to assume the debt that buying such land entails. Although the 30-year mortgages carry a 6 per cent rate of interest and a 4-year grace period, which are very favourable terms compared to commercial loans, the existence of a large mortgage on land precludes its use as collateral for a loan for working capital. In addition, technical assistance and credit have been in short supply, and it is rare for both to be provided at the same time.

With available technology, a farmer in El Salvador cannot support a family growing basic grains on a small plot of land. It has been estimated that as of the early 1990s, 1.4 ha of good land yielded a net income of no more than $270 a year from maize, from which the farmer would also have had to meet his mortgage payments after the grace period, while three to five hectares of land of poorer quality had such a low yield that net income would not have been much higher. Melons, tomatoes and vegetables required considerably more investment than basic grains but might have yielded a net income of $2,700 a year or more for farmers on land of the same size and quality. Permanent crops, such as coffee, citrus fruits, nuts and avocados, promised an even larger net income, but again their production required investment of considerable sums of money and a wait of three to five years from the time of planting to the first harvest.[12]

Moreover, the 12 per cent of land involved in the arms-for-land deal was subject to much the same difficulties as agriculture as a whole in El Salvador. Indeed, agricultural production suffered most from the violence of civil war and has been the slowest sector to recover (see table VIII.3). Agricultural prices in general have been depressed. Small farmers have lacked access to credit and the technical knowledge required to invest successfully in new crops. Large farmers have had access to credit or could invest their own sav-

9 See Graciana del Castillo, "Arms-for-land deal: lessons from El Salvador", in *Multidimensional Peacekeeping: Lessons from Cambodia and El Salvador*, M. Doyle and I. Johnstone, eds. (Cambridge University Press, 1996).

10 For details, see *The United Nations and El Salvador, 1990-1995* (United Nations publication, Sales No. E.95.I.12), pp. 27-29, 257-260 and 443-447.

11 See James K. Boyce and others, "Adjustment toward peace: economic policy and post-war reconstruction in El Salvador" (San Salvador, United Nations Development Programme), May 1995, pp. 43-61; and Graciana del Castillo, loc. cit.

12 See ECLAC, "La economía salvadoreña en el proceso de consolidación de la paz"..., pp. 62 and 72-76.

ings, but expected returns would have had to overcome a number of uncertainties. Evidently, land ownership has been a politically charged issue with important social and economic dimensions in El Salvador. The general agrarian reform that had been set in motion in 1980 had already constituted the most radical non-socialist redistribution of land in Latin America except for Mexico. Another discouragement of rural investment was that some former combatants who were landless and unemployed turned to banditry in the countryside, creating additional uncertainty.

When they do invest, farmers in El Salvador prefer projects with a quick return over long-term ventures, even if the latter promise a higher rate of return. For basic grains, for example, there is a relatively short time from planting to harvest, and production is recovering despite the set-back of the drought of 1994. In contrast, coffee and cotton output is stagnating. Similarly, poultry production has increased, whereas beef production continues to fall (see table VIII.3). It is no coincidence that a chicken reaches market weight much sooner than a steer, and price movements within the agricultural sector do not account for such differential performance (see table VIII.4).

In the original peace accords, it was envisaged that the legalization of the affected land tenure would be completed in 1992; by the end of 1995, however, the process was still not concluded,[13] and the political goals of the land programme had thus not yet been reached. Meanwhile, agriculture in general remained relatively depressed. In other words, despite the political importance of land and agriculture, the economic dynamism and the investment in the post-conflict period has largely been elsewhere in the Salvadoran economy.

Investment in El Salvador

In 1989, while the war continued, a newly elected Government took office promising to reverse many of the existing economic policies (with the important exception of land reform). In 1990, the central bank thus lifted restrictions on sale of foreign currency, and floated the official exchange rate. It quickly depreciated to a level close to the black market rate, but has since been man-

[13] See Graciana del Castillo, loc. cit.

Table VIII.3.
EL SALVADOR: GROWTH OF GDP BY INDUSTRIAL ORIGIN, 1991-1995

Percentage change in volume, 1990 prices					
	1991	1992	1993	1994	1995
GDP	3.6	7.5	7.4	6.0	6.3
Construction	10.3	6.4	8.3	10.1	6.0
Manufacturing	5.9	9.9	8.3	7.9	7.0
Agriculture	-0.3	8.0	-1.4	-2.4	5.3
Coffee	0.5	11.0	-9.6	-6.7	..
Cotton	-38.0	8.8	-11.3	-47.8	..
Cattle	-6.0	-3.0	-7.8	3.0	..
Poultry	6.0	8.7	-4.8	10.6	..
Basic grains	3.8	27.7	0.5	-15.0	..

Source: Banco Central de Reserva.

Table VIII.4.
EL SALVADOR: IMPLICIT PRICE DEFLATORS FOR COMPONENTS OF GDP, 1991-1994[a]

	1991	1992	1993	1994
GDP	112.7	122.6	138.7	153.5
Construction	105.5	147.8	171.4	191.9
Manufacturing	112.1	128.8	149.2	161.0
Agriculture	117.2	105.5	128.7	154.0
Coffee	103.3	69.4	82.8	..
Cotton	133.8	82.9	104.3	..
Cattle	118.4	124.6	130.4	..
Poultry	122.8	120.4	149.3	..
Basic grains	129.9	106.6	163.1	..

Source: UN/DESIPA, based on data provided by Banco Central de Reserva.
a 1990=100.

aged through central bank purchases and sales of foreign exchange in order to maintain a relatively constant nominal exchange rate (between 8 and 9 colones per dollar). In addition, the Government closed its marketing agencies for coffee and sugar, removed price ceilings from basic grains for domestic consumption, and reduced tariffs on imports. Reprivatization of the banking system began in 1991 (it was completed in November 1995).

For a time, the war appeared to intensify, with open guerrilla battles reaching the capital city of San Salvador for the first time in the offensive of November 1989. However, prospects for a negotiated settlement also began to improve.

Due to those political and economic developments, investor confidence strengthened. The ratio of gross private investment to GDP increased from less than 10 per cent in 1988 and 1989 to more than 11 per cent in 1990 and 12 per cent in 1991. After the signing of Peace Accords on 16 January 1992, private investment returned to its pre-conflict level (in excess of 13 per cent of GDP) and GDP growth increased to more than 6 per cent per annum. On 15 December 1992 the war officially ended, and the FMLN was certified as a political party. By 1994, private investment had risen to almost 15 per cent of GDP. Including government investment, the share was 18.5 per cent (see table VIII.5).

Private investment in El Salvador does not appear to be constrained by liquidity. On the contrary, according to one researcher, the country "suffers more from a lack of profitable investment opportunities than from a lack of financing for them. Formal sector institutions have an excess of loanable funds".[14] Since investment has been relatively strong that assessment is clearly an exaggeration, but there are areas of concern regarding private investment, not to mention questions about the adequacy of public investment in infrastructure.

One such concern is the impact of remaining uncertainties. In addition to the effect on farmers noted above, uncertainty affects the rest of the economy as well, with the result that investment is greatest in sectors where exit from the industry (and the country) is relatively easy. Thus, export processing zones, which employed only 4,200 workers in 1989, employed 62,000 workers in 1996, primarily in the manufacture of garments. While that is a very positive

14   See Colin Danby, "Challenges and opportunities in El Salvador's financial sector", *World Development*, vol. 23, No. 12 (December 1995), p. 2145.

Table VIII.5.
EL SALVADOR: SELECTED ECONOMIC INDICATORS, 1988-1995

	GDP growth	Consumer prices	Total investment	Government investment	Private investment	Workers' remittances
	(annual percentage change)		*(percentage of GDP)*			
1988	1.6	19.8	12.6	3.1	9.5	3.6
1989	1.1	17.6	13.3	3.5	9.8	3.5
1990	2.8	24.0	13.7	2.5	11.2	7.8
1991	3.6	14.4	15.2	2.8	12.3	8.1
1992	7.5	11.2	17.2	4.0	13.2	11.7
1993	7.4	18.6	17.9	4.0	13.9	11.3
1994	6.0	10.6	18.5	3.7	14.8	11.9
1995	6.3	10.1	..	..	..	11.6

Source: IMF and Banco Central de Reserva.

development, such investments are easily reversible: those jobs could be lost as quickly as they were created.

An additional concern is whether price signals to investors have been distorted by the so-called "Dutch disease", which can misdirect investment expenditure (see box VIII.1). Dutch disease is the real exchange rate appreciation caused by an abundant supply of foreign exchange, which in the case of El Salvador is the joint result of large inflows of migrants' remittances ($1.1 billion in 1995), substantial capital repatriation and continuing foreign assistance. Recorded remittances of emigrant workers increased sharply from less than 4 per cent of GDP in 1989 to nearly 8 per cent in 1990 and more than 11 per cent in 1992 (see table VIII.4).[15] In the 1980s, not only was the inflow of remittances smaller but its contribution to the supply of foreign currency was offset to a large extent by the demand for foreign exchange for capital flight.

In the 1990s, however, remittance inflows — along with private and official capital — finance imports and are added to central bank reserves. With the demand for imports easily met from the abundant foreign-exchange inflows, imports were under little price pressure, while the prices of non-tradables rose more strongly. The result was the "Dutch disease" appreciation of the real exchange rate, even while the nominal exchange rate remained unchanged.

A great incentive was thus created for investment in non-tradables, including services, residential housing and commercial buildings, rather than in agriculture and manufacturing. Indeed, construction is a leading sector in the economic recovery. The price of new construction, which has a large non-tradable component, has been increasing rapidly, as can be seen in table VIII.4.[16]

The central bank attempted to reduce the operation of Dutch disease by "sterilizing" the effect of its purchases of foreign exchange on the domestic money supply. It sold central bank bonds to absorb money in circulation and raised the reserve requirements of commercial banks, which reduced liquidity, as intended, but merely postponed the inevitable increase in the price of non-tradables, because domestic interest rates rose and attracted an even greater inflow of foreign currency.

The lesson of that experience is that the way to counter a real appreciation of the exchange rate is to address it directly and shift spending towards tradable

[15] Official data overstate the actual increase in remittances, because their increase to 8 per cent of GDP includes the effects of the abolition of exchange controls in 1990. Previously, many remittances were exchanged in the black market and thus went unrecorded (they financed capital flight, which also went unrecorded).

[16] Investors in Uganda, another post-conflict society, reportedly favour real estate over farms and factories because farms and factories are "more vulnerable to policy change than is the rental stream from residential (and to a lesser extent commercial) property" (see Paul Collier and Jan Willem Gunning, "War, peace and private portfolios", *World Development*, vol. 23, No. 2 (February 1995), p. 237). That is not generally the case in Central America, which has a long history of rent control and laws that make it difficult to evict tenants. Rent control in El Salvador dates from 1961; its existence makes the stream of rental income quite uncertain for a landlord. See Tova-Maria Solo, "Rebuilding the tenements: issues in El Salvador's earthquake reconstruction program", *Journal of the American Planning Association*, vol. 57, No. 3 (Summer 1991), p. 301.

Box VIII.1.

POST-CONFLICT "DUTCH DISEASE": THE ROLE OF WORKERS' REMITTANCES IN EL SALVADOR

Strong foreign-exchange inflows are not an unmitigated blessing. On the one hand, they give a country access to imports, which can be used to expand investment or increase consumption. On the other hand, they can depress production in export or import-competing activities, a factor called "Dutch disease".

Dutch disease occurs when foreign-exchange inflows exceed the outflow over a period and market forces then lower the domestic price of foreign exchange. If the exchange rate is not free to appreciate, an equivalent effect occurs indirectly (albeit with a lag) because the central bank buys up the excess foreign exchange at the set price and thereby puts more domestic money into the economy. With more money in the economy, domestic prices will rise, including wages and other costs of production. However, producers of tradables still have to compete with foreign goods whose prices have not risen, so they are less free to raise prices, which discourages their production. That kind of negative effect came to be called "Dutch disease" after the Netherlands faced such difficulties in the 1970s as a result of substantially increased foreign-exchange earnings from exports of natural gas.

El Salvador has experienced strong inflows of remittances, which have not only added to the nation's supply of foreign exchange but have also been of obvious benefit to the persons who received them. In El Salvador, workers' remittances go largely to low-income families, where they boost consumption more than savings or investment. Segundo Montes analysed a survey of households and found that one third of the families surveyed received remittances from at least one relative who had emigrated to the United States of America, and that those remittances represented, on average, 47 per cent of the family's income.[a]

If the remittances were spent entirely on additional imports, increased demand for foreign currency would offset the increased supply and there would be no pressure for the exchange rate to change: the inflow of foreign exchange would flow out almost immediately. In general, if all the remittances were spent on tradables (goods and services that can be exported or imported), there would be no Dutch disease.

But in fact it would be impossible for a family to spend additional income entirely on tradables. Suppose, for example, that a recipient of remittances purchases an imported television set. Only part of the purchase price represents a payment for imports; part is payment to the importer and merchant (wholesale and retail services, a non-tradable) and part is payment of import duties and sales taxes. Even if the Government spends all its increased tax revenue on imports, there will still be increased demand for wholesale and retail services, hence an increase in the relative price of non-tradables (real exchange-rate appreciation), giving rise to Dutch disease. That is an extreme example, however; there is ample reason to believe that a substantial share of remittances in El Salvador are spent directly on non-tradables.

The most important difficulty for policy makers in the face of Dutch disease is in assessing the sustainability of the inflows. If they were only temporary, then the disincentives to production of tradables would inappropriately shift investment towards the non-tradables sector. After the flows ended, the expansion of tradables production would be warranted but the capital stock would have been constructed with another emphasis, making the inevitable adjustment more difficult.

Even if the remittances were deemed a particular source of Dutch disease in El Salvador, the solution is not to discourage the inflow of remittances; the country would be poorer without them. Moreover, unlike loans and direct foreign investments, they are unrequited transfers to the economy. Indeed, policy could well seek to sustain the flow of remittances over the medium to long term. But Dutch disease is the net result of all the flows taken together, and policy might look to stretch out other capital inflows in order to contain excessive upward pressure on the real exchange rate.

At the same time, policy makers need to be concerned about the possibility of an abrupt fall in the inflow of foreign exchange. Such a fall would be more likely in capital flows, whose volatility is well known, or foreign aid, which can be unilaterally cut off, than in workers' remittances.[b] Even so, absent a continuing flow of new emigrants, remittance inflows would be expected to decline only slowly as migrants' links to their homeland became weaker.

[a] See Segundo Montes, op. cit., cited in Elisabeth Wood and Alexander Segovia, "Macroeconomic policy and the Salvadoran peace accords", *World Development*, vol. 23, No. 12 (December 1995), p. 2082.

[b] Elisabeth Wood and Alexander Segovia point out that remittances could drop off suddenly if the United States were to repatriate at once all the Salvadorans living there without immigrant visas (see Wood and Segovia, loc. cit.).

goods. Reduction of maximum import tariffs from 290 per cent to 20 per cent has helped, and tariffs are programmed to fall to a maximum of 15 per cent by 1996 and 6 per cent by the end of the century. But beyond that, the economic reality is that the developments that cause pressure for a real exchange-rate appreciation will also set in motion economic forces that will bring about changes in relative prices that are in any case equivalent to a nominal appreciation.

Indeed, real exchange rate appreciation is precisely what is required for adjustment when the pressures for appreciation are lasting ones. The difficulty is in distinguishing that situation from a more temporary foreign-exchange bonanza, as occurs when there is a surge of capital repatriation mainly into relatively liquid and reversible investments. Screening capital inflows to keep out "hot money" and temper the exchange rate appreciation in such circumstances is a policy approach that has received increasing attention in recent years.[17]

HAITI: A HESITANT PRIVATE RESPONSE

The collapse of the long-powerful Duvalier regime in February 1986 left Haiti with an impoverished population, a bankrupt State and a faltering economy. Between 1986 and 1991, five successive Governments were unable to reverse the situation. Indeed, the economic situation spiralled downward, with a further dramatic deterioration in economic and social conditions after the military coup in September 1991 that ousted the democratically elected Government of Jean-Bertrand Aristide. The international embargoes[18] and the freezing of development aid that followed exacerbated the economic difficulties.[19]

Real GDP declined an estimated 25 per cent between 1991 and 1994. Activity in export-processing plants — accounting for more than three quarters of total export revenue prior to the coup — came to an almost complete halt. Exports fell from close to $200 million in 1991 to about $60 million in 1994, and imports fell from over $400 million to about $170 million over the same period.[20] Output in the service sector decreased in line with the rest of the economy, while the tourist industry all but disappeared.[21]

Central government revenue declined from about 8 per cent of GDP in 1991 to 3.4 per cent in 1994, while expenditures increased, mainly in the form of increases in the wage bill. With virtually no external resources available, the fiscal deficit was financed by credit from the central bank and by the accumulation of external arrears.

Inflation doubled from an average of 18 per cent per annum in 1991-1993 to 36 per cent in 1994 (see table VIII.6), peaking in August 1994 at a 50 per cent annual rate. Inflation was fuelled by the vast increase in the money supply and was led by the increased prices of tradable goods owing to the sharp depreciation of the gourde (G), which lost half of its value against the United States dollar following the imposition of the 1991 international trade embargo.

Against that background, investment fell dramatically from more than 11 per cent of GDP in 1991 to less than 2 per cent in 1994 (see table VIII.6.); both public and private investment fell, resulting in a serious deterioration of the country's infrastructure and industrial base.

With the return of Haiti's democratically elected president in October 1994, the Government launched a major adjustment and reform effort aimed to secure macroeconomic stability as a first step in recovery and sustained development.

17 The literature on dealing with capital inflows that are potentially volatile and unpredictable has mushroomed. See, for example, *Coping with Capital Surges: the Return of Finance to Latin America*, Ricardo Ffrench-Davis and Stephany Griffith-Jones, eds., (Boulder, Colorado, Lynne Rienner Publishers, and Ottawa, International Development Research Centre, 1995); and *Securing Stability and Growth in Latin America: Policy Issues and Prospects for Shock-Prone Economies*, Ricardo Hausmann and Helmut Reisen, eds. (Paris, OECD, 1996).

18 The Organisation of American States imposed a trade embargo in 1991. In June 1993, the United Nations enacted an embargo on shipment of fuel and military equipment, which was widened in May 1994 to all trade except humanitarian imports.

19 Following the 1991 coup, donors froze $400 million of aid that was pledged to Haiti in July 1991; only humanitarian aid continued to flow in.

20 Workers' remittances, estimated to average $60 million a year during 1991-1994 (about 3 per cent of GDP in 1994), helped to finance the trade deficit.

21 Official statistics do not include the informal sector, which absorbed many of the people displaced from the formal economy. Indeed, the informal economy provides livelihoods, however meagre, for a significant share of the labour force; there is no formal social safety net in Haiti.

Table VIII.6.
HAITI: SELECTED ECONOMIC INDICATORS, 1990-1995[a]

	GDP growth	Consumer prices	Exchange rate	Total investment	Private investment	Public investment
	(annual percentage change)		*(gourde per dollar)*	*(percentage of GDP)*		
1990	-0.1	20.4	7.4	12.2	5.7	6.5
1991	-3.0	18.2	7.7	11.2	6.7	4.6
1992	-14.0	17.9	9.1	3.7	3.3	0.4
1993	-2.6	18.9	12.4	3.8	2.8	1.0
1994	-10.0	36.1	14.9	1.7	1.3	0.4
1995[b]	3.5	28.0	15.0	9.6	3.1	6.5

Source: Bank of the Republic of Haiti, IMF and World Bank.
a Fiscal years ending September 30.
b Preliminary estimate.

That effort was supported by the financial and technical assistance of the international community in the context of the Emergency Economic Recovery Programme (EERP) that was agreed with the Government in January 1995. Specific measures implemented by the Government included the abrogation of quantitative restrictions on imports; the reduction of tariffs; the elimination of the requirement that exporters surrender 40 per cent of their export receipts; the suspension of subsidies; the suspension of ceilings on interest rates; and the extension of the sales tax to banking services. The privatization of several State enterprises, another component of EERP, was postponed in 1995.

Meanwhile, donors' assistance helped to eliminate $82 million of arrears to multilateral agencies, clearing the way for emergency lending by IDB, IMF and the World Bank. In May 1995, Haiti reached a rescheduling agreement with its Paris Club creditors on concessional terms, eliminating the remaining external payments arrears to bilateral creditors. In addition, multilateral agencies and bilateral donors committed $1.7 billion for the period 1995-2000 to finance the economic recovery programme;[22] about one third of the funds were projected to be disbursed by the end of 1995.[23] Most of the funds went to balance-of-payments support; humanitarian assistance; and governance, including reform of the justice system, electoral support and modernization of public administration. Virtually no funds have yet been disbursed in support of the private sector, such as industrial restructuring or assistance to small credit institutions, and only limited amounts have been directed towards infrastructure.

By the end of the 1994-1995 fiscal year (September 1995), the stabilization programme was showing results: inflation had declined to an annual rate of 28 per cent from 36 per cent the previous year; tax revenue had increased from $59 million to $150 million, equivalent to 8 per cent of GDP, a great improvement if low by regional standards; and foreign-exchange reserves had surged to $121 million, quadrupling from the previous year and covering two and a half months of imports. In addition, GDP in the second half of 1995 recorded growth for the first time in five years. The expansion had been fuelled by an increase in government expenditure from $121 million in fiscal 1994 to $279 million in fiscal 1995, funded largely by foreign assistance. In addition,

22 An initial amount of $1.2 billion was increased to $1.7 billion by August 1995.

23 Based on Wendeline De Zan, "Haiti: donor commitment/disbursement estimates" (World Bank), mimeo, October 1995; the author's projections for disbursements in 1995, however, appear to have been over-optimistic.

spending by the United Nations mission and foreign aid missions boosted consumption and investment.

Nevertheless, financing of the fiscal deficit by the central bank, which had almost ceased in the first half of the 1994-1995 fiscal year, resumed later in the year due to an unexpected suspension in external financing.[24] However, the central bank was able to contain the new inflationary pressures and avoid excessive nominal devaluation of the gourde by "sterilizing" the deficit financing; that is, it sold a large amount of its foreign-exchange reserves (about $22 million between September and December 1995) and absorbed the unplanned additions to the money supply.

But that action has left the central bank in a difficult situation. The fiscal deficit is quite large — more than 7 per cent of GDP — so that its further monetization is likely to renew inflationary pressures unless an inflow of international aid or private capital replenishes the foreign-exchange reserves of the central bank.

The domestic financial system

The Haitian financial system consists of a central bank; 11 commercial banks; two mortgage banks; a private development foundation; and a wide-range of cooperatives, credit unions, farmers associations and non-governmental organizations. What the system does not do very well, however, is match small investors with appropriate investment funds, particularly in the agricultural sector.

The commercial banking system is relatively recent, dating from the 1970s; two of them — Banque Nationale de Credit and Banque Populaire Haitienne — are government-owned but targeted for privatization, while three others are branches of international banks.

With few exceptions, Haitian banks are very risk-averse and tend to limit lending to a small group of well-known, highly collaterized clients, even though they now have a large amount of deposits. As shown in table VIII.7, in September 1995 total deposits of commercial and mortgage banks amounted to G 9.3 billion (approximately $620 million), or about 30.4 per cent of GDP, the highest ratio in six years. At the same time, total loans outstanding were G 4.1 billion ($273 million), or only 34.3 per cent of total bank assets, down from 52.6 per cent in 1990. Cash accounts represented a hefty 52.5 per cent of total assets in September 1995, albeit down from 57.2 per cent the previous year.

Only three banks have agencies outside Port-au-Prince, an urban bias reflecting a preference for commerce and manufacturing, with agriculture receiving only a marginal share of loans, or an average less than 2 per cent of total loans in the period 1989-1994. That phenomenon can partly be explained by insecure land tenure in the agricultural sector, an issue that the Government is now seeking to address (see below). But effective rural lending also requires an outreach capability that is costly given the small size of most land-holdings, so that bankers prefer urban property and foreign-exchange deposits to guarantee loan repayment. Potential borrowers without such collateral have no access to bank credit.

The needs of rural small and medium-sized businesses are almost entirely provided by non-bank financial intermediaries. Many of them report demands

[24] Agreement with multilateral financial institutions on a structural adjustment credit of over $100 million, conditional on the implementation of reforms in State enterprises and public administration, was delayed for several months.

Table VIII.7.
HAITI: MAIN INDICATORS OF THE BANKING SYSTEM, 1990-1995[a]

Millions of gourdes						
	1990	1991	1992	1993	1994	1995[b]
Net loans to the private sector	1 763	2 118	2 239	2 833	2 999	4 127
Total assets	3 352	4 480	5 554	7 663	8 877	12 048
Total deposits	3 753	3 492	4 029	5 382	6 524	9 311
Memo items						
Ratio of loans to assets[c]	52.6	47.3	40.3	37.0	33.8	34.3
Ratio of deposits to GDP[c]	21.7	20.5	24.0	27.9	27.5	30.4

Source: Bank of the Republic of Haiti.
[a] Including all commercial banks, one savings bank and one mortgage bank; fiscal years ending 30 September.
[b] Preliminary estimate.
[c] Percentage.

that they cannot satisfy in the communities in which they operate. Some are non-governmental organizations, and current legislation prevents them from mobilizing savings, so that the scope of their operations depends on donor assistance.

Haitian bankers cite the uncertain political and economic climate, the absence of a functioning legal system, and government intervention — in particular the high reserve requirements — as the primary reasons that they do not pursue new clients. Yet interest rate ceilings were eliminated in May 1995, and there is a large spread between the average interest rate paid on savings (demand) deposits and that charged on loans: in 1994-1995, the two rates fluctuated from 3.5 to 5.0 per cent and from 16 to 18 per cent, respectively. On the other hand, since the rate of inflation exceeded 20 per cent, the cost of credit and the return to savers were both negative in real terms.

For the last 15 years, Haiti's central bank has relied on high reserve requirements to contain the inflationary impact of the monetization of budget deficits. Reserve requirements of about 50 per cent impose a heavy tax on financial savings and continue to be a major constraint on bank intermediation. Only the development of a market for government securities would allow the central bank to reduce significantly the reserve requirement, which is currently the main instrument for financing the fiscal deficit.

Large dollar inflows in 1995 were used partly for imports, but they were also partly spent locally and added to dollar accounts in Haitian banks, resulting in a near doubling of dollars held in the banks to about 20 per cent of total deposits. Those dollar accounts are not subject to reserve requirements, but only 50 per cent of such deposits have been lent to borrowers, mainly owing to a limited demand from qualified clients whose cash flow in dollars would adequately reduce the exchange-rate risk.

Investment in Haiti

Despite the economic progress achieved in the first year of the new Government, private investment has been slow to respond. Aside from shortcomings in the financial system as a financial intermediary, as discussed above, there are three broad reasons for the slow response: continued political and macroeconomic instability, a lack of clear property rights in agriculture and poor infrastructure.

By and large, private investors have taken a "wait and see" attitude. In the first place, although perceptions of security improved following the arrival of the multinational force in September 1994, the process of disarmament and reintegration of the disbanded army of 7,000 people and paramilitary forces was not quickly completed. In addition, considerable uncertainty surrounded the legislative and presidential elections of June and December 1995, respectively. However, the installation of a new President in February 1996, followed by a new Government and the announcement of their policy programmes, should give the signals that the business community is looking for and gradually restore business confidence.

In any event, the long decades of political and economic instability in Haiti have left domestic investors with a strong preference for projects that are reversible at a low cost. Commerce, for example, is preferred to manufacturing or agriculture because it is an activity that typically involves a smaller amount of fixed investment.

In the manufacturing sector, export processing attracted considerable investment in the past; like commerce, it is an activity that requires little machinery or equipment and is thus preferred in an uncertain environment. Firms in the sector assemble a number of products, primarily clothing but also toys, electronics and sporting goods, taking advantage of Haiti's low labour costs[25] and its proximity to the United States of America. A majority of firms are locally owned, although some are of United States origin. By the end of 1995, some 40 export-processing plants employed about 12,000 workers, down from 145 plants and 40,000 employees in 1991 but still on the rise, having closed down almost completely during the embargo period. The Government expects at most an additional 5,000 jobs in export processing by the end of 1996. Haitian authorities count on new arrivals and the reopening of local firms rather than the return of the companies that left the country for the Dominican Republic and Central America.

As in other post-conflict countries, investment in agriculture in Haiti has been restrained because it is almost completely irreversible and thus highly risky in an uncertain environment. An additional dimension in Haiti, however, is that few farmers have title to the land that they work. Haiti's agricultural sector is characterized by smallholdings — which account for almost 75 per cent of the cultivated land — and low productivity. The absence of clear property rights in agriculture has encouraged violent land conflicts and exploitation of land for quick gain, resulting in deforestation, soil erosion, flooding and desertification.

To tackle the issue of land tenure, the *Institut National pour la Reforme Agraire* was created in May 1995. The main objectives of the reform are to reduce the insecurity of land tenure, redistribute some State lands to peasant farmers, bring environmental protection concerns into land tenure reform, and consolidate and rationalize land holdings. Those are issues of high political sensitivity, however: limited progress has been achieved to date and little is expected in the near future.

Haiti's physical infrastructure was poor to begin with and has deteriorated significantly; its inadequacy is an important disincentive to investment. Several

25 The daily minimum wage was raised to G36 (about $2.40) in June 1995, from the level of G15 that had been in effect since October 1984.

large public utilities are financially distressed and fail to provide adequate service. Energy consumption in Haiti is the lowest in Latin America. The ineffectual state of electrical power production illustrates the nature of the situation. During 1995, out of an installed public electricity capacity of approximately 180 megawatts (MW), just over one third of that capacity was available on average, largely owing to the dilapidated conditions of the system due to lack of maintenance. Consequently, only two thirds of the estimated demand of about 100 MW could be met. Private firms had been forced to purchase and maintain their own generators in the face of recurring electric power shortages, which raised their fixed and operating costs. By the end of 1995, however, some improvements were made in maintenance and in the distribution system in the capital, although output remained limited. Power production was expected to increase further in early 1996, thanks to the installation of new generators and the repair of existing plants, funded by foreign aid.

The transport system also suffers from a decade of neglect and requires major rehabilitation. The antiquated port of Port-au-Prince is reputedly the most expensive port in the Caribbean, negatively affecting trade activity. Telecommunications are almost non-existent outside the capital. Haiti's telephone network consists of 55,000 lines for a population of 7 million (compared to 440,000 lines in the Dominican Republic for the same population size); this is the lowest penetration rate (0.8 per cent) in Latin America. Moreover, the quality of service is inadequate. Water and sanitation conditions, as well as the education and health systems, are also highly deficient. The lack of skilled labour seriously inhibits economic competitiveness.

The capacity of the Government to build or rebuild and to operate the economic infrastructure of Haiti is currently quite limited. Moreover, as elsewhere in the world, there is a greater appreciation of the potential benefits of private initiative in contestable markets for public utilities (see chaps. X and XI below). The Government is thus seeking to increase the role of the private sector through a restructuring plan developed in conjunction with several multilateral institutions, involving the privatization of some assets and for others the introduction of private management through management contracts, leases or other contractual arrangements. The plan will probably require a modification of the existing regulatory environment, tariff policies and quality standards. Foreign donors have committed over $400 million to support the rehabilitation of energy, transport and urban infrastructure.

In sum, since the restoration of constitutional order in October 1994, the international community has committed considerable financial and technical resources to the development of Haiti. So far, most resources have been directed towards balance of payments support, emergency humanitarian assistance and governance, including electoral support. As international cooperation moves from the emergency stage to a longer-term approach, assistance for development will take centre stage, particularly to improve capacity for efficient government operations. But the ultimate goal is to recharge the development potential of the economy as a whole, which means that priority must be given to the creation of a favourable environment for the development of private initiative, in the form of both small-scale farms and enterprises and larger establishments. It is a formidable task.

SOUTH AFRICA: POLITICAL BREAKTHROUGH, INVESTMENT INCREASE

South Africa has been experiencing a remarkable political transition from being a beleaguered State under apartheid to becoming a non-racialist, democratic country with multiple economic opportunities, what many in the country refer to as "the new South Africa".[26] The country is also facing an economic transition, and progress in the two are intertwined. But political stability ultimately depends on a more equal distribution of government services and economic opportunities and a lower unemployment rate. Indeed, one of the strongest incentives for political integration is that a major political crisis might drive the country into a violent conflict that nobody wants to contemplate. The goodwill that is created by the need to avoid such a scenario spills over into investment commitments, despite the kinds of uncertainty that normally accompany new political and economic departures and that delay investment elsewhere. The success of South Africa's political transition, the confidence that the Government is able to inspire in its policies and a number of economic factors have combined to bring about a swift increase in fixed investment.

The political transition was secured in 1993, when agreement was reached on a Government of National Unity, which was to be established after the election of April 1994. A Transitional Executive Council was installed in December 1993, which gave blacks a role in Government for the first time in the history of the country, and an interim constitution was adopted. After those developments, United Nations sanctions were repealed by the General Assembly in its resolution 48/1 of 8 October 1993.

According to various indicators, the prospects of a peaceful transition raised spirits in the country. The index of business confidence started an upward trend, and the financial rand started to strengthen at the end of 1992. South Africa had maintained a dual exchange rate, with a commercial rand for current transactions and a financial rand for capital transactions by foreigners. The financial rand had traded at a discount from the commercial rand, reflecting net disinvestment pressures internationally, and the discount had been shrinking during 1993.[27] Consumer confidence also commenced an upward trend in 1993, as reflected in an increase in private expenditures on durable and semi-durable goods, partly financed by the wider availability of consumer credit.

Despite some apprehension surrounding the April 1994 elections, the new Government was able to quickly reduce the level of political and economic uncertainty and gain the confidence of economic actors by, for example, keeping the budget deficit in check and adopting a pragmatic attitude towards privatization. Moreover, the rate of increase of consumer prices dropped in 1993 to a single-digit level for the first time in 19 years, and remained at that level in 1994 and 1995 despite weather-related fluctuations in food prices.

After the April 1994 elections, the amount of politically related violence declined — although crime increased — and in 1995, the number of man-days lost due to strikes reached its lowest point since 1988, while the business confidence index reached its highest level in 10 years.

The financial rand was smoothly abolished in March 1995, after the discount had been significantly reduced and foreign-exchange reserves had risen to $1.8 billion as of the end of February 1995, giving a further boost to confidence

[26] The following draws upon the data and analysis contained in the South African Reserve Bank, *Quarterly Bulletin*, various issues; and Macroeconomic Research Group, *Making Democracy Work: A Framework for Macroeconomic Policy in South Africa* (Bellville, South Africa, Centre for Development Studies, 1993).

[27] For discussion of financial flows to South Africa and the financial rand discount, see *World Economic and Social Survey, 1994* (United Nations publication, Sales No. E.94.II.C.1 and corrigendum), box IV.1.

in the Government's economic policy. Foreign-exchange controls have continued to be gradually loosened since then but have not been abandoned altogether. The business community in South Africa is calling for swift and complete removal of all remaining foreign-exchange controls on residents, but the central bank has resisted because it wants to avoid a sudden and large outflow of resident capital.

In other words, despite the generally positive atmosphere, considerable uncertainty resides just below the surface. Indeed, the value of the rand (R) dropped abruptly in February 1996, triggered by a false rumour that the President had suffered a heart attack and the expectation that the end of foreign-exchange controls was imminent. From the abolishment of the financial rand until that episode, the exchange rate had been quite stable; in fact, there had been some upward pressure in 1995 as a result of large capital inflows amounting to $6 billion, although appreciation of the rand had been partly contained by an increase in demand for foreign exchange by importers of machinery and equipment.

The real as well as the financial economy began to improve in 1993 (see table VIII.8): the South African economy ended a four-year long recession in May. GDP growth was at first primarily fuelled by a rapid recovery in the agricultural sector after a drought in 1992, but growth became broad-based rather quickly and has since been sustained. As a result, the capacity utilization rate rose from 77 per cent in September 1992 to 83 per cent in September 1995.

Exports have been particularly dynamic, stimulated by the recovery in the developed economies beginning in 1994, the improvement in the terms of trade beginning in mid-1992, and the lifting of sanctions. The volume of merchandise exports rose by 22 per cent in 1993 and by 8 per cent in 1994. They continued to rise in 1995, albeit at a slower rate owing to lower gold exports and the impact of a new drought on agricultural exports. The rise in exports has been especially fast for base metals, minerals, chemicals, machinery, and paper and pulp, with sales burgeoning to developing countries, such as Brazil, India, the Islamic Republic of Iran, Malaysia, the Republic of Korea and Zimbabwe. With the exception of Zimbabwe, however, exports to those countries increased from a very low base.[28]

Investment in South Africa

Gross domestic fixed investment (GDFI) in constant prices had recorded an almost continuous decline between 1982 and 1993 as a result of political uncertainty, slow economic growth, the intensification of economic sanctions and capital outflows. But real GDFI began to recover in the second quarter of 1993, although it declined again for the year as a whole. In the initial phase of the upturn, investment was largely limited to a number of large capital-intensive projects and investment by public enterprises, which have been extending telecommunication and electricity networks to deprived areas.

Real GDFI increased by 9 per cent in 1994 (see table VIII.8), with growth accelerating during the year: it grew by double digits during the last three quarters of 1994, and by more than 18 per cent in the last two quarters. Even in agriculture, GDFI increased in real terms in 1994 despite uncertainty surrounding the formulation of property rights to land in the new Constitution

[28] The share of exports to developing countries rose from 12 per cent in 1989 to 26 per cent during the first 10 months of 1995; for more than a third of South African exports, however, the destination is unrecorded.

Table VIII.8.
SOUTH AFRICA: SELECTED ECONOMIC INDICATORS, 1988-1995

	GDP growth	Consumer prices	Total investment	Public authorities investment	Public corporations investment	Private sector investment	Total investment	Private investment
			(annual percentage change)				(percentage of GDP)	
1988	4.2	12.7	12.6	-2.1	-6.4	17.7	19.8	13.2
1989	2.4	14.7	6.5	3.8	34.5	2.1	20.6	13.2
1990	-0.3	14.4	-2.3	-14.8	3.0	0.4	19.6	12.9
1991	-1.0	15.3	-7.4	-11.4	-10.4	-5.5	17.8	11.9
1992	-2.2	13.9	-5.3	-15.4	-6.4	-2.4	16.6	11.4
1993	1.3	9.7	-2.8	2.6	-13.4	-1.6	15.5	10.8
1994	2.7	9.0	8.7	-1.8	-2.1	13.3	16.0	11.7
1995[a]	3.3	8.7	10.4	-8.3	15.2	13.3	16.9	12.6

Source: UN/DESIPA, based on South African Reserve Bank, *Quarterly Bulletin* and other sources.
Note: Investment is gross domestic fixed investment.
[a] Preliminary estimate.

which was negotiated to meet a May 1996 deadline. In 1995, the increase in investment spread to nearly all sectors of the economy. Investment thus seems to be on a very positive track, although in view of the decade-long fall in real investment, the share of GDFI in GDP is still more than 10 percentage points below the high of the early 1980s.

A number of factors fuelled the rise in investment:[29] one was the improvement in the political situation; and another was the rise in GDP and capacity utilization, as noted above. Both factors, in combination with high interest rates, also attracted new foreign capital inflows, and in 1994, when other developing countries were beginning to experience smaller capital inflows, South Africa recorded its first surplus on capital account since 1984.

South Africa had earlier been outside the circle of countries with significant access to international capital for two reasons: the international sanctions and the residual effects of a debt crisis. South Africa had entered into its debt crisis when in September 1985 the Government announced that it would not repay principal on about half of its debt to foreign commercial banks (the so-called debt standstill). In September 1993, however, an agreement with its commercial creditors was reached on a final rescheduling of the outstanding debt. Under previous arrangements, South Africa repaid part of the frozen debt and continued to meet all its obligations on the debt outside the moratorium. Consequently, indicators of debt burden have all decreased substantially since 1985, and since 1992 South Africa has enjoyed a ratio of debt service to exports of about 10 per cent.

Another factor in the increase in investment has been Government policy to encourage particular types or locations of investment. For example, tax incentives have been offered for very large, capital-intensive projects. Section 37e of the Income Tax Act (valid until September 1993) was intended to encourage investment, by way of capital depreciation allowances, in projects aimed at adding value to primary commodities; in 1992 alone, investments worth R 11 billion ($3.9 billion) were approved for such projects which were also assisted

[29] For a statistical analysis of investment, see M. F. Bleaney, "Political uncertainty and private investment in South Africa", *The South African Journal of Economics*, vol. 62, No. 3 (September 1994), pp. 188-197 and Jonathan Garner, "Determinants of recent direct investment flows to South Africa", *Research Paper*, No. 8 (London, LSE Centre for the Study of the South African Economy and International Finance, November 1993).

by tariffs and subsidized inputs, such as electricity.

Construction on a number of those capital-intensive projects began in 1993 and 1994. For instance, the Alusaf aluminium smelter and the Columbus stainless steel mill together accounted for R 8.5 billion, approximately 12.5 per cent of GDFI in 1994. The projects typically entailed joint arrangements between one of the large South African conglomerates and the Industrial Development Corporation of South Africa Limited (IDC).[30]

Another driving force behind the investment revival has been the policy of the Government to invest in infrastructure in deprived areas. The Reconstruction and Development Programme (RDP) of the new Government focuses on a number of areas, such as health care, education, housing, telecommunications, electrification and water, in order to alleviate poverty, reduce inequality and rectify the apartheid legacy.[31] One of the more successful aspects of RDP is electrification. The State-owned electricity company ESKOM, which has excess generating capacity, electrified about 750,000 homes in the period from 1993 to 1995, funded by its own resources. In addition to ESKOM, local authorities are also establishing electricity connections the exact number of which is not known, which have stimulated the demand for durable consumer goods.

Finally, trade is fuelling investment, and investment is also fuelling trade since investment has a high import content. The lifting of sanctions has created new export possibilities, and investment has been particularly high in export-oriented sectors, such as the above-mentioned mineral-processing projects. Investment is also taking place as a result of increased and expected competition from imports and foreign direct investment.

After a long period of import-substitution policies behind protective walls during the apartheid era, the new Government is committed to a gradual liberalization of trade in order to improve the competitiveness of the South African economy. It has lowered tariffs on a number of products, and has subscribed to the agreements reached under the Uruguay Round of multilateral trade negotiations. The Government is phasing out the General Export Incentives Scheme, which will be terminated on 31 December 1997. A free-trade area with the European Union was also to be negotiated. Moreover, the Minister of Trade and Industry proposed in June 1995 to reduce tariffs in two of the most protected sectors, textiles and clothing and motor vehicles, over a period of 8 and 7 years, respectively, in the light of which significant restructuring programmes have been initiated in the two sectors. Thus, the Textile Federation plans to spend R 3 billion on capital goods, retraining and reorganization, and car manufacturers are intending to spend R 5 billion on new products and modernization in the next five years.

But however encouraging those investment plans and investment trends to date may be, there is a major concern in South Africa about whether they will contribute enough in one politically crucial dimension, the creation of employment. In particular, the employment created in the capital-intensive projects noted above has been relatively small even when direct and indirect employment creation are combined.[32]

The Government is increasingly concerned about the high unemployment rate, which was estimated at 33 per cent in 1995. Total employment declined by 7 per cent between 1989 and 1994, with two large sectors being particularly affected: manufacturing employment declined by 10 per cent between 1989

[30] IDC was established in 1940 to finance new industries and assist existing industries in expanding or restructuring, and has been a major instrument for industrial policy of the Government. In recent decades, IDC has been self-funded, and in 1995, it signed an $80 million three-year syndicated loan facility. Some 70 per cent of IDC financing between 1940 and 1993 was dedicated to the chemicals, metals and paper-related sectors.

[31] The shift towards social sectors and away from defence was started by the previous Government.

[32] It has been estimated, for example, that direct and indirect employment creation is three to five times as large in the light, labour-intensive industries, such as metal products and garments, as it is in the heavy, capital-intensive industries, such as chemicals and steel (see World Bank, Reducing Poverty in South Africa: Options for Equitable and Sustainable Growth, (Washington, D.C., 1994), p. 13; for a related discussion, see Raphael Kaplinsky, "Capital intensity in South African manufacturing and unemployment, 1972-1990", World Development, vol. 23, No. 2 (February 1995), pp. 179-192).

and December 1993 and has only increased slowly since then, while mining employment continues the decline that started in 1987.

The Government was expected to reveal in April 1996 a strategy for increasing the GDP growth rate to a sustainable annual rate of 6 per cent and creating 500,000 jobs per year by the year 2000. Among other things, the strategy is expected to increase substantially investment in education, training, infrastructure and the restructuring of industries and the public sector.

LESSONS FROM FOUR CASE STUDIES

The assumption in making a separate study of investment in countries that are emerging from periods of severe civil strife and war is that there are inherent and important differences between the individual experiences of those countries and other countries that have been discussed in this part of *World Economic and Social Survey*. Indeed, while the four countries studied in the present chapter are all developing countries and broadly subject to the same considerations as the six countries discussed in the previous chapter, they do have unique features as well.

Their greatest distinction is the absolute imperative to use public policy to knit together a society that has until recently been torn by conflict and that can return to a state of conflict at any time. The politics of decision-making about policy in such situations means that although it may be harder to attain than in non-conflict situations, a workable consensus is essential. That may limit the capacity of Governments to reach decisions, but then the legacy of years of conflict may also limit the ability of Governments to implement the decisions that they make.

International support seems to have been fundamental for strengthening post-conflict regimes. In the case of South Africa, for example, the genuine warmth with which South Africa was welcomed back into the community of nations not to mention international sporting circles, seems to have bolstered the capacity of the Government to act. But the economic wealth and level of institutional development in South Africa are also unique among the four case studies; in the other three countries, after the elimination of international sanctions and other economic barriers, direct financial assistance has been essential.

In most cases, in other words, the Government's ability to borrow or to tax the depressed income of its citizens is very limited. Aid relieves the fiscal budget constraint, allowing needed current expenditure, especially for increasing local security — and public investment in infrastructure. Some forms of foreign assistance — mine clearance is a prime example — can make an indispensable contribution to returning productive assets to their appropriate functioning, while allowing people to return to living more normal lives. Both current expenditure and investment that serves to reintegrate combatants into the economic mainstream have the double pay-off of yielding a direct economic benefit and reducing uncertainty that the peace can be maintained and deepened. Indeed, it is with that in mind that the United Nations employs the term "post-conflict peace-building".[33]

Revival of private investment in a post-conflict economy is not automatic. Liquidity, however, is seldom a binding constraint on private investment.

---

[33] See Boutros Boutros-Ghali, *An Agenda for Peace, 1995*, second edition (United Nations publication, Sales No. E.95.I.15), pp. 19-22, and 61 and 62.

On the contrary, during years of political turmoil and civil war, entrepreneurs typically transfer their wealth to stable countries, usually as very liquid assets, such as stocks, bonds or certificates of deposit; in extreme cases, they migrate with their wealth. Domestic and foreign investors who have shunned a society in conflict might be expected to embrace it upon the arrival of peace.

Before committing funds for investment, however, private investors not only look for peace but also for evidence of political stability and a climate that is attractive to investment. The resumption of private investment thus depends very much on the existence of peace and stability, but peace and political stability also depend on investment, which is in particular required to create productive employment for ex-combatants. Initially, much of that investment must be public investment, but private investment can also quickly come to play a role.

Macroeconomic stability is also important — sometimes even essential — but is not enough by itself to attract investment. Many decisions to invest are to a great extent irreversible; in such cases, once an entrepreneur commits funds to a project it is costly to withdraw if circumstances change. For that reason, investors tend to invest first in projects that are more easily wound up or moved, or where the short-term returns are very attractive, such as rehabilitation of housing and new housing construction, depending on the situation.

Investors abhor uncertainty — they will either avoid it or act in anticipation of profits high enough to compensate for it — and nothing creates more uncertainty than the possibility that policies may be reversed. Clearly defined property rights, for example, mean little unless there is a high probability that such rights will be respected in the future. Equally important is reliance on clear rules and regulations that limit the range for bureaucratic discretion in implementing policy. Investors expect to know that rules exist and that they are applicable to all firms operating in similar circumstances. The risk of policy reversal is greatest when an electorate is divided and without any consensus regarding basic economic rules of the game. All of which constitutes the political side to the economic policy of post-conflict peace-building.

On the economic side, the overall rate of inflow of foreign assistance, in conjunction with the inflows of private funds, raises macroeconomic considerations; that is, an inflow of foreign aid increases the supply of foreign exchange in the economy. If the flow is large relative to the size of the economy and is mainly spent on domestic, non-tradable goods and services, it can complicate the macroeconomic situation. The local currency will appreciate, if not nominally then at least in real terms through inflation. Private investment will then be directed excessively toward the production of non-tradables, particularly residential housing and commerce, rather than the export sector.

A sudden fall in international aid could precipitate the opposite effect: a sharp depreciation of the currency, requiring adjustment to a new set of relative prices, which would provide incentives for the production of exports and import substitutes. The point is that sharp fluctuations in the real exchange rate raise uncertainty about what the real exchange rate will be and thus have an adverse effect on private investment.

The obvious conclusion is that there needs to be a macroeconomic dimension to the programming of aid disbursements. By the same token, aid levels should be decreased slowly over time, rather than precipitously. As business confidence grows, private savings — some domestic, some foreign — should replace international aid as sources of investment finance, permitting a country's rate of investment to continue to be maintained or raised.

In sum, investment in a post-conflict economy tends to be directed to housing and commerce because of the high profitability of those sectors when large capital inflows appreciate the real exchange rate. Investment also tends to go into easily reversible projects because of the effect of uncertainty. The initial revival of investment thus manifests itself in a construction boom (both commercial and residential), commerce, light manufacturing and assembly (including export processing), and very short-term investments in agriculture (grains instead of permanent crops, poultry instead of beef cattle). The irreversibility of commitments to long-term projects in agriculture and manufacturing makes them more risky. Over time, however, they can also be expected to appear as responses to a combination of price incentives, clear rules and business confidence that policies will not be reversed in the future. The challenge for post-conflict societies is to move from the initial revival of investment to one that is mainly driven by private saving and that generates sustained, sustainable and well-distributed increases in incomes and output.

PART THREE

SOME DIMENSIONS OF ECONOMIC AND SOCIAL CHANGE

IX HOW MUCH DO WE KNOW ABOUT URBAN GROWTH IN THE LATE TWENTIETH CENTURY?

Among the unprecedented changes that have characterized the twentieth century, the increased tendency of the people of the world to live in urban areas is certainly one of the most salient. It is estimated that in 1900, when the world's population stood at 1.7 billion people, only 13 per cent of all persons on earth lived in areas that could be classified as urban.[1] According to current projections, by the year 2000 the world's population is expected to reach 6.2 billion people, nearly 48 per cent of whom will live in urban areas.[2] Consequently, not only has the twentieth century witnessed an unprecedented increase in the proportion of people living in urban areas but, in addition, the number of urban-dwellers has risen markedly, passing from 220 million in 1900 to an expected 2.9 billion by the year 2000. In terms of population dynamics, three distinct types of processes have contributed to the growth of the world's urban population, namely, the natural increase of the population living in urban areas, the fact that urban areas have been net gainers of population through migration, and the transformation of rural areas into urban settlements.

Natural increase results from the excess of births over deaths in a given population. During this century, natural increase has been high in many of the world's developing countries, especially as a result of the major reductions in mortality achieved through better means of combating key infectious and parasitic diseases. To the extent that reductions in mortality occurred earlier and were more widespread in urban than in rural areas, the former tended to grow more rapidly as a result of natural increase than the latter. However, in many developing countries, the decline in mortality has been followed, albeit with a considerable lag, by sizeable reductions in fertility that have tended to be more marked in urban than in rural areas. Consequently, in countries in which the transition from high to low fertility is fairly advanced, urban areas are likely to grow more slowly because of natural increase than their rural counterparts, though actual differences between the two will also depend on the distinct distributions by age of their respective populations.

The second process leading to urban population growth is perhaps the one that attracts the most attention because it involves the relocation of persons from rural to urban areas. However, the movement of persons between rural and urban areas is not unidirectional and always involves both flows from rural to urban areas and those from urban to rural areas. In terms of the growth of the urban population, it is the difference between rural-urban and urban-rural migration

[1] *Patterns of Urban and Rural Population Growth* (United Nations publication, Sales No. E.79.XIII.9 and corrigendum).

[2] *World Urbanization Prospects: The 1994 Revision* (United Nations publication, Sales No. E.95.XIII.12).

that matters and such a difference, which is usually positive, is denominated net rural-urban migration.

Lastly, the third key process leading both to the geographical and to the demographic expansion of urban areas is the transformation of rural areas into urban centres. Such transformation usually occurs as a result of changes in the patterns of settlement in a given location, changes that are often associated with the development of infrastructure, the expansion of productive activities not related to agriculture, or the growth of commercial and administrative activities. In many respects, it is the transformation of rural settlements into urban centres that underlies much of the urbanization trend that is reflected in the numbers cited above.

A wide range of factors contribute to urbanization and there are extensive writings on this subject. These encompass studies of particular countries or urban areas, as well as theoretical constructs that are intended to be of general validity. The purpose of the present chapter is not to contribute to the theoretical and empirical explanations of urbanization, but rather to describe what lies behind the statistical information and the United Nations projections on the subject. This chapter reviews the available data on the trends in urbanization, including decomposition by region and country and by different components; it also explains the methodology that is used to obtain these data and reviews its strengths and weaknesses. Urbanization is a critical dimension of development in every country of the world and the data are an indispensable starting-point for any examination of this process.

ESTIMATION AND PROJECTION OF WORLD URBAN POPULATION

Every two years, the Population Division of the United Nations Secretariat produces a complete set of estimates and projections of the overall number of urban-dwellers in each country of the world. The set of estimates has consistently covered a period beginning with 1950 and ending at different points according to the most recent information available for each country. The projection period, which reached the year 2000 in earlier publications, has recently been extended to the year 2025[3]. The production of a complete set of estimates of the urban population has been made possible by the wider availability of information derived from population censuses, which remain the major source of data on the size and geographical distribution of a country's population.

During most of this century, such a complete set of estimates of the size of the urban population in the world was not available. Estimates relative to the early parts of the century (1900 to 1925) were made in the 1970s,[4] but they only indicate general orders of magnitude. During the 1950s and 1960s, as population censuses began to be carried out on a more regular basis by increasing numbers of countries, the possibility of deriving a more comprehensive set of national estimates of the levels and trends of urbanization improved.

In general, the basic measures necessary to assess the dynamics of urbanization are (a) the level of urbanization, which is the proportion of a country's

3 *Patterns of Urban and Rural Population Growth* (United Nations publication, Sales No. E.79.XIII.9 and corrigendum); and *World Urbanization Prospects: The 1994 Revision* (United Nations publication, Sales No. E.95.XIII.12).

4 See John V. Grauman, "Orders of magnitude of the world's urban population in history", *United Nations Population Bulletin*, No. 8 - 1976 (United Nations publication, Sales No. E.76.XIII.3).

population living in urban areas and (b) the rate of urbanization, which is the average annual rate of change of the urban proportion. Estimates of the level of urbanization can be obtained from information on the total population of a country and that part of the population living in urban areas at a particular time. Estimates of the rate of urbanization require that the proportion of the population living in urban areas be available for at least two points in time (that is, from two censuses).

The procedure for using such information to derive projections, described in box IX.1, results in a logistic time path for the proportion urban that has 1 as a maximum asymptotic value but reaches this limit at a dampened rate. It provides a parsimonious means of projecting the urban population of the countries of the world on the basis of the minimal available information.[5] Although there have been no formal assessments of the accuracy of the results obtained, it is worth noting that when the world's urban population was first projected in the late 1970s using the United Nations method, the urban proportion of world population was expected to reach 46 per cent by 1990, a figure than can be compared with the 43 per cent urban presented as the global estimate for 1990 in the 1994 revision of *World Urbanization Prospects*.[6] Consequently, it would appear that the 1980 set of projections overestimated somewhat the rate of urbanization over the period 1960-1990 in comparison with the most recent data set.

It is important to note, however, that the estimates for 1990 presented in the 1994 revision are based on quite incomplete information. Out of the 222 countries or areas into which the world was divided in 1994, only 136 had information on the proportion urban referring to the period 1986-1993. Among the rest, for 67 countries the most recent information available referred to the period 1976-1985, for a further 17 it referred to 1966-1975 and for 2 it referred to years prior to 1965. Although the countries with recent information included the majority of those with large population sizes, lack of 1990 data for nearly 40 per cent of all countries or areas of the world cannot be discounted as a possible source of biases.

Another important point to bear in mind in analysing the results of the estimation and projection of the urban population is that there is no single operational definition of "urban" at the national level. The United Nations has compiled and published the definitions used for statistical purposes by the countries and areas constituting the world. In most cases (112 out of 222), the definitions available are based on administrative considerations equating urban areas with the capitals of provinces or with regions under the jurisdiction of certain types of local authority. However, in many such cases, the definitions provided are imprecise, as when they refer only to "urban centres", "towns with proclaimed legal limits", "localities designated" or "cities, urban agglomerations and urban communes".[7] In a further 53 cases, urban areas are distinguished from rural ones on the basis of population size and, in some cases, in terms of population density. However, the lower limit over which a settlement is considered urban varies between 200 and 50,000 persons. Thus, there is little homogeneity in the identification of urban settlements. In 32 countries or areas (including all the successor States of the former Union of Soviet Socialist Republics (USSR)), explicit mention is made of certain indicators of urban character, such as the proportion of the labour force employed in non-agricul-

5 See *Patterns of Urban and Rural Population Growth* (United Nations publication, Sales No. E.79.XIII.9 and corrigendum); and Department of International Economic and Social Affairs of the United Nations Secretariat, *Estimates and Projections of Urban, Rural and City Populations, 1950-2025: The 1982 Assessment* (ST/ESA/SER.R/58).

6 *World Urbanization Prospects: The 1994 Revision* (United Nations publication, Sales No. E.95.XIII.12). Moreover, the two sets of projections also differed in the estimates for 1960, the base year, with the 1980 set having a 1960 proportion urban of 33.9 per cent and the 1994 set having one of 34.2 per cent.

7 *World Urbanization Prospects: The 1994 Revision* (United Nations publication, Sales No. E.95.XIII.12).

Box IX.1.
THE ANALYTICS OF URBANIZATION PROJECTIONS

To derive the estimates and projections of the urban population of the world, the United Nations focuses on the ratio between the urban and the rural population of each country, a ratio whose growth rate over a particular period is the difference between the growth rates of the urban and rural populations. That is, if U_o and U_t represent the urban population as enumerated at times o and t, respectively, and R_o and R_t are the equivalent rural populations, then the annual average growth rate of the urban-to-rural ratio is defined as

$$g_t = [\ln (U_t/R_t) - \ln (U_o/R_o)]/t \qquad (1)$$

which is equivalent to

$$g_t = u_t - r_t \qquad (2)$$

where

$$u_t = [\ln (U_t/U_o)]/t \qquad (3)$$

and

$$r_t = [\ln (R_t/R_o)]/t \qquad (4)$$

with u_t and r_t denoting the growth rates of the urban and rural populations, respectively.

The projection procedure used by the United Nations involves the extrapolation of the value of g derived from the most recent data available for each country. It has been found empirically that the most important determinant of the difference between urban and rural growth rates (in other words, of the value of g) is net rural-urban migration and the reclassification of rural into urban areas. Moreover, both these factors point to a similar relationship between the growth of urbanization and the level of urbanization in the initial year. That is, as the level of urbanization rises, the pool of potential rural migrants to urban areas or of reclassifiable rural areas declines as a proportion of the urban population, and thus it is reasonable to expect the difference between the urban and rural growth rates to decline, as indeed it does.

Using the evidence derived from the censuses of 110 countries with a population of at least 2 million, a model for the long-term change in g is derived, in which the final value of g (denoted by g_f) over the projection period is a function of the urban proportion at the beginning of the projection period. To obtain appropriate values of g for each quinquennium over the projection period, a weighted average of g_o (the initial value of g) and g_f is calculated, with the weights adding to 1 and those applied to g_f starting at 0.2 and increasing by steps of 0.2. After five projection quinquenniums, g is set equal to g_f and maintained at that level until the year 2025.

Once values of g are available for each quinquennium of the projection period, the ratio of the urban to the rural population at the end of each quinquennium is estimated as follows:

$$U_{t+5}/R_{t+5} = (U_t/R_t) \exp(5g_t) \qquad (5)$$

so that the proportion urban can then be derived as

$$u_{t+5} = (U_{t+5}/R_{t+5})/[1 + (U_{t+5}/R_{t+5})] \qquad (6)$$

The projected proportion urban for each quinquennium having been calculated, it is applied to the projected size of the total population obtained independently in order to derive estimates of the size of the urban population in each country over the projection period.

tural activities or the availability of urban facilities (streets, water-supply systems, sewerage systems or electric lighting). Lastly, in 22 cases no definition of "urban" was provided and in another 3 all of the population was considered to be either urban or rural, depending on the circumstances.

In addition to estimating and projecting the size of the urban population of each country or area of the world, the United Nations also projects the sizes of specific cities or urban agglomerations. The procedure used is an extension of that described in box IX.1 to project the proportion urban and relies on projecting the proportion of a country's population living in a particular city.[8] Because the growth rates of specific cities tend to be subject to greater variability than those of the total urban population, the city projections are more likely to deviate from actual outcomes than those pertaining to the urban population as a whole. With these caveats in mind, the following sections provide an overview of the current state of urbanization in the world's different regions and of the developments expected during the next 20 years.

Counterurbanization and continued urbanization in the developed world

Developed countries are highly urbanized. It is estimated that in 1995, three quarters of the population in developed countries lived in urban areas and that by 2015 four out of every five persons living in developed countries will be city dwellers (see table IX.1). During 1975-1995, the rate of growth of the urban population in developed countries averaged 0.9 per cent per annum which, albeit low, still surpassed the rate of growth of the total population in the developed world by over 60 per cent. Because of the prevalence of low natural increase and relatively large losses due to net rural-urban migration, the rural population of developed countries has been decreasing at a rate of 0.4 per cent per year since 1975. In contrast, the urban areas of developed countries have been gaining, on average, 7.2 million people every year, a gain that is expected to decline to 5.8 million annually during 1995-2015.

According to the urbanization trends observed in developed countries until the middle of this century, it was thought that the increasing concentration of the urban population in the larger urban places was a natural concomitant of increases in the proportion of people living in urban areas. Yet, during the late 1960s, 1970s and early 1980s, a tendency towards population deconcentration was noticed in a number of developed countries. Berry[9] coined the term "counterurbanization" to denote the process by which the larger metropolitan areas lost population, at least in relative terms, to smaller urban regions. The widespread shift towards counterurbanization was first detected in the United States of America where, between the 1960s and 1970-1973, non-metropolitan areas registered a turnaround in net migration from net annual losses of 0.3 million to net annual gains of 0.4 million.[10] During the 1970s, the population in large metropolitan areas of the United States grew at half the rate of medium-sized and smaller metropolitan areas, with non-metropolitan areas outpacing the metropolitan aggregate.[11] Other studies confirmed that similar developments were occurring in different developed countries, including Australia,

[8] Full details can be found in Department of International Economic and Social Affairs of the United Nations Secretariat, *Estimates and Projections of Urban, Rural and City Populations, 1950-2025: The 1982 Assessment* (ST/ESA/SER.R/58).

[9] See B. J. L. Berry, "The counterurbanization process: urban America since 1970", in *Urbanization and Counterurbanization*, B. J. L. Berry, ed. (Beverly Hills, California, Sage, 1976). Fielding later provided a more rigorous definition of counterurbanization, according to which that phenomenon arises when there is a negative correlation between the net migration rate of places across the full settlement system and their respective population, where places are defined as relatively self-contained functional entities (see A. J. Fielding, "Counterurbanization in Western Europe", *Progress in Planning*, vol. 17, No. 1 (1982), pp. 1-52).

[10] See C. L. Beale, *The Revival of Population Growth in Non-metropolitan America* (Washington, D.C., Economic Research Service, U.S. Department of Agriculture, 1975).

[11] See W. H. Frey, "Perspectives on recent demographic change in metropolitan and non-metropolitan America", in *Population Change and the Future of Rural America*, D. L. Brown and L. Swanson, eds. (Washington, D.C., Economic Research Service, U.S. Department of Agriculture, 1992).

Table IX.1.
PROPORTION OF THE POPULATION RESIDING IN URBAN AREAS, AND RATE OF URBANIZATION, BY REGION AND COUNTRY

Percentage					
Region or country	Proportion urban (percentage)			Rate of urbanization	
	1975	1995	2015	1975-1995	1995-2015
World	37.7	45.2	55.5	0.9	1.0
More developed regions	69.8	74.9	81.0	0.4	0.4
Less developed regions	26.7	37.6	50.5	1.7	1.5
Least developed countries	14.2	22.4	35.9	2.3	2.4
Africa	25.2	34.4	47.2	1.6	1.6
Eastern Africa	12.3	21.7	34.1	2.8	2.3
Middle Africa	26.6	33.2	46.6	1.1	1.7
Northern Africa	38.6	45.9	57.3	0.9	1.1
Southern Africa	44.1	48.1	60.7	0.4	1.2
Western Africa	22.6	36.6	52.3	2.4	1.8
Asia	24.6	34.6	47.8	1.7	1.6
Developing Asia	22.1	33.0	46.8	2.0	1.7
Eastern Asia	25.1	36.9	51.7	1.9	1.7
China	17.3	30.2	46.9	2.8	2.2
Japan	75.7	77.6	82.0	0.1	0.3
South-central Asia	22.2	28.8	40.4	1.3	1.7
South-Eastern Asia	22.3	33.7	48.5	2.1	1.8
Western Asia	48.4	66.4	77.1	1.6	0.8
Europe	67.1	73.6	80.1	0.5	0.4
Eastern Europe	59.9	70.4	78.6	0.8	0.5
Northern Europe	81.7	83.7	87.4	0.1	0.2
Southern Europe	59.1	65.1	72.3	0.5	0.5
Western Europe	77.8	80.5	84.8	0.2	0.3
Latin America and the Caribbean	61.3	74.2	82.1	1.0	0.5
Caribbean	51.0	62.4	70.9	1.0	0.6
Central America	57.1	68.0	76.2	0.9	0.6
South America	64.2	78.0	85.7	1.0	0.5
Northern America	73.8	76.3	81.9	0.2	0.4
Oceania	71.8	70.3	72.1	-0.1	0.1
Australia-New Zealand	85.3	84.9	87.0	0.0	0.1

Source: Population Division, Department for Economic and Social Information and Policy Analysis of the United Nations Secretariat.
Note: The term "more developed regions" refers to all of Europe and Northern America, Australia, New Zealand and Japan. The term "less developed regions" refers to the rest of the world.

Denmark, France, Germany, Italy, Japan, Norway and the United Kingdom of Great Britain and Northern Ireland, though the scale and timing of the phenomenon, and to some extent its nature, differed from country to country.[12]

Despite the expectation that the shift away from concentration in the larger metropolitan areas towards medium-sized and small settlements would accelerate during the 1980s, recent evidence has failed to corroborate such a trend and suggests that the tendency towards population concentration in the larger urban places has returned. The most significant reversal seems to have taken place in the United States during the 1980s, though there is also evidence that the growth rates of the Paris agglomeration and of London have increased in recent years.[13]

Although the causes of both counterurbanization and the return of population concentration in larger metropolitan areas remain largely to be elucidated, several suggestions have been advanced.[14] On the one hand, the fertility declines registered during the 1960s, which tended to be more accentuated in metropolitan areas, contributed to reducing the growth of those areas relative to that of other urban centres. On the other hand, the growing levels of international migration, particularly during the late 1980s, coupled with the tendency of international migrants to settle in metropolitan areas, helped to accentuate the traditional form of population concentration. Yet, changes in internal migration remain the key element leading to counterurbanization and its reversal. The underlying causes of those changes include the new spatial division of labour stemming from the changing structure of corporate organization that has made possible the relocation of manufacturing away from major industrial centres. The successful development of economic activity based in rural areas, particularly that associated with energy resource development, agriculture and forestry, was also a factor contributing to counterurbanization during the 1970s, especially in the United States. Changing residential preferences associated with changes in the age structure of the population appear to have played a role as well. Lastly, government actions regarding infrastructure investment, including the expansion of transportation networks and the improvement of health and educational services in smaller communities; the support provided for agriculture, forestry and rural development in general; and the adoption of decentralization policies and "new town" development— all contributed to the fuelling of counterurbanization. However, the economic downturn that affected much of the developed world during the late 1970s and early 1980s weakened the commitment of Governments to those policies, and their subsequent deregulation of various elements of economic activity and service provision are likely to have renewed the advantages associated with the concentration of business, and consequently of population, in large metropolitan areas.

Latin America and the Caribbean: a highly urbanized region

In 1995, 74 per cent of the population of Latin America and the Caribbean lived in urban areas, a proportion comparable to that of the developed world. Latin America has traditionally been the most urbanized region of the developing world. In 1975, the 61 per cent of its population living in urban areas was equivalent to the corresponding proportion determined for developed countries

[12] See *Counterurbanization*, Anthony G. Champion, ed. (London, Edward Arnold, 1989).

[13] See Anthony G. Champion, "Population distribution patterns in developed countries", in *Population Distribution and Migration, Proceedings of the United Nations Expert Group Meeting on Population Distribution and Migration, Santa Cruz, Bolivia, 18-22 January 1993* (ST/ESA/SER.R/133) (United Nations publication, forthcoming); and *World Urbanization Prospects: The 1994 Revision* (United Nations publication, Sales No. E.95.XIII.12).

[14] See Anthony G. Champion, "Population distribution patterns in developed countries", in *Population Distribution and Migration, Proceedings of the United Nations Expert Group Meeting on Population Distribution and Migration, Santa Cruz, Bolivia, 18-22 January 1993* (ST/ESA/SER.R/133) (United Nations publication, forthcoming).

in 1960. Thus, Latin America experienced the same change in the level of urbanization in 20 years as developed countries experienced over the course of 35 years. During 1995-2015, both groups of countries are expected to follow similar urbanization paths, reaching similar levels of urbanization by 2015 (see table IX.1).

As in other developing regions, there is considerable variation in the level of urbanization of the different countries of Latin America and the Caribbean. In Antigua and Barbuda, Guyana, Haiti and Montserrat, over 60 per cent of the population still live in rural areas. At the other end of the spectrum, over 80 per cent of the population in countries like Argentina, Chile, Uruguay and Venezuela live in urban areas.

Although the rural population in Latin America and the Caribbean increased slightly during 1975-1995, nearly all population growth in the region occurred in urban areas (see table IX.2). Between 1995 and 2015, the rural population in Latin America is expected to decrease, implying that the expected population gains made by urban areas will surpass the total growth of the region's population (see table IX.3). Thus, the increase of urban areas in the region is expected to remain at about 8.4 million persons annually during 1995-2015, whereas the region's total population is expected to grow by a lower 8 million persons every year.

A salient characteristic of the distribution of the urban population of Latin America and the Caribbean is that it tends to be more concentrated in large cities than that of other major developing regions. Thus, in 1995, 20 per cent of Latin America's urban population resided in agglomerations of at least 5 million people, whereas only 16 per cent of the urban population of developing Asia and 8 per cent of that of Africa were concentrated in cities of that size (table IX.4). In addition, 52 per cent of Latin America's urban population resided in cities of less than half a million inhabitants in 1995, compared with 58 per cent both in Africa and in developing Asia. The tendency of the urban population to be highly concentrated in a single city is particularly marked in Argentina, Bolivia, Chile, Costa Rica, Cuba, the Dominican Republic, Panama, Peru, Puerto Rico and Uruguay, where over a quarter of the urban population lived in the capital city in 1995.

The tendency towards population concentration in a single city has been seen as a manifestation of economies of scale that contribute to increase economic efficiency and growth. Such concentration has generally been the result of a number of national policies favouring large cities as the preferred sites for industrial development and as the centres of finance and communications.[15] In Latin America and the Caribbean, the rate of growth of the population in major cities of the region generally peaked during the 1950s or 1960s, when fertility levels were still relatively high and industrialization was being fostered within a development model favouring import substitution. The evidence available suggests that the trend towards fertility reduction first took hold in the largest cities of each country and that, in general, fertility in the large urban agglomerations remains below the national average.[16] However, the reduction in net migration rates that has been recorded in certain large cities since the 1970s implies that natural increase has become their major source of population growth. Indeed, some major cities have seen their share of the urban population decline in recent years.[17] That is the case of Buenos Aires, Havana and

[15] See, for instance, Harry W. Richardson, "Population distribution policies", in *Population Distribution, Migration and Development, Proceedings of the Expert Group on Population Distribution, Migration and Development, Hammamet (Tunisia), 21-25 March 1983* (United Nations publication, Sales No. E.84.XIII.3); and Carlos Antonio De Mattos, "The moderate efficiency of population distribution policies in developing countries", and Economic Commission for Latin America and the Caribbean (ECLAC), "Population dynamics in the large cities of Latin America and the Caribbean", in *Population Distribution and Migration, Proceedings of the United Nations Expert Group Meeting on Population Distribution and Migration, Santa Cruz, Bolivia, 18-22 January 1993* (ST/ESA/SER.R/133) (United Nations publication, forthcoming).

[16] See ECLAC, "Population dynamics in the large cities of Latin America and the Caribbean", in *Population Distribution and Migration, Proceedings of the United Nations Expert Group Meeting on Population Distribution and Migration, Santa Cruz, Bolivia, 18-22 January 1993* (ST/ESA/SER.R/133) (United Nations publication, forthcoming).

[17] See Alfredo Lattes, "Population distribution in Latin America: Is there a trend towards population deconcentration", in *Population Distribution and Migration, Proceedings of the United Nations Expert Group Meeting on Population Distribution and Migration, Santa Cruz, Bolivia, 18-22 January 1993* (ST/ESA/SER.R/133) (United Nations publication, forthcoming).

Table IX.2.
ANNUAL GROWTH OF THE URBAN POPULATION, AND PROPORTION
OF TOTAL GROWTH OCCURRING IN URBAN AREAS, 1975-1995 AND
1995-2015

Region or country	Annual increment in urban areas (thousands)		Proportion of total population growth occurring in urban areas (percentage)	
	1975-1995	1995-2015	1975-1995	1995-2015
World	52 305	77 945	64	89
More developed regions	7 234	5 833	118	204
Less developed regions	45 071	72 112	59	85
Least developed countries	4 008	10 516	34	57
Africa	7 308	15 883	47	67
Eastern Africa	1 698	4 176	33	51
Middle Africa	764	2 041	41	64
Northern Africa	1 821	2 982	57	83
Southern Africa	501	1 021	54	86
Western Africa	2 524	5662	55	74
Asia	30 284	48 029	58	91
Developing Asia	29 649	47 722	57	90
Eastern Asia	12 482	16 647	76	141
China	10 472	15 347	71	140
Japan	636	308	94	723
South-central Asia	10 056	19 564	41	68
South-Eastern Asia	4 546	7 483	57	93
Western Asia	3 200	4 335	92	98
Europe	4 069	2 341	161	-8 917
Eastern Europe	2 322	1 045	202	-382
Northern Europe	279	327	124	189
Southern Europe	765	491	134	-1 390
Western Europe	703	478	120	436
Latin America and the Caribbean	8 076	8 419	100	106
Caribbean	424	478	99	104
Central America	2 065	2 396	86	97
South America	5 588	5 546	106	110
Northern America	2 335	2 946	87	114
Oceania	234	327	66	78
Australia-New Zealand	195	239	83	96

Source: Population Division, Department for Economic and Social Information and Policy Analysis of the United Nations Secretariat.
Note: The term "more developed regions" refers to all of Europe and Northern America, Australia, New Zealand and Japan. The term "less developed regions" refers to the rest of the world.

18 *World Urbanization Prospects: The 1994 Revision* (United Nations publication, Sales No. E.95.XIII.12).

19 See ECLAC, "Population dynamics in the large cities of Latin America and the Caribbean", in *Population Distribution and Migration, Proceedings of the United Nations Expert Group Meeting on Population Distribution and Migration, Santa Cruz, Bolivia, 18-22 January 1993* (ST/ESA/SER.R/133) (United Nations publication, forthcoming).

Montevideo since 1980, and a similar trend is expected for a number of other major Latin American cities during the 1990s.[18] According to recent census information, steep reductions in net migration gains have been experienced by Mexico City, Rio de Janeiro and Santiago (Chile).[19] At the same time, medium-sized and small urban centres have seen their population growth increase.

Asia: a region of extremes

In 1995, the population of developing Asia amounted to 3.3 billion persons, 58 per cent of the world's total population. The region as a whole has a great deal of heterogeneity, comprising as it does some of the most urbanized countries or areas in the world, such as Bahrain, Hong Kong, Israel, Kuwait, Qatar and Singapore with more than 90 per cent of their population living in urban areas, and some of the least urbanized, such as Bhutan, East Timor and Nepal with less than 14 per cent of their population classified as urban in 1995. In addition, Asia includes some of the most populous countries in the world, such as Bangladesh, China, India, Indonesia and Pakistan. These five countries have relatively low levels of urbanization (under 36 per cent) and their weight in terms of population size is largely responsible for producing a level of urbanization of only 35 per cent for the region as a whole (see table IX.1).

Despite its relatively low level of urbanization, Asia accounts for 46 per cent of the world's urban population, amounting to 1.2 billion persons in 1995, a number higher than the current urban population of the developed world (see table IX.3). In 1975, when the level of urbanization in developing Asia stood at only 22 per cent (see table IX.1), its urban population already amounted to 508 million persons or nearly 70 per cent of the number of urban-dwellers in developed countries. By 2015, developing Asia is expected to host slightly over 2 billion urban-dwellers, accounting for half of the world's urban population, and to have twice as many urban-dwellers as the developed world.

The high levels of urban population growth experienced by Asia have been accompanied by moderate levels of growth among the rural population. During 1975-1995, the urban population of developing Asia grew at an annual rate of 3.9 per cent and is expected to keep on growing at a level of 3.1 per cent annually during 1995-2015. The equivalent rates of growth of the rural population are 1.1 and 0.2 per cent, respectively. Thus, although Asia's rural population is expected to keep on growing well into the twenty-first century, a significant decline in its rate of growth is expected. Nevertheless, by 2015 the rural population of developing Asia is still expected to exceed that in urban areas by about 14 per cent or over 280 million persons, despite the fact that China is likely to experience a reduction in its rural population of about 87 million persons over the next 20 years.

The sizeable difference between the rate of growth of the urban population and that of the rural population of Asia is translated into a moderately high rate of growth in the urban share of population. Thus, during 1975-2015 developing Asia is expected to record the highest rate of urbanization among the major world regions, amounting to 1.9 per cent per year. Such an urbanization rate implies that the proportion of the population living in urban areas in developing Asia will more than double between 1975 and 2015, passing from 22 to 47 per cent.

Table IX.3.
TOTAL, URBAN AND RURAL POPULATION OF MAJOR AREAS AND SELECTED COUNTRIES IN THE WORLD

Millions

Region or country	Total population			Urban population			Rural population		
	1975	1995	2015	1975	1995	2015	1975	1995	2015
World	4 077	5 716	7 469	1 538	2 584	4 143	2 539	3 132	3 326
More developed regions	1 044	1 167	1 224	729	874	991	315	293	233
Less developed regions	3 033	4 550	6 245	809	1 710	3 153	2 224	2 839	3 092
Least developed countries	343	575	945	49	129	339	294	446	606
Africa	414	728	1 204	104	250	568	310	478	636
Eastern Africa	125	227	390	15	49	133	110	178	257
Middle Africa	45	82	146	12	27	68	33	55	78
Northern Africa	96	161	232	37	74	133	59	87	99
Southern Africa	29	47	71	13	23	43	16	25	28
Western Africa	118	211	364	27	77	190	91	134	174
Asia	2 406	3 458	4 516	592	1 198	2 159	1 814	2 260	2 357
Developing Asia	2 294	3 333	4 390	508	1 101	2 055	1 787	2 232	2 335
Eastern Asia	1 097	1 424	1 660	276	525	858	822	899	801
China	928	1 221	1 441	160	369	676	768	852	765
Japan	112	125	126	84	97	103	27	28	23
South-central Asia	886	1 381	1 954	197	398	789	689	983	1 165
South-Eastern Asia	324	484	645	72	163	313	252	321	332
Western Asia	99	168	257	48	112	198	51	57	59
Europe	676	727	726	454	535	582	223	192	145
Eastern Europe	286	309	303	171	217	238	115	91	65
Northern Europe	89	94	97	73	78	85	16	15	12
Southern Europe	132	144	143	78	94	103	54	50	40
Western Europe	169	181	183	132	146	155	38	35	28
Latin America and the Caribbean	320	482	641	196	358	526	124	124	115
Caribbean	27	36	45	14	22	32	13	13	13
Central America	78	126	176	45	86	134	34	40	42
South America	214	320	420	138	249	360	77	70	60
Northern America	239	293	345	177	223	282	63	69	62
Oceania	21	29	37	15	20	27	6	8	10
Australia-New Zealand	17	22	27	14	18	23	2	3	3

Source: Population Division, Department for Economic and Social Information and Policy Analysis of the United Nations Secretariat.
Note: The term "more developed regions" refers to all of Europe and Northern America, Australia, New Zealand and Japan.
The term "less developed regions" refers to the rest of the world.

As already noted, there are sharp differences in the levels of urbanization characterizing the different subregions of Asia. Data for Eastern Asia are largely dominated by China, a country that in 1995 constituted 35 per cent of Asia's total population and 31 per cent of Asia's urban population. During 1975-1995, partly as a result of the reclassification of rural into urban areas, China's rate of urbanization averaged 2.8 per cent annually and surpassed that recorded by other Asian countries. Because the extent of reclassification is expected to abate in the future, China's urbanization rate is projected to decrease to 2.2 per cent per year during 1995-2015, so that its share of the total urban population in Asia will remain nearly constant until 2015 at about 31 per cent. Despite its rapid urbanization rate, the population of China is expected to be only 47 per cent urban by 2015.

South-Eastern Asia is a fairly heterogeneous region that comprises some of the most dynamic economies in the Asian region as well as some of the region's least developed countries. Although its level of urbanization in 1975 was fairly low – 22 per cent – it grew at an annual rate of 2.1 per cent during 1975-1995, to reach 34 per cent. By 2015, 49 per cent of South-Eastern Asia's population is expected to live in urban areas, despite a decline in the rate of urbanization during 1995-2015. The rural population in the region, which grew at an annual rate of 1.2 per cent during 1975-1995, will continue to grow, albeit at a very low rate (0.2 per cent per year).

In 1995, South-central Asia was the second most populous subregion of Asia, comprising three of the most populous countries in the world: Bangladesh, India and Pakistan. Urbanization in South-central Asia has been traditionally low, with only 22 per cent of the population living in urban centres in 1975. Although the region is one of the few whose rate of urbanization is expected to increase between 1975-1995 and 1995-2015, by 2015 only 40 per cent of the population will likely live in urban areas. At 3.4 per cent annually during 1975-1995, the urbanization rate has been especially high in Bangladesh, one of the least urbanized countries of the subregion. Although that rate is expected to decrease to 2.8 per cent annually during 1995-2015, Bangladesh will still experience more than a threefold increase in the proportion urban (from 9 to 32 per cent) between 1975 and 2015. In comparison, India and Pakistan are expected to register more moderate gains, with the proportion urban rising from 21 to 37 per cent in India and from 26 to 49 per cent in Pakistan during the same period. One salient feature of South-central Asia is that its rural population is expected to keep on growing at relatively high rates. Thus, whereas the rural population of the region exceeded that of the developing countries in Eastern Asia by 85 million persons in 1995, it will surpass the latter by 364 million in 2015. South-central Asian countries are therefore faced with the double burden of accommodating a growing rural population as they cope at the same time with increasing levels of urbanization.

Western Asia, with 66 per cent of its population living in urban areas in 1995, is the only subregion of the continent with more than half of its population living in urban centres. However, there is also considerable variation within the subregion, with Oman having only 13 per cent of its population in urban areas and Kuwait having 97 per cent. Most of the population growth experienced by Western Asia has taken place in urban areas and this pattern is expected to continue. Between 1995 and 2015, the urban population of the region will increase by 78 per cent, whereas that in rural areas will barely rise by 4 per cent.

The process of urbanization in the most populous countries of Asia, by fostering population concentration, has given rise to some of the largest urban agglomerations in the developing world. Thus, in 1975, developing Asia included seven cities with at least 5 million people, compared with Latin America which included four and Africa which had one (see table IX.4). In fact, Asia was the only developing region with one city of more than 10 million inhabitants (Shanghai in China) in 1975. By 1995, there were 7 such cities in the developing countries of Asia (Beijing, Shanghai and Tianjin in China; Bombay and Calcutta in India; Jakarta in Indonesia; and Seoul in the Republic of Korea) and their number is expected to increase, by the year 2015, to 16 out of the anticipated total of 23 in all developing countries. Yet, the concentration of the urban population in megacities coexists with relatively high proportions of that population living in smaller urban centres. Thus, in 1995 about 58 per cent of all urban residents in Asia lived in cities of less than half a million persons and even by 2015 those cities are expected to account for 54 per cent of all urban-dwellers in the region.

Africa: a region of fast urban growth

Africa, with 34 per cent of its population living in urban areas in 1995, had a slightly higher level of urbanization than developing Asia. Africa's urbanization rate was lower than that experienced by the developing countries of Asia during 1975-1995 (1.6 versus 2 per cent per annum), but that difference is expected to become less accentuated during 1995-2015. By the end of that period, Africa is expected to have about the same proportion of its population living in urban areas (47 per cent) as developing Asia (see table IX.1). Just as in Asia, there is considerable variation in the level of urbanization of the subregions of Africa, with Eastern Africa having only 22 per cent of its population living in urban areas and Southern Africa having 48 per cent. Southern Africa is expected to remain the most urbanized subregion of the continent, followed closely by Northern Africa (their respective levels of urbanization by 2015 are likely to be 60 and 57 per cent). The other African subregions - Middle and Western Africa - are estimated to have 1995 levels of urbanization similar to the continental average (see table IX.1). A number of countries in Africa have very low proportions of their population living in urban areas (below 20 per cent), including Burundi, Eritrea, Ethiopia, Malawi, the Niger, Rwanda and Uganda, among which most belong to the group of least developed countries.

The urban population of Africa has been characterized by very high rates of growth, averaging 4.4 per cent annually during 1975-1995. High growth is expected to continue during 1995-2015 (at 4.1 per cent per annum), implying that Africa's urban population will be the fastest growing in the world. Urban population growth will be particularly rapid in Eastern Africa, where the average growth rate during 1995-2015 is expected to remain at 5 per cent per year. Relatively high rates of growth are also expected for the urban populations of Middle and Western Africa (4.6 and 4.5 per cent, respectively). Such high growth rates imply that the urban population of Africa is doubling every 15 or 16 years, so that it will increase more than fivefold between 1975 and 2015, passing from 104 million to 568 million (see table IX.3).

Table IX.4.
NUMBER OF URBAN AGGLOMERATIONS AND POPULATION IN THOSE
AGGLOMERATIONS BY SIZE CLASS AND MAJOR AREA, 1975, 1995
AND 2015

Class size	1975	1995	2015
A. World total			
10 million			
Number of agglomerations	4	15	27
Population in agglomerations (thousands)	58 330	207 551	449 661
As percentage of urban population	3.8	8.0	10.9
5 million to 10 million			
Number of agglomerations	18	23	44
Population in agglomerations (thousands)	136 399	167 438	281 732
As percentage of urban population	8.9	6.5	6.8
1 million to 5 million			
Number of agglomerations	157	287	472
Population in agglomerations (thousands)	305 802	552 400	940 990
As percentage of urban population	19.9	21.4	22.7
500,000 to 1 million			
Number of agglomerations	212	338	422
Population in agglomerations (thousands)	148 940	237 841	293 198
As percentage of urban population	9.7	9.2	7.1
Under 500,000			
Population in agglomerations (thousands)	888 876	1 419 223	2 177 766
As percentage of urban population	57.8	54.9	52.6
B. More developed regions			
10 million or more			
Number of agglomerations	2	4	4
Population in agglomerations (thousands)	35 651	66 176	71 212
As percentage of urban population	4.9	7.6	7.2
5 million to 10 million			
Number of agglomerations	8	6	8
Population in agglomerations (thousands)	62 173	44 475	56 162
As percentage of urban population	8.5	5.1	5.7
1 million to 5 million			
Number of agglomerations	75	102	120
Population in agglomerations (thousands)	145 275	204 220	239 703
As percentage of urban population	19.9	23.4	24.2
500,000 to 1 million			
Number of agglomerations	96	112	123
Population in agglomerations (thousands)	69 013	78 264	83 747
As percentage of urban population	9.5	9.0	8.5
Under 500,000			
Population in agglomerations (thousands)	417 173	480 835	539 798
As percentage of urban population	57.2	55.0	54.5

Table IX.4.
CONTINUED...

Class size	1975	1995	2015
C. Africa			
10 million or more			
Number of agglomerations	0	1	2
Population in agglomerations (thousands)	0	10 287	38 931
As percentage of urban population	0.0	4.1	6.9
5 million to 10 million			
Number of agglomerations	1	1	11
Population in agglomerations (thousands)	6 079	9 656	67 747
As percentage of urban population	5.8	3.9	11.9
1 million to 5 million			
Number of agglomerations	7	31	55
Population in agglomerations (thousands)	13 505	61 116	117 852
As percentage of urban population	13.0	24.4	20.8
500,000 to 1 million			
Number of agglomerations	19	33	53
Population in agglomerations (thousands)	14 006	24 153	36 941
As percentage of urban population	13.5	9.7	6.5
Under 500,000			
Population in agglomerations (thousands)	70 533	145 064	306 455
As percentage of urban population	67.7	58.0	54.0
D. Latin America and the Caribbean			
10 million			
Number of agglomerations	1	3	5
Population in agglomerations (thousands)	11 236	43 050	74 025
As percentage of urban population	5.7	12.0	14.1
5 million to 10 million			
Number of agglomerations	3	4	3
Population in agglomerations (thousands)	26 899	28 019	19 472
As percentage of urban population	13.7	7.8	3.7
1 million to 5 million			
Number of agglomerations	17	35	69
Population in agglomerations (thousands)	31 381	64 387	132 345
As percentage of urban population	16.0	18.0	25.2
500,000 to 1 million			
Number of agglomerations	24	52	66
Population in agglomerations (thousands)	15 907	36 886	45 824
As percentage of urban population	8.1	10.3	8.7
Under 500,000			
Population in agglomerations (thousands)	110 749	185 347	254 408
As percentage of urban population	56.5	51.8	48.4`

Table IX.4.
CONTINUED...

Class size	1975	1995	2015
D. Developing Asia			
10 million or more			
Number of agglomerations	1	7	16
Population in agglomerations (thousands)	11 443	88 038	265 493
As percentage of urban population	2.3	8.0	12.9
5 million to 10 million			
Number of agglomerations	6	12	22
Population in agglomerations (thousands)	41 248	85 288	138 351
As percentage of urban population	8.1	7.8	6.7
1 million to 5 million			
Number of agglomerations	58	119	228
Population in agglomerations (thousands)	115 641	222 678	451 090
As percentage of urban population	22.8	20.2	22.0
500,000 to 1 million			
Number of agglomerations	73	141	179
Population in agglomerations (thousands)	50 014	98 539	126 267
As percentage of urban population	9.9	9.0	6.1
Under 500,000			
Population in agglomerations (thousands)	324 889	639 656	1 109 264
As percentage of urban population	64.0	58.1	54.0

Source: Population Division, Department for Economic and Social Information and Policy Analysis of the United Nations Secretariat.

In comparison with other regions, the urban population in Africa tends to be more concentrated in smaller towns and urban centres. In 1995, 58 per cent of all urban-dwellers in Africa lived in cities of half a million people or less, and only two cities in the continent had more than 5 million inhabitants (Lagos and Cairo). Although the number of large cities is projected to increase during the coming decades, Africa will remain a continent of small and medium-sized urban centres. Even by 2015, over three fifths of the urban population in Africa will still live in cities with less than one million inhabitants (see table IX.4).

Lagos, one of the two largest urban agglomerations in Africa, was the first city in the continent to become one of the 10 largest urban agglomerations in the world. In 1950, Lagos was a relatively small urban centre with just 288,000 inhabitants but by 1970, growing at a rate of nearly 10 per cent per year, it had surpassed the 2 million mark. By 1995 the population of the city was estimated to have reached 10.3 million persons and it was expected to keep on growing at over 4 per cent annually for the next 20 years, reaching 24 million persons by 2015 (when it is expected to rank third among the world's largest cities).

In contrast to Lagos, Cairo was already a large city in 1950 when it had 2.4 million inhabitants. Although its growth rate declined from 4.3 per cent annually in the 1950s to about 2.3 per cent per year in the 1980s, by 1995 Cairo had 9.7 million inhabitants. During 1995-2015, Cairo's growth rate is expected to decline further to 2 per cent per annum, and by 2015, the city's population is expected to increase to 14.5 million persons. In that year, 19 per cent of Africa's urban population is expected to be living in the 13 cities having at least 5 million inhabitants, namely, Abidjan, Addis Ababa, Alexandria, Algiers, Cairo, Casablanca, Khartoum, Kinshasa, Lagos, Luanda, Maputo, Nairobi and Tripoli.

Not only is the urban population of Africa growing at relatively high rates, but that in rural areas is also increasing substantially. Indeed, Africa is the only major region whose rural population is projected to keep on growing at moderate rates beyond 2015. In 1995, 478 million persons or two thirds of Africa's population lived in rural areas, up from 310 million in 1975 (see table IX.3). By 2015, 636 million Africans will live in rural areas and will account for nearly one fifth of the total rural population of the world. Thus, most African countries are faced with the necessity of absorbing considerable increases in their rural population even as they experience rapid urban growth.

THE COMPONENTS OF URBAN GROWTH IN DEVELOPING COUNTRIES

As already noted, the growth of the urban population in a country is attributable to three types of processes: the excess of births over deaths in urban areas (natural increase); net rural-urban migration; and the reclassification of places from rural to urban as rural localities become urbanized. The United Nations estimates the size of these components of urban growth on the basis of information from consecutive censuses regarding the distribution of the population by place of residence (urban versus rural), age group and sex.

Estimation method and caveats

The estimation method used, which is described in detail in the publication entitled *Patterns of Urban and Rural Population Growth*,[20] begins with calculated probabilities of surviving from one census to the next. To estimate the relevant probabilities of survival between censuses, the data for the first census are adjusted so that they refer to a period exactly 10 years away from that of the data for the second census. The intercensal cohort survival ratios for the whole population of the country are then calculated and adjusted to reflect a pre-established mortality differential (constant at all ages) between rural and urban areas. In particular, it is assumed that the force of mortality (that is, the instantaneous rate of death) in rural areas exceeds that in urban areas by 25 per cent at all ages and that the mortality schedule for the country as a whole has the same shape as that for urban areas. The adjusted survival ratios are subsequently used to project the urban population classified by age group and sex from the first to the second date. Then the projected urban population is compared with the actual population enumerated in urban areas. The difference between the two is assumed to represent the effect of net migration and reclassification in the intercensal period or, as it is often interpreted, the net number of migrants surviving to the second census. This method makes no allowance for the effects of international migration, thus in effect assuming that

[20]   United Nations publication, Sales No. E.79.XIII.9 and corrigendum.

the population of the country is closed.

By reverse-projecting those surviving migrants to the mid-point of the intercensal period, an estimate of the net number of rural-urban migrants for the intercensal period is obtained.[21] However, for the first age group, 0-4, the estimate of the net number of migrants is obtained by applying the child/woman ratio of the urban population to the estimated net number of migrating women in the relevant age group. Once the net number of migrants is available, the net urban migration rate is obtained by dividing that number by the mid-period urban population, and the rate of natural increase of urban areas is obtained by subtracting the net migration rate from the observed growth rate of the urban population. Under these assumptions, the procedure permits the separation of two components of urban growth, namely, the part due to natural increase and the part due to both internal migration and reclassification. Without further information, however, it is not possible to distinguish the effects of migration from those of the reclassification of rural areas into urban areas.

Before discussing the application of this approach to urbanization trends, it is of interest to consider the types of biases that might result from violations of the assumptions made. If the mortality differential between urban and rural areas is larger than the 25 per cent assumed by the method, the urban mortality levels used in projecting the urban population over the relevant 10-year period will have been too high and will result in a projected urban population that is too small relative to the one that would be obtained using the correct mortality level. Hence, when the projected population is subtracted from the observed, the result will be an overestimate of the net number of migrants over the decade and therefore of the net migration rate. In addition, because the net migration rate and the rate of natural increase must add up to the growth rate of the urban population, the rate of natural increase will be underestimated. That is, an underestimate of the difference in mortality levels between urban and rural areas leads to an overestimate of the contribution of net rural-urban migration and reclassification to the growth of urban areas. If the mortality differential was less than 25 per cent, the opposite would result.

If a country's population is not closed, the contribution of international migration to the growth of urban areas may also bias the results obtained. The effect of net international migration depends on its distribution between rural and urban areas. When international migration is distributed between urban and rural areas in a manner proportional to their respective weights over the whole population, the estimates obtained will not be biased. However, if urban areas gain more than their share of international migrants over the period being considered, the observed urban population will be larger and the number of net internal migrants to urban areas will be overestimated. The effects of net international migration losses that are disproportionately concentrated in urban areas would be the reverse, leading to underestimates of net migration. Given that adequate estimates of the differential impact of international migration on rural and urban areas are generally not available, there is no basis on which adjustments could be made to prevent such biases from occurring.

Although the data requirements for the application of the method used to estimate the components of urban growth are modest, the information is either not available or inadequate for a large number of developing countries. Long intercensal intervals, delays in processing the information obtained, and

21 This estimation method assumes that both migration and the deaths of migrants are uniformly distributed over the intercensal period.

changes in the definitions of urban and rural areas between one census and the next are among the factors that hinder the derivation of reliable estimates of the components of urban growth. Table IX.5 indicates the availability of census data for all those countries for which the estimation method could be applied. As the table shows, information needed to estimate the components of urban growth for the 1960s, 1970s and 1980s was obtained for only one country in Africa (Botswana), nine countries in Latin America and three countries in Asia. For a considerably larger number of countries, information was available for at least one decade. In total, the components of urban growth could be estimated for 36 developing countries in the 1960s, 41 in the 1970s and 27 in the 1980s. However, in the cases marked by a footnote indicator in table IX.5, the method was applied to censuses that were separated by considerably more than 10 years and consequently the results obtained must be interpreted with caution. Among countries in the African region, the components of urban growth could be estimated in 17 cases, but for 9 of them the estimates refer only to one decade, making it impossible to obtain clear trends for the region. In the case of Latin America, better availability of census data has permitted the application of the estimation method to 22 countries, producing estimates for at least two decades for almost all of them. In Asia, estimates could be calculated for 16 countries, including the most populous ones – Bangladesh, China, India, Indonesia and Pakistan – although for China and Pakistan estimates were possible only for a single decade. Given the sparse availability of data, the assessment of trends since 1960 that will be presented here can only be taken as tentative. Nevertheless, the evidence presented provides the most complete picture available to date of the changing relevance of rural-urban migration and reclassification as opposed to natural increase in determining the growth of the urban population.

Natural increase versus other factors as determinants of urban growth

Table IX.6 presents a summary of the main estimates obtained. Focusing first on the percentage of urban growth attributable to internal migration and reclassification, it is clear that there is great variability among the countries covered by the estimates available: for the 1960s, estimates vary from 9 to 77 per cent, and for the 1970s the range of variation is from 13 to 66 per cent. In terms of the median value of the distribution of countries by percentage of urban growth attributable to migration and reclassification, there seems to have been a slight decline in the importance of that component, with the median passing from 41 per cent in the 1960s to 39 per cent during the 1980s. However, given the different coverage of countries from one decade to the next and the fact that countries of very different population sizes are being considered within each decade, the median may not be the best indicator of the relevance of migration and reclassification.

Table IX.5.
AVAILABILITY OF CENSUS DATA NEEDED TO ESTIMATE THE COMPONENTS OF URBAN GROWTH FOR EACH DECADE

Decade Region or country	1960s		1970s		1980s	
Africa						
Eastern Africa						
Kenya	--	--	1969	1979	--	--
United Republic of Tanzania	--	--	1967	1978	--	--
Zimbabwe	--	--	1969	1982	1982	1992
Northern Africa						
Egypt	--	--	1960	1976[a]	1976	1986
Libyan Arab Jamahiriya	1964	1973	1973	1984	--	--
Morocco	1960	1971	1971	1982	--	--
Sudan	--	--	1973	1983	--	--
Tunisia	1966	1975	1975	1984	--	--
Southern Africa						
Botswana	1964	1971	1971	1981	1981	1991
South Africa	1960	1970	--	--	--	--
Western Africa						
Burkina Faso	--	--	--	--	1975	1985
Côte d'Ivoire	--	--	--	--	1975	1988
Ghana	1960	1970	1970	1984[a]	--	--
Liberia	--	--	1974	1984	--	--
Mali	--	--	--	--	1976	1987
Senegal	--	--	--	--	1976	1988
Togo	1959	1970	--	--	--	--
Latin America						
Central America and the Caribbean						
Costa Rica	1963	1973	1973	1984	--	--
Cuba	1953	1970[a]	1970	1981	--	--
Dominican Republic	1960	1970	1970	1981	--	--
El Salvador	1961	1971	--	--	1971	1992[a]
Guatemala	1964	1973	--	--	--	--
Haiti	1950	1971[a]	1971	1982	--	--
Honduras	1961	1974	--	--	1974	1988[a]
Mexico	1960	1970	1970	1980	1980	1990
Nicaragua	1963	1971	--	--	--	--
Panama	1960	1970	1970	1980	1980	1990
Puerto Rico	1960	1970	1970	1980	1980	1990
South America						
Argentina	--	--	1960	1980[a]	1980	1991
Bolivia	--	--	--	--	1976	1992[a]
Brazil	1960	1970	1970	1980	1980	1991
Chile	1960	1970	1970	1982	1982	1992
Colombia	1964	1973	1973	1985	--	--
Ecuador	1962	1974	1974	1982	1982	1990
Guyana	1960	1970	--	--	--	--
Paraguay	1962	1972	1972	1982	1982	1992
Peru	1961	1972	1972	1981	1981	1993
Uruguay	1963	1975	1975	1985	--	--
Venezuela	1961	1971	1971	1981	1981	1990

Table IX.5.
CONTINUED...

Decade						
Region or country	1960s		1970s		1980s	
Asia						
Eastern Asia						
China	--	--	--	--	1982	1990
Republic of Korea	1960	1970	1970	1980	1980	1990
South-Eastern Asia						
Indonesia	1961	1971	1971	1980	1980	1990
Malaysia	--	--	1970	1980	--	--
Philippines	--	--	1970	1980	1980	1990
Thailand	--	--	1970	1980	1980	1990
Southern Asia						
Bangladesh	1961	1974	1974	1981	--	--
India	1961	1971	1971	1981	--	--
Iran (Islamic Republic of)	--	--	1966	1976	1976	1986
Nepal	1961	1971	1971	1981	--	--
Pakistan	--	--	1972	1981	--	--
Sri Lanka	1963	1971	--	--	--	--
Western Asia						
Iraq	1957	1965	1965	1977	1977	1987
Israel	--	--	1972	1983	--	--
Syrian Arab Republic	1960	1970	1970	1981	--	--
Turkey	1960	1970	1970	1980	--	--
Number of countries						
Africa	7		11		7	
Latin America	20		16		13	
Asia	9		14		7	
Total	36		41		27	

Source: Population Division, Department for Economic and Social Information and Policy Analysis of the United Nations Secretariat.
Note: The Symbol "--" indicates that the data available did not allow the estimation for the given decade to be carried out.
a   The two censuses were separated by considerably more than 10 years. The estimates presented refer to a 10-year period ending at the date of the second census. Because of the length of the original interval, the estimates obtained should be interpreted with caution.

Another way of assessing the relative impact of natural increase versus net migration/reclassification on the growth of the urban populations of the world's major regions is by using appropriate weights to aggregate country estimates. Thus, the estimated rural out-migration rates[22] may be weighted by the size of the rural population at the mid-point of the intercensal period to obtain a weighted estimate of the net number of rural-urban migrants during the period. Similarly, the estimates of urban natural increase may be weighted by the size of the urban population at the middle of the intercensal period to obtain the net gain of births over deaths. Using weights derived from the urban and rural estimates and projections prepared by the United Nations, weighted rural out-migration rates and weighted rates of natural increase by major region and decade can be obtained together with the relative contribution of each to the growth of urban populations at the regional and world levels. Table IX.7 shows the results obtained.

22 For convenience, the term "migration" is used as a shorthand for the net effect of migration and reclassification

Table IX.6.

ESTIMATES OF THE COMPONENTS OF URBAN GROWTH

Percentage

	Annual intercensal growth rate of urban areas			Annual urban rate of natural increase			Annual rate of urban growth from internal migration/reclassification			Proportion of urban growth attributable to internal migration/reclassification		
	1960s	1970s	1980s	1960s	1970s	1980s	1960s	1970s	1980s	1960s	1970s	1980s
Africa												
Eastern Africa												
Kenya	--	7.9	--	--	3.4	--	--	4.5	--	--	57.4	--
United Republic of Tanzania	--	12.6	--	--	4.8	--	--	7.8	--	--	61.9	--
Zimbabwe	--	5.4	5.9	--	2.2	2.9	--	3.3	3.0	--	60.0	50.7
Northern Africa												
Egypt	--	3.0[a]	2.8	--	2.1[a]	2.6	--	0.9[a]	0.2	--	31.5[a]	8.4
Libyan Arab Jamahiriya	13.9	6.5	--	5.9	4.5	--	7.9	2.0	--	57.2	30.2	--
Morocco	4.1	4.4	--	2.6	2.4	--	1.5	2.0	--	37.3	44.6	--
Sudan	--	4.9	--	--	3.8	--	--	1.1	--	--	22.9	--
Tunisia	4.7	3.2	--	2.3	2.3	--	2.4	0.9	--	52.0	27.8	--
Southern Africa												
Botswana	15.7	9.6	14.0	3.6	4.5	5.1	12.2	5.1	8.9	77.4	53.3	63.7
South Africa	3.4	--	--	2.5	--	--	0.9	--	--	26.1	--	--
Western Africa												
Burkina Faso	--	--	9.4	--	--	4.0	--	--	5.4	--	--	57.4
Côte d'Ivoire	--	--	5.3	--	--	4.0	--	--	1.3	--	-	24.5
Ghana	4.7	3.3[a]	--	2.7	2.5[a]	--	1.9	0.8[a]	--	41.5	23.6[a]	--
Liberia	--	6.2	--	--	4.1	--	--	2.1	--	--	34.5	--
Mali	--	--	4.4	--	--	2.2	--	--	2.2	--	--	49.5
Senegal	--	--	3.6	--	--	2.7	--	--	1.0	--	--	26.6
Togo	5.8	--	--	3.5	--	--	2.4	--	--	40.7	--	--
Latin America												
Central America and the Caribbean												
Costa Rica	4.9	3.1	--	2.8	2.2	--	2.1	1.0	--	42.9	31.2	--
Cuba	2.5[a]	2.4	--	2.0[a]	1.0	--	0.5[a]	1.3	--	20.7[a]	56.0	--
Dominican Republic	5.8	5.3	--	3.0	2.9	--	2.8	2.4	--	47.8	44.9	--
El Salvador	3.7	--	2.9[a]	2.9	--	1.5[a]	0.8	--	1.4[a]	21.8	--	47.3[a]
Guatemala	3.0	--	--	1.8	--	--	1.1	--	--	37.6	--	--
Haiti	4.0[a]	1.5	--	1.9[a]	1.3	--	2.2[a]	0.2	--	53.6[a]	13.2	--
Honduras	5.0	--	4.9[a]	2.5	--	3.0[a]	2.5	--	1.9[a]	49.5	--	38.9[a]
Mexico	4.9	4.3	2.8	3.3	3.1	1.9	1.6	1.3	0.9	32.0	29.1	31.2
Nicaragua	4.5	--	--	2.5	--	--	1.9	--	--	43.2	--	--
Panama	4.5	2.9	3.2	2.7	2.0	2.3	1.8	0.9	1.0	40.5	31.0	29.6
Puerto Rico	4.2	3.0	1.6	1.5	1.7	1.0	2.7	1.4	0.6	63.6	44.9	38.1

Table IX.6.
CONTINUED...

Percentage	Annual intercensal growth rate of urban areas			Annual urban rate of natural increase			Annual rate of urban growth from internal migration/reclassification			Proportion of urban growth attributable to internal migration/reclassification		
	1960s	1970s	1980s	1960s	1970s	1980s	1960s	1970s	1980s	1960s	1970s	1980s
South America												
Argentina	--	2.3 [a]	1.9	--	1.6 [a]	1.4	--	0.7 [a]	0.5	--	30.1 [a]	26.7
Bolivia	--	--	4.2 [a]	--	--	2.2 [a]	--	--	2.0 [a]	--	--	47.3 [a]
Brazil	5.1	4.3	2.9	2.6	2.3	1.8	2.5	2.1	1.1	48.3	47.2	37.5
Chile	3.0	2.8	1.8	2.0	2.0	1.7	1.0	0.7	0.1	34.3	26.6	6.6
Colombia	3.4	3.4	--	2.6	1.7	--	0.8	1.7	--	24.0	50.2	--
Ecuador	4.5	4.6	3.7	3.0	2.4	2.2	1.5	2.2	1.6	32.5	47.3	42.0
Guyana	8.8	--	--	2.5	--	--	6.3	--	--	71.6	--	--
Paraguay	3.1	3.8	4.7	2.1	2.0	2.8	1.1	1.8	1.9	33.8	47.3	41.2
Peru	4.9	3.5	2.8	2.9	2.4	2.0	2.1	1.1	0.8	41.8	32.2	29.3
Uruguay	0.7	1.0	--	0.6	0.6	--	0.1	0.4	--	8.8	40.8	--
Venezuela	4.1	3.9	3.0	3.2	3.0	2.4	0.9	1.0	0.6	21.1	24.5	20.1
Asia												
Eastern Asia												
China	--	--	4.6	--	--	1.3	--	--	3.3	--	--	71.9
Republic of Korea	6.2	5.0	4.1	2.5	2.2	1.9	3.8	2.8	2.3	60.3	56.3	55.0
South-Eastern Asia												
Indonesia	3.6	5.2	5.2	2.5	2.6	2.2	1.1	2.6	3.1	31.5	50.6	58.8
Malaysia	--	4.9	--	--	2.2	--	--	2.7	--	--	54.8	--
Philippines	--	4.3	4.9	--	2.6	2.4	--	1.7	2.6	--	40.2	52.4
Thailand	--	5.2	2.9	--	2.2	1.6	--	3.0	1.3	--	57.8	44.5
Southern Asia												
Bangladesh	6.6	10.6	--	2.7	3.7	--	3.9	7.0	--	58.6	65.6	--
India	3.2	3.7	--	2.2	2.0	--	1.0	1.7	--	31.3	45.1	--
Iran (Islamic Republic of)	--	4.8	5.3	--	2.7	3.8	--	2.1	1.6	--	43.2	29.6
Nepal	3.2	7.3	--	2.1	2.9	--	1.1	4.3	--	33.6	59.7	--
Pakistan	--	4.3	--	--	3.6	--	--	0.7	--	--	17.1	--
Sri Lanka	4.2	--	--	2.1	--	--	2.1	--	--	49.8	--	--
Western Asia												
Iraq	6.4	5.1	4.1	3.4	3.4	3.0	3.0	1.7	1.0	46.9	32.9	25.0
Israel	--	2.7	--	--	2.2	--	--	0.5	--	--	18.0	--
Syrian Arab Republic	4.9	4.0	--	3.3	3.2	--	1.5	0.8	--	31.1	20.9	--
Turkey	5.5	4.7	--	2.1	2.2	--	3.4	2.5	--	61.7	52.3	--
Minimum	0.7	1.0	1.6	0.6	0.6	1.0	0.1	0.2	0.1	8.8	13.2	6.6
Maximum	15.7	12.6	14.0	5.9	4.8	5.1	12.2	7.8	8.9	77.4	65.6	71.9
Number of countries	36	41	27	36	41	27	36	41	27	36	41	27
Mean	5.0	4.7	4.3	2.6	2.6	2.4	2.4	2.1	1.9	41.8	40.5	39.0
Median	4.5	4.3	4.1	2.5	2.4	2.2	1.9	1.7	1.4	41.1	43.2	38.9

Source: Population Division, Department for Economic and Social Information and Policy Analysis of the United Nations Secretariat.
Note: The Symbol "--" indicates that data were unavailable.
[a] The two censuses were separated by considerably more than 10 years. The estimates presented refer to a 10-year period ending at the date of the second census. Because of the length of the original interval, the estimates obtained should be interpreted with caution.

Table IX.7

ESTIMATES OF THE COMPONENTS OF URBAN GROWTH AT THE REGIONAL LEVEL

	1960s	1970s	1980s	1980s excluding China
Africa				
Urban population	18 135 000	38 831 000	32 858 000	
Rural population	31 277 000	89 368 000	58 461 000	
Urban natural increase	476 320	1 014 002	917 817	
Net number of rural-urban migrants	333 122	692 302	303 629	
Total net gain	809 443	1 706 304	1 221 447	
Proportion due to migration (percentage)	41.2	40.6	24.9	
Rate of natural increase of urban areas (percentage)	2.63	2.61	2.79	
Rural out-migration rate (percentage)	1.07	0.77	0.52	
Latin America				
Urban population	112 573 000	184 994 000	227 992 000	
Rural population	105 664 000	108 341 000	94 777 000	
Urban natural increase	3 036 246	4 223 178	4 223 886	
Net number of rural-urban migrants	2 032 718	2 871 882	2 161 934	
Total net gain	5 068 963	7 095 060	6 385 819	
Proportion due to migration (percentage)	40.1	40.5	33.9	
Rate of natural increase of urban areas (percentage)	2.70	2.28	1.85	
Rural out-migration rate (percentage)	1.92	2.65	2.28	
Asia				
Urban population	142 222 000	274 162 000	380 690 000	139 473 000
Rural population	612 806 000	873 718 000	1 067 651 000	238 694 000
Urban natural increase	3 285 794	6 552 978	6 518 400	3 433 705
Net number of rural-urban migrants	2 226 120	5 747 542	11 407 985	3 282 021
Total net gain	5 511 913	12 300 520	17 926 385	6 715 726
Proportion due to migration (percentage)	40.4	46.7	63.6	48.9
Rate of natural increase of urban areas (percentage)	2.31	2.39	1.71	2.46
Rural out-migration rate (percentage)	0.36	0.66	1.07	1.37
Developing World				
Urban population	272 930 000	497 987 000	641 540 000	400 323 000
Rural population	749 747 000	1 071 427 000	1 220 889 000	391 932 000
Urban natural increase	6 798 360	11 790 158	11 660 103	8 575 408
Net number of rural-urban migrants	4 591 960	9 311 726	13 873 548	5 747 584
Total net gain	11 390 319	21 101 884	25 533 651	14 322 992
Proportion due to migration (percentage)	40.3	44.1	54.3	40.1
Rate of natural increase of urban areas (percentage)	2.49	2.37	1.82	2.14
Rural out-migration rate (percentage)	0.61	0.87	1.14	1.47

Source: Population Division, Department for Economic and Social Information and Policy Analysis of the United Nations Secretariat.

As the table shows, different regions have experienced fairly different trends in natural increase and net rural out-migration rates. The most reliable estimates are those for Latin America where more countries have data for each decade. For that region, the rate of natural increase of urban areas has shown a tendency to decline from one decade to the next, a result that is consistent with trends in overall natural increase in the region. In Asia, the rate of natural increase of urban areas remained nearly constant during the 1960s and 1970s, but showed a marked decline during the 1980s. However, the 1980s estimate is the only one that contains data for China which, because of its size, is likely to affect the weighted average very substantially. For that reason, estimates for Asia excluding China are also presented. According to them, the rate of natural increase in the urban areas of the rest of Asia increased somewhat during the three decades considered. A similar trend is observed in Africa, whose estimates are the weakest because of the varying groups of countries with data for each decade. The estimates of the rate of natural increase in the urban areas of Africa can be conservatively interpreted as indicating that those rates are high and have varied little over the three decades. Once more, such an observation is consistent with what is known about trends in rates of natural increase for the region as a whole.

At the level of the developing world as a whole, the rate of natural increase of urban areas shows a moderately declining trend when China is excluded and a marked decline between the 1970s and the 1980s when China is included. In all cases, the rates of natural increase estimated for urban areas are similar to those estimated for the regions as a whole for the different periods considered. Since not all countries are included in the estimates presented here, differences can be expected. However, the overall consistency of the estimates obtained with those relative to whole regions lends them credence.

Of even greater interest are the estimated rural out-migration rates, which have not been available before. At the level of the developing world, they rise from 0.61 per cent in the 1960s to 1.14 per cent in the 1980s if China is included and to 1.47 per cent in the 1980s if China is excluded. However, the trends themselves are different for each of the major developing regions considered. Thus, in Africa, rural out-migration rates decline steadily from the 1960s to the 1980s, whereas in developing Asia they increase steadily (irrespective of whether China is included or not). In Latin America, in contrast, there is an increase of rural out-migration rates between the 1960s and the 1970s followed by a decline. Such trends are consistent with what is known about the economic situation of those major regions. In Africa, most economic indicators point to a deterioration of economic opportunities since the 1960s, and declining rural out-migration rates are consistent with such a scenario. It must be remembered, however, that because the rural population of Africa has been growing substantially, lower rates of rural out-migration need not mean lower numbers of net rural-urban migrants. Furthermore, the few African countries for which data are available are not necessarily representative of the continent as a whole. In fact, countries with very high rates of urban growth are underrepresented in the data used.

In Asia, the increasing rates of rural out-migration are consistent with the rising economic dynamism in the region. Furthermore, in countries such as China and Indonesia, relaxation of policies that effectively prevented rural-urban migration have contributed to rapid increases in that component of urban growth. It is important to stress, however, that rural out-migration rates in Asia were very low and are still only moderate. In contrast, rural out-migration rates in Latin America are high and their fluctuation over time is likely to be related to the declining economic opportunities that characterized the countries in the region during the 1980s.

The estimates obtained allow the calculation of the proportion of urban growth that is attributable to net internal migration and reclassification. Note, however, that because the rates of urban natural increase and the rural out-migration rates presented above have different denominators, it is not possible to obtain the percentage growth due to internal migration directly from them. Estimates of the actual number of persons added because of natural increase and gained through net rural-urban migration and reclassification were used to derive the percentages shown in table IX.7. Those percentages corroborate that, as concluded in an earlier study,[23] natural increase accounted for about 60 per cent of urban growth in the 1960s with internal migration and reclassification accounting for the other 40 per cent. During the 1970s there was a slight tendency for the contribution of internal migration and reclassification to increase, particularly because of its higher weight in Asia. Yet, at the level of the developing world as a whole, internal migration and reclassification accounted for about 44 per cent of urban growth. A major new finding is that by the 1980s, as fertility declines had become more evident in many countries and rural out-migration rates declined in Africa, internal migration and reclassification accounted for more than half of the urban growth (54 per cent) occurring in the developing world as a whole, but its contribution varied considerably from one region to another. Thus in the 1980s, whereas internal migration and reclassification accounted for only 25 per cent of urban growth in Africa and 34 per cent in Latin America, it was the source of 64 per cent of urban growth in developing Asia. China influenced these estimates very markedly. Without China, internal migration and reclassification accounted for about half of urban growth in other countries of Asia and, at the level of the developing world, were again responsible for 40 per cent of urban growth. However, in contrast with the 1960s, regional differences in the contribution of internal migration and reclassification to growth were marked.

Towards a contribution to policy

These findings have important implications for planners and policy makers. As the study carried out two decades ago[24] suggested, population growth in urban areas is highly determined by natural increase. These data further indicate that, especially in regions characterized by economic stagnation, the role played by natural increase has been strengthened. Consequently, if the population growth of urban areas is to be reduced significantly, more emphasis has to be placed on the reduction of fertility.

This conclusion runs counter to the frequent assumption that the control of urban growth hinges on the reduction of rural-urban migration. In fact, the estimates presented show that rural out-migration rates in both Africa and Asia have been on the low side. In addition, as other authors have reported,[25] there has been a positive and significant association between the estimated rural

[23] *Patterns of Urban and Rural Population Growth* (United Nations publication, Sales No. E.79.XIII.9 and corrigendum).

[24] Ibid.

[25] For example, see David Satterthwaite, "Health and environmental problems in the cities of developing countries", in *Population Distribution and Migration, Proceedings of the United Nations Expert Group Meeting on Population Distribution and Migration, Santa Cruz, Bolivia, 18-22 January 1993* (ST/ESA/SER.R/133) (United Nations publication, forthcoming).

out-migration rates and levels of gross domestic product (GDP) in developing countries during the three decades considered. Such an association suggests that higher rural out-migration and the reclassification of rural into urban areas that this migration sometimes masks are both related to higher levels of prosperity.

If, as recognized in the Programme of Action of the International Conference on Population and Development,[26] "the process of urbanization is an intrinsic dimension of economic and social development" (para. 9.1), its management, and not its retardation, should be the issue. As a new century approaches, the best information available suggests that the urban way of life will dominate the future. Much remains to be done, however, the better to document the processes underlying the urban transformation, especially those related to changes in productive systems and economic organization. The inertial forces characterizing demographic processes may allow us to produce serviceable forecasts from simple models, but the processes themselves are more complex and need to be better understood for policy-related purposes.

[26] *Report of the International Conference on Population and Development, Cairo, 5-13 September 1994* (United Nations publication, Sales No. E.95.XIII.18), chap. I, resolution 1, annex.

X HOW THE DEVELOPING WORLD GETS ITS ELECTRICITY

One of the major tasks that developing countries face today is to ensure reliable and affordable supplies of electric power for growing populations. Ready access to electricity for all households has come to represent a measure of economic and social progress and, to a degree, adequate power supplies are a requirement for that progress. Providing electricity to new communities and reducing interruptions in supply to existing users are traditional demands made of political figures. Indeed, there has been considerable dissatisfaction with the way that the electricity sector has been run in a large number of countries and with how investments have been planned.

The power sector is highly capital intensive, and substantial investment will be required to meet the rapidly rising demand for power. But this is not all. As Governments seek increased electric power, policy is increasingly turning to innovative investment schemes, more rational electricity pricing and more efficient supply and demand management. These issues are interrelated and, as time passes, it is becoming more and more critical to address them directly.

THE DEVELOPING COUNTRY POWER PROBLEM

Consumption of electricity in developing countries has doubled twice over the past two decades, requiring the construction of close to 100 medium-sized power stations each year. In many cases, however, large investments have not generated the quality of services expected. On average, 40 per cent of the power-generating capacity in developing countries is not available for production.[1] Frequent power cuts have resulted in substantial losses of industrial output in a large number of countries. Moreover, until a few years ago, environmental concerns were not a highly salient issue in power plant construction. Today, environmental concerns are very much in the public mind as regards both atmospheric pollution and the consequences of large hydroelectricity projects, such as the displacement of communities.

Together, these factors have led in two directions. One is a continuing demand for high levels of investment in the power sector. The other is a reassessment of the role of the State in the power sector in many countries and a movement away from direct government provision of electricity. It is part and parcel of a broader movement towards more indirect oversight of public utilities, which are increasingly becoming more autonomous and often privatized entities, albeit regulated ones.

[1] World Bank, *World Development Report, 1994* (Washington, D.C., 1994) p. 1.

Persistent growth in the demand for electricity

Despite the rapid growth of electric power consumption in the developing countries over the past few decades, the level of consumption is still quite low. It has yet to reach 2 billion people, living mainly in rural areas. Overall, electricity consumption per capita in the developing world is about one twelfth of what it is in the developed economies. It is highest in Latin America, among major developing economy regions, but even there it is only 17 per cent of the developed country average (see figure X.1). Per capita annual consumption of electricity in Africa is only one third of that in Latin America.

Electricity consumption depends on a combination of factors, chief among which are per capita income, the degree of urbanization and the extent of electrification (i.e., the percentage of households linked to an electrical grid). Latin America has the highest level of electrification, nearly 80 per cent of households having access to electricity. On the other hand, in Africa, only about 25 per cent of the population has access to electricity, and in some countries of sub-Saharan Africa, electrical power is available to only 5 per cent of all households.

The highest per capita consumption is to be found among the oil exporting countries of the Middle East and the newly industrialized economies of South-East Asia, reflecting their higher income and degree of urbanization (see table X.1). These factors are also reflected in the per capita consumption of other higher income countries, such as Argentina, Chile, Brazil, Malaysia, the Republic of Korea, South Africa and Thailand. By contrast, the current extremely low per capita consumption in the least developed countries (80 kilowatt hours a year) indicates the need and potential for substantial growth in electricity consumption in those countries.

Electricity has been the fastest growing form of energy end-use over the past few decades. While total commercial energy consumption in developing countries has grown by 5 per

Figure X.1
PER CAPITA ELECTRICITY CONSUMPTION, 1993

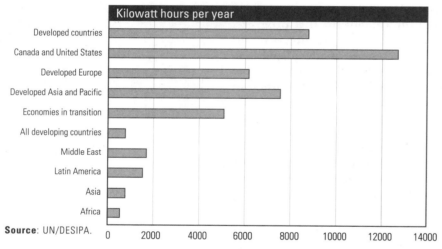

Source: UN/DESIPA.

Table X.1.
PER CAPITA ELECTRICITY CONSUMPTION IN DEVELOPING COUNTRIES, 1993

Kilowatt hours per year

High users		Low users	
Qatar	10 510	Chad	14
Kuwait	10 254	Cambodia	19
Israel	4 888	Burkina Faso	20
South Africa	3 830	Burundi	23
Republic of Korea	3 704	Ethiopia	25
Venezuela	3 399	Comoros	26
Argentina	1 903	Somalia	29
Malaysia	1 847	United Republic of Tanzania	32
Brazil	1 783	Mali	33
Chile	1 737	Uganda	34

Source: *1993 Energy Statistics Yearbook* (United Nations publication, Sales No. E/F.95.XVII.9).

cent a year since 1973, electricity consumption has grown by 7 per cent annually. In comparison, the demand for electricity in the developed countries, during the same period, rose by less than 3 per cent a year, albeit from a much higher base. Without the dampening effect of chronic shortages, developing country consumption could have increased even more rapidly.

The strength of the demand for increased electricity supplies may be seen in terms of implicit income elasticities. The rate of growth of demand for energy has generally been close to the rate of growth of GDP in the developing countries (i.e., the income elasticity of demand was 1). But the rate of growth of power usage has been close to 50 per cent faster than the rate of growth of GDP (elasticity of 1.5).

Figure X.2 illustrates the buoyancy in the demand for electricity in a different manner. Following very strong growth in the 1960s and early 1970s, the growth of total energy consumption decelerated and demand has since expanded at almost the same rate as GDP. This reflected energy conservation and efficiency improvements that followed the sharp rise of energy prices in 1973-1974 and 1979-1980. However, electricity consumption grew throughout this period at rates higher than those of GDP and commercial energy consumption. This was the case both in times of strong economic growth and in times of little or no growth, owing to the mechanization of industrial and agricultural production and the growth of electricity connection grids to households and service establishments.

Even so, electricity consumption in developing countries grew faster in the 1970s than it did in the 1980s and early 1990s. The rapid expansion of electricity in the 1970s took place while oil prices quadrupled in real terms. During that period, one might have expected the sharp rise in prices to substantially suppress consumption growth, particularly since electricity generation in most developing countries was heavily based on oil. While it is almost impossible to know with any degree of certainty how fast the growth in electricity use in developing countries would have been in the absence of the oil price changes of the 1970s, it appears that those shocks had little impact on the growth of electricity consumption. The most obvious explanation for that behaviour is that the increase in electricity costs due to the rises in oil prices were not quickly passed through to consumers but instead were absorbed by local power utilities through greater subsidies.

The aggregate relationship, in any case, is not the full story. Table X.2 presents information about the growth of both electricity use and national income for 18 developing countries (collectively they account for over four fifths of all developing country electricity use). Two generalizations were expected to apply to these data. One was that income elasticities of electricity demand would tend to be lower in countries with higher levels of economic development, as has generally been observed. While this hypothesis applies to the majority of countries in the table, it does not apply to them all. In particular, Argentina, Saudi Arabia, South Africa and Venezuela, in spite of having attained a relatively high level of GDP per capita, have continued to demonstrate large increases in electricity demand.

The second general relationship expected was that the income elasticity of electricity demand would vary positively with the rate of economic growth. In some cases, however, electricity demand continued to grow during periods of

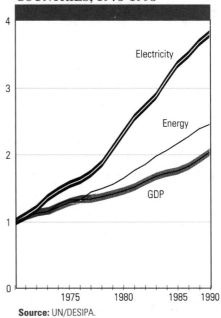

Figure X.2.

INCREASE IN GDP, ENERGY AND ELECTRICITY IN DEVELOPING COUNTRIES, 1975-1993*

Source: UN/DESIPA.

* All values are indexed to 1 in 1975.

Table X.2.
INCOME ELASTICITIES OF ELECTRICITY DEMAND IN DEVELOPING COUNTRIES

Country	Growth in electricity consumption	Growth in real GDP	Implied income elasticity of electricity demand	GNP per capita, 1984[a] (dollars)
	Average annual percentage change, 1975-1993			
Argentina	4.2	1.0	4.3	2 150
Brazil	6.9	2.8	2.5	1 700
Colombia	6.0	3.9	1.5	1 380
China	8.0	8.2	1.0	330
Egypt	8.3	5.9	1.4	640
India	7.8	4.2	1.9	280
Indonesia	14.9	5.6	2.6	590
Iran (Islamic Republic of)	8.3	1.1	7.8	3 750
Malaysia	10.0	6.6	1.5	2 120
Mexico	6.1	2.9	2.1	350
Pakistan	9.0	5.6	1.6	610
Philippines	2.5	2.8	0.9	2 240
Republic of Korea	11.4	7.5	1.5	2 040
Saudi Arabia	18.6	1.3	14.0	10 140
South Africa	4.5	1.5	3.0	2 354
Thailand	11.1	7.0	1.6	840
Turkey	8.5	3.7	2.3	1 100
Venezuela	7.0	2.1	3.4	4 250

Source: UN/DESIPA, and World Bank, *World Tables*, 1992.
[a]   Year chosen in mid-point of data range for elasticities; per capita figures are in accordance with World Bank Atlas methodology.

little or no economic growth (e.g., the Philippines in 1983-1985, and Saudi Arabia and the Islamic Republic of Iran in most of the 1980s). This indicates that in some countries, there are factors other than income that stimulate the growth in electricity demand. The main reasons for this disparity are price subsidies and government policies that facilitate access to and use of electricity.

Whenever possible, Governments of developing countries have promoted the use of electricity, both as a contributor to economic development and as a way to raise living standards. Similarly, some Governments have attempted to substitute readily available hydroelectricity for other forms of energy. For example, following the construction of the large Itaipu Dam, the Government of Brazil encouraged industrial customers to substitute hydropower (for which there was excess capacity) for imported fuel oil.[2] It is evident, therefore, that government promotion and subsidized pricing complemented rising income in contributing to the rapid rise of electricity use in developing countries over the past few decades.

[2]   Stephen Meyers and Jayant Sathaye, "Electricity use in developing countries: changes since 1970", *Energy*, vol. 14, No. 8 (August 1989), p. 436.

The production of electric power

The power stations that have been built in the developing world have relied primarily on relatively standardized technologies for electricity production. Figure X.3 shows the net installed capacity of electricity generating plants by type in 1993. About 67 per cent of capacity was thermal (i.e., using oil, gas or coal), 30.5 per cent hydropower, 2 per cent nuclear and 0.3 per cent geothermal. Other forms of new and renewable sources of energy, such as solar, wind and biomass are also being used to generate electricity in the developing world, but their contribution to overall electricity production remains negligible in spite of their potential use, particularly in rural areas.

The domestic availability of energy resources and the size as well as the location of the market weigh heavily in the choice of generating plants. For example, the availability of large-scale coal reserves have made coal-fired power plants particularly important in the power generation programmes of the electric utilities in China, India, Indonesia, South Africa and Turkey. In addition, because of its competitive price, a number of newly industrialized economies in South-East Asia rely heavily on imported coal for the generation of electricity. Coal at present thus accounts for about 45 per cent of power generation in developing countries, up from its level in the early 1970s.

In spite of its market competitiveness, however, coal use is expected to be limited in some countries because of concerns over environmental consequences, competition from natural gas, and financing difficulties in building new coal-fired capacity. Because of the high carbon and sulphur content of coal, its use has been the subject of global discussions on measures intended to reduce acid rain and mitigate the effects of global warming. Although fiscal mechanisms, such as carbon taxes have yet to be implemented in most countries, their proposals have led some power utilities in developed countries to move away from coal in favour of natural gas.[3] In developing countries, however, coal use will still grow very considerably, despite the environmental concerns, because of coal's availability and low cost.

The contribution of natural gas to the total power generation of developing countries currently stands at 7 per cent. However, natural gas use is set to grow very considerably owing to its environmental advantages over other fuels and relatively lower cost. Natural gas prices have fallen in real terms since the early 1980s, in parallel with the fall in oil prices. The growing importance of natural gas can also be attributed to the higher efficiency of combined

Figure X.3.
NET INSTALLED CAPACITY
OF ELECTRICITY GENERATING
PLANTS IN DEVELOPING
COUNTRIES, BY TYPE, 1993

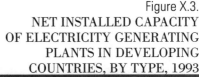

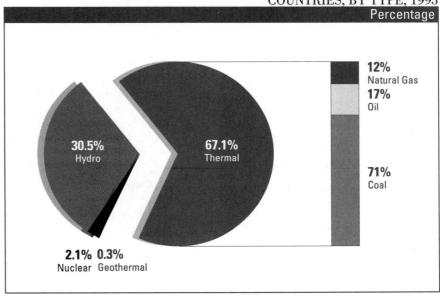

Source: UN/DESIPA.

3 International Energy Agency Coal Research, "Power station coal use: prospects to 2000", sample issue (January 1992).

cycle technology. In a combined cycle system, waste heat is recovered from a gas turbine to fuel a steam turbine, thereby reducing the heat content of a fuel that otherwise would have been lost in conventional, single cycle thermal power plants. The conversion efficiencies (the percentage of energy contained in the fuel that is converted into electricity) of combined cycle gas systems can reach 45 per cent, compared with about 30 per cent in conventional natural-gas-fired power plants. Such combined cycle plants are not only more efficient in the conversion of energy than the conventional oil-, gas- and coal-fired power plants, but they produce electricity at a much lower cost. [4] In addition, gas-fired power plants emit 20 to 50 per cent less carbon into the atmosphere than either oil- or coal-fired plants.

At present, oil accounts for only 11 per cent of electricity generation in the developing world, considerably down from its share in the early 1970s. Dependence on oil for the generation of power declined during the 1980s, particularly in the larger developing countries. However, a considerable number of smaller developing economies continue to rely exclusively on oil for their electric power generation.

The development of hydropower in the developing countries has increased rapidly over the past two decades, accounting for 31 per cent of their electricity supply in 1993 (the developing countries also accounted for one third of the world's hydropower). However, only a small part of the hydropower potential has been exploited so far, owing in part to a lack of large markets near some potential hydropower sites, as well as to environmental concerns. Nuclear power's overall contribution is small but significant in some countries or areas (e.g., Argentina, China, India, the Republic of Korea, South Africa and Taiwan Province of China).

In the medium term, traditional sources of energy for generating electric power will dominate capacity expansion. Cleaner burning coal technologies will be used more progressively, in the light of such international treaties, as the United Nations Framework Convention on Climate Change, among other things. Natural gas use for power generation will continue to expand in easily accessible markets, but the high costs associated with tapping and transporting large supplies of natural gas to remote areas may curtail the growth of the use of this clean-burning fuel. Oil will remain the primary fuel for incremental electricity capacity in the oil-exporting countries and in relatively small markets. Based on the resource potential, hydropower may contribute significantly to the supply of electricity in Africa and Asia.

In the longer run, more advanced power generation technologies will be able to produce electricity at lower costs and with a less adverse environmental impact. The most promising of these technologies —some of which are still in various stages of development and demonstration in Europe, Japan and the United States of America —include gas turbine/steam turbine combined cycles, atmospheric and pressurized fluid-bed combustion and integrated coal-gasification combined cycle power plants.

Power suppliers will also need to draw increasingly upon advances in technology that increase the technically feasible and economically competitive range of new and renewable sources of energy. Research and development in renewable energy over the past two decades have already led to substantial reductions in the costs of producing electricity from solar, wind and biomass energy, although they are generally still not competitive with traditional electricity production techniques. A large potential remains for further advances and cost reductions. At the present time, however, such energy sources can be used efficiently to supply electricity in rural

4 Thomas Johansson, and others, *Electricity* (Lund, Sweden, Lund University Press, 1989), p. 522.

areas, where costs of extending national electricity grids can be prohibitive. One of the most efficient ways to use renewable energy in rural areas is through decentralized electrification, which has been successful in several countries through private sector, cooperative, government and donor-supported initiatives.[5]

There is yet another source of increased electric power supplies that is already available and has become increasingly noted in recent years, namely cutting losses and improving the efficiency of existing plant capacities. On the basis of estimates of future investment requirements in the power sector of developing countries (see box X.1), a 5 per cent reduction in losses in the power sector of developing countries would reduce the need to expand capacity by nearly 4,000 megawatts a year and save over $6 billion annually. More savings could also be achieved through the use of more energy-efficient technologies in a number of energy end-use areas, such as lighting, heating and air conditioning.[6]

[5]   See, for example, *Proceedings of the Seminar on Sustainable Development of Rural Areas, Decentralized Electrification Issues, Marrakesh, Morocco, 13-17 November 1995*.

[6]   Thomas Johansson and others *Electricity* (Lund, Sweden, Lund University Press, 1989).

Box X.1.

CAPITAL EXPENDITURE FOR ELECTRIC POWER NEEDS

As development proceeds, the demand for electricity in developing countries will continue to rise rapidly. Improvements in energy efficiency and technological advances may cushion the growth in power needs, but this effect would be offset by growth in incomes and demographic factors. The single largest market for power generation is China, where growth in electricity consumption has averaged 8 per cent a year since 1980. Under one scenario, where GNP will grow on average by 8.5 per cent for the rest of the decade and then rise by 6.5 per cent a year between 2001 and 2010, the Chinese Government foresaw the need to raise power generation capacity by 15 gigawatts a year from 1995 to 1997 and by 20 gigawatts a year from 1998 to 2000.[a] Such an annual expansion, which would necessitate capital investment in the order of $20 billion a year, is equivalent to the total installed power capacity in such countries as Finland, the Netherlands or Switzerland. Even if this strong growth is sustained until 2010, China's per capita consumption would still be less than one fifth of that of the United States today. Other long-term forecasts estimate that electricity generation will need to grow by 6 per cent per year between 1990 and 2020 in order to sustain average annual GDP growth of 8 per cent.[b]

According to a World Bank study of the electric power expansion programmes in 70 developing and transition economies, including the eastern and central European countries of Hungary, Poland, Romania and the former Yugoslavia, demand for electricity in developing countries will grow at an average annual rate of 6.6 per cent between 1989 and 1999.[c] This would necessitate a power capacity expansion of 384 gigawatts, raising total capacity to 855 gigawatts in 1999 at a cumulative cost of $745 billion in 1989 dollars (almost $1 trillion in current dollars).

The World Energy Council expects investments in the power sector in developing countries to range between $2.4 and $4.4 trillion in 1990 dollars during the period 1990-2020.[d] This would account for between 64 and 79 per cent of all energy investments in developing countries over the same period.

At a conservative rate of 6 per cent a year, it is estimated that developing countries will require an additional 1,170 gigawatts of installed capacity during the period 1994-2010.[e] At an average overall system cost of around $1.6 billion per Gigawatt,[f] total investment will be in the order of $1.87 trillion, for an average of about $117 billion a year. At the same time, substantial investment will be needed to rehabilitate and replace older power plants reaching the limits of their operating lifetime. In addition, investment will also be needed to improve efficiency and reduce the impact of fossil fuel consumption on the environment.

[a]   K. Wu and B. Li, "Energy development in China", *Energy Policy*, vol. 23, No. 2 (1995), p. 175.
[b]   Todd M. Johnson, "Development of China's energy sector: reform, efficiency, and environmental impacts", *Oxford Review of Economic Policy*, vol. 11, No. 4 (1996), p. 123.
[c]   Edwin Moore and George Smith, *Capital Expenditures for Electric Power in the Developing Countries in the 1990s*, Industry and Energy Working Paper No. 21 (Washington, D.C., World Bank, 1990).
[d]   R.K. Pachauri and others "Financing energy development: the challenges and requirements of developing countries", Round Table Session 4: Financing Energy Development - Winners and Losers?, in *Proceedings of the Sixteenth Congress of the World Energy Council, Tokyo, 8-13 October 1995*.
[e]   There is, of course, considerable uncertainty about any long-term projection, and results will depend on assumptions made about key determinants of the forecast. Under this scenario, which is intended to provide one probable magnitude of future power needs in developing countries, it is assumed that the total growth in real income over the projection period will be much larger than the overall growth in electricity prices in real terms, so that the key source of the growth of electricity demand would be the value of income elasticity. The aggregate income elasticity of electricity demand in developing countries has been declining over the past few decades, averaging 1.5 over the period 1980 to 1993. It is assumed that the income elasticity of electricity demand in developing countries will continue to decline over the projection period so that it will average 1.2, and that overall GDP growth rate in developing countries will average 5 per cent a year.
[f]   Construction costs of power plants vary widely between countries. They depend on a number of factors, such as plant type (e.g., conventional versus nuclear), fuel inputs (oil, gas or coal) and plant site. For the purpose of this forecast, the average unit cost (including generation, transmission and distribution) for the power expansion for developing countries is assumed at around $1,600 per kilowatt of installed capacity.

Why the producers of electric power are changing

In any country, the electric power consumed by households, enterprises and Governments is typically taken almost completely from large-scale distribution networks that serve a region of some size or the whole country. The economies of scale in transportation and production of electrical energy are such that a single power plant can supply a substantial market. Indeed, electricity is a "tradable good" (actually, a service) that countries frequently supply across borders. In the light of the technical characteristics of the production and distribution of electricity, not to mention the importance of electric power as part of the essential infrastructure of an economy, Governments have frequently taken direct responsibility for the electric power sector, especially in developing countries.

As recently as a few years ago, the power sector in almost all developing countries was a state-owned and state-operated monopoly that was vertically integrated from electricity production to medium- and high-voltage electricity transmission, to conversion to low-voltage electricity for distribution to households. This is now changing, mainly because of dissatisfaction with the operation of government-run utilities. While the critical importance and the special character of the power sector give Governments an essential role in the oversight of the provision of its services, excessive intervention and subsidies have in many cases severely compromised the effectiveness of public power utilities.

Blackouts and brownouts are common experiences in most developing countries.[7] The value of industrial output lost owing to such disruptions of power supply can be very high. In India, for example, the loss of income due to power cuts and power shortages has been estimated to be equivalent to between 1 per cent and 3.5 per cent of annual GDP.[8] Frequent power cuts and voltage fluctuations also cause damage to electrical equipment. Often households as well as enterprises and governmental customers need to invest in voltage stabilizers and back-up generators to protect their electrical equipment.

In addition, developing country electric utilities have been subject to persistent, large transmission and distribution losses. While estimates of such losses vary, they all point to levels that are judged to be unacceptably high, ranging from about 15 to 25 per cent of net power generation. As shown in table X.3, such losses can exceed 20 per cent of total power generation, as in India and Pakistan, or over 15 per cent, as in Indonesia and the Philippines.[9] By con-

---

[7] The term "blackout" refers to periods when there is a total loss of load and the term "brownout" to periods when there is not enough power supply to meet the demand. In the latter situation, demand can be reduced through appeals for voluntary reductions in load or through imposed load reductions on a rotating basis.

[8] Arun P. Sanghvi, "Power shortages in developing countries", *Energy Policy*, June 1991.

[9] Distribution and transmission losses can be classified into three types: technical losses caused by passing the electrical current through the distribution and transmission lines; administrative losses due to poor systems of record-keeping billing, metering and bill collection; and losses resulting from illegal tampering with meters or unauthorized connection to the distribution network.

Table X.3.
PERFORMANCE INDICATORS IN THE POWER SECTOR IN SELECTED COUNTRIES, 1991

	Transmission and distribution losses (percentage of net generation)	Sales per employee (megawatt hour)
Public sector ownership		
India	23.5	204
Indonesia	16.9	523
Pakistan	22.2	219
Philippines	15.6	481
Thailand	10.0	492
Turkey	12.3	762
Private sector or commercialized		
Argentina	11.7	1 514
Chile	10.8	4 971
New Zealand	5.3	2 210
Norway	5.7	5 520
United Kingdom	8.4	1 965
United States	7.1	4 057

Source: Robert Bacon, *Appropriate Restructuring Strategies for the Power Generation Sector: The Case of Small Systems*, IEN Occasional Paper No. 3 (Washington, D.C., World Bank, May 1995).

trast, in New Zealand and Norway, less than 6 per cent of electricity generated is lost in transmission and distribution. The losses in developing countries are equivalent to about 75 gigawatts of capacity, or 300 billion kilowatt hours a year, representing a value of some $30 billion a year.[10]

Inadequate maintenance of power facilities has been another very costly and common practice in developing countries. Owing to inadequate maintenance and rehabilitation, it is estimated that in many of the least developed countries, electricity is being generated at a capacity utilization rate of only 25 per cent and in the developing countries as a whole at about 40 to 50 per cent. By comparison, utilization rates for the developed economies are about 80 per cent. Furthermore, it has been estimated that older power plants consume between 18 and 44 per cent more fuel per kilowatt hour than do power plants in systems operating at best-practice levels.[11]

It would often be cheaper to repair and rehabilitate ageing power stations than to construct new ones, but that rarely happens. Rehabilitation and upgrading can prolong the operational life of ageing power plants by 15 to 20 years and increase efficiency by up to 20 per cent. Inadequate maintenance shortens the operational life of power plants and reduces their effective capacity. Rehabilitation and maintenance of power plants would not only increase efficiency, but would also be cost effective ways of raising the effective installed capacity, reducing the need for new investment and cutting air pollution.

Another dimension of inefficiency in the power sector is labour productivity. Table X.3 shows labour productivity expressed as the output or sales per utility employee. The difference between government operated and other utilities has been dramatic. A power utility employee in Norway or Chile could be more than 20 times more productive than one in India or Pakistan. The main reason for the difference is staffing practices. For example, the state electric utilities of Botswana, Burundi, Mozambique, Papua New Guinea, Rwanda, Zambia and Zaire have fewer than 25 customers per employee. In Pakistan, state-owned utilities have on average 38 customers per employee. The Republic of Korea, however, has 292 customers per employee, the United States of America has 240, France has 222 and the United Kingdom of Great Britain and Northern Island has 153.[12] The point at issue, of course, is not whether the utility operates in a developed or a developing country, or even whether it is a private or state enterprise, but whether management has the incentive to raise productivity and curb costs. Privatization can be one mechanism for strengthening this incentive. A case in point: since being privatized, the power utility of the United Kingdom has cut its staff by 8,000 people, or 47 per cent.[13]

The above suggests that when the State owns a utility, performance often becomes a matter more of policy than of commercial necessity. However, when state-owned utilities are run along commercial lines, as in Australia, New Zealand, France or the Republic of Korea, their operational efficiency can be as high as that in the private sector. Moreover, the reason for state ownership has usually been that Governments could directly guide their own enterprise in a socially desirable direction, whereas large, private monopolies would operate differently. But government guidance can also be given indirectly, through regulation of a private utility. The experience of regulated monopolies, however, has been quite mixed.

[10] World Bank, *World Development Report, 1992* (Washington, D.C., 1992), p. 117.

[11] World Bank, *World Development Report, 1994* (Washington, D.C., 1994), p.5.

[12] See Jose R. Escay, *Summary Data Sheet of 1987 Power and Commercial Energy Statistics for 100 Developing Countries*, IEN Energy Series Paper No. 23 (Washington, D.C., World Bank, March 1990).

[13] See Bernard Tenenbaum and others, "Electricity privatization: structural, competitive and regulatory options", *Energy Policy*, vol. 20, No. 12, (December 1992), p. 1156.

Table X.4.
PRIVATIZATION STATUS OF SELECTED DEVELOPING COUNTRIES, 1995

Objectives			
Complete privatization		Argentina	Chile
Partial privatization	Ghana Pakistan Oman Tunisia Thailand Jamaica Costa Rica Indonesia	Malaysia The Philippines Colombia Jordan	
Commercialization/demonopolization	Mexico China India Turkey Côte d'Ivoire Guinea-Bissau Bolivia Peru Republic of Korea Morocco		
	Commercialization/ demonopolization	**Partial privatization**	**Near complete privatization**
			Status in 1995

Source: UN/DESIPA.

[14] See Robert Bacon, *Appropriate Restructuring Strategies for the Power Generation Sector: The Case of Small Systems*, IEN Occasional Paper No. 3 (Washington, D.C., World Bank, May 1995).

Rather, it appears that introducing competition in the provision of public services can be a more effective force for operational efficiency than ownership or traditional regulation. Regulated firms have even operated as government-protected monopolies. Studies of the performance of nearly monopolistic power distribution firms in England, Wales and Chile concluded that while privatization led to large gains in power generation, there was little or no increase in the productivity of the distribution companies after privatization relative to that prior to privatization.[14] The final customers still faced a single provider of electricity services.

In any event, reform of the power sector has clearly entered the agenda of policy planners in both developed and developing countries. Reforms range from corporatizing and commercializing the public utility without altering its ownership, to full or partial privatization. To date, only a small number of countries have fully implemented their reform programme and others are still in various stages of implementation (see table X.4).

Among developing countries, only Argentina and Chile have largely completed their power sector reform programme, while Bolivia, Costa Rica, Colombia, Ghana, Malaysia and Thailand are well advanced in their reforms. Other countries that have made modest beginnings on their way towards power sector reform include China, India, Indonesia, Jordan, Lebanon, Mexico, Pakistan, the Philippines and Tunisia. Other countries, such as Côte d'Ivoire and Guinea-Bissau have improved the performance of their national electric utilities through the adoption of the French approach based on a system of management contracts. For example, the introduction of a small management team under an expatriate management contract has improved efficiency and increased revenues of Guinea Bissau's national electric utility.[15] A number of other countries have barely begun to create a clear framework for power sector reforms despite a declared enthusiasm for the idea.

The reality is that the simplicity and attractiveness of "privatization" as a political slogan has to confront the complexity of an appropriate transfer of ownership from the State to the private sector. While there are benefits and opportunities that result from privatization, there are also a number of significant challenges.[16] Considerations, such as restructuring of the company, downsizing of the labour force, development of regulatory oversight capacity and social challenges, can be formidable. In cases where full privatization is not feasible, Governments have used a number of other options, including partial privatization, commercialization, corporatization or demonopolization to reduce state control and improve efficiency.[17] Moreover, there are a number of areas in which the private sector can participate even if the utility itself remains a state enterprise, ranging from collection, billing and maintenance to power generation, transmission and distribution.

THE DECISION-MAKING ENVIRONMENT IN THE POWER SECTOR

The general thrust of the reforms in the power sector has been to increase the autonomy of the managers of electric power utilities and create incentives and disincentives that encourage decisions in the socially and economically desired directions. Policy on the pricing of electricity is a major case in point.

Pricing: politics versus market forces

Throughout the developing world, electricity prices have lagged behind the costs of supply. The utilities, in other words, have depended heavily on governmental subsidies. A World Bank survey of power utilities in 60 countries found that price levels for nearly 80 per cent of the utilities did not cover the long-run average incremental cost of supply.[18] However, in recent years, electricity prices in some countries have begun to reflect supply costs in response to commercialization and privatization of the power sector.

The classic problem with the subsidization of electricity, or in the subsidization of any good or service, is that it encourages excessive consumption and thus artificially raises capacity needs. Subsidies provide a significant disincentive for energy efficiency in the industrial and commercial sectors, where typically 70 to 80 per cent of the total power supply is consumed. Usually, energy subsidies are advocated as a benefit for the poor. In practice, little of the subsidized electricity reaches lower-income households, as only a small segment of them have access to electricity, particularly in Africa. Because the poorest people often live in rural areas, they usually have to depend on more expensive and lower quality forms of energy.

15 The introduction of the expatriate management contract was a joint initiative of the Ministry of Cooperation of the Government of France, the United Nations Development Programme, the African Development Bank and the World Bank.

16 See Mongi Hamdi, "Integration and privatization of national oil companies", *Proceedings of the Sixteenth Congress of the World Energy Council, Tokyo, 8-13 October 1995.*

17 The aim of commercialization and corporatization is to provide power utilities the autonomy to operate on commercial principles (i.e., have the freedom to set prices on an economic cost-related basis) and to manage their own budgets, borrowing, procurement, employment and wages. Demonopolization refers to opening up the power sector to private utilities to operate in parallel with state-owned power utilities.

18 World Bank, *The World Bank's Role in the Electric Power Sector*, A World Bank Policy Paper (Washington, D.C., 1993), p. 25.

19   Anthony Churchill, "Money is not the problem: it is the answer", in *Proceedings of the Sixteenth Congress of the World Energy Council, Tokyo, 8-13 October 1995*.

But artificially low prices of electricity also deprive electric utilities of revenue and thus a measure of autonomy. Not only does this encourage the dependence of the utility on the Government, but it limits the ability of the utility to mobilize finance under its own name for capacity expansion. Indeed, according to the World Bank, the annual subsidies of electricity consumption are estimated at about $100 billion, which is roughly equivalent to annual investment requirements. [19]

The economic principles underlying more appropriate pricing of electricity are not that difficult to elucidate. First, Governments should give aid to the poor in a manner that least distorts prices and efficient resource allocation (optimally, through direct wealth transfers, such as rights to land for tenant farmers). Second, the price of electricity should reflect the "real" cost, that is the opportunity cost, of its provision. Third, if an electric utility were privatized and left to itself, it would not charge the appropriate price. It would charge a higher one that reflected its monopoly power, and therefore the price needs to be regulated and/or new sources of supply need to be fostered so that the market can be contested.

The difficulty in the power field is in putting principles into practice. Industrialized economies with regulated private power utilities support large cadres of lawyers and industry specialists that advocate with the authorities for one price or another. Utility regulation is itself a specialization in the field of economics. But the good need not be the prisoner of the best in this field as in any other in applied economics. There is a set of customary practices and there is learning by doing. The regular exchange of experiences among utility regulators and specialists would deepen the common understanding of what works best in reality.

The changing process of investment decisions

The evolving enterprise and market structure of the electric utility sector in developing countries is changing the way investment decisions are made in the sector. Investment decisions in public utilities have traditionally been identified through least-cost planning models. These models entail a number of steps that start with a forecast of electricity demand, followed by the identification of an investment plan that would enable power utilities to meet the forecast demand. Once the investment plan is identified, a number of scenarios are considered in order to minimize system operating costs, subject to supplying the projected load at some given standard of supply. These operating costs are then added to the capital costs (calculated separately) to estimate the overall costs of the plan. The final step involves soliciting bids to implement the agreed upon plan.

Now, however, as private power investments are increasing, least cost planning models are becoming less useful in identifying the best investment decisions. [20] The method that actually minimizes cost may now involve government policy makers in considering multiple proposals from potential private producers at an earlier stage of the planning process. Also, as an increasing number of plants would be feeding electricity into a national grid in a growing economy, there would be opportunities for introducing competition by considering the market based proposals of new firms.

20   Dennis Anderson, "Power sector investment: how market forces are challenging the least-cost plans", FPD Note No. 16 (Washington, D.C., World Bank, July 1994).

The point is that the availability of competing private producers adds a new dimension to the planning process. These producers are also willing to absorb technical and financial risks rather than transfer them to the host Government. Unlike least-cost planning models used by public utilities, where the least-costly programme is identified following an estimation of capacity and electricity requirements, in the private sector both capacity requirements and the choice of the plant are determined through competitive bidding.

The most important private power investment options available to developing countries are the build-own-operate-transfer (BOOT) and the build-own-operate (BOO) schemes. Under a BOOT arrangement, a private project company, or a joint venture with a minority equity participation of the host Government, is set up to raise funds and plan, design and construct the power plant. The company then runs the facility for a period of time, which is intended to be long enough to pay off the debt and make an acceptable return on the investment. At the end of this franchise period, normally 20 to 25 years, the operating company transfers ownership of the project to the host country. Under a BOO scheme, the private company or the consortium retains ownership. Among the potential benefits to be gained from either scheme is the expertise and the advanced technology that independent power producers usually bring with them. In addition, the private investors bring financial capital to the project. However, because the legal, institutional and financial arrangements are usually complex to negotiate, the number of projects that have been successfully launched is limited.

The factors that policy makers must take into account in electricity planning are more complicated than they might once have been, not least because of the increasing appreciation of the damage that earlier investments had done to the environment. While the decision-making process varies from one country to another, in most cases it involves a large number of actors, multiple criteria, policy instruments and impediments (see figure X.4). When the process works harmoniously, the participation of the actors involved in the decision — Governments, power utilities, international financial institutions, commercial

Figure X.4.
DETERMINANTS OF AN INVESTMENT DECISION

MULTIPLE ACTORS	MULTIPLE CRITERIA	INTEGRATED MULTILEVEL ANALYSIS	POLICY INSTRUMENTS	IMPEDIMENTS	FINAL AIM
International Institutions	Economic efficiency	Global level	International finance Technology transfer Treaties, protocols Guidelines	Uncertainties Lack of methodologies	
Multinational corporations					
International NGOs					
Commercial and development banks	Social equity	Macro level (national economy)	Laws Regulations Guidelines	Lack of infrastructures and skilled manpower	Feasible path to sustainable electricity sector development
Governments		Intermediate level (energy sector)	R&D Economic instruments	Inadequate institutions	
R&D Institutuions	Financial viability				
Utilities		Micro level (electricity subsector)	Timely plans Siting guidelines Licensing procedures Public participation Tariff-setting	Inadequate funding Lack of public acceptance and consistant political will	
Consumers					
Public interest groups	Other				

(vertical label: Environmental linkages)

Source: Mohan Munasinghe, "Efficient management of the power sector in developing countries", *Energy Journal*, February 1992.

banks, public interest groups —ensures that economic efficiency, adequate supply, social welfare and protection of the environment are given appropriate consideration. However, in the absence of a common understanding between the various actors and in the presence of conflicting views on the decision criteria, decision-making can be delayed and lead to power shortages.

Broader aspects of the role of government

The implication of the preceding discussion is that Governments need to address on the level of broad political understandings and the overall development framework the interrelationship between electricity supply and demand and the economic, environmental and social dimensions of development policies.[21] The result would be a broad sector policy that might serve to harmonize or at least sort out the priorities embodied in the multiple criteria shown in figure X.4. Not only would this speed up the decision-making process on electric power expansion, but it would clarify the national position for the potential actors.

This is part and parcel of a now widely recognized need for clarity and transparency in public policy. Governments have a critical role to play in establishing a proper legal and regulatory framework that would set out clear roles for government, power utility and consumers, redefining sector governance. The regulatory tasks should be performed by an independent regulatory authority that would hold the power sector accountable for performance.

Here, contemporary thinking emphasizes "incentive regulation":[22] measures that provide the sector with incentives and scope for efficient performance, transparency and openness, and clear articulation of reform objectives, including pricing, without compromising the public interest. Such regulatory approaches must also include mechanisms to ensure full compliance with the rules, clearly set out in advance. The issue is confidence about policy not being changed and methods to reduce the perceived risk to investors.

The purpose of regulation must not be lost sight of. While proper power sector reforms and regulation are needed to improve performance, hastily applied institutional changes, driven by a bias towards privatization, can be costly. The public has a legitimate concern in the area of electricity supply, ensuring for example that private monopolies are not simply substituted for public utilities. But a clearer role for the Government as policy maker, rather than producer, will avoid the confusion of roles that seems to have been the cause of much of the inefficiency in most publicly owned power utilities.

Power utilities should be provided with both incentives and autonomy to choose among various ways to achieve performance goals. Regardless of whether the ownership is public or private, the Government should be responsible for regulation and policies, while power utilities should be responsible for investment planning, construction and operation of power facilities. Indeed, ownership of power plants, the electric grid and distribution networks can be unbundled and can be public or private, albeit with governmental regulation and oversight.

21 Mohan Munasinghe and others "Incorporation of environmental and health impacts into policy, planning and decision-making for the electricity sector", Key Issues Paper No. 4, in *Proceedings of the Senior Expert Symposium on Electricity and the Environment, 13-17 May 1991, Helsinki, Finland.*

22 Witold Teplitz - Sembitzki, "Regulation, deregulation, or re-regulation - What is needed in the LDCs power sector?", *OPEC Bulletin*, February 1991, pp. 13-15

XI SHOULD WE WORRY ABOUT WATER?

The planet may be largely covered with water, but over 1 billion people were estimated to be without safe drinking water in 1994 and almost 3 billion (roughly half the world population) were without adequate sanitation in developing countries (see table XI.1). Not surprisingly, almost half of the world population (over 2.5 billion people) still suffered from diseases associated with insufficient or contaminated water at the beginning of the 1990s.[1] Furthermore, water-borne diseases contribute to the death of at least 4 million children in developing countries every year.[2]

As will be discussed further below, part of the problem is that freshwater is a product not only actually scarce in several regions, but also relatively costly to transport over long distances. In any case, water resources development frequently requires large investments and long time-horizons — not to mention high sunk costs of installing or expanding distribution networks — which cannot always be easily afforded by poorer countries with scarce financial resources. In addition, high rates of population growth will continue to put severe pressure on the ability of many developing countries to provide water supply and sanitation to their unserved population.

By the end of the century, there may be fewer people without potable water, but many more will be without sanitation, among the reasons for which is that sanitation costs more to introduce than safe water and is perceived as less vital for survival than freshwater-supplies themselves. In addition, the cost of supplying water to those who already receive it will likely rise appreciably in many parts of the world. The imbalance between the growing demand for water and an increasingly scarce (and polluted) supply along with the rising cost of expanding and modernizing water networks is making inefficient management of water resources extremely costly. The present chapter thus focuses on key dimensions of inefficient water resource management and concludes with a brief analysis of two new economic approaches to water resources management: efficient water pricing and market-based mechanisms for water transfers.

THE CURRENT SITUATION AND OUTLOOK FOR CLEAN WATER

Concern about clean water has been in the global agenda for at least two decades (the United Nations Water Conference took place in Mar del Plata, Argentina, in 1977). The General Assembly sought to focus attention on the issue, inter alia, through proclaiming the period 1981-1990 as the International

[1] See World Health Organization, *Our Planet, Our Health: Report of the WHO Commission on Health and the Environment* (Geneva, WHO, 1992) summary.

[2] See United Nations Children's Fund, *How To Achieve the Goals for Water Supply and Sanitation, A Document for Discussion, Dialogue and Debate* (New York, UNICEF, 1994), p. 2; and United Nations Environment Programme, *Poverty and the Environment: Reconciling short term needs with long-term sustainability goals* (Nairobi, UNEP, 1995), p. 47.

Table XI.1.

WATER SUPPLY AND SANITATION COVERAGE, BY DEVELOPING COUNTRY REGION, 1990-2000

(Millions of people)

	1990		1994		2000	
	Served	Unserved	Served	Unserved	Served	Unserved
Africa						
Safe water	288	345	326	380	384	447
Urban	135	66	153	85	181	129
Rural	153	279	173	295	203	318
Sanitation	229	404	243	462	265	566
Urban	130	71	131	107	133	177
Rural	99	333	112	355	132	389
Asia and the Pacific						
Safe water	1 653	1 129	2 349	626	3 081	197
Urban	576	140	690	149	862	197
Rural	1 077	989	1 659	477	2 219	0
Sanitation	748	2 034	770	2 205	801	2 477
Urban	400	316	469	371	570	489
Rural	348	1 718	301	1 834	231	1 988
Latin America and the Caribbean						
Safe water	346	93	376	97	420	103
Urban	282	32	306	42	342	58
Rural	64	61	70	55	78	45
Sanitation	304	136	296	176	285	238
Urban	262	52	254	94	242	159
Rural	42	84	42	82	43	79
Western Asia						
Safe water	56	16	71	10	90	8
Urban	39	6	51	1	65	0
Rural	17	10	20	9	25	8
Sanitation	47	25	55	26	65	32
Urban	31	14	36	16	43	22
Rural	16	11	19	10	22	10
Total						
Safe water	2 343	1 583	3 122	1 113	3 975	755
Urban	1 032	244	1 200	277	1 450	384
Rural	1 311	1 339	1 922	836	2 525	371
Sanitation	1 328	2 599	1 364	2 869	1 416	3 313
Urban	823	453	890	588	988	847
Rural	505	2 146	474	2 281	428	2 466

Sources: UN/DESIPA, based on the Report of the Secretary-General (A/50/213 - E/1995/87) entitled, "Progress made in providing water supply and sanitation for all during the first half of the 1990s".

Note: Information on service coverage provided by Governments of States Members of the United Nations; population data based on *World Population Prospects: The 1994 Revision* (United Nations publication, Sales No. E.95.XIII.16) and *World Urbanization Prospects: The 1994 Revision* (United Nations publication, Sales No. E.95.XIII.12). Owing to insufficient provision of information, data for Western Asia are estimated on the basis of trends from earlier years and may be considered to be of a more speculative nature.

Drinking Water Supply and Sanitation Decade. Broadly speaking, the main goal of the Decade was to promote a substantial improvement in the standards and levels of services in drinking water supply and sanitation, particularly in developing countries (see Assembly resolution 35/18 of 10 November 1980). Improvements in both types of services are closely intertwined because the lack of sanitation precludes the proper treatment of human waste which is, in turn, one of the main sources of unsafe water.

The International Drinking Water Supply and Sanitation Decade witnessed a significant expansion in the provision of potable water supply and sanitation, even though progress towards the ultimate goal of universal coverage in both services was hampered by unexpected and difficult economic developments in many developing countries, including external debt problems, macroeconomic adjustment requirements, disappointing economic growth and attendant constraints on public expenditure.[3]

Full coverage will still be far from attained in many areas during the present decade. According to available data, which are of uneven reliability, the share of population with access to safe water in developing countries rose from 60 to 74 per cent during the first half of the 1990s and it is forecast that that share will have increased even further by the end of the decade (see figure XI.1).[4] The situation with regard to sanitation, however, is deteriorating. Although an additional 100 million people will be provided with adequate sanitation during the 1990s, total coverage is expected to drop from 34 per cent of the population in the developing world in 1990 to 30 per cent in 2000, as the number of unserved people will also increase by over 600 million during the same period.

To make matters worse, even with impressive rates of progress in water-supply coverage during the first half of the 1990s, the number of people without access to safe water in urban areas increased, owing to the significant rates of population

3   See the report of the Secretary-General (A/45/327 of 13 July 1990) entitled "Achievements of the International Drinking Water Supply and Sanitation Decade 1981-1990".

4   The standards of management and those of water quality vary greatly around the world and therefore the number of actual connections to potable water supplies appears to be lower than the number reported in the official data of some countries. The figures in the text should thus be interpreted as representing an upper bound on actual coverage.

Figure XI.1
ACCESS TO SAFE WATER AND SANITATION IN DEVELOPING COUNTRIES, 1990-2000

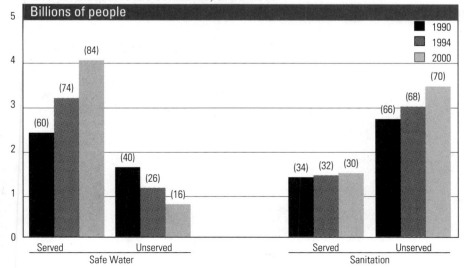

Source: UN/DESIPA, based on the report of the Secretary-General (A/50/213-E/1995/87) entitled "Progress made in providing safe water supply and sanitation for all during the first half of the 1990s".

Note: Numbers above bars are percentages of the relevant population.

growth in urban areas (see chap. IX). It is expected, however, that the situation will have worsened significantly in several respects by the end of the century. The number of urban-dwellers without access to safe water may increase by almost 60 per cent, from 244 million in 1990 to an estimated 384 million in 2000; and while the share of rural residents with access to safe water is expected to rise considerably during the 1990s, coverage in urban areas will drop to levels below those in 1990 (see figure XI.2). Sanitation coverage is meanwhile forecast to fall in both urban and rural areas. The number of urban-dwellers without access to adequate sanitation may almost double during this decade (see, also, table XI.1).

From a regional perspective, the urban water-supply crisis is likely to be worst in Africa, where percentage coverage will fall most markedly and where the number of unserved people will almost double between 1990 and 2000 (see figure XI.3). During the same period, the number of unserved urban residents will also increase by at least 80 per cent in Latin America and the Caribbean, and by 40 per cent in the Asia and Pacific region.

Securing a reliable supply of freshwater that is adequate in quality and quantity for all people is thus a fundamental challenge facing the world. It is being increasingly recognized, moreover, that the achievement of this goal may be undermined by a disruption in the water-supply of those who already enjoy access. As affirmed in the Dublin Statement on Water and Sustainable Development, one of the two main outputs of the 1992 International Conference on Water and the Environment: Development Issues for the Twenty-first Century:

"Scarcity and misuse of freshwater pose a serious and growing threat to sustainable development and protection of the environment. Human health and welfare, food security, industrial development and the ecosystems on which they depend, are all at risk, unless water and land resources are managed more effectively in the present decade and beyond than they have been in the past."[5]

5 The International Conference on Water and the Environment (ICWE) was held in Dublin, Ireland, in January 1992. It was convened by the World Meteorological Organization (WMO) on behalf of more than 20 organizations of the United Nations system involved in the field of water resources, and attended by participants from 114 member States, 14 intergovernmental bodies, 28 United Nations bodies and 38 non governmental organizations. ICWE provided the major input in the area of freshwater resources to the United Nations Conference on Environment and Development, held in Rio de Janeiro in 1992. (See *The Dublin Statement on Water and Sustainable Development and Report of the Conference* (Geneva, WMO, 1992). *The Dublin Statement and Report of the Conference* are also contained in document A/CONF/151/PC/112, annex I and annex II, respectively.

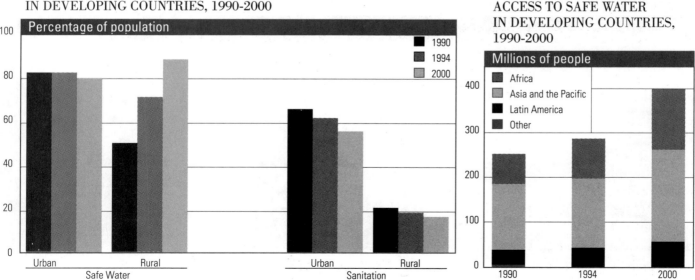

Figure XI.2
URBAN AND RURAL ACCESS TO SAFE WATER AND SANITATION
IN DEVELOPING COUNTRIES, 1990-2000

Figure XI.3
URBAN POPULATION WITHOUT
ACCESS TO SAFE WATER
IN DEVELOPING COUNTRIES,
1990-2000

Source: UN/DESIPA, based on the report of the Secretary-General (A/50/213-E/1995/87) entitled "Progress made in providing safe water supply and sanitation for all during the first half of the 1990s".

Roots of a threatened water crisis

The water crisis, if it indeed emerges, will be the result of four major tendencies. First of all, although freshwater is generally considered an abundant resource, its available supply is relatively scarce in many respects. While over two thirds of the Earth's surface is covered by 1.4 billion cubic kilometres of water, only 2.5 per cent of this volume is fresh, that is, suitable for drinking, irrigation and most industrial purposes (see figure XI.4). Moreover, no more than a third of this freshwater stock is available at less than extraordinary cost for human use in rivers, lakes and underground aquifers.[6] Furthermore, as the principle of sustainable development signifies, the amount of water available for human use should be determined not by the total volume of freshwater on Earth but by the volume of renewable freshwater stocks. Whenever rates of withdrawal exceed natural rates of recharge, human water use can be considered unsustainable. Such depletion of freshwater resources — notably of groundwater — is becoming increasingly common throughout the world.

The world's average annual renewable water supply is estimated at approximately 42,000 cubic kilometres, a figure representing a mere 0.1 per cent of total freshwater resources. This includes both water currently being withdrawn and water withdrawable under known technology at less than extraordinary cost. As table XI.2 shows, the availability of renewable freshwater resources also varies considerably among regions. For example, per capita availability in Oceania is 10 times greater than in Europe, whereas it is 9 times larger in Latin America than in Asia. Water availability problems are thus primarily regional ones. Indeed, in the densely inhabited and water-scarce north-eastern region of Brazil, it is irrelevant for human activities that most of the renewable freshwater stock of the sparsely populated Amazon River basin (which accounts for no less than 16 per cent of the world's renewable freshwater resources) goes unexploited.[7] The existence of the abundant water in the Ama-

Figure XI.4

DISTRIBUTION OF THE EARTH'S WATER RESOURCES

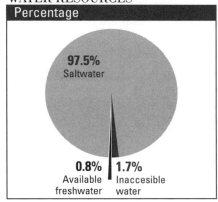

Percentage

97.5%
Saltwater

0.8%
Available
freshwater

1.7%
Inaccesible
water

Source: I.A. Shiklomanov, "Assessment of water resources and water availability in the world", mimeo (St. Petersbourg, Russian Federation, State Hydrologic Institute, 1995).

6   The bulk of the Earth's freshwater (69 per cent) is locked up in the polar regions and mountain glaciers (see I. A. Shiklomanov, "Assessment of water resources and water availability in the World", mimeo (St. Petersburg, Russian Federation, State Hydrologic Institute, 1995), p. 13).

7   See I. A. Shiklomanov, "Assessment of water resources and water availability in the World", mimeo (St. Petersburg, Russian Federation, State Hydrologic Institute, 1995), p. 29.

Table XI.2.

AVAILABILITY OF RENEWABLE FRESHWATER RESOURCES, BY REGION

(Millions of people)	Population, 1995 (millions)	Surface area (millions of square kilometres)	Renewable freshwater resources (cubic metres per year)		
			Annual average	Per capita, 1995	Per square kilometer
Africa	728.1	30.1	4 047.0	5.56	134.45
Asia	3 458.0	30.7	10 401.8	3.01	338.49
Europe	727.0	23.2	6 007.0	8.26	258.81
Latin America	482.0	20.6	13 120.0	27.22	637.20
North America	292.8	21.5	6 680.0	22.81	310.55
Oceania	28.5	9.0	2 402.0	84.14	268.38
World	5 716.4	135.1	42 657.8	7.46	315.77

Sources: UN/DESIPA, adapted from I. A. Shiklomanov, "Assessment of water resources and water availability in the world", mimeo (St. Petersburg, Russian Federation, State Hydrologic Institute, 1995); and *World Population Prospects: The 1994 Revision* (United Nations publication, Sales No. E.95.XIII.16).

Note: Latin America includes the Caribbean; Europe includes the whole of the Russian Federation; and the world total excludes Antarctica.

8   At the beginning of the 1990s, there were over 7,500 desalination plants in the world, with an annual capacity of 4,855 million cubic metres, that is, a mere 0.15 per cent of global water withdrawals. Almost half of this capacity was accounted for by only three Middle Eastern countries, namely, Saudi Arabia, Kuwait and the United Arab Emirates (see *World Resources Institute, World Resources 1992-93* (New York, Oxford University Press, 1992), p. 164).

9   Futuristic options like towing icebergs from the poles, also being beyond the means of most countries, would involve problems, not to mention such difficulties as might be created by exploiting the natural resources of the environmentally delicate and geopolitically sensitive polar regions.

10   Gershon Feder and Guy Le Moigne, "Managing water in a sustainable manner", *Finance and Development*, vol. 31, No. 2 (June 1994).

11   *World Population Prospects, The 1994 Revision* (United Nations publication, Sales No. E.95.XIII.16), annex table A.2 (population, medium variant).

12   Industrial water use is defined as encompassing freshwater withdrawals for manufacturing, mining and thermal electrical generation, whereas commercial water services include retail and recreation activities (see United Nations Industrial Development Organization "Global assessment of the use of freshwater resources for industrial and commercial purposes", mimeo (Vienna, UNIDO, 1995).

zon is even less relevant for the more distant water-short regions, such as Sahelian Africa or the Middle East. Strictly speaking, then, one cannot refer to an emerging "global" water crisis, but rather to a number of regional crises arising from imbalances between the local availability of renewable freshwater and the human demand for it.

One means suggested for overcoming unsustainable withdrawals of water is to increase freshwater supply by desalinating the vast stock of sea water. Although some desalination currently takes place, it is a highly capital- and energy-intensive activity and costs three to four times more than conventional freshwater withdrawals.[8] As a result of its high costs, desalination is used rarely and when it is used, it is often heavily subsidized by Governments. Thus, its use has largely been restricted to countries with abundant financial and/or energy resources. Even though costs are beginning to come down, desalination is likely to remain a relatively limited answer to local water shortages. In other words, it is highly unlikely that enough desalinating capacity would be created to make any significant contribution to ameliorating the building water-supply crisis.[9]

Outside the realm of exotic and non-competitive sources of potable water, the costs of adding new water-supplies have been rising. Most cities naturally first developed easily available and cheaper water sources, and so the unit costs of new water projects tend to be higher than the cost of existing supplies. In Amman (Jordan), for example, while the average incremental cost of the original water-supply network (based on groundwater pumping) had been $0.41 per cubic metre, this cost rose to $1.33 per cubic metre when physical shortages of groundwater led to the use of surface water.[10] The costs of expanding or modernizing existing urban water-supply networks are also rising because of higher water quality standards resulting from health considerations or consumer pressure. Higher project costs will also contribute to increasing delays in implementing new water projects, even though those projects may be urgently required to satisfy rising demand.

The second major tendency that could lead to a water crisis is to be found on the demand side. It is evident that freshwater resources will be increasingly challenged by a significant growth in world population, from an estimated 5.7 billion in 1995 to over 8 billion in 2025 and almost 10 billion in 2050.[11] Moreover, between 1995 and 2025, 96 per cent of global population growth is expected to take place in urban areas, mostly in developing countries (see chap. IX). As noted above, urban areas are also likely to suffer the most serious water-supply shortages in the years and decades to come.

The rapid growth of water use by industry and services adds to this problem.[12] In several rapidly industrializing areas, manufacturing and commercial water use are expected to increase 10-fold between 1990 and 2025. This is not surprising, given that the share of industrial water use in total water withdrawals in industrialized countries is over six times the share in developing countries (see figure XI.5). As the latter industrialize, they are also likely to experience a considerable rise in industrial water use.

It is generally agreed, as a rough rule-of-thumb, that when a country's annual renewable freshwater resources fall to around 1,700 cubic metres per capita, it will begin to become "water-stressed", and that, when this rate drops below 1,000 cubic metres per capita, that country is likely to suffer "chronic water

Figure XI.5
WATER USE, BY COUNTRY GROUP

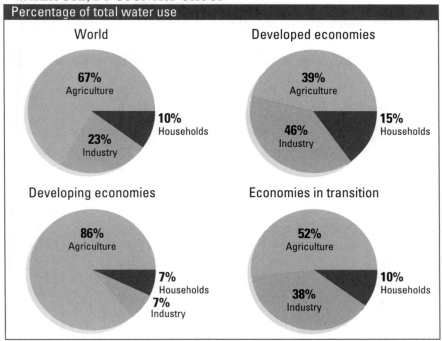

Percentage of total water use

World

67%
Agriculture

10%
Households

23%
Industry

Developed economies

39%
Agriculture

15%
Households

46%
Industry

Developing economies

86%
Agriculture

7%
Households

7%
Industry

Economies in transition

52%
Agriculture

10%
Households

38%
Industry

Source: World Resources Institute, *World Resources, 1994-1995* (New York, Oxford University Press, 1994).

scarcity", that is, to have its water availability then considered a severe constraint on socio-economic development.[13] Although these scarcity thresholds can obviously be affected by changes in the composition of production and consumption, efficiency of water use and climate patterns, they are commonly used as warning signals by many organizations of the United Nations system.[14]

According to these thresholds, no less than 30 States Members of the United Nations are likely to experience chronic water scarcity by 2025 (see table XI.3).[15] Overall, at least 50 countries are expected to be water-stressed by 2025, including many developing countries with large populations (China will be close to the water-stress threshold by 2025 and at it by 2050). As figure XI.6 illustrates, several highly populated developing countries that had abundant per capita water resources only a few decades ago are water-stressed or will be so within the next few decades. Moreover, because of uneven geographical distribution of surface water, groundwater and rainfall — together with the high cost of pumping water over long distances — several countries with abundant water resources at the national level frequently experience severe water shortages in certain regions, such as, for example, north-eastern Brazil, northern Ethiopia and north-western India, not to mention the south-western United States of America.

[13] These water scarcity thresholds were originally calculated on the basis of the understanding that 100 litres per day (36.5 cubic metres per year) were the minimum per capita requirement for basic household needs so as to maintain good health and that, in moderately developed countries, 5 to 20 times that amount was needed to satisfy the requirements of agriculture, industry and energy generation (see M. Falkenmark and others, "Macro-scale water scarcity requires micro-scale approaches: aspects of vulnerability in semi-arid development", *Natural Resources Forum*, vol. 13, No. 4 (November 1989), pp. 258-267)

[14] See, for example, United Nations Environment Programme, *Freshwater Pollution*, UNEP Global Environment Monitoring System (GEMS) Environment Library, No. 6 (Nairobi, UNEP, 1991); World Bank, *World Development Report, 1992: Development and the Environment* (New York, Oxford University Press, 1992); *Report on the World Social Situation, 1993* (United Nations publications, Sales No. E.93.IV.2); and Food and Agriculture Organization of the United Nations, *Water Sector Policy Review and Strategy Formulation* (Rome, FAO, 1995).

[15] There are no data on available freshwater resources for 26 (out of 185) States Members of the United Nations, a few of which may also be water-stressed. It is worth noting that several water-stressed countries (such as Egypt, Mauritania, the Syrian Arab Republic and Pakistan) obtain a significant share of their renewable water resources from other countries.

Table XI.3.

TOTAL ANNUAL RENEWABLE FRESHWATER RESOURCES, AND ANNUAL RENEWABLE FRESHWATER RESOURCES PER CAPITA, 1950, 1995, 2025 AND 2050, OF COUNTRIES LIKELY TO BE CLOSE TO OR TO HAVE EXCEEDED THE WATER SCARCITY THERESHOLD, IN 2025

(Cubic metres)

	Total annual renewable freshwater resources	Annual renewable freshwater resources, per capita			
		1950	1995	2025	2050
Kuwait	0	0.0	0.0	0.0	0.0
Bahrain	0	0.0	0.0	0.0	0.0
Qatar	20	800.0	36.3	25.0	22.5
Saudi Arabia	2 200	687.3	123.0	51.6	36.1
Libyan Arab Jamahiriya	700	680.3	129.5	54.3	36.6
Malta	30	96.2	82.0	71.1	68.3
Yemen	2 500	579.2	172.4	74.2	50.2
United Arab Emirates	300	4 285.7	157.6	101.4	87.6
Jordan	1 420	1 147.9	261.1	117.9	84.2
Barbados	50	237.0	190.8	161.8	153.8
Singapore	600	587.1	210.7	178.8	181.6
Kenya	14 800	2 362.3	523.7	233.6	160.5
Burundi	3 600	1 465.8	563.1	266.9	188.8
Cape Verde	200	1 369.9	510.2	272.1	208.6
Israel	2 150	1 709.1	382.0	275.4	240.8
Djibouti	300	4 838.7	519.9	284.4	213.8
Tunisia	4 350	1 232.3	489.0	327.3	278.7
Oman	2 000	4 386.0	924.6	328.2	199.9
Rwanda	6 300	2 971.7	792.3	398.8	289.6
Malawi	9 000	3 123.9	808.7	402.7	267.4
Algeria	19 100	2 182.1	683.6	420.0	343.1
Somalia	11 500	3 743.5	1 243.2	540.5	358.7
Egypt	58 100	2 661.0	923.2	597.1	494.9
Comoros	1 020	5 896.0	1 562.0	619.7	410.6
South Africa	50 000	3 654.2	1 205.8	704.7	554.8
Morocco	30 000	3 350.8	1 110.0	738.0	626.9
Haiti	11 000	3 373.2	1 532.0	837.9	592.5
Iran (Islamic Republic of)	117 500	6 947.3	1 746.4	951.0	720.4
Lesotho	4 000	5 449.6	1 951.2	958.8	683.1
Cyprus	900	1 821.9	1 212.9	970.9	894.6

Table XI.3.
CONTINUED...

(Cubic metres)	Total annual renewable freshwater resources	Annual renewable freshwater resources, per capita			
		1950	1995	2025	2050
Water scarcity threshold in 2025					
Syrian Arab Republic	35 500	10 157.4	2 421.4	1 059.5	751.9
Lebanon	4 800	3 326.4	1 595.2	1 085.0	925.0
Peru	40 000	5 241.1	1 682.1	1 090.2	912.8
Afghanistan	50 000	5 581.6	2 482.5	1 104.7	833.9
Madagascar	40 000	9 458.5	2 709.5	1 162.1	785.5
Zimbabwe	23 000	8 424.9	2 042.4	1 171.6	863.9
Belgium	12 500	1 446.9	1 236.0	1 201.1	1 241.6
United Republic of Tanzania	76 000	9 637.3	2 560.2	1 208.4	834.0
Korea (Republic of)	66 120	3 248.0	1 469.5	1 215.0	1 171.2
Togo	11 500	8 653.1	2 779.1	1 226.4	839.2
Nigeria	308 000	9 351.8	2 756.9	1 292.0	909.9
Burkina Faso	28 000	7 662.8	2 713.4	1 293.1	839.2
Poland	56 200	2 263.9	1 464.0	1 352.8	1 302.3
Uganda	66 000	13 859.7	3 099.0	1 373.4	915.0
Ghana	53 000	10 816.3	3 036.7	1 395.2	966.0
Mauritius	2 200	4 462.5	1 969.6	1 485.5	1 330.1
India	2 085 000	5 831.2	2 228.2	1 497.8	1 271.4
Pakistan	468 000	11 844.2	3 331.0	1 643.1	1 226.8
Mozambique	58 000	9 357.9	3 624.1	1 650.6	1 112.3
Mauritania	7 400	8 969.7	3 254.2	1 665.5	1 217.7
Water stress threshold in 2025					
Sri Lanka	43 200	5 626.5	2 353.7	1 725.9	1 523.8
Armenia	8 270	6 072.0	2 297.9	1 750.6	1 578.2
Ukraine	86 800	2 344.4	1 689.4	1 781.8	1 837.0
Dominican Republic	20 000	8 499.8	2 556.6	1 791.5	1 518.9
China	2 800 000	5 047.2	2 292.3	1 834.7	1 743.5

Sources: UN/DESIPA, based on World Resources Institute, *World Resources, 1994-95* (New York Oxford University Press, 1994); and *World Population Prospects: The 1994 Revision* (United Nations publication, Sales No. E.95.XIII.16).

Figure XI.6
ANNUAL RENEWABLE FRESHWATER IN SELECTED COUNTRIES,
1950-2050

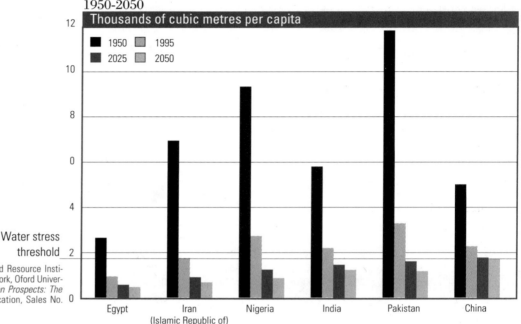

Source: UN/DESIPA, based on World Resource Institute, *World Resources, 1994-95* (New York, Oford University Press, 1994); and *World Population Prospects: The 1994 Revisions* (United Nations publication, Sales No. E.95.XIII.16).

The third factor that is all too often pushing towards water shortages is the increasing pollution of freshwater sources by untreated household sewage, industrial effluent, agricultural run-offs and inappropriate land-use patterns. Indeed, major industrial water pollutant loads in 2025 might increase three to five times the 1990 level, depending on plausible alternative economic development and energy growth scenarios.[16]

Water pollution is becoming a particularly costly problem in heavily populated urban areas in developing countries. Freshwater sources near many urban centres have become so severely contaminated that more distant sources have had to be developed at a considerable cost. In Shanghai, for example, water intakes had to be relocated more than 40 kilometres upstream at a cost of about $300 million.[17] In addition, increasing water demand by rapidly growing cities has in many cases led to overpumping of underground aquifers at a rate well above their natural rate of recharge. This is not only unsustainable in the long run, but also contributory to land subsidence in parts of several large cities. In Mexico City, for instance, water is currently being pumped over an elevation of 1,000 metres through a 140-kilometre pipeline because increasing land subsidence and deteriorating water quality have restricted the use of the city's aquifer.[18]

Last but not least, it is worrisome to note the degree of inefficient water resources management. The issue was highlighted in Agenda 21,[19] which expressed concern about the "fragmentation of responsibilities for water resources development" (para. 18.6) and the lack of integrated water resources planning and management. In many countries, water resources are developed and managed more or less independently at different levels of jurisdiction

[16] UNIDO, "Global assessment of the use of freshwater resources for industrial and commercial purposes", mimeo (Vienna, UNIDO, 1995), p. 3.

[17] J. Briscoe and H. A. Garn, "Financing water supply and sanitation under Agenda 21", *Natural Resources* Vol 19, No. 1 (February 1995), pp. 59-70.

[18] C. Casasús, "Privatizing the Mexican water industry", *Journal of the American Water Works Association*, March 1994, pp. 69-73.

[19] *Report of the United Nations Conference on Environment and Development, Rio de Janeiro, 3-14 June 1992*, vol. I, *Resolutions Adopted by the Conference* (United Nations publication, Sales No. E.93.I.8 and corrigendum), resolution 1, annex II. See also *Earth Summit: Agenda 21: The United Nations Programme of Action from Rio* (United Nations publication, Sales No. E.93.I.11), chap. 18.

(national, regional and local) and along the lines of separate sectors, such as agriculture, industry, hydropower generation, municipal water-supply, navigation, inland fisheries, recreation and so forth. Such fragmentation fails to take advantage of the multisectoral nature of water resources development and often leads to inefficient use of scarce water resources. Furthermore, inefficient water management is often closely associated with widespread underpricing of water and thus with a certain disregard for its economic value. There is therefore a policy dimension to the inefficiency question that warrants discussion.

The policy basis of inefficient water resources management

In many countries, political and social considerations have tended to overrule pricing policies that would promote more efficient water use. In addition, scarce public funds are allocated to develop new water sources — many of which are not financially or environmentally sound. In other words, water pricing subsidies and disregard for efficient demand management not only contribute to wasteful consumption, but also often lead to costly investments in otherwise unnecessary storage facilities and water distribution infrastructure.

Subsidization of publicly supplied water is a particularly serious problem in agriculture because agriculture tends to absorb the bulk of supply (see figure XI.5), often for low-efficiency and low-value uses. In the State of Arizona (in the south-western United States), for example, publicly supplied water is used to irrigate land producing wheat that yields values of about $33 per 1,000 cubic metres. In cities of the same State, the direct economic value of the same volume of water can be as high as $302.[20] In neighbouring California, water prices for irrigated agriculture are so low that it is profitable to grow low-value crops (such as corn for silage) even in very arid areas.

Widespread underpricing of irrigation water can be questioned not only because it tends to encourage production of low-value crops and wasteful water use, but also because it absorbs scarce public investment resources. There is much evidence that irrigation projects have become one of the most heavily subsidized of economic activities. For instance, a study of 18 major public irrigation projects in the western United States showed that the estimated subsidy ranged from 57 to 97 per cent of the full cost of supply, with a median of 85 per cent.[21] Another study estimated that average irrigation subsidies in six Asian countries covered no less than 90 per cent of total operation and maintenance costs.[22] Because of improper pricing of irrigation water, the percentage of capital and even operation and maintenance costs recovered from users is so low that very high levels of public subsidies are required to sustain irrigation facilities. Inadequate cost recovery, in turn, tends to reduce public funds available for investments in new irrigation projects or improvements in current ones.

Given artificially low water prices, it is no surprise that the predominant method of irrigation in many parts of the world is the flood system — that is, the pumping of water from open ditches between rows of crops until it soaks into the soil. This method is not only the most water-intensive (compared with more efficient sprinkler systems or drip irrigation), but also vulnerable to the greatest waste of water by evaporation. It is estimated that, on average, as much as 55 per cent of the water used for irrigation is lost to evaporation and other inefficiencies (see figure XI.7). Furthermore, without adequate drainage,

[20] See FAO, *Water Sector Policy Review and Strategy Formulation* (Rome, FAO, 1995), p. 72.

[21] At present, Californian farmers can pay as little as $3.50 per acre-foot of water, compared with a "water bank" buying price of around $125 per acre-foot (see M. T. Kanazawa, "Water subsidies, water transfers and economic efficiency", *Contemporary Economic Policy*, April 1994, pp. 112-122).

[22] FAO, *Water Sector Policy Review and Strategy Formulation* (Rome, FAO, 1995), pp. 10-11.

23 Waterlogging, the result of excessive watering of land that has a limited natural drainage capacity, increases soil salinity, as plants extract pure water, and evaporation from the soil surface leaves dissolved salts and minerals (that were present in the irrigation water) in the soil.

24 See FAO, *Water Sector Policy Review and Strategy Formulation* (Rome, FAO, 1995), p. 11.

25 See Feder and Le Moigne, loc. cit., section on "Underpricing of water and lack of cost recovery".

26 See John Briscoe, "Poverty and water supply: how to move forward", *Finance and Development,* vol. 29, No. 4 (December 1992); and Briscoe and Garn, loc. cit.

27 S. Cairncross and J. Kinnear, "Water vending in urban Sudan", *Natural Resources Forum,* vol. 7, No. 4 (November 1991), pp. 267-273.

28 See J. Karp, "Water, water, everywhere", *Far Eastern Economic Review,* June 1995, pp. 54-61. There is also evidence that in several Asian countries even very poor farmers pay relatively high prices for irrigation water supplied by informal sector traders (see World Bank, *Water Resources Management, A World Bank Policy Study* (Washington, D.C., World Bank, 1993).

29 See, for example, N. Spulber and A. Sabaggi, *Economics of Water Resources: From Regulation to Privatization* (Boston, Massachusetts, Kluwer, 1994), which shows how groups of consumers may be defined, based on economic, social or regional criteria, for the purpose of their receiving water vouchers or lump-sum credits through social security and the taxation system.

Figure XI.7
AVERAGE IRRIGATION

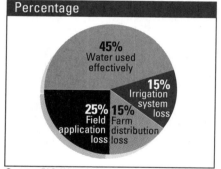

Source: FAO, Water for Life (Rome, FAO, 1994)

the flood system often leads to decreasing yields because of waterlogging and salinization.[23] At least a quarter of all irrigated land in developing countries is affected by salinization.[24]

In addition, public water companies often provide subsidized water services to urban households, particularly in developing countries and countries with economies in transition. A recent review of public urban water-supply projects financed by the World Bank in these countries shows that water prices cover only about a third of the cost of supply.[25] As in the agricultural sector, underpricing of urban water services is often accompanied by wasteful consumption patterns and, in many countries, occasional interruptions of supply or rationing. In addition, access to government subsidies by public water authorities also makes feasible low operating efficiency, be it in terms of low labour productivity, poor financial performance or disregard for unacceptably high levels of unaccounted-for water use resulting from the failure to repair leaks or limit illegal connections.

Furthermore, while such subsidies are often justified on the grounds that lower-income groups cannot afford to pay for water, there is evidence that it is usually wealthier and more influential groups that benefit disproportionately from government subsidies, since public water-supply networks in many developing countries tend to exclude services to the poorest urban-dwellers. Several studies show that, in many developing countries, subsidized urban water supply and sanitation are provided disproportionately to politically more influential middle- and higher-income groups which, in effect, pre-empt the inadequate supplies.[26] Other studies also show that large numbers of urban poor depend on private water vendors and pay a much higher price than wealthier consumers served by public piped water. In Khartoum, for example, private water vendors have charged between 30 and 120 times the rate per cubic metre paid by residents with a piped supply.[27] In low-income neighbourhoods of several Asian cities, water sold by private vendors costs between 20 and 100 times more than what middle-class residents pay for the same amount of piped water.[28] In any case, more efficient water pricing can be accompanied by social policy to better target subsidies on the true low-income groups; in other words, a policy of economic pricing does not necessarily imply that the poor should pay the full cost of water.[29]

In the presence of a growing scarcity of public funding, failure to charge more realistic prices for water has often been accompanied by insufficient investment in the modernization, expansion and even maintenance of water and sewerage infrastructure. Lack of adequate investment, in turn, has had adverse impacts on coverage of low-income groups, water-quality standards, human health and environmental balance. This vicious circle of heavy subsidization, inefficient operation, inadequate service expansion and insufficient investment cries out for re-examination by policy makers.

NEW ECONOMIC APPROACHES TO EFFICIENT WATER RESOURCE ALLOCATION

In response to the problems associated with inefficient patterns of water allocation among competing uses, Agenda 21, in its chapter 18, synthesized the consensus view on integrated approaches to the development, management and use of water resources. In addition, new, experimental economic approaches to scarce water resources management are emerging in various parts of the world. Among the innovative policies that countries have increasingly been introducing to promote a more efficient water resource allocation, two options deserve to be highlighted: (a) pricing policies aimed at improving water use efficiency or cost recovery and (b) market-based mechanisms for transferring water from low-value to higher-value uses.

Water pricing

Prices that reflect the economic value of water are particularly important because they encourage more efficient consumption and allocation of scarce water resources among different uses. It can be argued that efficient pricing of water should basically be determined in relation to its opportunity cost — that is, its value in the best alternative use. In other words, water should be available to a particular use only if its opportunity cost is lower than the value of that use. However, determining the opportunity cost of water requires detailed information about complex variables, such as the market value of future demand, pollution costs and investment alternatives, that are not always available, particularly in developing countries.[30] In any case, political and social considerations seem to allow only a gradual move towards the adoption of a price for water that equals its opportunity cost, not least because of the extensive degree of underpricing, particularly in the agricultural sector.

As a result, there has been an increasing emphasis on pricing policies linked to the cost of water-supply, as a first step, away from heavy subsidization towards politically infeasible opportunity cost pricing. In fact, according to a recent United Nations inter-agency water sector policy review, there are only two effective pricing principles that are practical: one based on the cost of provision of water and the other on its market price.[31] The motive of the first principle (the second will be discussed further below) is primarily to stress the importance of cost recovery by water companies in order to reduce pricing subsidies, operating inefficiency and inadequate investment. Thus, as discussed by Serageldin,[32] several countries are now beginning to set water prices that cover the cost of services in order to ensure the financial autonomy of their water companies and the sustainability of their operations.

Charging prices that ensure the financial autonomy of water companies is relatively easier in urban areas because of their greater concentration of consumers that can be metered and their generally high concentration of higher-value uses. Given the potentially large economies of scale in urban areas and, in developing countries, the existence of inefficient and small-scale private vendors that charge high water prices anyway, there are many opportunities to expand and improve piped water services at water prices that recover at least the cost of operation and maintenance.

In fact, in some recent experiences of urban water privatization, water companies have also been able to recover the fixed capital costs of new infrastructural investments by increasing water prices. One example from the developed economies that emphasizes full-cost pricing by a public utility is the English and Welsh model of full privatization of water-supply through the sale of shares to the public. It has shown that, contrary to conventional policy, a whole water-

30 See R. K. Sampath, "Issues in irrigation pricing in developing countries", World Development, vol. 20, No. 7 (1992), pp. 967 977; and World Bank, *Water Resources Management, A World Bank Policy Study* (Washington, D.C., World Bank, 1993), pp. 42-43.

31 FAO, *Water Sector Policy Review and Strategy Formulation* (Rome, FAO, 1995), pp. 18-26.

32 See I. Serageldin, *Toward Sustainable Management of Water Resources* (Washington, D.C., World Bank, 1995), pp. 18-26.

supply system (collection, purification, delivery and sewerage) can be owned and operated satisfactorily by private firms (provided, of course, that an effective regulatory machinery is in place to prevent excessive monopoly profits and to ensure that adequate infrastructural investments are carried out with reasonable profit returns).

However, the English and Welsh model of full privatization may not be suitable to most countries, particularly developing countries and economies in transition, because of their underdeveloped capital markets, restricted share-ownership base and limited capacity to regulate, and because of political opposition to the possibility of transferring ownership of such an essential public service to foreign investors.

Consequently, most recent experiences of water privatization have been based on long-term leases or concessions, as pioneered in France, where private companies are currently responsible for approximately three-quarters of water-supply. A leasing contract generally involves transferring the management, operation and maintenance of a water-supply system from a public water authority to the private sector for a fixed period of time (usually 10-20 years). In Guinea, for example, less than two years after contracts to supply water to the main cities were awarded to private water companies, the fee collection rate had increased from 15 to 70 per cent and services had improved considerably.[33]

Under a "concessionary contract" (that is, a contract that grants an operating concession), the private firm also becomes responsible for financing, building and operating new facilities to meet additional water demand over the concession period (usually 20-30 years), at the end of which all facilities are returned to the public water authority. An important feature of concessionary contracts is thus that increased water charges are also aimed at financing at least part of the capital (as well as operating) costs.[34] When private sector involvement is limited to the building and management of new water and sewerage facilities, the concession is often called a build-operate-transfer (BOT) contract.

Long-term concessions and BOT contracts have recently been awarded to private consortia, invariably led by French or British water companies, in places spread around the world, such as Buenos Aires, Mexico City, the Czech Republic, Malaysia, Ho Chi Minh City and several southern Chinese cities. For example, at the end of 1994, a joint venture between a local government authority in southern China and a leading French water company began a 30-year concession to run the water-supply system in the city of Tanzhou. It became the country's first water utility to be partly owned and managed by foreign private investors. This venture reflected how one local government authority had chosen to undertake costly improvements in water infrastructure that were necessary to support the city's rapid demographic and industrial growth. Many more contracts of this type are in the pipeline in several developing, industrialized and transition countries that have never before experimented with urban water privatization.

In agriculture, where economically efficient pricing is often hindered by the difficulty of measuring the volume each farmer consumes, there has also been increasing interest in cost-recovery schemes. The degree of subsidization has been quite large, even in industrialized countries, as public irrigation pricing

33 Feder and Le Moigne, loc. cit., p. 26.

34 Although state subsidies are often reduced, they are not totally eliminated and range from hidden subsidies -- such as the writing off of debt accumulated by public water authorities, as in the case of England and Wales (see F. Neto, "Privatization and regulation of water utilities: a comparative study of the English and French models", *DESIPA Working Paper Series* (New York, UN/DESIPA, forthcoming) -- to outright government subsidies to contain water price rises, such as exist in Malaysia (see V. Subramaniam, "Privatization of water supplies: the Malaysian experience", Aqua, vol. 42, No. 5 (1993), pp. 310-313).

has generally been set to cover only a small part of operation and maintenance costs.[35] Given the extent of subsidization and underpricing of irrigation services and the large size and long-term horizon of some infrastructural investments, the immediate objective of increased pricing in several countries has thus been to enhance the recovery of operating costs, leaving aside fixed (capital) costs for the time being.

Pricing of irrigation services include (a) direct pricing based on volume of water consumed, (b) quasi-direct pricing based on duration of delivery, delivery turns (that is, rotating of their access by users) or area irrigated and (c) indirect instruments, such as additional land taxes based on the value of agricultural output or taxes on fuel used by pumps.[36] Agricultural water use, however, is rarely priced on a volumetric basis, usually because consumption cannot be easily measured (notably groundwater). In any case, volumetric pricing of irrigation services to a large number of small farmers is usually impractical, if not infeasible. For example, it would be very costly to measure individual water consumption in large irrigation projects in South Asia given that, in many cases, hundreds of thousands of farmers receive a variable quality of service in areas even larger than 1 million hectares.[37]

A new approach increasingly being used to deal with this problem entails measuring and pricing water delivered to an ad hoc rural water user association, which then becomes responsible for recovering costs from users through indirect charging methods.[38] Besides improving cost recovery, this approach often contributes to improved coordination and cooperation between farmers and irrigation agencies, and thus to greater accountability of irrigation managers to water users. For example, evidence from the Republic of Korea shows that the establishment of such ad hoc associations has led to full user participation in water resources management.[39] Such innovative cost-recovery schemes can clearly contribute to ensuring the financial autonomy of the water-supply agency and to reducing pricing subsidies. However, because they are not fully based on volumetric pricing, and because subsidies are not totally eliminated, these schemes may not do enough to ensure efficient water reallocation from lower- to higher-value uses.

Water markets

Although water transfers within a sector are common in many parts of the world, transfers from low-value agricultural uses to high-value urban ones in order to increase aggregate economic benefit are still rare. In theory, this could be carried out in any of three ways, namely, through (a) administrative reallocation by national or provincial legislation ("command and control"), (b) raising water prices so that low-value users are encouraged to release extra amounts to higher-value ones ("opportunity cost pricing") and (c) trading among users in a free or regulated market.

The first approach, where water allocations are decided through administrative means, leaves allocation decisions to bureaucratic bodies that are never adequately informed about the relative costs and benefits faced by water users. The reallocation of water tends to be an antagonistic and cumbersome process that generally responds to changes in cost and demand conditions only with long lags, if at all. Consequently, allocation decisions tend to be ambiguous

[35] M. T. Kanazawa, "Water subsidies, water transfers and economic efficiency", *Contemporary Economic Policy*, April 1994, pp. 112-122; and Organisation for Economic Cooperation and Development, *Pricing of Water Services* (Paris, OECD, 1987).

[36] Delivery turns can be based on continuous flow (with water flowing through an irrigation canal at certain times and each farm free to consume as much as it needs) or a rotation system, under which water is delivered to users in turns, which usually depend on unpredictable annual river flows rather than known volumes (see M. W. Rosegrant and H. P. Binswanger, "Markets in tradable water rights: potential for efficiency gains in developing country water resource allocation", *World Development*, vol. 22, No. 11 (1994), pp. 1,613-1,625; and OECD, *Pricing of Water Services* (Paris, OECD, 1987), pp. 89-97).

[37] See World Bank, *Water Resources Management* (Washington, D.C., World Bank, 1993) p. 73.

[38] FAO, *Water Sector Policy Review and Strategy Formulation* (Rome, FAO, 1995), p. 73.

[39] Sampath, loc. cit., p. 975.

and hinder economically efficient use of water. Given that opportunity cost pricing can be accomplished easily only in the context of well-defined property rights and actual market transactions as well as other factors, the second approach is not much different from the first.

The challenge is to replace the largely administrative approach to water allocation with one that recognizes the unitary nature of the resource and its economic value, and distinguishes between public responsibility for the resource and the users' responsibility to manage its use. That there are many theoretical aspects of market-based water allocation methods that are potentially attractive is indicated by but a few examples: Water transfers are truly voluntary and hence tend to defuse political conflict; they ensure the mobility of water entitlement from less efficient to economically more efficient uses of water; they provide improved incentives to adopt water-saving technology and practices; they are decentralized and increase users' involvement in water resource management; they reduce environmental problems through more efficient resource utilization; and, last but not the least, they encourage efficient investment behaviour in water users. Despite the apparent theoretical attractiveness of water markets, their practical implementation is difficult to achieve, since a wide range of factors — physical (geographical, climatic, infrastructural and so forth), legal and administrative, cultural and psychological, to name just the most important ones — limit water rights transfers by raising the transactions costs that market exchanges must overcome.

A "sticks-and-carrots" combination of all three mechanisms mentioned above is present in a 1992 federal law of the United States which, inter alia, reallocates water away from California's Central Valley Project, a huge network comprising dams and miles of canals that transport water from northern California to the centre of the State's farm industry in the central valley. First of all, the law reserves 800,000 acre-feet of water — roughly 10 per cent of the water the project delivers in a year of normal rainfall — to rivers, estuaries, reservoirs and wildlife reserves, primarily to restore fish and waterfowl habitats. Second, it reduces federal subsidies and introduces a tiered pricing system designed to reduce wasteful consumption and encourage conservation. Third, the law allows farmers to sell excess water-supplies at market rates to urban water utilities.

This piece of legislation has emerged from the century-old battle over water rights in California between farmers, who use about 85 per cent of the State's water-supply, and household and industrial users, who have been facing severe water rationing, particularly during recent droughts. As a result, an intersectoral market in water is beginning to emerge. For example, in some transactions between the Imperial Valley irrigation system and the city of Los Angeles, farmers have agreed to adopt more economical irrigation methods or to improve existing irrigation infrastructure in order to free water for sale to the city.[40]

In theory, one of the main economic advantages of such water markets is increased productive efficiency, as owners of water rights are encouraged to chose more efficient ways of using water in order to derive financial gain through the sale of the surplus.[41] In addition, because water markets promote a more efficient use of existing supplies, they tend to reduce the amount of investment necessary to develop new supplies.

---

[40] Some types of improvements involve reducing the loss of water by investing in canal linings, with urban users bearing the cost. However, as Larry D. Simpson notes, an increase in total economic welfare might be achieved only if the salvaged water would otherwise be lost to beneficial use (see "Are 'water markets' a viable option?", *Finance and Development*, vol. 31, No. 2 (June 1994).

[41] See Larry D. Simpson, "Are 'water markets' a viable option?", *Finance and Development*, vol. 31, No. 2 (June 1994), subsection on "Advantages of water markets: increased efficiency".

Although there is evidence to show that some of these efficiency improvements are occurring in parts of the western United States, there also exist restrictive state water trading laws that undermine the satisfactory operation of free water markets.[42] In fact, water rights transactions are usually conducted through private contracts (in other words, without public bidding), albeit with oversight by government agencies, which often fixes ranges within which water prices can move. In other words, certain basic conditions for the effective functioning of markets, such as large numbers of buyers and sellers and well-defined property rights, are missing from most United States water markets. As a result, although market-like exchanges of water rights have generated some localized efficiency gains, water-intensive agriculture using inefficient irrigation methods has, on the whole, largely continued.

A possibly better water market model for countries to consider is that of Chile. Chile is a relatively dry country that has long metered water use, albeit with subsidies for low-income households. It is thus not surprising that Chile was the first country to adopt a comprehensive water law that established a detailed system of tradable property rights.[43] Its 1981 Water Code defines water rights that confer ownership and are transferable and independent of land use or ownership.

Under the Water Code, water is a public good with the right to use granted to private parties. Water rights are considered private assets which, subject to the Civil Code, can be sold or mortgaged separately from land. The right to use water is an actual or real right that confers ownership. The owner is entitled to use water, obtain benefits from it, and dispose of it. After the initial granting of a right, the State does not interfere with the process of water allocation and the future distribution of rights among users is left to the markets.

Although the most frequent transaction in the water market occurs between neighbouring farmers, there are a considerable number of purchases of rights from farmers by urban water companies, particularly in order to supply water to new housing developments or new industry. In order to enter into such deals, farmers are encouraged to use irrigation water more efficiently so that they can sell a small portion of their rights. For example, a farmer who increases irrigation water use efficiency by 30 per cent on a 40-hectare grape plantation can sell shares in water rights equivalent to 24 litre/second (enough to irrigate about 12 hectares annually) for $7,000-$10,000. In fact, farmers often sell a portion of their water rights to higher-value agricultural users as well.

What have been the results of the market allocation of water so far? Market allocation of water, and particularly the existence of secure property rights, appear to have made a noticeable contribution to the overall growth in the value of Chile's agricultural production during the last 15 years. The effects of the water market cannot be fully separated, however, from the effects of other economic reforms, especially trade liberalization and establishing of secure land rights.[44] This notwithstanding, the market mechanism did succeed in reducing the need for expensive new hydraulic infrastructure (the impressive growth in agricultural production has been accomplished without sizeable investments in irrigation infrastructure), improving overall irrigation efficiency and reducing the number of conflicts over water allocation. In addition, recent research has demonstrated that the market mechanism does produce substantial economic gains-from-trade both in inter- and intrasectoral transactions.[45]

[42] See, for example, R. G. Cummings and V. Nercessiantz, "The use of water pricing to enhance water use efficiency in irrigation: case studies from Mexico and the United States", in *Water Policy and Water Markets: Selected Papers and Proceedings from the World Bank's Ninth Annual Irrigation and Drainage Seminar, Annapolis, Maryland, December 8-10, 1992*, World Bank Technical Paper, No. 249, Guy Le Moigne and others, eds. (Washington, D.C., World Bank, 1994), pp. 79-95.

[43] See R. Gazmuri, "Chile's market-oriented water policy: institutional aspects and achievements", in *Water Policy and Water Markets: Selected Papers and Proceedings from the World Bank's Ninth Annual Irrigation and Drainage Seminar, Annapolis, Maryland, December 8 10, 1992*, World Bank Technical Paper, No. 249, Guy Le Moigne and others, eds. (Washington, D.C., World Bank, 1994), pp. 65-77; and M. W. Rosegrant and H. P. Binswanger, "Markets in tradable water rights: potential for efficiency gains in developing country water resource allocation", World Development, vol. 22, No. 11 (1994), pp. 1,613-1,625.

[44] See Robert R. Hearne and K. William Easter, *Water allocation and Water Markets: An Analysis of Gains-from-Trade in Chile*, World Bank Technical Paper, No. 315 (Washington, D.C., World Bank, 1995).

[45] Ibid.

The mechanism is not free from problems, particularly regarding intersectoral water allocations and conflict resolution, and sales and transfers of water rights separate from land have been infrequent, involving only a relatively small proportion of water users and relatively little reallocation.[46]

In sum, water trading can be considered a more politically feasible and economically effective instrument of water transfers than either administrative reallocation or full opportunity cost pricing. Governments have usually avoided the compulsory reallocation of water from low-value agricultural uses to higher-value urban and industrial ones on political grounds, not to mention those involving concerns about food security and possible compensation costs.[47] Furthermore, while the imposition of volumetric pricing in agriculture is usually regarded by farmers as a type of expropriation of the acquired right to a "free good", the establishment of formal water markets actually formalizes existing water rights and is therefore more feasible politically.

CONCLUSION

The conclusion of a major review of water reuse in the early 1980s — namely, that there is plenty of water in the world, but that it is either situated in the wrong place or available at the wrong time as well as relatively costly to transport[48] — is relevant here. Its differentiation by location implies that freshwater is primarily a local or regional product and thus that water scarcity cannot be considered a global environmental problem — in the same manner as, for example, stratospheric ozone depletion — even if there is a worldwide series of regional water crises. However, the situation as regards regional scarcity problems has, if anything, deteriorated significantly during the past decade and is expected to worsen even further in the near future. This calls for policies aimed at promoting more efficient water use and a more efficient allocation of scarce water resources among different uses, especially in water-short regions.

The importance of economic instruments of water demand management, such as appropriate pricing and water markets, is basically determined by the relative value of water. There have been obstacles to the introduction of full opportunity cost pricing and cost-recovery strategies, however important these strategies may be to ensuring the financial viability of water-supply companies and reducing the pressure on budgets of pricing subsidies. They are not, in any case, the only tools available for allocating water efficiently among different uses. Water markets can be a feasible and effective mechanism of water reallocation. As water becomes increasingly scarce in many regions, water trading could play a greater role both in improving water use efficiency and in transferring water to higher-value uses.

As in any structural economic adjustment, moving towards more efficient water use may displace workers and disrupt existing production. It may threaten, in particular, irrigated agriculture, and the challenge in that sector is to move towards means of irrigation that are more efficient or crops that are less water-intensive. This may even mean contraction of the agricultural sector; but the central goal must be to raise employment and production in the economy as a whole — in a sustainable manner and with appropriate attention to income distribution — and thereby raise overall living standards and efficiency.

[46] See Carl Jonathan Bauer, "Against the current? Privatization, markets, and the State in water rights: Chile, 1979-1993", unpublished dissertation, (Berkeley, California, University of California at Berkeley, 1995).

[47] As agricultural users would undoubtedly oppose such administrative reallocations, public authorities might have to negotiate with the users and possibly find a way of compensating them at least partially for the loss of their subsidy (see M. W. Rosengrant and H. P. Binswanger, "Markets in tradable water rights: potential for efficiency gains in developing country water resource allocation", World Development, vol. 22, No. 11 (1994), pp. 1,613-1,625).

[48] See J. Messer, "International development and trends in water reuse", in Water Reuse, E. J. Middlebrooks, ed. (Ann Arbor, Michigan, Ann Arbor Science Publishers, 1982). (Waste-water reuse could actually be a promising alternative source of water if enough treatment facilities were built and strict health standards were met, particularly before using such water directly in irrigation.)

XII BUSINESS SERVICES IN INTERNATIONAL TRADE

One of the tasks that macroeconomists set for themselves is to explain — even forecast — the total flow of international trade of a country, that is, the total of goods and services that are transferred between the domestic economy and the rest of the world. The central interest is in the total purchases by foreign residents of local production and by local residents of foreign production. The reason is that together these transactions bear on total expenditure in the domestic economy and thus on total production and employment therein. With certain major exceptions — such as shipping, travel and construction — most services have been considered "non-tradables" and the trade as considered in national income and balance-of-payments analyses was focused almost exclusively on merchandise trade. In recent years, however, more services have become increasingly "tradable", have entered into international trade in greater volumes and warrant an increasing focus of attention by macroeconomists.

Many of these services can be classified as "business services". They comprise a heterogeneous group of activities, which include communications, financial services, software development, database management, computer services, royalties for the use of proprietary information or designs, accounting services, construction and engineering, advertising, legal services, management and technical consulting. With the explosion of communications technology and the spread of liberalized trade policies, the effective size of various services markets spilled over borders and some have become global. Indeed, the relatively new "information age" activities loom large in the growth of the trade in business services, much as they so loomed in the growth of trade in manufactures.[1]

The present chapter surveys the development of international trade in these business services in recent years and demonstrates why analysts of this activity from a trade-cum-macroeconomic perspective must be particularly aware of the partial nature of their viewpoint.

DIMENSIONS OF THE GROWTH OF TRADE IN BUSINESS SERVICES

Selling services across borders is not the only — and often not the most prevalent — means for residents of one country to provide services to residents of another. The establishment of a subsidiary in one country by an enterprise from another country is in many sectors a more typical means, as when a foreign-owned banking affiliate provides retail banking services in a second

1 On the international trade in "new" manufactured products, see *World Economic and Social Survey, 1995* (United Nations publication, Sales No. E.95.II.C.1), chap. XI.

[2] The statistical classification and data on international trade in services and merchandise used in this chapter are largely those of the International Monetary Fund (IMF), as compiled from balance-of-payments statistics. To the extent possible, the data follow the guidelines of the recently revised *Balance of Payments Manual*, 5th ed. (Washington, D.C., IMF, 1993), as embodied in the monthly IMF computer tapes of *Balance of Payments Statistics* (beginning with the December 1995 issue). The data pertain to the value of exports and cover a sample of 86 countries for which data were available for the full period for the five major categories of services shown in the tables and figures.

[3] See Commission of the European Communities, IMF, Organization for Economic Cooperation and Development (OECD), United Nations and World Bank, *System of National Accounts, 1993* (United Nations publication, Sales No. E.94.XVII.4).

country. In fact, direct investment has been the primary means of foreign participation in markets for business services that were once local by nature. It is still a major means for delivering services abroad, but, increasingly, so is trade.

The increasing tradability of services is not, however, immediately obvious from the basic data on international trade.[2] In 1994, the most recent year for which relatively complete information is available, the global value of trade in all types of services was 22 per cent of the value of merchandise trade. This was virtually the same as the 1970 proportion, which was 21 per cent (see figure XII.1). In 1980, moreover, services were only 19 per cent of the value of trade in merchandise, although it should be noted that petroleum prices, having been unusually high that year, artificially depressed the proportion.

The explanation of the relative constancy in the share of services in international trade lies in the difference in the rates of growth, over the past quarter century, of the value of trade in the main types of services. The value of transportation services in international trade grew more slowly than the average of trade in all goods and services from 1970 to 1980 and from 1980 to 1994. Indeed, the average cost of transportation services fell dramatically over this period. One rough indication is that it was 9 per cent of the value of merchandise trade in 1970 but 8 per cent in 1980 and about 6.5 per cent in 1994. This reflected, in part, technical change and economies of scale that became feasible under the new technologies (as in bulk cargo carriers, very large tankers and containerized shipping), as well as the lower costs of moving people.

While the growth of travel earnings was slower than the average growth of total trade in goods and services in the 1970s, it has been relatively more rapid in the period since 1980. ("Travel" under balance-of-payments accounting — or "tourism" in the System of National Accounts[3] — entails the expenditures, in the "exporting" country, of foreign visitors.) This seems partly to reflect the greater ability to travel of an increasing proportion of the world's population, and also the increase in business travel that has accompanied the transnational spread of corporations.

In contrast to travel and transportation, however, business services are the one major category of traded services whose international sales grew more rapidly than the total value of trade in goods and services both in the 1970s and in the period since. By 1994, they had become the largest category of services trade, accounting for 42 per cent of the total, with a total value of exports of almost $410 billion.

In developing as well as developed economies, trade in business services grew faster than other service components and faster than merchandise trade in the past 14 years. The developed economies thus almost doubled the share of business services in total services exports between 1970 and

Figure XII.1.
WORLD TRADE IN GOODS AND SERVICES, 1970, 1980 AND 1994

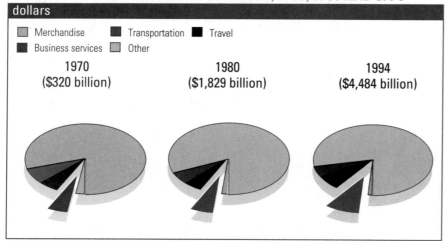

dollars

☐ Merchandise   ■ Transportation   ■ Travel
■ Business services   ☐ Other

1970
($320 billion)

1980
($1,829 billion)

1994
($4,484 billion)

Source: UN/DESIPA, based on data of IMF (sample of 86 countries).

Table XII.1.

STRUCTURE OF WORLD SERVICES EXPORTS, 1970 AND 1994

Percentage of total trade in services

	1970			1994		
	World	Developed economies	Developing economies	World	Developed economies	Developing economies
Transportation	35.1	36.3	23.1	23.2	23.3	23.1
Travel	27.0	25.6	37.1	30.0	28.2	39.7
Business services	27.0	28.0	19.8	42.0	43.7	32.6
Government services[a]	10.9	9.5	20.0	4.8	4.8	4.6
Total services	100.0	100.0	100.0	100.0	100.0	100.0

Source: UN/DESIPA, based on data of IMF (sample of 86 countries).
a Mainly expenditures of Governments (or international organizations) in other countries (for example, to maintain embassies or consulates).

Table XII.2.

WORLD EXPORTS OF BUSINESS SERVICES, BY REGION, 1980-1994

Billions of dollars

	1980	1985	1990	1994
World	112.7	141.0	310.1	409.6
Developed economies	99.4	127.1	281.4	361.4
Developing economies	13.3	14.0	28.7	48.2
Oil exporting economies	3.1	2.8	4.8	5.2
Non-oil exporting countries	10.2	11.2	23.9	43.0
East and South-East Asia[a]	6.1	6.8	14.0	28.5
Other Asia	1.6	2.6	6.4	9.3
Latin America and the Caribbean	4.0	3.2	5.3	8.2
Africa	1.6	1.4	3.0	2.2

Source: UN/DESIPA, based on data of IMF.
a Excluding China, owing to unavailability of data for full time-series.

1994, while in the developing countries, the share of business services rose from one fifth to one third (see table XII.1).

The major exporters of business services

The export of business services is mainly provided by the developed economies, which accounted for 88 per cent of the total trade in 1994 (see table XII.2). The world's top seven suppliers, in order of size, were the United States of America, the Netherlands, France, Japan, the United Kingdom of Great Britain and Northern Ireland, Germany and Italy. Together they account for two thirds of world exports of business services. The United States was the largest individual exporter, with $66 billion in 1994. The exports of France and the Netherlands were also quite substantial at $47 billion and $48 billion, respectively.

The developed economies have also been the largest international buyers of business services, although their exports exceeded their imports by $25 billion-$40 billion a year in the 10 years ending in 1994. Among the seven largest exporters, the United States, the United Kingdom, France and the Netherlands are net exporters, while Germany, Italy and Japan are net importers. This does not necessarily mean that the first group of countries are consistently more competitive suppliers of these services, since provision through direct investment is an alternative to export. It means no more and no less than that, for whatever combination of reasons, the first group are net exporters and the second net importers of traded services.

The United States recorded the largest surplus ($26.5 billion in 1994), which was more than two thirds of the total surplus of the developed economies. Large surpluses in royalties and licence fees and software were major contributing factors. Germany and Japan, on the other hand, have been in chronic deficit in business services trade, their deficits amounting in 1994 to $10 billion and $13 billion, respectively, mainly owing to their large imports of producer services (that is, services used as inputs into the production process). For France, Italy and the Netherlands, a sizeable surplus in construction and engineering has been notable. Among other developed economies, about half — including Austria, Belgium, Denmark, Greece, the Netherlands, Sweden and Switzerland — were net exporters.

The developing economies exported $48 billion in business services in 1994, an amount smaller than that of the United States alone. Most — but not all — developing countries lack the requisite labour, research and development capacity and modern information infrastructures that are essential for competitiveness in these services. The developing countries as a whole have been in deficit of around $2 billion - $7 billion per year in the past decade. The largest net earners of business service export revenues have been Singapore, Turkey and the Philippines ($6.3 billion, $3.6 billion and $1.7 billion, respectively, in 1994), while Brazil, Thailand and several oil exporting countries have been relatively large net importers (each with deficits in business services trade of at least $1 billion), the latter group of countries especially of oil-related services and construction.[4]

Although the level of business services exports of the developing countries is small, it has been growing increasingly rapidly. There are no simple ways to

4   The difference between the developed country surplus of $25 billion -$40 billion a year on trade in business services and the developing country deficit of $2 billion - $7 billion per year reflects the degree of incompleteness in the coverage of the data. Not only are the imports of business services of developing countries incompletely reported, but the substantial net imports of the transition economies are only partially recorded (they are not included in the database used in this chapter). Exports of business services are probably also under-recorded globally, as considerable activity takes place between affiliates of a single company in different countries and this is imperfectly registered.

measure this, since services data are usually given in value terms and exchange rates of major currencies have had large swings; however, figure XII.2 shows the average growth rates of business services as measured in special drawing rights (SDRs), a basket of currencies. Indeed, the figure shows that the growth of these exports from developing countries seems to have been less affected by the recession of the early 1990s in the industrialized countries than were the business services exports of the developed countries.

The main thrust in the growth of developing country exports of business services came from the dynamic economies of East and South-East Asia, where the dollar value of exports grew almost 12 per cent annually, a figure significantly higher than that for Latin America (5 per cent) and Africa (2 per cent). Among the top 30 countries in world trade in business services, 11 were developing countries, of which 5 were Asian economies, namely, the Republic of Korea, Malaysia, the Philippines, Singapore and Thailand. They accounted for more than half of the total business service exports from the developing countries in 1994. Singapore led with an export value of almost $12 billion and a surplus in business services trade of over $6 billion. In contrast, the Republic of Korea, Malaysia and Thailand are large importers of business services and persistently run a deficit on the business services account.

Three Latin American countries, Brazil, Chile and Mexico, are also among the world's top 30 exporters, but large imports in Brazil and Mexico have left these two countries with a net deficit of $1 billion - $2 billion each. Although small in scale, certain Caribbean islands have also participated in business services exports, in particular in the area of offshore data entry (for example, Barbados, Jamaica, Saint Lucia and Grenada),[5] while other countries have been significant providers of traditional offshore financial-market activities.

Africa's business service exports were less than a fifth of those in East and South-East Asia in 1994. Africa's deficit of $20 billion - $35 billion a year accounted for about two thirds of its overall deficit in services trade. Most of Africa's skill-intensive business services are either imported from developed economies or provided by foreign affiliates and professionals from these countries.

Just as intraregional links in merchandise trade are not well developed in Africa, so, also, is intraregional trade in business services limited, and in the same manner. However, increasing regional efforts to establish a continental communication network and other regional cooperation efforts may begin to promote greater intra-African trade in business services.

The major services exported

Information-related services — telecommunications, software development, computer services and data processing — have been the most dynamic category of business services. World expenditures on information services were estimated to have reached $325 billion in 1995,[6] reflecting advances in information technologies and their applications to a wide range of business activities. In addition, increased ability to "outsource" these services — to contract them out to independent suppliers — and a surge in demand for the services associated with the restructuring and re-engineering of industries have raised international trade in such services significantly.

The services are provided in a variety of forms: for example, either embod-

Figure XII.2.
GROWTH OF WORLD TRADE IN BUSINESS SERVICES, 1981-1994

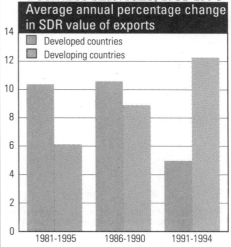

Average annual percentage change in SDR value of exports

■ Developed countries
■ Developing countries

Source: UN/DESIPA, based on data of IMF.

5 See *World Economic and Social Survey, 1995* (United Nations publication, Sales No. E.95.II.C.1), Chap. XIV, sect. entitled "Labour and technology: transformation of two industries" ("Data processing").

6 United States Department of Commerce, *U.S. Global Trade Outlook, 1995-2000* (Washington, D.C., 1995), p. 175.

ied in merchandise or disembodied, and sold either directly to final users or through intermediaries, with purchaser and seller either in physical proximity or remote access, and either in individual or in package deals. Moreover, the global structure of the information-related services industry is in great flux. The technologies in the different services are converging (that is, they are using digital signals to transmit voice, video and data) and this is spawning a wide range of new services firms, while existing firms merge, integrate vertically and diversify.

The United States is the main provider of information services, having held in 1994 a 46 per cent share of the international market, a larger share than that of the Western European economies taken together (32.5 per cent).[7] The United States holds a technological lead and provides a wide range of products which mostly have already been tested in its large, sophisticated domestic market. It also benefits from the dominant usage of English. United States exports of telecommunications, computer services and database services, excluding shipments to foreign affiliates, grew at about 10 per cent annually during 1986-1994 and reached $6 billion in 1994.[8] European countries and Japan are major importers. European countries, however, are competitive in various segments of the market and have been expanding to other regions rapidly.

There is a large gap in terms of skill and technology with respect to these services between the developed and developing countries. Information services in most developing countries are still in their infancy and most core parts are imported from the developed economies; but as the usage of computers spreads and communication infrastructure improves, demand for those services is increasing rapidly, indeed, at 10-15 per cent annually in many developing countries. Their exports — mainly, labour-intensive activities in dynamic economies in Asia — are also growing fast. Indeed, opportunities for exports of such services have been opening in recent years, as firms in the developed economies expand their outsourcing of these services to developing countries.

Communication services

Communication services are an especially important part of the information market. Internationally, as within many domestic economies, supplies have traditionally been less than competitive in the sense that customer charges, especially in the case of telephone services, have included significant and differential economic rents, as well as costs of service delivery. The standard mechanism has been one where national authorities (state telecommunications companies or national regulators) establish prices for international connections to the domestic system, as a result of which the charges can be quite different for a telephone call over comparable equipment from one country to either of two other countries despite their being an equal distance from the first.

In any event, the total revenue of the developed economies from sales of public telecommunication services was estimated to be $395 billion in 1992.[9] The United States accounted for about 41 per cent of the total in 1992. Telephone service is the main segment of communication services, but new services such as cable television, "value-added" services (including a variety of specialized services that can be accessed through the regular telephone network or via special carrier network), data transmission and mobile telephones constitute very dynamic sectors. The convergence of technologies, as noted

7   Ibid., p. 174.

8   Computation based on data from United States Department of Commerce, Survey of Current Business, September 1995, p. 76.

9   OECD, Communications Outlook, 1995 (Paris, 1995), p. 22.

above, and deregulation are expected to heighten competition, stimulate growth and bring about a substantial development of the market. Alliances among firms that specialize in different components of these services have already begun to intensify.

Total revenue in communication services in the developed economies grew about 9 per cent annually during 1990-1993. Growth in the United States was somewhat below this figure, at 6 per cent, although it has the dominant position. The rapid increase in demand for communication services is attributed to falling communication cost, increasing transportability of services and expanding digital communication networks as well as increased international trade and investment. Liberalization and deregulation in this sector, leading to more competitive pricing, have also stimulated the growth of demand.

Among developing economies, East and South-East Asia is the most dynamic region in the telecommunications sector. Export revenues in a number of countries in the region grew very rapidly in the past decade, albeit from a low base. China's revenues from international telecommunications also grew rapidly, indeed, by 56 per cent per year in this period, reflecting China's growing integration into the international economy.

Many developing countries have been installing digital communication systems and a number of those with the necessary technological base and skilled human resources may be able to leapfrog the mainly analog systems to a higher stage of technological sophistication directly. Given the huge cost of building a dominant communication network, however, firms in developing countries are making strategic alliances with firms in the developed economies to secure access to global communication networks.

The Asian experience is nevertheless not typical. In particular, development of the communications sector is at an early stage in Africa, although efforts have begun there to strengthen telecommunication infrastructures and connect their systems to world networks.

Computer software

With the growing connections of personal computers to networks and the application of new technologies to other industries, demand for software is increasing rapidly. As the interface among different systems becomes more complex, a share of business is shifting from hardware to software services. Global economic expansion also feeds demand.

Software is one of the especially confusing, grey areas in international trade between merchandise and services. While software that is written explicitly for a foreign customer is clearly a service export, packaged software that is mass-marketed might seem to be more in the nature of merchandise, and it is often recorded as such in trade accounts; however, as the value of packaged software greatly exceeds the cost of the physical product, owing to its being of the nature of intellectual property, it is more properly classified as a service export.[10]

In any event, world revenue from packaged software grew over 15 per cent annually in the first half of the 1990s, reaching $95 billion in 1995.[11] The United States is the dominant supplier in the world software market, having provided about 75 per cent of the $70 billion world total of packaged software in 1993.[12] Its foreign sales of packaged software were estimated at $24 billion in 1993, compared with purchases of only $4 billion from foreign vendors. The

[10] Indeed, the software is actually licensed for use by the purchaser, and not sold, as the fine print on the envelopes containing programme diskettes in packaged software makes clear.

[11] Data provided by the United States Department of Commerce in February 1996.

[12] United States Department of Commerce, *U.S. Global Trade Outlook, 1995-2000* (Washington, D.C., 1995), p. 135.

shares of Western Europe and Japan remain small, but competition is intensifying. Indeed, it has driven down software prices substantially.

Software industries in several dynamic economies in Asia and a number of economies in Latin America (including Argentina, Brazil, China, Hong Kong, India, Mexico, the Republic of Korea, the Philippines, Singapore and Taiwan Province of China) have exhibited a very rapid growth in the past decade, albeit from a very small base. However, software production is still relatively small in volume and rudimentary, even though some of these economies have become significant producers of hardware. Most sophisticated software is imported. Countries in Latin America, such as Argentina, Brazil and Mexico, have been trying to establish information industries and their software production grew rapidly during the 1980s.[13] However, this production was mainly in less sophisticated areas, such as administrative and accounting applications. In many African countries, personal computers have been introduced only recently and while some after-sale services are being performed, software services are generally small.

One notable development in the past decade is that a number of developing countries, including Brazil, China, India, Mexico and the Philippines, have experienced a surge in exports of labour-intensive computer services, including data entry and programming. This reflected the surge in outsourced demand for these services and a shortage of computer professionals in the developed economies.

India is a case in point. Domestic software production is growing rapidly and software is being exported. In fiscal 1994/95, India's domestic software sales increased 54 per cent to 11 billion Indian rupees (Rs) and software exports grew by 50 per cent to about $500 million.[14] Endowed with a pool of well-qualified computer professionals whose wages are less than a fifth of those in developed economies, India can be highly competitive in this sector, where labour cost is a major part of total production cost. The Indian Government has also provided incentives to encourage foreign investment inflow and exports. All in all, India's software industry is going through a rapid transformation from data processing based on low-cost labour to more sophisticated software development projects. To take advantage of these opportunities, an increasing number of foreign firms have been moving towards India and other countries with comparable situations.

Financial services

Developments in the information sector have also stimulated the growth of other business service sectors, perhaps most notably that part of the financial services industry whose operations are closely dependent upon the transmission and processing of information. These services include banking, insurance and securities exchanges. The technical possibility of the remote processing of information and the falling cost of information transmission, together with liberalization and deregulation in financial markets, led to the rapid globalization of financial services and the emergence of new, complicated — even customized — financial instruments. Through global communication networks, massive international financial trading can now occur routinely with remote places and at any time around the clock.

Thus, trade in financial services has rapidly expanded since the late 1980s.

[13] See Carlos M. Correa, "Informatics in Latin America: promises and realities", *Journal of World Trade*, vol. 23, No. 2 (April 1989), pp. 81-96.

[14] As per information of National Association of Software and Services Companies, Delhi, as provided to *Financial Times*, 6 December 1995.

In the developed economies, this process has progressed at a much faster pace than in the developing countries. Virtually all banks in the developed economies are now linked to international information networks either through their own networks or by leasing of network services from others. Financial services provided by resident banks of major industrialized economies to foreign customers almost doubled during 1987-1990.[15] United States exports of financial services grew 10 per cent annually in the past decade.

Developing countries generally lag far behind the developed countries in both technological applications and the liberalization of the financial sector. In the past decade, however, in an increasing number of developing countries, particularly in Asia, financial markets have been liberalized substantially and this has facilitated the inroads of financial firms from the developed economies. In many developing countries, however, concern about the infancy of their financial industries, costs of accessing global financial networks and the poor state of communication infrastructure have inhibited the integration of their financial markets into the international market.

Other services

In addition to dynamic "information age" services, there is also considerable international trade in more traditional business service sectors. One such sector is construction and engineering, where a combination of two different types of human resources are required: highly skilled professionals and semi-skilled labour.[16] Because of this, international contracts are often in the form of joint ventures between firms in developed and developing countries.

For the component that requires highly skilled professionals, such as consulting engineering, the developed countries dominate the market. On the basis of the revenues of the top 225 firms, contractors of the developed countries account for 89 per cent of total international construction revenue of $92 billion in 1994. Japan has the largest share (20 per cent), followed by the United States, France, the United Kingdom and Germany (with shares of 16, 13, 12 and 11 per cent, respectively).[17] Competition among developed countries is stiff. Among developing countries, China, which is competitive in labour-intensive projects, has emerged as a major exporter. In 1994, it earned almost $3 billion, an amount close to the revenue of the largest exporter, the Republic of Korea. Its technical sophistication is growing rapidly.

Among regional markets of developing countries, East and South-East Asia is most dynamic. Construction contracts for this region range widely from infrastructure projects, such as powerplants and transportation systems, to chemical plants, refineries, other manufacturing facilities and large buildings. Countries in the region import key parts of the construction from multinational companies, owing to inadequate domestic expertise and financial resources; but some of these countries also export construction services, as noted above.

In sub-Saharan Africa, owing to unavailable expertise, poor equipment, low technology, inadequate financing and foreign exchange constraints, local consultancy and engineering services are generally not internationally competitive and major parts of consulting projects go to European consultants.[18]

In other components of business services, such as legal services, accounting, medical services, broadcasting, cinema and advertising, cross-border transactions are constrained by regulatory barriers, ranging from restrictions

15   United Nations Conference on Trade and Development (UNCTAD), *The Tradability of Banking Services: Impact and Implications* (United Nations publication, Sales No. E.94.II.A.12)), table VI.2.

16   Activities of semi-skilled labour are often classified not as business services, but rather as labour exports, migrants transfers or workers' remittances, depending on both the length of time the workers are overseas and their residency status. This is yet another factor complicating interpretation of report.

17   *Engineering-News Record*, 28 August 1995, p. 36.

18   See G. K. Ikiara, W. N. Nyangena and M. I. Muriira, "Services in Kenya" (UNCTAD, Coordinated African Programme of Assistance on Services, August 1994), pp. 31-34.

on qualifications required before a foreign provider is allowed to perform a service in a country, to outright prohibition for reasons of national security, public health and cultural protection. Technological barriers in the same services, however, have been reduced significantly, inter alia, through advances in information technologies, and such trade has indeed been growing.

DETERMINANTS OF TRADE IN BUSINESS SERVICES

The growth of international trade in business services is part and parcel of the growth of services in economic activity globally. In 1970, services (including construction) accounted for 55 per cent of the combined gross product of developed and developing countries. By 1990, the share had risen to 65 per cent, owing almost entirely to the growth of the category of services that includes the ones that have entered into international trade.[19] Although the economic importance of services has risen highest in the developed economies, the expansion has also strongly affected developing countries. The growing role of services arises not only out of the growing demand for services by consumers, which accompanies rising incomes, but also from the increasing demand by firms for producer services. Furthermore, the conservation of materials and the miniaturization of products have been conducive to an increase in the share of services embodied in industrial output. In addition to these general factors, there are other specific determinants of the dynamism of international trade in business services.

Factors in the growth and spread of international business services trade

For business services to be traded internationally, they have first to be provided as a separate, identifiable business activity and second to be offered for sale across borders. Technical change has fostered the viability of separable and specialized business service firms that can interact over long distances. In addition to technical change, the spread of transnational corporations around the world and the relaxation of regulations and trade barriers have also made for greater international trade in these services.

Large corporations have been prominent in overseas industrial production for a century or more; so, too, have large business service firms, particularly in banking and insurance;[20] but whereas the industrial investments were typically related to international trade in one way or another, the services investments were more in the nature of a foreign entity establishing itself in a host country and providing a service to the local market (the exception, of course, being international trade financing). Now, however, services investments are more like industrial ones: trade is a key part of the story.

The reasons for the change seem grounded in the wave of technical change (still going on) that has multiplied the number of separable business services, often reduced the cost of providing them on a large scale and allowed them to be produced at a distance from the customer. In some cases these business services have become standardized (allowing, for example, use of "off-the-shelf" accounting software) and in some other cases the opportunities for customized services have been enhanced (for example, through contracting with a foreign firm of computer programmers to design a customized accounting system).

19 That is to say, the shares in gross domestic product (GDP) of construction, and wholesale and retail trade (about 5.5 and 18.5 per cent, respectively) were virtually unchanged, while that of transportation and communications had risen only half a percentage point (to about 5.5 per cent); however, the share of "other services" had risen from 26.5 to almost 35 per cent of gross product (estimates of Macroeconomics Division, UN/DESIPA).

20 A classic study of this phenomenon is found in Mira Wilkins, *The Emergence of the Multinational Enterprise*, Cambridge, Massachusetts, Harvard University Press, (1970).

The "information revolution" is at the centre of the entire process, particularly in the form of computerization and the transmission of computer-readable information over digital networks. The continuing rush of technical innovation in this area and its quick diffusion have revolutionized the speed and volume of information transfers several times in a generation.

The number of business service activities that have to be carried out "face to face" continues to decline; the opportunities for a finer division of labour continue to grow. Firms find themselves closing down their own in-house capacity to provide particular services and purchasing them from independent suppliers instead. As communications capacities swell, the suppliers that might once have had to be in the same city as the customer can increasingly be located anywhere on the planet. With rapid technical change occurring in the information and communication networks, the performance of an increasing number of services is no longer critically dependent on physical presence. Such disembodiment now takes place in a context where services are simply transmitted over the wire to users.[21] Indeed, there is a strong competitive pressure to reduce costs by unbundling segments of producer services and relocating them to other places within one country or to other countries where complementary inputs are cheaper or where demand for the separated services has significant potential.[22]

As the technological barrier to international trade in services has been falling, so too have policy barriers, although many still exist. Currently, the level of artificial barriers in business service trade is much higher than in merchandise trade. Barriers take the form of direct control of cross-border movement of services, restrictions on service-related investment, and discouragement of trade through administrative procedures, taxes and ownership standards. Market pressures to reduce these barriers have come both from firms wishing to provide the services to a market they cannot yet access and from potential buyers of the services. Such pressures have put liberalization of this trade high in the agenda in an increasing number of countries.

A case in point is financial services. International sales of financial services — for example, buying and selling of securities for foreign clients and research into the performance of locally listed companies for foreign stock traders — accompanied the liberalization of the financial flows in national markets in developed and developing countries. For the most part, the service trade in this area is closely associated with direct investment by foreign financial institutions. In the case of the Republic of Korea, the number of foreign bank branches increased from 16 in 1975 to 98 in 1995 and the number of affiliates and branches of foreign securities and insurance companies increased from 7 in 1980 to 78 in 1995.[23]

Transnational service firms could sell in a foreign market without investing there directly, but investment and sales of services through their own entities seem to be a preferred modality. In any event, it is clearly the case that the role of services firms — in this case, a larger classification than just business services — has grown substantially as a share of direct foreign investment. In the case of Canada, France, the United Kingdom and the United States, about half of the total stock of foreign investment by national enterprises was in the services sector, reflecting in each case the growing presence of the sector over time (see table XII.3). Services also figure prominently in the foreign invest-

[21] See Jagdish N. Bhagwati, "Splintering and disembodiment of services and developing nations", *The World Economy*, vol. 7 (June 1984), pp. 133-143.

[22] Up to a point: that is to say, there are fashions in management and some observers discern a move back towards centralizing tendencies in corporate organization.

[23] Data provided by Bank of Korea, January 1996.

24 A major part of the direct investment in services in developing countries is in offshore financial centres and flag-of-convenience countries; but even if these investments are excluded, the share of services in total direct investment in the developing countries has generally increased over time (see *Transnational Corporations in World Development: Trends and Prospects* (United Nations publication, Sales No. E.88.II.A.7), table XX1.6.

ments that these countries host. In the cases of Germany, Italy and Japan, about two thirds of the stock of foreign investment was in services. Investments by foreign services firms in these economies have also been very strong, albeit less so in Japan. A similar trend can be seen in the developing countries.[24]

There are no simple theories of international trade in business services

The discussion in this chapter might be quite discouraging to the macro-economist who wants to explain the export and import of business services. The conventional theories of trade in merchandise are more straightforward than the comparable theory for trade in business services would have to be. The reason is only partly that business services are a very heterogeneous collection of activities. There is a more fundamental problem, over and above the issue of heterogeneity, namely, that the services can be provided in more ways than goods can be, and for each way, in proportions that are the result of a myriad of factors.

At the heart of many internationally traded business services is an intangible asset — a "piece" of intellectual property — that gives the providing firm a competitive advantage in selling the service. If the firm licenses its product (or trade mark), it receives royalties, which are counted as an export of a business service. If it invests directly in a foreign country, it receives investment income, constituting another category of flow and one with a different time path. If it incorporates its technology or trade mark into a product that is exported, this is recorded as an export of a good in the balance of payments. These are merely three ways of extracting an economic rent from the intellectual property.

The point may be clarified with an example. Suppose that we want to measure trade and specialization in a specific sub-industry, say, word-processing programmes. If a company ships its software and manuals for sale abroad, this may be recorded as a merchandise export. If it sells these materials to a computer company that preloads them, then exports the computer, this is included in the value of the exported machine. If it sends just one copy of the software to a foreign firm that pays royalties in order to make further copies for sale or to preload in computers, this will show up in the balance of payments as an export of a business service. Finally, if the firm opens an overseas branch, the economic rents on sale of the software would be recorded as part of the revenues of the branch and will be a determinant of its profits which, when repatriated, enter the balance of payments as investment income.

In sum, it appears that the economist seeking an explanation for business services trade would need to include in that explanation the determinants of the substitutability of the goods, services and investment modes for capturing the economic rents. Moreover, the rents can often be increasingly timebound, even ephemeral, owing to the possibility of a rapid erosion of the superiority of the technology and knowledge.[25] Thus, analysing the flow of business services as if that flow were independent of the flow of related goods, direct investment and even technological sequences might not suffice; indeed, such an approach can be a problem for the analysis of trade in particular goods as well. It is always a problem, however, for the analysis of trade in business services, and to ignore it would be to act like the three blind men in the parable who, from where they stood, described an elephant according to the parts they could touch...

25 See James R. Melvin, Trade in Services (Nova Scotia, The Institute for Research on Public Policy, 1989), pp. 42-43.

Table XII.3.

SHARE OF SERVICES IN STOCK OF FOREIGN DIRECT INVESTMENT OF SEVEN MAJOR INDUSTRIALIZED ECONOMIES

Percentage

	1975	1980	1993
Canada			
Inward stock	25	25	32
Outward stock	28	26	49
France			
Inward stock	60	62	59
Outward stock	40	44	52
Germany			
Inward stock	34	40	53
Outward stock	47	48	69
Italy			
Inward stock	29	31	58
Outward stock	40	31	65
Japan			
Inward stock	18	22	44
Outward stock	40	44	66
United Kingdom			
Inward stock	..	28	41
Outward stock	..	35	45
United States			
Inward stock	36	45	53
Outward stock	29	39	51

Source: Data of UNCTAD, January 1996.

STATISTICAL TABLES

ANNEX
STATISTICAL TABLES

This annex contains the main sets of data on which the analysis provided in the *World Economic and Social Survey*, 1996 is based. The data are presented in greater detail than in the text and for longer time periods, and incorporate information available as of 15 April 1996.

The annex, like the *Survey* itself, was prepared by the Macroeconomics Division of the Department for Economic and Social Information and Policy Analysis of the United Nations Secretariat. The annex is based on information obtained from the Statistics Division and the Population Division of that Department, as well as from the United Nations regional commissions, the International Monetary Fund (IMF), the World Bank, the Organisation for Economic Cooperation and Development (OECD), the United Nations Conference on Trade and Development (UNCTAD) and national and private sources. Estimates for the most recent years were made by the Macroeconomics Division in consultation with the regional commissions.

Forecasts are based on the results of the March-April 1996 forecasting exercise of Project LINK, an international collaborative research group for econometric modelling, headquartered in the Macroeconomics Division. The LINK itself is a global model that links together the trade and financial relations of 79 country or regional models that are managed by over 40 national institutions and by the Division. The models assume that the existing or officially announced macroeconomic policies as of 15 April are in effect. The primary linkages are merchandise trade and prices, as well as interest and exchange rates of major currency countries. The model generates a consistent solution by an iterative process, and thus key exchange rates, interest rates and a complete matrix of trade flows and price changes are determined endogenously. The one significant exception is the international price of crude oil, which is derived using a satellite model of the oil sector; in this case, the average price of the Organization of the Petroleum Exporting Countries (OPEC) basket of seven crude oils is expected to remain at its 1995 level in 1996 and fall by about 3 per cent in 1997.

COUNTRY CLASSIFICATION

The country classification in the *Survey* divides the world into three major groups: developed economies, economies in transition and developing countries, as defined in the explanatory notes that appear at the beginning of the *Survey*. The groups are under review in the light of the major geopolitical and economic changes that have taken place.

The group of developed economies, comprising 23 countries, is further subdivided for analytical purposes into the following overlapping classifications: the major industrialized countries, which consist of the seven largest economies in terms of gross domestic product (GDP), namely Canada, France, Germany, Italy, Japan, the United Kingdom of Great Britain and Northern Ireland and the United States of America; Western Europe; the European Union; and North America. Data cover the 15 current members of the European Union for all years. North America includes Canada and the United States.

The group of economies in transition is subdivided into three subgroups: one is Central and Eastern Europe, also called Eastern Europe for short, which comprises Albania, Bulgaria, the Czech Republic, Hungary, Poland, Romania and Slovakia; a second group is the Commonwealth of Independent States (CIS), including Azerbaijan and Georgia; and the third comprises the Baltic States (Estonia, Latvia and Lithuania). In some cases, data are shown for the former Soviet Union until 1991 and for the aggregate of the successor States of the USSR from 1992 so as to facilitate analysis of trends over time. Data for individual successor States of the Soviet Union will be included in the annex as sufficient time-series become available.

Developing countries are grouped mainly by region, according to their geographical location (see the explanatory notes). For analytical purposes, a distinction is also made between capital-surplus countries and capital-importing countries (for country composition, see the explanatory notes). The capital-surplus countries are a group of petroleum exporters that at one point were major suppliers of financial capital to the world and whose very heavy dependence on oil revenues warrants maintaining them as a separate analytical grouping, even though most of them have become substantial net importers of financial capital. All other developing countries are included in the group of capital importing developing countries. The latter are further subdivided into energy exporters and energy importers. A country is defined as an energy exporter if it meets the following twin criteria: (a) its primary energy production (including coal, lignite, crude petroleum, natural gas, hydropower and nuclear electricity) exceeds its consumption by at least 20 per cent; and (b) its energy exports are equivalent to at least 20 per cent of its total exports (Myanmar, Yemen and Zaire meet these two criteria, but are not included in the group because they are least developed countries).

Energy-importing developing countries are further differentiated as belonging either to a group of four exporters of manufactures, that is, the four Asian economies considered to constitute the first generation of successful exporters of manufactures (Hong Kong, the Republic of Korea, Singapore and Taiwan Province of China), or to a group of other countries.

Finally, two other analytical groupings are sometimes employed. One is sub-Saharan Africa, which groups together all the African countries south of the

Sahara desert, excluding Nigeria and South Africa. The intent in this grouping is to focus on the smaller African economies; moreover, the data of the latter two countries would overwhelm the data of the smaller economies and give a distorted picture of the region in terms of GDP, population, international trade and so forth.

The other group is the least developed countries. Unlike the other groupings, which are created by the Secretariat for the convenience of economic and social analysis, the countries included in the list of least developed countries are decided by the General Assembly, on the basis of the recommendations of the Committee for Development Planning, which reviews criteria for identifying the least developed countries and considers the classification of individual cases. In its most recent resolution on the matter (resolution 49/133 of 19 December 1994), the Assembly added Angola and Eritrea to the list and graduated Botswana from it. Thus, there are at present 48 countries on the list.[1] The basic criteria for inclusion in the list pertain to being below certain thresholds with regard to per capita GDP, an economic diversification index and an "augmented physical quality of life index".[2]

DATA QUALITY

There is a growing demand from both the public and the private sector for timely and reliable statistics that can be used for economic and social analysis and decision-making in the present environment of rapid internationalization and information dissemination. Statistical information that is consistent and comparable across time and countries is of vital importance when monitoring structural adjustment, discussing welfare, environmental policy and poverty, or assessing emerging markets and economies. In addition, the multifaceted nature of these and other current issues, such as the high mobility of capital and people, and economic regionalization, call for an integrated as well as a selective approach to national and international data.

At the level of establishing international norms for definition and presentation of data, the 1993 revision of the System of National Accounts (SNA)[3] and the latest edition of the IMF *Balance of Payments Manual*[4] (the IMF Manual) highlight the changes within the economic and social context underlying statistical data during the past two decades, and constitute a major step forward in efforts to incorporate those changes into an integrated and harmonized system of statistics. The 1993 SNA strives to have concepts, definitions and classifications that are interrelated at both the macro- and micro-levels. Concepts in the IMF Manual have been harmonized, as closely as possible, with those of the 1993 SNA and with the Fund's methodologies pertaining to money and banking and government finance statistics. In addition, through a system of satellite accounts, which are semi-integrated with the central framework of the SNA, it is possible to establish linkages between national accounts data and other particular fields of economic and social statistics, such as the environment, health, social protection and tourism. The fact that the experts have failed to agree on a set of standards to define formal and informal activities, consumer and producer subsidies, education and other aspects of investment in human capital shows the methodological and material limits to capturing and quantifying all occurrences and changes. However, both the 1993 SNA and the IMF

1   Afghanistan, Angola, Bangladesh, Benin, Bhutan, Burkina Faso, Burundi, Cambodia, Cape Verde, Central African Republic, Chad, Comoros, Djibouti, Equatorial Guinea, Eritrea, Ethiopia, Gambia, Guinea, Guinea-Bissau, Haiti, Kiribati, Lao People's Democratic Republic, Lesotho, Liberia, Madagascar, Malawi, Maldives, Mali, Mauritania, Mozambique, Myanmar, Nepal, Niger, Rwanda, Samoa, Sao Tome and Principe, Sierra Leone, Solomon Islands, Somalia, Sudan, Togo, Uganda, United Republic of Tanzania, Tuvalu, Vanuatu, Yemen, Zaire and Zambia.

2   Report of the Committee for Development Planning on its twenty-ninth session *(Official Records of the Economic and Social Council, 1994, Supplement No. 2)* (E/1994/22), chap. V.

3   Commission of the European Communities, IMF, OECD, United Nations and World Bank, *System of National Accounts, 1993* (United Nations publication, Sales No. E.94.XVII.4).

4   IMF, *Balance of Payments Manual*, 5th ed. (Washington, D.C., IMF, 1993).

Manual will serve as guideposts for countries that wish to update, review or improve their statistical reporting.

As Governments begin to report their data on the basis of these standards, those data will be incorporated into the statistics in this annex. For the time being, however, the reader should be aware of the deep-rooted weaknesses underlying some of the national and international statistics that are perforce used in this *Survey* and other international publications. Inconsistency of coverage, definitions and data-collection methods among reporting countries sometimes mars the easy interpretation of data published by international agencies.

Another perennial problem is late, incomplete or non-reporting of data. Although adjustments and estimations are possible and are made in selected cases, in an era where economic and social indicators are closely tracked and extensively used, there is a need for timely reporting not only on an annual basis, but also on a quarterly or even more frequent basis, where applicable. It is worth noting, in this regard, the considerable progress made by some developing and transition economies in publishing annual and quarterly data on a timely and regular basis, whereas major lacunae have developed in the case of other economies in transition, in conflict or at war.

On the one hand, a widespread source of inaccuracy is the use of out of-date benchmark surveys and censuses or old models and assumptions about behaviour and conditions that no longer apply. On the other hand, when statistical administrations seek to improve their estimates using new sources of data, updated surveys and input-output tables in a sporadic fashion, there can be frequent breaks in the series. National income estimates are especially subject to significant revisions of the order of 10-30 per cent.[5]

National accounts and related indicators mainly record market transactions conducted through monetary exchange. Barter, production by households, subsistence output and informal sector activities are not always recorded. Generally, all but the last category have a larger share of total activity in low-income countries and lead to an underestimation of production of up to 40 per cent of national output. As the degree of underestimation varies across countries, output comparisons may give faulty results. In addition, as the non-market sector is absorbed into the mainstream of production over time through increasing monetization, the extent of output growth will be overstated based on the extent of this shift (see "Data definitions and conventions" below for illustrations of difficulties of the type noted here).

It is no exaggeration to say that weaknesses at the national level become major analytical handicaps when comparisons are made between countries or groupings of countries at a given time or over a period of time. Missing, unreliable or incompatible country data necessitate considerable estimation and substitution on the part of international organizations to retain consistent country composition of aggregated data over time. Furthermore, the absence of reliable GDP estimates for many developing countries and the transition economies requires analysts to resort to very approximate estimates in preparing country aggregations, as GDP weights underlie many data series.

Besides GDP, there are serious problems with other types of statistics that are commonly cited, such as unemployment, consumer price inflation and the volume of exports and imports. Cross-country comparisons of unemployment must be made with caution owing to differences in definition among countries.

5   Wilfred Beckerman, "National income", in *The New Palgrave: The World of Economics*, John Eatwell, Murray Milgate, and Peter Newman, eds., (New York, The Macmillan Press, Limited, 1991), p. 486.

For this reason in particular, table A.6 employs the standardized definitions of unemployment rates which, in certain cases, differ substantially from national definitions.

Consumer price indices are among the oldest of the economic data series collected by Governments, but are still surrounded by controversy even in countries with the most advanced statistical systems, owing in particular to changes in the quality of goods and consumer behaviour that are often not captured because of infrequent consumer spending surveys and revisions to sample baskets of commodities.

There are no clear-cut solutions to many of the problems noted above, and even when there are, inadequate resources allocated to the improvement of statistical systems and reporting can perpetuate statistical shortcomings. In this light, it is advisable to approach economic and social indicators as presented in this *Survey* as approximations and estimations, especially at the aggregate level.

DATA DEFINITIONS AND CONVENTIONS

Aggregate data are either sums or weighted averages of individual country data. Unless otherwise indicated, multi-year averages of growth rates are expressed as compound annual rates of change. The convention followed is to identify the *period of change* in a multi-year growth rate and omit the base year; for example, the 10-year average growth rate of a variable in the 1980s would be identified as the average annual growth rate in 1981-1990. Year-to-year growth rates are expressed as annual percentage changes.

Historical data presented in the statistical annex may differ from those in previous editions because of updating, as well as changes in the availability of data for individual countries.

Output

The growth of output in each group of countries is calculated from the sum of GDP of individual countries measured at 1988 prices and exchange rates. That is to say, national currency data for GDP in 1988 were converted into dollars (with adjustments in selected cases)[6] and were extended forward and backward in time using changes in "real" GDP for each country. The method is believed to supply a reasonable set of aggregate growth rates for a period of about 15 years, centred on 1988. In other words, the base year has to be moved from time to time to reflect the changed composition of production and expenditure over long periods.

National data on "real GDP" are utilized to build the aggregate output figures and thus national practices are followed in defining real GDP for each country. It would be fortuitous if individual countries also chose 1988 as the base year for their accounts, but in general they have not.

In the case of the United States, the base year itself has now a very different meaning. That is, United States GDP data have recently been recalculated in terms of a "chain-weighted" index. Instead of estimating the GDP for several years in the prices of the base year and then calculating the growth rate between years from these estimates, the growth rate of real GDP in the United

6 When individual exchange rates seem outside the bounds of "realism", alternative exchange rates are substituted. Averages of the exchange rates in relevant years might be used, or the exchange rate of a more normal year might be adjusted according to relative inflation rates since the time the exchange rate was deemed "correct".

States for any year is now the average of the GDP growth calculated in the prices of that year and the growth rate calculated in the prices of the previous year. A series of "real GDP" of the United States is then calculated by applying these growth rates to the dollar value of GDP in the base year, which is currently 1992.[7]

Developed economies

Up to and including the *World Economic Survey, 1992*,[8] the *Surveys*, in order to be as current as possible, published either GDP or gross national product (GNP) data (depending on which data series was released first) as indicators of economic activity in developed market economies. However, because of the improved availability of GDP data, as of the *World Economic Survey, 1993*,[9] the *Survey* has used GDP as its measure of aggregate output for all countries.

Beginning in 1991, aggregate economic growth data for Germany includes the former German Democratic Republic. Because official data for the level of GDP in post-reunification Germany began with 1991, the first year for which a growth rate could be calculated from official data was 1992. The growth rate in 1991, as shown in table A.2, was a weighted average of official and estimated GDP growth rates in the two parts of Germany, with the weighting based on the level of GDP in 1991, as published by the *Statistisches Bundesamt* (Federal Statistical Office) of Germany.

Economies in transition

Starting with the *World Economic Survey, 1992*, there was a switch to GDP from net material product as the measure of aggregate output of economies in transition. For the purpose of arriving at an analytically useful time-series in real and nominal terms, adjustments were made, notably in the case of the former Soviet Union, to the GNP data published in terms of local currency. In many instances, there were neither fully reliable national accounts data nor meaningful exchange rates for the 1980s, and this continued into the 1990s in several cases. Thus, a set of weights had to be estimated from fragmentary data (and a series of approximate growth rates of GDP in constant prices was constructed for the Soviet Union for 1981-1990).

Subsequently, new data became available that warranted updating the estimates of the weighting scheme. The data pertain directly to 1990, but as 1988 has been retained temporarily as the base year, the new data have been used to revise the 1988 weights, beginning with *World Economic and Social Survey, 1995*. In the previous exercise, as there were not economically meaningful market exchange rates for the transition economies in 1988, an effort was made to extrapolate a study of purchasing power parities (PPPs) in 1980 among the member countries of the former Council for Mutual Economic Assistance. In 1994, however, the European Comparison Programme published a set of estimates of GDP for 1990, valued at PPPs (see below), which followed upon a study of the same nature of all the member countries of OECD.[10] In addition, in 1993, a revised version of the "Penn World Table" (PWT Mark 5.5) was released, containing estimates of GDP in terms of 1985 PPPs for countries that had not participated in the International Comparison Programme (ICP) exercise for that year, and new estimated growth rates of GDP in PPP terms for all the countries through the 1980s also were made available.[11]

[7] See Charles Steindel, "Chain-weighting: the new approach to measuring GDP", *Current Issues in Economics and Finance*, Federal Reserve Bank of New York, December 1995; for details, see United States Department of Commerce, *Survey of Current Business*, January/February 1996, pp. 1-118.

[8] United Nations publication, Sales No. E.92.II.C.1 and corrigenda.

[9] United Nations publication, Sales No. E.93.II.C.1.

[10] See *International Comparison of Gross Domestic Product in Europe, 1990* (United Nations publication, Sales No. E.94.II.E.23); and OECD, *Purchasing Power Parities and Real Expenditures*, vol. I (Paris, OECD, 1992).

[11] See Robert Summers and Alan Heston, "The Penn World Table (Mark 5): an expanded set of international comparisons, 1950-1988", *Quarterly Journal of Economics*, vol. 106, No. 2 (May 1991), pp. 327-368. These data were made available on diskette by the National Bureau of Economic Research, Cambridge, Massachusetts, United States of America.

Estimates of GDP in 1990 for Czechoslovakia, Hungary, Poland, Romania and the Soviet Union were arrived at by using the OECD study to obtain GDP per capita figures in 1990 using "international dollars" and multiplying by 1990 population estimates. *World Economic and Social Survey* estimates of the growth of real GDP in 1989 and 1990 were used to extrapolate backwards to 1988 GDP levels, which were than deflated to 1988 prices using the revised PWT (albeit in terms of the 1985 base year). As Bulgaria and the German Democratic Republic had not participated in any ICP exercise, their 1988 base year GDP weights were estimated using a transitive approach (through the ratios with GDP estimates for Hungary in 1988).

In addition to the general caveat as to the overall reliability, consistency and comparability of data, the extent of economic activity not captured by national statistics has become an especially acute concern in some countries. The proliferation of new modes of production, transactions and entities has rendered the previous institutional and methodological framework for statistics inadequate. This produced major inconsistencies in officially reported data. A comprehensive reform of national statistical systems has thus been under way in the Russian Federation and in other States of the former USSR. As a result, important revisions to several data series have been released. Further revisions of past and current performance are expected, and it is likely that they will more accurately reflect market economic activity in its totality, in particular its currently unreported components. It therefore bears repeating more than ever that the statistical information provided, especially for many of the successor States of the Soviet Union, as well as for other countries in transition, must be treated as tentative estimates subject to potentially large revision.[12]

Developing countries

Beginning with the *World Economic Survey, 1993*, estimates of the growth of output in developing countries have been based on the data of 93 countries, accounting for an estimated 99 per cent of the population of all developing countries. GDP expressed in national currency in 1988 is converted to dollars. In cases where the conversion at the official exchange rate yielded unrealistic results, adjustments were made.

It has to be borne in mind that the veracity of estimates of output and of other statistical data of developing countries is related to the stage of development of their statistical systems. As these improve, revisions to the data can be expected. For example, in 1994, Turkey recalculated its GNP going back to 1968 by using new data, such as results of recent surveys, and incorporating some items and economic subsectors that could not be included in previous annual national accounts.[13] In Africa in particular, there is a wide divergence in the values of the economic aggregates provided by different national and international sources for many countries. Data for the countries in Asia and Europe as well as in Africa in which civil strife and war exist should be interpreted as indicating only rough orders of magnitude. In addition, in countries experiencing high rates of inflation and disequilibrium exchange rates, substantial distortions can invade national accounts data. For this reason, among others, Argentina revised its 1980s GDP by some 30 per cent.

[12] See *World Economic and Social Survey, 1995* (United Nations publication, Sales No. E.95.II.C.1), "Data caveats and conventions" in the statistical annex, pp. 289-293.

[13] State Institute of Statistics, Prime Ministry (Ankara, 1994), Republic of Turkey, *Gross National Product: Concepts, Methods and Sources*, State Institute of Statistics, pp. iii-iv.

Alternative aggregation methodologies for calculating world output

The *World Economic and Social Survey* utilizes a weighting scheme derived from exchange rate conversions of national data in order to aggregate rates of growth of output of individual countries into regional and global totals, as noted above. This is similar to the approach followed in other international reports, such as those of the World Bank. IMF, however, particularly in its *World Economic Outlook*, now follows a different approach. In May 1993, it adopted a weighting scheme for aggregation in which the country weights are derived from national GDP in "international dollars", as converted from local currency using PPPs as exchange rates. OECD followed IMF and adopted the alternate method in December 1993 in its *OECD Economic Outlook*. The question of which approach to use still seems controversial.[14]

The motivation for PPP weights was the belief that when aggregating production in two countries, a common set of prices should be used to value the same activities in both countries, which is frequently not the case when market exchange rates are used to convert local currency values of GDP. The PPP approach revalues gross production (actually, expenditure) in different countries in a single set of prices. The PPP conversion factor is in principle the number of units of national currency needed to buy goods and services equivalent to what can be bought with one unit of currency of the numéraire country, the United States. In principle as well as in practice, however, PPPs are difficult to calculate because goods and services are not always directly comparable across countries, making direct comparisons of their prices correspondingly difficult. This is particularly the case for several services such as health care and education, where output itself is hard to measure, let alone prices.

One significant problem in employing such PPP estimates for calculating the relative sizes of countries is that the most recently completed set of PPP prices, which was for 1985, covered a set of only 64 countries.[15] Estimates for a new benchmark year (1993) covering a larger set of countries will be published later in 1996 or in early 1997 by ICP, whose activities are coordinated by the Statistics Division of the Department for Economic and Social Information and Policy Analysis of the United Nations Secretariat.

This notwithstanding, certain regularities had been observed, on the one hand, between GDP and its major expenditure components when measured in market prices and on the other, between GDP and its components measured in "international" prices as derived in the ICP exercise. On that basis (and using other, very partial data on consumer prices) a technique was devised to approximate PPP levels of GDP and its major expenditure components for countries that had not participated in ICP, the results having come to be known among economists and statisticians as the Penn World Tables.[16]

Neither the PPP approach nor the exchange-rate approach to weighting country GDP data can be applied in a theoretically pure or fully consistent way. The data requirements for a truly global ICP are enormous, although in each round the ICP coverage grows. Similarly, since a system of weights based on exchange rates presumes a world of foreign exchange markets and domestic economies under competitive and liberal conditions, its application has been constrained by exchange controls and severe distortions of market prices in many countries. However, the global trend towards liberalization and the goal

14 See *World Economic and Social Survey, 1995...*, pp. 293-296.

15 See World Comparisons of Real Gross Domestic Product and Purchasing Power, 1985: *Phase V of the International Comparison Programme*, Series F, No. 64 (United Nations publication, Sales No. E.94.XVII.7).

16 See Summers and Heston, op. cit.

of full convertibility where it does not yet exist may make possible a more consistent application over time of the exchange-rate method. Even so, the methods are conceptually different and thus yield different measures of world output growth.

The differences in output growth measures can be seen in table A.1 below for the periods 1981-1990 and 1991-1995. The estimates employ the same individual country GDP data and data are employed for the same number of countries in both sets of averages. The columns differ only in the weights used to form the averages, which are shown in the table below, of output and per capita output in the base year.[17]

[17] The PPP data are taken from the Penn World Table (Mark 5.6a). This source is not used for the economies in transition because estimates of their GDP per capita are implausibly high for 1988. On the other hand, per capita GDP for China was reduced by nearly 60 per cent in PWT 5.6a compared with PWT 5.5. While this number is more in line with other estimates, the revision underlines the large degree of uncertainty surrounding some of the estimates of GDP on a PPP basis.

OUTPUT AND PER CAPITA OUTPUT IN THE BASE YEAR

	GDP (billions of dollars)		GDP per capita (dollars)	
	Exchange rate basis 1988	PPP basis 1988	Exchange rate basis 1988	PPP basis 1988
World	19 547	22 329	3 875	4 427
Developed economies of which:	14 091	12 409	17 875	15 741
United States	4 900	4 854	19 992	19 804
European Union[a]	5 224	4 720	14 415	13 024
Japan	2 898	1 843	23 638	15 033
Economies in transition[b]	2 217	2 217	5 779	5 779
Developing countries	3 239	7 703	836	1 989
By region:				
Latin America	863	1 856	2 069	4 450
Africa	397	734	704	1 304
West Asia	430	509	3 482	4 125
South and East Asia	972	2 708	619	1 726
China	438	1 553	390	1 384
Mediterranean	140	342	1 800	4 410
By analytical grouping:				
Capital-surplus countries	368	384	3 863	4 031
Capital-importing countries	2 871	7 319	760	1 938
Four exporters of manufactures	357	542	5 088	7 720
Other	2 514	6 777	678	1 828
Memo items				
Sub-Saharan Africa	113	254	348	781

Source: UN/DESIPA.
a The German Democratic Republic is included in western Germany beginning with 1991.
b For the economies in transition, GDP is valued at PPPs only.

Clearly, the world economy has grown faster when country GDPs are valued at PPP conversion factors, although the growth rates for the different groupings of countries are generally not much different when data are converted at PPP rather than at exchange rate factors. This is easy to explain: the Asian developing countries, which account for a large share of the GDP of the developing countries, are growing more rapidly than the rest of the world and their weight under PPPs is higher than it is under the exchange rate scheme. The influence of China is particularly important. In 1988, the total GDP of all developing countries excluding China was 2.2 times larger when valued at PPPs rather than exchange rates, but China's GDP was 3.5 times larger. Thus, the GDP of the developing countries excluding China valued at exchange rates grew between 1991 and 1995 at about the same rate as GDP valued at PPPs, that is, 3.6 per cent versus 3.8 per cent. When China is included, however, the growth rates are 4.8 and 5.5 per cent, respectively.

International trade

The main source of data for tables A.15 and A.16 is the IMF *Direction of Trade* database, while tables A.17 and A.18 are drawn from the more detailed trade data in the United Nations External Trade Statistics Database (COMTRADE).

Trade values in table A.19 are largely based on customs data for merchandise trade converted into dollars using average annual exchange rates and are mainly drawn from IMF, International Financial Statistics. These data are supplemented by balance-of-payments data in certain cases. Estimates of dollar values of trade for the years up to 1990 in the case of the economies in transition were based on the research undertaken in the Economic Commission for Europe (ECE). Data for the most recent years include estimates by the regional commissions and the Department for Economic and Social Information and Policy Analysis of the United Nations Secretariat.

For developed market economies and economies in transition, the growth of trade volumes are aggregated from national data, as collected by ECE, IMF and the Department for Economic and Social Information and Policy Analysis. Implicit unit value indices in table A.20 are calculated from value and volume measures. Terms of trade are defined as the ratio of export to import unit values.

As of 1 January 1993, customs offices at the borders between States members of the European Union (EU), which used to collect and check customs declarations on national exports and imports, were abolished as the Single Market went into effect. A new system of data collection for intra-EU trade, called INTRASTAT, has been put in place. INTRASTAT relies on information collected directly from enterprises and is linked with the system of declarations of value-added tax (VAT) relating to intra-EU trade to allow for quality control of statistical data. There remains, nevertheless, a discontinuity owing to the changes in methodology.

Concerning the economies in transition, two factors preclude the presentation of estimates for trade values and volumes as other than tentative: first, the switch, which occurred mainly in 1991, from intraregional trade at rather arbitrarily set prices in transferable roubles to trade at world market prices in convertible currency; and second, the inadequacy of the data-collection systems in the region. These largely affect the reliability of calculations of changes in unit values.

Unit values of exports for groupings of developing countries are estimated from weighted averages of export prices of commodity groupings at a combination of three- and four-digit Standard International Trade Classification (SITC) levels, based on COMTRADE (the weights reflect the share of each commodity or commodity group in the value of the region's total exports). Unit values of imports for groupings of the developing countries are estimated from weighted averages of export unit values of groupings of supplier countries (the weights reflect the shares of each supplier group in the value of the region's imports).[18]

International finance

The *Survey* includes standardized tables on the net transfer of financial resources of developed and developing countries, in addition to those on balance of payments on current account, external debt and particular financial flows. Net transfer is measured in two ways, based on either of two definitions, according to the derivation contained in the *World Economic Survey, 1986*.[19]

One definition covers the concept of net transfer on an expenditure basis, which can be related in broad terms to the System of National Accounts. This net transfer measure concerns the implicit financing of the balance of trade in goods, services, compensation of employees and transfers related to labour income (largely, workers' remittances). Algebraically, if X represents exports of goods, services, compensation of employees and transfers, and M represents the corresponding import variable, then the net transfer on an expenditure basis is defined as $-(X-M)$. A positive net transfer means that total expenditure in the economy on domestic production and imports exceeds the value of output produced domestically (including net foreign earnings of labour).

The second concept is of net transfer on a financial basis, which is defined as net flow of capital minus net payment of interest and dividends. Capital is so defined as to include official grants, private grants (other than workers' remittances), direct investment[20] and all credit flows, including use of IMF resources. This treatment embodies one – but not the only – standard approach to the balance of payments. It incorporates a definition of the current account as the balance of payments on goods, all services and private transfers, and also treats borrowing from IMF as a credit flow, whereas in some other treatments such borrowing is considered part of the change in reserves.

The link between the two definitions of net transfer is net change in reserves, that is, net transfer on a financial basis minus net increase in reserves equals net transfer on an expenditure basis. The concept of net transfer on an expenditure basis in effect makes no distinction between reserve changes and other capital flows, lumping them all together as constituting the means of financing the net transfer. The concept of net transfer on a financial basis in effect focuses attention on the composition of the financial flows of all actors other than the central bank of the country concerned.

18 Owing to the aforementioned change in United States methodology for calculating real values in terms of chain-weighted indices instead of fixed-year weights, the unit values and volumes of trade have been revised significantly, which has also caused significant revisions in the volume and unit value estimates of developing-country trading partners.

19 United Nations publication, Sales No. E.86.II.C.1, annex III.

20 Direct investment is defined on an actual cash flow basis, which is consistent with the practice of a large number of developing countries in reporting such data; that is to say, direct investment excludes reinvested earnings and correspondingly, direct investment income also excludes reinvested earnings.

LIST OF TABLES

IV. THE INTERNATIONAL OIL MARKET

I . GLOBAL OUTPUT AND MACROECONOMIC INDICATORS

Table A.1.
WORLD POPULATION, OUTPUT AND PER CAPITA GDP, 1980-1995

	Growth of GDP (annual percentage change)				Growth rate of population (annual percentage change)		Population (millions)		GDP per capita Exchange-rate basis (1988 dollars)	
	Exchange-rate basis (1988 dollars)		PPP basis							
	1981-1990	1991-1995	1981-1990	1991-1995	1981-1990	1991-1995	1980	1995	1980	1995
World	2.9	1.4	3.2	2.5	1.7	1.6	4 392	5 639	3 548	3 900
Developed economies of which:	2.9	1.5	2.9	1.6	0.6	0.6	753	824	14 984	19 665
United States	2.9	1.9	2.9	1.9	0.9	1.1	228	263	17 215	21 385
European Union[a] (15)	2.3	1.3	2.3	1.3	0.3	0.4	355	372	12 390	16 039
Japan	4.1	1.3	4.1	1.3	0.6	0.3	117	125	18 193	27 129
Economies in transition[b]	2.0	-7.7	2.0	-7.7	0.7	0.2	361	391	4 823	3 639
Developing countries by region:	3.1	4.8	4.0	5.5	2.1	1.9	3 278	4 424	780	988
Latin America	1.2	2.7	1.2	2.8	2.1	1.9	353	475	2 182	2 092
Africa	2.0	1.6	2.1	1.8	2.9	2.9	448	686	765	657
West Asia	-1.3	2.3	-0.5	2.8	4.0	2.9	90	153	5 736	3 328
South and East Asia	6.0	6.0	5.6	5.6	2.1	2.0	1 322	1 802	464	817
China	9.0	11.3	9.0	11.3	1.5	1.1	999	1 221	202	664
Mediterranean	2.1	-0.9	2.5	-0.3	1.8	1.4	67	86	1 716	1 573
by analytical grouping:										
Capital-surplus countries	-2.2	1.5	-1.8	1.8	4.2	2.4	68	115	7 127	3 622
Capital-importing countries	4.0	5.2	4.4	5.7	2.1	1.9	3 210	4 309	646	918
Four exporters of manufactures	8.0	7.0	8.0	6.9	1.2	1.0	63	75	2 982	7 578
Other	3.5	4.9	4.1	5.6	2.1	1.9	3 147	4 233	599	799
Memo items:										
Sub-Saharan Africa	1.8	1.0	1.7	1.3	3.1	3.1	255	401	380	304
Fifteen heavily indebted countries	1.1	2.2	1.2	2.2	2.2	2.0	472	651	1 857	1 684
Least developed countries	2.0	2.0	2.5	2.7	2.5	2.9	363	536	261	238

Source: UN/DESIPA.

a The former German Democratic Republic is included in Germany beginning in 1991.
b For the economies in transition, GDP is valued at PPPs.

Table A.2.
DEVELOPED ECONOMIES: RATES OF GROWTH OF REAL GDP, 1986-1996

Annual percentage change[a]

	1986	1987	1988	1989	1990	1991	1992	1993	1994	1995[b]	1996[c]
All developed economies	2.8	3.2	4.4	3.6	2.5	✦ 0.7	1.6	0.7	2.7	2.0	2
Major industrialized countries	2.9	3.2	4.6	3.6	2.5	✦ 0.7	1.7	0.8	2.6	1.8	2
Canada	3.3	4.3	4.9	2.5	-0.2	-1.8	0.8	2.2	4.6	2.2	2
France	2.5	2.3	4.5	4.3	2.5	0.8	1.4	-1.5	2.9	2.2	1
Germany	2.2	1.4	3.7	3.3	4.7	✦ 1.2	2.1	-1.1	2.9	1.9	1
Italy	2.9	3.1	4.1	2.9	2.1	1.3	0.9	-0.7	2.1	3.0	1¾
Japan	2.6	4.1	6.2	4.7	4.8	4.3	1.1	-0.2	0.5	0.9	2
United Kingdom	4.3	4.8	5.0	2.2	0.4	-2.0	-0.5	2.3	3.9	2.5	2
United States	3.0	2.9	3.8	3.4	1.3	-1.0	2.7	2.2	3.5	2.0	2¼
Other industrialized countries	2.5	3.3	3.5	3.7	2.6	0.6	0.9	0.1	3.0	3	2
Memo items:											
Western Europe	2.8	2.8	4.0	3.4	2.7	✦ 0.6	1.0	-0.5	2.9	2.4	1½
European Union (15)	2.8	2.9	4.1	3.4	2.7	✦ 0.6	1.0	-0.5	2.9	2.4	1½

Source: UN/DESIPA, based on *IMF, International Financial Statistics*.
✦ Indicates discontinuity in the series: from 1991, Germany includes eastern *Länder*.
a Data for country groups are weighted averages, where weights for each year are GDP valued at 1988 prices and exchange rates.
b Partly estimated.
c Forecast, based on Project LINK.

Table A.3.
ECONOMIES IN TRANSITION: RATES OF GROWTH OF REAL GDP, 1986-1996

Annual percentage change[a]

	1986	1987	1988	1989	1990	1991	1992	1993	1994	1995[b]	1996[c]
Economies in transition[d]	3.5	2.6	4.5	2.1	-6.1	✦ -8.6	-12.0	-6.9	-8.9	-1.8	2
Eastern Europe[d]	3.2	2.2	2.7	0.1	-11.1	✦-10.6	-3.0	1.0	3.9	5.9	5
Albania	5.6	-0.8	-1.4	9.8	-13.1	-29.4	-6.0	11.0	7.4	6.0	5
Bulgaria	4.2	6.1	2.6	-1.4	-9.1	-6.9	-5.7	-3.7	2.2	2.5	3½
Former Czechoslovakia	1.8	0.8	2.6	1.3	-1.2	-14.2	-6.4				
Czech Republic								-0.9	2.6	4.8	5½
Slovakia								-4.1	4.8	7.4	5¾
Hungary	1.5	3.8	2.7	3.8	-3.3	-11.9	-3.0	-0.8	2.9	2.0	2¾
Poland	4.2	2.0	4.4	0.2	-11.6	-7.0	2.6	3.8	5.0	7.3	5¾
Romania	2.3	0.8	-0.5	-5.8	-8.2	-12.9	-8.8	1.3	3.5	6.9	5½
Former Soviet Union	3.6	2.8	5.3	3.0	-4.0	-8.0					
CIS							-14.1	-9.6	-14.6	-5.7	¼
Russian Federation							-14.5	-8.7	-12.6	-4.0	½
Baltic States							-31.6	-14.4	1.8	1.5	2
Estonia							-14.8	-7.8	4.0	3.0	2½
Latvia							-34.9	-14.9	0.6	-1.6	¼
Lithuania							-35.0	-17.0	1.5	3.1	3¼

Sources: UN/DESIPA and ECE.
✦ Indicates discontinuity in the series.
a Country group aggregates are averages weighted by GDP in 1988 dollars (for methodology, see *World Economic Survey, 1992* (United Nations publication, Sales No. E.92.II.C.1 and corrigenda), annex, introductory text.
b Partly estimated.
c Forecast, partly based on Project LINK.
d Including the former German Democratic Republic until 1990.

Table A.4.

DEVELOPING COUNTRIES: RATES OF GROWTH OF REAL GDP, BY COUNTRY GROUP, 1986-1996

Annual percentage change

	1986	1987	1988	1989	1990	1991	1992	1993	1994	1995[a]	1996[b]
All developing countries	3.2	4.1	4.5	3.5	3.1	3.4	4.9	5.0	5.5	5.2	5 ½
By region:											
Latin America	4.2	3.0	0.7	1.0	-0.1	2.9	2.2	3.0	4.6	0.9	2½
Africa	1.5	0.6	2.7	3.0	2.2	1.4	0.9	0.4	2.5	2.7	4¼
West Asia	-6.4	-0.8	0.0	3.2	1.9	-0.2	5.7	2.6	0.6	3.1	3
South and East Asia	6.2	7.0	8.5	6.3	6.6	5.4	5.2	5.5	6.7	7.1	6¾
China[c]	8.5	11.1	11.3	4.3	3.9	8.0	13.2	13.4	11.8	10.2	9
Mediterranean	5.5	1.1	0.8	0.4	1.1	-5.6	-1.4	0.1	-3.2	5.6	3½
By analytical grouping:											
Capital-surplus countries	-8.0	-1.8	-1.1	3.6	1.4	-1.4	5.3	2.1	-0.6	2.3	2½
Capital-importing countries	5.1	5.0	5.2	3.5	3.3	4.1	4.9	5.3	6.2	5.5	5½
Net energy exporters	1.0	1.7	3.5	3.0	5.1	4.6	4.3	2.1	3.7	2.1	4¼
Net energy importers	6.4	6.0	5.7	3.7	2.8	3.9	5.0	6.3	6.9	6.4	6
Four exporters of manufactures	10.8	12.0	9.6	6.5	7.2	7.8	5.7	6.2	7.6	7.6	6¾
Other	5.7	5.0	5.0	3.1	1.9	3.1	4.9	6.3	6.7	6.1	6
Memo items											
Sub-Saharan Africa	2.6	0.6	2.9	1.5	1.2	0.4	0.1	-0.7	1.8	3.1	5
Fifteen heavily indebted countries	4.1	2.4	1.2	1.3	-0.2	2.2	1.4	2.2	4.7	0.8	2¾
Least developed countries	3.0	1.1	1.6	1.9	2.0	0.6	2.4	1.1	2.5	3.3	4¾

Source: UN/DESIPA.
a Preliminary estimates.
b Forecast, partly based on Project LINK.
c Data for 1986-1989 are government estimates.

Table A.5.

DEVELOPED ECONOMIES: INVESTMENT, SAVING AND NET TRANSFERS, 1980-1994

Percentage of GDP

		Gross domestic investment	Gross domestic saving			Net financial transfer
			Total	Government saving	Private saving	
Total[a]	1980	23.4	23.6	0.9	22.7	-0.2
	1985	21.6	22.0	-0.6	22.5	-0.4
	1990	22.2	22.2	1.2	21.0	0.0
	1991	21.3	22.1	0.6	21.4	-0.8
	1992	20.6	21.8	-0.4	22.2	-1.1
	1993	20.1	21.6	-0.4	22.0	-1.4
Major industrialized countries[a]	1980	23.3	22.7	0.8	21.8	0.6
	1985	21.6	21.1	-0.7	21.9	0.5
	1990	22.0	22.0	1.1	20.9	-0.0
	1991	21.2	22.0	0.7	21.3	-0.8
	1992	20.6	21.8	-0.3	22.1	-1.1
	1993	20.3	21.6	-0.3	21.8	-1.3
	1994	20.8	21.9	..	..	-1.1
of which:						
Germany, western	1980	23.4	22.8	2.4	20.4	0.5
	1985	19.6	23.1	2.6	20.5	-3.5
	1990	21.4	27.2	1.3	25.9	-5.8
	1991	21.8	27.6	1.1	26.5	-5.8
	1992	20.8	27.7	1.5	26.2	-6.9
	1993	19.0	26.6	0.8	25.9	-7.7
	1994	19.7	27.6	..	..	-7.9
Japan	1980	32.2	31.3	3.2	28.2	0.9
	1985	28.2	31.5	4.9	26.6	-3.4
	1990	32.8	33.5	9.0	24.5	-0.7
	1991	32.5	34.3	9.5	24.8	-1.8
	1992	31.1	33.5	8.4	25.1	-2.4
	1993	29.9	32.3	6.6	25.7	-2.3
	1994	28.8	31.0	..	..	-2.1
United States	1980	20.2	19.7	-0.1	19.8	0.5
	1985	20.7	18.0	-2.4	20.4	2.7
	1990	17.4	16.2	-1.9	18.0	1.2
	1991	15.8	15.5	-2.7	18.2	0.3
	1992	16.0	15.5	-3.7	19.2	0.5
	1993	16.5	15.5	-2.8	18.3	1.0
	1994	17.7	16.3	..	..	1.4

Sources: OECD, *National Accounts*; and national information supplied to the Statistics Division/DESIPA.

a   National data converted to dollars for aggregation at annual average exchange rates.

Table A.6.
DEVELOPED ECONOMIES: UNEMPLOYMENT RATES, 1986-1996[a]

Percentage of total labour force

	1986	1987	1988	1989	1990	1991	1992	1993	1994	1995[b]	1996[c]
All developed economies	7.6	7.2	6.7	6.2	6.0	6.7	7.4	8.0	7.9	7.6	7¾
Major industrialized countries	7.1	6.7	6.1	5.7	5.6	6.2	6.8	7.1	7.0	6.8	7
Canada	9.5	8.8	7.7	7.5	8.1	10.2	11.3	11.2	10.3	9.5	9½
France	10.4	10.5	10.0	9.4	8.9	9.4	10.4	11.6	12.3	11.6	11½
Germany[d]	6.4	6.2	6.2	5.6	4.9	4.2	4.6	7.9	8.4	8.2	10½
Italy	10.5	10.9	11.0	10.9	10.3	9.9	10.5	10.2	11.1	12.2	11
Japan	2.8	2.8	2.5	2.3	2.1	2.1	2.2	2.5	2.9	3.1	3
United Kingdom	11.2	10.3	8.5	7.1	6.8	8.8	10.1	10.4	9.5	8.7	8
United States	6.9	6.1	5.4	5.2	5.4	6.6	7.3	6.7	6.0	5.6	5¾
Other industrialized countries	10.2	9.8	9.3	8.4	8.1	8.9	10.1	12.0	12.3	11.6	11½
Memo items:											
Western Europe	9.9	9.7	9.1	8.3	7.6	8.0	8.9	10.6	11.0	10.7	10¾
European Union (15)	10.3	10.0	9.4	8.5	7.8	8.2	9.1	10.8	11.2	10.9	11

Source: UN/DESIPA, based on data of OECD.

a   For the seven countries shown and ten others, unemployment data are standardized by OECD for comparability among countries and over time, in conformity with the definitions of
the International Labour Office (see OECD, *Standardized Unemployment Rates: Sources and Methods* (Paris, 1985)); national definitions and estimates are used for other countries.
b   Partly estimated.
c   Forecast.
d   Prior to January 1993, western Germany only

Table A.7.
DEVELOPED ECONOMIES: CONSUMER PRICE INFLATION, 1986-1996[a]

Annual percentage change

	1986	1987	1988	1989	1990	1991	1992	1993	1994	1995[b]	1996[c]
All developed economies	2.2	2.8	3.2	4.4	5.0	4.3	3.1	2.6	2.3	2.4	2¼
Major industrialized countries	1.8	2.6	3.0	4.2	4.8	4.2	2.9	2.5	2.1	2.3	2
Canada	4.1	4.4	4.0	5.1	4.7	5.6	1.5	1.9	0.2	2.2	1¼
France	2.6	3.3	2.8	3.4	3.4	3.2	2.4	2.1	1.7	1.7	2¼
Germany, western	-0.2	0.3	1.3	2.7	2.7	3.5	4.0	4.1	3.0	1.7	1¼
Italy	5.8	4.7	5.1	6.2	6.5	6.3	5.1	4.5	4.0	5.4	4
Japan	0.6	0.1	0.7	2.2	3.1	3.3	1.7	1.2	0.7	-0.1	¼
United Kingdom	3.5	4.1	4.8	7.8	9.5	5.9	3.7	1.6	2.5	3.4	2¾
United States	1.8	3.7	4.0	4.9	5.4	4.2	3.1	2.7	2.6	3.0	2¾
Other industrialized countries	4.8	4.2	4.2	5.2	6.1	5.2	4.0	3.7	3.1	3.3	3
Memo items:											
Western Europe	2.9	3.0	3.3	4.8	5.5	4.9	4.0	3.4	3.0	3.0	2½
European Union (15)	2.9	2.9	3.3	4.9	5.5	4.9	4.0	3.4	3.1	3.1	2¾

Source: UN/DESIPA, based on IMF, *International Financial Statistics*.

a   Data for country groups are weighted averages, where weights for each year are consumption expenditure for the year valued at 1988 prices and exchange rates.
b   Partly estimated.
c   Forecast.

Table A.8.
MAJOR DEVELOPED ECONOMIES: FINANCIAL INDICATORS, 1985-1995

	1985	1986	1987	1988	1989	1990	1991	1992	1993	1994	1995
Growth of real money[a] *(percentage change)*											
Canada	3.1	4.9	3.9	5.6	8.3	4.4	1.9	8.2	9.7	7.3	4.2
France	1.0	2.3	3.5	2.7	-0.6	-0.7	-4.1	-0.8	1.2	5.4	1.5
Germany	5.7	3.2	4.0	4.2	2.6	14.9	2.4	3.4	8.1	0.5	3.3
Italy	1.7	0.6	1.5	1.0	4.8	1.1	2.0	0.8	2.8	1.4	-7.6
Japan	7.2	7.4	11.1	9.4	9.7	5.8	0.4	-1.5	1.7	2.6	3.7
United Kingdom	5.3	18.7	15.3	10.0	12.2	3.9	-4.5	5.0	1.5	3.7	4.4
United States	5.0	7.7	0.2	2.2	1.5	2.3	-1.5	-0.2	-0.7	-1.9	0.7
Short-term interest rates[b] *(percentage)*											
Canada	9.8	8.2	8.5	10.4	12.1	11.6	7.4	6.8	3.8	5.5	5.7
France	9.9	7.7	8.0	7.5	9.1	9.9	9.5	10.4	8.8	5.7	6.4
Germany	5.2	4.6	3.7	4.0	6.6	7.9	8.8	9.4	7.5	5.4	4.5
Italy	15.3	13.4	11.5	11.3	12.7	12.4	12.2	14.0	10.2	8.5	10.5
Japan	6.5	4.8	3.5	3.6	4.9	7.2	7.5	4.6	3.1	2.2	1.2
United Kingdom	10.8	10.7	9.7	10.3	13.9	14.7	11.7	9.6	5.5	4.8	6.0
United States	8.1	6.8	6.7	7.6	9.2	8.1	5.7	3.5	3.0	4.2	5.8
Long-term interest rates[c] *(percentage)*											
Canada	11.0	9.5	10.0	10.2	9.9	10.9	9.8	8.8	7.8	8.6	8.3
France	10.9	8.6	9.4	9.1	8.8	10.0	9.1	8.6	6.9	7.4	7.6
Germany	6.9	5.9	5.8	6.1	7.1	8.9	8.6	8.0	6.3	6.7	6.5
Italy	13.0	10.5	9.7	10.2	10.7	11.5	13.2	13.3	11.3	10.6	12.2
Japan	6.3	4.9	4.2	4.3	5.1	7.4	6.5	4.9	3.7	3.7	2.5
United Kingdom	10.6	9.9	9.5	9.4	9.6	11.1	9.9	9.2	7.9	8.1	8.3
United States	10.6	7.7	8.4	8.9	8.5	8.6	7.9	7.0	5.8	7.1	6.6
General government financial balances[d] *(percentage)*											
Canada	-6.8	-5.4	-3.8	-2.5	-2.9	-4.1	-6.6	-7.4	-7.3	-5.3	-4.4
France	-2.9	-2.7	-1.9	-1.7	-1.2	-1.6	-2.2	-4.0	-6.1	-6.0	-5.0
Germany[e]	-1.2	-1.3	-1.9	-2.2	0.1	-2.1	-3.3	-2.8	-3.5	-2.6	-3.1
Italy	-12.6	-11.6	-11.0	-10.7	-9.9	-10.9	-10.2	-9.5	-9.6	-9.0	-7.4
Japan	-0.8	-0.9	0.5	1.5	2.5	2.9	3.0	1.5	-1.4	-3.5	-3.9
United Kingdom	-2.8	-2.4	-1.4	1.0	0.9	-1.2	-2.6	-6.1	-7.8	-6.9	-5.0
United States	-3.1	-3.4	-2.5	-2.0	-1.5	-2.5	-3.2	-4.3	-3.4	-2.0	-1.6

Source: UN/DESIPA, based on data of IMF, *International Financial Statistics,* and OECD, *Economic Outlook.*

a Real money is here defined as broad money (denoted by M2 and comprising currency outside banks and demand deposits plus time, savings and foreign currency deposits of resident sectors other than central government) deflated by GDP deflators. Growth rates measure changes from year-end to year-end (1995 data are partly estimated).
b Money market rates.
d Surplus (+) or deficit (-) as a percentage of nominal GNP or GDP; 1995 data are OECD estimates.
c Yield on long-term government bonds.
e Data up to end-1990 are for western Germany only.

Table A.9.

MAJOR DEVELOPED MARKET ECONOMIES: EFFECTIVE EXCHANGE RATES, BROAD MEASUREMENT, 1985-1995[a]

1990=100

	1985	1986	1987	1988	1989	1990	1991	1992	1993	1994	1995
Nominal effective exchange rates											
Canada	87.2	81.9	84.2	90.8	97.4	100.0	103.1	98.1	94.1	89.7	88.6
France	86.1	90.1	91.6	91.3	91.8	100.0	99.7	104.9	109.3	113.0	118.1
Germany	73.1	81.7	88.4	89.9	91.1	100.0	101.2	106.9	112.5	116.8	125.1
Italy	84.2	87.8	89.8	89.2	92.8	100.0	101.0	100.7	86.7	86.2	79.1
Japan	63.9	84.2	94.8	106.9	104.4	100.0	111.7	120.4	148.6	166.5	177.4
United Kingdom	98.6	92.5	92.7	99.8	98.3	100.0	102.3	100.3	93.2	95.6	92.3
United States	95.0	87.4	85.0	86.4	94.8	100.0	104.3	107.5	116.7	122.9	123.5
Real effective exchange rates											
Canada	96.1	91.0	93.6	101.8	105.0	100.0	97.6	91.4	88.5	87.8	92.0
France	95.3	99.6	101.6	98.8	95.8	100.0	97.9	101.6	103.1	102.6	103.2
Germany	88.1	96.7	101.0	99.7	96.7	100.0	97.9	100.6	100.9	99.7	104.9
Italy	87.1	90.0	91.6	90.1	93.1	100.0	101.0	98.3	85.0	83.3	81.1
Japan	94.7	111.2	114.5	120.4	112.1	100.0	104.8	106.6	121.6	126.4	127.0
United Kingdom	96.5	92.3	93.5	100.4	98.2	100.0	103.0	99.8	91.7	92.6	89.8
United States	131.8	116.7	105.7	97.9	101.9	100.0	101.2	101.0	103.3	100.6	95.6

Source: Morgan Guaranty Trust Company, *World Financial Markets*.

[a] Indices based on a "broad" measure currency basket of 22 OECD currencies and 23 developing-economy currencies. The real effective exchange rate, which adjusts the nominal index for relative price changes, gauges the effect on international price competitiveness of the country's manufactures due to currency changes and inflation differentials. A rise in the index implies a fall in competitiveness and vice versa. The relative price changes are based on indices most closely measuring the prices of domestically produced finished manufactured goods, excluding food and energy, at the first stage of manufacturing. The weights for currency indices are derived from 1990 bilateral trade patterns of the corresponding countries.

Table A.10.
ECONOMIES IN TRANSITION: OUTPUT AND DEMAND INDICATORS, 1985-1995

Annual percentage change

	1985	1986	1987	1988	1989	1990	1991	1992	1993	1994	1995[a]
Industry, gross product											
Central and Eastern Europe[b]	3.7	4.7	3.2	3.5	-1.1	-17.6	♦-18.9	-8.5	0.6	7.6	7.5
Albania						-7.5	-37.0	-44.0	-10.0	-2.0	5.1
Bulgaria	3.2	4.7	6.0	3.2	2.2	-16.8	-27.8	-15.0	-6.9	4.1	5.2
Former Czechoslovakia	3.5	3.2	2.5	2.1	0.8	-3.7	-23.0	-7.9	-	-	-
Czech Republic						-3.5	-21.8	-10.6	-5.1	2.3	9.5
Slovakia						-4.0	-25.4	-13.8	-10.6	6.4	8.7
Hungary	0.7	1.9	3.5	-0.3	-1.0	-9.6	-18.2	-9.7	4.0	9.5	4.8
Poland	4.5	4.7	3.4	5.3	-0.5	-24.2	-11.9	3.9	5.6	13.0	6.9
Romania	3.9	7.3	2.4	3.1	-5.3	-23.7	-22.8	-21.9	1.3	3.3	8.9
Former Soviet Union and successor States[c,d]	3.4	4.4	3.8	3.9	1.7	-1.2	-7.8	-18.0	-12.0	-23.0	-3.0
Agriculture, gross product											
Central and Eastern Europe[b]	-1.7	2.5	-3.2	2.8	-0.2	-3.4	♦ -2.9	-14.0	-0.2	-1.3	5.7
Albania						-6.9	-24.0	-15.0	15.0	..	..
Bulgaria	-11.9	11.7	-3.5	0.9	1.2	-6.0	-0.3	-12.0	-18.2	0.8	1.6
Former Czechoslovakia	-1.6	0.6	0.9	2.9	1.7	-3.9	-8.4	-12.7	-	-	-
Czech Republic						-2.3	-8.9	-12.1	-2.3	-5.6	3.1
Slovakia						-7.2	-7.4	-13.9	-8.1	9.1	2.2
Hungary	-5.5	2.4	-2.0	4.3	-1.3	-4.8	-6.2	-20.0	-9.7	2.4	2.5
Poland	0.7	5.0	-2.3	1.2	1.5	-2.2	-1.6	-12.8	1.5	-4.0	9.0
Romania	0.7	-5.5	-8.9	5.8	-5.0	-2.9	1.0	-13.8	12.4	0.2	4.9
Former Soviet Union and successor States[c,d]	0.1	5.3	-0.5	1.7	1.3	-2.8	-7.0	..	..	-13.0	-8.0
Gross investment											
Central and Eastern Europe[b]	4.2	4.7	3.1	2.1	-1.5	-13.2	♦-14.8	0.8	-1.6	6.7	8.3
Albania						-14.8	..	..	..	..	..
Bulgaria	6.2	13.7	0.3	4.5	-10.1	-18.5	-19.9	-1.5	-9.0	-2.0	-1.0
Former Czechoslovakia	5.4	1.4	4.4	4.1	1.6	6.1	-27.2	4.7	-	-	-
Czech Republic						6.5	-17.7	3.8	-7.7	7.8	12.6
Slovakia						5.3	-20.0	6.4	-3.5	-7.4	4.9
Hungary	-3.0	6.5	9.8	-9.1	7.0	-9.6	-11.9	-1.3	2.7	10.4	6.5
Poland	6.0	5.1	4.2	5.4	-2.4	-10.1	-4.1	0.7	2.2	6.6	9.2
Romania	1.6	1.1	-1.4	-2.2	-1.6	-38.3	-25.8	-1.1	0.7	15.3	12.1
Former Soviet Union and successor States[c,d]	3.0	8.3	5.7	6.2	4.7	1.0	-12.0	-39.0	-10.0	-25.0	-13.0

Sources: UN/DESIPA and ECE, 1988 prices and exchange rates based on national data.

♦ Indicates discontinuity in the series.
[a] Preliminary estimate.
[b] Until 1990, including the former German Democratic Republic.
[c] Excluding Estonia, Latvia and Lithuania.
[d] Data for 1995 represent the Russian Federation only.

Table A.11.
DEVELOPING COUNTRIES: INVESTMENT, SAVING AND NET TRANSFERS, 1980-1994
Percentage of GDP

	Gross domestic investment				Gross domestic saving				Net transfer of resources			
	1980	1985	1990	1994	1980	1985	1990	1994	1980	1985	1990	1994
All developing countries[a]	25.7	23.4	24.7	25.8	28.3	24.2	25.7	25.7	-2.6	-0.8	-1.0	0.2
by region:												
Latin America	24.8	19.2	19.7	19.6	23.6	23.9	22.0	18.6	1.2	-4.7	-2.3	1.1
Africa	25.6	20.1	20.2	19.6	27.3	20.7	19.1	16.2	-1.7	-0.6	1.1	3.3
West Asia	24.5	21.2	22.0	21.5	46.6	20.2	24.6	22.4	-22.0	1.0	-2.6	-0.9
South and East Asia[b]	26.3	24.3	29.1	29.5	24.2	24.6	28.6	29.6	2.1	-0.3	0.5	-0.2
Mediterranean	22.5	21.5	25.7	21.9	14.4	17.8	22.0	22.8	8.2	3.7	3.6	-0.9
by analytical grouping:												
Capital-surplus countries	24.0	21.2	23.5	20.3	52.0	22.1	27.8	27.7	-28.0	-0.9	-4.4	-7.4
Capital-importing countries	25.9	23.7	24.9	26.1	24.5	24.5	25.5	25.5	1.4	-0.8	-0.7	0.6
Energy exporters	26.8	21.8	22.2	24.4	29.5	24.6	23.8	21.6	-2.7	-2.8	-1.6	2.7
Energy importers	25.5	24.6	25.6	26.7	22.0	24.5	26.0	26.7	3.5	0.1	-0.4	-0.0
Four exporters of manufactures	34.3	26.2	31.3	32.1	29.9	32.3	34.5	35.4	4.4	-6.0	-3.2	-3.3
Other countries	24.4	24.4	24.2	25.0	21.0	23.2	23.8	24.0	3.4	1.2	0.3	1.0
Memo items:												
Sub-Saharan Africa	20.0	17.4	18.1	19.1	13.2	15.0	12.3	12.3	6.8	2.4	5.8	6.8
Fifteen heavily indebted countries	24.8	18.2	19.8	19.6	24.6	23.1	22.2	18.5	0.2	-4.8	-2.4	1.1
Least developed countries	17.3	14.6	16.1	15.5	8.0	6.6	7.6	9.1	9.2	8.1	8.5	6.4
Selected developing countries												
Argentina	25.3	17.6	14.0	19.9	23.8	23.1	19.7	17.6	1.4	-5.5	-5.7	2.3
Bangladesh	14.9	12.9	12.8	14.0	2.1	2.0	2.9	7.9	12.8	10.9	9.9	6.1
Brazil	23.3	19.2	21.5	16.5	21.1	24.4	23.2	18.3	2.3	-5.2	-1.7	-1.8
China	30.1	38.6	33.2	42.6	30.0	34.7	37.3	45.3	0.2	3.9	-4.1	-2.7
Côte d'Ivoire	26.5	12.6	9.3	12.5	20.4	25.8	14.6	25.3	6.2	-13.1	-5.4	-12.7
Egypt	27.5	26.7	21.9	17.5	15.2	14.5	6.8	5.9	12.4	12.1	15.1	11.6
India	20.9	23.9	25.7	23.0	17.4	20.8	22.8	21.6	3.5	3.1	2.8	1.4
Indonesia	24.3	26.2	30.9	29.1	37.1	27.9	31.5	30.3	-12.8	-1.8	-0.5	-1.3
Kenya	29.2	26.0	24.3	20.6	18.1	24.9	19.1	23.8	11.1	1.1	5.2	-3.2
Mexico	27.2	21.2	21.9	24.5	24.9	26.3	20.7	19.2	2.3	-5.1	1.2	5.3
Morocco	24.2	27.1	25.2	21.2	13.7	18.1	19.2	16.0	10.5	9.0	6.0	5.2
Nigeria	22.2	9.0	13.6	10.1	32.3	12.6	28.3	11.0	-10.1	-3.7	-14.7	-0.9
Peru	29.0	18.4	15.5	22.2	31.4	24.9	16.2	20.0	-2.4	-6.5	-0.7	2.2
Republic of Korea	32.0	29.6	36.9	38.4	24.8	30.9	36.4	39.2	7.3	-1.3	0.5	-0.8
South Africa	28.3	20.1	17.1	17.7	36.5	29.2	23.1	19.7	-8.2	-9.1	-6.0	-1.9
Thailand	29.1	28.2	41.1	40.1	22.9	25.5	33.6	32.5	6.3	2.7	7.5	7.6
Tunisia	29.4	26.6	27.1	24.3	24.0	20.4	20.0	22.0	5.4	6.1	7.0	2.3
Turkey	21.9	21.0	25.5	21.6	14.1	17.8	21.9	22.8	7.8	3.2	3.6	-1.2
Zambia	23.3	14.9	17.3	9.2	19.3	14.1	17.8	-7.5	4.0	0.8	-0.5	16.6

Source: UN/DESIPA, based on World Bank, *World Tables*, and United Nations Secretariat estimates.

a Excluding the former Yugoslavia.
b Excluding China.

Table A.12.

DEVELOPING COUNTRIES: MAJOR CATEGORIES OF FOREIGN EXCHANGE EARNINGS, 1980-1992

Percentage share in total exports of goods and services

	Manufactures 1980	1985	1992	Non-fuel primary commodities 1980	1985	1992	Fuels trade balance 1980	1985	1992	Services[a] 1980	1985	1992	Workers' remittances 1980	1985	1992
All developing countries[b] **by region:**	17.6	29.2	48.1	18.0	18.0	13.6	34.0	18.3	7.6	11.8	14.3	16.1	2.7	3.2	2.5
Latin America	12.5	20.2	27.3	30.1	30.2	28.8	15.1	16.7	8.7	14.0	14.1	19.7	0.7	1.2	3.8
Africa	8.0	9.2	26.9	16.9	15.8	15.7	44.3	35.9	27.2	10.6	13.0	21.3	5.0	8.0	9.6
West Asia	4.7	9.7	15.7	1.4	2.7	3.6	80.5	51.5	47.7	7.1	11.0	11.4	0.9	1.5	1.1
South and East Asia[c]	39.6	50.0	61.4	24.8	17.0	10.2	-3.6	-2.1	-3.1	16.0	16.4	14.7	3.6	3.3	1.2
Mediterranean	25.7	40.5	39.5	39.1	21.5	13.8	-65.5	-27.2	-12.1	29.2	27.3	37.7	35.2	12.7	9.4
By analytical grouping															
Capital-surplus countries	2.2	4.2	6.9	0.5	1.0	1.9	89.1	64.6	62.1	5.1	6.9	6.0	..	..	..
Capital-importing countries	23.4	33.5	52.1	24.6	21.0	14.7	13.1	10.2	2.2	14.4	15.6	17.1	3.7	3.8	2.8
Energy exporters	5.3	7.5	30.2	18.0	13.6	14.5	58.8	38.1	27.6	10.7	12.6	18.9	3.1	3.9	4.9
Energy importers	35.0	47.0	58.9	28.9	24.8	14.8	-16.0	-4.2	-5.6	16.7	17.2	16.6	4.0	3.7	2.1
Four exporters of manufactures	64.6	71.5	69.1	9.8	7.3	5.0	-10.9	-9.5	-4.7	17.6	14.6	13.2	0.1	0.2	0.2
Other countries	17.0	24.8	42.6	40.4	40.6	30.4	-19.0	0.7	-7.1	16.2	19.5	22.0	6.4	6.8	5.3
Memo items															
Sub-Saharan Africa	8.0	8.6	16.1	48.7	35.5	43.1	13.7	13.9	15.7	17.5	17.3	22.4	2.8	5.4	4.3
Fifteen heavily indebted countries	12.1	20.6	28.8	28.4	28.7	26.5	27.4	22.3	12.1	12.4	13.5	19.1	1.5	1.8	3.3
Selected developing countries															
Argentina	16.5	17.2	19.9	52.6	58.0	49.2	-7.2	1.7	3.9	16.7	15.9	15.8	..	..	..
Bangladesh	52.0	52.4	66.8	23.6	24.7	15.0	-19.2	-28.1	-20.8	16.7	18.7	18.5	20.2	29.8	33.2
Brazil	33.4	39.2	50.5	51.6	42.7	35.4	-44.7	-14.1	-10.5	7.4	7.1	8.0	0.2	0.1	4.2
China	41.9	44.6	79.7	31.3	23.9	15.4	14.2	23.3	1.2	9.1	10.3	10.9	3.1	0.6	0.3
Egypt	5.1	2.5	8.9	11.6	5.4	5.2	29.2	14.0	10.0	36.7	39.5	61.6	41.4	47.0	44.7
India	40.0	38.2	59.4	27.6	23.5	17.5	-50.6	-27.1	-26.2	23.9	24.9	19.1	22.6	16.7	8.4
Indonesia	2.6	10.3	42.5	27.6	18.7	17.0	69.5	56.9	24.2	1.5	4.2	8.9	..	0.3	0.6
Malaysia	16.7	23.8	56.5	48.9	35.6	19.4	10.5	19.0	7.6	8.3	11.5	11.7	..	..	0.4
Morocco	17.3	27.7	33.2	52.6	38.1	25.1	-26.7	-31.3	-15.2	25.0	31.4	35.6	32.2	30.6	32.9
Republic of Korea	69.7	83.6	78.1	7.6	5.0	4.1	-29.3	-19.4	-14.3	20.8	16.9	13.9	0.4	0.8	0.8
Saudi Arabia	0.6	2.3	6.5	0.2	0.3	1.0	94.6	60.4	65.9	5.3	8.4	6.0	..	..	..
South Africa	16.9	18.3	56.0	23.1	23.9	16.7	2.7	6.9	4.9	7.4	7.7	10.6	..	..	..
Thailand	21.3	27.1	51.4	54.5	41.7	23.6	-32.6	-19.6	-7.0	17.4	20.0	20.0	..	..	..
Tunisia	23.8	26.9	48.1	7.8	7.8	7.9	13.2	11.7	2.0	32.9	35.8	32.0	9.5	10.0	9.4
Turkey	21.3	42.7	41.5	56.8	23.8	15.7	-98.2	-29.9	-13.8	19.4	22.9	33.4	56.4	15.0	11.9
Venezuela	1.5	7.7	8.3	3.9	9.1	7.1	83.5	66.2	61.0	4.1	5.8	9.0	..	..	..

Source: UN/DESIPA, based on World Bank, *World Tables, 1995* and other sources.

a   Including receipts from transportation, travel and business services but not investment income or workers' remittances.

b   Excluding the former Yugoslavia.

c   Excluding China

Table A.13.
DEVELOPING COUNTRIES: INFLATION, 1986-1996[a]

Annual percentage change

	1986	1987	1988	1989	1990	1991	1992	1993	1994	1995[b]	1996[c]
All developing countries[d]	32.5	53.3	115.9	291.8	499.9	73.6	130.1	269.7	125.7	20.0	16
by region:											
Latin America	96.1	156.0	375.0	1002.3	1746.8	228.8	427.4	921.9	397.9	25.5	23
Africa	14.2	26.7	14.5	18.7	14.5	18.6	22.7	20.7	24.3	21.5	17
West Asia	17.1	19.8	18.9	15.5	8.5	13.4	15.1	13.2	18.5	28.2	14
South and East Asia	6.2	5.6	7.1	6.4	8.2	10.6	8.2	6.3	7.9	7.8	8
China	7.1	8.7	18.8	18.3	3.0	3.5	6.3	14.6	24.2	16.9	10
Mediterranean	32.0	36.0	68.1	58.6	55.9	61.1	65.0	61.3	98.3	86.6	65
by analytical grouping:											
Capital-surplus countries	10.8	17.7	18.6	14.8	6.2	12.9	16.2	13.8	20.5	32.9	16
Capital-importing countries	40.2	65.9	145.7	376.0	651.5	94.0	166.8	347.8	157.2	19.1	17
Energy exporters	35.0	48.4	46.3	25.0	20.0	19.8	19.2	17.7	20.4	28.0	27
Energy importers	42.2	72.3	182.4	505.4	883.8	121.3	221.1	469.1	207.5	15.8	13
Four exporters of manufactures	2.1	2.5	5.2	5.6	7.3	8.1	6.0	4.7	5.8	4.8	5
Other	54.1	91.4	230.8	642.1	1 122.6	152.2	279.7	595.7	262.4	18.8	15
Memo items:											
Sub-Saharan Africa	11.4	78.2	3.9	17.5	18.5	24.2	26.6	26.4	38.3	21.2	16
Fifteen heavily indebted countries[d]	87.5	145.0	348.4	927.3	1621.0	212.6	398.5	858.1	372.0	26.6	23

Source: UN/DESIPA, based on IMF, *International Financial Statistics*.

a   Weights used are GDP in 1988 dollars.
b   Preliminary estimates based on data for part of the year.
c   Forecast.
d   Excluding the former Yugoslavia and Zaire.

Table A.14.
SELECTED DEVELOPING COUNTRIES OR AREAS: REAL EFFECTIVE EXCHANGE RATES, BROAD MEASUREMENTS, 1985-1995[a]

1990 = 100

	1985	1986	1987	1988	1989	1990	1991	1992	1993	1994	1995
Argentina	124.5	107.1	94.4	104.8	86.4	100.0	117.8	115.7	117.3	113.6	111.1
Brazil	70.7	62.0	61.7	67.4	82.9	100.0	80.8	73.5	82.7	94.5	100.7
Chile	128.0	110.8	105.8	98.7	101.9	100.0	106.1	113.7	113.9	113.9	120.3
Mexico	125.8	90.0	92.7	112.3	107.6	100.0	106.1	107.7	116.6	111.9	78.6
Venezuela	170.9	164.0	119.4	135.5	115.7	100.0	99.8	100.7	104.0	108.9	138.8
Hong Kong	101.8	92.0	88.3	89.8	96.1	100.0	105.1	110.7	118.0	122.5	124.6
Indonesia	176.6	135.9	104.8	101.9	102.8	100.0	100.7	99.5	101.4	100.2	98.8
Malaysia	153.7	125.6	118.1	105.5	103.0	100.0	99.0	106.3	109.5	105.8	105.1
Philippines	128.5	101.5	98.1	100.3	106.3	100.0	97.0	105.7	97.2	104.3	102.9
Republic of Korea	104.6	89.2	88.5	96.3	107.9	100.0	97.4	88.3	85.8	84.0	85.5
Singapore	116.6	98.4	90.8	90.2	95.6	100.0	102.4	105.1	106.0	109.0	110.0
Taiwan Province of China	99.9	91.2	97.0	100.6	107.1	100.0	97.4	95.9	92.7	91.0	91.4
Thailand	120.8	102.6	96.9	97.4	100.4	100.0	102.3	98.6	99.9	99.3	98.9
Turkey	78.2	80.3	84.3	87.2	95.4	100.0	97.2	89.1	92.6	76.2	81.1

Source: Morgan Guaranty Trust Company, *World Financial Markets*.

a   Measured against a broad currency basket of 22 OECD currencies and 23 developing-economy currencies (mostly Asian and Latin American). The real effective exchange rate, which adjusts the nominal index for relative price changes, gauges the effect on international price competitiveness of the country's manufactures due to currency changes and inflation differentials. A rise in the index implies a fall in competitiveness and vice versa. The relative price changes are based on indices most closely measuring the prices of domestically produced finished manufactured goods, excluding food and energy, at the first stage of manufacturing. The weights for currency indices are derived from 1990 bilateral trade patterns of the corresponding countries.

II . INTERNATIONAL TRADE

Table A.15.

DIRECTION OF TRADE: EXPORTS (F.O.B.), 1980-1995

Origin		World[b]	Developed market economies[c]	Economies in transition	Developing countries (total)	Latin America	Africa	West Asia	South and East Asia	Other Asia[d]
		Billions of dollars	Percentage							
World[b]	1980	1 835.1	67.7	4.3	25.5	6.1	3.1	4.2	7.1	1.1
	1985	1859.9	69.2	4.9	24.3	4.3	2.3	3.7	7.6	2.1
	1990	3383.3	72.5	2.9	23.3	3.8	1.8	2.2	9.7	1.5
	1994	4198.6	66.3	3.7	28.6	5.2	1.5	2.0	12.9	3.1
	1995[e]	4942.1	65.9	4.1	28.8	4.9	1.5	1.8	13.4	3.2
Developed economies[c]	1980	1241.7	69.1	3.1	25.1	5.9	3.6	4.5	5.7	1.1
	1985	1286.2	72.9	2.5	22.8	4.4	2.5	3.7	6.2	2.0
	1990	2452.2	76.4	2.3	20.1	3.9	1.9	2.2	7.5	0.9
	1994	2785.6	70.9	3.1	24.8	5.5	1.5	2.1	10.1	1.8
	1995[e]	3257.3	70.6	3.3	25.2	5.2	1.6	1.9	10.8	1.8
Economies in transition	1994	154.6	54.2	32.5	12.8	0.9	0.5	1.4	2.5	3.1
	1995[e]	201.6	52.1	34.7	12.8	0.9	0.5	1.4	3.2	2.7
Developing countries	1980	468.5	67.9	3.0	27.5	7.1	1.9	3.3	11.0	0.8
	1985	452.5	62.8	5.6	28.1	4.4	1.9	3.5	11.6	2.4
	1990	786.9	62.0	3.3	32.6	3.9	1.7	2.3	16.5	3.3
	1994	1199.8	56.8	1.3	39.6	4.9	1.4	1.8	21.1	6.2
	1995[e]	1425.3	56.6	1.3	39.8	4.9	1.4	1.6	21.1	6.6
of which:										
Latin America	1980	111.6	66.1	3.4	28.6	20.9	1.5	1.7	1.1	0.6
	1985	80.8	72.2	3.1	22.4	12.5	2.2	2.3	1.6	1.6
	1990	129.3	70.8	1.4	26.1	16.0	0.8	1.6	3.1	0.7
	1994	219.0	70.0	0.6	28.1	19.0	0.6	0.9	3.5	1.0
	1995[e]	243.9	70.0	0.8	28.0	18.3	0.6	0.9	3.9	1.2
Africa	1980	56.6	82.9	2.7	13.2	3.1	4.9	0.9	1.5	0.5
	1985	43.3	81.2	2.1	15.1	4.2	4.5	0.8	1.5	0.6
	1990	61.4	81.0	1.3	16.5	1.5	7.4	1.1	3.2	0.5
	1994	61.7	78.7	0.8	19.3	2.5	8.9	1.0	4.2	0.6
	1995[e]	72.1	78.1	0.9	19.8	2.3	9.0	0.9	4.0	1.2
West Asia	1980	76.2	75.2	0.4	22.0	2.9	1.3	3.1	10.5	0.1
	1985	68.7	59.9	2.6	33.7	5.1	2.0	5.0	12.7	0.1
	1990	75.7	61.2	2.5	30.7	3.8	1.6	4.8	11.2	0.3
	1994	83.9	51.8	1.4	35.4	3.0	1.8	4.3	18.4	1.1
	1995[e]	89.1	51.1	1.3	36.2	3.0	1.8	3.7	19.7	1.7
South and East Asia	1980	129.6	61.5	2.9	34.7	2.3	2.1	3.7	20.1	2.1
	1985	141.7	60.4	2.1	36.2	1.6	1.5	3.0	19.9	6.3
	1990	328.8	59.7	1.6	37.4	1.6	1.2	1.7	20.5	7.4
	1994	540.8	52.1	1.0	45.6	2.4	1.1	1.2	23.6	12.3
	1995[e]	662.2	52.0	1.0	45.6	2.5	1.0	1.3	23.0	12.8
Other Asia[d]	1980	19.9	44.8	6.1	45.6	2.0	0.4	2.1	38.9	2.1
	1985	39.6	40.9	8.3	48.6	1.8	1.5	5.3	37.9	1.6
	1990	52.4	34.6	4.3	59.3	1.0	1.9	1.5	51.4	0.8
	1994	129.8	51.4	2.4	45.4	2.4	0.8	1.3	37.0	1.0
	1995[e]	158.6	51.9	2.2	45.4	2.5	0.9	1.1	36.6	1.0

Source: UN/DESIPA, based on data of IMF, *Direction of Trade Statistics.*

[a] Shares of trade to destinations do not add up to 100 per cent owing to incomplete specification of destinations in underlying data.
[b] Including data for economies in transition; before 1994, data for economies in transition are incomplete.
[c] Including South Africa.
[d] Including data for China, Democratic People's Republic of Korea, Mongolia and Viet Nam.
[e] Estimates.

Table A.16.
DIRECTION OF TRADE: IMPORTS (F.O.B.), 1980-1995

Origin		World[b]	Developed market economies	Economies in transition	Developing countries *(total)*	Latin America	Africa	West Asia	South and East Asia	Other Asia[d]
		Destination[a]								
World[b]		Billions of dollars								
	1980	1910.7	1221.9	79.1	580.3	105.0	71.2	166.1	118.1	20.2
	1985	1951.1	1319.3	95.2	522.3	114.3	57.5	77.1	140.5	32.0
	1990	3495.3	2494.9	98.6	873.1	157.1	71.2	109.0	285.6	91.1
	1994	4323.3	2917.8	164.3	1188.9	201.2	64.0	97.9	443.2	197.8
	1995[e]	5183.2	3489.5	218.1	1427.8	237.1	73.7	109.7	554.6	238.8
Developed economies[c]		Percentage								
	1980	64.0	65.4	34.9	62.9	63.2	74.3	68.6	55.7	73.7
	1985	67.6	70.8	34.8	60.6	65.1	75.0	66.4	56.2	67.4
	1990	71.4	74.7	50.9	61.6	70.9	71.3	70.7	56.3	48.1
	1994	67.5	71.2	55.5	60.5	71.8	67.5	69.6	53.2	53.8
	1995[e]	67.3	71.3	54.4	60.2	69.7	68.2	68.7	53.9	52.4
Economies in transition	1994	3.8	3.1	33.3	1.7	0.6	1.2	2.4	0.7	4.5
	1995[e]	4.2	3.4	35.0	1.7	0.7	1.5	2.6	0.8	4.2
Developing countries	1980	30.4	30.9	12.3	30.4	33.8	21.6	22.3	41.7	16.5
	1985	26.8	25.8	18.1	29.2	32.0	20.5	24.1	40.4	25.2
	1990	25.0	22.5	16.3	32.4	27.1	23.5	23.9	41.1	44.4
	1994	27.5	24.7	10.7	35.8	25.6	27.1	24.1	44.6	39.6
	1995[e]	27.5	24.7	10.2	36.3	27.6	26.2	24.6	44.0	41.1
of which:										
Latin America	1980	5.5	5.5	2.7	5.8	15.0	2.5	0.8	1.2	2.5
	1985	5.9	6.2	2.6	4.9	18.2	3.5	3.0	2.1	4.1
	1990	4.5	4.7	1.8	4.0	17.8	1.9	2.6	1.6	2.2
	1994	4.7	5.0	0.9	4.2	16.8	1.9	1.9	1.3	1.8
	1995[e]	4.6	5.0	0.9	4.0	16.2	1.7	2.1	1.3	2.0
Africa	1980	3.7	4.5	1.5	1.5	1.4	5.2	0.9	0.7	0.5
	1985	2.9	3.4	0.8	1.9	5.0	4.9	0.6	0.9	0.7
	1990	2.0	2.3	0.8	1.4	1.2	7.2	1.1	0.7	0.6
	1994	1.5	1.8	0.3	1.0	0.7	7.8	0.8	0.5	0.3
	1995[e]	1.4	1.7	0.3	0.9	0.6	7.7	0.7	0.4	0.6
West Asia	1980	8.7	8.7	4.8	9.3	8.7	7.3	7.2	12.8	0.4
	1985	4.0	3.5	3.2	5.1	5.1	4.0	5.4	6.5	0.3
	1990	3.1	2.8	3.7	4.1	4.1	2.4	5.6	4.5	0.7
	1994	2.3	2.0	0.9	3.0	1.3	2.7	5.4	3.5	1.0
	1995[e]	2.1	1.9	0.8	2.8	1.2	2.6	4.5	3.3	1.5
South and East Asia	1980	6.2	6.1	1.2	7.3	1.1	2.6	4.3	14.7	3.4
	1985	7.2	6.8	1.8	8.7	1.0	2.9	5.2	16.4	14.0
	1990	8.2	6.9	2.0	12.2	1.9	5.3	5.9	16.6	33.3
	1994	10.3	8.7	2.2	14.9	4.1	9.0	6.5	19.3	23.2
	1995[e]	10.7	8.9	2.7	15.8	5.9	8.1	8.5	19.8	24.5
Other Asia[d]	1980	1.1	0.7	2.1	2.1	0.5	1.2	1.1	5.1	1.6
	1985	1.6	1.1	2.4	2.9	0.9	1.1	0.8	7.6	1.1
	1990	2.6	1.8	2.8	5.0	0.6	1.7	1.3	10.3	1.0
	1994	4.6	3.7	1.6	6.9	1.1	1.6	1.7	13.0	1.1
	1995[e]	4.6	3.7	1.5	7.0	1.7	2.0	2.0	12.4	1.2

Source: UN/DESIPA, based on data of IMF, *Direction of Trade Statistics*

[a] Shares of trade to destinations do not add up to 100 per cent owing to incomplete specification of destinations in underlying data.
[b] Including data for economies in transition; before 1994, data for economies in transition are highly incomplete.
[c] Including South Africa.   [d] Including data for China, Democratic People's Republic of Korea, Mongolia and Viet Nam.   [e] Estimates

Table A.17.

COMMODITY COMPOSITION OF WORLD TRADE: EXPORTS, 1980-1994

Billions of dollars and percentage

Exporting country group	Total exports (billions of dollars)			Primary commodities Food			Agricultural raw materials			Fuels			Ores and metals		
	1980	1990	1994	1980	1990	1994	1980	1990	1994	1980	1990	1994	1980	1990	1994
World (billions of dollars)	2000.9	3416.4	4208.1	221.1	294.1	352.3	73.9	124.8	145.5	480.8	357.5	324.4	93.5	50.1	48.8
World (percentage share)				(100)	(100)	(100)	(100)	(100)	(100)	(100)	(100)	(100)	(100)	(100)	(100)
Developed economies[a]	1258.9	2410.8	2851.6	64.4	67.5	65.3	61.2	66.3	61.1	18.3	28.7	30.8	67.5	51.3	49.3
Economies in transition[b]	155.2	182.6	151.0	4.4	3.1	2.8	8.8	5.8	7.3	8.8	13.6	10.0	5.2	6.9	6.3
Developing countries	586.8	799.9	1177.4	31.2	28.7	31.0	30.0	26.4	32.0	72.9	57.7	59.1	27.3	40.9	43.3
Latin America	107.8	134.3	189.0	14.2	10.9	11.0	4.6	6.6	7.7	9.5	10.3	8.9	10.9	14.4	15.7
Africa	94.9	102.0	98.4	4.6	4.4	4.1	4.0	3.1	3.2	14.9	13.4	12.0	6.0	13.9	13.5
West Asia	211.0	110.5	123.5	1.2	1.1	1.4	1.3	0.4	0.6	41.5	22.4	24.8	1.2	0.7	0.6
South and East Asia	141.6	391.5	650.1	8.0	10.0	11.8	17.1	14.6	16.7	6.3	10.1	11.7	6.4	10.0	11.7
Other Asia[c]	20.4	62.1	121.0	2.3	2.4	3.1	2.1	2.4	2.6	0.6	1.5	1.3	1.2	1.4	1.6

Exporting country group	Manufactures Textiles			Chemicals			Machinery and transport			Metals			Other		
	1980	1990	1994	1980	1990	1994	1980	1990	1994	1980	1990	1994	1980	1990	1994
World (billions of dollars)	96.0	219.2	289.6	140.7	300.9	389.6	513.1	1219.1	1610.1	114.1	178.3	201.8	221.1	514.3	602.0
World (percentage share)	(100)	(100)	(100)	(100)	(100)	(100)	(100)	(100)	(100)	(100)	(100)	(100)	(100)	(100)	(100)
Developed economies[a]	61.3	46.2	37.3	87.1	82.8	80.3	85.0	83.0	77.6	85.7	73.1	64.2	80.1	68.9	64.0
Economies in transition[b]	5.0	2.3	3.2	5.5	3.8	3.5	9.0	3.9	1.2	6.8	6.0	13.1	5.2	7.2	3.9
Developing countries	33.7	46.6	54.2	7.4	12.6	15.3	6.0	12.7	20.8	7.5	20.3	22.7	14.7	24.1	32.8
Latin America	2.2	1.7	2.3	2.0	2.2	2.5	1.0	1.2	2.9	1.6	8.2	7.3	1.7	2.5	4.2
Africa	1.2	3.3	2.9	0.6	2.0	1.6	0.1	0.7	0.5	0.2	2.8	2.5	0.5	0.4	0.7
West Asia	1.5	4.7	5.1	1.0	1.5	1.4	0.3	0.3	0.4	0.4	2.0	2.8	0.6	0.3	0.2
South and East Asia	23.1	33.6	36.1	2.3	5.9	8.7	3.9	9.8	15.8	4.0	5.9	8.1	9.9	16.5	20.0
Other Asia[c]	4.8	7.7	12.3	0.8	1.2	1.6	0.1	0.9	1.4	0.6	1.1	1.5	1.2	2.4	5.3

Source: Statistics Division/DESIPA.

[a]   Including South Africa.
[b]   Data for 1994 include trade flows between the States of the former USSR. Prior to 1992, these flows were considered internal.
[c]   Including China, Democratic People's Republic of Korea, Mongolia and Viet Nam; China accounts for more than 90 per cent of amounts shown.

Table A.18.
COMMODITY COMPOSITION OF WORLD TRADE: IMPORTS, 1980-1994
Billions of dollars and percentage

Importing country group	Total imports (billions of dollars)			Primary commodities											
				Food			Agricultural raw materials			Fuels			Ores and metals		
	1980	1990	1994	1980	1990	1994	1980	1990	1994	1980	1990	1994	1980	1990	1994
World (billions of dollars)	2000.9	3416.4	4208.1	221.1	294.1	352.3	73.9	124.8	145.5	480.8	357.5	324.4	93.5	50.1	48.8
World (percentage share)				(100)	(100)	(100)	(100)	(100)	(100)	(100)	(100)	(100)	(100)	(100)	(100)
Developed economies[a]	1336.0	2448.9	2773.3	61.4	69.3	68.9	68.3	70.4	64.4	75.3	70.8	65.2	79.1	70.1	66.3
Economies in transition[b]	144.0	155.1	143.7	10.3	6.1	6.5	7.5	3.9	4.0	3.9	5.7	5.3	5.5	6.3	4.7
Developing countries	504.0	812.4	1287.5	27.3	24.3	23.9	24.0	26.0	29.3	18.9	23.5	28.3	13.2	22.9	28.4
Latin America	126.1	136.4	220.9	6.0	4.2	5.0	3.1	3.7	4.9	6.7	4.1	4.4	3.1	3.0	3.4
Africa	84.4	97.4	99.4	6.0	5.3	4.8	2.3	5.0	4.6	1.6	2.0	1.9	1.4	3.4	3.3
West Asia	96.5	106.7	110.0	5.6	4.2	2.5	2.1	0.9	-0.8	2.0	3.3	4.0	1.5	3.5	4.8
South and East Asia	150.7	420.2	737.6	7.0	8.9	8.2	10.5	12.4	12.9	7.4	12.7	14.3	5.1	12.0	14.6
Other Asia[c]	22.8	57.0	125.0	1.7	1.9	3.5	4.1	4.1	7.7	0.1	1.6	3.9	0.7	1.1	2.6

Importing country group	Manufactures														
	Textiles			Chemicals			Machinery and transport			Metals			Other		
	1980	1990	1994	1980	1990	1994	1980	1990	1994	1980	1990	1994	1980	1990	1994
World (billions of dollars)	96.0	219.2	289.6	140.7	300.9	389.6	513.1	1219.1	1610.1	114.1	178.3	201.8	221.1	514.3	602.0
World (percentage share)	(100)	(100)	(100)	(100)	(100)	(100)	(100)	(100)	(100)	(100)	(100)	(100)	(100)	(100)	(100)
Developed economies[a]	69.7	67.9	61.8	63.8	67.5	64.6	59.5	70.7	65.5	56.3	70.9	62.5	72.2	78.9	74.0
Economies in transition[b]	6.8	4.3	4.3	7.4	4.3	3.9	8.7	4.4	2.6	9.3	3.5	4.3	5.5	3.7	2.0
Developing countries	23.1	27.3	33.7	28.5	27.2	30.7	31.3	24.3	31.4	33.9	24.9	33.0	22.0	17.2	23.8
Latin America	3.6	2.7	4.3	8.0	1.2	0.5	7.8	4.5	6.1	6.4	2.9	3.5	4.9	5.2	4.1
Africa	4.4	3.8	8.3	4.7	1.2	0.8	6.2	2.8	2.1	6.4	2.2	1.9	3.9	3.2	1.6
West Asia	5.8	2.8	1.5	4.2	2.1	0.8	6.9	3.0	2.5	8.7	12.2	4.4	5.6	0.8	4.2
South and East Asia	7.3	12.9	11.0	8.7	18.9	22.2	8.1	12.8	18.5	8.5	7.8	22.8	6.2	7.0	12.2
Other Asia[c]	1.1	5.2	8.6	1.6	3.8	6.4	1.3	1.4	2.3	2.3	0.3	0.6	0.7	0.6	1.0

Source: Statistics Division, DESIPA.

[a] Including South Africa.
[b] Data for 1994 include trade flows between the States of the former USSR. Prior to 1992, these flows were considered internal.
[c] Including China, Democratic People's Republic of Korea, Mongolia and Viet Nam; China accounts for more than 90 per cent of amounts shown.

Table A.19.

WORLD TRADE: CHANGES IN VALUE AND VOLUME OF EXPORTS AND IMPORTS, BY MAJOR COUNTRY GROUP, 1986-1996

Annual percentage change	1986	1987	1988	1989	1990	1991	1992	1993	1994	1995[a]	1996[b]
Dollar value of exports											
World	10.2	17.2	13.8	8.1	14.3	2.3	6.5	-0.2	13.1	19.1	7
Developed economies of which:	16.1	16.6	14.4	7.1	15.3	2.0	5.9	-3.0	12.1	19.1	4¾
North America	2.5	11.0	24.8	10.5	7.3	5.3	6.1	4.7	11.1	14.5	9
Western Europe	21.5	20.1	10.8	6.7	20.7	-0.5	5.6	-7.9	13.1	22.9	3¾
Japan	19.0	9.7	14.5	3.4	5.0	9.5	8.0	6.6	9.6	11.6	2½
Economies in transition	5.2	4.1	-0.8	-1.5	-4.2	*-14.6	6.1	♦4.8	17.5	17.6	..
Central and Eastern Europe	5.6	2.7	0.5	-3.2	-3.2	*-8.7	-1.0	♦4.0	19.6	8.8	10
Former Soviet Union[c]	4.7	5.6	-2.2	0.4	-5.2	-21.0	15.2	5.6	15.3	27.4	..
Developing countries	-7.1	22.0	14.6	12.8	14.2	5.1	8.2	6.5	15.0	19.2	12¾
Latin America	-16.2	11.3	13.8	10.0	8.1	-2.0	2.7	4.5	15.6	23.7	10
Africa	-16.1	13.3	-0.5	10.4	24.5	-5.0	-3.4	-7.0	3.7	12.5	8½
West Asia	-24.7	17.3	0.1	24.3	24.7	-10.0	4.1	-0.8	1.3	7.2	6
South and East Asia	8.1	30.4	23.6	12.1	10.4	14.0	12.6	10.7	17.0	21.2	15½
China	13.1	27.5	20.5	10.6	18.1	15.8	18.1	13.5	31.9	22.9	10½
Mediterranean	-4.0	21.6	12.9	3.8	9.9	1.4	-4.2	-3.4	8.5	10.0	12
Memo items:											
Net energy exporters	-28.2	12.0	1.2	20.5	16.3	-7.3	10.7	2.2	1.9	8.1	11
Net energy importers	7.7	24.0	21.5	10.6	9.3	10.4	10.6	9.0	18.1	13.9	12
Dollar value of imports											
World	9.7	16.5	14.0	8.5	14.0	3.2	6.4	-1.8	12.6	18.0	7½
Developed economies of which:	12.6	18.2	13.0	8.3	14.9	0.7	4.4	-6.0	12.8	17.8	5½
North America	8.0	10.5	10.7	7.1	4.5	-1.1	7.9	8.7	13.8	11.3	6
Western Europe	18.2	22.2	12.4	7.8	20.8	1.5	3.9	-13.4	11.9	20.4	4¾
Japan	-2.2	18.4	24.1	11.9	12.2	0.7	-1.6	3.6	13.9	22.1	10¾
Economies in transition	7.6	0.6	-2.5	2.4	7.4	♦0.8	-11.0	♦1.2	2.2	22.4	..
Central and Eastern Europe	13.2	0.7	-2.7	-2.2	3.1	♦1.8	7.7	♦5.3	12.4	27.8	20
Former Soviet Union[c]	1.5	0.5	-2.2	7.9	12.0	-0.2	-30.1	-5.3	-15.6	9.9	..
Developing countries	0.5	14.9	19.5	9.9	12.3	11.0	13.3	7.6	13.4	18.2	12
Latin America	1.9	8.9	11.3	6.1	11.5	16.3	19.8	8.2	16.1	10.7	8½
Africa	3.1	2.4	14.0	1.4	11.8	-2.0	7.0	-4.7	7.9	17.5	8
West Asia	-10.5	7.4	3.3	4.9	3.7	11.2	16.7	-9.8	0.6	-0.8	5
South and East Asia	4.3	28.0	29.9	15.0	16.5	13.8	11.6	9.9	18.3	23.6	13
China	1.5	0.7	27.9	7.0	-9.8	19.6	26.3	27.9	11.2	14.2	19½
Mediterranean	-2.1	17.6	4.4	11.9	32.9	-11.2	-3.6	15.3	-12.2	26.4	17½
Memo items:											
Net energy exporters	-11.4	3.4	12.1	6.8	9.3	16.4	17.0	-7.2	4.3	0.3	12½
Net energy importers	4.7	18.7	21.6	11.1	13.5	10.0	12.5	11.9	15.3	21.6	11½

Table A.19 (continued)

	1986	1987	1988	1989	1990	1991	1992	1993	1994	1995[a]	1996[b]
Volume of exports											
World	4.1	5.3	7.3	7.3	5.4	◆ 3.8	4.5	2.9	10.2	8.7	7¾
Developed economies of which:	1.7	4.5	7.9	6.9	5.0	3.1	3.9	1.2	9.7	7.5	5½
North America	3.2	8.1	15.9	7.7	6.6	4.9	6.8	4.9	10.0	9.3	8¼
Western Europe	1.8	4.3	6.0	7.5	4.2	2.2	3.3	0.4	11.0	7.4	5
Japan	-0.7	0.4	5.9	4.3	5.3	2.5	1.5	-2.5	1.7	6.0	2½
Economies in transition	4.0	2.4	4.5	-1.5	-9.5	..	..	..	..	..	..
Central and Eastern Europe	-0.7	1.7	4.3	-2.9	-6.2	◆ -9.3	-0.1	◆ 0.3	19.1	9.5	8
Former Soviet Union[c]	10.0	3.3	4.8	0.0	-13.1	..	..	..	..	..	..
Developing countries	11.9	8.5	6.3	10.7	9.1	8.7	5.6	7.6	11.1	12.2	12¾
Latin America	-1.5	4.8	5.7	7.1	2.8	4.9	3.1	7.6	9.2	16.2	11¾
Africa[d]	18.4	1.1	0.4	5.0	14.6	7.6	-4.7	-4.0	2.0	4.5	9½
West Asia	41.2	-7.2	11.2	8.8	2.1	3.4	3.7	9.7	4.7	-0.2	6
South and East Asia	19.0	18.2	13.0	10.9	7.5	16.0	10.1	11.5	14.2	14.9	16
China	17.9	11.8	10.0	8.4	14.4	18.3	15.4	14.2	29.1	17.1	10¾
Mediterranean	-4.2	10.8	0.9	2.6	8.4	2.9	-5.9	-2.7	3.9	3.6	12¾
Memo items:											
Net energy exporters	20.7	-5.3	5.5	9.0	-2.1	3.8	11.0	5.9	-1.5	1.7	11¾
Net energy importers	14.5	13.9	10.2	9.2	6.8	13.0	8.7	9.8	14.3	7.8	12½
Volume of imports											
World	4.5	5.7	8.2	7.4	4.6	◆ 4.6	5.4	2.8	10.3	8.5	7¼
Developed economies of which:	7.5	6.6	7.4	7.2	4.6	2.5	4.2	0.2	10.6	8.0	5
North America	11.6	3.9	5.3	4.3	1.4	-0.9	7.9	9.6	13.0	8.6	5
Western Europe	6.1	7.7	6.8	8.0	6.2	3.9	3.3	-4.4	8.8	7.4	5
Japan	9.5	9.2	17.9	7.9	5.7	4.0	-0.4	2.9	13.7	10.3	6¼
Economies in transition	-0.3	2.4	-0.8	2.4	0.2	-5.2	-5.2	-13.8	..	..	...
Central and Eastern Europe	4.6	3.5	3.4	0.2	-8.9	◆ 2.3	5.9	◆ 5.9	10.8	11.0	10
Former Soviet Union[c]	-5.1	1.1	-5.8	5.3	10.6	-12.2	-35.0	..	..	..	..
Developing countries	-4.3	3.5	12.5	8.6	5.5	12.5	11.0	9.1	10.1	9.7	12¼
Latin America	0.2	0.7	4.7	4.0	5.6	18.0	19.1	9.9	13.4	3.6	8½
Africa[d]	-7.8	-12.9	6.3	1.2	2.8	0.6	6.0	-1.2	2.4	2.1	7¼
West Asia	-16.1	-4.9	-1.7	3.2	-6.2	13.3	14.6	-6.2	-1.4	-9.4	5½
South and East Asia	1.6	15.0	21.9	13.2	10.1	14.3	8.8	10.2	14.8	15.6	13¼
China	-6.4	-8.4	19.0	6.1	-14.1	20.0	23.2	27.5	7.3	6.4	20
Mediterranean	-4.7	2.6	1.4	9.7	17.6	-8.5	-5.1	23.3	-13.7	13.5	18½
Memo items:											
Net energy exporters	-16.8	-6.4	5.7	5.2	1.8	17.4	15.3	-5.3	1.9	-7.0	12¾
Net energy importers	1.3	6.6	14.4	9.5	6.1	11.2	10.2	13.0	12.0	13.2	11¾

Source: UN/DESIPA, based on data of IMF and United Nations and estimates of ECE from national data.
Note: As of 1993, transactions between the Czech Republic and Slovakia are recorded as foreign trade.

◆ Indicates break in the series.
a Preliminary estimates.
b Forecast.
c CIS countries since 1992.
d Excluding South Africa.

Table A.20.

WORLD TRADE: CHANGES IN PRICES OF EXPORTS AND IMPORTS AND TERMS OF TRADE, BY MAJOR COUNTRY GROUP, 1986-1996

Annual percentage change in dollar-based indices

	1986	1987	1988	1989	1990	1991	1992	1993	1994	1995[a]	1996[b]
Unit value of exports											
World	6.3	11.3	6.0	0.7	8.6	*-1.3	2.0	-3.3	2.6	9.3	-½
Developed economies of which:	14.0	11.7	6.0	0.2	9.9	-1.0	2.0	-4.4	2.2	10.9	-¾
North America	-0.8	2.6	7.6	2.6	0.7	0.4	-0.6	-0.2	1.0	4.7	¾
Western Europe	19.3	15.1	4.6	-0.8	15.8	-2.6	2.2	-8.3	1.8	14.4	-1¼
Japan	19.8	9.3	8.1	-0.8	-0.3	6.8	6.4	9.3	7.7	5.3	0
Economies in transition	1.1	1.6	-5.1	0.1	5.9	..	..	..	..	..	..
Central and Eastern Europe	6.4	1.0	-3.6	-0.3	3.2	* 0.7	-0.9	*-0.1	1.2	..	..
Former Soviet Union[c]	-4.8	2.2	-6.7	0.4	9.1	..	..	..	..	..	..
Developing countries	-16.7	12.2	5.6	3.9	6.7	-4.9	2.5	-1.1	3.7	6.4	0
Latin America	-15.0	6.2	7.7	2.7	5.2	-6.6	0.5	2.9	5.7	6.4	-1½
Africa[d]	-35.6	11.3	-2.4	8.8	14.2	-10.7	-1.9	-6.9	1.9	7.9	-1½
West Asia	-46.8	26.5	-9.9	14.1	22.2	-13.0	0.4	-9.6	-3.2	7.3	0
South and East Asia	-9.2	10.4	9.4	1.1	2.7	-1.9	2.3	-0.7	2.5	5.4	-¼
China	-4.0	14.0	9.3	2.0	3.3	-2.2	2.4	-0.5	2.2	5.0	-¼
Mediterranean	0.2	9.7	11.9	1.2	1.4	-1.5	1.9	-0.7	4.5	6.1	-½
Memo items:											
Net energy exporters	-40.5	18.3	-4.1	10.6	18.9	-10.8	-0.3	-3.5	3.4	6.4	-¾
Net energy importers	-5.9	9.0	10.2	1.3	2.4	-2.3	1.8	-0.8	3.3	5.6	-½
Unit value of imports											
World	5.0	10.3	5.2	1.1	9.1	*-1.3	0.9	-4.6	2.2	8.3	¼
Developed economies of which:	4.8	10.6	5.3	1.0	9.9	-1.7	0.3	-6.2	2.0	9.0	½
North America	-3.1	6.3	5.2	2.6	3.2	-0.3	0.0	-0.9	0.7	2.5	1
Western Europe	11.6	13.4	5.3	-0.2	13.7	-2.2	0.7	-9.4	2.9	12.1	-¼
Japan	-10.7	8.4	5.2	3.8	6.1	-3.2	-1.2	0.7	0.2	10.6	4¼
Economies in transition	7.9	-1.6	-1.5	0.0	7.1	..	..	..	..	..	..
Central and Eastern Europe	8.2	-2.7	-5.8	-2.3	13.1	*-0.5	1.8	*-0.6	1.4	..	..
Former Soviet Union[c]	6.9	-0.6	3.8	2.4	1.4	..	..	..	..	..	..
Developing countries	4.6	11.0	6.1	1.5	6.8	-1.0	2.3	-1.2	2.9	7.5	-¼
Latin America	1.7	8.1	6.3	2.1	5.6	-1.4	0.6	-1.5	2.4	6.8	0
Africa[d]	9.2	13.3	4.9	1.0	12.3	-2.8	1.7	-5.4	1.9	10.9	-¾
West Asia	6.8	13.0	5.1	1.7	10.5	-1.8	2.0	-3.8	2.1	9.5	-½
South and East Asia	2.7	11.2	6.6	1.6	5.8	-0.4	2.6	-0.3	3.0	6.9	-¼
China	8.5	10.0	7.4	0.9	5.1	-0.5	2.5	0.4	3.6	7.3	-¼
Mediterranean	2.7	14.6	3.0	2.0	13.0	-3.0	1.6	-5.7	1.7	11.4	-¾
Memo items:											
Net energy exporters	6.5	10.5	6.2	1.5	7.4	-0.9	1.5	-1.9	2.3	7.8	0
Net energy importers	3.4	11.4	6.3	1.7	7.0	-1.1	2.2	-1.0	3.0	7.5	-¼

Table A.20 (continued)

	1986	1987	1988	1989	1990	1991	1992	1993	1994	1995[a]	1996[b]
Terms of trade											
Developed economies	8.8	0.8	0.8	-0.8	-0.1	✦ 0.6	1.7	2.0	0.3	1.7	-1¼
of which:											
North America	2.4	-3.4	2.4	0.0	-2.5	0.7	-0.6	0.6	0.3	2.2	- ¼
Western Europe	6.9	1.7	-0.6	-0.4	1.9	-0.4	1.4	1.2	-1.0	2.1	-1
Japan	34.2	0.9	2.8	-4.4	-6.1	10.3	7.6	8.5	7.3	-4.8	-4
Economies in transition	-6.3	3.3	-3.6	0.0	-1.1	..	..	..	..	..	..
Central and Eastern Europe	-1.7	3.8	2.4	2.1	-8.8	✦ 1.2	-2.6	✦ 0.4	-0.2	..	..
Former Soviet Union[c]	-10.9	2.9	-10.0	-1.9	7.6	..	..	..	..	..	..
Developing countries	-21.2	1.5	2.0	0.8	-1.7	-1.9	0.2	0.1	0.8	-1.0	¼
Latin America	-16.3	-1.9	1.3	0.6	-0.4	-5.2	-1.1	-1.4	3.3	-0.4	-1½
Africa[d]	-41.0	-1.7	-7.0	7.7	1.7	-8.1	-3.5	-1.6	0.0	-2.6	-¾
West Asia	-50.1	11.9	-14.3	12.3	10.5	-11.3	-1.6	-5.9	-5.3	-1.9	½
South and East Asia	-11.5	-0.8	2.6	-0.3	-2.9	-1.3	-0.3	-0.6	-0.5	-1.5	0
China	-11.6	3.7	1.8	1.1	-1.7	-1.7	-0.2	-0.9	-1.4	-2.2	¼
Mediterranean	-2.4	-4.3	8.6	-0.7	-10.2	1.6	0.2	5.3	2.7	-4.7	¼
Memo items											
Net energy exporters	-44.1	6.9	-9.7	8.8	10.5	-9.7	-1.7	-1.6	1.1	-1.3	-½
Net energy importers	-9.0	-2.4	3.7	-0.4	-4.3	-1.2	-0.5	0.1	0.3	-0.2	-¼

Source: UN/DESIPA, based on data of United Nations and IMF.
Note: As of 1993, transactions between the Czech Republic and Slovakia are recorded as foreign trade.

✦   Indicates break in the series.
a   Preliminary estimates.
b   Forecast.
c   CIS countries since 1992.
d   Excluding South Africa.

Table A.21.

INDICES OF PRICES OF NON-FUEL PRIMARY COMMODITIES
EXPORTED BY DEVELOPING COUNTRIES, 1985-1995

1990 = 100

		Food	Tropical beverages	Vegetable oil-seeds and oils	Agricultural raw materials	Minerals and metals	Combined index Dollar	Combined index SDR	Prices of manufactures[a]	Real prices of commodities[b]	Memo item: crude petroleum[c]
1985		66	161	135	74	68	79	105	63	125	124
1986		73	200	84	76	65	82	95	76	108	58
1987		77	131	99	88	76	84	88	85	99	76
1988		101	132	130	96	111	106	107	92	116	64
1989		107	113	115	95	111	106	113	91	117	78
1990		100	100	100	100	100	100	100	100	100	100
1991		93	92	108	94	91	93	93	100	93	84
1992		91	79	116	92	87	91	87	103	88	83
1993		92	84	116	89	74	87	85	97	90	73
1994		101	147	145	101	84	102	97	99	103	70
1995		107	148	160	115	101	113	101	107	105	76
1994	I	105	95	130	94	74	95	93	96	99	61
	II	100	124	137	98	80	97	94	98	99	70
	III	98	197	145	103	87	106	99	102	104	75
	IV	102	173	164	109	97	110	102	102	108	73
1995	I	105	164	162	122	103	115	104	106	108	77
	II	103	160	156	123	99	112	97	110	102	80
	III	109	142	160	105	103	112	100	108	104	72
	IV	111	127	162	109	99	111	101	108	103	75

Sources : UNCTAD, *Monthly Commodity Price Bulletin*; and United Nations, *Monthly Bulletin of Statistics*.

a   Unit value of exports of manufactures from developed economies.
b   Dollar index deflated by unit values of manufactured exports of developed economies.
c   OPEC oil price, which is the average spot price of a basket of seven OPEC country crudes (Saharan Blend, Minas, Bonny Light, Arab Light, Dubai, T. J. Light and Isthmus).

III. INTERNATIONAL FINANCE AND FINANCIAL MARKETS

Table A.22.

WORLD BALANCE OF PAYMENTS ON CURRENT ACCOUNT, BY COUNTRY GROUP, 1985-1995[a]

Billions of dollars

	1985	1986	1987	1988	1989	1990	1991	1992	1993	1994	1995[b]
Developed economies	-37.2	-3.5	-29.3	-22.6	-43.5	-58.9	-3.0	22.1	94.0	64.4	65.5
Major developed economies of which:	-35.9	1.3	-23.7	-15.9	-21.3	-34.0	9.4	32.1	63.3	30.4	20.1
Germany[c]	24.0	48.7	57.2	61.8	69.7	63.4	10.5	-1.8	9.6	3.7	10.6
Japan	50.1	87.0	88.6	81.7	59.8	39.9	84.1	120.3	134.5	133.2	115.4
United States	-111.0	-137.0	-154.1	-114.3	-90.6	-72.5	-28.4	-43.2	-80.3	-131.9	-139.3
Other industrialized countries	-1.3	-4.8	-5.6	-6.7	-22.2	-24.8	-12.4	-10.0	30.7	34.0	45.3
Economies in transition[d]	3.1	2.9	7.7	3.8	-2.9	-11.3	♦ -4.1	-7.5	-6.2	-8.5	2.2
Central and Eastern Europe	3.0	0.2	0.4	0.9	-2.1	-6.5	♦ -3.3	-2.1	-9.1	-5.2	-8.9
Former Soviet Union	0.1	2.7	7.3	2.9	-0.8	-4.8	♦ -0.8	-5.5	2.9	-2.9	13.4
Developing countries	-30.3	-46.8	-8.3	-25.8	-20.1	-2.7	-72.7	-79.1	-109.2	-78.9	-85.7
Capital-surplus countries	2.9	-3.4	-2.1	-5.0	3.4	9.5	-59.0	-20.6	-21.1	-3.2	-0.3
Capital-importing countries	-33.2	-38.5	-8.2	-21.3	-23.9	-22.7	♦ -44.6	-62.2	-93.7	-78.7	-88.7
Energy exporters	-4.5	-19.3	-1.7	-16.8	-8.8	2.0	-20.1	-33.6	-38.5	-46.1	-24.9
Energy importers	-28.7	-19.2	-6.5	-4.5	-15.0	-24.7	-24.5	-28.6	-55.2	-32.7	-63.8
Four exporters of manufactures	11.0	23.3	31.1	31.7	27.4	18.4	14.0	15.6	20.7	16.9	9.2
Other	-39.7	-42.5	-37.6	-36.2	-42.4	-43.1	-38.5	-44.2	-75.9	-49.6	-73.0
World residual[e] of which:	64.4	47.4	29.9	44.6	66.5	72.8	79.6	64.4	21.4	22.2	18.0
Trade residual (imports, f.o.b.)	-21.1	-20.3	-39.0	-48.3	-31.8	-27.3	-22.3	-39.4	-70.0	-86.3	-83.7
Services and private transfers	85.5	67.7	68.9	92.9	98.4	100.0	101.9	103.8	91.4	108.5	101.7

Source: UN/DESIPA, based on data of IMF and other national and international sources.

♦   Indicates break in series.
a   Balance on goods, services and private transfers.
b   Preliminary estimate.
c   Including transactions of the former German Democratic Republic as from July 1990.
d   Balance in convertible currencies; total including the former German Democratic Republic until 1990;
     data excluding the trade among members of the former Czechoslovakia and the Commonwealth of Independent States.
e   Unreported trade, services and private transfers, as well as errors and timing asymmetries in reported data.

Table A.23.
CURRENT ACCOUNT TRANSACTIONS: DEVELOPED ECONOMIES, 1985-1995[a]

Billions of dollars

	1985	1986	1987	1988	1989	1990	1991	1992	1993	1994	1995[b]
All developed economies											
Goods: exports (f.o.b.)	1263.4	1469.3	1717.6	1976.6	2118.7	2435.6	2480.8	2633.5	2543.5	2851.7	3402.3
Goods: imports (f.o.b.)	-1304.3	-1478.6	-1746.7	-1984.8	-2152.3	-2472.6	-2468.7	-2593.4	-2441.4	-2755.8	-3290.0
Trade balance	-40.9	-9.3	-29.0	-8.2	-33.5	-37.0	12.1	40.1	102.1	95.9	112.2
Net services, income and private transfers	3.7	5.8	-0.2	-14.4	-10.0	-21.9	-15.1	-17.9	-8.1	-31.5	-46.8
of which:											
Investment income	1.3	-2.1	-1.4	1.4	4.5	-4.3	-8.7	-11.1	-3.0	-19.5	-18.9
Current account balance	-37.2	-3.5	-29.3	-22.6	-43.5	-58.9	-3.0	22.1	94.0	64.4	65.5
Major developed economies											
Goods: exports (f.o.b.)	937.0	1083.7	1253.9	1450.8	1559.1	1771.1	1814.6	1928.0	1886.9	2102.2	2441.0
Goods: imports (f.o.b.)	-976.2	-1083.8	-1266.7	-1445.0	-1568.8	-1784.2	-1791.6	-1881.9	-1808.6	-2032.6	-2370.9
Trade balance	-39.2	-0.1	-12.8	5.8	-9.7	-13.1	23.0	46.1	78.3	69.6	70.1
Net services, income and private transfers	3.3	1.5	-10.9	-21.7	-11.6	-20.9	-13.6	-14.0	-15.0	-39.2	-50.0
of which:											
Investment income	15.7	13.5	14.1	20.1	25.8	26.3	21.3	25.1	22.7	9.1	6.5
Current account balance	-35.9	1.3	-23.7	-15.9	-21.3	-34.0	9.4	32.1	63.3	30.4	20.1
of which:											
Germany[c]											
Goods: exports (f.o.b.)	182.7	241.5	291.5	322.8	340.9	412.0	403.7	430.6	382.6	430.1	508.1
Goods: imports (f.o.b.)	-154.2	-186.8	-223.4	-246.5	-265.9	-343.4	-385.2	-408.5	-342.7	-381.7	-442.8
Trade balance	28.5	54.8	68.1	76.3	75.0	68.6	18.5	22.1	39.9	48.3	65.3
Net services, income and private transfers	-4.6	-6.0	-10.9	-14.5	-5.4	-5.2	-8.0	-23.9	-30.4	-44.6	-54.7
of which:											
Investment income	3.3	4.8	4.1	4.6	11.8	18.2	19.8	16.9	14.1	7.7	1.8
Current account balance	24.0	48.7	57.2	61.8	69.7	63.4	10.5	-1.8	9.6	3.7	10.6
Japan											
Goods: exports (f.o.b.)	174.0	205.6	224.6	259.8	269.5	280.3	306.6	330.9	351.3	384.2	427.3
Goods: imports (f.o.b.)	-118.0	-112.8	-128.2	-164.8	-192.7	-216.8	-203.5	-198.5	-209.7	-238.3	-292.5
Trade balance	56.0	92.8	96.4	95.0	76.9	63.6	103.1	132.4	141.6	145.9	134.8
Net services, income and private transfers of which:	-5.9	-5.8	-7.8	-13.3	-17.1	-23.7	-18.9	-12.1	-7.0	12.7	-19.4
Investment income	6.8	9.5	16.7	21.0	23.4	23.2	26.7	36.2	41.4	41.0	45.1
Current account balance	50.1	87.0	88.6	81.7	59.8	39.9	84.1	120.3	134.5	133.2	115.4
United States											
Goods: exports (f.o.b.)	215.9	223.4	250.2	320.2	362.2	389.3	416.9	440.3	458.7	504.5	576.8
Goods: imports (f.o.b.)	-338.1	-368.4	-409.8	-447.2	-477.3	-498.3	-491.0	-536.4	-590.1	-668.9	-749.8
Trade balance	-122.2	-145.1	-159.6	-127.0	-115.1	-109.0	-74.1	-96.1	-131.4	-164.3	-173.0
Net services, income and private transfers	11.1	8.1	5.5	12.6	24.6	36.5	45.6	52.9	51.1	32.4	33.7
of which:											
Investment income	8.1	15.1	14.8	29.4	28.3	20.8	19.1	21.9	15.5	17.9	13.8
Current account balance	-111.0	-137.0	-154.1	-114.3	-90.6	-72.5	-28.4	-43.2	-80.3	-131.9	-139.3
Other industrialized countries											
Goods: exports (f.o.b.)	326.4	385.7	463.7	525.9	559.7	664.5	666.2	705.5	656.7	749.5	961.3
Goods: imports (f.o.b.)	-328.1	-394.8	-479.9	-539.8	-583.5	-688.4	-677.1	-711.6	-632.8	-732.2	-919.1
Trade balance	-1.7	-9.1	-16.3	-14.0	-23.8	-23.9	-10.8	-6.1	23.8	26.3	42.1
Net services, income and private transfers	0.4	4.4	10.7	7.2	1.6	-1.0	-1.5	-3.9	6.9	7.7	3.2
of which:											
Investment income	-14.3	-15.6	-15.6	-18.7	-21.3	-30.6	-30.1	-36.2	-25.7	-28.6	-25.4
Current account balance	-1.3	-4.8	-5.6	-6.7	-22.2	-24.8	-12.4	-10.0	30.7	34.0	45.3

Source: UN/DESIPA, based on IMF, World Trade Organization and national sources.

a   Balance on goods, services and private transfers.
b   Preliminary estimates.
c   Including transactions of the former German Democratic Republic as from July 1990.

Table A.24.

CURRENT ACCOUNT TRANSACTIONS: ECONOMIES IN TRANSITION, 1985-1995[a]

Billions of dollars

	1985	1986	1987	1988	1989	1990	1991	1992	1993	1994	1995[b]
Economies in transition[c]											
Goods: exports (f.o.b.)	91.4	91.5	97.7	99.4	101.1	100.9	*90.8	98.3	*107.3	125.2	149.3
Goods: imports (f.o.b.)	-82.2	-83.5	-87.2	-88.2	-95.6	-113.4	*-111.2	-99.0	*-104.5	-106.5	-129.8
Trade balance	9.2	8.0	10.5	11.1	5.5	-12.5	*-20.4	1.4	2.8	18.7	19.5
Net services, income and private transfers	-6.1	-5.1	-2.8	-7.3	-8.4	1.2	*16.3	-8.9	-9.0	-27.2	-17.3
Current account balance	3.1	2.9	7.7	3.8	-2.9	-11.3	*-4.1	-7.5	-6.2	-8.5	2.2
Central and Eastern Europe[c]											
Goods: exports (f.o.b.)	34.1	31.5	34.3	37.4	38.8	41.9	*44.1	44.6	*46.4	55.5	60.4
Goods: imports (f.o.b.)	-28.3	-28.8	-32.2	-34.4	-37.6	-48.4	*-46.3	-51.8	*-57.4	-65.0	-83.1
Trade balance	5.8	2.7	2.1	2.9	1.2	-6.5	*-2.2	-7.2	-11.0	-9.5	-22.7
Net services, income and private transfers	-2.8	-2.5	-1.7	-2.0	-3.3	0.0	*-1.1	5.1	1.9	4.3	13.8
Current account balance of which:	3.0	0.2	0.4	0.9	-2.1	-6.5	*-3.3	-2.1	-9.1	-5.2	-8.9
Former Czechoslovakia											
Goods: exports (f.o.b.)	3.9	4.3	4.5	5.0	5.4	5.9	11.3	12.3			
Goods: imports (f.o.b.)	-3.2	-4.1	-4.6	-5.1	-5.0	-6.8	-11.0	-14.0			
Trade balance	0.7	0.2	-0.1	-0.1	0.4	-0.9	0.3	-1.7			
Net services, income and private transfers	-0.0	0.2	0.2	0.2	-0.1	0.7	-0.3	2.3			
Current account balance	0.7	0.4	0.1	0.1	0.3	-0.2	0.0	0.6			
Czech Republic											
Goods: exports (f.o.b.)									10.4	12.0	14.3
Goods: imports (f.o.b.)									-10.6	-12.8	-18.1
Trade balance									-0.2	-0.8	-3.8
Net services, income and private transfers									0.0	0.1	2.1
Current account balance									-0.2	-0.7	-1.7
Slovakia											
Goods: exports (f.o.b.)									3.1	4.2	5.6
Goods: imports (f.o.b.)									-4.0	-4.7	-6.1
Trade balance									-0.9	-0.5	-0.5
Net services, income and private transfers									0.5	1.2	0.7
Current account balance									-0.4	0.7	0.2
Hungary											
Goods: exports (f.o.b.)	4.2	4.2	5.0	5.5	6.4	6.4	10.2	10.7	8.9	10.6	12.6
Goods: imports (f.o.b.)	-4.1	-4.7	-5.0	-5.0	-5.9	-6.0	-11.4	-11.1	-12.7	-14.5	-15.3
Trade balance	0.1	-0.5	-0.0	0.5	0.5	0.4	-1.2	-0.4	-3.8	-3.9	-2.7
Net services, income and private transfers	-0.9	-1.0	-0.9	-1.3	-1.9	-0.3	1.4	0.7	0.4	-0.0	0.2
Current account balance	-0.8	-1.5	-0.9	-0.8	-1.4	0.1	0.2	0.3	-3.4	-3.9	-2.5
Poland											
Goods: exports (f.o.b.)	5.8	6.2	6.9	7.9	8.3	11.3	14.9	13.2	14.2	17.3	23.2
Goods: imports (f.o.b.)	-4.6	-5.1	-5.9	-7.0	-8.4	-9.9	-15.5	-16.1	-18.8	-21.6	-29.4
Trade balance	1.2	1.1	1.0	0.9	-0.1	1.4	-0.6	-2.9	-4.6	-4.3	-6.2
Net services, income and private transfers	-1.7	-1.7	-1.4	-1.5	-1.7	-2.1	-0.8	2.6	2.3	3.4	2.5
Current account balance	-0.5	-0.6	-0.4	-0.6	-1.8	-0.7	-1.4	-0.3	-2.3	-0.9	-3.7
Former Soviet Union[d]											
Goods: exports (f.o.b.)	57.3	60.0	63.4	62.0	62.3	59.0	46.7	53.7	56.7	65.4	83.3
Goods: imports (f.o.b.)	-53.9	-54.7	-55.0	-53.8	-58.0	-65.0	-64.9	-45.4	-43.0	-36.3	-39.9
Trade balance	3.4	5.3	8.4	8.2	4.3	-6.0	*-18.2	8.3	13.7	29.1	43.4
Net services, income and private transfers	-3.3	-2.6	-1.1	-5.3	-5.1	1.2	17.4	-13.8	-10.8	-32.0	-30.0
Current account balance	0.1	2.7	7.3	2.9	-0.8	-4.8	-0.8	-5.5	2.9	-2.9	13.4

Source: UN/DESIPA, based on IMF and ECE.

* Indicates break in series.
a Balance in convertible currencies on goods, services and private transfers; data excluding trade among members of the former Czechoslovakia and the Commonwealth of Independent States.
b Preliminary estimates.
c Including transactions of the former German Democratic Republic until 1990.
d From 1992, data for the Commonwealth of Independent States.

Table A.25.

CURRENT ACCOUNT TRANSACTIONS: DEVELOPING COUNTRIES, 1985-1995[a]

Billions of dollars

	1985	1986	1987	1988	1989	1990	1991	1992	1993	1994	1995[b]
All developing countries *(129 economies)*											
Goods: exports (f.o.b.)	500.2	464.6	576.1	663.6	745.1	849.1	891.8	978.6	1034.7	1191.2	1415.7
Goods: imports (f.o.b.)	-447.4	-443.0	-518.5	-618.4	-685.2	-772.4	-861.3	-972.1	-1055.7	-1191.3	-1421.5
Trade balance	52.7	21.6	57.6	45.3	59.8	76.2	30.6	6.6	-21.1	-0.1	-5.9
Net services, income and private transfers	-83.0	-68.5	-65.9	-71.1	-80.0	-79.4	-103.1	-85.6	-88.1	-78.0	-79.8
of which:											
Investment income	-50.6	-44.6	-49.2	-52.0	-55.0	-53.2	-55.8	-55.0	-55.3	-59.8	-64.6
Current account balance	-30.3	-46.8	-8.3	-25.8	-20.1	-2.7	-72.6	-79.1	-109.2	-78.1	-85.7
Totals by region											
Latin America											
Goods: exports (f.o.b.)	99.2	88.9	101.5	117.4	130.4	143.9	144.0	153.1	164.2	189.7	229.5
Goods: imports (f.o.b.)	-68.4	-72.1	-81.1	-93.5	-102.2	-115.2	-131.5	-160.8	-176.0	-207.0	-232.5
Trade balance	30.8	16.8	20.4	23.9	28.2	28.7	12.5	-7.7	-11.9	-17.3	-3.0
Net services, income and private transfers	-35.9	-37.9	-33.2	-36.3	-39.9	-34.5	-32.8	-30.0	-34.9	-34.6	-33.1
of which:											
Investment income	-37.0	-34.1	-32.1	-35.8	-40.7	-35.8	-33.0	-33.1	-35.9	-33.6	-39.1
Current account balance	-5.2	-21.1	-12.8	-12.4	-11.7	-5.8	-20.2	-37.7	-46.7	-51.9	-36.0
Africa											
Goods: exports (f.o.b.)	82.8	67.0	76.4	77.2	84.2	103.9	99.2	96.8	90.7	93.9	105.0
Goods: imports (f.o.b.)	-67.7	-62.3	-69.2	-77.2	-80.0	-89.8	-89.8	-93.8	-90.5	-95.4	-108.7
Trade balance	15.1	4.7	7.2	0.0	4.1	14.1	9.4	3.1	0.2	-1.5	-3.7
Net services, income and private transfers	-18.6	-17.0	-17.1	-17.3	-18.9	-19.8	-18.3	-13.6	-12.3	-14.8	-11.8
of which:											
Investment income	-11.7	-11.5	-14.4	-15.0	-15.7	-17.7	-16.9	-13.9	-12.9	-12.1	-11.9
Current account balance	-3.6	-12.3	-9.9	-17.3	-14.8	-5.7	-8.9	-10.5	-12.1	-16.3	-15.5
West Asia											
Goods: exports (f.o.b.)	99.8	69.3	87.3	88.2	108.5	132.7	119.4	131.1	126.0	130.9	140.3
Goods: imports (f.o.b.)	-77.0	-69.5	-75.9	-78.6	-83.6	-90.5	-102.7	-135.1	-109.3	-102.3	-110.2
Trade balance	22.9	-0.2	11.3	9.6	25.0	42.2	16.7	-4.0	16.7	28.6	30.1
Net services, income and private transfers	-32.7	-16.2	-18.6	-20.8	-24.2	-28.2	-54.5	-23.4	-42.5	-39.6	-35.9
of which:											
Investment income	13.5	16.7	13.3	14.4	15.6	13.7	9.8	8.0	4.7	2.5	1.3
Current account balance	-9.8	-16.4	-7.3	-11.2	0.8	14.0	-37.8	-27.4	-25.7	-11.0	-5.8
South and East Asia											
Goods: exports (f.o.b.)	196.7	217.9	286.1	352.9	393.1	437.2	497.1	566.7	624.8	741.1	899.6
Goods: imports (f.o.b.)	-206.1	-214.0	-264.3	-339.6	-384.9	-432.1	-494.9	-563.3	-633.7	-745.8	-915.6
Trade balance	-9.4	3.9	21.8	13.3	8.2	5.1	2.2	3.4	-8.9	-4.6	-16.1
Net services, income and private transfers	-5.6	-2.5	-2.2	-3.9	-6.7	-5.5	-5.8	-6.5	-9.8	1.2	-12.3
of which:											
Investment income	-12.7	-11.2	-12.3	-11.3	-10.6	-10.0	-12.4	-13.4	-12.7	-14.2	-16.1
Current account balance	-15.0	1.4	19.5	9.4	1.5	-0.4	-3.6	-3.1	-18.8	-3.4	-28.4

Table A.25 (continued)

Totals by trade grouping	1985	1986	1987	1988	1989	1990	1991	1992	1993	1994	1995[b]
Surplus energy exporters *(8 economies)*											
Goods: exports (f.o.b.)	94.9	62.5	77.5	76.6	94.8	118.6	105.2	115.0	106.5	110.4	117.4
Goods: imports (f.o.b.)	-63.9	-54.9	-58.9	-61.1	-68.0	-71.7	-82.0	-89.6	-80.6	-70.0	-73.9
Trade balance	31.0	7.6	18.2	15.5	26.8	46.9	23.2	25.4	25.9	40.5	43.4
Net services, income and private transfers	-28.1	-15.9	-18.7	-20.0	-23.1	-26.9	-51.1	-42.3	-41.4	-39.8	-40.4
of which:											
Investment income	15.8	18.6	16.0	17.5	18.1	16.3	12.3	10.8	7.7	5.4	3.6
Current account balance	2.9	-8.3	-0.1	-4.5	3.7	20.0	-28.0	-16.9	-15.5	0.7	3.0
Deficit energy exporters *(19 economies)*											
Goods: exports (f.o.b.)	127.3	96.8	118.4	124.1	147.7	183.8	187.1	198.4	209.7	237.2	285.9
Goods: imports (f.o.b.)	-95.1	-85.9	-91.8	-111.6	-122.7	-146.3	-169.6	-193.6	-207.9	-239.4	-268.8
Trade balance	32.2	10.9	26.6	12.5	25.0	37.6	17.5	4.8	1.8	-2.2	17.1
Net services, income and private transfers	-36.7	-30.2	-28.3	-29.4	-33.8	-35.6	-37.6	-38.5	-40.3	-43.9	-41.9
of which:											
Investment income	-26.1	-22.2	-25.0	-26.6	-30.1	-30.7	-31.8	-32.6	-33.4	-35.1	-35.4
Current account balance	-4.5	-19.3	-1.7	-16.8	-8.8	2.0	-20.1	-33.6	-38.5	-46.1	-24.9
Energy-importing countries *(102 economies)*											
Goods: exports (f.o.b.)	278.0	305.3	380.2	463.0	502.6	546.7	599.6	665.2	718.5	843.5	1012.4
Goods: imports (f.o.b.)	-288.4	-302.2	-367.8	-445.7	-494.6	-554.4	-609.7	-688.9	-767.3	-882.0	-1078.8
Trade balance	-10.5	3.1	12.4	17.3	8.0	-7.7	-10.1	-23.7	-48.8	-38.4	-66.4
Net services, income and private transfers	-18.3	-22.3	-18.9	-21.7	-23.0	-16.9	-14.4	-4.8	-6.3	5.7	2.5
of which:											
Investment income	-40.3	-41.1	-40.2	-42.8	-43.0	-38.7	-36.4	-33.2	-29.6	-30.1	-32.8
Current account balance	-28.7	-19.2	-6.5	-4.5	-15.0	-24.7	-24.5	-28.6	-55.2	-32.7	-63.8
Four exporters of manufactures *(4 economies)*											
Goods: exports (f.o.b.)	108.6	131.2	177.1	228.2	246.1	266.9	304.6	343.8	377.5	435.9	526.0
Goods: imports (f.o.b.)	-99.8	-111.4	-150.3	-199.2	-224.6	-256.1	-298.1	-339.0	-372.0	-435.5	-532.2
Trade balance	8.8	19.8	26.8	29.6	21.5	10.8	6.5	4.8	5.5	0.4	-6.2
Net services, income and private transfers	2.2	3.5	4.3	2.1	5.9	7.6	7.5	10.8	15.2	16.5	15.4
of which:											
Investment income	-2.6	-0.4	-0.5	1.8	3.4	4.5	4.8	5.2	4.3	3.2	3.7
Current account balance	11.0	23.3	31.1	31.7	27.4	18.4	14.0	15.6	20.7	16.9	9.2

Source: UN/DESIPA, based IMF, and national and other sources.

[a] Balance on goods, services and private transfers.
[b] Preliminary estimate.

Table A.26.

NET TRANSFER OF FINANCIAL RESOURCES OF INDUSTRIALIZED COUNTRIES, 1985-1995

Billions of dollars

	1985	1986	1987	1988	1989	1990	1991	1992	1993	1994	1995[a]
United States											
Net capital flow	125.9	142.0	158.0	123.7	130.6	104.0	52.6	62.7	115.7	145.3	185.4
Current grants: private[b]	-4.2	-4.4	-4.4	-5.5	-5.8	-5.9	-6.6	-6.2	-6.8	-8.5	-9.0
Current grants: official	-13.4	-14.0	-12.5	-13.0	-13.4	-20.4	20.7	-18.8	-19.4	-19.0	-13.7
Capital transfers[c]	0.2	0.2	0.2	0.2	0.2	0.3	0.3	0.4	-0.2	-0.6	0.1
Direct investment[d]	21.2	26.4	47.3	52.1	51.5	53.0	27.1	4.6	9.3	27.2	23.2
Portfolio	68.5	81.5	61.7	66.0	73.6	-6.8	11.8	25.1	-31.4	90.8	141.4
Medium- and long-term loans	8.0	-5.1	-0.6	11.7	3.2	18.9	8.5	-1.4	1.6	2.4	1.4
Short-term capital[e]	22.7	26.0	70.3	25.3	-32.7	20.3	19.6	85.4	126.5	67.2	35.4
Errors and omissions	22.9	31.4	-4.0	-13.0	54.0	44.5	-28.9	-26.4	36.0	-14.3	6.7
Use of IMF credit	0.0	0.0	0.0	0.0	0.0	0.0	0.0	0.0	0.0	0.0	0.0
Net dividends and interest	5.3	3.1	-8.0	2.3	-6.9	-14.3	-21.4	-19.6	-31.8	-36.4	-56.7
Net transfer of resources (financial basis)	131.2	145.1	150.0	125.9	123.7	89.6	31.2	43.1	83.9	108.8	128.7
Use of official reserves[f]	-3.8	0.3	9.2	-3.9	-25.3	-2.2	5.8	3.9	-1.4	5.3	-9.8
Net transfer of resources (expenditure basis)	127.4	145.4	159.2	122.0	98.4	87.4	37.0	47.0	82.5	114.2	118.9
United Kingdom											
Net capital flow	-5.1	4.4	29.3	38.5	29.1	36.3	27.4	13.8	17.7	12.7	18.6
Current grants: private[b]	0.4	0.1	-0.2	-0.5	-0.5	-0.5	-0.5	-0.5	-0.4	-0.4	-0.4
Current grants: official	-4.4	-3.3	-5.4	-5.9	-7.0	-8.2	-1.9	-8.6	-7.4	-7.8	-8.1
Capital transfers[c]	0.0	0.0	0.0	0.0	0.0	0.0	0.0	0.0	0.0	0.0	-0.8
Direct investment[d]	-3.5	-3.7	-9.0	-5.3	3.7	24.5	9.5	4.3	-3.3	1.7	9.9
Portfolio	-8.6	-14.9	48.2	10.6	-29.7	-7.9	-22.9	-2.7	-56.3	75.0	-31.3
Medium- and long-term loans	2.0	6.7	2.2	4.3	9.4	11.8	24.2	5.7	22.4	-7.6	14.8
Short-term capital[e]	8.0	12.7	-2.5	25.2	49.4	15.6	19.4	7.1	66.6	-56.1	31.3
Errors and omissions	0.9	6.8	-4.0	10.0	3.6	1.0	-0.3	8.5	-3.8	8.0	3.1
Use of IMF credit	0.0	0.0	0.0	0.0	0.0	0.0	0.0	0.0	0.0	0.0	0.0
Net dividends and interest	1.3	2.0	-0.3	-2.5	-2.9	-10.0	-10.7	-1.8	-5.0	-0.8	-5.3
Net transfer of resources (financial basis)	-3.8	6.4	29.0	36.0	26.2	26.3	16.7	12.0	12.7	11.9	13.3
Use of official reserves[f]	-0.6	-1.4	-20.2	-4.9	8.8	-0.1	-5.0	2.6	-1.1	-1.6	0.6
Net transfer of resources (expenditure basis)	-4.4	5.0	8.8	31.1	35.0	26.2	11.7	14.6	11.6	10.3	13.9
Germany[g]											
Net capital flow	-24.5	-47.1	-42.0	-83.5	-74.2	-62.1	-25.7	33.6	-28.7	-5.3	2.5
Current grants: private[b]	-4.0	-5.8	-6.5	-7.2	-8.1	-10.6	-11.3	-6.3	-5.8	-5.7	-7.4
Current grants: official	-6.3	-7.7	-10.7	-12.1	-12.5	-15.1	-29.2	-24.6	-24.8	-27.6	-27.9
Capital transfers[c]	-0.2	-0.0	-0.1	-0.0	0.1	-1.3	-0.7	0.7	0.5	0.7	-2.3
Direct investment[d]	-3.6	-7.5	-7.8	-10.0	-7.5	-17.2	-17.5	-16.4	-12.0	-11.5	-23.9
Portfolio	1.8	23.4	3.8	-36.8	-2.4	-1.8	25.0	30.8	116.3	-33.6	18.0
Medium- and long-term loans	1.0	6.3	12.5	-16.2	2.9	-6.5	-21.8	8.3	9.2	4.3	23.6
Short-term capital[e]	-16.4	-57.1	-32.4	-3.7	-51.3	-24.5	21.9	29.1	-99.8	71.5	19.7
Errors and omissions	3.0	1.4	-0.9	2.6	4.6	14.8	8.0	11.9	-12.4	-3.4	2.7
Use of IMF credit	0.0	0.0	0.0	0.0	0.0	0.0	0.0	0.0	0.0	0.0	0.0
Net dividends and interest	2.1	1.4	3.9	3.6	11.1	13.7	17.7	15.9	13.2	1.5	-0.3
Net transfer of resources (financial basis)	-22.4	-45.7	-38.1	-79.9	-63.1	-48.4	-8.0	49.5	-15.5	-3.8	2.2
Use of official reserves[f]	-2.2	-5.5	-21.5	15.4	-2.8	-7.3	6.0	-37.2	14.2	2.0	-18.4
Net transfer of resources (expenditure basis)	-24.7	-51.2	-59.6	-64.5	-65.9	-55.8	-2.0	12.4	-1.3	-1.8	-16.2

Table A.26 (continued)

	1985	1986	1987	1988	1989	1990	1991	1992	1993	1994	1995[a]
Japan											
Net capital flow	-48.6	-73.1	-52.8	-67.2	-74.0	-48.0	-92.0	-121.6	-110.0	-111.4	-9.9
Current grants: private[b]	-0.7	-0.9	-2.1	-2.0	-1.5	-1.5	-1.3	-2.0	-3.1	-3.5	-4.5
Current grants: official	-0.9	-1.2	-1.6	-2.1	-2.8	-4.1	-11.2	-2.6	-3.0	-4.0	-4.9
Capital transfers[c]	0.0	0.0	0.0	0.0	0.0	0.0	0.0	0.0	0.0	0.0	0.0
Direct investment[d]	-5.8	-14.3	-18.4	-34.7	-45.2	-46.3	-29.4	-14.5	-13.6	-17.1	-22.2
Portfolio	-40.3	-101.4	-94.4	-66.1	-28.8	-4.8	39.7	-28.7	-63.8	-48.8	-52.2
Medium- and long-term loans	-15.7	-15.8	-24.3	-29.6	-16.0	7.7	25.3	12.2	-2.0	-16.1	-17.0
Short-term capital[e]	11.1	57.9	91.6	64.2	42.1	21.9	-107.4	-75.5	-24.2	-4.2	76.9
Errors and omissions	3.8	2.5	-3.7	3.1	-21.8	-20.9	-7.7	-10.5	-0.3	-17.8	14.1
Use of IMF credit	0.0	0.0	0.0	0.0	0.0	0.0	0.0	0.0	0.0	0.0	0.0
Net dividends and interest	6.8	9.5	16.7	21.0	23.4	23.2	26.7	36.2	41.4	41.0	45.1
Net transfer of resources (financial basis)	-41.8	-63.6	-36.1	-46.2	-50.6	-24.8	-65.3	-85.4	-68.6	-70.4	35.2
Use of official reserves[f]	0.6	-14.8	-37.9	-16.5	12.8	6.6	6.6	-0.6	-27.7	-25.3	-110.0
Net transfer of resources (expenditure basis)	-41.2	-78.4	-74.0	-62.7	-37.8	-18.2	-58.7	-86.0	-96.2	-95.7	-74.8
Other industrialized countries											
Net capital flow	5.5	6.7	57.7	58.9	75.0	124.7	58.1	8.7	-27.2	-33.8	-40.4
Current grants: private[b]	1.0	0.6	1.3	2.0	1.5	0.9	-0.7	-2.2	0.9	0.4	-0.6
Current grants: official	-4.7	-9.0	-9.7	-10.3	-12.6	-14.6	-16.0	-17.2	-6.4	-22.2	-18.1
Capital transfers[c]	0.8	0.5	0.9	1.6	2.3	4.0	6.2	6.0	5.7	4.9	6.8
Direct investment[d]	-10.2	-9.8	-10.3	-7.9	-16.2	-16.0	-12.6	-0.9	2.7	-10.9	11.3
Portfolio	17.0	18.1	23.1	36.0	60.9	66.3	52.7	52.7	165.7	-106.5	21.2
Medium- and long-term loans	5.2	2.8	19.2	3.6	18.6	21.5	38.1	22.4	46.1	1.8	18.9
Short-term capital[e]	7.0	11.4	33.2	41.3	33.2	83.1	-9.9	-55.9	-215.7	105.9	-76.6
Errors and omissions	-10.6	-8.0	0.2	-6.8	-12.9	-20.5	0.3	3.7	-26.3	-7.3	-3.2
Use of IMF credit	0.0	-0.0	-0.3	-0.5	0.0	0.0	0.0	0.0	0.0	0.0	0.0
Net dividends and interest	-26.1	-29.7	-37.8	-46.7	-51.6	-69.5	-71.5	-83.2	-69.2	-76.4	-70.6
Net transfer of resources (financial basis)	-20.6	-23.0	19.8	12.2	23.3	55.2	-13.4	-74.6	-96.4	-110.2	-111.0
Use of official reserves[f]	0.6	-3.7	-43.4	-27.5	-19.1	-53.6	-0.5	35.6	-1.9	-15.1	-17.1
Net transfer of resources (expenditure basis)	-20.0	-26.8	-23.6	-15.3	4.2	1.6	-13.9	-39.0	-98.3	-125.3	-128.1

Source: UN/DESIPA, based on data of IMF and national sources.

a   Preliminary estimate.
b   Excluding workers' remittances.
c   Including debt forgiveness.
d   Net of reinvested earnings.
e   Including items unidentified by maturity.
f   Additions to reserves are shown as negative numbers.
g   Including transactions of the former German Democratic Republic as from July 1990.

Table A.27.

NET TRANSFER OF FINANCIAL RESOURCES OF CAPITAL-IMPORTING DEVELOPING COUNTRIES, 1985-1995

Billions of dollars

	1985	1986	1987	1988	1989	1990	1991	1992	1993	1994	1995[a]
All countries[b]											
Transfer through direct investment											
Net investment flow	8.3	6.1	9.3	15.4	17.4	16.8	22.7	30.9	46.8	58.7	63.6
Direct investment income: net	-8.7	-7.9	-8.9	-9.9	-11.5	-12.9	-12.6	-13.7	-16.2	-17.0	-17.8
Net transfer	-0.4	-1.7	0.5	5.5	5.9	3.9	10.1	17.2	30.6	41.7	45.8
Transfer through medium- and long-term foreign private borrowing											
Net credit flow	13.5	9.1	4.3	12.0	3.2	10.8	14.7	27.5	31.6	36.9	38.0
Interest paid	-38.9	-34.3	-33.5	-38.7	-32.6	-29.3	-28.1	-27.4	-24.8	-29.4	-42.3
Net transfer	-25.5	-25.2	-29.2	-26.8	-29.4	-18.6	-13.5	0.1	6.8	7.5	-4.3
Transfer through net stock transactions, short-term borrowing and domestic outflows[c]											
Net transfer	-11.4	-6.8	-13.5	-22.3	-10.9	-2.5	21.7	24.6	36.8	1.6	29.3
Transfer through private grants: net	3.7	4.7	5.0	6.2	4.8	6.3	7.9	9.5	9.0	7.9	8.0
Transfer through official flows											
Official transfers (grants)	10.8	10.3	11.7	12.3	13.3	17.6	17.7	15.8	12.7	10.4	10.4
Net official credits	19.0	18.5	16.0	13.5	20.1	22.2	20.6	16.3	17.4	10.4	35.9
Interest paid	-12.8	-15.7	-16.5	-17.9	-18.1	-20.6	-21.9	-22.1	-23.2	-24.5	-31.1
Net transfer	17.0	13.1	11.2	7.9	15.4	19.2	16.4	10.0	7.0	-3.7	15.2
Total net transfer (financial basis)	-16.5	-16.1	-26.0	-29.5	-14.3	8.2	42.6	61.4	90.2	55.0	94.0
Use of official reserves[d]	-0.8	12.0	-8.0	-2.9	-15.4	-36.4	-47.8	-47.2	-42.9	-19.4	-56.0
Total net transfer (expenditure basis)	-17.3	-4.1	-34.0	-32.4	-29.7	-28.1	-5.2	14.2	47.3	35.6	38.0
Africa											
Grants:											
Private	1.1	1.4	1.2	1.2	1.3	1.3	1.7	2.0	2.0	1.2	1.7
Official	4.5	4.9	5.7	6.2	7.4	9.8	9.5	8.7	6.4	4.3	3.7
Net direct investment	0.3	-0.4	-0.7	-0.2	2.3	-0.6	0.2	0.8	0.1	1.5	0.2
Foreign official credit	2.1	1.6	2.4	1.3	2.2	1.0	1.6	1.2	-0.1	0.4	-0.8
Foreign private credit[e]	-3.7	-1.4	-0.8	-0.2	-2.4	-4.6	-5.2	-5.3	-3.2	-3.1	-4.4
Short-term borrowing and domestic outflows[c]	-2.7	0.1	-6.0	-3.0	-5.0	-4.8	-3.0	-1.1	2.6	0.7	3.0
Total net transfer (financial basis) of which:	1.8	6.2	1.8	5.4	5.8	2.5	5.2	6.3	5.7	3.8	1.8
Net capital flow	11.5	15.0	13.2	17.8	18.9	16.7	19.5	17.8	16.6	13.6	11.4
Use of official reserves[d]	-4.6	1.5	0.2	1.6	-1.6	-7.6	-6.5	-4.1	-2.7	1.9	-0.0
Total net transfer (expenditure basis)	-2.8	7.6	2.0	7.0	4.2	-5.1	-1.3	2.2	3.0	5.8	1.8

Table A.27 (continued)

	1985	1986	1987	1988	1989	1990	1991	1992	1993	1994	1995[a]
Sub-Saharan Africa											
Grants:											
Private	0.8	0.7	1.0	1.0	0.9	1.1	1.5	1.8	1.8	1.8	2.0
Official	3.3	3.9	4.7	5.3	6.1	6.1	5.7	6.2	4.5	4.4	4.3
Net direct investment	-0.3	-0.5	-0.6	-0.6	-0.6	-1.5	-0.4	-1.1	-1.1	-1.1	-1.2
Foreign official credit	1.5	1.6	2.6	2.5	2.5	2.7	2.2	2.7	2.3	1.9	1.8
Foreign private credit[e]	-1.2	-0.8	-0.9	-0.2	-0.5	-0.7	-0.2	-0.5	-0.3	-1.2	-2.0
Short-term borrowing and domestic outflows[c]	-0.2	1.0	-0.6	0.7	-1.9	0.9	0.3	0.9	1.1	-0.3	1.4
Total net transfer (financial basis) of which:	3.9	6.0	6.1	8.6	6.5	8.5	9.1	10.1	8.3	5.6	6.2
Net capital flow	8.2	10.6	11.4	14.4	12.6	15.3	15.5	16.0	13.3	10.3	10.3
Use of official reserves[d]	-0.8	-0.0	-0.1	-0.8	-0.2	-0.4	-0.4	0.8	0.4	1.0	1.5
Total net transfer (expenditure basis)	3.1	6.0	6.0	7.8	6.3	8.1	8.7	10.8	8.7	6.6	7.7
Asia											
Grants:											
Private	1.0	1.6	1.9	2.6	1.1	1.1	1.7	3.0	3.0	2.6	2.3
Official	4.5	4.7	4.5	4.8	4.3	3.7	4.1	3.9	3.4	4.1	4.3
Net direct investment	-1.2	0.4	2.2	5.7	4.6	6.7	9.1	10.4	27.8	32.2	41.6
Foreign official credit	3.2	0.7	0.9	0.3	4.5	2.3	6.4	4.8	2.9	-3.3	-5.4
Foreign private credit[e]	3.1	-0.2	-9.7	-5.3	-5.3	-2.3	1.0	6.8	-2.2	11.7	25.5
Short-term borrowing and domestic outflows[c]	9.0	6.6	7.8	-9.9	-2.6	-3.4	15.7	-5.1	6.6	-9.4	-16.9
Total net transfer (financial basis) of which:	19.7	13.9	7.7	-1.9	6.6	8.1	38.0	23.9	41.5	37.9	51.3
Net capital flow	32.3	24.9	19.7	9.1	16.5	17.7	49.9	36.7	53.7	51.5	66.6
Use of official reserves[d]	3.1	-21.7	-36.3	-14.3	-18.7	-19.2	-44.7	-29.2	-29.7	-54.7	-35.3
Total net transfer (expenditure basis)	22.7	-7.9	-28.6	-16.2	-12.1	-11.1	-6.8	-5.3	11.8	-16.8	16.0

Table A.27 (continued)

	1985	1986	1987	1988	1989	1990	1991	1992	1993	1994	1995[a]
Latin America											
Grants:											
Private	1.1	1.1	1.2	1.7	1.6	2.9	3.8	3.8	3.4	3.1	3.4
Official	2.5	1.5	2.1	2.0	2.2	3.4	2.3	2.6	2.0	1.8	1.6
Net direct investment	0.8	-1.1	0.5	2.3	-0.9	-1.0	3.6	5.4	3.5	5.1	1.1
Foreign official credit	2.2	0.8	-1.4	-1.7	-0.9	0.3	-7.1	-9.0	-6.7	-11.3	14.8
Foreign private credit[e]	-22.8	-21.8	-18.8	-23.5	-22.1	-9.9	-7.0	-4.0	7.9	2.5	-8.8
Short-term borrowing and domestic outflows[c]	-11.6	-0.2	-0.2	-10.6	-5.6	-7.2	11.7	31.9	22.7	-0.1	13.0
Total net transfer (financial basis) of which:	-27.7	-19.6	-16.6	-29.8	-25.7	-11.4	7.3	30.7	32.7	1.1	25.2
Net capital flow	7.2	12.5	14.6	4.3	11.4	22.5	37.9	61.5	65.2	30.9	60.0
Use of official reserves[d]	-2.9	7.7	-1.5	8.0	-1.6	-15.7	-16.3	-22.3	-18.4	5.3	-24.8
Total net transfer (expenditure basis)	-30.6	-11.9	-18.1	-21.8	-27.3	-27.1	-8.9	8.4	14.3	6.4	0.4
Fifteen heavily indebted countries											
Grants:											
Private	1.1	1.4	1.6	1.8	2.0	3.6	3.5	3.8	3.2	3.3	3.3
Official	1.0	0.5	0.8	0.9	1.2	2.4	2.2	2.4	1.3	1.3	1.2
Net direct investment	1.6	-0.5	0.8	3.1	1.9	0.6	4.9	6.8	5.6	8.2	4.6
Foreign official credit	0.2	-0.3	-2.3	-4.0	-2.7	-2.1	-17.0	-8.6	-7.6	-12.7	8.2
Foreign private credit[e]	-25.9	-25.2	-21.5	-26.6	-25.2	-13.2	-10.3	-8.8	7.7	4.1	-4.1
Short-term borrowing and domestic outflows[c]	-15.1	-3.7	-5.9	-12.8	-9.5	-5.1	18.5	26.4	19.9	-4.2	10.0
Total net transfer (financial basis) of which:	-37.1	-27.8	-26.5	-37.6	-32.3	-13.7	1.7	22.0	30.1	0.0	23.2
Net capital flow	-34.3	-24.7	-23.0	-33.5	-27.1	-8.8	7.6	28.4	40.1	10.1	34.2
Use of official reserves[d]	-3.3	5.8	-2.2	6.5	-4.5	-19.7	-15.5	-21.4	-19.8	16.3	-23.9
Total net transfer (expenditure basis)	-40.5	-22.0	-28.7	-31.1	-36.8	-33.4	-13.8	0.6	10.3	16.3	-0.7

Source: UN/DESIPA, based on IMF, OECD and World Bank and United Nations Secretariat estimates.

Note: Direct investment is net of reinvested earnings (cash flow approach); official credits include use of IMF credit; interest includes IMF charges; private grants include net flow of gifts from overseas residents (excluding workers' remittances) and grants by non-governmental organizations.

a Preliminary estimate.

b Sample of 93 countries (principal difference from data in Table III.1 is omission of certain countries, mainly from Asia, for which full financial data were not available.

c Calculated as a residual (including short-term trade financing, normal outflows and "capital flight", arrears of interest due, stock transactions and other flows captured in balance-of-payments data as errors and omissions and presumed to be financial flows).

d Additions to reserves are shown as negative numbers.

e Medium- and long-term foreign borrowing

Table A.28.
OFFICIAL RESERVES AND COVERAGE OF CURRENT EXPENDITURES OF CAPITAL-IMPORTING DEVELOPING COUNTRIES, 1985-1995

	1985	1986	1987	1988	1989	1990	1991	1992	1993	1994	1995[a]
Level of reserves[b] *(billions of dollars)*											
All countries	129.8	148.9	195.5	195.5	229.2	278.4	341.8	364.1	425.6	503.8	568.1
Energy exporters	38.6	34.3	44.5	31.8	37.3	53.8	73.0	83.8	102.4	85.1	96.9
Energy importers	91.2	114.6	151.0	163.8	191.9	224.6	268.8	280.4	323.2	418.6	471.2
Four exporters of manufactures	38.5	62.8	96.0	104.0	109.4	115.7	130.9	140.0	152.8	177.0	191.6
Other	52.7	51.8	55.1	59.8	82.5	108.9	137.8	140.4	170.4	241.6	279.6
Memo items											
Latin America	41.2	33.4	38.2	31.1	33.4	48.6	66.2	89.1	109.3	105.3	130.2
Sub-Saharan Africa	4.0	5.0	5.8	6.3	6.9	8.2	9.5	9.1	10.0	11.8	13.3
Fifteen heavily indebted countries	40.9	34.4	38.7	32.9	38.1	57.2	74.5	92.4	112.8	110.4	134.2
Coverage of current expenditures[c] *(months of import coverage)*											
All countries[d]	2.6	2.5	2.7	2.4	2.5	2.9	3.5	3.5	3.9	4.2	4.1
Energy exporters	2.7	2.8	3.5	2.1	2.3	2.8	3.4	3.5	4.1	3.0	2.9
Energy importers	2.6	2.4	2.3	2.6	2.6	3.0	3.6	3.4	3.8	4.8	4.7
Memo items											
Latin America	3.8	3.1	3.1	2.2	2.2	2.9	3.7	4.3	4.9	4.2	4.9
Sub-Saharan Africa	1.4	1.5	1.6	1.6	1.7	1.8	2.2	2.0	2.5	3.2	3.2
Fifteen heavily indebted countries	3.1	2.7	2.8	2.1	2.2	2.9	3.7	4.2	4.7	4.1	5.5

Source: UN/DESIPA, based on IMF and national estimates.

a   Partly estimated.
b   Total reserves, end of period (with gold valued at SDR 35 per ounce).
c   Expenditures on goods and services (including interest payments) for given year relative to total reserves at end of year.
d   Sample of 93 countries.

Table A.29.

NET IMF LENDING TO DEVELOPING COUNTRIES, BY FACILITY, 1985-1995

Billions of dollars

	1985	1986	1987	1988	1989	1990	1991	1992	1993	1994	1995
Regular facilities	1.1	0.0	-3.9	-4.0	-3.0	-1.6	-1.2	-0.1	-0.2	-0.9	12.6
Repayment terms:											
3-5 years (Credit tranche)	0.6	1.3	-0.6	-0.4	-0.2	-1.7	0.2	1.4	-0.2	0.1	12.5
3.5-7 years (SFF/EAP)[a]	0.6	-1.0	-2.7	-2.7	-2.8	-0.7	-0.8	-1.5	-1.5	-1.5	-1.7
4-10 years (Extended Fund Facility)	-0.0	-0.2	-0.5	-0.9	0.1	0.7	-0.7	-0.0	1.5	0.5	1.8
Concessional facilities	-0.3	-0.5	-0.2	-0.3	0.9	0.2	1.1	0.8	0.2	0.9	1.5
In order created:											
Trust Fund[b]	-0.3	-0.6	-0.7	-0.7	-0.5	-0.4	-0.1	0.0	-0.1	-0.0	-0.0
SAF[c]	-	0.1	0.5	0.3	0.7	0.1	0.2	0.0	-0.1	-0.2	-0.1
ESAF[c]	-	-	-	-	0.8	0.5	0.9	0.7	0.4	1.1	1.6
Additional facilities[d]	-0.5	-1.9	-1.1	-0.4	0.2	-0.8	1.2	-0.9	-0.2	-0.9	-1.6
In order created:											
Compensatory financing[e]	-0.4	-1.8	-1.1	-0.4	0.2	-0.8	1.2	-0.9	-0.2	-0.9	-1.6
Buffer stock[f]	-0.2	-0.2	-0.1	-0.0	0.0	0.0	0.0	0.0	0.0	0.0	0.0
STF [g]									0.0	0.0	0.1
Total	0.3	-2.4	-5.2	-4.7	-1.9	-2.3	1.0	-0.2	-0.2	-0.8	12.5
Memo items:											
Selected characteristics of higher conditionality lending agreements											
Number initiated during year	26	31	25	28	23	13	24	17	13	26	19
Average length (months)	16	22	26	25	25	19	22	26	24	25	23
Total amount committed (billions of dollars)	3.4	4.0	4.4	5.4	13.8	1.9	6.4	7.1	3.0	6.6	23.2

Source: IMF, *International Financial Statistics and IMF Survey.*

[a] The Supplementary Financing Facility (SFF) (1979-1981) and the Enhanced Access Policy (EAP) (1981-present) have provided resources from funds borrowed by IMF from member States, on which the Fund pays a higher interest rate than the remuneration paid to countries that have a net creditor position with the Fund. Thus, users of SFF and EAP resources have paid a higher interest rate than that on drawings from ordinary resources, which are partly subsidized (for example, in fiscal 1981/82: 6.3 per cent versus 14.8 per cent for SFF and 13.2 per cent for EAP; by 1985/86, the spread was much reduced: 7 per cent versus 9.4 per cent and 9.2 per cent). However, up to a 3 percentage point subsidy was made available for IDA-eligible countries and up to half that for countries with GDP per capita above International Development Association (IDA) limits but under the maximum for Trust Fund eligibility, in order to reduce interest on SFF drawings towards the rate on ordinary drawings. There has been no subsidy on EAP drawings.
[b] Mainly using resources from IMF gold sales, the Trust Fund lent during 1977-1981 under one-year adjustment programmes. Eligibility was based on maximum per capita income criteria and loans had 10-year maturities, with repayments beginning in the sixth year. The interest rate was 0.5 per cent per year.
[c] The Structural Adjustment Facility (SAF) and the Enhanced Structural Adjustment Facility (ESAF) (the first financed mainly from Trust Fund reflows and the second from loans and grants) have made loans to IDA-eligible countries with protracted balance-of-payments problems; funds are disbursed over 3 years (under Policy Framework Paper arrangements), with repayments beginning in 5.5 years and ending in 10 years; the interest rate is 0.5 per cent.
[d] All having final maturity of 7 years and repayments beginning in 3.5 years.
[e] Compensatory Financing Facility from 1963 to 1988; Compensatory and Contingency Financing Facility from August 1988.
[f] Helps to finance buffer stock purchases under approved international buffer stock arrangements; established June 1969.
[g] See description in table A.30 below

Table A.30.

NET IMF LENDING TO ECONOMIES IN TRANSITION: BY FACILITY, 1985-1995

Billions of dollars

	1985	1986	1987	1988	1989	1990	1991	1992	1993	1994	1995
Regular facilities	-0.1	-0.2	-0.6	-0.5	-0.3	0.3	2.1	1.9	0.1	0.2	4.4
Repayment terms:											
3-5 years (Credit tranche)	-0.1	-0.2	-0.4	0.0	0.0	0.5	1.1	1.8	0.1	0.5	4.9
3.5-7 years (SFF/EAP)	-0.0	-0.1	-0.2	-0.4	-0.3	-0.1	0.3	0.0	-0.0	-0.3	-0.0
4-10 years (Extended Fund Facility)							0.8	0.1	0.0	0.0	-0.5
Concessional facilities (ESAF)									0.0	0.0	0.1
Additional facilities											
Compensatory financing	-0.1	-0.1	0.0	0.0	0.0	0.0	1.5	-0.1	0.0	-0.7	-0.6
STF									2.0	2.7	1.0
Total	-0.3	-0.3	-0.6	-0.5	-0.3	0.3	3.6	1.8	2.1	2.2	4.8
Memo items:											
Selected characteristics of											
lending agreements											
Number initiated during year	0	0	0	1	0	2	5	7	9	8	11
Average length (months)	0	0	0	12	0	12	12	12	18	18	13
Total amount committed	0.0	0.0	0.0	0.4	0.0	1.0	4.9	2.2	1.6	2.1	9.2

Source: Data of IMF, International Financial Statistics.
Note: The Systemic Transformation Facility (STF), created in 1993 on a temporary basis, assists economies in transition with severe balance-of-payments problems arising from dis-continuance of trade arrangements under planning. For members that have not yet had a standby arrangement, drawings can be made be in two tranches in support of a written statement of policy reform intentions, the second 6-18 months after the first, assuming satisfactory progress towards an upper credit tranche arrangement (repayment terms are the same as for the Extended Facility). See table A.29 above for description of other facilities.

Table A.31.

FUNDS RAISED ON INTERNATIONAL CREDIT MARKETS, 1985-1995

Billions of dollars

	1985	1986	1987	1988	1989	1990	1991	1992	1993	1994	1995
World total	279.1	321.4	303.7	371.9	385.3	361.4	432.5	458.3	625.8	669.7	832.2
grouped by borrower:											
Developed economies	230.5	285.2	260.2	330.3	345.0	312.4	374.0	398.4	537.3	580.3	726.9
Economies in transition	5.3	3.9	3.7	4.3	4.7	4.7	1.7	1.5	6.2	3.6	6.5
Developing countries	30.1	22.2	27.8	26.9	22.7	28.9	42.2	37.5	61.6	73.5	81.1
Multilateral institutions	13.2	10.1	11.9	10.5	12.9	15.4	14.7	20.9	20.7	12.4	17.7
grouped by instrument:											
Bonds	169.1	228.1	180.8	229.7	255.8	229.9	308.7	333.7	481.0	428.6	460.7
International bonds	136.5	187.7	140.5	178.9	212.9	180.1	258.2	276.1	394.6	368.4	371.2
Foreign and special placements	32.5	40.4	40.3	50.8	42.9	49.8	50.6	57.6	86.4	60.2	89.4
Loans	110.1	93.3	122.9	142.2	129.5	131.5	123.8	124.6	144.8	207.7	371.6
Bank loans	61.1	63.2	91.7	125.6	121.2	124.5	116.0	117.9	136.7	236.2	368.4
Other facilities	48.9	30.0	31.2	16.6	8.4	7.0	7.7	6.7	8.2	4.9	3.1

Source: OECD, *Financial Statistics Monthly.*

Table A.32.
NET ODA FROM MAJOR SOURCES, BY TYPE, 1975-1994

Donor group or country	Growth rate of ODA[a] (1993 prices and exchange rates) 1975-1984	Growth rate of ODA[a] (1993 prices and exchange rates) 1985-1994	ODA as percentage of GNP 1994	Total ODA (millions of dollars) 1994	Bilateral Grants[b]	Bilateral Technical cooperation	Bilateral Loans	Multilateral United Nations	Multilateral IDA	Multilateral Other
Total DAC countries	4.69	1.39	0.30	59152	59.5	21.7	10.3	7.3	7.8	15.1
Total EU	4.99	2.38	0.42	30420	58.2	22.0	9.5	6.0	6.3	20.1
Austria	7.06	4.45	0.33	655	54.0	15.6	27.8	4.7	8.4	5.2
Belgium	3.04	-2.93	0.32	726	59.4	14.2	0.6	5.8	0.0	34.3
Denmark	6.36	4.45	1.03	1446	60.9	12.8	-5.4	19.1	5.7	19.6
Finland	10.77	1.95	0.31	290	73.4	10.7	0.0	16.6	0.7	9.0
France[c]	5.33	2.90	0.64	8466	70.8	26.4	7.3	1.9	5.1	14.8
Germany	4.79	0.61	0.34	6818	52.1	31.2	8.7	4.2	10.3	24.7
Ireland	20.06	5.20	0.25	109	51.4	30.3	0.0	8.3	5.5	34.9
Italy	10.35	4.11	0.27	2705	24.6	4.7	43.2	7.0	0.1	25.1
Luxembourg	-	18.15	0.40	59	67.8	3.4	0.0	6.8	0.0	25.4
Netherlands	7.34	0.68	0.76	2517	76.8	23.9	-9.2	11.1	7.7	13.6
Portugal	-	25.71	0.35	308	47.7	21.8	22.1	1.0	3.9	25.3
Spain	-	18.70	0.28	1305	19.7	6.8	45.7	4.0	0.3	30.2
Sweden	4.20	2.90	0.96	1819	75.4	17.5	0.1	14.7	5.7	4.1
United Kingdom	0.16	1.39	0.31	3197	56.6	21.3	-1.4	4.8	9.5	30.6
Australia	2.40	0.72	0.35	1088	74.3	26.9	0.0	8.7	7.8	9.2
Canada	3.61	1.83	0.43	2250	63.6	18.0	-0.4	11.3	9.0	16.4
Japan	6.83	1.70	0.29	13239	40.0	16.6	32.2	5.1	11.6	11.1
New Zealand	1.43	0.00	0.24	110	77.3	35.5	0.0	6.4	7.3	9.1
Norway	11.43	2.52	1.05	1137	72.3	13.5	0.5	18.4	6.8	2.0
Switzerland	8.29	2.93	0.36	982	74.2	28.0	-0.4	11.6	10.7	4.0
United States	2.64	-1.52	0.15	9927	83.6	28.2	-10.2	11.4	6.9	8.3
Arab countries of which:	..	..	..	..	———	..	———	———	..	———
Saudi Arabia	..	..	..	317	———	55.5	———	———	44.5	———
Kuwait	..	..	..	555	———	89.0	———	———	11.0	———
United Arab Emirates	..	..	..	100	———	92.0	———	———	8.0	———
Other developing countries:	..	..	..	..	———	..	———	———	..	———
China	..	..	..	..	———	..	———	———	..	———
India		..	..	28	———	53.6[d]	———	———	46.4[e]	———
Republic of Korea	..	..	0.37	140	———	42.9[d]	———	———	57.1[e]	———
Taiwan Province of China	..	..	0.03	79	———	89.9	———	———	10.1	———

Source: UN/DESIPA, based on OECD, *Development Co-operation*, 1995.

a   Average annual rates of growth, calculated from average levels in 1973-1974, 1983-1984 and 1993-1994.
b   Including technical cooperation.
c   Excluding flows from France to the Overseas Departments, namely Guadeloupe, French Guiana, Martinique and Réunion.
d   Total bilateral: grants and loans.
e   Total multilateral: United Nations, IDA and "other", including technical cooperation.

Table A.33.

REGIONAL DISTRIBUTION OF ODA FROM MAJOR SOURCES, 1983-1994

Donor group or country	All developing countries		Latin America		Africa		West Asia		South and East Asia		Mediterranean	
	1983-1984	1993-1994	1983-1984	1993-1994	1983-1984	1993-1994	1983-1984	1993-1994	1983-1984	1993-1994	1983-1984	1993-1994
Millions of Dollars, two-year average												
Total ODA[a] *(net)*	30631.4	58197.3	2933.2	5481.9	10435.2	21958.9	3753.4	3759.3	8348.3	16460.6	347.0	2481.2
DAC countries, bilateral	19161.2	39837.8	2132.2	4131.3	6766.7	13628.1	1642.8	2572.8	5293.6	11558.6	264.5	1365.8
Australia	571.0	761.4	1.5	1.0	58.4	60.4	3.1	2.8	478.3	643.9	0.3	1.0
Austria	131.8	470.3	8.4	30.5	75.0	98.7	7.2	21.4	24.7	144.6	6.3	153.0
Belgium	280.8	446.9	17.8	51.0	183.0	230.1	1.4	2.5	31.3	61.8	7.0	-1.3
Canada	943.8	1508.2	130.8	143.2	332.9	321.1	4.2	11.9	284.6	277.4	0.3	5.4
Denmark	229.6	776.9	4.0	41.4	128.1	376.4	2.9	4.8	70.7	132.1	-0.1	-0.1
Finland	100.4	227.2	6.6	17.9	64.4	88.0	0.7	6.0	19.4	57.7	-0.2	7.1
France[b]	3157.6	6374.3	107.6	245.0	1241.9	3873.2	48.6	116.9	506.8	1319.0	14.8	64.5
Germany	1984.5	4295.1	222.6	483.5	799.1	1480.9	115.2	140.5	544.9	1120.1	30.0	464.4
Ireland	14.3	49.0	0.0	0.7	0.0	32.7	0.0	0.6	0.0	2.6	0.0	1.8
Italy	536.8	1853.1	45.3	289.6	357.8	934.4	17.8	44.5	23.1	309.3	28.8	121.6
Japan	2426.3	8770.2	234.8	780.3	371.5	1349.8	59.1	328.6	1621.1	5298.3	30.0	15.3
Luxembourg	0.0	34.8	0.0	7.4	0.0	17.0	0.0	0.2	0.0	2.9	0.0	1.4
Netherlands	845.4	1727.8	164.5	343.6	301.7	533.8	16.2	69.8	239.9	174.7	0.1	137.6
New Zealand	45.7	79.4	0.1	0.7	0.2	2.9	0.1	0.0	43.0	64.6	0.0	0.2
Norway	318.3	740.3	11.3	48.6	172.5	337.6	2.8	14.0	91.7	127.3	3.1	64.6
Portugal	0.0	202.9	0.0	0.5	0.0	201.1	0.0	0.2	0.0	0.5	0.0	0.5
Spain	0.0	892.8	0.0	439.9	0.0	172.9	0.0	9.0	0.0	223.1	0.0	1.6
Sweden	525.8	1344.1	32.5	126.1	254.9	487.5	3.5	29.2	161.6	248.1	-0.2	112.3
Switzerland	218.3	664.3	29.9	76.4	96.5	198.0	4.8	21.0	50.3	152.3	1.3	30.5
United Kingdom	821.1	1572.1	60.8	114.1	281.6	571.7	11.0	35.3	297.9	403.7	0.7	117.2
United States	6010.0	7048.0	1054.0	890.5	2047.5	2260.0	1344.5	1714.0	804.5	796.0	142.5	68.0
DAC countries, multilateral	7442.1	17304.8	795.1	1352.3	2627.3	7906.4	227.1	762.8	2834.0	4969.6	41.9	955.5
Total DAC	26603.2	57142.6	2927.3	5483.6	9394.0	21534.5	1869.8	3335.5	8127.6	16528.2	306.3	2321.3
Arab countries, bilateral[c]	3797.9	831.6	-1.9	0.6	923.4	274.6	1844.3	341.8	166.7	-56.6	40.0	160.7
Arab countries, multilateral	230.3	223.1	7.8	-2.3	117.9	149.8	39.4	82.0	54.1	-11.1	0.7	-0.8

Source: UN/DESIPA calculations based on OECD, *Geographical Distribution of Financial Flows to Aid Recipients.*

a Excluding ODA provided by centrally planned economies, owing to measurement difficulties.
Donor total includes unallocated amounts and hence is larger than the sum of the amounts per regions.
b Excluding flows from France to the Overseas Departments, namely Guadeloupe, French Guiana, Martinique and Réunion.
c Approximately 35-40 per cent of Arab bilateral aid is geographically unallocated, depending on the year

Table A.34.
RESOURCE COMMITMENTS OF MULTILATERAL DEVELOPMENT INSTITUTIONS, 1985-1995[a]

Millions of dollars	1985	1986	1987	1988	1989	1990	1991	1992	1993	1994	1995
Financial institutions	23809	24960	26640	27636	32410	34766	39859	39771	39530	40639	44050
African Development Bank	1154	1640	2140	2194	2841	3191	3445	2982	2518	1434	669
Asian Development Bank	1845	2044	2508	3220	3760	4095	4914	5226	5426	3864	5759
Caribbean Development Bank	50	67	41	58	73	109	111	71	71	56	110
European Bank for Reconstruction and Development							66	1071	1925	2436	3283
Inter-American Development Bank	3102	3057	2408	1738	2694	4005	5661	6246	6191	5298	7454
of which: Inter-American Investment Corporation					15	67	102	158	124	43	36
International Fund for Agricultural Development	131	147	233	244	277	323	281	331	383	364	414
World Bank Group	17527	18005	19310	20182	22765	23043	25381	23844	23016	27187	26361
International Bank for Reconstruction and Development	12952	13593	14066	14411	16251	15176	17021	15551	15098	16427	15950
of which: International Development Association	3541	3373	3841	4350	4924	6300	7160	6310	5345	7282	5973
International Finance Corporation	1034	1039	1403	1421	1590	1567	1200	1983	2573	3478	4438
Operational agencies of the United Nations system	2037	1966	1957	2493	2542	2754	3628	3683	3374	3476	3099
United Nations Development Programme[b]	572	689	702	833	897	1042	1134	1027	1031	1036	1014
United Nations Population Fund	141	116	134	169	194	211	212	164	206	278	340
United Nations Children's Fund	452	248	330	454	498	545	947	917	655	769	649
World Food Programme	872	913	791	1037	953	956	1335	1575	1482	1393	1096
Total commitments	25846	26926	28597	30129	34952	37520	43487	43454	42904	44115	47149
Memo item: Commitments in units of 1990 purchasing power[c]	41025	35429	33644	32749	38409	37520	42188	43135	44231	44561	44064

Source: Annual reports and information supplied by individual institutions.

[a] Loans, grants, technical assistance and equity participation, as appropriate; all data are on a calendar-year basis.
[b] Including United Nations Development Programme (UNDP)-administered funds.
[c] Total commitments deflated by the United Nations index of manufactured export prices in dollars of developed economies: 1990=100.

Table A.35.

EXTERNAL DEBT AND DEBT INDICATORS FOR ECONOMIES IN TRANSITION, 1985-1995

External debt (billions of dollars)	1985	1986	1987	1988	1989	1990	1991	1992	1993	1994	1995[a]
Russian Federation/ former Soviet Union[b]											
Total external debt	28.3	30.7	38.3	42.2	53.9	59.8	67.6	79.0	83.9	94.2	..
Long-term debt	21.4	23.3	29.7	31.0	35.7	48.0	55.0	65.9	75.6	84.3	..
Concessional	0.0	0.0	0.0	0.0	0.0	1.3	2.0	2.6	6.1	6.6	..
of which: bilateral	0.0	0.0	0.0	0.0	0.0	1.3	2.0	2.6	6.1	6.5	..
Official, non-concessional	0.4	0.4	1.4	1.9	2.3	6.1	9.1	11.1	23.5	33.8	..
Bilateral	0.4	0.4	1.3	1.7	2.0	5.7	8.7	9.6	19.6	28.1	..
Multilateral	0.0	0.0	0.1	0.2	0.2	0.4	0.4	0.5	1.4	1.5	..
IMF	0.0	0.0	0.0	0.0	0.0	0.0	0.0	1.0	2.5	4.2	..
Private creditors	21.0	22.9	28.4	29.1	33.5	40.6	43.8	52.2	46.0	43.8	..
of which:											
Bonds[c]	0.0	0.0	0.0	0.3	1.5	2.0	2.0	1.9	1.7	1.9	..
Commercial banks[c]	11.9	13.3	14.8	15.6	18.2	18.8	17.2	18.0	15.3	15.6	..
Short-term debt	6.9	7.4	8.6	11.2	18.2	11.8	12.6	13.1	8.3	10.0	
Central and Eastern Europe											
Total external debt	62.7	72.0	83.7	80.9	82.8	91.2	100.8	96.2	100.9	104.1	106.0
Long-term debt	53.6	60.4	69.9	64.4	65.5	73.5	85.4	84.2	90.0	95.0	96.0
Concessional	7.1	4.6	4.9	4.7	3.8	4.2	4.0	13.4	13.1	11.7	11.9
of which: bilateral	7.0	4.5	4.9	4.7	3.7	4.1	4.0	13.3	12.9	11.3	11.4
Official, non-concessional	18.0	23.1	25.8	23.0	24.3	29.4	41.8	33.6	34.9	37.0	36.0
Bilateral	13.5	17.5	19.7	18.3	20.7	24.7	31.4	21.3	21.5	21.7	22.2
Multilateral	2.8	3.8	4.8	3.9	3.1	3.9	5.8	7.2	8.2	9.8	10.4
IMF	1.6	1.7	1.3	0.8	0.5	0.8	4.6	5.2	5.2	5.4	3.5
Private creditors	28.6	32.7	39.1	36.6	37.4	39.9	39.6	37.2	42.0	46.3	48.1
of which:											
Bonds[c]	0.6	1.0	1.8	2.6	3.7	5.4	7.1	7.8	12.0	28.5	30.7
Commercial banks[c]	20.9	24.4	28.7	26.4	27.6	28.8	27.8	24.9	23.5	8.8	8.6
Short-term debt	9.0	11.6	13.8	16.6	17.3	17.7	15.4	12.0	10.9	9.1	10.0
of which:											
Hungary											
Total external debt	14.0	16.9	19.6	19.6	20.4	21.3	22.6	22.0	24.2	28.0	..
Long-term debt	10.9	13.4	16.5	16.2	17.1	18.3	20.4	19.7	22.2	25.6	..
Concessional	0.8	0.7	0.2	0.1	0.1	0.1	0.1	0.1	0.2	0.3	..
of which: bilateral	0.8	0.6	0.1	0.0	0.0	0.0	0.0	0.1	0.1	0.2	..
Official, non-concessional	1.5	2.0	2.1	2.3	2.4	3.0	5.0	4.9	4.9	5.1	..
Bilateral	0.1	0.1	0.1	0.1	0.1	0.1	0.5	0.6	0.6	0.6	..
Multilateral	0.4	0.8	1.2	1.6	1.8	2.5	3.3	3.2	3.1	3.3	..
IMF	1.0	1.0	0.8	0.6	0.5	0.3	1.3	1.2	1.2	1.1	..
Private creditors	8.6	10.8	14.2	13.9	14.6	15.3	15.3	14.7	17.1	20.2	..
of which:											
Bonds[c]	0.6	1.0	1.8	2.5	3.4	4.7	6.0	6.8	10.1	13.4	..
Commercial banks[c]	6.4	8.2	10.7	9.9	10.2	9.6	8.1	6.4	5.1	3.9	..
Short-term debt	3.0	3.5	3.1	3.4	3.3	2.9	2.2	2.3	2.0	2.4	

Table A.35 (continued)

	1985	1986	1987	1988	1989	1990	1991	1992	1993	1994	1995[a]
Poland											
Total external debt	33.3	36.6	42.6	42.1	43.1	49.2	53.6	48.6	45.3	42.2	..
Long-term debt	29.7	31.9	36.0	33.6	34.5	39.6	46.0	44.1	42.7	41.3	..
Concessional	6.1	3.7	4.5	4.4	3.5	3.8	3.7	12.9	12.5	10.7	..
of which: bilateral	6.1	3.7	4.5	4.4	3.5	3.8	3.7	12.9	12.5	10.7	..
Official, non-concessional	12.9	17.0	18.9	17.4	20.1	24.4	31.2	20.9	20.8	21.8	..
Bilateral	12.2	16.1	18.0	16.7	19.6	23.4	29.4	18.9	18.6	18.5	..
Multilateral	0.6	0.9	0.9	0.7	0.5	0.5	0.9	1.2	1.5	2.0	..
IMF	0.0	0.0	0.0	0.0	0.0	0.5	0.9	0.8	0.7	1.3	..
Private creditors	10.8	11.1	12.6	11.7	10.9	11.3	11.1	10.3	9.4	8.8	..
of which:											
Bonds[c]	0.0	0.0	0.0	0.0	0.0	0.0	0.0	0.0	0.0	7.3	..
Commercial banks[c]	7.7	8.8	9.9	9.2	9.0	9.8	9.7	9.1	8.6	0.4	..
Short-term debt	3.6	4.7	6.6	8.5	8.6	9.6	7.6	4.5	2.7	0.8	

Debt indicators (Percentage)

Ratio of external debt to GNP

Russian Federation/former Soviet Union	7.8	7.5	8.2	7.6	9.0	9.9	12.2	16.4	19.3	25.4	..
Central and Eastern Europe of which:	32.5	33.8	40.9	38.8	37.5	43.5	52.4	46.8	46.9	44.4	41.9
Bulgaria	22.0	29.1	29.4	39.6	48.0	57.1	125.0	117.9	113.7	105.7	..
Former Czechoslovakia	12.5	13.5	14.3	15.7	17.7	20.2	29.6	24.3	27.3	29.7	..
Hungary	70.6	74.3	78.1	71.4	73.4	67.2	70.7	61.7	65.0	70.1	..
Poland	48.7	51.4	69.8	63.9	54.5	88.4	72.8	58.8	53.5	46.8	..
Romania	14.8	13.5	17.4	7.3	2.6	3.1	7.5	12.5	16.2	18.3	

Ratio of external debt to exports

Russian Federation/former Soviet Union[d]	41.8	45.9	52.3	57.8	72.7	73.8	124.5	186.0	162.0	159.7	..
Central and Eastern Europe of which:	105.0	114.8	123.4	116.2	116.7	145.9	181.4	134.3	140.9	128.1	142.0
Bulgaria	32.3	57.5	71.5	84.7	114.2	239.7	332.9	240.4	246.9	189.9	..
Former Czechoslovakia	36.4	39.6	42.1	45.8	52.7	63.9	76.1	42.1	46.5	54.6	..
Hungary	139.4	153.4	162.8	161.3	159.4	186.3	185.6	176.1	226.4	256.8	..
Poland	278.7	264.2	306.7	270.3	291.9	264.5	351.8	299.9	283.8	215.7	..
Romania	62.2	64.7	56.6	23.4	9.3	17.3	40.8	59.0	71.0	74.0	..

Ratio of debt service to exports

Russian Federation/former Soviet Union[d]	8.1	11.8	11.9	11.3	12.3	14.6	24.9	3.1	4.5	6.2	..
Central and Eastern Europe of which:	17.1	17.4	17.3	19.2	16.0	12.8	12.4	13.0	12.7	17.1	21.7
Bulgaria	9.9	15.2	17.2	22.2	29.1	30.3	7.4	8.2	5.9	13.8	..
Former Czechoslovakia	8.8	8.5	8.3	9.6	10.3	10.5	12.0	9.0	7.0	12.6	..
Hungary	36.8	37.9	31.2	28.9	27.9	37.0	32.8	39.8	41.4	52.2	..
Poland	17.1	13.1	14.8	11.3	10.4	5.2	6.4	9.1	10.5	15.8	..
Romania	18.3	18.4	21.4	32.7	16.5	1.1	2.3	8.4	5.4	7.9	..

Source: UN/DESIPA, based on data of IMF and World Bank.

a   Estimate.
b   In 1992, the Russian Federation assumed the debt of the former Soviet Union.
c   Government or government-guaranteed debt only.
d   Merchandise exports only.

Table A.36.

EXTERNAL DEBT OF CAPITAL-IMPORTING DEVELOPING COUNTRIES, 1985-1995

Billions of dollars

	1985	1986	1987	1988	1989	1990	1991	1992	1993	1994	1995[a]
All countries[b]											
Total external debt	934.2	1026.5	1157.7	1153.0	1167.8	1284.3	1347.4	1404.7	1482.2	1603.1	1476.6
Long-term debt	793.2	890.2	1008.0	997.9	996.7	1080.4	1120.4	1150.6	1204.6	1307.3	1155.5
Concessional	167.1	191.3	229.2	240.0	278.6	307.1	328.6	341.1	360.2	394.5	..
Bilateral	124.5	142.9	172.2	179.7	212.5	231.9	244.9	251.8	263.5	283.5	..
Multilateral[c]	42.6	48.4	56.9	60.3	66.1	75.2	83.7	89.3	96.7	111.1	..
Official, non-concessional	164.2	202.0	244.0	240.9	215.5	271.7	284.3	286.5	293.1	312.0	..
Bilateral	66.8	81.2	97.8	102.4	107.3	114.1	120.9	125.9	126.1	136.3	..
Multilateral	61.3	83.0	107.8	106.2	79.6	127.3	134.5	133.8	140.8	149.6	..
IMF	36.1	37.8	38.5	32.3	28.6	30.3	28.8	26.7	26.1	26.1	35.8
Private creditors	461.8	496.9	534.8	517.0	502.6	501.6	507.6	523.0	551.3	600.8	652.3
of which:											
Bonds[d]	34.8	37.8	40.6	43.6	46.1	103.7	110.4	121.4	155.0	209.8	..
Commercial banks[d]	244.8	272.5	300.2	296.5	286.5	210.6	202.9	193.9	174.3	141.6	..
Short-term debt	141.1	136.3	149.7	155.0	171.2	204.0	227.0	254.1	277.6	295.8	321.1
Memo items											
Principal arrears on long-term debt	16.4	23.9	28.0	37.4	41.7	52.4	56.2	64.1	68.8	78.4	90.8
Interest on long-term debt	6.2	8.7	15.1	18.1	29.0	39.6	42.4	39.0	38.0	35.2	34.9
Latin America											
Total external debt	410.0	430.4	471.4	458.1	454.2	476.5	490.6	504.7	531.0	562.4	606.7
Long-term debt	364.4	393.8	426.4	409.0	394.6	399.0	402.9	409.2	432.0	457.0	494.3
Concessional	33.9	36.3	42.3	44.9	46.3	49.1	52.2	54.1	56.2	59.7	..
Bilateral	28.9	30.8	36.5	38.9	40.1	42.4	45.2	46.8	48.5	51.2	..
Multilateral	5.1	5.5	5.8	5.9	6.2	6.7	7.0	7.3	7.7	8.5	..
Official, non-concessional	61.2	75.4	95.0	98.1	100.4	116.4	120.9	121.1	123.2	125.3	..
Bilateral	20.7	23.6	31.0	37.0	38.9	45.0	48.4	51.8	51.8	52.0	..
Multilateral	25.9	35.4	45.9	44.8	45.9	53.3	55.4	54.5	57.5	59.9	..
IMF	14.5	16.3	18.1	16.3	15.6	18.1	17.1	14.8	13.9	13.4	26.8
Private creditors	269.3	282.2	289.1	266.0	247.9	233.5	229.8	234.0	252.6	272.1	281.4
of which:											
Bonds[d]	17.8	17.6	16.8	18.1	19.1	76.0	79.1	81.8	108.9	156.4	..
Commercial banks[d]	173.5	189.0	200.8	190.3	178.6	102.7	97.4	95.4	76.1	40.0	..
Short-term debt	45.7	36.5	45.0	49.2	59.6	77.5	87.7	95.6	99.0	105.3	112.4
Memo items											
Principal arrears on long-term debt	6.9	9.6	12.6	15.3	18.6	25.3	25.0	25.5	22.5	21.5	22.5
Interest arrears on long-term debt	2.7	3.5	8.3	8.6	16.6	25.7	27.7	21.4	15.6	9.6	7.0

Table A.36 (continued)

	1985	1986	1987	1988	1989	1990	1991	1992	1993	1994	1995[a]
Africa											
Total external debt	198.3	224.0	258.3	262.0	268.9	279.7	283.0	278.5	281.8	303.5	282.0
Long-term debt	160.8	185.1	226.3	230.3	234.4	244.8	248.7	241.9	240.3	259.8	235.6
Concessional	48.1	55.4	66.1	69.2	73.1	79.6	87.5	91.3	96.1	106.1	..
Bilateral	34.3	39.0	45.5	46.8	47.9	51.1	55.5	57.3	59.0	63.1	..
Multilateral[c]	13.9	16.4	20.6	22.3	25.2	28.4	32.0	34.0	37.1	43.0	..
Official, non-concessional	47.0	60.4	75.2	74.0	76.6	79.2	81.5	79.3	77.9	87.6	..
Bilateral	28.9	38.7	48.3	48.3	51.3	51.8	53.2	51.6	49.1	56.9	..
Multilateral	10.0	14.2	18.8	18.3	18.7	21.2	22.6	22.7	23.8	24.9	..
IMF	8.1	7.6	8.1	7.4	6.6	6.1	5.7	5.0	5.0	5.8	3.6
Private creditors	65.7	69.2	84.9	87.1	84.7	86.1	79.7	71.2	66.3	66.0	69.1
of which:											
Bonds[d]	5.6	5.0	5.2	4.7	4.5	3.6	3.1	5.1	2.9	3.3	..
Commercial banks[d]	20.5	22.1	30.9	32.8	31.4	30.8	28.9	22.4	21.4	21.4	..
Short-term debt	37.5	38.9	32.1	31.7	34.5	34.9	34.3	36.6	41.5	43.7	46.4
Memo items:											
Principal arrears on long-term debt	8.2	13.3	13.3	19.9	19.9	22.2	22.0	25.3	30.9	34.8	41.7
Interest arrears on long-term debt	3.3	5.1	6.6	8.9	11.1	11.6	11.7	13.9	17.8	20.1	21.2
Sub-Saharan Africa											
Total external debt	79.6	93.0	112.4	114.5	120.3	135.9	141.4	144.3	149.0	156.0	159.0
Long-term debt	70.2	83.0	100.1	100.9	103.7	115.9	119.7	120.4	122.1	130.2	132.3
Concessional	27.9	33.4	41.7	44.0	47.4	55.3	60.3	63.2	66.8	73.5	..
Bilateral	17.4	20.4	24.8	25.3	25.9	29.4	30.9	31.7	32.5	33.7	..
Multilateral[c]	10.5	13.0	16.9	18.7	21.5	25.9	29.5	31.5	34.3	39.8	..
Official, non-concessional	22.5	27.5	33.9	33.0	32.3	35.7	34.8	33.8	32.4	34.7	..
Bilateral	11.7	14.9	19.2	19.3	20.6	23.7	23.8	23.7	22.7	25.5	..
Multilateral	4.7	6.2	8.1	7.7	7.0	7.5	7.2	6.9	6.8	6.1	..
IMF	6.0	6.4	6.6	6.0	4.7	4.4	3.8	3.2	3.0	3.1	0.9
Private creditors	19.9	22.0	24.5	23.9	24.1	24.9	24.6	23.3	22.9	21.9	..
of which:											
Bonds[d]	0.4	0.5	0.5	0.4	0.4	0.3	0.3	0.2	0.2	0.2	..
Commercial banks[d]	6.7	7.4	8.2	7.8	8.0	8.5	8.1	7.7	7.7	7.7	..
Short-term debt	9.4	10.0	12.3	13.6	16.6	20.1	21.7	23.9	26.8	25.8	26.7
Memo items:											
Principal arrears on long-term debt	4.2	5.6	8.2	11.0	13.7	16.8	20.7	23.2	26.7	28.2	32.6
Interest arrears on long-term debt	1.9	2.6	3.8	5.4	7.4	8.9	10.9	12.5	15.2	15.9	16.6

Table A.36 (continued)

	1985	1986	1987	1988	1989	1990	1991	1992	1993	1994	1995[a]
Asia											
Total external debt	254.6	290.6	332.3	337.0	377.9	421.6	463.3	504.8	545.0	612.6	670.4
Long-term debt	206.1	241.5	273.3	275.0	312.6	347.4	376.1	406.7	437.0	489.1	534.0
Concessional	66.2	77.7	94.4	99.3	131.5	149.7	158.2	166.1	178.4	198.0	..
Bilateral	44.2	53.3	66.6	69.9	99.6	112.6	116.7	121.2	129.7	142.0	..
Multilateral[c]	22.0	24.4	27.9	29.3	31.9	37.1	41.5	44.8	48.7	56.0	..
Official, non-concessional	39.6	47.0	51.8	48.9	49.9	56.9	62.7	68.3	75.8	82.1	..
Bilateral	11.6	12.6	11.8	10.8	10.8	11.5	13.5	17.1	20.2	22.0	..
Multilateral	18.0	23.7	30.5	31.3	33.6	39.9	43.6	44.5	48.6	53.8	..
IMF	10.0	10.6	9.5	6.9	5.6	5.5	5.6	6.7	7.0	6.3	4.3
Private creditors	100.4	116.8	127.0	126.8	131.2	140.8	155.2	172.4	182.8	208.9	245.4
of which:											
Bonds[d]	11.1	14.9	17.9	17.4	17.3	18.2	21.7	25.6	30.0	35.6	..
Commercial banks[d]	37.4	44.8	48.6	51.3	54.0	54.6	55.6	55.8	58.7	60.0	..
Short-term debt	48.5	49.1	59.0	62.0	65.3	74.2	87.1	98.1	108.0	123.5	136.4
Memo items											
Principal arrears on long-term debt	0.8	0.1	0.8	0.8	1.5	2.2	4.7	7.3	7.8	11.1	12.9
Interest arrears on long-term debt	0.1	0.0	0.0	0.2	0.9	1.5	1.9	2.2	2.3	2.7	2.9
Least developed countries											
Total external debt	54.1	63.5	77.4	81.8	86.1	96.1	100.4	103.7	106.8	115.1	117.3
Long-term debt	47.9	57.1	69.4	72.4	75.1	83.2	86.1	87.7	90.5	97.2	98.7
Concessional	33.5	39.6	48.9	52.6	55.4	62.1	66.1	68.9	72.8	79.0	77.7
Bilateral	21.3	24.8	30.3	32.1	32.5	34.6	35.3	35.9	36.9	38.3	34.3
Multilateral[c]	12.3	14.8	18.6	20.5	22.9	27.5	30.8	33.0	35.9	40.7	43.4
Official, non-concessional	13.8	17.1	19.9	19.1	18.9	20.3	19.2	18.0	17.0	17.5	20.3
Bilateral	8.3	10.8	13.0	12.9	13.6	15.4	15.3	15.0	14.4	15.3	18.9
Multilateral	1.5	2.1	2.2	2.0	1.8	1.7	1.1	0.6	0.3	0.0	0.0
IMF	4.0	4.2	4.7	4.2	3.5	3.2	2.8	2.4	2.2	2.3	1.4
Private creditors	9.1	10.7	13.0	13.3	13.5	14.3	14.1	13.7	13.5	13.5	13.5
of which:											
Bonds[d]	0.0.	0.0	0.0	0.0	0.0	0.0	0.0	0.0	0.0	0.0	0.0
Commercial banks[d]	2.6	2.9	3.4	3.2	3.2	3.4	3.0	2.9	2.9	3.0	3.0
Short-term debt	6.3	6.4	7.9	9.4	11.0	12.9	14.3	16.0	16.3	17.9	18.6
Memo items:											
Principal arrears on long-term debt	4.0	5.1	7.6	9.7	11.8	14.7	17.9	19.9	22.8	26.0	30.3
Interest arrears on long-term debt	1.8	2.3	3.5	4.5	6.2	7.6	9.1	10.4	12.2	14.1	15.1

Source: UN/DESIPA, based on data of IMF, OECD and World Bank.

[a] Estimate.
[b] Debt of 122 economies, drawn primarily from the data of the Debtor Reporting System of the World Bank (107 countries).
For non-reporting countries, data are drawn from the Creditor Reporting System of OECD (15 economies), excluding, however, non-guaranteed bank debt of offshore financial centres, much of which is not the debt of the local economies.
[c] Including concessional facilities of IMF.
[d] Government or government-guaranteed debt only

Table A.37.

DEBT INDICATORS AND DEBT-SERVICE PAYMENTS FOR CAPITAL-IMPORTING DEVELOPING COUNTRIES, 1985-1995

	1985	1986	1987	1988	1989	1990	1991	1992	1993	1994	1995[a]
Debt indicators *(percentage)*											
Ratio of external debt to GNP											
All countries of which:	44.1	47.0	49.3	43.8	40.1	39.1	39.5	38.1	37.5	37.0	31.6
Latin America	62.2	63.7	65.7	56.7	50.1	44.9	45.5	42.7	40.0	37.1	39.6
Africa	57.8	66.7	72.8	72.0	73.6	70.4	72.4	69.7	71.0	76.4	65.0
Asia	26.0	28.6	30.4	26.3	26.6	27.2	27.8	27.9	28.6	28.5	26.8
Memo items:											
Sub-Saharan Africa	75.9	77.7	87.0	86.9	91.3	98.9	103.0	108.3	114.2	135.8	120.9
Least developed countries	58.4	63.6	71.1	75.2	76.6	82.6	86.0	91.5	91.9	98.5	89.8
Ratio of external debt to exports											
All countries of which:	179.9	198.8	185.6	158.6	143.2	138.9	138.9	132.4	130.2	122.8	98.8
Latin America	326.1	392.7	384.7	332.5	293.2	277.3	281.8	276.0	274.5	258.4	254.0
Africa	208.9	262.3	273.1	263.9	252.4	223.1	229.5	218.7	232.9	248.7	223.6
Asia	101.9	105.6	94.0	78.0	78.0	77.4	76.7	73.5	71.8	67.7	63.1
Memo items											
Sub-Saharan Africa	259.7	302.5	338.8	327.7	320.7	327.1	352.0	356.6	386.0	384.5	366.3
Least developed countries	281.5	358.3	372.4	375.5	356.0	368.0	408.2	412.8	436.6	435.3	410.8
Ratio of debt service to exports											
All countries of which:	23.5	24.5	21.8	19.9	17.3	15.7	14.6	14.5	14.6	12.9	12.9
Latin America	38.6	44.4	38.2	39.6	32.1	26.3	26.2	28.9	30.0	27.5	30.3
Africa	26.1	29.1	23.8	26.0	24.3	24.0	23.2	22.3	22.4	19.0	19.6
Asia	15.7	15.5	15.4	11.7	10.7	9.9	8.8	8.6	9.2	8.1	7.7
Memo items											
Sub-Saharan Africa	21.3	24.8	23.1	22.3	19.3	17.7	17.6	15.3	14.4	16.7	19.3
Least developed countries	15.9	22.1	17.6	17.2	16.1	14.1	14.6	11.2	11.2	11.3	16.8

Table A.37 (continued)

	1985	1986	1987	1988	1989	1990	1991	1992	1993	1994	1995[a]
Debt-service payments *(billions of dollars)*											
All countries											
Total debt service	122.2	126.5	135.8	144.9	141.3	144.9	142.0	153.6	166.1	168.8	192.8
Interest payments	67.7	63.1	62.0	70.7	66.4	65.1	66.8	64.5	64.0	72.0	86.4
of which:											
non-concessional	65.2	60.1	58.9	67.1	62.4	59.9	61.6	58.5	57.5	64.7	..
Latin America											
Total debt service	48.5	48.6	46.8	54.5	49.8	45.2	45.6	52.8	58.0	59.9	72.3
Interest payments	35.0	30.4	28.6	33.2	25.7	22.4	23.9	22.8	22.9	27.0	35.1
of which:											
non-concessional	34.6	29.9	28.1	32.6	25.3	21.5	23.0	21.9	21.9	25.9	..
Africa											
Total debt service	24.7	24.8	22.5	25.8	25.9	30.1	28.6	28.3	27.0	23.2	24.7
Interest payments	10.9	10.5	9.4	11.2	11.6	12.4	11.6	11.1	9.5	10.3	11.1
of which:											
non-concessional	10.4	9.9	8.9	10.5	10.8	11.3	10.8	9.7	8.1	8.5	10.2
Asia											
Total debt service	39.3	42.7	54.4	50.7	51.9	54.2	53.3	59.0	69.6	73.4	81.8
Interest payments	17.2	17.2	18.7	20.2	23.5	24.0	25.5	24.8	26.5	29.7	34.5
of which:											
non-concessional	15.9	15.6	17.0	18.2	21.2	21.2	22.4	21.5	22.8	25.6	..
Memo items											
Sub-Saharan Africa											
Total debt service	6.5	7.6	7.7	7.8	7.2	7.4	7.1	6.2	5.6	6.8	8.4
Interest payments	3.0	3.2	3.0	3.2	3.0	3.1	3.1	2.7	2.4	2.8	2.6
of which:											
non-concessional	2.7	2.9	2.7	2.8	2.6	2.7	2.6	2.2	1.9	2.2	..
Least developed countries											
Total debt service	3.1	3.9	3.7	3.7	3.9	3.7	3.6	2.8	2.7	3.0	4.8
Interest payments	1.4	1.5	1.4	1.6	1.4	1.4	1.5	1.2	1.2	1.3	1.3
of which:											
non-concessional	1.1	1.1	1.0	1.1	1.0	0.9	0.9	0.6	0.6	0.6	0.6

Source: UN/DESIPA, based on data of IMF, OECD and World Bank.

a   Preliminary estimate.

Table A.38.

DEBT RESTRUCTURING WITH OFFICIAL CREDITORS, 1985-1995

	1985	1986	1987	1988	1989	1990	1991	1992	1993	1994	1995
Number of agreements											
Developing countries, total	22	19	17	15	24	17	14	16	10	14	17
Middle-income countries	9	3	4	3	6	1	2	4	1	2	1
Lower-middle-income countries	4	6	6	4	6	7	9	4	3	6	7
Low-income countries	9	10	7	8	12	9	3	8	6	6	9
Memo items:											
Sub-Saharan Africa	10	15	9	9	16	9	6	9	4	10	9
Amounts rescheduled[a] *(millions of dollars)*											
Developing countries, total	6457	12183	19969	9362	18600	6075	44308	12522	3394	14020	14163
Middle-income countries	3789	2201	6670	6721	6016	200	1825	7287	57	293	1030
Lower-middle-income countries	1692	7502	10962	1342	9312	3320	34150	2628	2615	11360	11130
Low-income countries	976	2480	1987	973	2518	2445	390	2607	722	1007	2003
Memo items:											
Sub-Saharan Africa	1192	9466	2904	1299	10330	3374	1810	3687	633	5289	3117
Average consolidation period *(years)*											
Developing countries, total	1.2	1.2	1.2	1.3	1.4[b]	1.5	..[c]	1.9	2.3	1.4	2.1[d]
Middle-income countries	1.1	1.2	1.1	1.4	1.6	1.4	0.8	1.5	-	0.5	3.0
Lower-middle-income countries	1.2	1.2	1.4	1.4	1.4	1.4	..[c]	1.5	3.1	1.8	1.9
Low-income countries	1.3	1.2	1.2	1.2	1.3[b]	1.7	1.2	2.1	2.1	1.2	2.1
Memo items:											
Sub-Saharan Africa	1.2	1.2	1.2	1.2	1.3[b]	1.6	1.2	2.0	2.3	1.4	2.1

Source: UNCTAD, based on Paris Club Agreed Minutes.

Note: In 1995, Paris Club creditors introduced new concessional debt-relief measures for poor, severely indebted countries, known as the "Naples terms". For the major features of current Paris Club rescheduling terms, see: the report of the Secretary-General, entitled: "The developing countries' debt situation as of mid-1995" (A/50/379) of 31 August 1995, paras. 12-16 and table 2.

a   Including previously rescheduled debt.
b   Excluding Equatorial Guinea.
c   Owing to the menu options for Egypt, it is not possible to calculate consolidation periods and maturity averages for 1991.
d   Excluding Bolivia and Uganda which obtained a 67 per cent Naples terms stock reduction agreement.

Table A.39.
DEBT-RESTRUCTURING AGREEMENTS WITH COMMERCIAL BANKS: ALL DEVELOPING COUNTRIES, 1985-1995

	1985	1986	1987	1988	1989	1990	1991	1992	1993	1994	1995
Number of agreements	14	12	19	10	4	5	0	1	-	1	1
Amounts rescheduled[a] (billions of dollars)	72.7	89.7	79.7	6.8	5.4	-	-	0.2	-	0.2	3.2
Average consolidation period (years)	2.8	4.0	6.5	3.3	7.3	-	4.0	..	-	..	..
Average repayment terms											
Maturity (years)	11	10	15	19	16	13	-	13	-	..	..
Grace (years)	4	4	5	7	5	4	-	3	-	..	..
Spread over LIBOR (percentage)	1.5	1.3	1.0	0.8	0.9	0.8	-	0.8	-	..	..

Concluded debt and debt-service reduction agreements *(billions of dollars)*

	1990				1991	1992	
	Mexico	Philippines	Costa Rica	Venezuela	Uruguay	Philippines	Nigeria
Debt reduction							
Debt buyback	-	1.3	1.0	1.4	0.5	1.3	3.3
Discount bonds	20.6	-	-	1.8	-	-	-
Debt-service reduction	22.4	-	0.5	10.3	0.4	2.6	2.0
New money	4.4	-	-	6.1	0.4	0.5	-
Total debt restructured	48.1[b]	1.3	1.5[c]	19.6	1.3	4.4	5.3
Total financing required	7.0	0.7	0.2	2.4	0.5	1.2	1.7
of which: own resources	1.2	0.05	0.04	0.4	0.3	1.0	1.7

	1993			1994		1995	
	Argentina	Jordan		Brazil	Dominican Republic		Ecuador
Debt reduction							
Debt buyback	-	..			0.3		
Discount bonds	6.6	0.2		4.0	0.5		2.6
Debt-service reduction	12.2	..		4.0	0.7		1.9
New money	-	..		4.0	..		..
Total debt restructured	27.0[d]	0.9		*46.6	1.2		7.8
Total financing required	4.0	0.15		4.6	0.2		0.7
of which: own resources	0.8	0.15		4.6	0.2		0.1

Sources: World Bank, *World Debt Tables 1996, vol. I* (Washington, D.C., World Bank, 1996); and IMF.

a   Including previously rescheduled debt.
b   Including portion ($693 million) not committed to any option.
c   Overdue interest amounting to $114 million was converted into bonds by those banks that chose the buyback option.
d   Total including $8.3 billion past-due interest.

IV. THE INTERNATIONAL OIL MARKET

Table A.40.
WORLD OIL DEMAND, 1986-1996[a]

Millions of barrels per day

	1986	1987	1988	1989	1990	1991	1992	1993	1994	1995	1996[b]
Developed economies	35.7	36.4	37.5	37.9	38.0	38.2	38.9	39.1	40.0	40.4	41.0
North America	18.1	18.5	19.2	19.3	18.9	18.6	19.0	19.2	19.7	19.8	20.1
Western Europe	12.4	12.5	12.7	12.8	13.0	13.4	13.6	13.6	13.7	13.9	14.1
Pacific[c]	5.2	5.3	5.6	5.9	6.1	6.2	6.3	6.3	6.6	6.7	6.7
Economies in transition	10.7	10.8	10.8	10.6	10.1	9.7	8.5	7.1	6.2	6.2	6.2
Central and Eastern Europe	1.8	1.8	1.8	1.8	1.7	1.4	1.4	1.3	1.4	1.4	1.5
Former Soviet Union[d]	9.0	9.0	9.0	8.8	8.4	8.2	7.1	5.7	4.8	4.8	4.7
Developing countries	15.4	16.1	16.8	17.5	18.3	19.0	20.2	21.5	22.4	23.5	24.5
Latin America	4.8	5.0	5.0	5.1	5.2	5.3	5.5	5.7	5.9	6.0	6.2
Africa	1.7	1.8	1.9	1.9	2.0	2.0	2.0	2.0	2.1	2.1	2.2
West Asia	3.0	3.1	3.1	3.1	3.3	3.4	3.6	3.9	4.0	4.1	4.1
South and East Asia	3.9	4.2	4.6	5.0	5.6	5.9	6.5	7.0	7.4	8.0	8.5
China[d]	2.0	2.1	2.3	2.4	2.3	2.5	2.7	3.0	3.1	3.3	3.5
World total[e]	61.8	63.3	65.1	66.1	66.4	66.9	67.5	67.6	68.5	70.0	71.6

Source: UN/DESIPA, based on International Energy Agency, *Monthly Oil Market Report*, various issues.
a   Including deliveries from refineries/primary stocks and marine bunkers, and refinery fuel and non-conventional oils.
b   Estimate.
c   Australia, Japan and New Zealand.
d   Based on estimates of apparent domestic demand derived from official production figures and quarterly trade data.
e   Totals may not add up because of rounding.

Table A.41.
WORLD CRUDE OIL PRODUCTION, 1986-1996[a]

Millions of barrels per day

	1986	1987	1988	1989	1990	1991	1992	1993	1994	1995	1996
Developed economies	16.9	16.8	16.7	15.9	15.9	16.3	16.6	16.8	17.6	18.0	18.9
Economies in transition	12.8	13.0	12.9	12.6	11.8	10.7	9.2	8.2	7.5	7.4	7.5
Developing countries	31.1	31.4	33.9	36.3	38.0	38.5	40.0	41.1	41.9	43.1	43.7
OPEC[b]	19.8	19.7	21.8	23.8	25.1	25.3	26.5	27.0	27.3	27.8	27.8
Non-OPEC developing countries[b]	11.3	11.7	12.1	12.5	12.9	13.2	13.5	14.1	14.6	15.3	15.9
Processing gains[c]	1.1	1.2	1.2	1.3	1.3	1.3	1.3	1.4	1.4	1.5	1.5
World total	62.0	62.4	64.8	66.1	67.0	66.8	67.1	67.4	68.4	70.0	71.6

Source: UN/DESIPA, based on International Energy Agency, *Monthly Oil Market Report*, various issues.

a   Including crude oil, condensates, natural gas liquids (NGLs), oil from non-conventional sources and other sources of supply.
b   Ecuador is included in OPEC through 1992 and in non-OPEC developing countries starting in 1993.
c   Net volumetric gains and losses in refining process (excluding net gain/loss in the economies in transition and China) and marine transportation losses

Table A.42.
OPEC CRUDE OIL PRODUCTION, 1995

Thousands of barrels per day

	Jan.	Feb.	March	April	May	June	July	Aug.	Sept.	Oct.	Nov.	Dec.	1995	Memo Item: 1994
Algeria	750	750	750	750	800	800	800	750	800	800	780	780	778	748
Gabon	340	340	340	345	345	345	345	350	350	350	350	350	346	324
Indonesia	1 350	1 330	1 330	1 330	1 330	1 323	1 330	1 340	1 340	1 340	1 350	1 350	1 337	1 321
Iran (Islamic Republic of)	3 530	3 770	3 289	3 600	3 575	3 645	3 585	3 610	3 495	3 795	3 600	3 355	3 571	3 583
Iraq	540	540	540	540	540	540	550	550	550	550	550	550	545	506
Kuwait[a]	2 000	2 000	2 000	2 000	2 000	2 000	2 000	2 000	2 030	2 000	2 000	2 000	2 002	2 000
Libyan Arab Jamahiriya	1 400	1 400	1 400	1 400	1 400	1 400	1 400	1 400	1 405	1 405	1 370	1 370	1 396	1 392
Nigeria	1 860	1 850	1 850	1 920	1 920	1 850	1 810	1 850	1 900	1 920	1 940	1 960	1 886	1 877
Qatar	420	420	410	420	420	420	420	420	420	420	430	445	422	399
Saudi Arabia[a]	8 000	8 000	8 000	8 000	8 000	8 000	8 000	8 000	8 000	8 000	8 000	8 000	8 000	8 000
United Arab Emirates	2 200	2 200	2 174	2 175	2 180	2 180	2 180	2 170	2 160	2 180	2 180	2 180	2 180	2 180
Venezuela	2 500	2 500	2 500	2 510	2 580	2 700	2 700	2 750	2 750	2 750	2 800	2 800	2 653	2 456
Total	24 890	25 100	24 583	25 010	25 090	25 210	25 120	25 190	25 200	25 510	25 350	25 140	25 116	24 786

Source: *Middle East Economic Survey*, 15 January 1996.

a   Including share of the neutral zone.

Table A.43.
VALUE OF OIL EXPORTS OF OPEC MEMBER COUNTRIES, 1960-1995[a]

Millions of dollars

	1960	1970	1980	1985	1988	1989	1990	1991	1992	1993	1994	1995[b]
Algeria	106	681	12 647	9 170	4 988	7 000	9 588	8 464	7 885	6 902	6 361	6 900
Gabon	9	62	1 745	1 629	779	1 200	1 967	1 740	1 712	1 506	1 668	1 800
Indonesia	221	446	12 850	7 670	5 189	6 059	6 481	5 745	5 850	4 560	5 219	5 500
Iran (Islamic Republic of)	723	2 358	13 286	15 590	9 210	10 809	14 567	15 280	15 700	14 241	15 068	16 300
Iraq	445	788	26 296	10 685	9 312	11 876	9 463	380	326	364	328	350
Kuwait	855	1 619	18 353	9 453	6 839	9 306	6 386	875	6 224	9 986	10 396	11 260
Libyan Arab Jamahiriya	9	2 356	21 387	10 524	6 397	7 500	9 800	10 025	9 200	7 607	7 141	7 730
Nigeria	13	716	25 290	12 353	6 267	7 470	13 200	12 150	11 690	11 024	10 025	10 860
Qatar	103	227	5 406	3 068	1 709	1 955	2 960	2 187	3 200	2 594	2 419	2 650
Saudi Arabia	682	2 418	105 813	24 180	20 206	24 096	40 128	43 656	47 560	41 353	37 530	40 700
United Arab Emirates	1	513	19 558	11 842	7 352	11 300	15 600	14 765	14 490	12 086	12 200	13 200
Venezuela	1 983	2 371	17 562	12 956	8 158	10 001	13 953	12 305	11 208	10 565	10 343	11 600
Total	5 150	14 555	275 993	129 120	86 402	107 572	144 642	129 223	136 247	126 049	116 050	128 850

Source: *OPEC Annual Statistical Bulletin*, various issues.

a   Where appropriate, petroleum product exports are included. Data for some countries may include exports of condensate.
    Starting in 1980, Saudi Arabia data exclude natural gas liquids.
b   Preliminary estimate by UN/DESIPA.

UNITED NATIONS PUBLICATIONS
United Nations, Room DC2-0853, New York, New York 10017, U.S.A.

UNITED NATIONS PUBLICATIONS
Palais des Nations, 1211 Geneva 10, Switzerland

Printed in U.S.A. • 93139—June 1996—5,875
ISBN 92-1-109131-4 • Sales Number E.96.II.C.1
E/1996/60 • ST/ESA/247